THE (MKTG) SOLUTION

LAMB HAIR MCDANIEL BOIVIN GAUDET SHEARER   FOURTH CANADIAN EDITION

PRINT

MKTG delivers all the key terms and all the content for the **Principles of Marketing** course through a visually engaging and easy-to-review print experience.

DIGITAL

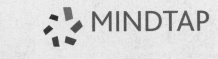 MINDTAP

MindTap enables you to stay organized and study efficiently by providing a single location for all your course materials and study aids. Built-in apps leverage social media and the latest learning technology to help you succeed.

1 Open the Access Card included with this text.

2 Follow the steps on the card.

3 Study.

Student Resources

- Enhanced interactive ebook
- Chapter-opening video animations
- Video cases
- *Concept-in-Action* video interviews with Canadian marketing professionals
- Practice quizzing
- Concept maps
- Homework assignments
- Pathbrite online portfolio

Students: **nelson.com/student**

Instructor Resources

- Access to all student resources
- Engagement tracker
- Instructor companion site
- PowerPoint® slides
- Updated test bank
- LMS integration

Instructors: **nelson.com/instructor**

NELSON

MKTG, Fourth Canadian Edition

by Charles W. Lamb, Joe F. Hair, Carl McDaniel, Marc Boivin, David Gaudet, and Janice Shearer

Vice President, Product Solutions:
Claudine O'Donnell

Publisher, Digital and Print Content:
Alexis Hood

Executive Marketing Manager:
Amanda Henry

Content Manager:
Lisa Berland

Photo and Permissions Researcher:
Julie Pratt

Production Project Manager:
Jennifer Hare

Production Service:
MPS Limited

Copy Editor:
Wendy Thomas

Proofreader:
Aditi Rai, MPS Limited

Indexer:
Edwin Durbin

Design Director:
Ken Phipps

Higher Education Design PM:
Pamela Johnston

Cover Design:
Courtney Hellam

Compositor:
MPS Limited

Library and Archives Canada Cataloguing in Publication Data

Lamb, Charles W., author
    MKTG / by Charles W. Lamb, Joe F. Hair, Carl McDaniel, Marc Boivin, David Gaudet, Janice Shearer. — Fourth Canadian edition.

Title from cover.
Includes bibliographical references and index.
ISBN 978-0-17-672368-2 (softcover)

    1. Marketing—Textbooks.
2. Marketing—Management—Textbooks. 3. Textbooks.
I. McDaniel, Carl D., author
II. Shearer, Janice, author
III. Hair, Joe F., author
IV. Boivin, Marc, 1973-, author
V. Title. I. Title: Marketing.

HF5415.L34 2018   658.8
C2017-907049-5

ISBN-13: 978-0-17-672368-2
ISBN-10: 0-17-672368-4

MKTG

BRIEF CONTENTS

CONTENTS

Part 1
MARKETING—LET'S GET STARTED

My Life Graphic/Shutterstock.com

Part 1 Case: From Analysis to Action 69

Part 2 ANALYZING MARKETING OPPORTUNITIES

6 Consumer Decision Making   94

7 Business Marketing   116

Courtesy of Tylko

Part 3 PRODUCT DECISIONS

11 Developing and Managing Products 194

12 Services and Nonprofit Organization Marketing 212

13 Setting the Right Price 232

Part 4 Case: Pricing Decisions 251

Part 5
DISTRIBUTING DECISIONS

14 Marketing Channels and Supply Chain Management 254

15 Retailing 274

Part 5 Case: Distribution Decisions 293

Part 6
PROMOTION DECISIONS

16 Marketing Communications 296

17 Advertising, Public Relations, and Direct Response 316

1 | An Introduction to Marketing

LEARNING OUTCOMES

1-1 Define marketing

1-2 Describe the evolution of marketing

1-3 Define key marketing terms

1-4 Explain why marketing matters

"Marketing is dead."

—Kevin Roberts, CEO of Saatchi & Saatchi (top advertising agency)[1]

1-1 WHAT IS MARKETING?

Marketing is a word that elicits much opinion and discussion. It is often defined by what it is not rather than by what it actually is. Marketing is one of the most misused words in business today. It is often reduced to a few words that are attached to the activities of marketing: sales, advertising, and promotion.

Sometimes marketing is seemingly written off entirely, as can be seen by the quote at start of this chapter from Kevin Roberts of Saatchi & Saatchi, a global communications and advertising company. Could this be true? Do we not need to worry about marketing anymore? Far from it. Without marketing, there is no customer. Most departments in a firm—whether accounting or finance or operations—are internally focused on achieving goals related to their functional area. Marketing's sole focus is on the customer and understanding what makes them tick. Without

marketing the activities that develop an offering in order to satisfy a customer need

need a state of being where we desire something that we do not possess but yearn to acquire

marketing to identify a customer to create revenues and profit, there is no need for an accounting department or manufacturing facility.

So it has become a marketer's job to understand the customer, and in doing so, transition marketing from something that used to be considered an afterthought to a key component in an organization. Being able to bring an external customer-based approach, marketing can inform other parts of the organization to focus on the needs of customers when undertaking any action or decision. Marketing is far from dead and, in fact, has never been so alive.

1-1a What Is Marketing?

Marketing is about understanding the **needs** of the customer. No other aspect of business has this focus. Marketing helps to shape the products and services of a firm, based on an understanding of what the customer is looking for. Marketing is about engaging in a conversation with that customer and guiding the delivery of what is required to satisfy those needs.

The goal of marketing is summarized nicely by the marketing concept. At its core, the marketing concept

Marketing

is about offering the customer what they are looking for. It includes the following:

- Focusing on customer wants and needs so that the organization can distinguish its offerings from those of its competitors.
- Integrating all the organization's activities, including production, to satisfy customers' wants.
- Achieving long-term goals for the organization by satisfying customers' wants and needs legally and responsibly.

Kevin Roberts was in fact not speaking of the demise of marketing in the provocative quote, but rather its rebirth. He implored marketing practitioners to change the way in which marketing is applied. He tasked his audience with seeing marketing differently and moving marketing from "interruption to interaction."[2]

Marketing is becoming a conversation with the customer rather than a distraction. Companies are finding innovative ways in which to lead this conversation, and with access to more tools (Instagram, SnapChat), consumers are now, more than ever, able to talk back.

Marketing is not dead. Marketing is constantly changing, along with the customer it continually strives to better understand. We are heading into a new era of marketing—one that is reflective of the digital, online, and engaged world around us. Without marketing, there is no understanding this world.

1-2 THE EVOLUTION OF MARKETING

The misconceptions surrounding marketing come from the evolution of how marketing has been used in firms for more than a century. In their seminal article in the *Journal of Public Policy and Marketing*, renowned researchers William Wilkie and Elizabeth Moore described how today's marketing has resulted from many shifts in both the field of marketing and society. The authors note that the past century of marketing thought "has experienced periodic shifts in dominance of prevailing modes of thinking."[3] Numerous terms and ideologies are used to describe these shifts in thinking, and below are a few of the orientations in marketing that have been part of these periodic shifts. It is important to investigate some prior perspectives on marketing to provide a better understanding of how marketing is perceived today and why there is so much confusion around what truly constitutes marketing.

1-2a The Production Orientation

The **production orientation** focuses on marketing as a messenger. Marketing is seen as a way to let customers know about products and assumes that those customers will beat a path to the producer's door.

This perspective can best be described as the "field of dreams" orientation, thanks to the movie of the same name in which a character states, "If you build it, they will come." The production orientation focuses on products because of a lack of product options in the marketplace. Companies are free to create whatever products they deem appropriate, and customers have to accept what is offered.

1-2b The Sales Orientation

The **sales orientation** is highlighted by the increased power of customer choice. Companies

Henry Ford of the Ford Motor Company once stated, "Any customer can have a car painted any colour that he wants, so long as it is black." Ford was describing the line of Model T cars that were available to the customer. His perspective is a great example of the production orientation way of thinking.

Stocksearch/Alamy Stock Photo

no longer simply produce a product and expect willing customers to be waiting to buy whatever they are selling. Sales techniques were established and evolved to convince consumers to buy, giving consumers choice and ensuring companies focused on creating market share and building sales volume in a highly competitive environment.

Sales pitches are encouraged under this orientation, in which savvy salespeople use their understanding of human nature to convince customers to purchase their products. Answer the door at home to a company using the sales orientation, and you may see a well-dressed person attempting to sell vacuum cleaners or encyclopedias.

The need to coax the customer is paramount in the sales orientation. Behind this belief, companies place resources, specifically sales materials (brochures, print ads, etc.) that are used in great quantities to encourage sales of their products. Companies respond to a marketplace with more competition by overwhelming customers with promotional activities that focus on the hard sell.

Today, some companies still believe in the importance of hard selling to customers. Companies are still

production orientation a focus on manufacturing and production quantity in which customers are meant to choose based on what is most abundantly available

sales orientation hard selling to the customer, who has greater choice thanks to more competition in the marketplace

Old Visuals/Alamy Stock Photo

using aggressive sales tactics to entice customers, which is why consumers associate marketing with selling and why marketing is often considered intrusive.

The majority of companies and marketers do not subscribe to a marketing approach heavy only on selling. While sales makes up an important part of the marketing offering, it is only one part of the promotional tools available to today's marketer. Management thinker and innovator Peter Drucker put it best: "There will always, one can assume, be a need for some selling. But the aim of marketing is to make selling superfluous. The aim of marketing is to know and understand the customer so well that the product or service fits him and sells itself. Ideally, marketing should result in a customer who is ready to buy."[4]

1-2c The Marketing Company Orientation

The **marketing company orientation** is highlighted by the coordination of marketing activities—advertising, sales, and public relations—into one department in an organization. Much of how a marketing department is organized is based on the need to include those elements. The job of this department is to better understand the customer rather than just trying to sell to them.

As society evolves and consumers become more sophisticated, products and services previously seen as exclusive and out of reach are now seen as possible purchases. In this orientation, customers are grouped into market segments, with marketing professionals tasked with understanding their customer before making their move.

A term that is important in many orientations, and very much so in a marketing company orientation, is the *marketing concept*. The marketing concept focuses on linking the needs of customers with the competencies of an organization seeking to meet those needs.

In bringing the elements of the marketing company orientation together, it becomes clear that marketing and persuasion are intermixed. Marketing professionals focus on how to be shrewder about convincing customers to buy. Emotions are tied to basic-need products, higher-order benefits are attached to everyday products, and the customer is as much of a target of focus as the product.

However, this stage in the marketing orientation process is not devoid of any counteraction from the customer. Consumers are becoming shrewd themselves, as they begin to ask for more from the companies providing them products and services. While consumers are focused on aspects of value and service, they begin to seek out new ways to satisfy their needs. As seen by the prominence of the sharing phenomenon, through companies like Uber and Airbnb, consumers flock towards new offerings that satisfy their needs in ways not considered before. Companies can no linger simply focus on persuasion to a passive customer. The customer begins to demand more from the companies that serve them, both for them and for society at large.

1-2d Societal Marketing Orientation

It is apparent when we distill the marketing concept down to a basic idea (give customers what they want) that its pursuit can have potentially unsavoury consequences (what if what they want isn't good for them?). Dealing with this challenge created the **societal marketing orientation**, where looking at not only what the customer wants but also what society wants becomes a dual emphasis.

Societal marketing examines the longer-term impacts on the customer and the environment when customers seek to satisfy needs. New movements, such as recycling and waste reduction, sought out companies' solutions to deal with greater consumerism. Health issues relating to product use are at the forefront of this orientation, with greater awareness of the safety and dietary issues attached to products. This orientation brings a greater

marketing company orientation a strong emphasis on the marketing concept and development of a more comprehensive approach to understanding the customer

societal marketing orientation looking not only at the customer but expanding marketing efforts to include aspects from the external environment that go beyond a firm's customers, suppliers, and competitors

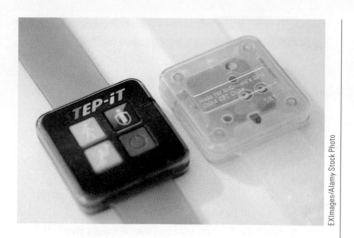

government involvement in consumer needs and wants. Thanks to better customer education and extremely strict promotional restrictions, sales of products like cigarettes have dropped drastically. Industries and companies are placing an emphasis on self-regulation before more strict government involvement created bottom-line and public relations issues.

A signpost for change in societal marketing was the Happy Meal. McDonald's signature meal has long been a target for critics who argue that the fast-food giant has used it to attract young customers. In 2011, the Happy Meal began to offer more nutritious options, such as yogurt and a "mini" size of fries (31 grams). In 2012, apple slices were offered as a replacement for french fries. In 2013, McDonald's announced it would provide health information on the Happy Meal boxes that touts healthier food choices.

In 2016, McDonald's offered a rather unusual toy in its Happy Meals. In conjunction with the 2016 Rio Olympics, McDonald's offered a "Step-iT," a fitness tracker for kids. The device was in the form of a watch that children could wear to monitor the steps they take each day. This offer was clearly aimed at responding to concerns over the types of toys on offer at the food retailer. A recent study by the Robert John Wood Foundation showed that McDonald's most often targeted children with toys and movie tie-ins, rather than food. The Step-iT was an attempt to allay these concerns; however, the resulting fallout from the Step-iT distracted from any focus on the health of this new toy. The plastic wristband on the Step-iT was found to cause rashes and other skin irritations. This forced McDonald's to recall 3.9 million units.[5] The company offered a free replacement toy, yogurt tube, or apple slices as a replacement—no french fries or Chicken McNuggets to solve this problem.

1-2e Relationship Marketing Orientation

Today, the relationship marketing orientation is about developing a real and sustainable relationship with the customer. As Kevin Roberts (he of the "marketing is dead" proclamation) said, marketing has to go from "interruption to interaction."[6] This phrase means that marketing can no longer look for a one-off sale; marketing has to focus on taking steps to truly engage with the customer. Engagement is the focus of this orientation, aided by the use of two essential customer-based strategies: customer satisfaction and relationship marketing.

CUSTOMER SATISFACTION Customer satisfaction is the customer's evaluation of a good or service in terms of whether that good or service has met the customer's needs and expectations. Failure to meet a customer's needs and expectations results in the customer's dissatisfaction with the good or service.[7] Keeping current customers satisfied is just as important as attracting new customers—and a lot less expensive. One study showed that reducing customer attrition by just 5 to 10 percent could increase annual profits by as much as 75 percent.[8] A 2 percent increase in customer retention has the same effect on profits as cutting costs by 10 percent.[9] Firms that have a reputation for delivering high levels of customer satisfaction tend to do things differently from their competitors. When top management is obsessed with customer satisfaction, employees throughout the organization are more likely to understand the link between how they perform their job and the satisfaction of customers. The culture of such an organization focuses on delighting customers rather than on selling products.

RELATIONSHIP MARKETING Relationship marketing is a strategy that focuses on keeping and improving relationships with current customers. This strategy assumes that many consumers and business customers prefer to keep an ongoing relationship with one organization rather than to switch continually among providers in their search for value. Disney is a good example of an organization focused on building long-term relationships with its customers. Disney managers understand that their company creates products and experiences that become an important part of people's lives and memories. This understanding has made Disney a leader in doing "right by the customer"—starting with the front-line cast members who interact directly with

customer satisfaction
customers' evaluation of a good or service in terms of whether it has met their needs and expectations

relationship marking a strategy that focuses on keeping and improving relationships with current customers

the public and encompassing all employees in all departments, who assess each decision based on how it will affect the customers and their relationship with the Disney brand.

CUSTOMER RELATIONSHIP MANAGEMENT

An important result of the relationship marketing orientation has been the concept of customer relationship management (CRM). While born as a data-mining system to help marketers understand each customer on an individual level, CRM best serves the ultimate goal of meeting the needs of customers and building relationships.

A key aspect of relationships—and any CRM system—is trust. To build trust, companies have to be willing to share their stories with customers and listen to and act on what customers desire. Doing this has not always been possible when companies use data mining from various sources, but it is possible with social and mobile marketing.

Creating a 24/7/365 relationship with customers is now possible, if companies are willing to plug in to the online world, an arena not only for exchange but also for true communication.

In the days of Henry Ford, door-to-door salesmen, and real-life Mad Men, there was never the opportunity to understand and target individual customers. However, this goal is now possible. Just head to a popular social media site, and you will find an interactive world with endless potential.

An important chapter in this text (Chapter 9) is all about CRM and will pull all the pieces together and show the possibility of truly evolving from "interruption to interaction."

1-3 KEY MARKETING TERMS

Now that we have seen the past and given an indication of the future of marketing, it is important to cover some of the fundamental aspects of marketing that every student of marketing should know. These ideas will form the basis of all remaining chapters and will provide you with the necessary tools to discuss and learn about marketing.

1-3a Exchange

One desired outcome of marketing is an **exchange**—people giving up one thing to receive another thing they would rather have. Normally, we think of money as the medium of exchange. We "give up" money to "receive"

the goods and services we want. Exchange does not, however, require money. Two people may barter or trade such items as baseball cards or oil paintings.

CUSTOMER VALUE Customer value is the relationship between benefits and the sacrifice necessary to obtain those benefits. Customer value is not simply a matter of high quality. A high-quality product that is available only at a high price will not be perceived as good value, nor will bare-bones service or low-quality goods selling for a low price. Instead, customers value goods and services that are of the quality they expect and are sold at prices they are willing to pay. Value can be used to sell both a Mercedes-Benz and a $3 frozen dinner.

MARKET SEGMENTS Market segments are groups of individuals, families, or companies that are placed together because it is believed that they share similar needs. As we saw in the discussion of the evolution of marketing earlier in this chapter, segmentation has gone from not being done at all to being done at an almost individual level. Market segments form the core of marketing efforts because they represent the source of customer needs.

To target specific market segments, much has to be done to research the lives, trends, and needs of a particular group. Later in the book, we will look at how marketing research (Chapter 5), consumer

exchange people giving up one thing to receive another thing they would rather have

customer value the relationship between benefits and the sacrifice necessary to obtain those benefits

CHAPTER 1: An Introduction to Marketing

The Force is with Disney

A recent example of Disney's relationship marketing was the case of an eight-year-old boy with autism who visited Disney World's Hollywood Studios theme park in Florida in June 2013. The boy, Josiah, had been looking forward to participating in the Jedi Training Academy—and just as he was to enter the stage to "fight" Darth Vader, the Florida skies opened up, and the rest of the event was rained out. Josiah was crestfallen, and his mother was worried he would retreat into his own world. The mother, Sharon Edwards, rushed over to the Disney employee playing the "Jedi Master" and explained the situation. The actor, David Piggott, told her in a hushed voice to meet him at the side of the building.

David, still in character as the Jedi Master, handed Josiah a lightsabre signed by Darth Vader. Josiah was ecstatic; he had gone from devastation to elation in minutes thanks to a kind act by this Disney employee.

Sharon decided she had to share this experience, so she wrote a post in her blog called "The Most Beautiful Ruined Moment," describing their encounter with an employee who went beyond his duty to make a memorable moment for her son. Soon, the blog was being passed around social media and on autism family support websites, and within days her blog had hundreds

Courtesy of Sharon Edwards and David Piggott

of thousands of views. As word spread, new media began to get involved, and the story travelled around the world. Sharon had been worried that the publicity from this incident might get David Piggott (the Jedi Master) in trouble for not following protocol. Instead, Disney responded by saying that it will be using this incident as an example of "good customer relations."

Sources: John I. Carney, "A Jedi Master and the Blog Side of the Force," *Times-Gazette*, June 19, 2013, www.t-g.com/story/1979291.html (accessed September 2013); and Sharon Edwards, "The Most Beautiful Ruined Moment," June 13, 2013, http://writeshesays.wordpress.com/2013/06/13/the-most-beautiful-ruined-moment/ (accessed September 2013).

decision making (Chapter 6), and business marketing (Chapter 7) help provide the necessary tools to develop strong market segments (Chapter 8).

BUILDING RELATIONSHIPS Attracting new customers to a business is only the beginning. The best companies view new-customer attraction as the launching point for developing and enhancing a long-term relationship. Companies can expand their market share in three ways: attracting new customers, increasing business with existing customers, and retaining current customers. Building relationships with existing customers directly addresses two of the three possibilities and indirectly addresses the other.

THE MARKETING MIX The marketing mix—also known as the 4Ps of marketing—refers to product, price, place, and promotion. Each of the 4Ps must be studied and developed to create a proper strategy to go after a market segment:

- **Product** relates to the tangible and intangible aspects of a company's offering. A product could be a can of soup or a virtuoso ballet performance; both

Research In Motion—A Cautionary Tale

In the early 2000s, Research In Motion (RIM) was touted as an unbelievable success story. BlackBerrys were omnipresent and seen in the hands of world leaders (Barack Obama) and celebrities (Kim Kardashian). With a security system beyond reproach and a messaging system that was as simple as it was addicting, the Blackberry and Research In Motion had arrived. So what went wrong? Look at the magazine photo below that shows a BlackBerry beside ancient relics, showing it as a relic.

Among the many things that went wrong was RIM's lack of interest in researching and understanding customer needs. The BlackBerry was created to provide security and messaging—but what did consumers want? In 2007, research was showing that consumers were looking for "candy bar phones" that would have a simple user interface and a single touch screen. What did BlackBerry put out to market? The Pearl Flip, a flip phone that consumers were no longer interested in. A member of RIM's customer base management team noted the interaction between the sales team that wanted the candy bar phone and the company's development team: "All the sales guys were like…we asked you for big screens, touchscreens, more of these candy bar styles. And they were like 'Yeah, but we came up with this really cool technology about the hinge. Look at how this works.' There is probably still a warehouse full of them." In the end, customers stopped buying BlackBerrys, and app makers stopped producing applications for BlackBerry devices.

Bloomberg Businessweek

How BlackBerry Became A Relic

Used with permission of Bloomberg L.P. Copyright © 2017. All rights reserved.

Andrew Twort/Alamy Stock Photo

Research In Motion focused too much on its platform and security features and forgot about the customer. The makers of the BlackBerry failed to see that consumers, not businesses, would lead the smartphone market in the future. Consumers were looking for touch screens and a fully interactive communication device. RIM gave consumers keyboards and security features they did not ask for. There was never an attempt to evolve with customers and their changing needs. Blackberry suffered from the "Field of Dreams" belief—if you build it, they will come. Soon customers might have to visit a museum to see what a BlackBerry looks like.

Source: Felix Gillette, Diane Brady, and Caroline Winter, "The Rise and Fall of BlackBerry: An Oral History," *BusinessWeek*, December 5, 2013, www.businessweek.com/articles/2013-12-05/the-rise-and-fall-of-blackberry-an-oral-history (accessed August 4, 2014).

companies will need to look at what needs are being satisfied and how to best package all the aspects of the offering so that the consumer will be satisfied.

- **Price** relates to the quantifying of a value in exchange for a company's offering. Competition is a significant issue here, as are customer perception and economic factors. Setting the right price is all about taking those factors into consideration and making the best decision that satisfies the bottom line and the customer.

- **Place** relates to much of the behind-the-scenes activities of making an offering available to the customer. This is the world of channels and logistics, where decisions made on how to get a company's product to market could be more important than the product itself.

- **Promotion** relates to what most people believe marketing to be about. These are the most visible activities of marketing, the ones that get into the news and

CUSTOMER VALUE

Marketers interested in customer value

- offer products that perform
- earn trust through loyalty programs
- avoid unrealistic pricing by communicating clearly
- give consumers the facts and the opportunity to learn more
- offer an organization-wide commitment to service and after-sales support
- partner with consumers to co-create experiences that consumers want

the faces of customers. Trying to find the right balance of what techniques to use (including advertising) is a constant challenge, as is keeping a consistent feel and look.

1-4 WHY MARKETING MATTERS

Given that this chapter started out by proclaiming the death of marketing, the question that needs to be asked is *Why does marketing matter?* Here are a few compelling reasons.

1-4a Marketing Is Part of Every Company

No matter what discipline in business you choose to pursue, you will have customers. If you do not concern yourself with the customer, you will cease to have any (just ask BlackBerry).

All companies, from multinationals to independent consultants, need to be customer focused. We know now that marketing provides this customer focus; therefore, understanding marketing means understanding your customer.

Successful companies have a strong understanding of the importance of marketing. Apple, the incredibly successful technology firm, created a three-point marketing philosophy when it was founded in 1977. The first point of that philosophy is the most telling: "Empathy—we will truly understand [the customer's] needs better than any company." This fundamental belief lies at the core of many successful organizations, including Apple.[10]

1-4b Marketing Is a Rewarding Career

Marketing can provide both financial and personal rewards. Marketing graduates have the flexibility of seeking employment in any industry, profit or nonprofit, public or private. This is because there is an inherent need for marketing in any organization that has a customer—whether final consumers or businesses' customers.

Careers in marketing are varied and offer many opportunities to those looking for a constantly evolving and changing marketplace. There are entry level positions like marketing coordinators and marketing analysts; these positions offer an opportunity for aspiring marketers to learn the skill set necessary to be successful in marketing. These are often challenging roles that are rewarded with greater opportunity and responsibility. As you become versed in the world of marketing, more senior level positions become available. Job titles like marketing manager, project manager, and vice president of marketing all display the importance of leadership and management while still applying the basic concepts of marketing along with advance techniques of analysis and strategy.

A great advantage to a career in marketing lies in the variety of industries in which marketing jobs are present. Although there are many jobs in the areas of advertising, product management, and marketing research, there are also many opportunities to apply the concepts of marketing to various situations. Numerous marketing opportunities can be found in government (at the municipal level especially), but also in sports, the arts, and nonprofit worlds. There is no shortage of opportunity in the field of marketing—finding the right opening often comes down to how well students can learn the material (like reading a textbook like this) and combine that with skills that are invaluable in creating a career in marketing.

To excel and advance in the field of marketing, strong communication and analytical skills are essential. Now that we know that marketing forms a fundamental part of any organization, a good marketer will understand the importance of working with other departments to ensure customer needs are met. As well, managers in marketing will deal constantly with uncertainty, so being able to analyze diverse and often divergent information will be key in becoming a successful marketing professional.

1-4c Marketing Provides an Important Skill Set

Even if your career aspirations are not in the field of marketing, you will still need to sell yourself to a future employer. Skills developed when learning marketing—how to understand needs, research trends, create an offering, and communicate benefits—all relate back to a person's job search.

Brett Wilson, who is quoted on his views of marketing in the picture on this page, is a successful Canadian entrepreneur and former panellist on the television show *Dragons' Den*. He has noted the importance of marketing as part of the skill set of any aspiring businessperson. When asked about his best business advice, Wilson stated, "Study marketing, entrepreneurship, and philanthropy. The incredible relevance of these courses merits mention. You cannot over-study these life-enhancing courses at any stage in your career." [11]

1-4d Marketing Is Part of Everyday Life

The tasks in marketing, as we have seen in this chapter, go well beyond a simple advertisement or sales call. Marketing includes important tasks that may not always be associated with marketing—such as distribution—that ensure that the products are on store shelves or delivered from a favourite website.

Being informed about marketing means being an informed consumer. Most Canadians' lives are full of activities and tasks that will have them confronting marketing messages from numerous organizations. By learning about marketing, you will be better able to discern a good message from a bad one and hold those companies that are targeting you to a higher standard.

Malcolm Taylor/Getty Images

Marketing, in my mind, is invaluable and underrated by most people. [12]—Brett Wilson

You now have the necessary background and understanding of marketing. Turn the page to start learning about what marketing has to offer.

STUDY TOOLS

IN THE BOOK, YOU CAN:

✔ Rip out the Chapter in Review card at the back of the book.

ONLINE, YOU CAN:

✔ Stay organized and efficient with a single online destination with all the course material and study aids you need to succeed.

Go to nelson.com/student to access the digital resources.

SIDE LAUNCH
BREWING COMPANY
CONTINUING CASE

Side Launch Brewing Company

Beer Is Everywhere People Are

"Find out where people are going—and buy land before they get there." This quotation attributed to American Cherokee leader and Confederate Colonel William Penn Adair is from more than 150 years ago. Perhaps never, though, has a more poignant mantra for marketing been captured in one phrase.

For Side Launch Brewing Company, the award-winning craft brewery based in Collingwood, Ontario, being the best beer where people are going is a parallel philosophy. If marketing is about the discovery and satisfaction of customer needs, Side Launch, as founder Garnet Pratt suggests, wants to be the beer companion that marks these occasions, both good and bad, that accompany people through the milestones of their life. "When you think about the journey of your adult life, beer is just there, humbly being a part of it. Weddings, funerals, graduations, and birthdays. It's there even in your more routine activities. It's also waiting for you after you've mowed the lawn or had a hard day at work. It's there when you're among friends, or alone, it's just there. If you're a beer drinker, why wouldn't you want that beer to be the best beer?"

Marketing is accomplished when value is exchanged. Value is the solution to a need. But needs, as we'll discuss throughout the book, are not always obvious, nor do we even always know we have them. They sometimes knock us over the head with a direct and vivid message: "I'm hungry—feed me." But sometimes those needs will be encrypted in feelings that are less obvious: "I'm vulnerable—comfort me."

The latter is one of an infinite number of reasons for the rapid growth in popularity of craft beer. "The beer market has changed," asserts Chuck Galea, VP Sales and Marketing, "primarily because beer drinkers have changed. They are more sophisticated and know what really good beer tastes like. People now choose a beer to go along with a season, or an occasion, or even a food group. It's the new wine, you know, where there are beer tastings and beer food pairings. And Side Launch is right there now. We're getting in people's hands, they're trying us, they're liking us, and they're helping to tell our story."

Founding brewer Michael Hancock refers to his beers as "accessible." "My tagline for our Dark Lager is that it's the dark beer for people who don't think they like dark beer. Our Wheat Beer often appeals to people

who may not even like beer; you know, it was called 'banana beer' when it first came out as it had a totally different flavour profile due to the low level of hops." Michael knows of what he speaks—being one of the true pioneers of wheat beer brewing in all of North America. "Michael is the keeper of quality," adds Dave Sands, VP Operations, who has a pedigree of beer industry expertise, stemming from a formal postsecondary brewing education and over 12 years working with the two biggest beer conglomerates in the world (Anheuser-Busch InBev and Molson-Coors). "We start with the basis of a quality culture, which sets a level of expectation among the basic things. You find the best ingredients from the best suppliers and mix them with the highest standards of production—it's like cooking—you're going to end up with a fundamentally better product."

You'll be reading about Side Launch in a continuing case study throughout this book, as we view each chapter concept through the lens of Side Launch Brewing Company. You'll learn how, as Garnet puts it, Side Launch makes a product that is "approachable and drinkable" but is also "made well, and packaged well, delivered well, and sold well." But don't just take her word for it. Witness the wild 300 percent growth over its first three years, tuck in a handful of nationally sought-after beer awards, and mix in a healthy dose of consistently high beer reviews among the most influential ratings sites, and you'll soon see that the story of Side Launch is a story in marketing.

Questions

1. What is the "need" being satisfied through the sale of beer?

2. Is there anything different about the product (beer) that the Side Launch Brewing Company makes that pursues a more specific need?

3. What are some of the initial things you might consider to be a part of the Side Launch value proposition?

Side Launch Brewing Company

2 | The Marketing Environment, Social Responsibility, and Ethics

LEARNING OUTCOMES

2-1 Discuss the external environment of marketing, and explain how it affects a firm

2-2 Describe the competitive factors that affect marketing

2-3 Describe the regulatory factors that affect marketing

2-4 Describe the economic factors that affect marketing

2-5 Describe social factors that affect marketing

2-6 Explain the importance to marketing managers of current demographic trends

2-7 Describe technological factors that affect marketing

2-8 Discuss corporate social responsibility

2-9 Describe the role of ethics and ethical decisions in business

"Nothing is more important than preparation."

—Simon Sinek[1]

2-1 THE EXTERNAL MARKETING ENVIRONMENT

One of the most important roles of marketing managers is overseeing the development of the marketing mix. Recall from Chapter 1 that a marketing mix is the unique combination of product, place (distribution), promotion, and price strategies. (The marketing mix is also addressed in Chapter 3.) The marketing mix is, of course, under the firm's control and is designed to appeal to a specific group of potential buyers—the target market. A **target market** is a defined group of potential customers that managers feel is most likely to buy a firm's product.

Over time, firms adjust the marketing mix to reflect the changing needs and composition of the target market, brought on by the changes in the environment in which consumers live, work, and make purchasing decisions. Also, as markets mature, some new consumers become part of the target market; others drop out. Those who remain may have different tastes, needs, incomes, lifestyles, and buying habits than the original target consumers. They, along with their behaviours, will also be affected by fluctuations in the economy and changes in socio-political and technological events, as well as offerings from other competitors.

target market a group of people or organizations for which an organization designs, implements, and maintains a marketing mix intended to meet the needs of that group, resulting in mutually satisfying exchanges

Controllable and uncontrollable variables affect the target market, whether it consists of consumers or business purchasers. Although companies can control the marketing mix, as well as other internal activities of the business such as operations and finance, they cannot control elements in the external environment that continually evolve, thus moulding and reshaping the target market. Marketing managers can only shape and reshape the marketing mix to react to the external environment, in an attempt to influence the target market. However, they may not be as much at the mercy of the external environment as first perceived.

2-1a Understanding the External Environment

By understanding the external environment, marketing managers and the firms they work for can intelligently plan for the future. However, the environment neither rests nor takes time off. It is in constant motion—sometimes wreaking havoc like a hurricane, resulting in threats to a firm. At other times, it brings sunshine and blue sky as far as the eye can see, giving firms valuable opportunities. But it is possible to foresee most of these external forces. Many organizations assemble a team of specialists to continually collect and evaluate environmental information—a process called *environmental scanning.*

The factors within the external environment that are important to marketing managers can be classified as competitive, regulatory, economic, social, and technological factors. Often referred to as the CREST model, this scanning tool is shown in Exhibit 2.1.

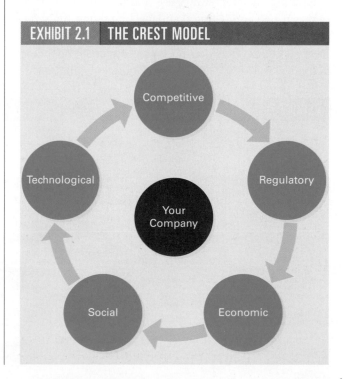

EXHIBIT 2.1   THE CREST MODEL

Competitive

Regulatory

Economic

Social

Technological

Your Company

CHAPTER 2: The Marketing Environment, Social Responsibility, and Ethics

2-2 COMPETITIVE FACTORS

The competitive environment encompasses the competitors a firm must face, both directly and indirectly, the relative size of the competitors, and the degree of interdependence within the industry. Management has little control over the competitive environment confronting a firm. In the 1979 *Harvard Business Review* article "How Competitive Forces Shape Strategy," business guru Michael Porter identified the five forces of competition² (see Exhibit 2.2) to assist in planning defence against such competition:

- **Direct competitors:** Competitors most closely matching a firm's product offering.

- **Substitutes:** Competitors whose products can satisfy the same need, but in different ways.

- **New entrants:** Competitors who might emerge due to entry barriers present in the industry.

- **Suppliers:** Business partners, such as materials producers, competing for profit margins from the firm and thus motivated to charge the highest price for goods or services provided.

- **Buyers:** Business partners, such as retailers, competing for profit margins from the firm and thus motivated to pay less for goods or services purchased from the firm.

The five forces of competition demonstrate how competition is not always for market share, as it is between two competing companies targeting the same market. It is also about competition over dollars, as seen in Exhibit 2.2, between a company and its suppliers and buyers. Either way, as Canadian population growth slows, costs rise, available resources tighten, and firms must work harder to maintain both their profits and their market share, regardless of the form of the competitive market. Firms are turning more and more to innovation across all parts of the marketing mix to chisel out some kind of advantage.

This creates a double-edged sword for companies in gathering information on any form of competition. Their competitors are leveraging the power of big data, analytics, and social media to gather information about their customers—and then relate to them across a host of different platforms, most of which are open for public viewing. The problem is that when the company gathers intelligence on its competitors, it is also being viewed by its competitors, creating an obvious dilemma. Firms *must* use social media to tell their story and build community, but in doing so they leave themselves wide open to being viewed by competitors.

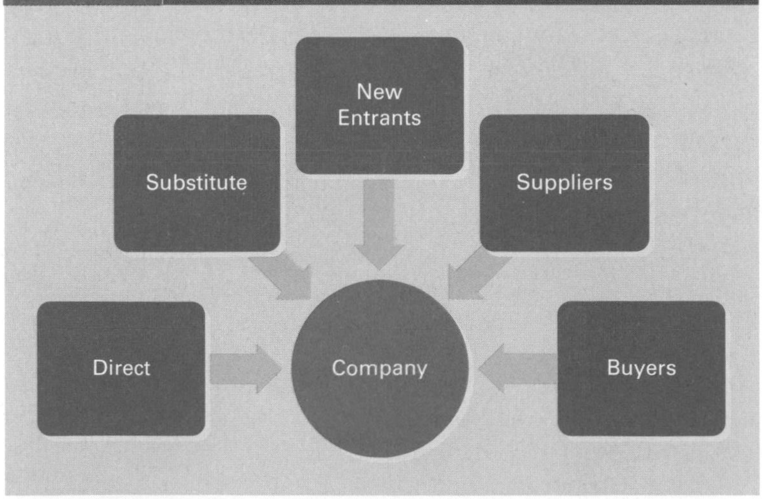

2-3 REGULATORY FACTORS

Every aspect of the marketing mix is subject to laws and restrictions created by regulators. It is the duty of marketing managers and their legal counsel not only to understand these laws and conform to them today, but also to track and predict the shaping and reshaping of laws. Failure to comply with regulations can have major consequences for a firm. Sometimes just sensing trends and taking corrective action before a government agency acts can help avoid the negative effects of regulation.

Marketers must balance caution with risk. It is all too easy for a marketing manager—or sometimes a lawyer—to say no to a marketing innovation that actually entails little risk. For example, an overly cautious lawyer could hold up sales of a desirable new product by warning that the package design could prompt a copyright infringement suit. Thus marketers need a thorough understanding of the laws established by the various levels of government and regulatory agencies to govern marketing-related issues.

It is also important to note that regulations don't just fall from the sky unexpectedly. They are, in fact, shaped by human beings who respond to events that affect them personally. Distracted driving laws, for instance, would never have come into place if innocent people weren't being seriously harmed. The fact that injury and death were resulting from distracted driving gave way to public outcry and eventually to distracted driving laws.

EXHIBIT 2.2 | FORCES OF COMPETITION

EXHIBIT 2.3 | SPECIALIZED FEDERAL LEGISLATION AFFECTING BUSINESS

Legislation	Major Provisions
Competition Act	Promotes the efficiency and adaptability of the Canadian economy. Expands opportunities for Canadian participation in world markets, while at the same time recognizing the role of foreign competition in Canada. Ensures that small and medium-sized enterprises have an equitable opportunity to participate in the Canadian economy. Provides consumers with competitive prices and product choices.
Consumer Packaging and Labelling Act	Requires prepackaged consumer products to bear accurate and meaningful labelling information to help consumers make informed purchasing decisions. It prohibits false or misleading representations and sets out specifications for mandatory label information.
Trade-marks Act	Regulates and protects trade names and trademarks.
Textile Labelling Act	Requires that textile articles bear accurate and meaningful labelling information to help consumers make informed purchasing decisions. It prohibits false or misleading representations and sets out specifications for mandatory label information.
Health Canada's Food and Drugs Act & Regulations	Establishes standards for the safety and nutritional quality of all foods sold in Canada.
Motor Vehicle Safety Act	Regulates the safety standards for the manufacture and importation of motor vehicles.
Personal Information Protection and Electronic Documents Act	Supports and promotes electronic commerce by protecting personal information that is collected, used, or disclosed in certain circumstances, by providing for the use of electronic means to communicate or record information or transactions.
Privacy Act	Governs the personal information handling practices of federal government institutions. Applies to all the personal information the federal government collects, uses, and discloses—whether about individuals or federal employees.

Source: Zikmund/D'Amico/Browne/Anthony/Monk/Donville. Effective Marketing, 1E. © 2008 Nelson Education Ltd. Reproduced by permission. www.cengage.com/permissions; Competition Bureau (https://www.competitionbureau.gc.ca; accessed January 17, 2017); Health Canada (https://www.canada.ca/en/health-canada.html; accessed January 17, 2017); Justice Laws Website (https://www.laws-lois.justice.gc.ca; accessed January 17, 2017); Office of the Privacy Commissioner of Canada (https://www.priv.gc.ca (accessed January 17, 2017).

2-3a Federal Legislation

The federal legislation affecting how business is conducted in Canada is administered by the **Competition Bureau**, an independent agency of Industry Canada. This bureau encompasses several branches and is responsible for enforcing laws covering such areas as bankruptcy, trade practices, competition, credit, labelling and packaging, copyrights, hazardous products, patents, and trademarks.[3] Some of the specialized federal legislation that affects businesses and business dealings is listed in Exhibit 2.3.

2-3b Provincial and Territorial Laws

In Canada, our constitution divides legal jurisdictions between the provincial or territorial legislatures and the federal government, thus allowing each level of government to legislate in the areas for which it has been given responsibility. For example, Québec's Bill 101 restricts the use of the English language in certain advertising and promotion material. A national company, such as Tim Hortons, may have to alter its advertising and store signage in Québec to be in compliance. Alberta allows the sale of alcoholic beverages by retailers, whereas Ontario has provincially run Liquor Control Board of Ontario (LCBO) outlets. Airlines, on the other hand, are under federal jurisdiction, and the provinces do not have direct powers to regulate airline companies. Marketing managers, especially those working for national companies, must be aware of the differences in each province's and territory's legal environment, and they also need a sound understanding of federal legislation that affects their industry.

2-3c Self-Regulation

Instead of facing explicit legislation from either the provincial, territorial, or federal governments, many business groups in Canada have formed associations that police themselves. This arrangement is called **self-regulation**. One such association is Advertising Standards Canada (ASC), established by Canada's advertising industry to monitor honesty and fairness in advertising. Advertising is a very visible form of communication strategy, and some firms come under fire from consumer groups regarding deception in their advertising. The ASC provides clear ethical guidelines to both advertisers and advertising agencies in its document "The Canadian Code of Advertising Standards."[4] Another group, the Canadian Association of Broadcasters (CAB), has established a code of ethics for its member television and radio stations. The

Competition Bureau the federal department charged with administering most marketplace laws

self-regulation programs voluntarily adopted by business groups to regulate the activities of their members

Canadian Marketing Association (CMA) has made great strides in developing guidelines and ethical practices for its thousands of member marketing firms.

CONSUMER PRIVACY A marketing manager must also be aware of the increasingly important area of consumer privacy, especially because of the vast amounts of data that almost any firm can collect and store by using the latest cloud technology. Everything from customer information to survey data is valuable to companies, but privacy issues need to be addressed. Firms should be able to justify the type of information they have and how it is to be used. Other issues of note are the security of information storage and the sale or transfer of information to others. Increasingly, and largely as a result of pressure from consumers' groups, governments are looking at developing, or have already developed, privacy legislation.

Canada's federal government, like the governments of many other countries, already has legislation relating to privacy. The Privacy Act (PA) and the Personal Information Protection and Electronic Documents Act (PIPEDA) were put in place to protect the privacy of our personal information and to ensure that its collection, use, and disclosure are both legal and ethical. The latest protection, established in July 2014 by the federal government to improve and protect consumer privacy, is referred to as the Canadian Anti-Spam Legislation (CASL). Its intent is to deter the most damaging and deceptive forms of spam. The CASL, which is enforced by the Canadian Radio-television and Telecommunications Commission (CRTC), the Competition Bureau, and the Privacy Commissioner, undergoes review and updates as deemed necessary. Canadian consumers are concerned about their privacy, but most are unaware of the details of this legislation. Therefore, marketers must be proactive in ensuring consumer privacy.

2-4 ECONOMIC FACTORS

In addition to competitive and regulatory factors, marketing managers must understand, forecast, and react to the economic environment. The three economic areas of greatest concern to most marketers are consumers' incomes, inflation, and recession.

2-4a Consumers' Incomes

As disposable (or after-tax) incomes rise, more families and individuals can afford the "good life." The median total family income in Canada was $78,870 in 2014; that means half of all Canadian households earned less than and the other half earned more than that amount.[5]

Education is the primary determinant of a person's earning potential. According to Human Resources and Skills Development Canada, the benefits of higher education include higher earnings, greater savings and assets, higher growth in earnings, and higher income during retirement. In addition, higher education reduces the risk of experiencing low income and unemployment. The benefits of higher education are consistent across all provinces.[6]

Along with willingness to buy, or ability to buy, income is a key determinant of target markets. The marketer who knows where the money is knows where the markets are. If you are seeking a location for a new Louis Vuitton retail store, a brand that caters to high-income–earning consumers, you would probably concentrate on areas where residents have incomes that are significantly higher than the median.

In Canada, 25.2 percent of households spend more than 30 percent of their income on shelter, far exceeding the affordable housing standards. Once many Canadians have paid for their essential living expenses, they are left with little or no spare cash. As a result, many Canadians have turned to credit to buy the things they want. Credit gives middle- and lower-income consumers the financial flexibility that only the rich used to enjoy. Since the 1990s, the median income for Canadian households has risen less than median household spending. How can the typical family afford to live? The result has been an increase in household debt. As of 2016, the average Canadian is now $1.65 in debt for every dollar they earn.[7] This situation has led to the growth of off-price retailers and the demand by Canadian shoppers for low prices. Debt, of course, means that consumers must eventually use their income to make interest payments instead of buying more goods and services. The compounding nature of interest payments, combined with the consumer behavioural trait

SpeedKingz/Shutterstock.com

of credit-based spending, can have serious negative results on individuals, which leads to reduced spending—which is bad for businesses in general.

2-4b Purchasing Power

Rising incomes don't necessarily mean a higher standard of living. Increased standards of living are a function of purchasing power. **Purchasing power** is measured by comparing income to the relative cost of a set standard of goods and services in different geographic areas, usually referred to as the cost of living. Another way to think of purchasing power is income minus the cost of living (i.e., expenses). In general, a cost-of-living index takes into account the costs of housing, food and groceries, transportation, utilities, healthcare, and miscellaneous expenses, such as clothing, services, and entertainment. The cost of living is generally higher in major urban markets. For example, a worker living in Toronto must earn nearly three times as much to have the same standard of living as someone in Sydney, Nova Scotia.

When income is high relative to the cost of living, people have more **discretionary income.** That means they have more money to spend on nonessential items (in other words, on wants rather than needs). This information is important to marketers for obvious reasons. Consumers with high purchasing power can afford to spend more money without jeopardizing their budget for such necessities as food, housing, and utilities. They also have the ability to purchase higher-priced necessities, such as a more expensive car, a home in a more expensive neighbourhood, or a designer handbag versus a purse from a discount store.

2-4c Inflation

Inflation is a measure of the decrease in the value of money, generally expressed as the percentage reduction in value since the previous year, which is the rate of inflation. Thus, in simple terms, an inflation rate of 5 percent means 5 percent more money is needed today to buy the same basket of products that was purchased last year. If inflation is 5 percent, you can expect that, on average, prices have risen about 5 percent over prices in the previous year. Of course, if pay raises are matching the rate of inflation, then employees will be no worse off with regard to the immediate purchasing power of their salaries.

Inflation pressures consumers to make more economical purchases and still maintain their standard of living. When managers create marketing strategies to cope with inflation, they must realize that, despite what happens to the seller's cost, buyers will not pay more for a product than the subjective value they place on it. No matter how compelling the justification might be for a 10 percent price increase, marketers must always examine the impact of the price increase on demand. Many marketers try to hold prices level as long as is practical. (See Chapter 13 for more information on the strategies marketers use during periods of high inflation.)

2-4d Recession

A **recession** is a period of economic activity characterized by negative growth. More precisely, a recession occurs when the gross domestic product falls for two consecutive quarters. The recession that began in December 2007 affected Canada less than the rest of the world. Statistics Canada's official report on the 2008–2009 slump shows it was a recession that was milder than two previous economic dips. Canada experienced a recession that was less severe and shorter than in the other G7 nations, and our financial institutions ended up in a much better position than those in the United States, where many required government aid to stay afloat. The effects of the 2008 recession are still being felt in high unemployment rates as the imbalances sparked by the event remain unaddressed.[8] However, rich Canadians report being financially better off after the 2008 recession than before.[9] To cope during the recession, many consumers switched to store brands, which on average cost less than manufacturers' brands. More consumers began using coupons than ever before, and group coupon sites started springing up all over. In a recession, consumers consider the price–value relationship deliberately before making purchases.

purchasing power a comparison of income versus the relative cost of a set standard of goods and services in different geographic areas

discretionary income the amount of money people have to spend on nonessential items

inflation a measure of the decrease in the value of money, expressed as the percentage reduction in value since the previous year

recession a period of economic activity characterized by negative growth, which reduces demand for goods and services

© iStockphoto.com/s-cphoto

The Canadian Press/Jonathan Hayward

Recessions can sometimes be isolated geographically as well. When world oil prices began to plunge in mid-2014, so too did the economy of the province of Alberta, which relied heavily on the oil industry. From 2014 to 2016, Alberta's GDP fell by 6.5 percent.[10] To add insult to injury, wildfires in 2016 led to the evacuation of over 80,000 residents of Fort McMurray, Alberta, and temporarily shut down production of oil sands operations. The cost of the shutdown alone shaved another 0.33 percent off Alberta's GDP and was significant enough to make a minor dent in the Canadian GDP.[11] The wildfires are a good example of an **environmental factor**. Environmental factors are often treated separately, as part of the natural environment. Like any of the environmental forces described here, the natural environment cannot be controlled by firms. That said, natural disasters, aside from the obvious human toll, usually end up affecting the economic environment, which is why we are discussing them here. Either way, in cases of geographically isolated peaks and valleys in the economy, national brands in particular have to manage their marketing strategy accordingly, providing one plan for the isolated area, and another for the rest of the country.

2-5 SOCIAL FACTORS

Social change is perhaps the most difficult external variable for marketing managers to forecast, influence, or integrate into marketing plans. Social factors include demographics, as well as our attitudes, values, and lifestyles. Social factors influence the products people buy, the prices paid for products, the effectiveness of specific promotions, and how, where, and when people expect to purchase products. In addition, in most cases, other environmental forces of concern to marketers often begin with social forces.

2-5a Marketing-Oriented Values

A *value* is a strongly held and enduring belief. Our values are key determinants of what is important and not important, what actions we take or do not take, and how we behave in social situations. Our values are typically formed through our interactions with family, friends, and other influencers, such as teachers, religious leaders, and politicians. The changing environment can also play a key role in shaping our values. Four basic values strongly influence attitudes and lifestyles of Canadian consumers:

- **Self-sufficiency:** Every person should stand on his or her own two feet.
- **Upward mobility:** Success should come to anyone who gets an education, works hard, and plays by the rules.
- **Work ethic:** Hard work, dedication to family, and frugality are moral and right.
- **Fairness:** No one should expect to be treated differently from anybody else.

These core values hold for a majority of Canadians today and have led to the perception that Canadians are trustworthy, family oriented, conservative, and increasingly eco-conscious. Canadian society is known to be tolerant and respectful of other cultures.

Values also influence our buying habits. Today's consumers are demanding, inquisitive, and discriminating. No longer willing to tolerate products that break down, we insist on high-quality goods that save time, energy, and often calories. Shoppers rank the characteristics of product quality as (1) reliability, (2) durability, (3) easy maintenance, (4) ease of use, (5) a trusted brand name, and (6) a low price. As shoppers, we are also concerned about nutrition and want to know what's in our food, and many of us have environmental concerns.

2-5b The Growth of Component Lifestyles

Canadian consumers today are piecing together **component lifestyles**. A lifestyle is a mode of living; it is the way we decide to live our lives. In other words, we choose products and services that meet our diverse needs and interests rather than conforming to traditional stereotypes.

In the past, a person's profession—for instance, banker—defined his or her lifestyle. Today, a person can be a banker and also a gourmet cook, a fitness enthusiast,

environmental factors
noncontrollable factors caused by natural disasters, which negatively or positively affect organizations

component lifestyles
mode of living that involves choosing goods and services that meet one's diverse needs and interests rather than conforming to a single, traditional lifestyle

a dedicated single parent, and an Internet guru. Each of these lifestyles is associated with different goods and services and represents a target audience. Component lifestyles increase the complexity of consumers' buying habits. The unique lifestyles of every consumer can require a different marketing mix.

2-5c Families Today

The Vanier Institute of the Family defines the family today as "any combination of two or more persons who are bound together over time by ties of mutual consent, birth and/or adoption or placement and who, together, assume responsibilities for variant combinations of some of the following:

- Physical maintenance and care of group members
- Addition of new members through procreation or adoption
- Socialization of children
- Social control of members
- Production, consumption, distribution of goods and services
- Affective nurturance—love"[12]

Despite a great deal of media coverage on the changing role of the family, it isn't so much the *role* of the family that has changed but the *makeup* of the family. Canadian families have an unprecedented level of diversity. Some men and women are raising children on their own without a partner; others are living together

Annette Shaff/Shutterstock.com

unmarried, with or without children; and gay and lesbian couples are caring for each other and raising children together. In addition, some adult children are following a trend of returning to the nest and living with their parents, and an increasing number of people are living alone.[13] Families today still demonstrate how, as individuals, we accept responsibility for each other.[14]

We face significant challenges in how we carry out our family responsibilities. For families today, two key resources are required—time and money—and they are both in short supply. To meet financial obligations it is common for couples to work and even, in some cases, hold multiple jobs. This situation results in further time poverty and affects the consumption choices that a family makes. The recent developments in technology combined with the time poverty of Canadian families has led to an increase in the use of social media not only as a communication tool but also as an information-gathering and shopping tool. Decision makers in families are increasingly using the Internet to do chores, plan trips, research products, find health information, read the news, seek out specials, and get coupons or participate in group savings. Consumers freely share the information they find with everyone in their personal networks.

2-6 DEMOGRAPHIC FACTORS

Another variable in the external environment and one extremely important to marketing managers is **demography**—the study of people's vital statistics, such as their age, race and ethnicity, and location. Demographics are significant because they are strongly related to consumer behaviour in the marketplace.

We turn our attention now to a closer look at age groups, their impact, and the opportunities they present for marketers. Why does tailoring the merchandise to particular age groups matter? One reason is that each generation enters a life stage with its own tastes and biases, and tailoring products to what customers value is key to sales. The cohorts have been named Generation Z, Generation Y/Millennials, Generation X, and baby boomers. You will find that each cohort group has its own needs, values, and consumption patterns.

2-6a Generation Z

Members of **Generation Z**, increasingly referred to as snowflakes (because they have been called "special and unique" by

demography the study of people's vital statistics, such as their age, race and ethnicity, and location

Generation Z people born between 1995 and 2009

their parents), are preadolescents and early adolescents born between 1995 and 2009. With attitudes, access to information, brand consciousness, technical sophistication well beyond their years, and purchasing power to match, these young consumers increasingly represent an attractive segment for marketers of all kinds of products.

The number of Gen Zs (also called tweens) who own cellphones has increased significantly over the years, with cellphone ownership among Grade 4 students at 25 percent and 50 percent for those in Grade 7.[15] This age group represents the fastest-growing segment in the cellphone market.[16] Add to this the dollar amounts that parents will spend on their tweens, and one grasps the importance and potential of this market. Gen Zs overwhelmingly (92 percent) recognize television commercials for what they are—just advertising—and indicate that they tune out ads simply because they are boring. Despite tweens' tech-savvy attitude, major social network sites, such as Facebook, are off limits to tweens under age 13 because of privacy and safety concerns. However, a national survey found that one-third of under-aged students surveyed in 2014 claimed they had a Facebook account anyway.[17]

The older Gen-Zers, those born between 1995 and 2000, represent just over 2.1 million people in Canada. As a group, they are extremely important to marketers because they wield significant purchasing power and are key influencers in family purchases. Teenagers are avid shoppers, spending on fashion, makeup, food, and entertainment. They are computer savvy, heavy users of social media, and active digital music and movie downloaders.

2-6b Generation Y

Those designated by demographics as **Generation Y** were born between 1979 and 2000. They began hitting their purchasing power around the turn of the millennium—hence the increasingly familiar cohort term of *Millennials.* Though Gen-Yers represent a smaller group than the baby boomers, whose birthdates span nearly 20 years, they are plentiful enough to put their own footprints on society. You will also note that inconsistencies within the study of demography often result in age overlap, as we note here, where the last four years of Gen Y overlap with the first four years of Gen Z.

Environics, a national research firm, estimates there are over 9 million Gen-Yers in Canada,

Generation Y people born between 1979 and 2000

accounting for over 27 percent of the country's population. But while Gen Yers are smaller in population than the baby boomer segment, Environics predicts the Yers will soon overtake baby boomers because boomers will be decreasing due to mortality.[18] Gen-Yers range from new career entrants to those in their late 30s. Those starting their careers are already making major purchases, such as cars and homes, and have a heightened sense of social responsibility. A survey conducted by Leger Marketing found a growing attitude among young Canadians of expecting their employer to be aware of their impact on the environment, and one-third reported they would quit their job over the environmental policies of their company.[19] Gen-Yers have been referred to as "trophy kids" as a result of their high expectations in the workforce and their increased sense of entitlement, which leads to a desire for a better work–life balance. Most Gen-Yers are the children of baby boomers and so are sometimes referred to as echo boomers. Because of economic necessity, many baby boomers in Canada are working well into their retirement age, thus shrinking the employment opportunities for Gen-Yers. As a result, Gen-Yers are facing unstable employment opportunities and struggling to establish themselves professionally. Those who have launched their careers often find themselves working side by side with baby boomers. The workplace dynamics of this demographic integration have not created widespread issues, according to an IBM Institute for Business Value study, which concluded both cohorts had similar values and goals, thus minimizing negative effects.[20]

Demographic patterns and economic realities make it still commonplace to find baby boomers and Gen Yers doing essentially the same job in the same company.

When the traditional "job hunt" fails to fulfill Gen-Yers with a dream career, they are more likely to be entrepreneurial. They have grown up in the face of a global financial crisis and significant meltdown in the financial markets. They are thus able to work with an uncertainty that other generations can't. They have the ability to network and can use social media to their advantage. They have seen people all around them forced out of work and are able to reinvent themselves as freelancers or consultants.

Researchers have found Gen-Yers to be

- **Impatient:** Because they have grown up in a world that has always been automated, they expect instant gratification.

- **Family oriented:** Gen-Yers had relatively stable childhoods and grew up in a very family-focused era, so they tend to have a stronger family orientation than the generation that preceded them.

- **Inquisitive:** Gen-Yers tend to want to know why things happen, how things work, and what they can do next.

- **Opinionated:** Gen-Yers have been encouraged to share their opinions by everyone around them. As a result, they feel that their opinions are always needed and welcomed.

- **Diverse:** Gen Y is the most ethnically diverse generation the nation has ever seen, so they're much more accepting overall of people who are different from themselves.

- **Good managers of time:** Their entire lives have been scheduled—from playdates to hockey to dance—so they've picked up a knack for planning along the way.

- **Savvy:** Having been exposed to the Internet and 24-hour cable TV news at a young age, Gen-Yers are not easily shocked. They're much more aware of the world around them than earlier generations were.[21]

- **Connected:** Gen-Yers use social networks, such as Facebook and Twitter, for both communication and commerce.

- **Life-balance seekers:** Having watched their baby boomer parents burn out from work, many Gen-Yers are more inclined to take care of themselves holistically, especially when raising their own families.

Finally, older Millennials are now parenting and are breaking the cycle of "helicopter parenting" initiated by the youngest of today's baby boomers and

GeorgeRudy/iStock/Thinkstock

Gen-Yers pursue balance in life, often integrating their children into activities that cultivate this value.

almost the entire Generation X cohort.[22] This will likely pave the way for more independent future generations of Canadians.

2-6c Generation X

Generation X—people born between 1966 and 1978—consists of more than 7 million consumers across Canada, including Justin Trudeau, who was sworn in as Canada's prime minister in 2015 at age 43. It is the first generation of latchkey children—products of dual-career households or, in roughly half the cases, of divorced or separated parents. Gen-Xers have been bombarded by multiple media since their cradle days; thus, they are savvy and cynical consumers.

Their careers launched and their families started, Gen-Xers are at the stage in life when a host of demands are competing for their time—and their budgets. As a result, Gen X spending is quite diffuse: food, housing, transportation. Time is at a premium for harried Gen-Xers, so they're outsourcing the

Generation X people born between 1966 and 1978

Generation X is smaller than and often overshadowed by the generations before and after it, but Gen-Xers have plenty of spending power as they raise families and progress in their careers.

Due to the volatility of Canada's economy since 2008, and lost retirement savings related to the recession, which began that year, many baby boomers have elected to stay in their careers for prolonged periods.

tasks of daily life, which include responsibilities such as housecleaning, dog walking, and lawn care. Because of demands on their time, Gen-Xers spend much more on personal services than any other age group.[23] Many Gen-Xers work from home.

Gen-Xers face the reality, however, that the generation ahead of them, having experienced a financial recession, which started in late 2007, may opt not to retire, thereby affecting the Gen-Xers' ability to maximize their income. In addition, as an impending pension crisis looms, the Gen-Xers may find themselves funding the retirement years of the baby boomers.[24] Although Gen-Xers are making and spending money, companies still sometimes tend to ignore them, focusing instead on the larger demographic groups—the baby boomers and Gen-Yers.

2-6d Baby Boomers—A Mass Market

Baby boomers make up the largest demographic segment of today's Canadian population. There are nine million **baby boomers** (people born between 1947 and 1965). The oldest have already turned 70. There are now more people 65 and over in Canada than there are aged 15 and younger.[25] With average life expectancy increasing, more and more Canadians over the age of 50 consider middle age to be a new start on life. People now in their 50s may well work longer than any previous generation; more men and women, given better health and uncertain economic cycles, are working in their careers longer than ever before.

The boomers' incomes will continue to grow as they keep working, especially those born toward the end

baby boomers people born between 1947 and 1965

of the cohort. In general, baby boomers are active and affluent, but a subsegment of boomers worry about the future and their own financial security.[26] Many retired boomers suffered major losses to their retirement savings during the financial crisis of 2008 that started in the banking sector. Younger baby boomers who are still employed are facing the financial challenges of high debt, reduced incomes, and the need to support their adult children who are still struggling to be self-sufficient after the recession years.[27] Nielsen research indicates that over the next decade, Canadian households will be smaller. With a tougher economy, those smaller households will spend less, and the shrinking economy will affect the salaries of the Gen-Yers and Gen-Xers. Despite the fact that baby boomer lifestyles, product preferences, and consumer behaviour may not seem in vogue, established firms and startups must maintain a keen focus on this cohort in addition to satisfying the needs of subsequent demographic groups. They are a powerful demographic (as they have always been) with a spending power of more than $1 trillion.

2-6e Population Shifts in Canada

Canada is a large country with a relatively small population that was, historically, spread out between rural and urban areas. Since the mid-1970s, however, the population has shifted out of rural areas so that now over 82 percent of Canadians are considered to be urban dwellers. The majority of these persons live in census metropolitan areas (CMAs), regions defined by Statistics Canada as comprising one or more municipalities situated around a major urban core, with a total population of at least 100,000.[28]

According to Statistics Canada, the Canadian population topped 36 million in October 2015.[29] More than 50 percent of the Canadian population lives in four major urban regions in Canada: the Golden Horseshoe in Ontario, Montreal and surrounding area, British Columbia's Lower Mainland, and the Calgary–Edmonton corridor. A Statistics Canada study observed that new parents and those between the ages of 25 and 44 were more likely than any others to move from an urban central municipality to a surrounding municipality or suburb.[30] Most of Canada's population growth comes from immigration, and 2015–2016 was a banner year for this growth with over 320,000 immigrants, close to 10 percent of whom were Syrian refugees.[31] The majority of immigrants are settling within Canada's largest urban centres, namely Toronto, Montréal, and Vancouver.[32] As a result, these urban core areas are the focus of many marketing programs by firms that are interested in reaching a large national yet very multicultural market.

2-6f Ethnic and Cultural Diversity

Multiculturalism refers to the peaceful and equitable coexistence of different cultures, rather than one national culture, in a country. More than 200 different languages are spoken in Canada and the trend in Canada is toward greater multiculturalism.

The largest urban centres or census metropolitan areas in Canada experience the greatest impact of multiculturalism. The *National Post* published the results of a report that found that in 2012, 20 percent of Canada's population spoke a foreign language at least periodically, with Chinese languages dominating this statistic, followed by Punjabi. Tellingly, the same study showed that over two million people speak neither of Canada's official languages at home.[33] These findings have major implications for any marketing program. Companies such as CIBC and Kruger have altered their advertising campaigns to reflect their changing customer profile and to provide information in other languages.[34] The service sector, in particular, has had to adapt quickly to this change in Canada's demographic makeup. A visit to a local bank or hospital in any urban centre will demonstrate the different needs that must be met in a culturally diverse population and the variety of languages that the services should be offered in. Consider, for example, that as stated in the study reported on by the *National Post*, more than 1.8 million people in the city of Toronto speak an "immigrant language."

The cultural diversity of our country and the trend to multiculturalism will require multicultural marketing

More and more foreign-born Canadians are using their native languages at home, rather than either English or French.

right at home. More than 20 percent of the visible minority population is under 15 years of age. This group will have a great impact in the decade ahead. Many of these young people can understand and converse in multiple languages and have adapted elements of numerous cultures into their lifestyle. These cultures influence their response to marketing messages and ultimately determine their buying behaviour. What does being a Canadian really mean to a marketer?

Recent immigrants to Canada are tech savvy. Young people from various cultures use the Internet for accessing information and making purchases, which has spawned new strategies for using the Internet to reach the diverse youth markets. Every cultural group has access to websites that cater to their specific culture—such as social networks, products, events, and links to their native country. These culture-specific websites present opportunities for firms to target specific ethnic groups.

2-7 TECHNOLOGICAL FACTORS

Technology is a critical factor in every company's external environment. Our ability, as a nation, to maintain and build wealth depends in large part on the speed and effectiveness with which we invent and adopt machines and technologies that lift productivity.

multiculturalism refers to the peaceful and equitable coexistence of different cultures, rather than one national culture, in a country

External technology is important to managers for two reasons. First, by acquiring a technology, a firm may be able to operate more efficiently or create a better product. Second, a new technology may render existing products obsolete, as in the case of the traditional film-based camera being replaced by digital camera technology. Staying technologically relevant requires a great deal of research and a willingness to adopt new technologies.

2-7a Research

Basic research (or pure *research*) attempts to expand the frontiers of knowledge but is not aimed at a specific, pragmatic problem. Basic research aims to confirm an existing theory or to learn more about a concept or phenomenon. For example, basic research might focus on high-energy physics. **Applied research**, in contrast, attempts to develop new or improved products.

2-7b Technology and the Future of Businesses

Of all the external environmental forces, technology is the fastest changing with, perhaps, the most significant impact on businesses. New technologies will create not only new industries but also new ways to develop products, compete, and meet customer needs. Such is the accelerated rate of technology that the very topics written here in this textbook will likely be "old news" by the time it ends up in your hands. With that disclaimer out of the way, here are five of Fast Company's Top Twelve Tech Trends of 2017.[35]

1. **Smart building materials:** Sensors will become prevalent in construction of houses and highways, both to maximize cost efficiency and to develop environmental sustainability.

2. **Synthetic food and cellular agriculture:** Plant proteins will be re-engineered into food that mimics meat, and the ability to grow food in a lab will be possible.

3. **Virtual reality vs. live performance:** Expensive live performances will be displaced by low-cost/high-engagement options from the home.

Distracted driving? How long before this becomes a familiar sight on Canadian roads? The driverless (autonomous) cars are coming.

riopatuca/Shutterstock.com

You won't have to be at the ACC to see Beyoncé's concert there—and you'll get a richer experience from your home.

4. **Autonomous driving:** Driverless cars (and trucks) will begin entering the marketplace. The goal—saving over one million lives per year currently lost to human error while driving.

5. **Spaces as participants:** Using sensors, places such as hospital rooms and public transit seating will be monitored to assess how people use these spaces, leading to improved design, greater efficiency, and better value for consumers.

2-8 CORPORATE SOCIAL RESPONSIBILITY

Corporate social responsibility (CSR) is a business's concern for social and environmental welfare. But really, CSR is the culmination of decades of accrued forces of the collective external environment (CREST), as explained so far in this chapter (see Exhibit 2.4). Since the end of World War II, these forces have accelerated along parallel tracks, helping businesses grow rapidly, but ultimately converging to a point where the advancement of society, caused largely through the growth of companies, has left the planet in a state of depleted resources, alarming environmental concerns, and wealth inequality. With due awareness and concern of these and other related issues, society has forced companies to pursue the **triple bottom line**—profitability, care for the planet, and care

basic research pure research that aims to confirm an existing theory or to learn more about a concept or phenomenon

applied research an attempt by marketers to use research to develop new or improved products

corporate social responsibility a business's concern for society's welfare

triple bottom line a business philosophy seen as the pursuit of profit while also benefiting society and the environment

EXHIBIT 2.4 CORPORATE SOCIAL RESPONSIBILITY

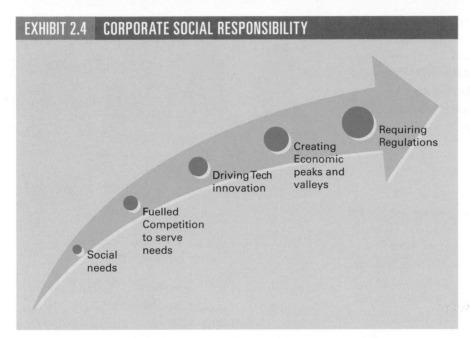

- Social needs
- Fuelled Competition to serve needs
- Driving Tech innovation
- Creating Economic peaks and valleys
- Requiring Regulations

for people. Thus, at a high level, CSR has evolved into a core value of any successful company, while at a nuts and bolts level, it is indeed a cost of doing business.

The integrated forces of the CREST environment have ultimately resulted in a very high standard of living in the developed world, while at the same time, drying up the earth's resources, creating a wealth divide, and risking environmental sustainability. This process of **social acceleration**, fuelled by the business cycle, has resulted in the need to implement heightened regulations of business practices regionally, federally, and internationally to protect people and the planet from the blind pursuit of profit by business. It has also introduced a permanent ethical dimension to business,

summed up by the concept of corporate social responsibility.

Total corporate social responsibility has four components: economic, legal, ethical, and philanthropic.[36] The **pyramid of corporate social responsibility** portrays economic performance as the foundation for the other three responsibilities (see Exhibit 2.5). At the same time that a business pursues profits (economic responsibility), however, it is also expected to obey the law (legal responsibility); to do what is right, just, and fair (ethical responsibilities); and to be a good corporate citizen (philanthropic responsibility). These four components are distinct but together constitute the whole. This reminds us that, at its roots, in its DNA, a business must be profitable in order to accommodate not only the needs of its customers and owners, but also the needs of society and the environment. Viewed this way, the pyramid of corporate social responsibility has, in effect, morphed into a cycle of corporate social responsibility.

2-8a Growth of Social Responsibility

The social responsibility of businesses is growing around the world and has become more than simply a fashionable expression. A 2015 study of CSR practices conducted by the *Harvard Business Review* on 142 executives attending Harvard Business School over a four-year period found a

EXHIBIT 2.5 PYRAMID OF CORPORATE SOCIAL RESPONSIBILITY

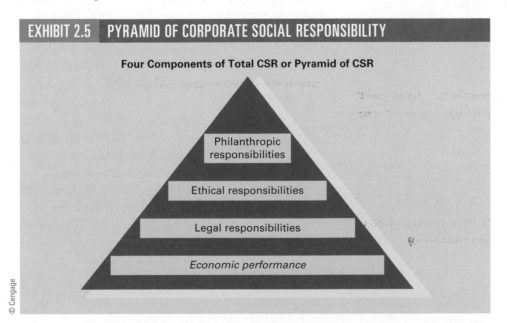

Four Components of Total CSR or Pyramid of CSR

- Philanthropic responsibilities
- Ethical responsibilities
- Legal responsibilities
- Economic performance

© Cengage

social acceleration the concept of exponentially rapid growth starting with human desire for improved products, spurring competitive pursuit of market share, driving innovation and technology, resulting in higher standard of living, but with new socio-environmental problems

pyramid of corporate social responsibility a model that suggests corporate social responsibility is composed of economic, legal, ethical, and philanthropic responsibilities and that the firm's economic performance supports the entire structure

wide array of differing definitions and degrees of CSR implementation. In their summarizing article, "The Truth About CSR," researchers concluded that "most companies practice a multifaceted version of CSR that runs the gamut from pure philanthropy to environmental sustainability to the active pursuit of shared value. Moreover, well-managed companies seem less interested in totally integrating CSR with their business strategies and goals than in devising a cogent CSR program aligned with the company's purpose and values."[37]

In Canada social responsibility has become increasingly professionalized and integrated across all levels within most organizations. According to Imagine Canada, a national program supporting public and corporate charitable giving, businesses have moved beyond simply writing a cheque to a more engaged and integrated approach to social responsibility that includes in-kind gifts, employee volunteerism, and sponsorships.[38]

Firms are realizing that corporate social responsibility isn't easy or quick. It works only when a firm engages a long-term strategy and effort and the strategy is coordinated throughout the organization. It doesn't always come cheap, and the payoff, both to society and to the firm itself, isn't always immediate. But consumers will patronize firms that are socially responsible.

2-8b Green Marketing

An outgrowth of the social responsibility movement is **green marketing**—the development and marketing of products designed to minimize negative effects on the physical environment. Not only can a company aid the environment through green marketing, but green marketing can often help the bottom line. Environmentally aware consumers tend to earn more and are more willing to pay a premium for green products.

To protect consumers from companies capitalizing on the green movement without substance, the Canadian Competition Bureau launched a guide that provides the

Stephen Mcsweeny/Shutterstock.com

The Canadian Press/Don Denton

business community with green marketing guidelines. While the guide is not law, the Competition Bureau will pursue deceptive environmental claims, fine violators, or remove products from store shelves. The guide suggests that environmental claims should be clear, specific, accurate, and not misleading, and that all environmental claims should be verified and substantiated.

A company known for its green marketing practices is S. C. Johnson & Son. This company developed the Greenlist process, which requires that its scientists evaluate all the company's product ingredients to determine their impact on the environment and to reformulate products to reduce that impact.[39] The use of this patented process led to the reformulation of Windex, resulting in a greener and more effective product.

2-9 ETHICAL BEHAVIOUR IN BUSINESS

Social responsibility and ethics go hand in hand. **Ethics** refers to the moral principles or values that generally govern the conduct of an individual or a group. Ethics can also be viewed as the standard of behaviour by which conduct is judged. Standards that are legal may not always be ethical, and vice versa. Laws are the values and standards enforceable by the courts. Ethics consists of personal moral principles and values, rather than societal prescriptions.

Defining the boundaries of ethicality and legality can be difficult. Often, judgment is needed to determine whether an action that may be legal is an ethical or unethical act. Also, judgment is required to determine whether an unethical act is legal or illegal.

green marketing the development and marketing of products designed to minimize negative effects on the physical environment

ethics the moral principles or values that generally govern the conduct of an individual or a group

Morals are the rules people develop as a result of cultural values and norms. Culture is a socializing force that dictates what is right and wrong. Moral standards may also reflect the laws and regulations that affect social and economic behaviour. Thus, morals can be considered a foundation of ethical behaviour.

Morals are usually characterized as good or bad. *Good* and *bad* have different connotations, including effective and ineffective. A good salesperson makes or exceeds the assigned quota. If the salesperson sells a new stereo or television set to a disadvantaged consumer—knowing full well that the person can't keep up the monthly payments—is the salesperson still considered to be good? What if the sale enables the salesperson to exceed his or her quota?

Good and bad can also refer to conforming and deviant behaviours. Any doctor in Canada who charges extra fees for fast-tracking patients on waiting lists for provincially funded procedures would be considered unprofessional. Such a doctor would not be conforming to the norms and laws of the medical profession or to the laws regarding universal healthcare set by our provincial or territorial legislatures and federal government. Bad and good are also used to express the distinction between criminal and law-abiding behaviour. And finally, different religions define good and bad in markedly different ways. A Muslim who eats pork would be considered bad, as would a fundamentalist Christian who drinks whisky.

2-9a Morality and Business Ethics

Today's business ethics consist of a subset of major life values learned since birth. The values business people use to make decisions have been acquired through family and educational and religious institutions.

Ethical values are situation specific and time oriented. Nevertheless, everyone must have an ethical base that applies to conduct in the business world and in personal life. One approach to developing a personal set of ethics is to examine the consequences of a particular act. Who is helped or hurt? How long-lasting are the consequences? What actions produce the greatest good for the greatest number of people? A second approach stresses the importance of rules. Rules come in the form of customs, laws, professional standards, and common sense. "Always treat others as you would like to be treated" is an example of a rule.

The last approach emphasizes the development of moral character within individuals. Ethical development can be thought of as having three levels:[40]

- *Preconventional morality,* the most basic level, is childlike. It is calculating, self-centred, even selfish, and is based on what will be immediately punished or rewarded.

- *Conventional morality* moves from an egocentric viewpoint toward the expectations of society. Loyalty and obedience to the organization (or society) become paramount. A marketing decision maker at this level would be concerned only with whether the proposed action is legal and how it will be viewed by others.

- *Postconventional morality* represents the morality of the mature adult. At this level, people are less concerned about how others might see them and more concerned about how they see and judge themselves over the long run. A marketing decision maker who has attained a postconventional level of morality might ask, "Even though it is legal and will increase company profits, is it right in the long run?"

2-9b Ethical Decision Making

Ethical questions rarely have cut-and-dried answers. Studies show that the following factors tend to influence ethical decision making and judgments:[41]

- **Extent of ethical problems within the organization:** Marketing professionals who perceive fewer ethical problems in their organizations tend to disapprove more strongly of unethical or questionable practices than those who perceive more ethical problems. Apparently, the healthier the ethical environment, the more likely marketers will take a strong stand against questionable practices.

- **Top-management actions on ethics:** Top managers can influence the behaviour of marketing professionals by encouraging ethical behaviour and discouraging unethical behaviour.

- **Potential magnitude of the consequences:** The greater the harm done to victims, the more likely marketing professionals will recognize the behaviour as unethical.

- **Social consensus:** The greater the degree of agreement among managerial peers that an action is harmful, the more likely marketers will recognize the action as unethical.

- **Probability of a harmful outcome:** The greater the likelihood that an action will result in a harmful outcome, the more likely marketers will recognize the action as unethical.

> **morals** the rules people develop as a result of cultural values and norms

The World's Top CSR Companies, 2016

Forbes Magazine published the following list produced by the Reputation Institute (RI), which conducts annual studies to determine how people feel about brands with whom they interact. The research produces an aggregate weighted average score, but is based almost entirely on perception of people—that is, how responsible people believe firms to be. RI surveyed 240,000 people across 15 countries to arrive at the following list.

Ranking	Company	Score	Ranking	Company	Score
1	Google	75.4	11	Canon	72.5
2	Microsoft	75.1	12	Johnson & Johnson	71.7
3	The Walt Disney Company	74.7	13	Sony	71.5
4	BMW	73.9	14	Michelin	71.4
5	Lego	73.8	15	Ferrero	71.3
6	Daimler	73.3	16	Adidas	71.2
7	Apple	73.3	17	Nintendo	70.8
8	Rolls-Royce	73.1	18	Nestlé	70.0
9	Rolex	73.0	19	IKEA	69.6
10	Intel	72.9	20	Samsung	69.8

Source: Forbes, The Companies with the best CSR Reputations in the World in 2016, http://www.forbes.com/sites/karstenstrauss/2016/09/15/the-companies-with-the-best-csr-reputations-in-the-world-in-2016/#3bba794a7b83.

- **Length of time between the decision and the onset of consequences:** The shorter the length of time between the action and the onset of negative consequences, the more likely it is that marketers will perceive the action as unethical.

- **Number of people to be affected:** The greater the number of persons affected by a negative outcome, the more likely it is that marketers will recognize the behaviour as unethical.

2-9c Ethical Guidelines

Many organizations have become more interested in ethical issues. Companies of all sizes have developed a **code of ethics** as a guideline to help marketing managers and other employees make better decisions.

code of ethics a guideline to help marketing managers and other employees make better decisions

Creating ethics guidelines has several advantages:

- The guidelines help employees identify the business practices their firm recognizes as being acceptable.

- A code of ethics can be an effective internal control on behaviour, which is more desirable than external controls, such as government regulation.

- A written code helps employees avoid confusion when determining whether their decisions are ethical.

- The process of formulating the code of ethics facilitates discussion among employees about what is right and wrong, which ultimately leads to better decisions.

Businesses must be careful, however, not to make their code of ethics too vague or too detailed. Codes that are too vague give little or no guidance to employees in their day-to-day activities. Codes that are too detailed encourage employees to substitute rules for judgment.

For instance, if employees are involved in questionable behaviour, they may use the absence of a written rule as a reason to continue their behaviour, even though their conscience may be telling them otherwise. Following a set of ethical guidelines will not guarantee the "rightness" of a decision, but it will improve the chances that the decision will be ethical.

Although many companies have issued policies on ethical behaviour, marketing managers must still put the policies into effect. They must address the classic "matter of degree" issue. For example, marketing researchers often resort to deception to obtain unbiased answers to their research questions. Asking for a few minutes of a respondent's time is dishonest if the researcher knows the interview will last 45 minutes. Not only must management post a code of ethics, but it must also give examples of what is ethical and unethical for each item in the code. Moreover, top management must stress to all employees the importance of adhering to the company's code of ethics. Without a detailed code of ethics and top management's support, creating ethical guidelines becomes an empty exercise. The Canadian Marketing Association's code of ethics outlines its purpose.

WHAT'S EXPECTED OF CANADIAN MARKETERS

The [Canadian Marketing Association's] Code of Ethics and Standards of Practice . . . is designed to establish and maintain standards for the conduct of marketing in Canada.

Marketers acknowledge that the establishment and maintenance of high standards of practice are a fundamental responsibility to the public, essential to winning and holding consumer confidence, and the foundation of a successful and independent marketing industry in Canada.

Members of the Canadian Marketing Association recognize an obligation—to the consumers and the businesses they serve, to the integrity of the discipline in which they operate, and to each other—to practise to the highest standards of honesty, truth, accuracy, fairness, and professionalism.

Source: From "Code of Ethics and Standards of Practice," Canadian Marketing Association, www.the-cma.org.

STUDY TOOLS

IN THE BOOK, YOU CAN:

✔ Rip out the Chapter in Review card at the back of the book.

ONLINE, YOU CAN:

✔ Stay organized and efficient with a single online destination with all the course material and study aids you need to succeed.

Go to nelson.com/student to access the digital resources.

SIDE LAUNCH
BREWING COMPANY
CONTINUING CASE

Side Launch Brewing Company

Yeast Gone Wild

In August 2016, at the peak of Ontario cottage country's most drink-worthy time of year, a craft brewery's worst nightmare came true. Through its own quality assurance testing, Side Launch noticed something wrong with a batch of its celebrated Wheat Beer. "It had been turning sour," founding brewer Michael Hancock vividly recalls. "We were able to determine that it was a brew that had been in the market for three or four weeks, and specifically [involved] cans which had not been refrigerated." Through Michael's excessively detailed documentation, which follows every drop as it goes through the Side Launch brewing process, they were able to correlate the release date of the beer with the batch of yeast used, to narrow down the problem. "We knew that it was the second generation of a particular yeast that was introduced in April or May and had an infection of some kind."

A side note here is necessary for clarification. Brewer's yeast is one of the four main ingredients of beer (along with grain, hops, and water). It is, by definition, a fungus, one that is used in the fermentation process, and it is commonly re-used up to four times before it is disposed of. Thus, because it is "living," infection is not uncommon. Finding out which batch is infected, however, is a bit of a needle in a haystack proposition. "We built a family tree— it took up most of the lab—and we could quickly predict which brews would likely be sour or go sour." Determining the source of the problem allowed Side Launch to calculate exact locations of where the infected beer had gone.

"As the whole thing was unfolding," recalls founder Garnet Pratt, "I remember looking at Michael and . . . and we've had our differences before, but in this case we both knew in this instance that there was only one thing we could do—recall product and make it square with our customers." In all, 380 hectolitres of beer were lost, the majority of which had already gone to market, but a significant amount was disposed of onsite due to suspected contamination related to the yeast issue.

Needless to say, the episode resulted in a substantial financial loss to the company. It also serves to demonstrate the concepts covered in this chapter— the marketing environment, and the role that ethics and social responsibility play within this orbit. First, Side Launch lacked the resources and sophistication to identify the problem before the beer went to market. That's a weakness, which they have since corrected. Second, the leadership, once made aware of the situation, made a sound ethical decision to bite the bullet, take the loss, and do the right thing. A strength to be sure, and one for which Side Launch was widely praised. Third, society's demand for transparency, regulators'

requirement for quality of consumer goods, and the buzzing technology that is social media, were all threats in this case—uncontrollable and potentially damaging. Yet as with many threats, how a firm reacts can flip them into opportunities, which is exactly what Side Launch did in this case.

"We used social media and traditional media to spread the word, and we set up a QA email account and encouraged people to write in to us. I personally handled at least 50 of those," recalls Michael.

Today, sitting inconspicuously on a desk in the brewery's lab is a small cylinder-shaped instrument no larger than a household blender. It is a DNA tester, which is able to identify things like yeast infections within hours of beer coming off the assembly line. The Wheat recall of 2016 forced Side Launch to look at its operations and ask, "How can we avoid this in the future?" It also demonstrates how honest SWOT analysis is not merely an annual exercise, rather it is done all the time. In this case, it revealed a weakness—lack of immediate testing—which directed Side Launch to a solution, cloaked in the opportunity of an affordable testing tool.

Questions

1. The case refers to society's demand for transparency as a threat. Threats are generally negative occurrences for a firm. Why is transparency here treated as a threat?

2. Bad beer, as opposed to, say, bad lunch meat, does not pose a health threat, but rather tends to taste inferior or outright awful. Thus, unlike other packaged food and beverage products, there was no regulation compelling Side Launch to recall the Wheat Beer. So why did the company proceed with this costly recall?

3. Use of the DNA tester at Side Launch would be considered a strength—it serves to enhance the quality of the beer product. But the tester itself, prior to its use by Side Launch, introduced what type of opportunity for the company?

Side Launch Brewing Company

3 | Strategic Planning for Competitive Advantage

LEARNING OUTCOMES

3-1 Explain the importance of strategic planning

3-2 Develop an appropriate business mission statement

3-3 Describe how to conduct business portfolio analysis

3-4 Summarize how business planning is used for competitive advantage

3-5 Discuss marketing planning and identification of target markets

3-6 Describe the elements of the marketing mix

3-7 Explain why implementation, evaluation, and control of the marketing plan are necessary

3-8 Identify several techniques that help make strategic planning effective

"The one who follows the crowd never gets ahead of the crowd."

—Travis Kalanick, Co-founder, Uber[1]

3-1 THE IMPORTANCE OF STRATEGIC PLANNING

Business **planning** in general is the process of anticipating future events and determining strategies to achieve organizational objectives in the future. This should happen in an organization at the strategic and tactical levels.

Strategic planning is the leadership and managerial process of establishing the organization's objectives and then determining how to achieve them given internal resources and the evolving **marketing environment**. The goal of strategic planning is long-run profitability and growth.

> **planning** the process of anticipating future events and determining strategies to achieve organizational objectives in the future
>
> **strategic planning** the managerial process of creating and maintaining a fit between the organization's objectives and resources and evolving market opportunities

Thus strategic decisions require long-term commitments of resources. A strategic error can threaten a firm's survival. On the other hand, a good strategic plan can help protect and grow the firm's resources.

Organizations are increasingly becoming complex, and modern businesses, especially large corporations, constitute a set of diverse business interests spread over several business areas and markets. These diverse businesses within a corporation are linked by common corporate goals and interdependent business strategies that must be coordinated to obtain maximum advantage for the business and its customers. In a large business setting, strategic planning is a complex set of activities that takes place at three levels: (1) corporate, (2) business, and (3) marketing. The corporate strategic planning takes place at the highest level of an organization and sets the direction and scope of the overall corporation through its mission statement, the identification of key business opportunities and constraints, and the allocation of resources.

Corporate planning leads to objectives for business- and marketing-level planning that address issues related to when, where, how, and against whom to compete. Business planning is undertaken at the **strategic business unit (SBU)** level, which is a subgroup of a single business or a collection of related businesses within the larger organization. A properly defined SBU should have a distinct mission and specific target market, control over its resources, its own competitors, and plans independent of the other SBUs in the organization. The goal of business-level planning is to formulate strategies that deal with issues related to the competitive advantage a business intends to achieve through various means—including, for example, the supply chain, strategic partnerships, and the development and capitalization of distinctive competencies. The marketing planning activities are aimed at target market and marketing mix considerations that cover, for example, product lines, branding, pricing, and communication strategies. The corporate planning guides business and marketing planning; however, at the same time the corporate planning is also based on input from the other two lower levels.

Strategic decisions are made at all three levels, whereas tactical decisions are limited to the implementation of marketing plans at the lowest operational level. A strategic decision is a decision that is wider in scope and

long term in its orientation, whereas a tactical decision is narrower in scope and is short term. Strategic decisions, like that of Mountain Equipment Co-op (MEC) to add several new locations across Canada between 2017 and 2020, affect an organization's long-run course, its allocation of resources, and ultimately its financial success. In contrast, a tactical decision, such as changing the package design for Iögo, probably won't have a big impact on the long-run profitability of the company. What constitutes a long- and short-term orientation is relative and varies from industry to industry. For example, a long-term decision in the auto industry may cover five to seven years, whereas a long-term decision in the tech industry may cover 12 to 24 months. However, the decisions that an organization makes at the tactical and business levels directly link to and flow from the strategic decisions made at the highest level within the organization. For example, an organization might make a strategic decision to increase its presence in a particular market. This decision may result in one of its SBUs expanding its

marketing environment
The entire set of situational conditions, both internal (strengths and weaknesses) and external (opportunities and threats), within which a business operates

strategic business unit (SBU) a subgroup of a single business or a collection of related businesses within the larger organization

IÖGO (pronounced "you go") is a Canadian brand of yogurt. Iögo is available in eight lines and comes in over 40 flavours.

Helen Sessions/Alamy Stock Photo

market share through new product introductions as a result of brand or line extensions.

How do companies go about developing strategic marketing? How do leaders know how and when to implement the long-term goals of the firm? The answer is a strategic plan that addresses all three levels of planning (see Exhibit 3.1). Strategic planning spawns a marketing plan, which is a written document that acts as a guidebook of marketing analysis and activities for the marketing manager. In this chapter, you will learn the importance of marketing analysis, strategic planning, and preparing a marketing plan. And it all begins by setting a company's mission statement.

3-2 CORPORATE PLANNING— DEFINING THE BUSINESS MISSION

The foundation of any strategic direction, much less the marketing plan it spawns, is the firm's **mission statement**, which answers the question "What value do we provide for customers?" The way a firm defines— and lives—its mission profoundly affects the firm's long-run resource allocation, profitability, and survival. The mission statement is based on a

mission statement a statement of the firm's value based on a careful analysis of benefits sought by present and potential customers and an analysis of existing and anticipated environmental conditions

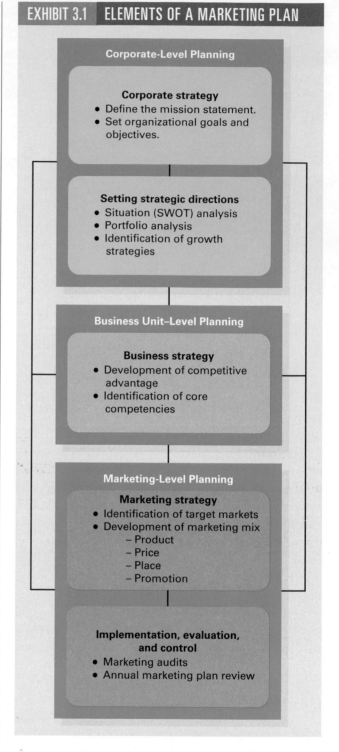

EXHIBIT 3.1 ELEMENTS OF A MARKETING PLAN

Corporate-Level Planning

Corporate strategy
- Define the mission statement.
- Set organizational goals and objectives.

Setting strategic directions
- Situation (SWOT) analysis
- Portfolio analysis
- Identification of growth strategies

Business Unit–Level Planning

Business strategy
- Development of competitive advantage
- Identification of core competencies

Marketing-Level Planning

Marketing strategy
- Identification of target markets
- Development of marketing mix
  - Product
  - Price
  - Place
  - Promotion

Implementation, evaluation, and control
- Marketing audits
- Annual marketing plan review

careful analysis of benefits sought by present and potential customers and an analysis of existing and anticipated environmental conditions. The firm's mission statement establishes boundaries for all subsequent decisions, objectives, and strategies. Thus a mission statement should focus on the market or markets the organization is attempting to serve rather than on the goods or services offered. Otherwise, a new technology may quickly make the goods or services obsolete and the mission statement irrelevant to company functions.

 Mission statements that are stated too narrowly define a business by its goods and services rather than by the benefits that customers seek. On the other hand, missions stated too broadly will provide neither focus for strategic planning nor the differentiation that customers are often attracted to. Care must be taken to state the business a firm is in, and to emphasize the distinct benefits that customers seek, before the foundation for the marketing plan is set.

The organization may also need to develop a mission statement and objectives for a strategic business unit (SBU). Thus a large firm such as Procter & Gamble may have marketing plans for each of its SBUs, which include beauty, hygiene, homecare, and health and grooming.

3-3 STRATEGIC DIRECTIONS— DESIGNING THE BUSINESS PORTFOLIO

To set an organization's strategic direction, businesses must thoroughly understand their current environment and any potential environment in which they will be operating. This goal is accomplished by conducting a **SWOT analysis** of an organization's internal environment of strengths (S) and weaknesses (W) in the context of its external environment of opportunities (O) and threats (T). Exhibit 3.2 provides an outline of a SWOT analysis.

3-3a Conducting a SWOT Analysis

When examining internal strengths and weaknesses, marketers should focus on three key organizational categories—financial, management, and marketing. The

EXHIBIT 3.2	SWOT ANALYSIS		
		Strengths	**Weaknesses**
Internal	Financial		
	Management		
	Marketing		
		Opportunities	**Threats**
External	Competitive		
	Regulatory		
	Economic		
	Social		
	Technological		

financial category, for instance, would include things like cash on hand and access to funding. Management would cover production costs, HR processes, and supply chain management. Marketing would be made up of value of offerings, number of customers, brand reputation, pricing strategy, distribution, and communication—in other words, anything within the four Ps. In fact, the very practice of strategic planning and SWOT analysis could be viewed as either a strength or weakness depending upon how or even if a company chooses to use the SWOT tool in the first place. For example, a perceived weakness of Canada's second-largest airline, WestJet, might be its lack of penetration into global destinations, making it less of an international player than Air Canada. Meanwhile, a strength is its reputation for creating a unique and pleasant customer experience, with its on-flight crew sharing their passion for their job with WestJet's "guests," as they are called. All participants in the SWOT analysis must be able to step back from their biased view of the company and provide a rigorous and honest depiction of what works and what doesn't.

When examining external forces of opportunities and threats, marketers must analyze aspects of the marketing environment. This process is called **environmental scanning**—the collection and interpretation of information about forces, events, and relationships in the external environment that may affect the future of the organization or the implementation of the marketing plan. These are inherently uncontrollable by the firm. That is, the company neither initiates them nor stops them—rather, companies can only prepare to act upon them. Environmental scanning is at its best when it foresees business opportunities and threats at an early stage so that trends identified may be acted upon to either make or save money. For example, Canadian lending institutions such as RBC must be acutely aware of the economic environment as it influences regulations made by the Bank of Canada concerning lending rates. The financial collapse in 2008 slowed the Canadian economy so much that the federal government was forced to use tactics such as near-zero prime lending rates to help restore consumer confidence in buying homes.

The five most often studied macro-environmental forces are competitive, regulatory, economic, social, and technological. These forces were examined in detail in Chapter 2.

SWOT analysis identifying internal environment of strengths (S) and weaknesses (W) as well as external opportunities (O) and threats (T)

environmental scanning the collection and interpretation of information about forces, events, and relationships in the external environment that may affect the future of the organization or the implementation of the marketing plan

SWOT analysis helps identify the strategic direction the firm should follow. That is, if done properly, SWOT analysis findings will often be so compelling that firms can proceed with confidence with a growth strategy.

EXHIBIT 3.3	ANSOFF'S STRATEGIC OPPORTUNITY MATRIX	
	Current Product	**New Product**
Current Market	Market Penetration	Product Development
New Market	Market Development	Diversification

© Cengage

3-3b Strategic Alternatives—Linking SWOT to Growth Strategies

Once an organization fully identifies strengths, weaknesses, opportunities, and threats, certain ideas will emerge in the form of alternative growth strategies. These can be easily categorized using Ansoff's strategic opportunity matrix (see Exhibit 3.3), which matches products with markets. The grid produces the following four options:

- **Market penetration:** A firm using the market penetration alternative tries to increase market share among existing customers by selling more of its current products. Tim Hortons' annual "Roll Up the Rim" campaign is not just a great promotional strategy, it's an annual market penetration strategy that drives loyal and even passive customers to drink even more coffee.

- **Market development:** Market development involves attracting new customers to existing products. Ideally, new uses for old products stimulate additional sales among existing customers while also bringing in new buyers. For example, Tim Hortons provides a catering service that essentially offers its regular line of sandwiches to the corporate market, rather than limiting its business to consumers at the restaurant.

- **Product development:** A product development strategy entails the creation of new products for current markets. Pushed not only by evolutionary social taste preferences, but by competitors like McDonald's, Tim Hortons must constantly be aware of up-and-coming food trends in quick-service restaurants and be able to spring into action with the trends that are suitable for its operations. It regularly introduces new soups, sandwiches, and sides, as well as new doughnut flavours and baked goods.

- **Diversification:** Diversification is a strategy of increasing sales by introducing new products into new markets. By far the riskiest of the four strategies, diversification, though, is often necessary to combat competitive forces or to take advantage of new social trends. Tim Hortons' implementation of espresso machines in its stores in 2017 was no doubt an attempt to woo Starbucks customers into its restaurants by way of a new line of coffees.[°]

SELECTING A STRATEGIC ALTERNATIVE Selecting which alternative to pursue depends on the overall company philosophy and culture. Clearly the goal of for-profit companies is just that—profit. However, a firm may face a situation, as identified through SWOT, in which it's necessary to place profit at a lower priority and choose a strategy that may not reap profits in the near term. Companies generally have one of two philosophies about when they expect profits. Even though market share—the percentage of sales in a market owned by a company—and profitability are compatible long-term goals, companies might pursue profits right away or first seek to build market share and/or awareness, before going after profit.

The four strategic alternatives supported by Ansoff's matrix generally befit any given situation. However, marketers should have both the SWOT matrix and Ansoff's matrix visible on a large whiteboard, where they can pivot back and forth between the two. They often need to prioritize between where there is the greatest gain and where there is the least harm. For instance, in assessing whether to grow by penetration, product development, market development, or diversification, a firm needs to look at what jumps out of the SWOT analysis most urgently. Is there an underused strength that needs to be fully leveraged? A craft brewery, for example, may be constantly running out of a particular beer. Ramping up production of this product and selling more of it to the brewery's current customers may be the most effective and profitable strategy—that is, market penetration. On the other hand, that same brewery, noting the growth in demand for ciders in the female market, may decide that it should leverage its strengths of operations and distribution and develop a cider (new product) for women (new market), thereby arriving at a diversification strategy.

market penetration
a marketing strategy that tries to increase market share among existing customers, using existing products

market development
a marketing strategy that involves attracting new customers to existing products

product development
a marketing strategy that entails the creation of new products for current customers

diversification a strategy of increasing sales by introducing new products into new markets

---

[°] © Cengage

Either way, firms cannot run away with an idea that seems obvious upon completion of SWOT, any more than they should jump at a growth strategy from Ansoff's matrix, without pushing the two tools together and critically thinking through all options.

 ## 3-4 BUSINESS PLANNING FOR COMPETITIVE ADVANTAGE

Once an organization has thoroughly scanned its internal and external environment via SWOT analysis and considered the most appropriate growth strategy by combining SWOT with Ansoff's matrix, it needs to begin outlining *how* to go about implementing and executing the strategy. At this stage, more detailed planning is required at the strategic business unit (SBU) level as to how a business will achieve a sustainable competitive advantage, which will allow it to succeed among its competitors. Leaders of SBUs must identify the **core competencies** that will help them attain a competitive advantage. In other words, SWOT must be conducted at an SBU level as well to identify SBU-related factors not evident in the corporate analysis.

3-4a Competitive Advantage

A **competitive advantage** is a set of unique features of a company and its products that are perceived by the target market as significant and superior to the competition and thus results in customers choosing one firm over its competitors. There are a variety of competitive advantage strategies to pursue, most of which fall into the category of cost, product differentiation, or niche strategies.

3-4b Cost Competitive Advantage

As you will learn in Chapter 13 when we look at the concept of price, nothing drives demand quite like a low price. And nothing enables low prices more than low costs. Thus establishing a low-cost operation is one of the most obvious and controllable competitive advantage strategies. This can result from obtaining inexpensive raw materials, creating an efficient scale of plant operations, designing products for ease of manufacture, controlling overhead costs, and avoiding marginal customers. Having a **cost competitive advantage** means being the low-cost competitor in an industry while maintaining satisfactory profit margins. A cost competitive advantage enables a firm to deliver superior customer value. Walmart is the world's leading value-priced department store. Its value to customers results from providing a large selection of merchandise at low prices. Walmart is able to keep its prices down not only because it has

EXHIBIT 3.4 COST COMPETITIVE ADVANTAGE

- Experience Curves
- Efficient Labour
- No-Frills Goods and Services
- Government Subsidies

+

Cost Competitive Advantage

- Product Design
- Re-engineering
- Production Innovations
- New Methods of Service Delivery

strong buying power in its relationships with suppliers, but also because of its extremely efficient supply chain management.

Goods producers soon learn that the combined efficiencies in acquiring raw materials and human resources, among other factors, lead to cost leadership as well (see Exhibit 3.4).

Costs can be reduced in a variety of ways.

- **Experience curves:** **Experience curves** demonstrate that costs decline at a predictable rate as experience with a product increases. The experience curve effect encompasses a broad range of manufacturing, marketing, and administrative costs. Experience curves reflect learning by doing, technological advances, and economies of scale. Firms use historical experience curves as a basis for predicting and setting prices. Experience curves allow management to forecast costs and set prices based on anticipated costs as opposed to current costs. The experience curve was conceived by the Boston Consulting Group in 1966.

core competencies key unique strengths that are hard to imitate and underlie the functioning of an organization

competitive advantage the set of unique features of a company and its products that are perceived by the target market as significant and superior to the competition

cost competitive advantage being the low-cost competitor in an industry while maintaining satisfactory profit margins

experience curves curves that show costs declining at a predictable rate as experience with a product increases

- **Efficient labour:** Labour costs can be an important component of total costs in low-skill, labour-intensive industries, such as product assembly and apparel manufacturing. Many Canadian manufacturers have gone offshore to achieve cheaper manufacturing costs. Many Canadian companies are also outsourcing activities such as data entry and other labour-intensive jobs.

- **No-frills goods and services:** Marketers can lower costs by removing frills and options from a product or service. Jetlines, for example, aims to be to the Canadian airline that WestJet was when it launched in the mid-1990s. Jetlines offers low fares with no frills. The assumption is that low prices give Jetlines a higher load factor and greater economies of scale, which, in turn, mean even lower prices.

- **Government subsidies:** Governments may provide grants and interest-free loans to target industries. Ottawa's ongoing support of the Canadian auto industry, through programs like the Automotive Innovation Fund, help to demonstrate this concept.

- **Product design:** Cutting-edge design technology can help offset high labour costs. BMW is a world leader in designing cars for ease of manufacture and assembly. Reverse engineering—the process of disassembling a product piece by piece to learn its components and obtain clues as to the manufacturing process—can also mean savings. Reverse-engineering a low-cost competitor's product can save research and design costs.

- **Re-engineering:** Re-engineering entails fundamental rethinking and redesign of business processes to achieve dramatic improvements in critical measures of performance. It often involves reorganizing from functional departments, such as sales, engineering, and production, to cross-disciplinary teams. Uber, the global, ride-sharing juggernaut, launched by Calgarian Garrett Camp, realizes one of its biggest costs is one that seemed unavoidable—paying the drivers. However, the driverless car breakthrough has not been lost on Uber, which piloted the technology in Pittsburgh in 2017. When it is fully piloted and vetted by regulators, it is hard to imagine Uber not fully embracing this technology due to the massive reduction in the costs of human drivers. What happens to them, however, is the subject of a separate discussion.

- **Production innovations:** Production innovations, such as new technology and simplified production techniques, help lower the average cost of production. Technologies such as computer-aided design and computer-aided manufacturing (CAD/CAM) and increasingly sophisticated robots help companies, such as Boeing, Ford, and General Electric, reduce their manufacturing costs.

- **New methods of service delivery:** While all banks, not to mention household utility service providers, have gone paperless with statements and billing, Tangerine, a subsidiary of Scotiabank, has gone to the extreme of cost reduction by implementing a network replacing expensive bricks-and-mortar buildings with cafés and pop-up kiosks, driving its younger target market toward a total mobile banking experience.*

3-4c Product Differentiation Competitive Advantage

Because cost competitive advantages are subject to continual erosion (costs can be pushed only so low), product differentiation tends to provide a longer-lasting competitive advantage. The durability of this strategy tends to make it more attractive to many top managers. A **product/service differentiation competitive advantage** exists when a firm provides a unique benefit that is valuable to buyers beyond simply offering a low price. Examples are brand names, a strong dealer network, product reliability, image, or service. A great

The Canadian Press/Mario Beauregard

product/service differentiation competitive advantage
the provision of a unique benefit that is valuable to buyers beyond simply offering a low price

* © Cengage

example of a company with a strong product differentiation competitive advantage in all of these categories is Apple. Apple's advantage is built around one simple idea—innovation.

3-4d Niche Competitive Advantage

A **niche competitive advantage** seeks to target and effectively serve a single segment of the market (see Chapter 8). For small companies with limited resources that potentially face giant competitors, carving out a niche strategy may be the only viable option. A market segment that has good growth potential but is not crucial to the success of major competitors is a good candidate for developing a niche strategy. Many companies using a niche strategy serve only a limited geographic market. Other companies focus their product lines on specific types of products, as is the case with the Canadian company Freshii, whose mission is to "help people all over the world live healthier and better lives by making healthy food convenient and affordable."[2] Since becoming a publicly traded company in early 2017, Freshii's sharp focus on a core market segment clearly differentiates it from other quick-service restaurants (QSR) that happen to include healthier menu options alongside standard fast-food fare, such as McDonald's or Tim Hortons.

3-4e Building Sustainable Competitive Advantage

The key to having a competitive advantage is the ability to sustain that advantage. A **sustainable competitive advantage** is an advantage that cannot be copied by the competition. Examples of companies with a sustainable competitive advantage are Rolex (high-quality watches), Harry Rosen stores (customized service), and Cirque du Soleil (top-notch entertainment). When a company or organization doesn't have a competitive advantage, target customers don't perceive any reason to patronize one organization over its competitors.

> **niche competitive advantage** the advantage achieved when a firm seeks to target and effectively serve a single segment of the market
>
> **sustainable competitive advantage** an advantage that cannot be copied by the competition

No Competition

It's hard to find a direct competitor for Montreal's Cirque du Soleil, for several reasons:

- The performers tell a story that goes beyond the acrobatic acts using animals that other circuses focus on.

- The show employs more than 4000 people from 50 countries.

- Each stage show has a life of 10 to 12 years.

- The company has run over 40 shows in over 400 cities on every continent except Antarctica, entertaining over 160 million people.

- More than 300 seamstresses, engineers, and makeup artists sew, design, and build custom materials for exotic shows with such names as *Kooza, Ka, Joya,* and *Amaluna,* and its most recent introduction, *Volta.*

All this plus an Emmy Award–winning series on Bravo make Cirque du Soleil a tough act to follow. (In marketing terms, that means sustainable competitive advantage has been achieved.)

Christopher Leggett/Alamy Stock Photo

Source: Cirque du Soleil, "Cirque du Soleil to Create Opening Ceremony for Toronto 2015 Pan Am Games," September 24, 2013, www.toronto2015.org/news/archive/cirque-du-soleil-to-create-opening-ceremony-for-toronto-2015-pan-am-games/74 (accessed June 6, 2014).

The notion of competitive advantage means that a successful firm will stake out a position unique in some manner from its rivals. Imitation by competitors indicates a lack of competitive advantage and almost ensures mediocre performance. Moreover, competitors rarely stand still, so it is not surprising that imitation causes marketers to feel trapped in a seemingly endless game of catch-up. They are regularly surprised by the new accomplishments of their rivals.

Companies need to build their own competitive advantages rather than copy a competitor. The sources of tomorrow's competitive advantages are the skills and assets of the organization. Skills are functions, such as customer service and promotion, that the firm performs better than its competitors. Assets include patents, copyrights, locations, and equipment and technology that are superior to those of the competition. Marketing leaders should continually focus the firm's skills and assets on sustaining and creating competitive advantages.

Remember, a sustainable competitive advantage is only as sustainable as the speed with which competitors can imitate a leading company's strategy and plans. Imitation requires a competitor to identify the leader's competitive advantage, determine how it is achieved, and then learn how to duplicate it.

3-5 MARKETING PLANNING—SETTING THE OBJECTIVES AND IDENTIFYING THE TARGET MARKET

After the corporate level and SBU level, the third level of planning is aimed at developing **marketing strategy**, which involves the activities of selecting and describing one or more target markets and developing and maintaining a marketing mix that will produce mutually satisfying exchanges with target markets.

3-5a Setting Marketing Plan Objectives

Before the details of a marketing plan can be developed, objectives for the plan must be stated. Without objectives, a firm has no basis for measuring the success of its marketing plan activities.

marketing strategy the activities of selecting and describing one or more target markets and developing and maintaining a marketing mix that will produce mutually satisfying exchanges with target markets

marketing objective a statement of what is to be accomplished through marketing activities

A **marketing objective** is a statement of what is to be accomplished through marketing activities. To be useful, stated objectives should meet five criteria, easily developed through the *SMART* method. First, objectives should be *specific*, meaning that they must be worded in a way that leaves little guessing or generality. Second, they need to be *measurable*, using a unit of measure, such as dollar amount, so that a level of achievement can be literally witnessed. Third, objectives must be attainable, or realistically within the reach of the firm. Fourth, they should be relevant to the organization, in that they are on-brand or parallel to the firm's mission. Finally, they should be time-bound, by assigning some sort of time window for the objective to be achieved. It is tempting to state that the objective is "to be Canada's leading publisher of post-secondary marketing textbooks." However, what is "leading" for one firm might mean selling 10,000 units, whereas another firm might view "leading" as having cutting-edge digital textbook supplements. "Leading" in this statement is neither specific nor measurable. We therefore have no idea whether it is attainable, nor do we know when the objective should be met. A SMART objective might read, "Achieve sales of 10,000 units of the *Introduction to Marketing* textbook to post-secondary business students, by June 1, 2019." Objectives are the main intersection of a firm's marketing strategies. Specifically, objectives flow from the situational analysis and mission statement, and drive the decisions made for the future in the marketing plan.

Carefully specified objectives serve several functions. First, they communicate marketing management philosophies and provide direction for lower-level marketing managers so that marketing efforts are integrated and pointed in a consistent direction. Objectives also serve as motivators by creating goals for employees to strive toward. When objectives are attainable and challenging, they motivate those charged with achieving the objectives. Additionally, the process of writing specific objectives forces executives to clarify their thinking. Finally, objectives form a basis for control; the effectiveness of a plan can be gauged in light of the stated objectives.

3-5b Target Market Strategy

A **market segment** is a group of individuals or organizations that share one or more characteristics. As we'll see in Chapter 8, a segment isn't necessarily the same as a target, until it can be established that one of these characteristics is an actual need for the product being offered. For example, parents of babies and toddlers might be a target of The Children's Place, but the same retailer would not be targeting parents of teenagers.

The target market strategy identifies the market segment or segments on which to focus. This process begins with a **market opportunity analysis (MOA)**—the description and estimation of the size and sales potential of market segments that are of interest to the firm and the assessment of key competitors in these market segments. After the firm describes the market segments, it may choose to target one or more of these segments. Marketers use three general strategies for selecting target markets.

Target markets can be selected by appealing to the entire market with one marketing mix, concentrating on one segment, or appealing to multiple market segments using multiple marketing mixes. The characteristics, advantages, and disadvantages of each strategic option are examined in Chapter 8. Target markets could be individuals who are concerned about sensitive teeth (the target of Sensodyne toothpaste) or young urban professionals needing inexpensive transportation on demand (Car2Go).

The Canadian Press/Richard Lam

Target market for Lululemon: Educated women (and men) who practise yoga and other activities to reduce stress and lead a healthier life and who also want to look stylish and feel comfortable.

Any market segment that is targeted must be fully described. Geographics, demographics, psychographics, and buyer behaviour should be assessed. Buyer behaviour is covered in Chapters 6 and 7. If segments are differentiated by ethnicity, multicultural aspects of the marketing mix should be examined. If the target market is international, it is especially important to describe differences in culture, economic and technological development, and political structure that may affect the marketing plan. Global marketing is covered in more detail in Chapter 4.

3-6 THE MARKETING MIX

The term **marketing mix** refers to a unique blend of product, price, place (distribution), and promotion strategies (often referred to as the **four Ps**) designed to produce mutually satisfying exchanges with a target market. The marketing manager can control each component of the marketing mix, but the strategies for all four components must be blended to achieve optimal results. Any marketing mix is only as good as its weakest component. The best promotion and the lowest

> **market opportunity analysis (MOA)** the description and estimation of the size and sales potential of market segments that are of interest to the firm and the assessment of key competitors in these market segments
>
> **marketing mix** a unique blend of product, price, place, and promotion, strategies designed to produce mutually satisfying exchanges with a target market
>
> **four Ps** product, price, place, and promotion, which together make up the marketing mix

price cannot save a poor product. Similarly, excellent products with poor placing, pricing, or promotion will likely fail.

Variations in marketing mixes do not occur by chance. Astute marketers devise marketing strategies to gain advantages over competitors and best serve the needs and wants of a particular target market segment. By manipulating elements of the marketing mix, marketing managers can fine-tune the customer offering and achieve competitive success.

3-6a Product Strategies

Typically, the marketing mix starts with the product P, as this is essentially where marketing starts. The product is the literal satisfaction of the discovered need. The heart of the marketing mix, the starting point, is the product offering and product strategy. Without knowing the product to be marketed, it is difficult to design a pricing strategy, place strategy, or decide on a promotion campaign.

The product includes not only the physical unit but also its package, warranty, after-sale service, brand name, company image, value, and many other factors. A Godiva chocolate has many product elements: the chocolate itself, a fancy gold wrapper, a customer satisfaction guarantee, and the prestige of the Godiva brand name. We buy products not only for what they do (their benefits) but also for what they mean to us (their status, quality, or reputation).

Products can be tangible goods, such as computers; ideas, such as those offered by a consultant; or services, such as medical care. To be successful, products must offer customer value. Product decisions are covered in Chapters 10 and 11, and services marketing is detailed in Chapter 12.

3-6b Pricing Strategies

Price is what a buyer must give up to obtain a product. Thus it is often viewed in a subconscious (or conscious) calculation of value by a consumer. It is often the most flexible of the four marketing mix elements because it is the quickest element to change. Marketers can raise or lower prices more frequently and easily than they can change other marketing mix variables. Price is an important competitive weapon and is very important to the organization because price multiplied by the number of units sold equals total revenue for the firm. Pricing decisions are covered in Chapter 13 and its online appendix.

implementation the process that turns a marketing plan into action assignments and ensures that these assignments are executed in a way that accomplishes the plan's objectives

3-6c Place (Distribution) Strategies

Place, or distribution, strategies are concerned with making products available when and where customers want them. Would you rather buy a kiwi fruit at the 24-hour grocery store within walking distance or fly to New Zealand to pick your own? A part of the place P is physical distribution, which involves all the business activities concerned with storing and transporting raw materials or finished products. The goal is to ensure products arrive in usable condition at designated places when needed. Place strategies are covered in Chapters 14 and 15.

3-6d Promotion Strategies

Elements of the promotional mix, or integrated marketing communications (IMC), include advertising, direct marketing, public relations, sales promotion, personal selling, and digital marketing. Promotion's role in the marketing mix is to introduce, facilitate, or sustain conversation and community between companies and their customers. It does this by informing, educating, persuading, and reminding consumers of the benefits of an organization or a product. A good promotion strategy can dramatically increase sales. Good promotional strategies, however, are not the same as costly promotional strategies. Despite higher campaign budgets in the 2016 U.S. presidential election, Republican leadership hopefuls Jeb Bush and Marco Rubio were overwhelmingly defeated by Donald Trump on his way to become the 45th president of the United States. Trump's win may forever be regarded as an example of a promotional campaign where message and target marketing outstripped quantity. Each element of the promotion P is coordinated and managed with the others to create a promotional blend or mix. These integrated marketing communications activities are described in Chapters 16, 17, 18, and 19. Technology-driven aspects of promotional marketing are covered in Chapter 5.

 3-7 # MARKETING PLAN IMPLEMENTATION, EVALUATION, AND CONTROL

3-7a Implementation

Implementation is the process that turns a marketing plan into action assignments and, in theory, ensures that these assignments are executed in a way that accomplishes the plan's objectives. Implementation activities may involve detailed job assignments, activity descriptions, timelines, budgets, and lots of communication. Although implementation is essentially "doing what you said you were going to do," many organizations repeatedly experience failures in strategy implementation. Brilliant marketing plans are doomed to fail if they are not properly implemented. Strategies that envision lofty and ambitious growth for a firm cannot be supported by the strength of their potential alone. They must be supported by tangible tactics, which provide the building blocks to strategies. The detailed implementation plan should be communicated both in written form and in the form of a project planning device, most commonly demonstrated in a Gantt chart.

3-7b Evaluation and Control

After a marketing plan is implemented, it should be evaluated. **Evaluation** involves gauging the extent to which marketing objectives have been achieved during the specified time. Four common reasons for failing to achieve a marketing objective are unrealistic marketing objectives, inappropriate marketing strategies in the plan, poor implementation, and changes in the environment after the objective was specified and the strategy was implemented. It is important to note here that both implementation and evaluation are written into a marketing plan before the plan is approved, as a means of demonstrating to executives, who sign off on these plans, that there is follow-through on the plan's objectives.

Once a plan is chosen and implemented, its effectiveness must be monitored. **Control** provides the mechanisms both for evaluating marketing results in light of the plan's objectives and for correcting actions that do not help the organization reach those objectives within budget guidelines. Firms need to establish formal and informal control programs to make the entire operation more efficient.

Perhaps the broadest control device available to marketing managers is the **marketing audit**—a thorough, systematic, periodic evaluation of the objectives, strategies, structure, and performance of the marketing organization. A marketing audit helps management allocate marketing resources efficiently.

 Although the main purpose of the marketing audit is to develop a full profile of the organization's marketing effort and to provide a basis for developing and revising the marketing plan, it is also an excellent way to improve communication and raise the level of marketing consciousness within the organization. A marketing audit is a useful vehicle for selling the

FOUR CHARACTERISTICS OF A MARKETING AUDIT

- **Comprehensive:** covers all major marketing issues facing an organization and not just trouble spots.
- **Systematic:** takes place in an orderly sequence and covers the organization's marketing environment, internal marketing system, and specific marketing activities. The diagnosis is followed by an action plan with both short-run and long-run proposals for improving overall marketing effectiveness.
- **Independent:** normally conducted by an inside or outside party who is independent enough to have top management's confidence and to be objective.
- **Periodic:** for maximum benefit, should be carried out on a regular schedule instead of only in a crisis.

Source: © Cengage

philosophy and techniques of strategic marketing to other members of the organization.

3-8 EFFECTIVE STRATEGIC PLANNING

Effective strategic planning requires continual attention, creativity, and management commitment. Strategic planning should not be an annual exercise, in which managers go through the motions and forget about strategic planning until the next year. It should be an ongoing process because the environment is continually changing and the firm's resources and capabilities are continually evolving.

Sound strategic planning is based on creative thinking. Marketers should challenge assumptions about the firm and the environment and establish new strategies. And above all, the most critical element in successful strategic planning is top management's support and participation.

evaluation gauging the extent to which the marketing objectives have been achieved during the specified period

control provides the mechanisms both for evaluating marketing results in light of the plan's objectives and for correcting actions that do not help the organization reach those objectives within budget guidelines

marketing audit a thorough, systematic, periodic evaluation of the objectives, strategies, structure, and performance of the marketing organization

SIDE LAUNCH
BREWING COMPANY
CONTINUING CASE

Side Launch Brewing Company

Born to Grow

This chapter fuses two of the most important concepts not only in marketing, but in business: analysis (via the SWOT tool) and strategic growth (via Ansoff's Growth Matrix). Organizations are born to grow. Those that do not follow through on this pull of inertia are destined to fail. Growth, though, is often haphazardly implemented by founders, managers, or entrepreneurs who fail to connect the findings of SWOT with a well-thought-out growth strategy. We've covered the four main components of SWOT; we look now at the four main components of the growth matrix, once again using Side Launch as our storyline.

Three years into Side Launch's existence, founder Garnet Pratt encountered the type of good problem most entrepreneurs dream about—demand for her company's beer was soaring, and growth opportunities seemed to be everywhere. Sales of Side Launch had grown 100 percent in each of those years, and at the time of this writing, it was poised to grow by another 40 percent year over year from 2016 to 2017. "That is staggering growth," she said, "to be growing at 40 percent when the industry is growing at 20 percent. And we have all been feeling it, but it is a good problem to have. I'd rather that than having a bunch of beer in the refrigerator that won't sell."

Keeping up with increasing demand for the four core brands created by Side Launch—Wheat, Pale Ale, Dark Lager, and Mountain Lager—will, by default, result in growth by market penetration. "At this point, it's the only logical strategy," asserts Dave Sands, VP Operations. "And with these four core beers, we have covered a large cross-section of craft beer consumers," chimes in brewer Michael Hancock.

Side Launch also realizes that other growth strategies exist. "We develop new flavour profiles regularly throughout the year in limited quantities," explains Michael. Technically, this is product development strategy, but in the case of Side Launch, it is more about living up to brand and category DNA than it is a deliberate attempt to grow. The exquisitely on-brand names of these specially produced beers, "The Ships of Collingwood" and "Man Overboard," show leadership and innovation as a brewer. "It's important that we don't chase trends," rationalizes Michael, "but at the same time it is important, there's no question, for a reputable craft brewer to be innovative, while at the same time being grounded in the traditional values which result in a really good-tasting beer."

"It's easy in any consumer goods business to get caught up in chasing trends and growing at the peril of your core portfolio," explains Dave. "Ultimately, whether you're big or small, you have to do both. Take care of the products that got you to where you are and pay the bills, but be open and forward looking to what's next." The brewery's operations manager then makes an interesting comparison between brewing beer and preparing food. "I look at production brewing [of the four core Side Launch brands] like baking—proven recipes and ingredients, precisely controlled, deliberate, time consuming, and let's face it, not very sexy or exciting if you do it right. The product development is like cooking. Taking an idea, finding some ingredients we like, tinkering, testing, adjusting, and hopefully ending up with something tasty. But this is a small-volume opportunity."

For now, the Side Launch strategy of expanding its share within that growing craft beer market seems the only logical strategy. The linkage here between SWOT and the growth matrix can thus be summed up by Garnet's description of her brand's greatest strength—"Being true to style and authentic"—and by Michael's identification of the opportunity—"The market for craft is huge and growing and just waiting to be tapped, when you consider the core number of craft consumers, and those in transition." Extracting your biggest findings from SWOT will almost always lead you to the most viable and profitable strategy for growth.

Questions

1. Using Ansoff's Growth Matrix, which growth strategy is Side Launch employing as it attempts to "grow in the craft beer market"?

2. The Side Launch products stemming from its "Ships of Collingwood" and "Man Overboard" series represent what type of growth strategy?

3. What would be an example of a diversification strategy for Side Launch?

Side Launch Brewing Company

4 | Developing a Global Vision

LEARNING OUTCOMES

4-1 Discuss the importance of global marketing

4-2 Discuss the impact of multinational firms on the world economy

4-3 Describe the external environment facing global marketers

4-4 Identify the various ways of entering the global marketplace

4-5 List the basic elements involved in developing a global marketing mix

4-6 Discover how the Internet is affecting global marketing

"There is no locality on the web—every market is a global market."

—Ethan Zukerman[1]

4-1 REWARDS OF GLOBAL MARKETING

Today, global revolutions are underway in many areas of our lives: management, politics, communications, and technology. The word "global" has assumed a new meaning, referring to a boundless mobility and competition in social, business, and intellectual arenas. **Global marketing**—marketing that targets markets throughout the world—has become an imperative for business.

Canadian managers must develop a global vision not only to recognize and react to international marketing opportunities but also to remain competitive at home. Often a Canadian firm's toughest domestic competition comes from foreign companies. As an example, consider the impact of fashion retailers like Zara, H&M, and Uniqlo on the Canadian retailing environment. Moreover, a global vision enables a manager to understand that customer and distribution networks operate worldwide, blurring geographic and political barriers and making them increasingly irrelevant to business decisions. In summary, having a **global vision** means recognizing and reacting to international marketing opportunities, using effective global marketing strategies, and being aware of threats from foreign competitors in all markets.

World merchandise trade volume is expected to continue to demonstrate growth year over year, but the strength of the growth is weakening. This weakness in world merchandise trade is driven by a slowing GDP, and decelerated trade growth in both North America and developing countries. As product development costs continue to rise, the role of the digital economy and e-commerce continues to dominate, and life cycles of products continue to shorten, the contraction in world trade adds another layer of challenges to the already challenging demands placed on marketers today.[2] But instead of fearing change, marketing winners relish its unrelenting pace.

global marketing marketing that targets markets throughout the world

global vision a recognition of and reaction to international marketing opportunities using effective global marketing strategies and being aware of threats from foreign competitors in all markets

Adopting a global vision can be very lucrative for a company. COM DEV, a space engineering company located in Cambridge, Ontario, has grown to be one of the most sophisticated space technology companies with over 80 percent of all commercial communication satellites ever launched containing COM DEV technology. The James Webb Space telescopes' (the successor to the Hubble) Fine Guidance Sensor, its Near InfaRed Imager, and its Slitless Spectrograph were built by COM DEV, and as production continues on the Webb, COM DEV is being awarded lucrative contracts.[3] Another company with a global vision is McCain Foods Limited. McCain is a privately owned company established in 1957 in Florenceville, New Brunswick. McCain employs over 19,000 people worldwide on 6 continents working with over 3200 farmers. One of McCain's business strategies is to create a single aligned global organization, which has resulted in reported sales of more than $6 billion annually.[4]

Although a company may have a global vision, it doesn't always automatically mean success. In 2013 the retailer Target entered the Canadian market with great fanfare and consumer anticipation. Almost two years from the opening of the first Canadian store, Target Canada filed for creditor protection, costing the company billions of dollars, putting almost 18,000 people out of work, and most importantly negatively affecting the Target brand image. There are many reasons for the failure, including new and inexperienced employees, a lack of understanding of the competitiveness of the food and general merchandise industry in Canada, and the use of nonproprietary technology that was not suited to the complexities of the Canadian supply chain. The U.S. retailer has not completely abandoned Canada however. In the fall of 2015, Target launched a pilot project to ship goods ordered online to Canadians. "The company that lost billions, suffered a humiliating defeat here and endured an ordeal that left its employees drained, exhausted and ultimately jobless, titled the website for Canuck shoppers 'Target loves Canada.'"[5]

As the Target story suggests, global marketing is not a one-way street in which Canadian companies sell their wares and services throughout the world and still have the Canadian market all to themselves. Foreign competition in the domestic market, once relatively rare, is now found in almost every industry. In fact, in many industries, Canadian businesses have lost significant market share to imported products. In electronics, clothing, cameras, automobiles, fine china, tractors, leather goods, and a host of other consumer and industrial products, Canadian companies have struggled at home to maintain their market shares against foreign competitors.

4-1a Importance of Global Marketing to Canada

Canada's reliance on international commerce will increase as global markets become easier for Canadian firms to access. Globalization also means that foreign firms will find Canada an appealing market for their products and services. As the world continues to shrink through advances in technology and telecommunications, improved and less costly transportation, and a reduction in trade barriers, the trend toward increased globalization will certainly continue. Canada's future growth will largely depend on our ability to effectively compete in the global marketplace.

In Canada in 2015, exports represented 30.1 percent of **gross domestic product (GDP)**—the total market value of all goods and services produced in a country for a given period—and imports were 33.8 percent of GDP. Canada's share of the value of global trade has been affected by the developing countries. In 2014, Canada ranked as the 11th largest exporter and the 12th largest importer. Our largest trading partner, by far, is the United States (see Exhibit 4.1), which is the destination for almost 74 percent of our exports and the source of just over 60 percent of our imports.[6] Crude petroleum continues to be the number one export, representing almost 20 percent of all exports, followed by cars, which account for just over 10 percent. Clearly, the United States is important to our economy and prosperity. However, Canada's overreliance on the United States has led all levels of government to encourage firms of all sizes to seek new opportunities in almost every region of the world. These efforts continue to bear fruit, as Asian economies increase their share of trade with Canadian businesses.

Where once the global domain was restricted to large multinationals, today distribution and communications technology has opened the door for all firms, irrespective of size. Small and medium-sized businesses around the globe see the benefits of global trade and are active players. Canadian small and medium-sized businesses, however, have not ventured globally to the same degree as others internationally. While small and medium-sized businesses account for almost 95 percent of all businesses in Canada and generate approximately 40 percent of Canada's GDP, only

gross domestic product (GDP) the total market value of all goods and services produced in a country for a given period

outsourcing the practice of using an outside supplier, generally where the productions costs are lower, to complete the work

inshoring returning jobs to Canada

EXHIBIT 4.1	CANADA'S TOP TEN EXPORT MARKETS, 2015
Country	Export Value (in millions of Canadian dollars)
1. United States	$402,173
2. China	$20,221
3. United Kingdom	$15,952
4. Japan	$9,772
5. Mexico	$6,594
6. India	$4,321
7. South Korea	$4.027
8. Hong Kong	$3,914
9. Germany	$3,612
10. Netherlands	$3,556

Source: Innovation, Science and Economic Development Canada (2015). Trade Data Online report, Canadian Total Exports, Total for all Products, Canada, Top 10 countries for 2015, in millions of dollars. Reproduced with the permission of the Minister of Innovation, Science and Economic Development Canada, 2017.

10 percent are exporters, and since the recession the return to export markets has been slow.[7]

JOB OUTSOURCING AND INSHORING The notion of **outsourcing** (sending Canadian jobs abroad) has been highly controversial for several decades. Many executives have said that it leads to corporate growth, efficiency, productivity, and revenue growth. Most companies see cost savings as a key driver in outsourcing. But outsourcing also has its negative side: job losses to the local economy, a loss of intellectual capital to the outsourced country, a loss in manufacturing capacity, and reliance on the outsourced countries' regulations and relations with Canada. Increased fuel and transportation costs associated with long-distance shipping, coupled with the lower Canadian dollar, have given impetus to **inshoring,** returning production jobs to Canada. In addition, rapid consumer product innovation has led to the need to keep product designers, marketing researchers, logistic experts, and manufacturers in close proximity so they can work as a team, further supporting inshoring. If your product story centres on "made in Canada," then inshoring supports this positioning. An increasing number of Canadians are influenced in their purchase decisions by source of production. Providing local or Canadian-made products is growing in popularity as a product differentiator, and Canadians are willing to pay a premium for locally produced goods. In fact, a study released by the Business Development Bank of Canada reported that 97 percent of Canadians decide to buy locally to support the local economy.[8]

THE IMPACT OF EXPORTS

Although some countries may depend more on international commerce than Canada does, the impact of exports on the Canadian economy is still considerable:

- Exports in 2016 were US$390 billion or just under 25 percent of the total Canadian economic output.
- Trade is equal to over 60 percent of Canada's GDP.
- One in five Canadian jobs is a result of exports.
- If Canada did not export, October 21 represents the day in the year that average Canadians would stop working.
- After October 21,
  - there would be 3.3 million fewer jobs,
  - the unemployment rate would reach over 25 percent,
  - Canadian GDP and incomes would plummet,
  - and workers in all sectors and all Canadians would feel the consequences.[9]
- Seventy-eight percent of exports were to the partners in the North American Free Trade Agreement.
- Eight percent of exports were to Europe.
- Eleven percent of exports were to Asia.[10]

BENEFITS OF GLOBALIZATION According to traditional economic theory, globalization relies on competition to drive down prices and increase product and service quality. Businesses go to the countries that operate most efficiently and those that have the technology to produce what is needed. Thus globalization expands economic freedom, spurs competition, and raises the productivity and living standards of people in countries that open themselves to the global marketplace. For less developed countries, globalization also offers access to foreign capital, global export markets, and advanced technology while breaking the monopoly of inefficient and protected domestic producers. Faster growth, in turn, reduces poverty, encourages democratization, and promotes higher labour and environmental standards. Although

government officials may face more difficult choices as a result of globalization, their citizens enjoy greater individual freedom. In this sense, globalization acts as a check on governmental power by making it more difficult for governments to abuse the freedom and property of their citizens.

Globalization deserves credit for helping lift many millions out of poverty and for improving standards of living for low-wage families.

4-2 MULTINATIONAL FIRMS

Many large Canadian companies are global marketers, and many have been very successful. A company that is heavily engaged in international trade, beyond exporting and importing, is called a multinational corporation. **Multinational corporations** move resources, goods, services, and skills across national boundaries without regard to the country in which the headquarters is located.

Multinationals often develop their global business in stages. In the first stage, companies operate in one country and sell into others. Second-stage multinationals set up foreign subsidiaries to handle sales in one country. In the third stage, they operate an entire line of business in another country. The fourth stage has evolved primarily because of the Internet and involves mostly high-tech companies. For these firms, the executive suite is virtual. Their top executives and core corporate functions may be located in different countries, wherever the firms can gain a competitive edge through the availability of talent or capital, low costs, or proximity to their most important customers. A multinational company may have several worldwide headquarters, depending on the locations of certain markets or technologies.

The role of multinational corporations in developing nations is a subject of controversy. Multinationals' ability to tap financial, physical, and human resources from all over the world and combine them economically and profitably can be of benefit to any country. They also often possess and can transfer the most up-to-date technology. Critics, however, claim that often the wrong kind of technology is transferred to developing nations. Usually, it is **capital intensive** (requiring a greater expenditure for equipment than for labour) and thus does not substantially increase

> **multinational corporations** companies that are heavily engaged in international trade, beyond exporting and importing
>
> **capital intensive** using more capital than labour in the production process

employment. A *modern sector* then emerges in the nation, employing a small proportion of the labour force at relatively high productivity and income levels and with increasingly capital-intensive technologies. In addition, multinationals sometimes push for very quick production turn-around times, which have led to long hours and dangerous working conditions. In 2013, a Bangladesh garment factory collapsed, and more than 1100 people died as they rushed to meet production quotas for firms, including Loblaw Companies Ltd.[11] Other critics say that multinational firms take more wealth out of developing nations than they bring in, thus widening the gap between rich and poor nations.

To counter such criticism, more and more multinationals are taking a proactive role in being good global citizens. Sometimes multinationals are spurred to action by government regulation, other times the action is an attempt to protect their good brand name. In the aftermath of the Bangladesh factory collapse, the Retail Council of Canada committed to updating guidelines for best practices and educational materials and resources for its members in regards to foreign production. The Coca-Cola Company has committed to enabling the economic empowerment of 5 million women entrepreneurs across the company's value chain by 2020. To date over 1.2 million women have been trained.[12]

4-2a Global Marketing Standardization

Traditionally, marketing-oriented multinational corporations have used a strategy of providing different product features, packaging, advertising, and so on, in each country where they operate. McDonald's global success is—believe it or not—based on variation rather than standardization. McDonald's changes its salad dressings and provides self-serve espresso for French tastes, bulgogi burgers in South Korea, falafel burgers in Egypt, beer in Germany, and sake in Japan.

In contrast to the idea of tailoring marketing mixes to meet the needs and wants of consumers in different countries, **global marketing standardization** involves producing uniform products that can be sold in the same way all over the world. Most smartphones and tablets, for example, are standardized globally except for the language displayed. Communication and technology have made the world smaller so that almost all consumers everywhere want all the things they have heard about, seen, or experienced. Global

global marketing standardization production of uniform products that can be sold the same way all over the world

marketing standardization presumes that the markets throughout the world are becoming more alike, so, by practising uniform production, companies should be able to lower production and marketing costs and increase profits.

Today, many multinational companies use a combination of global marketing standardization and variation. The idea is to determine which product modifications are necessary from country to country while trying to minimize those modifications. While Coca-Cola products are sold in over 160 countries, only three Coca-Cola brands are standardized, and one of them, Sprite, has a different formulation in Japan. Although McDonald's is often considered a good example of a company practising multidomestic standardization, as we just mentioned, it varies its menu for different markets.

Companies with separate subsidiaries in other countries can be said to operate using a multidomestic strategy. A multidomestic strategy occurs when multinational firms enable individual subsidiaries to compete independently in domestic markets. For example, Colgate-Palmolive markets Axion paste dishwashing detergent in developing countries, and La Croix detergent was custom created for the French market.

Nevertheless, some multinational corporations are moving beyond multidomestic strategies toward a degree of global marketing standardization. Toothpaste and Nike shoes are marketed the same ways globally, using global market standardization.

4-3 EXTERNAL ENVIRONMENT FACING GLOBAL MARKETERS

A global marketer or a firm considering global marketing must consider the external environment. Many of the same environmental factors that operate in the domestic market also exist internationally. These factors include culture, economic and technological development, political structure and actions, demographic makeup, and natural resources.

4-3a Culture

Central to any society is the common set of values shared by its citizens that determines what is socially acceptable. Culture underlies the family, the educational system, religion, and the social class system. The network of social organizations generates overlapping roles and status positions. These values and roles have a tremendous effect on people's preferences and thus on marketers'

REUTERS/Stringer

Jon Le-Bon/Shutterstock.com

options. The sensitivity to a country's culture is critical to a success. Swedish furniture retailer IKEA has 21 stores across China. Like other multinational retailers, IKEA is hoping to capitalize on the growing Chinese economy and it has done so like no other. IKEA found success in China because it undertook to understand the Chinese culture and adapted its marketing strategy accordingly. IKEA stores show the furniture in small apartment-style displays, similar to the tiny spaces most Chinese families live in. Further, because the Chinese consumer thinks nothing of sitting on the display couches for long periods of time in conversation with friends, napping on the beds, or sharing a brown bag lunch on a display kitchen, IKEA chose to encourage such behaviour. This 12-year investment in understanding the Chinese consumer and adapting retailing accordingly has resulted in China representing the fastest-growing market for IKEA.[13]

Language is another important aspect of culture. Marketers must take care in translating product names, slogans, instructions, and promotional messages so as not to convey the wrong meaning. Schweppes Tonic Water's expansion into the Italian market faced challenges because of a campaign that translated the name into "water from the toilet."[14] Free translation software, such as babelfish.com or Google Translate, allows users to input text in one language and output in another language. But marketers must still take care!

Each country has its own customs and traditions that determine business practices and influence negotiations with foreign customers. In many countries, personal relationships are more important than financial considerations. Negotiations in Japan often include long evenings of dining, drinking, and entertaining; only after a close personal relationship has been formed do business negotiations begin.

Making successful sales presentations abroad requires a thorough understanding of the country's culture. Germans, for example, don't like risk and need strong reassurance. A successful presentation to a German client must emphasize three points: (1) the bottom-line benefits, (2) strong service support, and (3) product guarantee. In southern Europe, it is an insult to show a price list. Without negotiating, you will not close the sale. Meanwhile, the English want plenty of documentation for product claims and are less likely to simply accept the word of the sales representative. Compared with managers in other countries, managers in Scandinavian and Dutch companies are more likely to approach business transactions as Canadian managers do.

4-3b Economic and Technological Development

A second major factor in the external environment facing the global marketer is the level of economic development in the countries where it operates. In general, complex and sophisticated industries are found in developed countries, and more basic industries are found in less developed nations. Average family incomes are higher in the more developed countries compared with those in the less developed markets. Larger incomes mean greater purchasing power and demand, not only for consumer goods and services but also for the machinery and workers required to produce consumer goods.

According to the World Bank, the average **gross national income (GNI) per capita** for the world in 2015 was US$10,433.[15] GNI is a country's GDP together with its income received from other countries (mainly interest and dividends) less similar payments made to other countries. The 2015 GNI per capita of Canada was $47,500, behind that of the United States, which was $54,980. The country with the highest GNI per capita in 2015 was Bermuda at $106,140. Of course, there are many poor countries: Burundi, with a GNI per capita of $260; Ethiopia at $590; and Malawi at $350, for example.[16] GNI per capita is one measure of the ability of a country's citizens to buy various goods and services. A marketer

gross national income (GNI) per capita one measure of the ability of a country's citizens to buy various goods and services

with a global vision can use this data to aid in measuring market potential in countries around the globe.

Not only is per capita income a consideration when going abroad, but so is the cost of doing business in a country. Although it is not the same as the cost of doing business, we can gain insights into expenses by examining the cost of living in various cities. Singapore is the most expensive place to live in the world. Sixteen ounces of local cheese will cost US$10 while a bottle of table wine will set you back just over US$25.[17]

4-3c The Global Economy

A global marketer today must be fully aware of the intertwined nature of the global economy. In the past, the size of the U.S. economy was so large that global markets tended to move up or down depending on its health. For example, the U.S. housing market collapse and speculative financing led to a major global recession in 2008. This is still true today. Slow growth in America and even slower growth in Europe and Japan have hampered global economic progress. Even China's growth rate is lower today than in recent years. Politics continues to play a role in how multinationals serve their markets in countries like China and Russia. Despite politics, the BRIC (Brazil, Russia, India, and China) countries will play an increasingly important role in the global economy for years to come. By 2020, Brazil's market will top US$1.6 trillion. The consumer markets in India and China are together projected to top US$10 trillion in 2020.[18] While it is still too early to tell what the impact of Brexit will be on the world economy, it is certainly a key factor in a multinational's decision making. The lesson for the global marketer is clear: forecasting global demand and economic growth requires an understanding of what is happening economically in countries around the globe.

DOING BUSINESS IN CHINA AND INDIA The two countries of growing interest to many multinationals are India and China because of their huge economic potential. They have some of the highest growth rates in the world and are emerging as megamarkets. China and India also have the world's largest populations, two of the world's largest geographic areas, greater linguistic and sociocultural diversity than any other country, and among the highest levels of income disparity in the world—some people are extremely poor whereas others are very rich. Given this scale and variety, there is no average Chinese or Indian customer.

There are more consumers trading up to higher-priced, higher-quality products in emerging markets than there are in developed nations. This holds especially true for big-ticket items like housing, cars, and large appliances.

Seventy percent of consumers in China and 67 percent of consumers in India cite "brand name and reputation" as key reasons for trading up to higher-priced goods and services.[19]

Both India and China have exploded in spending power, particularly in the upper classes. In 2015, China accounted for about 20 percent or US$16 billion of global luxury sales. This was a softening of sales from expectations, largely due to China's slower economic growth, weaker currency, and a change in consumer demand. While branding is still important to the Chinese consumer, there is a growing emphasis on quality. Unique, high-end niche products and customization are becoming key consumption drivers.[20]

Canada and China have a strong trade relationship but a unique one in that it is based more on imports than exports. This situation is more typically seen between a poor developing country and a rich developed country. This flipped trade relationship is a result of Canada's strong resource wealth and China's strong manufacturing ability. Canada imports largely manufactured goods from China, while natural resources account for more than a third of Canadian exports to China.[21]

In a continued effort to diversify our trading partners, Canada is working to improve trade relations with the emerging markets, including the BRIC countries.

4-3d Political Structure and Actions

Political structure is a third important variable facing global marketers. Government policies run the gamut from no private ownership and minimal individual freedom to little central government and maximum personal freedom. As rights of private property increase, government-owned industries and centralized planning tend to decrease. But rarely will a political environment be at one extreme or the other. More often, countries combine multiple elements into a unique political and economic identity. India, for instance, is a republic whose political ideology includes elements of socialism, monopoly capitalism, and competitive capitalism.

A recent World Bank study found that less regulation fosters the strongest economies. The least regulated and most efficient economies are concentrated among countries with well-established common-law traditions, such as Australia, Canada, New Zealand, the United Kingdom, and the United States. With less regulation, starting a new business—the future lifeblood of any economy—is easier, quicker, and less costly, thereby improving the competitiveness of that economy and the potential for creating jobs.[22]

It is not uncommon for international politics to affect business laws. In 2010 Google pulled out of China due to intense government censorship. Six years after they left, they were preparing to re-enter by working collaboratively with the Chinese government to offer an app store for Android devices that would include only government-approved apps. While the re-entry into China offers Google access to a large number of Internet users, it demonstrates that international politics can affect business laws but in this case not the level of consumer freedom of information for the Chinese consumer that Google had ultimately hoped for.[23]

Russia has also attacked Canadian companies in the wake of political disagreement. In 2014 Russia seized the Crimea peninsula, a Ukrainian territory. This military involvement in Ukraine was considered a violation of Ukraine's sovereignty and territorial integrity. In response, Canada and many in the international community imposed sectoral sanctions on Russia. Russia then ordered a ban on billions of dollars' worth of fruits, vegetables, meat, fish, and milk and dairy products from Canada, the United States, and the European Union. Given the size of Russia and the power it wields as a consumption nation, prices for the banned products fell drastically. Unexpectedly and overnight, farmers and manufacturers lost millions of dollars in sales. For example, in the late summer and early fall of 2013, exports of fresh, chilled, or frozen pork to Russia totalled $64 million. During the same period one year later, the export value of those same products measured $7 million.[24]

LEGAL CONSIDERATIONS Closely related to and often intertwined with the political environment are legal considerations. Many of the following legal structures are designed to either encourage or limit trade:

- **Tariff:** a tax levied on the goods entering a country.

- **Quota:** a limit on the amount of a specific product that can enter a country. Companies request quotas as a means of protection from foreign competition.

- **Boycott:** the exclusion of all products from certain countries or companies. Governments use boycotts to exclude products from countries with which they have a political dispute.

- **Exchange control:** a law compelling a company earning foreign exchange from its exports to sell it to a control agency, usually a central bank. A company wanting to buy goods abroad must first obtain foreign currency exchange from the control agency. For instance, Avon Products drastically cut back new production lines and products in the Philippines because exchange controls prevented the company from converting pesos to dollars to ship back to the home office. The pesos had to be used in the Philippines.

- **Market grouping** (*also known as a common trade alliance*): occurs when several countries agree to work together to form a common trade area that enhances trade opportunities.

- **Trade agreement:** an agreement to stimulate international trade. Not all government efforts are meant to stifle imports or investment by foreign corporations. The Uruguay Round of trade negotiations is an example of an effort to encourage trade. The largest Latin American trade agreement is **Mercosur**, made up of Argentina, Bolivia, Brazil, Chile, Colombia, Ecuador, Paraguay, Peru, Uruguay, and most recently Venezuela. The elimination of most tariffs among the trading partners has resulted in trade revenues of over US$16 billion annually. The economic boom created by Mercosur will undoubtedly cause other nations to seek trade agreements on their own or to enter Mercosur.

URUGUAY ROUND AND DOHA ROUND The **Uruguay Round** is an agreement that has dramatically lowered trade barriers worldwide. Adopted in 1994, the agreement has been signed by 148 nations. It is the most ambitious global trade agreement ever negotiated. The agreement has reduced tariffs by one-third worldwide—a move that is expected to raise global income by US$235 billion annually. Perhaps most notable is the recognition of new global realities. For the first time, an agreement covers services, intellectual property rights, and trade-related investment measures, such as exchange controls.

A NEW TRADE ORGANIZATION The **World Trade Organization (WTO)** replaced the old **General Agreement on Tariffs and Trade (GATT)**, which was created in 1948. The GATT contained extensive loopholes that enabled countries to avoid the trade-barrier reduction agreements—a situation similar to obeying the law only if you want to! Today, all WTO members must fully comply with all agreements under the Uruguay Round. The WTO also has an effective dispute settlement procedure with strict time limits to resolve disputes.

Mercosur the largest Latin American trade agreement, made up of Argentina, Bolivia, Brazil, Chile, Colombia, Ecuador, Paraguay, Peru, Uruguay, and Venezuela

Uruguay Round an agreement created by the World Trade Organization to dramatically lower trade barriers worldwide

World Trade Organization (WTO) a trade organization that replaced the old General Agreement on Tariffs and Trade (GATT)

General Agreement on Tariffs and Trade (GATT) a trade agreement that contained loopholes that enabled countries to avoid trade-barrier reduction agreements

Canada Goose is a family business started in 1957 by a Polish immigrant and is today run by Dani Reiss, the grandson of this immigrant entrepreneur. With the total value of the apparel business on a steady decline—between 2007 and 2011 apparel manufacturing GDP declined 8.5 percent—Canada Goose is an anomaly. It would certainly be less expensive to produce the clothing offshore but for Canada Goose, the location of manufacturing is intricately tied to the brand's positioning. Reiss said, "When people around the world own a Canada Goose jacket, one of the things that make them feel special about the product is that I think they feel they own a piece of Canada."[25]

The Canadian Press/AP Photo/Mark Lennihan

The trend toward globalization has resulted in the creation of additional agreements and organizations: the North American Free Trade Agreement, the Central America Free Trade Agreement, the European Union, the World Bank, the International Monetary Fund, and the G20, a group of the largest and fastest-growing top 20 economies of the world.

NORTH AMERICAN FREE TRADE AGREEMENT

At the time it was instituted, the **North American Free Trade Agreement (NAFTA)** created the world's largest free trade zone. The agreement was reached by Canada, the United States, and Mexico, with a combined population of almost 450 million and a combined economy of US$17 trillion. Canada, the largest U.S. trading partner, entered a free trade agreement with the United States in 1988, so the main impact of NAFTA was to open the Mexican market to Canadian and U.S. companies. When the treaty went into effect, it removed a web of Mexican licensing requirements, quotas, and tariffs that limited transactions in Canadian and U.S. goods and services.

The real question is whether NAFTA will continue under the new Trump Republican administration.

Despite the fact that since the agreement was signed all three countries have benefitted from the deal, Trump campaigned on eliminating NAFTA, which superseded the pre-existing Canada-U.S. Free Trade Agreement (FTA) of 1989. The FTA had removed most tariffs from goods traded between the United States and Canada, but it did not include Mexico. Should NAFTA be eliminated, the FTA would still exist, as it was never repealed, so the impact on trade between Canada and the United States may not be seriously affected. Mexico has thrived under NAFTA, yet its advantage as a low-cost producer is being lost today to countries such as India and China. American and Canadian businesses complain that Mexico has a dysfunctional judicial system, unreliable power supplies, poor roads, high corporate tax rates, and unfriendly labour relations. These complaints have given companies pause when considering investing in Mexico; will the elimination of NAFTA seriously harm Canadian trade numbers?

CANADA AND FREE TRADE AGREEMENTS

Apart from the free trade agreement with the United States and Mexico (NAFTA), Canada is continually improving its mutually beneficial trade relations with other countries. Canada has either signed free trade agreements (FTAs) or is in discussion with many countries worldwide in an effort to increase export/import opportunities.[26]

On October 30, 2016, Prime Minister Justin Trudeau signed the historic and long-awaited **Canadian-European Union Comprehensive Economic and Trade Agreement (CETA).** CETA is a progressive

North American Free Trade Agreement (NAFTA) an agreement among Canada, the United States, and Mexico that created the world's largest free trade zone at that time

Canadian-European Union Comprehensive Economic and Trade Agreement (CETA) a progressive free trade agreement, which covers almost all sectors, and aspects of Canada-EU trade in order to eliminate or reduce barriers

free trade agreement, which covers almost all sectors and aspects of Canada–EU trade in order to eliminate or reduce barriers. It is expected that the European Union and Canada will ratify about 95 percent of the agreement by mid-2017. Ratification will result in the removal of tariffs on 95 percent of the goods and services Canada now sells to Europe, and the agreement will see the elimination of many nontariff barriers to business currently in existence. Once it is fully implemented, it is expected that CETA will create jobs and economic growth, as it will make doing business in Canada easier and more accessible. It is interesting to note that one provision of the agreement provides a framework to approve the recognition of qualifications of regulated professions, making it easier for professionals to work both within Canada and within the EU member countries.[27]

EUROPEAN UNION One of the world's most important free trade zones is the **European Union (EU)**, which now encompasses most of Europe. More than a free trade zone, it is also a political and economic community with a common currency. It guarantees the freedom of movement of people, goods, services, and capital between member states. It also maintains a common trade policy with outside nations and a regional development policy. The EU represents member nations in the WTO. Recently the EU began moving into foreign policy.

The primary goal of the EU is to create a unified European market. Other goals include instituting a common foreign policy, security policy, and defence policy and a European citizenship, whereby any EU citizen can live, work, vote, and run for office anywhere in the member countries. The EU is creating standardized trade rules and coordinated health and safety standards.

FRANCOIS LENOIR/AFP/Getty Images

Duties, customs procedures, and taxes have been standardized. The standardized rules have helped to create an estimated 2.5 million jobs since 1993.

The European Union currently has 28 member states: Austria, Belgium, Bulgaria, Croatia, Cyprus, Czech Republic, Denmark, Estonia, Finland, France, Germany, Greece, Hungary, Ireland, Italy, Latvia, Lithuania, Luxembourg, Malta, the Netherlands, Poland, Portugal, Romania, Slovakia, Slovenia, Spain, Sweden, and the United Kingdom. However, in June 2016 the United Kingdom voted 52 percent to leave the EU. This action, known as Brexit, led to the resignation of David Cameron and the instalment of Theresa May as Britain's new prime minister. Prime Minister May, although against Brexit, has publicly stated she will support the will of the people. To execute Brexit, she invoked Article 50 of the Lisbon Treaty, giving Britain and the EU two years to agree to the terms of the separation. Many questions exist as a result of Brexit, both for Britain and EU members, including two key questions: What happens to British citizens working in the EU and what happens to EU citizens living in Britain? The Brexit vote caused a sharp decline in the value of the British pound. There is much to be watched as the next few years unfold.[28]

The recent financial crisis in Greece demonstrates the challenges of a large currency union such as the EU where member nations maintain responsibility for their own fiscal policies. Unable to devalue its currency to boost sales of products without injuring other member nations, Greece turned to member states for a bailout. Such situations continue to exist with other member nations as the European economic crisis continues.

The EU is the largest economy in the world, with a GDP of US$18 trillion and a population of over 500 million. It is an attractive market with huge purchasing power. But despite the objective

European Union (EU)
a free trade zone encompassing 28 European countries

EXHIBIT 4.2	CANADA'S TOP TEN IMPORT MARKETS, 2016
Country	**Import Value (in billions of U.S. dollars)**
United States	297.7
China	15.8
United Kingdom	12.9
Japan	8.1
Mexico	5.8
South Korea	3.3
Germany	3.1
India	3.0
France	2.6
Belgium	2.3

Source: World's Top Exports, www.worldstopexports.com/canadas-top-import-partners.

of creating a unified European market, many regulations still are not standardized and with more than 15 different languages and individual national customs, Europe will always be far more diverse than North America, and product differences will continue. Marketers thus will not be able to produce a single European product for a generic European consumer.

An entirely different type of problem facing global marketers is the possibility of a protectionist movement by the EU against outsiders. For example, France has a strict quota on Japanese cars to protect French automakers Renault and Peugeot, which would be negatively affected if the quota did not exist.

THE WORLD BANK AND INTERNATIONAL MONETARY FUND

Two international financial organizations are instrumental in fostering global trade. The **World Bank** offers low-interest loans to developing nations. Originally, the purpose of the loans was to help these nations build infrastructure, such as roads, power plants, schools, drainage projects, and hospitals. Now the World Bank offers loans to help developing nations relieve their debt burdens. To receive the loans, countries must pledge to lower trade barriers and aid private enterprise. In addition to making loans, the World Bank is a major source of advice and information for developing nations.

The **International Monetary Fund (IMF)** was founded in 1945, one year after the creation of the World Bank, to promote trade through financial cooperation and eliminate trade barriers in the process. The IMF makes short-term loans to member nations that are unable to meet their budgetary expenses. It operates as a lender of last resort for troubled nations such as Greece. In exchange for these emergency loans, IMF lenders frequently extract significant commitments from the borrowing nations to address the problems that led to the crises. These steps may include curtailing imports or even devaluing the currency. Greece, while working with both the IMF and the EU, has raised taxes to unprecedented levels, cut government spending (including pensions), and implemented labour reforms such as reducing minimum wage as part of its austerity measures to receive loans from the IMF and the EU.

World Bank an international bank that offers low-interest loans, advice, and information to developing nations

International Monetary Fund (IMF) an international organization that acts as a lender of last resort, providing loans to troubled nations, and also works to promote trade through financial cooperation

Group of Twenty (G20) a forum for international economic development that promotes discussion between industrial and emerging-market countries on key issues related to global economic stability

The **Group of Twenty (G20)** finance ministers and central bank governors was established in 1999 to bring together industrialized and developing economies to discuss key issues in the global economy. The G20 group accounts for over 80 percent of world GDP and two-thirds of the world population. The group is a forum for international economic development that promotes discussion between industrial and emerging-market countries on key issues related to global economic stability. By contributing to the strengthening of the international financial system and providing opportunities for discussion on national policies, international cooperation, and international financial institutions, the G20 helps to support growth and development across the globe. The members of the G20 are shown in Exhibit 4.3.

Members of the G20 met in Hamburg, Germany in July 2017. Agenda topics included climate change, free trade, and help for migrants and refugees, as well as the previous summit agenda topics of economic growth, international trade, and financial market regulations. Encouragingly, the 2017 G20 agenda also included a dis-

Artefficient/Shutterstock.com

EXHIBIT 4.3	MEMBERS OF THE G20		
Argentina	European Union	Italy	Saudi Arabia
Australia	France	Japan	South Africa
Brazil	Germany	Mexico	Turkey
Canada	India	Republic of Korea	United Kingdom
China	Indonesia	Russia	United States

© Cengage

cussion on women's economic empowerment; a private-public loans program entitled the Women Entrepreneurs Finance Initiative (We-Fi) was also announced at the summit. The program is designed to support women-owned small and medium-sized businesses in developing countries. Canada contributed $20 million to the initial fund of US$325 million.[29]

4-3e Demographic Makeup

The world's wealth is not evenly distributed. The wealth of the richest 1 percent of the population is now equal to the wealth of the poorest 50 percent. In 2015, Asia-Pacific (Japan and China) over took North America as the number one wealth market. If past trends continue, it is anticipated that over the next decade Asia-Pacific will grow to represent two-fifths of the world's **high-net-worth individual (HNWI)** wealth, more than that of Europe, Latin America, the Middle East, and Africa combined. HNWIs are individuals with more than $1 million in liquid financial assets. Over 60 percent of HNWI populations are concentrated in four countries: United States, Japan, Germany, and China. Canada ranks eighth in the HNWI population.[30]

Two primary determinants of any consumer market are wealth and population. The three most densely populated nations in the world are China, India, and Indonesia. For marketers, though, that fact alone is not particularly useful; they also need to know whether the population is mostly urban or rural. Countries with a higher population living in urban settings represent more attractive markets.

Another key demographic consideration is age. A wide age gap separates the older populations of the industrialized countries from the vast working-age populations of developing countries. This gap has enormous implications for economies, businesses, and the competitiveness of individual countries. While Europe and Japan struggle with pension schemes and the rising cost of healthcare, China, Brazil, and Mexico reap the rewards of a demographic dividend: falling labour costs, a healthier and more educated population, and the entry of millions of women into the workforce. The demographic dividend is a gift of falling birthrates, which causes a temporary bulge in the number of working-age people. Population experts have estimated that one-third of East Asia's economic miracle can be attributed to a beneficial age structure. But the miracle occurred only because the governments had policies in place to educate the people, create jobs, and improve health.

4-3f Natural Resources

A final factor in the external environment that has become more evident in the past decade is the shortage of natural resources. Petroleum shortages have created huge amounts of wealth for oil-producing countries such as Norway, Saudi Arabia, and the United Arab Emirates. Both consumer and industrial markets have blossomed in these countries. Other countries, such as Indonesia, Mexico, and Venezuela, were able to borrow heavily against oil reserves in order to develop more rapidly. On the other hand, industrial countries such as Japan, the United States, and much of Western Europe have experienced an enormous transfer of wealth to the petroleum-rich nations. The high price of oil has created inflationary pressures in petroleum-importing nations. Now, however, new technologies like fracking are facilitating the economic recovery of oil and gas from the tar sands of Canada and shale rock of America. This will significantly reduce demand for foreign oil.

Steep declines in the price of oil in 2014 and 2015 had a very negative effect on Canada's oil producers—particularly shale oil companies. This change has had a very real impact on Canada's national income.

Petroleum is not the only natural resource that affects international marketing. Warm climate and lack of water mean that many of Africa's countries will remain importers of foodstuffs. Vast differences in natural resources create international dependencies, huge shifts of wealth, inflation and recession, export opportunities for countries with abundant resources, and even a stimulus for military intervention.

> **high-net-worth individuals (HNWI)**
> individuals who have $1 million in liquid financial assets

Kokhanchikov/Shutterstock.com

The shortage of natural resources has become a major issue in the external environment in the last decade.

4-4 GLOBAL MARKETING BY THE INDIVIDUAL FIRM

A company should consider entering the global marketplace only after its management has a solid grasp of the global environment. Companies decide to *go global* for a number of reasons. Perhaps the most important reason is to earn additional profits. Managers may feel that international sales will result in higher profit margins or more added-on profits. A second stimulus is that a firm may have a unique product or technological advantage not available to other international competitors. Such advantages should result in major business successes abroad. In other situations, management may have exclusive market information regarding foreign customers, marketplaces, or market situations not known to others. Although exclusivity can provide an initial motivation for international marketing, managers can expect that competitors will catch up with their firm's temporary information advantage. Finally, saturated domestic markets, excess capacity, and potential for economies of scale can also be motivators to go global. Economies of scale mean that average per-unit production costs fall as output is increased.

Many firms form multinational partnerships—called strategic alliances—to assist them in penetrating global markets (strategic alliances will be examined in Chapter 7). Five other methods of entering the global marketplace are, in order of risk, exporting, licensing and franchising, contract manufacturing, the joint venture, and direct investment (see Exhibit 4.4).

4-4a Exporting

When a company decides to enter the global market, exporting is usually the least complicated and least risky method of entry. **Exporting** is selling domestically produced products to buyers in another country. China is currently the world's largest exporter, followed by the United States and then Germany. Canada ranks 12th overall with exports accounting for more than 30 percent of Canadian GDP. Canada's largest export is oil. Over 75 percent of our exports are to the United States and Mexico.[31] A company can sell directly to foreign importers or buyers. Exporting is not limited to huge corporations. Smaller Canadian companies have found many export market opportunities for their products and services. Canada is renowned for production of high-quality icewine, because our climate is ideal for it, and in 2015 over $18.6 million of icewine was exported with over 33 percent of those exports going to China.[32] Instead of selling directly to foreign buyers, a company may decide to sell to intermediaries located in its domestic market. The most common intermediary is the export merchant, also known as a **buyer for export**, which is usually treated as a domestic customer by the domestic manufacturer. The buyer for export assumes all risks and sells internationally for its own account. The domestic firm is involved only to the extent that its products are bought in foreign markets.

A second type of intermediary is the **export broker**, who plays the traditional broker's role by bringing buyer and seller together. The manufacturer still retains title and assumes all the risks. Export brokers operate primarily in agricultural products and raw materials.

Export agents, a third type of intermediary, are foreign sales agent-distributors who live in the foreign country and perform the same functions as domestic

---

exporting selling domestically produced products to buyers in another country

buyer for export an intermediary in the global market that assumes all ownership risks and sells globally for its own account

export broker an intermediary who plays the traditional broker's role by bringing buyer and seller together

export agents intermediaries who act like manufacturers' agents for exporters; the export agents live in the foreign market

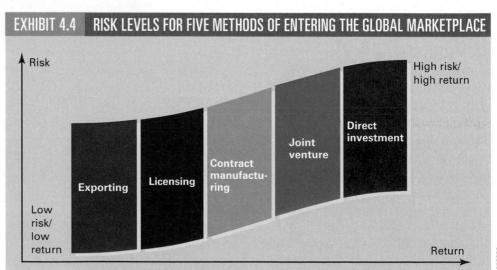

EXHIBIT 4.4   RISK LEVELS FOR FIVE METHODS OF ENTERING THE GLOBAL MARKETPLACE

Risk

Low risk/low return — Exporting — Licensing — Contract manufacturing — Joint venture — Direct investment — High risk/high return

Return

© Cengage

manufacturers' agents, helping with international financing, shipping, and so on. Export Development Canada provides help for Canadian firms seeking agents or distributors in almost every country. A second category of agents resides in the manufacturer's country but represents foreign buyers. This type of agent acts as a hired purchasing agent for foreign customers operating in the exporter's home market.

4-4b Licensing and Franchising

Another effective way for a firm to move into the global arena with relatively little risk is to sell a licence to manufacture its product to someone in a foreign country. **Licensing** is the legal process whereby a licensor allows another firm to use its manufacturing process, trademarks, patents, trade secrets, or other proprietary knowledge. The licensee, in turn, pays the licensor a royalty or fee agreed on by both parties. Because licensing has many advantages, companies—both big and small—have eagerly embraced the concept.

A licensor must ensure it can exercise sufficient control over the licensee's activities to ensure proper quality, pricing, distribution, and so on. Licensing may also create a new competitor in the long run, if the licensee decides to void the licence agreement. International law is often ineffective in stopping such actions. Two common ways of maintaining effective control over licensees are shipping one or more critical components from Canada or registering patents and trademarks locally to the Canadian firm, not to the licensee. Garment companies maintain control by delivering only so many labels per day; they also supply their own fabric, collect the scraps, and complete accurate unit counts.

Franchising is a form of licensing that has grown rapidly in recent years. Over half of all international franchises are for fast-food restaurants and business services.

4-4c Contract Manufacturing

Firms that do not want to become involved in either licensing or global marketing may choose to engage in **contract manufacturing**, which is private-label manufacturing by a foreign company. The foreign company produces a certain volume of products to specification, with the domestic firm's brand name on the goods. The domestic company usually handles the marketing. Thus the domestic firm can broaden its global marketing base without investing in overseas plants and equipment. After establishing a solid base, the domestic firm may switch to a joint venture or to direct investment. One company using contract manufacturing is Joe Fresh.

In February 2011 Tim Hortons signed a master licence agreement with The Apparel Group to open restaurants in the United Arab Emirates.

To produce good-quality and fashionable garments, Joe Fresh contracts production of the goods to factories overseas. The factory collapse in Bangladesh that killed over 300 people in spring 2013 is a poignant example of the risks associated with this retailer's desire for inexpensive production.

4-4d Joint Venture

Joint ventures are similar to licensing agreements. In an international joint venture, the domestic firm either buys part of a foreign company or joins with a foreign company to create a new entity. Skechers, the global leader in casual and performance footwear, has been available in China for over 15 years through a third-party distributor. During that period, as a result of creative marketing efforts and controlled distribution in over 55 Skechers stores, Skechers established a strong brand presence and product availability. In November 2016, Skechers announced it was moving into a joint venture relationship with Luen Thai Enterprises. As a result of the additional market insights that Luen Thai Enterprises will offer, Skechers believes that this joint venture will take the brand to a level beyond that which it has achieved in the past 15 years of the brand's globalization strategy.[33]

licensing the legal process whereby a licensor agrees to let another firm use its manufacturing process, trademarks, patents, trade secrets, or other proprietary knowledge

contract manufacturing private-label manufacturing by a foreign company

joint venture a domestic firm's purchase of part of a foreign company or a domestic firm joining with a foreign company to create a new entity

Honda Canada's Alliston, Ontario, plant opened in 1986, making it the first plant built in Canada by a Japanese car manufacturer. Alliston now has two more Honda plants supplying cars and engines for Japan, the United States, South America, and other countries.

Joint ventures can be very risky. Many fail; others fall victim to a takeover, in which one partner buys out the other. Sometimes joint venture partners simply can't agree on management strategies and policies. When a joint venture is successful, however, both parties gain valuable skills from the alliance.

4-4e Direct Investment

Active ownership of a foreign company or of overseas manufacturing or marketing facilities is **direct foreign investment**. Direct investors have either a controlling interest or a large minority interest in the firm. Thus they hold both the greatest potential reward and the greatest potential risk. Sometimes firms make direct investments because they can find no suitable local partners. Also, direct investments avoid the communication problems and conflicts of interest that can arise with joint ventures. Other firms simply don't want to share their technology, which they fear may be stolen or ultimately used against them by a newly created competitor. Toyota Manufacturing Corporation has invested heavily in the manufacturing of its automobiles here in Canada to take advantage of the quality manufacturing occurring in our auto sector.

A firm may make a direct foreign investment by acquiring an interest in an existing company or by building new facilities. It might do so because

direct foreign investment
active ownership of a foreign company or of overseas manufacturing or marketing facilities

it has difficulty either transferring some resource to a foreign operation or sourcing that resource locally. One important resource is personnel, especially managers. If the local labour market is tight, the firm may buy an entire foreign firm and retain all its employees instead of paying higher salaries than competitors.

4-5 THE GLOBAL MARKETING MIX

To succeed, firms seeking to enter into foreign trade must adhere to the principles of the marketing mix. Information gathered on foreign markets through research is the basis for the four Ps of global marketing strategy: product, place (distribution), promotion, and price. Marketing managers who understand the advantages and disadvantages of different ways of entering the global market and the effect of the external environment on the firm's marketing mix have a better chance of reaching their goals.

The first step in creating a marketing mix is developing a thorough understanding of the global target market. Often this knowledge can be obtained through the same types of marketing research used in the domestic market (see Chapter 5). However, global marketing research is conducted in vastly different environments. Conducting a survey can be difficult in developing countries, where telephone ownership is growing but is not always common, and mail delivery is slow or sporadic. Drawing samples that are based on known population parameters is often difficult because of the lack of data. Moreover, the questions a marketer is able to ask may differ in other cultures. In some cultures, people tend to be more private than in Canada and will not respond to personal questions on surveys.

4-5a Product Decisions

With the proper information, a good marketing mix can be developed. One important decision is whether to alter the product or the promotion for the global marketplace. Other options are to radically change the product or to

EXHIBIT 4.5	CANADA'S TOP FIVE EXPORTS, 2015 ($ BILLION)	
1. Crude oil and crude bitumen		77.8
2. Motor vehicles for passenger transport (other than buses/public transport)		60
3. Machines, engines, pumps		31.1
4. Gems, precious metals		19
5. Electronic equipment		13.2

Source: World's Top Exports, http://www.worldstopexports.com/canadas-top-exports.

adjust either the promotional message or the product to suit local conditions.

ONE PRODUCT, ONE MESSAGE The strategy of global marketing standardization, which was discussed earlier, means developing a single product for all markets and promoting it the same way throughout the world. Procter & Gamble uses the same product and promotional themes for Head & Shoulders in China as it does in North America. This advertising brings attention to a person's dandruff problem, which can be an issue in a nation of predominantly black-haired people. Head & Shoulders is one of the best-selling shampoos in China. Procter & Gamble (P&G) markets its rich portfolio of personal care, beauty, grooming, health, and fabric products in more than 180 countries. The firm has 20 brands that sell more than $1 billion annually around the world. Some brands, such as Duracell batteries, are heavily standardized. P&G has moved away from standardization for other brands, however. Its Axe line of male grooming products uses a constantly running sociological study in order to keep its video ads up to date with the latest trends among young men. Axe's promotion, bottle size, and pricing also change according to which country is being targeted.[34]

Global media—especially satellite and cable TV networks, such as CNN International, MTV Networks, and British Sky Broadcasting—make it possible to beam advertising to audiences unreachable a few years ago. Eighteen-year-olds in Paris often have more in common with 18-year-olds in Halifax than with their own parents. They buy the same products, go to the same movies, listen to the same music, and sip the same colas. Global media companies allow advertisers to run unified campaigns across nations.

TOP 10 GLOBAL BRANDS

1. Apple
2. Google
3. Coca-Cola
4. Microsoft
5. Toyota
6. IBM
7. Samsung
8. Amazon
9. Mercedes-Benz
10. GE

Source: Interbrand, Interbrand's Best Global Brands 2016, http://interbrand.com/best-brands/best-global-brands/2016/ranking/.

Unchanged products may fail simply because of cultural factors. In Russia Campbell's Soups failed because families prefer to make soup from scratch. Despite cultural hurdles, numerous multinational firms are applying uniform branding to products around the world. Sometimes the desire for absolute standardization must also give way to practical considerations and local market dynamics. For example, the European version of Diet Coke is known as Coca-Cola Light, as Europeans use the word "light" to denote something low in calories. Sometimes, even if the brand name differs by market, managers can create a strong visual relationship by uniformly applying the brandmark and graphic elements on packaging.[35]

PRODUCT INVENTION In the context of global marketing, product invention can be taken to mean either creating a new product for a market or drastically changing an existing product. For example, more than 100 unique Pringles potato chip flavours have been invented for international markets. Prawn Cocktail (the United Kingdom), Seaweed (Japan), Blueberry (China), Cinnamon Sweet Potato (France), and Bangkok Grilled Chicken Wing (Thailand) are some of the many Pringles flavours available outside the United States.[36] Chinese consumers found Oreo cookies "too sweet," while Indian consumers said that they were "too bitter." In response, Kraft changed the recipe in each country and created a new Green Tea Oreo flavour for China.

PRODUCT ADAPTATION Another alternative for global marketers is to slightly alter a basic product to meet local conditions. McDonald's global success is built on this strategy.

Sometimes marketers can simply change the package size. In India, Unilever sells single-use sachets of Sunsilk shampoo for 2 to 4 cents. Unilever's Rexona brand deodorant sticks sell for 16 cents and up. On electronic products, power sources and voltage must be changed. It may be necessary, for example, to change the size and shape of the electrical plug.

4-5b Promotion Adaptation

Another global marketing strategy is to maintain the same basic product but alter the promotional strategy. Bicycles are mainly pleasure vehicles in Canada. In many parts of the world, however, they are a family's main mode of transportation. Thus promotion in these countries should stress durability and efficiency. In contrast, Canadian advertising may emphasize escaping and having fun.

Some cultures view a product as having less value if it has to be advertised. In other nations, claims that seem commonplace by Canadian standards may be viewed negatively or even not allowed. Germany does not permit advertisers to state that their products are the best or better than those of competitors, a description used in Canadian advertising. Language barriers, translation problems, and cultural differences have generated numerous headaches for international marketing managers. For example, a toothpaste claiming to give users white teeth was especially inappropriate in many areas of Southeast Asia, where the well-to-do chew betel nuts and black teeth are a sign of higher social status.

4-5c Place (Distribution)

Solving promotional and product problems does not guarantee global marketing success. The product still needs to be adequately distributed. For example, Europeans do not play sports as much as Americans do, so they do not visit sporting-goods stores as often. Realizing this, Reebok started selling its shoes in about 800 traditional shoe stores in France. In just one year, the company doubled its French sales.

Channel members vary globally. For example, Taiwanese convenience stores are quite different from convenience stores found in Canada. Beyond the staple snacks, they provide an array of services such as dry cleaning, train and concert ticket reservations, traffic fine and utility payment, hot sit-down meals, mail drop-off, and book pickup. They also deliver items as varied as refrigerators and multicourse banquets. As you might expect, heavy convenience store patronage is the norm in Taiwan.[37] Starbucks success in China came about because it recognized that the Chinese consumer tended to visit coffee shops in large groups to meet, linger, and socialize. Recognizing the role that the coffee shop played in daily living, Starbucks created larger stores with furniture that could be moved around to accommodate large group seating for the China market.[38]

Innovative distribution systems can create a competitive advantage for savvy companies. Planes taking tourists by day to Kenya's Nairobi Airport return to their European hubs by night crammed with an average 25 metric tons apiece of fresh beans, bok choy, okra, and other produce that was harvested and packaged just the day before.

In many developing nations, channels of distribution and the physical infrastructure are inadequate. Both inadequate and poorly maintained highways, distribution centres, and storage facilities mean that a significant portion of food products may spoil while being transported from the farm to the market, resulting in higher costs and shortages. A global marketer must consider the impact of such infrastructure issues on their strategy to ensure that they can be competitive.

4-5d Pricing

Once marketing managers have determined a global product and promotion strategy, they can select the remainder of the marketing mix. When creating a final price, exporters must not only cover their production costs but must also consider transportation costs, insurance, taxes, and tariffs. In addition, marketers must also determine what customers are willing to spend on a particular product and ensure that their foreign buyers will pay the price. The retail price for a Starbucks coffee in China is higher than in Canada. This is likely a result of the lower volume of coffee sales in China, relative to Canada; China ranks 67th in coffee consumption in the world, compared to Canada, which ranks 12th.[39] But it also drives an air of prestige for the brand, which is key to the prestige-brand-conscious consumer of middle-class China.[40]

Because developing nations lack mass purchasing power, selling to them often poses special pricing problems. Sometimes a product can be simplified to lower the price. The firm must not assume that low-income countries are willing to accept lower quality, however. L'Oréal was unsuccessful selling cheap shampoo in India, so the company targets the rising class. It now sells a $17 Paris face powder and a $25 Vichy sunscreen. Both products are very popular.

EXCHANGE RATES The exchange rate is the price of one country's currency in terms of another country's currency. If a country's currency *appreciates*, less of that country's currency is needed to buy another country's currency. If a country's currency *depreciates*, more of that currency will be needed to buy another country's currency.

Appreciation and depreciation affect the prices of a country's goods. If the Canadian dollar depreciates relative to the Japanese yen, Canadian residents will need to pay more dollars to buy Japanese goods. To illustrate, suppose the dollar price of a yen is $0.012 and that a Toyota is priced at 2 million yen. At this exchange rate, a Canadian resident pays $24,000 for a Toyota ($0.012 × 2 million yen = $24,000). If the dollar depreciates to $0.018 to 1 yen, however, the Canadian resident will have to pay $36,000 for the same Toyota.

As the dollar depreciates, the prices of Japanese goods rise for Canadian residents, so they buy fewer Japanese goods—thus Canadian imports may decline. At the same time, as the dollar depreciates relative to the yen, the yen appreciates relative to the dollar. This means prices of Canadian goods fall for the Japanese, so they buy more Canadian goods—and Canadian exports rise.

Currency markets operate under a system of **floating exchange rates.** Prices of different currencies float up and down on the basis of the demand for and the supply of each currency. Global currency traders create the supply of and demand for a particular country's currency on the basis of that country's investment, trade potential, and economic strength.

DUMPING Dumping is generally considered to be the sale of an exported product at a price lower than that charged for the same or a like product in the home market of the exporter. This practice is regarded as a form of price discrimination that can potentially harm the importing nation's competing industries. Dumping may occur as a result of exporter business strategies that include (1) trying to increase an overseas market share, (2) temporarily distributing products in overseas markets to offset slack demand in the home market, (3) lowering unit costs by exploiting large-scale production, and (4) attempting to maintain stable prices during periods of exchange rate fluctuations.

Historically, the dumping of goods has presented serious problems in international trade. As a result, dumping has led to significant disagreements among countries and diverse views about its harmfulness. Some trade economists view dumping as harmful only when it involves the use of predatory practices that intentionally try to eliminate competition and gain monopoly power in a market. They believe that predatory dumping rarely occurs and that antidumping rules are a protectionist tool whose cost to consumers and import-using industries exceeds the benefits to the industries receiving protection.

COUNTERTRADE Global trade does not always involve cash. Countertrade is a fast-growing way to conduct global business. In **countertrade**, all or part of the payment for goods or services is in the form of other goods or services. Countertrade is thus a form of barter (swapping goods for goods), an age-old practice whose origins have been traced back to cave dwellers.

One common type of countertrade is straight barter. The Malaysian government purchased 20 diesel-electric locomotives from General Electric in exchange for a supply of 200,000 metric tons of palm oil. Sometimes, countertrade involves both cash and goods. General Motors sold locomotive and diesel engines to Yugoslavia in exchange for $4 million and Yugoslavian cutting tools.[41] Another form of countertrade is the compensation agreement. Typically, a company provides technology and equipment for a plant in a developing nation and agrees to take full or partial payment in goods produced by that plant.

4-6 THE IMPACT OF THE INTERNET

In many respects, "going global" is easier than it has ever been. Opening an e-commerce site on the Internet immediately puts a company in the international marketplace. Sophisticated language translation software can make any site accessible to people around the world. Global shippers, such as UPS, FedEx, and DHL, help solve international e-commerce distribution complexities. Currency conversion software allows companies to post prices in Canadian dollars, then ask their customers what currency they want to use for payment. But despite much advancement, the promises of borderless commerce and the global Internet economy are still being restrained by the

floating exchange rates prices of different currencies move up and down based on the demand for and the supply of each currency

dumping the sale of an exported product at a price lower than that charged for the same or a like product in the home market of the exporter

countertrade a form of trade in which all or part of the payment for goods or services is in the form of other goods or services

If a country's currency depreciates, more of that currency will be needed to buy another country's currency.

otnaydur/Shutterstock.com

CHAPTER 4: Developing a Global Vision

old rules, regulations, and culturally based habits. Lands' End is not allowed to mention its unconditional refund policy on its e-commerce site in Germany because German retailers, which normally do not allow returns after 14 days, sued and won a court ruling blocking mention of it. Canadians are more and more likely to rely on credit cards when completing purchase transactions. In 2015, 42 percent of all payment transactions by Canadians were by credit card, making online shopping easy and convenient.[42] Japan, however, is for the most part still a cash-transaction–based culture, making online shopping difficult. Recognizing this as a cultural challenge, Amazon offers "cash on delivery," where Japanese customers pay the post carrier upon delivery.

4-6a Social Media and Global Marketing

Almost half of the 7.476 billion people around the globe are Internet users, and one-third of them are active on social media. Almost 34 percent of these social media users access their social media sites via their mobile phone. In fact, between 2016 and 2017 social media usage via mobile phones grew by 30 percent, outpacing total social media usage growth. The Asia-Pacific consumer is driving this growth, suggesting that mobile enhanced digital marketing campaigns represent an opportunity area for reaching this global segment.[43] Because Facebook, YouTube, Instagram and other social media are popular around the world, firms both large and small have embraced social media marketing. In May of 2015, shoe company TOMS donated one pair of shoes for every person who took a picture of their bare feet and shared it on Instagram with the hashtag #withoutshoes. This campaign reached thousands of consumers who were unaware of TOMS. It also reinforced TOMS's key differentiator in the competitive casual shoe category: the donation of a pair of shoes for every pair of shoes sold. The campaign has become an annual campaign for TOMS. As a result of the #withoutshoes campaign held in May 2016, 27,435 children in 10 countries received free shoes.

Biltwell Inc. is a manufacturer and seller of parts and accessories to customize motorcycles. To engage and maintain the passion for the brand among motorcycle enthusiasts, Biltwell uses its Facebook fan page quite effectively. Biltwell fans from around the world are invited to show how they customize Biltwell helmets by posting a picture of their "helmet art" on the Biltwell Facebook page.

Blogs and other social media sites help global marketers gather consumer intelligence quickly to be in a position to continually alter and adapt their messages and

strategies. Global marketers use social media not only for understanding consumers but also to build their brands as they expand internationally. Uniqlo, the Japanese apparel retailer, opened its first two stores in Canada in late 2016. Because of the power of the Internet, Uniqlo was already a known retailer to many Canadians, leading to lineups on opening day. The Internet and social media bring every company from every corner of the world into consumers' homes. Even the smallest company today can be a global marketer!

Given the global nature of social media, marketing managers of social media campaigns must be vigilantly aware of the cultural norms of the many countries in which the campaign can be viewed. Social media campaigns must transcend a variety of cultural boundaries in the hopes of ensuring acceptance of the message globally. Bic South Africa posted an ad on Facebook to celebrate National Women's Day. The ad carried the copy "Look like a girl, act like a lady, think like a man, work like a boss." Women around the world, not just in South Africa, took offence.[44] Such reactions can significantly hurt a brands reputation amongst its target consumer.

The Globalized Beer Drinker

"Globalization" is not only a view outward from a firm to the planet's opportunity. It is often a firm's view of itself through the lens of the world. If that sounds backwards, consider the situation of Side Launch Brewing Company, competing within the space of craft beer, which by definition must contain itself to a volume limit in order to qualify as a "craft brewer"—so it has no interest in building a national, never mind a global, brand. "We could meet our sales quota by selling to China," claims founder Garnet Pratt. "But why? That's just selling beer for the sake of selling beer. That's not us." That said, because globalization is not just about growing internationally but also about international competitors infringing on its turf, it is in Side Launch's best interest to have one eye on global trends in order to seize opportunities or thwart threats.

The biggest threat stemming from the globalization trend is, perhaps surprisingly, from macro beer companies, but it's not in the way that might be expected. Based on his wealth of experience with some of those global brands, VP Operations Dave Sands explains, "Many national and international brewing companies have tried to launch craft styles and/or craft portfolios from within their organizations with very limited success, due in part to a negative or skeptical consumer perception of the quality of the products." The solution to this conundrum, the large brewers have decided, is to simply buy up the little guys. "As can be seen with the recent industry trends, acquisition is seemingly the only way the big brewers have been able to participate in the craft part of the segment."

But aside from the big bad macro beer companies acquiring little vulnerable craft companies and competing head on with Side Launch, something over which they have zero control, Side Launch has other concerns with globalization. "With our present model, any exporting comes with a huge risk," cautions brewer Michael Hancock. "Our beer is unpasteurized, which on one hand makes it better tasting, but on the other hand makes it prone to spoiling if not properly refrigerated. So even shipping beer outside of Ontario, and maintaining our reputation, can be very, very risky."

Having said all of this, one could make the argument that the idea of craft beer is due to the concept of globalization. The pattern of North Americans spending time in Europe, consuming European beers, then returning to North America with the desire to find something that doesn't taste like a generic macro brand is the undeniable genesis of craft. "I didn't invent dark lager, it came from Germany," admits Michael. "I was one of the first in North America to make a wheat beer, but it was this notion of introducing a well-established European brewing technique to North Americans. And people loved it."

Thus, for reasons of position and reputation, Side Launch will not pursue a globalization growth strategy. And yet it is because of globalization that Side Launch must rely heavily on its reputation to defend against the threat presented by big beer craft acquisitions, and it must keep a keen eye on global trends, to ensure it is attending to the needs of an increasingly global beer drinker. "People will say to me," begins VP Sales and Marketing Chuck Galea, "'Ahh, you know your beer reminds me of my trip to Munich and sitting on a patio there enjoying a truly German lager.'"

Questions

1. Although global marketing is a logical, if not necessary, pursuit for some companies in certain industries, discuss some of the barriers that would make it difficult for Side Launch to go in this direction.

2. Research some of the multinational brewing companies and identify Canadian-based breweries that have become acquired by these large global firms.

3. While Canada's liquor retail outlets offer products from all over the world, including beer, what is the main advantage offered to small independently owned breweries such as Side Launch within their home provinces?

Side Launch Brewing Company

Part 1 Case
From Analysis to Action

The Canadian Coffee Competition

Like the "double-double," the Canadian coffee market was a category made to order for Tim Hortons. Socially we were gathering more and more at corner cafés, and Tim's, founded in 1964, had established itself as the category king long before Starbucks laid down stakes in the 1990s. However, concern began brewing for Tim's when McDonald's decided to put forth a concerted effort to cash in on coffee by creating the McCafé brand in 2009.

The impact was felt immediately as Tim's market share of fresh brewed coffee in Canada began to erode, although by mid-2017, 8 out every 10 cups consumed outside the home were still coming from Tim Hortons. That said, the demand for coffee in Canada, which built the Tim Hortons brand in the first place, was by the late 2010s clearly being contested by Tim's, McDonald's, and the omnipresent Starbucks.

The story of how this came to be—the opportunity that each contestant saw in the coffee market, the decisions they made to dive in, and those they continue to make to grab an edge—will unfold as leaders of these brands keep one eye on their competition and one eye on percolating consumer trends. For marketing students wondering about the real-life applicability of marketing theory, read on as we combine two cornerstone concepts of marketing—SWOT analysis and Ansoff's opportunity matrix—and compare how they are used within the strategic chess game going on between the major players in Canada's competitive coffee landscape.

While every single market competitor in every single industry *should* be practising these marketing fundamentals constantly, the evidence does not always show this to be happening. By mid-2017, the once dominant Tim Hortons was fine-tuning its coffee business in the wake of news showing same-store sales were on the slide. While it would have been difficult for those caught in a typical Tim Hortons in-store or drive-through lineup to notice that business had slowed at all, a glance toward the nearest McDonald's McCafé might have proved otherwise. It would have also, no doubt, supported the decision by Tim Hortons to ratchet up its once untouchable way of doing coffee.

One thing SWOT teaches us is that every opportunity and threat has an epicentre—an origin from which a small, sometimes unnoticeable crack becomes a gaping chasm. By dividing the O and T in SWOT into five subcategories—competition, regulation, economics, social, and technological (CREST) forces—we see how one force might arise on its own but quickly trigger others before creating a flywheel that becomes an entity that business leaders are forced to deal with. The trick, however, is to notice, prepare, and act before that flywheel becomes too powerful to overcome.

The flywheel in the case of Canada's coffee landscape might be traced to, of all places, Italy. It was there that Howard Schultz, would-be CEO and Starbucks brand architect, noted there was a "third place" in the daily routine of people—a gathering spot between work and home—that was embedded in the European culture. He gambled that North Americans would embrace this concept as well and in 1987 purchased Starbucks and set off to create a category that was neither a restaurant nor a coffee shop, but a "third place."

Twenty years later, McDonald's had a separate business unit with a visible in-store "third place" presence—complete with the requisite fireplaces and WiFi—and Tim Hortons was introducing, with the assistance of a major marketing communications push, the "perfectly uncomplicated latte" of its own in order to create its own "third place" environment.

Focusing solely on Tim Hortons for a moment (we are a Canadian publication after all), a high-level glimpse at its SWOT analysis for the year ending 2016 might have looked something like that shown in the table below.

While extensively more detail would have been written into an actual SWOT performed by Tim Hortons leadership in the mid-2010s, the 12 factors noted in Exhibit P1.1 would have been enough to prompt Tim Hortons to cobble together a growth matrix resembling something similar to that shown in the table below.

Reviewing their options, the leadership of Tim Hortons might have evaluated them in a way similar to the following.

- *Market penetration:* Making more of the same coffee for the same coffee customers represents a no-gainer, based upon current leadership in the space, with little if any room to grow.

- *Product development:* Creating a new coffee product or product line, targeted at Tim's large and loyal customers and potentially luring new customers, keeping up with consumer trends, and defending its position as Canada's coffee brand, represents a significant growth opportunity.

- *Market development:* Pursuing a new customer, a Starbucks customer for instance, would be difficult to achieve given Starbucks' domination of the "third place" category and therefore presents no significant growth opportunity

- *Diversification:* Developing a new product, as Starbucks did when it began selling wine and beer in Canada in 2016, would seem simply too risky… if not preposterous for the "family" image of Tim Hortons.

The process outlined above artificially condenses and compresses the process of SWOT analysis and growth opportunity evaluation into a simplistic series of tables and bullet points. Months of research involving deep dives into extensive data and analytics would have had to be waded through in order to come to similar conclusions. But then again, we have the luxury of hindsight and armchair marketing advice. The point is, marketing is a strategic process that fuels the engine that makes businesses tick.

At the time of this writing, Tim Hortons was pushing its franchisees to order $12,000 espresso machines across Canada to support the "perfectly uncomplicated latte" campaign. McDonalds McCafés were continuing their aggressive push into territories of both Tim Hortons and

EXHIBIT P1.1	TIM HORTONS SWOT ANALYSIS—2016 (HYPOTHETICAL)
Strengths	**Weaknesses**
• Canadian market leader • Access to capital • Value pricing	• Perception of "blue collar" appeal • Unsophisticated coffee offerings • Lineups
Opportunities	**Threats**
• "Bourgeois" reputation of Starbucks and its customer base • Social demand for specialty coffees • Technological methods for cost-effective specialty coffee production	• Ubiquity and growth of the specialty coffee market and associated products • McDonald's launch of McCafé, with value-priced specialty coffees • Shift in demographics, and growing preference for specialty coffees

EXHIBIT P1.2	TIM HORTONS OPPORTUNITY MATRIX—2016 (HYPOTHETICAL)	
	Current Products	**New Products**
Current Markets	Market Penetration Open more restaurants, make more coffee, sell more coffee to same customers. The safest growth strategy.	Product Development Create new product(s) for loyal Tim Hortons customers, who want something different.
New Markets	Market Development Pursue a different or untapped market, currently unserved by Tim Hortons.	Diversification Develop a new product for a new market—the riskiest of all growth strategies.

Starbucks, essentially employing a market penetration strategy. As for Starbucks? Well, it was not so casually continuing to fortify its position as leaders in the "third place" category but with the aforementioned addition of alcoholic beverages was developing a new product line for a new market segment—a classic diversification growth strategy.

Your job, now that time has passed since this writing, is to report back with your observations on how these combatants, and any others, have fared in the great Canadian coffee showdown.

SOURCES

Calum Marsh. "With Its 'Uncomplicated Latte' Is Tim Hortons Risking Its Blue Collar Brand?" *National Post,* May 4, 2017, http://news.nationalpost.com/life/food-drink/with-its-uncomplicated-latte-is-tim-hortons-risking-its-blue-collar-brand (accessed May 10, 2017).

Al Ramadan, Dave Peterson, Christopher Lochhead, and Kevin Maney. *Play Bigger: How Pirates, Dreamers, and Innovators Create and Dominate Markets.* New York: HarperCollins, 2016.

Hollie Shaw. "Tim Hortons, Burger King Owner's Same Store Sales Decline as It Battles McDonald's," *Financial Post,* April 26, 2017, http://business.financialpost.com/news/retail-marketing/tim-hortons-burger-king-and-popeyes-sales-fall-in-their-home-markets-but-earnings-beat-expectations (accessed April 28, 2017).

Marina Strauss. "The $12,000 Espresso Machine: Tim Hortons Brews up New Plan in Coffee Wars," *Globe and Mail,* updated December 12, 2016, www.theglobeandmail.com/report-on-business/tim-hortons-to-roll-out-new-premium-espresso-options/article33302351 (accessed May 10, 2017).

QUESTIONS

1. How are the three coffee brands featured in this article (Tim Hortons, Starbucks, and McCafé) faring today in market share in Canada? Search them online, paying particularly close attention to coverage in the *National Post* and *Globe and Mail*.

2. Have any additional competitive forces emerged into the Canadian coffee competition that have altered the landscape in any way? List and explain.

3. What other forces of the marketing environment have affected the progress of each of the three coffee brands in Canada?

4. What, if any, new growth strategies have any of the three coffee brands employed?

5 | Marketing Research

LEARNING OUTCOMES

5-1 Explain the role of marketing research

5-2 List the steps in the marketing research process

5-3 Discuss the impact of technology on marketing research

5-4 Describe when to conduct marketing research

> *"It's a digital world out there! Everything from TV, to phone, to in-store shopping and transportation modes, are somehow connected. The marketing research world is no exception, and in fact must be at the heart of it. That's where the consumer lives."*
>
> —Tamer El Araby, Managing Director, Nielsen Insights[1]

5-1 THE ROLE OF MARKETING RESEARCH

Marketing research is about gathering information about customers, their needs, and the marketplace in which they operate. The challenge can be great, as that marketplace is constantly changing, and customers are not always clear (whether intentionally or not) about what their needs are or how they would like them satisfied.

Marketing research is about bringing clarity to unknown aspects of a marketplace. It should not be used simply to try to reinforce a belief, but rather as a means to better understand the connections between marketing actions and customer needs. As famed advertising executive David Ogilvy once said, "Some people use research like a drunkard uses a lamppost: for support, not illumination."[2]

Marketing research is a process, like any other

marketing research the process of planning, collecting, and analyzing data relevant to a marketing decision

type of research. There is an unknown element—a problem—that needs to be investigated. Investigating the problem requires a plan. There are tools to use to assess the problem and seek out potential solutions—but instead of beakers and lab equipment, marketers use a myriad of tools like observation, surveys, and focus groups. Once those tools have been used to gather data, the data are then processed into information to help solve the problem.

An important note about marketing research is that despite the methodical process, it does not solve the problem on its own. Marketing research is used to help make decisions; it is not the only basis for a decision. It is invaluable in helping companies better understand their customers, the marketplace, and the inherent challenges of meeting customer needs.

How can marketing research information be used to help make decisions? There are three functional roles that marketing research can play in an organization:

1. *Descriptive role*—presenting factual statements. For example, What are the historic sales trends in the

industry? What are consumers' attitudes toward a product and its advertising?

2. *Diagnostic role*—explaining relationships within data. For example, What is the impact on a product's sales if the colour of the packaging is changed?

3. *Predictive role*—predicting results of a marketing decision (what if?). For example, What is the impact of a new product introduction on market share?

A good marketing research program will attempt to balance these three roles and provide the best information related to the problem.

The best way to understand the role of marketing research is to see it as an overarching activity that supports the many marketing activities of a firm. The American Marketing Association has used the same definition for marketing research for a decade: "Marketing research is the function that links the consumer, customer, and public to the marketer through information—information used to identify and define marketing opportunities and problems; generate, refine, and evaluate marketing actions; monitor marketing performance; and improve understanding of marketing as a process."[3]

This definition shows the impact that marketing research can have when done properly. To conduct marketing research properly, you must understand the process behind it.

5-2 THE MARKETING RESEARCH PROCESS

The marketing research process is a scientific approach to decision making that maximizes the chance of receiving accurate and meaningful results. Exhibit 5.1 traces the six steps in the research process and provides the basis from which marketing research is undertaken.

5-2a Step 1: Identify the Problem

Identifying the problem is the most important stage of the entire marketing research process. Without a defined problem statement, marketing research will be nothing more than a series of tasks without direction or purpose. This first stage is best explained by a phrase used in information technology: "garbage in, garbage out"; the integrity of the output (results) is dependent on the integrity of the input (the problem).

This means that a researcher should first determine whether there is enough information to clearly define a problem before embarking on the full marketing research

EXHIBIT 5.1 THE MARKETING RESEARCH PROCESS

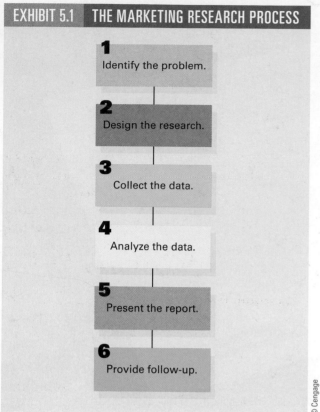

1 Identify the problem.

2 Design the research.

3 Collect the data.

4 Analyze the data.

5 Present the report.

6 Provide follow-up.

© Cengage

objective. A **marketing research objective** is developed to provide insightful decision-making information. It is the specific information needed to solve a marketing research issue. Managers must combine this information with their own experience and other information to make a proper decision.

Marketing research objectives are developed as a series of questions that seek to clarify what decision makers needed to know to make a marketing decision. If the research problem focuses on factors that determine how a customer chooses a restaurant, then some key questions to ask are the following:

- What is the demographic profile of the restaurant's patrons?

- What external factors (time, expense) are influencing the public's willingness to dine out?

- How important is branding to diners in the restaurant industry?

Once these objectives have been created, researchers can then determine the overall approach necessary to meet the research objectives and answer the research question. Marketing research objectives must consider the internal and external environments to ensure that a well-informed decision can be made.

5-2b Step 2: Design the Research

The **research design** specifies how to go about answering the questions and achieving the objectives. This stage is about deciding on the type of study that will be conducted and the tools and techniques that will be used to gather and analyze the collected data. The research design is about creating a roadmap for the research process.

TYPES OF RESEARCH DESIGN To gather the necessary information to answer the research question, a researcher must decide on the type of research design to use. There are two types of research design: exploratory and conclusive.

Exploratory research is done to help explore the problem further, looking for a context in which the research will be conducted. Because the parameters of exploratory research are not always clearly defined, researchers have more flexibility in how the research is conducted. This is a process of informal discovery, where looking for key relationships and variables is more important than attempting to solve a research problem. There are a number of different methods of exploratory research: focus groups, expert interviews, literature search, and case studies.

process. Decision makers must be able to diagnose the right situation for conducting marketing research. We'll discuss this further in the section titled When to Conduct Marketing Research later in the chapter.

The first task in this step is to differentiate between a management decision and a research problem. A management decision is often a big-picture dilemma facing a marketing manager—in other words, what do they need to *do*? A research problem is a statement that identifies what information is to be gathered—in other words, what do they need to *know*? Consider these examples:

- *Management decision:* What should be done about a restaurant's slow sales?

- *Research problem:* What factors go into a customer's decision to dine at a particular restaurant?

Once this difference has been established, a marketing researcher can then move forward to create the marketing research

marketing research objective specific statement about the information needed to solve the research question

research design a plan that specifies how to answer the research question and achieve the research objectives by laying out the research tools and techniques necessary to collect and analyze data

exploratory research an informal discovery process that attempts to gain insights and a better understanding of the management and research problems

Conclusive research is, as its name suggests, more focused on developing conclusions and courses of actions. Often conclusive research can help to verify the insights provided by exploratory research—findings from exploratory methods (e.g., focus groups) can help develop conclusive methods (e.g., surveys). Descriptive research uses exclusively primary research methods.

There are two kinds of conclusive research: descriptive and causal. **Descriptive research**, by far the more common type of conclusive research used in business, attempts to describe marketing phenomena and characteristics. **Causal research** focuses on the cause and effect of two variables and attempts to find some correlation between them. This type of conclusive research is used often in academic and research environments.

THE RESEARCH DESIGN PROCESS In deciding on a research design, it should be noted that this is not an "either–or" situation where only one type of research design can be chosen. The best way to consider research design is as a process, described in Exhibit 5.2. Researchers should use exploratory research to provide clarity and structure to the problem while also examining if there are existing studies that might help in identifying key variables. Then the researcher can choose, depending on the results of exploratory research, which type of conclusive research (descriptive or causal) will best solve the research problem.

EXHIBIT 5.2 THE RESEARCH DESIGN PROCESS

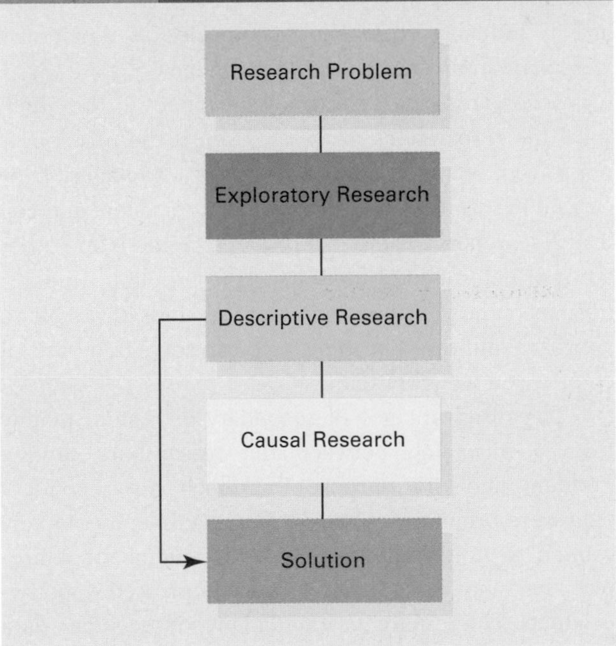

Often researchers will first attempt to solve the problem by using descriptive research methods like surveys. However, if there are still outstanding issues or the problem was not solved with descriptive research, then causal research would be used.

5-2c Step 3: Collect the Data

Now that the research design has been chosen, it is time to collect the data by using that design. An important early decision at this stage of the process is what mix of secondary and primary research will be used.

SECONDARY VERSUS PRIMARY RESEARCH

The temptation for researchers is to begin collecting their own data to answer their research question. But it is vital that there be an examination of what data already exist.

Secondary data are data that already have been collected by another entity (government, industry association, company). The key thing to remember is that secondary research was collected for another purpose, meaning that it will be very unlikely that secondary data on their own will answer your research question. There are exceptions to every rule, however, as you can see by reading the following example about Campbell's Soup.

Campbell used U.S. government data on nutritional and eating habits and created the famous "Soup Is Good Food" campaign. Little else was done in the way of primary research, and the campaign became synonymous with Campbell's Soup for decades.

Much has changed today, however, with Campbell's approach to marketing research. The company recently completed two years of primary research into studying how skin moisture and heart rate change when consumers look at pictures of soup and logo designs. The results of this biometrics research: bigger and clearer pictures of steaming soup and fewer spoons on the packaging of Campbell's Soup products.[4]

Primary research is research that is new and created by the researcher. A number of techniques can be used to generate primary data, all of which can be tailored to meet the specific research needs of an organization. While this research is more expensive

conclusive research a more specific type of research that attempts to provide clarity to a decision maker by identifying specific courses of action

descriptive research a type of conclusive research that attempts to describe marketing phenomena and characteristics

causal research a type of conclusive research that focuses on the cause and effect of two variables and attempts to find some correlation between them

secondary data data previously collected for any purpose other than the one at hand

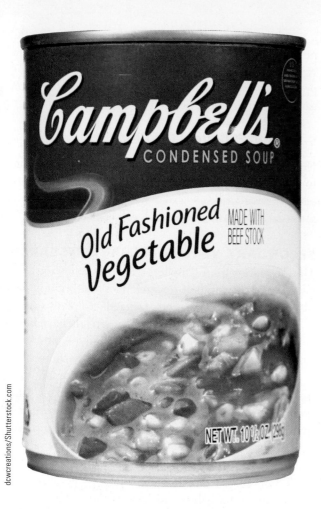

dcwcreations/Shutterstock.com

SECONDARY DATA COLLECTION There are two main sources of secondary data: sources inside the organization conducting the research and external sources that are publicly available, sometimes at a price.

Secondary information originating from within the company includes documents such as annual reports, reports to shareholders, product-testing results (perhaps made available to the news media), the company's own marketing data, and house periodicals prepared by the company for communication to employees, customers, or others. Often this information is incorporated into a company's internal database.

Innumerable outside sources of secondary information also exist. These are principally business data summaries prepared by government departments and agencies (federal, provincial or territorial, and local), such as Statistics Canada. Still more data are available from online journals and research studies available from research and marketing associations, such as the Marketing Research and Intelligence Association (MRIA) and the Canadian Institute of Marketing (CIM).

Trade and industry associations also publish secondary data that can be found in business periodicals and other news media that regularly publish studies and articles on the economy, specific industries, and even individual companies. The unpublished summarized secondary information from these sources includes internal reports, memos, or special-purpose analyses with limited circulation. Economic considerations or priorities in the organization may preclude publication of these summaries. In addition, information on many topics, such as a Nielsen PRIZM segmentation, industry trends, and brands, can be derived from polls, focus groups, surveys, panels, and interviews and is available from such companies as Environics Research Group and other sources online.

Secondary data save time and money if they help solve the researcher's problem. Even if the problem is not solved, secondary data have other advantages. They can aid in formulating a clear research problem and can lead researchers to potential research methods and other types of data needed for solving the problem. In addition, secondary data can pinpoint the kinds of people to approach and their locations, and can serve as a basis of comparison for other data.

The disadvantages of secondary data stem mainly from a mismatch between the researcher's unique problem and the purpose for which the secondary data were originally gathered. For example, a company wanted to determine the market potential for a fireplace log made of coal rather than compressed wood by-products. The researcher found plenty of secondary data

and time-consuming than secondary research, it has the distinct advantage of achieving the research objectives specified in step 1 of the research process.

Researchers have to balance the positives and negatives of both secondary and primary research when collecting data (Exhibit 5.3).

EXHIBIT 5.3	ADVANTAGES AND DISADVANTAGES OF PRIMARY AND SECONDARY DATA
Advantages of Secondary Data	**Disadvantages of Secondary Data**
Inexpensive	Collected for another purpose
Clarifies problem	Questionable sources
Fast to collect	Quickly outdated
Advantages of Primary Data	**Disadvantages of Primary Data**
Focuses on solving a specific problem	Expensive
Sources are known	Time-consuming
Results more accurate	Requires specific skills sets

Return of the Census— Long-Form Edition

After a brief hiatus, the long-form census in Canada returned in 2016. The goal of the long form is to ask Canadians about their needs as they relate to government services. It has become an invaluable tool to reveal gaps of service across Canada so they can be filled in. It is considered a public duty to fill out the long-form census if asked, and there are potential punishments for not completing the form. However, in 2011, filling in the long-form census was not considered mandatory, resulting in response rates that fell to 68.6 percent. This rate meant that fewer reliable conclusions could be made from the data; data from 1100 communities across Canada were not published because of low response rates.

Some of the decisions that are made based on the long-form census relate to public transportation, schools, and infrastructure. The long-form census asks questions regarding mental health, housing needs, housing repairs, and responsibilities for paying for basic needs. When the information from the 2016 long-form census is released in late 2017, it will become clear what, if any, gaps there were in the data collected in 2011.

The Canadian Press/Lars Hagberg

Sources: Hannah Jackson, "The Long-Form Census Is Back, It's Online – and This Time, It's Mandatory," CBC News, May 2, 2016, http://www.cbc.ca/news/politics/mandatory-census-mail-out-1.3557511; "It's as Canadian as … the Long-Form Census," Globe Editorial, *Globe and Mail*, May 9, 2016, http://www.theglobeandmail.com/opinion/editorials/its-as-canadian-as-the-long-form-census/article29945412/.

on total wood consumed as fuel, quantities consumed in each province and territory, and types of wood burned. Secondary data were also available on consumer attitudes and purchase patterns of wood by-product fireplace logs. The wealth of secondary data provided the researcher with many insights into the artificial-log market. Yet the researchers could not locate information on whether consumers would buy artificial logs made of coal.

The quality of secondary data may also pose a problem. Secondary data sources do not often give detailed information that would enable a researcher to assess the data's quality or relevance. Whenever possible, a researcher needs to address these important questions: Who gathered the data? Why were the data obtained? What methodology was used? How were classifications (such as heavy users versus light users) developed and defined? When was the information gathered?

PRIMARY DATA COLLECTION Primary data, or information collected for the first time, are used for solving the particular issue under investigation. The main advantage of primary data is that they will answer a specific research question that secondary data cannot answer. For example, suppose Pillsbury has two new recipes for refrigerated dough for sugar cookies. Which one will consumers like better? Secondary data will not help answer this question. Instead, targeted consumers must try each recipe and evaluate the taste, texture, and appearance of each cookie.

Moreover, primary data are current and researchers know the source. Sometimes researchers gather the data themselves rather than assigning projects to outside companies. Researchers also specify the methodology of the research. Secrecy can be maintained because the information is proprietary. In contrast, much secondary data is available to all interested parties either for free or for relatively small fees.

Gathering primary data is expensive; costs can range from a few hundred dollars for a limited exploratory study comprising a few

primary data information that is collected for the first time and is used for solving the particular problem under investigation

focus groups to several million for a nationwide survey research study. Because primary data gathering is so expensive, firms may reduce the number of in-person interviews they conduct and use an online study instead. Larger companies that conduct many research projects might use another cost-saving technique. They *piggyback* studies, or gather data on two different projects by using one questionnaire.

Nevertheless, the disadvantages of primary data gathering are usually offset by the advantages. Gathering primary data is often the only way of helping to solve a research problem. Because of the variety of techniques now available for research, including surveys, observations, and experiments, primary research can address almost any marketing question.

© iStockphoto.com/todd olson

QUALITATIVE AND QUANTITATIVE RESEARCH

Primary research is collected through either qualitative or quantitative research methods. (See Exhibit 5.4.) Qualitative research is best used when a researcher still needs to clear up aspects of the research problem or requires a better understanding of a research situation. Quantitative research methods are best used when a researcher wants specific numbers and the ability to analyze the data to provide statistical conclusions.

The difference between qualitative and quantitative research methods brings us back to research design (step 2) and the three types of design: exploratory, descriptive, and causal. Exploratory research includes the collection of secondary data and qualitative data collection. Descriptive research seeks to describe phenomena that are observed and collected. Causal research looks for relationships and interactions between variables that are identified before research begins. Both descriptive and causal research are included under quantitative data collection.

QUALITATIVE DATA COLLECTION METHODS

depth interview an interview that involves a discussion between a well-trained researcher and a respondent who is asked about attitudes and perspectives on a topic

focus group a small group of recruited participants engaged in a nonstructured discussion in a casual environment

DEPTH INTERVIEWS A **depth interview** involves interviewing people one on one, at their offices or homes, concerning products or services, a process that is very costly. First, individuals must be identified and loc-

ated, which can be expensive and time-consuming. Once a qualified person is located, the next step is to get that person to agree to be interviewed and to set a time for the interview.

An interviewer must take the time to set up interviews and arrange to have the discussion taped and transcribed. This type of survey requires the very best interviewers because they are frequently conducting interviews on topics that they may not know much about.

FOCUS GROUPS A **focus group** is a small group of recruited participants engaged in a nonstructured discussion in a casual environment. Often recruited by random telephone screening, a small group of individuals possessing desired characteristics forms a focus group. These qualified consumers are usually offered a monetary incentive to participate in a group discussion. Compensation can range from around $20 for groups recruited from the general public to several hundred dollars for participants in more exclusive groups (e.g., senior executives).

The meeting place is usually a room that resembles a typical business meeting room with a large conference table in the centre. The room is equipped with audio and video taping capabilities (which the participants are aware of). One wall of the focus group room has a one-way mirror that allows the client to view the

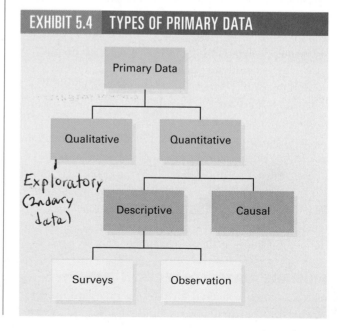

EXHIBIT 5.4   TYPES OF PRIMARY DATA

EXHIBIT 5.5 — CHARACTERISTICS OF TRADITIONAL FORMS OF SURVEY RESEARCH

Characteristic	In-Home Personal Interviews	Mall Intercept Interviews	Central-Location Telephone Interviews	Self-Administered and One-Time Mail Surveys	Mail Panel Surveys
Cost	High	Moderate	Moderate	Low	Moderate
Time span	Moderate	Moderate	Fast	Slow	Relatively slow
Use of interviewer probes	Yes	Yes	Yes	No	Yes
Ability to show concepts to respondent	Yes (also taste tests)	Yes (also taste tests)	No	Yes	Yes
Management control over interviewer	Low	Moderate	High	n/a	n/a
General data quality	High	Moderate	High to moderate	Moderate to low	Moderate
Ability to collect large amounts of data	High	Moderate	Moderate to low	Low to moderate	Moderate
Ability to handle complex questionnaires	High	Moderate	High, if computer-aided	Low	Low

proceedings. A moderator sits at the head of table and leads the discussion with the participants.

The discussion is guided and directed by the moderator, who uses a moderator's guide (a series of questions developed by the researchers) to discuss a variety of topics in an open discussion. Focus groups can be used to gauge consumer response to a product or promotion and are occasionally used to brainstorm new product ideas or to screen concepts for new products.

Focus groups are a popular technique with companies, as the format and discussion are often engaging and entertaining for clients watching the proceedings from behind the one-way mirror. But focus groups should never be confused with quantitative data collection methods like surveys. The unstructured nature of focus group discussions allows for very few conclusive statements. The opinions, no matter how passionately presented in a focus group session, are still those of only a handful of people.

QUANTITATIVE DATA COLLECTION METHODS

SURVEY RESEARCH The most popular descriptive technique for gathering primary data is **survey research**, in which a researcher interacts with people to obtain facts, opinions, and attitudes. Exhibit 5.5 summarizes the characteristics of traditional forms of survey research.

IN-HOME PERSONAL INTERVIEWS Although in-home personal interviews often provide high-quality information, they tend to be very expensive because of the interviewers' travel time and costs. Therefore, in-home personal interviews are rapidly disappearing from North American and European researchers' survey toolboxes. This method is, however, still popular in many countries around the globe.

MALL INTERCEPT INTERVIEWS The **mall intercept interview** is conducted in the common area of a shopping mall or in a market research office within the mall. To conduct this type of interview, the research firm rents office space in the mall or pays a significant daily fee. One drawback is that it is difficult to get a representative sample of the population, as not every consumer type comes to the mall at the same time, and many shoppers are often in a hurry, making them reluctant to participate in a survey. One advantage is the ability of the interviewer to probe when necessary—a technique used to clarify a person's response and ask for more detailed information.

Mall intercept interviews must be brief. Only the shortest interviews are conducted while respondents are standing. Usually, researchers invite respondents to their office for interviews, which are generally less than 15 minutes long. The overall quality of mall intercept interviews is about the same as that of telephone interviews.

survey research the most popular technique for gathering primary data, in which a researcher interacts with people to obtain facts, opinions, and attitudes

mall intercept interview interviewing people in the common areas of shopping malls

Increasingly, marketing researchers are applying computer technology in mall interviewing. One technique that uses this is **computer-assisted personal interviewing**. The researcher conducts in-person interviews, reads questions to the respondent from a computer screen, and directly keys the respondent's answers into the computer. A second approach is **computer-assisted self-interviewing**. A mall interviewer intercepts and directs willing respondents to nearby computers. Each respondent reads questions from a computer screen or iPad and directly keys his or her answers into a computer. The third use of technology is fully automated self-interviewing. Respondents are guided by interviewers or independently approach a centrally located computer station or kiosk, read the questions from a screen, and directly key their answers into the station's computer.

TELEPHONE INTERVIEWS Telephone interviews cost less than personal interviews, but the cost is rapidly increasing because of respondents' refusals to participate. Most telephone interviewing is conducted from a specially designed phone room called a **central-location telephone (CLT) facility**. A phone room has many phone lines and individual interviewing stations and may include monitoring equipment and headsets. The research firm typically will interview people nationwide from a single location. The Canadian National Do Not Call List (Bill C-37) does not apply to survey research. However, with more Canadians choosing not to have home phones, and with a greater difficulty of acquiring cellular telephone numbers, the success of telephone interviews has been greatly reduced. Without access to a large enough sample size of telephone numbers, some CLT facilities have found it challenging to meet requirements for survey validity.

Most CLT facilities offer computer-assisted interviewing. The interviewer reads the questions from a computer screen and enters the respondent's data directly into the computer, saving time. Hallmark Cards found that interviewers could administer a printed questionnaire for its Shoebox Greeting cards in 28 minutes. The same questionnaire administered with computer assistance took

Surveys where respondents select an answer from a list or rate the intensity of their response on a scale are relatively easy to evaluate.

only 18 minutes. The researcher can stop the survey at any point and immediately print out the survey results, allowing the research design to be refined as necessary.

MAIL SURVEYS Mail surveys have several benefits: relatively low cost, elimination of interviewers and field supervisors, centralized control, and actual or promised anonymity for respondents (which may draw more candid responses). A disadvantage is that mail questionnaires usually produce low response rates because certain elements of the population tend to respond more than others. In order to improve response rates for mail surveys, it is vital that follow-up is conducted, which should include no more than three instances where contact is made to a mail respondent to encourage completion.[5] The resulting sample may therefore not represent the general population. Another serious problem with mail surveys is that no one probes respondents to clarify or elaborate on their answers.

Mail panels offer an alternative to the one-shot mail survey. A mail panel consists of a sample of households recruited to participate by mail for a given period. Panel members often receive gifts in return for their participation. Essentially, the panel is a sample used several times. In contrast to one-time mail surveys, the response rates from mail panels are high. Rates of 70 percent (of those who agree to participate) are not uncommon.

QUESTIONNAIRE DESIGN All forms of survey research require a questionnaire. Questionnaires ensure that all respondents will be asked the same series of questions. Questionnaires include three basic types of questions: open-ended, closed-ended, and scaled-response. An **open-ended question** encourages an answer phrased in the respondent's own words. Researchers receive a

computer-assisted personal interviewing technique in which the interviewer reads the questions from a computer screen and enters the respondent's data directly into a computer

computer-assisted self-interviewing technique in which the respondent reads questions on a computer screen and directly keys his or her answers into a computer

central-location telephone (CLT) facility a specially designed phone room used to conduct telephone interviewing

open-ended question an interview question that encourages an answer phrased in the respondent's own words

Avocado	1	Olives (black/green)	6
Cheese (Monterey Jack/cheddar)	2	Onions (red/white)	7
Guacamole	3	Peppers (red/green)	8
Lettuce	4	Pimento	9
Mexican hot sauce	5	Sour cream	10

EXHIBIT 5.6 OBSERVATIONAL SITUATIONS

Situation	Example
People watching people	Observers stationed in supermarkets watch consumers select frozen pizza; the purpose is to see how much comparison shopping people do at the point of purchase.
People watching phenomena	Observers stationed at an intersection count traffic moving in various directions.
Machines watching people	Movie or video cameras record behaviour as in the people-watching-people example above.
Machines watching phenomena	Traffic-counting machines monitor traffic flow.

rich array of information that is based on the respondent's frame of reference (e.g., "What do you think about the new flavour?"). In contrast, a **closed-ended question** asks the respondent to make a selection from a limited list of responses. Closed-ended questions can either be what marketing researchers call dichotomous (e.g., "Do you like the new flavour? Yes or No") or *multiple choice*. A **scaled-response question** is a closed-ended question designed to measure the intensity of a respondent's answer.

Closed-ended and scaled-response questions are easier to tabulate than open-ended questions because the response choices are fixed. On the other hand, unless the researcher designs the closed-ended question very carefully, an important choice may be omitted. For example, suppose a food study asked this question: "Besides meat, which of the following items do you normally add to a taco that you prepare at home?" A respondent may then answer, "I usually add a green, avocado-tasting hot sauce" or "I cut up a mixture of lettuce and spinach." How would you code these replies? As you can see, the question needs both an "other" category and a place for respondents to elaborate on their answers.

Good questions address each of the previously set research objectives. Questions must also be clear and concise, and ambiguous language must be avoided. The answer to the question "Do you live within ten minutes of here?" depends on the mode of transportation (maybe the person walks), driving speed, perceived time, and other factors. Language should also be clear. Thus, jargon should be avoided, and wording should be geared to the target audience. A question such as "What is the level of efficacy of your preponderant dishwasher soap?" would probably be greeted by blank stares. It would be much simpler to say "Are you (1) very satisfied, (2) somewhat satisfied, or (3) not satisfied with your current brand of dishwasher soap?"

Stating the survey's purpose at the beginning of the interview may improve clarity, but it may also increase the chances of receiving biased responses. Many times respondents will try to provide answers that they believe are "correct" or that the interviewer wants to hear. To avoid bias at the question level, researchers should avoid using leading questions and adjectives that cause respondents to think of the topic in a certain way.

Finally, to ensure clarity, the interviewer should avoid asking two questions in one; for example, "How did you like the taste and texture of the Betty Crocker coffee cake?" This should be divided into two questions, one concerning taste and the other texture.

OBSERVATION RESEARCH Observation is categorized as another method of descriptive quantitative research, but instead of asking questions to respondents, **observation research** depends on watching what people do. In order to qualify as descriptive, observation must be completed in a structured manner, with data being collected and tracked by participant. Specifically, observation is the systematic process of recording the behavioural patterns of people, objects, and occurrences with or without questioning them. A marketing researcher uses the observation technique and witnesses and records information as events occur or compiles evidence from records of past events. While there are observation methods that are more qualitative in nature, the focus often is on using observation as a means to supplement and complement a quantitative research program. Carried a step further, observation may involve watching people or phenomena and may be conducted by human observers or machines. For example, a machine may be used to track a person's eye movements to see how and what they read in a magazine or on a website. Examples of these various observational situations are shown in Exhibit 5.6.

Two common forms of people-watching-people

closed-ended question an interview question that asks the respondent to make a selection from a limited list of responses

scaled-response question a closed-ended question designed to measure the intensity of a respondent's answer

observation research watching people or phenomena in a controlled manner, through either human or machine methods.

Mystery shoppers are tasked with (and paid for!) assessing a company's operations without its staff realizing their true intentions. Mystery can be a helpful aspect of a retailer's overall marketing research efforts.

research are mystery shoppers and one-way mirror observations. **Mystery shoppers** are researchers posing as customers who gather observational data about a store (i.e., are the shelves neatly stocked?) and collect data about customer–employee interactions. The interaction is not an interview, and communication occurs only so that the mystery shopper can observe the actions and comments of the employee. Mystery shopping is, therefore, classified as an observational marketing research method even though communication is often involved. One-way mirror observations allow researchers to see how consumers react to products or promotions.

ETHNOGRAPHIC RESEARCH Ethnographic research comes to marketing from the field of anthropology. The technique is becoming increasingly popular in commercial marketing research. **Ethnographic research**, or the study of human behaviour in its natural context, involves observation of behaviour and physical setting. Ethnographers, such as Canadian-based marketing research firm Environics, directly observe the population they are studying. As "participant observers," ethnographers can use their intimacy with the people they are studying to gain richer, deeper insights into culture and behaviour—in short, learning what makes people do what they do. While ethnographic research in anthropology often use qualitative methods of data collection (e.g., semi-structured interviews), there is a greater prevalence of the use of more quantitative methods such as surveys and questionnaires.[6]

The key focus for ethnographic research is to watch people in their "natural setting," much like anthropologist Jane Goodall's seminal work with chimpanzees. In the marketing world, Procter & Gamble (P&G) sends researchers to people's homes for extended periods of time to see how customers do household chores such as laundry and vacuuming. In a famous case, P&G discovered the design and use for the now-famous Swiffer Mop from conducting ethnographic research by observing people mopping their floors. The key finding from watching this mundane chore: people spent more time cleaning their mop than cleaning their floor. Promotions for Swiffer often focus on the time saving benefit of using the product instead of conventional methods of cleaning.[7]

EXPERIMENTS An **experiment** is a causal method a researcher can use to gather primary data. The researcher alters one or more variables—price, package design, shelf space, advertising theme, advertising expenditures—while observing the effects of those alterations on another variable (usually sales). The best experiments are those in which all factors are held constant except the ones being manipulated. The researcher can then observe, for example, how sales change as a result of changes in the amount of money spent on advertising.

There are two types of settings for experimental design: laboratory and field. A laboratory environment can be any situation where the researcher can create and control a set of variables to measure. An example of laboratory testing is a test store or simulated supermarket, where shoppers interact in a real or virtual environment that simulates a shopping experience. A field environment is much less controllable than a laboratory; however, field experiments provide a more realistic

mystery shoppers
researchers posing as customers who gather observational data about a store

ethnographic research
the study of human behaviour in its natural context; involves observation of behaviour and physical setting

experiment a method a researcher uses to gather primary data to determine cause and effect

EXHIBIT 5.7 TYPES OF SAMPLES

	Probability Samples
Simple Random Sample	Every member of the population has a known and equal chance of selection.
Stratified Sample	The population is divided into mutually exclusive groups (by gender or age, for example); then random samples are drawn from each group.
Cluster Sample	The population is divided into mutually exclusive groups (by geographic area, for example); then a random sample of clusters is selected. The researcher then collects data from all the elements in the selected clusters or from a probability sample of elements within each selected cluster.
Systematic Sample	A list of the population is obtained—e.g., all persons with a chequing account at XYZ Bank—and a skip interval is obtained by dividing the sample size by the population size. If the sample size is 100 and the bank has 1000 customers, then the skip interval is 10. The beginning number is randomly chosen within the skip interval. If the beginning number is 8, then the skip pattern would be 8, 18, 28, etc.
	Nonprobability Samples
Convenience Sample	The researcher selects the easiest population members from which to obtain information.
Judgment Sample	The researcher's selection criteria are based on personal judgment that the elements (persons) chosen will likely give accurate information.
Quota Sample	The researcher finds a prescribed number of people in several categories—e.g., researcher selects a specific number of business students, arts students, science students, etc., so that each group has a specific number represented in the study. Respondents are not selected on probability sampling criteria.
Snowball Sample	Additional respondents are selected on the basis of referrals from the initial respondents. This method is used when a desired type of respondent is difficult to find—e.g., persons who have taken round-the-world cruises in the last three years are asked to refer others they know who have taken long cruises and could be involved in the research study. This technique employs the old adage "Birds of a feather flock together."

environment in which a respondent will display relevant behaviours and attitudes.

SPECIFYING THE SAMPLING PROCEDURES

Once the researchers decide how they will collect primary data, their next step is to select the sampling procedures to use. A firm can seldom interview or take a census of all possible users of a new product. Therefore, a firm must select a sample of the group to be interviewed. A **sample** is a subset from a larger population.

Several questions must be answered before a sampling plan is chosen. First, the population of interest must be defined. It should include all the people whose opinions, behaviours, preferences, attitudes, and so on are of interest to the marketer. For example, in a study whose purpose is to determine the market for a new canned dog food, the population might be defined to include all current buyers of canned dog food.

After the population has been defined, the next question is whether the sample must be representative of that population. If the answer is yes, a probability sample is needed. Otherwise, a nonprobability sample might be considered (see Exhibit 5.4).

PROBABILITY SAMPLES A **probability sample** is a sample in which every element in the population has a known statistical likelihood of being selected. Its most

desirable feature is that scientific rules can be used to ensure that the sample represents the population.

One type of probability sample is a **random sample**—a sample arranged in such a way that every element of the population has an equal chance of being selected as part of the sample. For example, suppose a university is interested in receiving a cross-section of student opinions on a proposed sports complex to be built using student activity fees. If the university can acquire an up-to-date list of all the enrolled students, it can draw a random sample by using random numbers from a table (found in most statistics books) to select students from the list. Common forms of probability and nonprobability samples are shown in Exhibit 5.7.

NONPROBABILITY SAMPLES Any sample in which little or no attempt is made to have a representative cross-section of the population can be considered a **nonprobability sample**. Therefore, the probability of each sampling unit being selected is not known. A common

sample a subset from a larger population

probability sample a sample in which every element in the population has a known statistical likelihood of being selected

random sample a sample arranged in such a way that every element of the population has an equal chance of being selected as part of the sample

nonprobability sample any sample in which little or no attempt is made to have a representative cross-section of the population

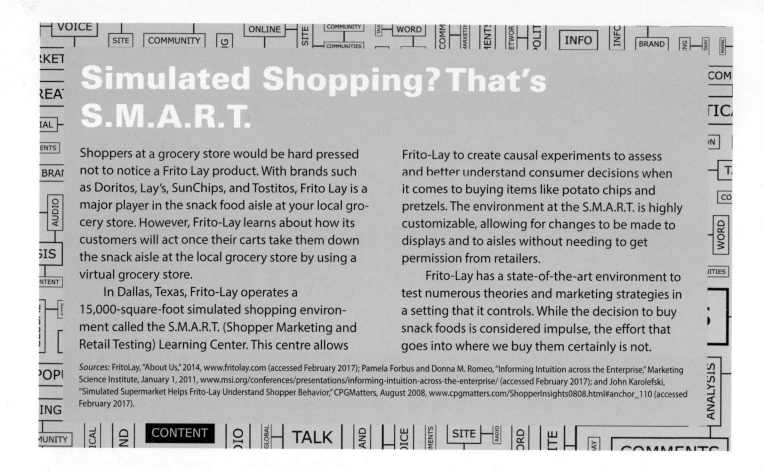

Simulated Shopping? That's S.M.A.R.T.

Shoppers at a grocery store would be hard pressed not to notice a Frito Lay product. With brands such as Doritos, Lay's, SunChips, and Tostitos, Frito Lay is a major player in the snack food aisle at your local grocery store. However, Frito-Lay learns about how its customers will act once their carts take them down the snack aisle at the local grocery store by using a virtual grocery store.

In Dallas, Texas, Frito-Lay operates a 15,000-square-foot simulated shopping environment called the S.M.A.R.T. (Shopper Marketing and Retail Testing) Learning Center. This centre allows Frito-Lay to create causal experiments to assess and better understand consumer decisions when it comes to buying items like potato chips and pretzels. The environment at the S.M.A.R.T. is highly customizable, allowing for changes to be made to displays and to aisles without needing to get permission from retailers.

Frito-Lay has a state-of-the-art environment to test numerous theories and marketing strategies in a setting that it controls. While the decision to buy snack foods is considered impulse, the effort that goes into where we buy them certainly is not.

Sources: FritoLay, "About Us," 2014, www.fritolay.com (accessed February 2017); Pamela Forbus and Donna M. Romeo, "Informing Intuition across the Enterprise," Marketing Science Institute, January 1, 2011, www.msi.org/conferences/presentations/informing-intuition-across-the-enterprise/ (accessed February 2017); and John Karolefski, "Simulated Supermarket Helps Frito-Lay Understand Shopper Behavior," CPGMatters, August 2008, www.cpgmatters.com/ShopperInsights0808.html#anchor_110 (accessed February 2017).

---

form of a nonprobability sample is the **convenience sample**, which uses respondents who are convenient, or readily accessible, to the researcher—for instance, employees, friends, or relatives.

Nonprobability samples are acceptable as long as the researcher understands their nonrepresentative nature. Because of their lower cost, nonprobability samples are the basis of much marketing research.

TYPES OF ERRORS

Whenever a sample is used in marketing research, two major types of error may occur: measurement error and sampling error. **Measurement error** occurs when the information desired by the researcher differs from the information provided by the measurement process. For example, people may tell an interviewer that they purchase Crest toothpaste when they do not. Measurement error generally tends to be larger than sampling error.

Sampling error occurs when a sample does not represent the target population. A sampling error can be one of several types. A **nonresponse error** occurs when the sample interviewed differs from the sample drawn. This error happens because the original people selected to be interviewed either refused to cooperate or were inaccessible.

Frame error, another type of sampling error, arises when the sample drawn from a population differs from the target population. For instance, suppose a telephone survey is conducted to find out Calgary beer drinkers' attitudes toward Molson Canadian. If a Calgary telephone directory is used as the frame (the device or list from which the respondents are selected), the survey will contain a frame error. Not all Calgary beer drinkers have a phone, others may have unlisted phone numbers, and often young adults have only a cellphone. An ideal sample (for example, a sample with no frame error) matches all important characteristics of the target population to be surveyed. Can you suggest a perfect frame for Calgary beer drinkers?

Random error occurs when the selected sample is an imperfect representation of the overall population.

convenience sample a form of nonprobability sample using respondents who are convenient, or readily accessible, to the researcher—for example, employees, friends, or relatives

measurement error an error that occurs when the information desired by the researcher differs from the information provided by the measurement process

sampling error an error that occurs when a sample does not represent the target population

frame error a sample drawn from a population that differs from the target population

random error a type of sampling error in which the selected sample is an imperfect representation of the overall population

Random error represents how accurately the chosen sample's true average (mean) value reflects the population's true average (mean) value. For example, we might take a random sample of beer drinkers in Calgary and find that 16 percent regularly drink Molson Canadian beer. The next day we might repeat the same sampling procedure and discover that 14 percent regularly drink Molson Canadian beer. The difference is due to random error. Error is common to all surveys, yet it is often not reported or is under-reported. Typically, the only error mentioned in a written report is a sampling error.

5-2d Step 4: Analyze the Data

After collecting the data, the marketing researcher proceeds to the next step in the research process: data analysis. The purpose of this analysis is to interpret and draw conclusions from the mass of collected data. The marketing researcher tries to organize and analyze those data by using one or more techniques common to marketing research: one-way frequency counts, cross-tabulations, and more sophisticated statistical analysis. Of these three techniques, one-way frequency counts are the simplest. One-way frequency tables simply record the responses to a question. For example, the answers to the question "What brand of microwave popcorn do you buy most often?" would provide a one-way frequency distribution. One-way frequency tables are always used in data analysis, at least as a first step, because they provide the researcher with a general picture of the study's results. A **cross-tabulation** shows the analyst the responses to one question in relation to the responses to one or more other questions. For example, what is the association between gender and the brand of microwave popcorn bought most frequently, as shown in Exhibit 5.8?

Researchers can use many other more powerful and sophisticated statistical techniques, such as proportion testing, measures of association, and regression analysis. A description of these techniques goes beyond the scope of this book but can be found in any good marketing research textbook. The use of sophisticated statistical techniques depends on the researchers' objectives and the nature of the data gathered.

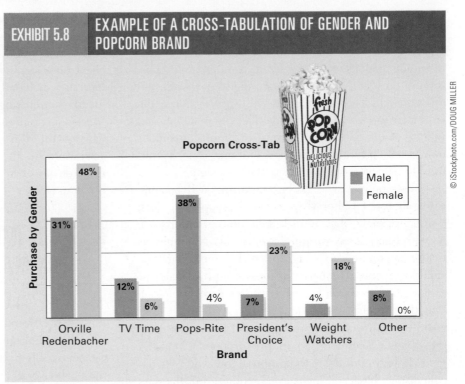

EXHIBIT 5.8 — **EXAMPLE OF A CROSS-TABULATION OF GENDER AND POPCORN BRAND**

© iStockphoto.com/DOUG MILLER

5-2e Step 5: Present the Report

After data analysis has been completed, the researcher must prepare the report and communicate the conclusions and recommendations to management. This is a key step in the process. If the marketing researcher wants managers to carry out the recommendations, he or she must convince the managers that the results are credible and justified by the data collected.

Researchers are usually required to present both written and oral reports on the project. They should begin with a clear, concise statement of the research issue studied, the research objectives, and a complete but brief and simple explanation of the research design or methodology employed, including the nature of the sample and how it was selected. A summary of major findings should come next. The way in which this section is written is very important, as this is the part of the report that will build a case as to how the marketing research will help solve the research problem. Staying away from technical jargon is vital; the report has to be written in an accessible manner for the manager who will be making a decision based on the information provided. The findings can be presented in a number of formats, including cross-tabulations tables, line charts, and flow charts. Having a mix of writing and visuals will

> **cross-tabulation** a method of analyzing data that shows the analyst the responses to one question in relation to the responses to one or more other questions

keep the attention of the reader and provide for a more compelling presentation than writing alone.

The conclusion of the report should also present recommendations to management. Any research report should present limitations that might have affected the research. These limitations will warn or advise the readers of any issues that could affect the reliability and validity of the research. Awareness of these limitations may also help future researchers and may serve as cautions to managers when making their decision.

Most people who enter marketing will become research users rather than research suppliers. Thus, they must know what items to take note of in a report. As with many items we purchase, quality is not always readily apparent, and a high price does not guarantee superior quality. The basis for measuring the quality of a marketing research report is the research proposal. Was the correct type of data collection methods used given the nature of the problem? Did the report meet the objectives established in the proposal? Was the methodology outlined in the proposal followed? Are the conclusions based on logical deductions from the data analysis? Do the recommendations seem prudent, given the conclusions?

5-2f Step 6: Provide Follow-Up

The final step in the marketing research process is to follow up. The way in which follow-up is conducted will depend on whether the marketing researcher was an internal or external provider.

Internal providers of marketing research will have the opportunity for greater interaction and feedback into the report and research efforts. They should be prepared to answer any questions and be available to discuss the project and its ramifications. The internal researcher should keep track of the project that relates to the research. Questions to ask include the following:

- Was sufficient decision-making information included?

- What could have been done to make the report more useful to management?

A good rapport is essential between the internal marketing researcher and the manager who authorized the project. Often, these individuals must work together on many studies throughout the year.

External marketing research providers will not have the same level of access to the decision makers as someone who works within an organization. For the external provider, managing the client is a very important part of the research process and can ensure that there is the possibility of future work with that client. The external researcher may be asked to be part of implementing aspects of the research report. If they are not part of this process, it is important to agree with the client on a follow-up schedule. Often postreport meetings are included in research contracts, with some meetings occurring years after the final report has been handed in. A fundamental question to ask a client is whether the research has been conducted properly and accurately. In other words, did the researcher solve the research problem and help in making a management problem clearer?

5-3 THE IMPACT OF TECHNOLOGY ON MARKETING RESEARCH

Technology is pervasive in our lives. You may be reading these words from your laptop, tablet, or cellphone. Marketing research must keep up with technology to meet the needs of both those looking to conduct research and those who would be the subjects of such research.

There are two main areas in which technology and marketing research have combined: online and mobile devices. There are now focus groups online, surveys on cellphones, and virtual repositories of data being used in ways unimaginable a few years ago.

We also must be aware of the public's reduced use of and reliance on tried-and-true marketing research tools, like telephone interviewing and mail surveys. Researchers are scrambling to keep up with a digital revolution that threatens to leave them behind unless they incorporate the new technological reality into their methods and activities.

Now, however, the rapid development of online secondary data resources has eliminated much of the drudgery associated with the collection of secondary data. However, a key problem remains: source accuracy.

Students often turn to Google or other search engines as a starting point for secondary research. This can lead them to websites and sources that may or may not be appropriate for a school report. If you would like to start a lively debate in your class about secondary sourcing, just mention Wikipedia!

A good rule of thumb for testing the accuracy of online sources is CARS. This acronym stands for *credibility* (author's credentials), *accuracy* (timeliness), *reasonableness* (balanced and objective argument), and *support* (corroboration of findings).[8]

Let's now look at some of the ways technology is changing marketing research.

5-3a Online Surveys

According to a 2015 Pew Global study, the percentage of adult Canadians with Internet access reached the 90 percent mark for the first time.[9] Greater Internet access means a larger sample from which to recruit survey respondents. Better online survey tools have been the result of this improved access, and websites like Survey Monkey allow even the most untrained marketing researcher to develop a survey and put it online.

The huge growth in the popularity of Internet surveys is the result of many advantages:

- **Rapid development, real-time reporting:** Internet surveys can be broadcast to thousands of potential respondents simultaneously. Respondents complete surveys simultaneously; then results are tabulated and posted for corporate clients to view as the returns arrive. Survey results can be in a client's hands in significantly less time than would be required for traditional surveys.

- **Dramatically reduced costs:** The Internet can cut costs significantly and provide results in half the time required for traditional telephone surveys. Traditional survey methods are labour-intensive efforts incurring costs related to training, telecommunications, and management. Electronic methods eliminate these costs completely. While costs for traditional survey techniques rise proportionally with the number of interviews desired, electronic solicitations can grow in volume with little increase in project costs.

- **Improved respondent participation:** Internet surveys take half as much time to complete as phone interviews, can be accomplished at the respondent's convenience (after work hours), and can be much more stimulating and engaging. As a result, Internet surveys enjoy much higher response rates.

- **Contact with the difficult-to-reach:** Certain groups—doctors, high-income professionals, top management in Global 2000 firms—are among the most surveyed individuals on the planet and the most difficult to reach. Many of these groups are well represented online. Internet surveys provide convenient "anytime, anywhere" access that makes it easy for busy professionals to participate.

5-3b Online Research Panels

A panel is a group of respondents who agree to be polled by a

Feng Yu/Shutterstock.com. Bank note image used with the permission of the Bank of Canada.

Companies can now purchase online focus group software, which can be very cost-efficient, and depending on the provider it can be free. This compares quite favourably to conventional focus groups, which can cost thousands of dollars.

marketing research firm about a series of products and services. This is not a one-time occurrence like other surveys—panellists are involved over a long period. This method allows research firms to build large pools of individuals who are available to respond quickly to the demands of online marketing research. Internet panels have grown rapidly, with marketing research companies boasting of millions of people in many countries who form their online research panels.

Thanks to the ease of use of online surveys, participants can complete Internet panels quickly and efficiently. Those participants come from all walks of life. TNS Canada, a marketing and opinion research firm, offers online panels of more than 100,000 Canadians ranging from a teen panel to a doctor panel. TNS boasts over one million panel members in the United States and over 500,000 in Europe.[11]

Charity Starts Online

Online panels are an effective tool not only for marketing research companies and for-profit firms—charities are now going online to seek out panellists. Charities can gain valuable information from access to online panels, including getting feedback on fundraising programs, determining donor profiles, and assessing the effectiveness of marketing campaigns. Charities can either hire a marketing research firm or create their own panel. Good Works Co. is an Ottawa-based firm that started out helping charities better execute direct mail campaigns. Good Works focuses on helping charities build meaningful long-term relationships with donors by giving them access to online panels. Good Works labels online panels as "a hot new trend in market research." Charities are also being encouraged to create their own online panels. If a charity creates a panel of donors, not only does it have access to potential fundraising sources, but the panel itself could also be a source of income as external marketing research firms are often looking for stable and dynamic online panels.

Sources: Good Works, "Donor Research," 2014, http://goodworksco.ca/what-we-do/donor-research.aspx (accessed February 2017); and UKFundrasing, "Three Reasons Why Charities Should Build a Market Research Panel," October 30, 2013, www.fundraising.co.uk/blog/2013/10/30/three-reasons-why-charities-should-build-marketresearch-panel (accessed February 2017).

5-3c Online Focus Groups

The exploratory research method of focus groups has also found a home online. A number of organizations are currently offering this new means of conducting focus groups. The process is fairly simple. The research firm builds a database of respondents via a screening questionnaire on its website. When a client comes to a firm with a need for a particular focus group, the firm goes to its database and identifies individuals who appear to qualify. The firm sends an email to these individuals, asking them to log on to a particular site at a particular time scheduled for the group. Like in-person focus groups, firms pay respondents an incentive for their participation. However, the two types of focus groups are not alike when it comes to costs. Beyond providing the moderator and the online capabilities for supporting the focus group session, research firms save on a number of costs for online focus groups compared to in-person focus groups. Items like room rentals, food costs, and travel reimbursement are all non-issues for online focus groups, providing a real cost savings along with convenience as key benefits of going online for focus groups.

The firm develops a moderator's guide similar to the one used for a conventional focus group, and a moderator runs the group by typing in questions online for all to see. The group operates in an environment similar to that of a chat room so that all participants see all questions and all responses. The firm captures the complete text of the focus group and makes it available for review after the group has finished.

5-3d Mobile Marketing Research

Readers will likely not be surprised to discover that a 2015 survey found that more Canadian householders subscribe to mobile wireless services than to a landline for the first time ever.[12]

And it is the increased use of smartphones that has allowed people to complete many more activities with the use of their mobile device. A recent Google study showed that consumers use their smartphones to research products, seek out information from offline advertisements, and make purchases. More than one-third of respondents in the Google survey stated they would give up their television before giving up their smartphone.

These trends we have just outlined have created a greater focus on conducting marketing research by using customers' mobile devices. Research firms can develop applications that can be downloaded by respondents, which can allow for participation in surveys, focus groups, and panels. Respondents can provide insights through videos, photos, and messages sent from the phone, creating a dynamic and almost instant connection with the respondent. However, this interaction has created concerns over privacy and security of information, prompting the European Society for Opinions and Market Research (ESOMAR) to create a comprehensive set of guidelines relating to mobile marketing research. It has been predicted that smartphone marketing research will become commonplace in developed nations around the world.[13]

5-3e Social Media Marketing Research

With the changes created by the Internet and mobile devices, it is not hard to see how social media might become part of the discussion on technology and marketing research. The online and mobile technologies allow for greater communication and sharing among customers.

With two-thirds of Canadians who use the Internet being regular social media users[14] and 78 percent of smartphone users connecting to social media,[15] marketing researchers are beginning to listen. Numerous social media sites can be tapped by marketing researchers, from the more popular (Facebook, Twitter, LinkedIn) to specialized social media networks. There are social media analytical tools that firms are selling to help keep track of all the conversations going on in social media about companies, brands, perceptions, and attitudes—a veritable gold mine for companies and researchers.

The challenge with social media marketing research is trying to find a way to measure the chatter going on in social media. HootSuite provides a means of helping companies manage social media websites and better track what is being said about a brand or marketing campaign. From their Vancouver head office, HootSuite provides companies with a dashboard from which data from a number of social media sites can be tracked and analyzed.

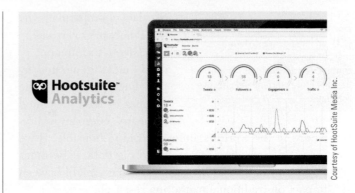

The Hootsuite Dashboard provides a centralized hub for social media analytics. Companies can see the progress (or lack thereof) it's making in social media efforts. It can be localized to a particular social media outlet or generalized by providing information on referrals and revenues from social media efforts. Having a centralized location provides great value to companies that have a myriad of activities, actions, and interactions taking place in social media environments that can be volatile and overwhelming at times.

5-3f The Rise of Big Data

As you have learned in this chapter, collecting data is an important part of the marketing research process. With the introduction of the various technologies we have outlined, one of the greatest challenges is how to deal with all the data that are generated from these new sources of information.

The term **big data** refers to the very large volume of data that companies have access to as the result of the recent advancements in technology. Big data is a relatively new concept originating from the early 2000s. How big data gets differentiated from data management from the past is through what are called the three "Vs" of big data: volume, velocity, and variety. *Volume* refers to the amount of data being held, and these numbers can be staggering. Facebook, for example, stores more than 250 billion images. *Velocity* refers to how quickly this volume of data is entering a system. For Facebook to maintain its current services offering a site for billions of pictures, it must process up to 900 million photos per day. This requires a lot of velocity. *Variety* refers to the various forms and formats in which the data are going to arrive in velocity and volume. Companies like Facebook have to be prepared for the inundation of more than just photos: there are also video files, audio files, URLs, and other forms

> **big data** large amounts of data collected from interactions with customers that reveal trends and patterns

of data bombarding the social network every day.[16]

Given the amount of data that is generated by just Facebook alone, the amount of data generated by every company everywhere in the world is almost incomprehensible. If we focus on marketing research and big data, it becomes important to discuss how all of this data might have an impact on traditional marketing research.

It has been stated that companies will soon no longer be required to conduct surveys, focus groups, or interviews. Instead, they can simply wait for big data to come down the pipe and then figure out a system to analyze volume, velocity, and variety. Companies have access to website feedback, customer service information, and other external data and could conceivably use this information alone to make business decisions that would have previously been reserved for marketing research.

While it is clear that big data could be quite disruptive to marketing research, it is also clear that there is room for both big data and marketing research in trying to help firms make better decisions. For example, a company could glean from big data that customers purchased a certain amount of their products, and there could be demographic information tied into those purchases based on credit card and customer database information. But what is still missing from this picture is *why* they bought the product. The "why" aspect could only definitively be answered by conducting some form of marketing research that would ask the customer directly, via surveys, focus groups, or other traditional methods of marketing research. As anthropologist Tom Boellstorff noted, "Huge volumes of data may be compelling at first glance, but without an interpretive structure they are meaningless."[17]

Therefore, in order to bring meaning to big data and its role in marketing research, it will be vital to search for an interpretive structure. The question is, does this structure already exist?

 5-4 WHEN TO CONDUCT MARKETING RESEARCH

You don't have to be a rocket scientist to admit you don't know what you don't know. However, too often company decision makers do not heed Werner von Braun's advice when trying to solve a problem.

Marketing research is a process, and the first step in that process is the most important. Understanding the problem is a key to determining what next steps (if any) are necessary. As information is gathered, it may become clear that marketing research may not be necessary. This can only be determined once a researcher has explored the problem. Some firms with big brands and large budgets, like Procter & Gamble, can afford to cut down on the marketing research done to introduce new products in markets where they control a large part of the market share. However, most firms can benefit from conducting marketing research.

Gathering the right information can require a great deal of time and expense. However, the potential expense to a company when introducing a new product or entering a new market without the right information can be catastrophic. Even if a firm can afford to do only some secondary research, the value of the information to the decision process is immense. With technology making this information more accessible and the data more detailed, it is incumbent upon any business decision maker to include some aspect of the research process in their decision-making process.

Marketers can use information from an external environmental analysis (see Chapter 2) in combination with marketing research data to help in making important strategic decisions. Since competitive advantage is a significant goal in any business, being able to understand other companies can be of great value, especially in highly competitive industries. **Competitive intelligence (CI)** helps managers assess their competitors and their vendors and create a more efficient and effective company. Intelligence is analyzed information. It becomes decision-making intelligence when it has implications for the organization. For example, a primary competitor may have plans to introduce a product with performance standards equal to a company's current product but with a 15 percent cost advantage. The new product will reach the market in eight months. This intelligence has important decision-making and policy consequences for management. Competitive intelligence and environmental scanning combine to create marketing intelligence.

We leave this chapter with another look to the stars—this time with the words of the first man on the moon, Neil Armstrong: "Research is creating new knowledge." And we all know what kind of power knowledge can provide.[18]

Food Data Is Good Data

Canadians from coast to coast have been telling a complete stranger what they had for dinner, lunch, or a snack. And this complete stranger couldn't be happier. That stranger is one of Canada's most well-known marketing research companies: Ipsos Canada. This full disclosure of food consumption is being operated as a panel that assesses the continually changing world of eating habits among Canadians. What results is a glut of data that can then be used, once paid for, by food companies looking to find the next great Canadian food trend. This panel has created a window into the eating habits of Canadians, be the teenagers from a small town or Baby Boomers living in a large metropolitan area. The Ipsos data has led to some very interesting findings (see sidebar, "Snack foods, by generation").

These data paint a picture for large food organizations, such as Starbucks and General Mills. By having data from a firm like Ipsos, which not only gathers the data but also puts it into some order and structure, firms are better able to make decisions on how they will approach their vastly different food customers. Food retailers have made decisions from data like these, such as adjusting the size of stores to meet the needs of Millennials who tend to live in city centres and don't have access to a car. This big amount of data is very filling, but food companies can't seem to get enough.

Snack foods, by generation

Generation Z kids:
Yogurt is almost two times as likely to be consumed by a Gen Z kid as a snack – illustrating the parental influence over how and what this group eats. Also interesting: This group is much less likely to snack on nuts, probably because so many schools have enacted rules against them.

Generation Z teens:
This group is 1.3 times more likely to snack on rice cakes or rice-based chips or crackers – possibly owing to their more health-conscious mentality.

Millennials:
Protein bars and other meal replacement bars – products such as Luna bars – are 1.2 times more popular with millennials. "They're quite expensive, but they have a very specific purpose, they're very functional and have fewer ingredients," Ipsos Canada's Kathy Perrotta said.

Generation X:
Aside from the Gen Z kids, the Gen X group is least likely to indulge in less healthy snacks. But when they do, they're 1.2 times more likely than other groups to turn to cake.

Boomers:
Like the Gen Xers, the baby boomers have a sweet tooth and are 1.5 times more likely than others to turn to baked goods (a category that includes everything outside of traditional cakes and brownies).

Source: Ipsos FIVE

Reproduced by permission of Ipsos Marketing.

Source: Ann Hui, "In Today's Market, Your Food Chooses You," *The Globe and Mail*, October 11, 2016, http://www.theglobeandmail.com/news/national/how-the-food-industry-is-using-canadians-changing-eating-habits-to-market-to-different-generations/article32316327/.

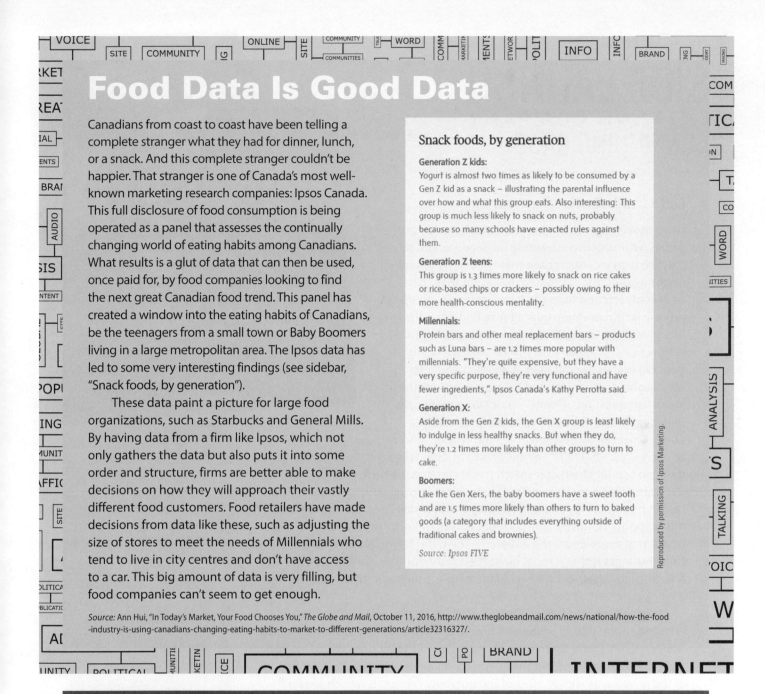

STUDY TOOLS

IN THE BOOK, YOU CAN:

✔ Rip out the Chapter in Review card at the back of the book.

ONLINE, YOU CAN:

✔ Stay organized and efficient with a single online destination with all the course material and study aids you need to succeed.

Go to nelson.com/student to access the digital resources.

SIDE LAUNCH
BREWING COMPANY
CONTINUING CASE

Side Launch Brewing Company

Data in Absentia

Deep observation and analysis of SWOT provide companies with ongoing marketing intelligence, and this practice is an essential component of a firm's overall marketing information system (MIS). But these data, commonly referred to as secondary research, normally provide little more than quantitative findings—the kind that gives firms like Side Launch an idea, for instance, of how many Ontarian beer drinkers are switching from big brands to craft beer. It doesn't delve into key insights companies need to know to answer the important question of "why"—as in "Why are people switching to craft?" or perhaps more interesting to Chuck Galea, VP Sales and Marketing, "Why don't some beer drinkers switch to craft?" For answers to questions like this, firms can guess, or they can conduct market research to get closer to the truth.

With Side Launch, however, like many start-ups, a directed marketing research project is a luxury of funding it simply does not have (at the time of this writing). "Honestly," admits founder Garnet Pratt, "we are not at the size where that even enters the equation." The bitter financial reality of many a small business is that it must navigate its way through complicated questions, fusing together observable forces of the marketing environment and a lot of experiential know-how.

"With those four beers," explains Michael Hancock, founding brewer, referring proudly to the four core brands brewed year-round at Side Launch, "I deliberately made them to cover four really different beer styles." He adds, with admirable pride, "And they're pretty damn easy to sell." Certainly sales of these beers, as well as sales of the quarterly seasonals (which always sell out), is a vivid measurement of the positive response by the market. For something more qualitative and yet still affordable, Side Launch will pay a lot of attention to how the press and bloggers are representing their beers to the public. Ratings sites such as Ratebeer.com and Untappd.com also provide a peek into the "why" as opposed to just the "what," but they alone do not answer unique market research problems Side Launch may encounter.

All of this is not to suggest Side Launch Brewing Company has no need for a scientific market research investment. "We're at a stage," admit both Garnet and Chuck. "Gaining some knowledge on brand recognition at this point would be really valuable," they concur. For now, however, with sharply increasing growth, supported by the collective experiential knowledge of

NEL

the industry between Michael, Dave (VP Operations), and Chuck, Side Launch has little choice but to hold the fort with what it has created and rely on the most important metric of all—sales data—to prove their case. "We know right now," adds Garnet confidently, "that the four styles of beer that we sell year-round all sell very well and all have their significant strengths. And so our strategy going forward, our primary focus, is to produce as much of those as we can sell, to grow those brands within our established market, and then make prudent geographic expansions as warranted to incite growth." That prudence, one expects, will eventually involve the kind of fact checking that only a structured marketing research project can assure.

Questions

1. What is the biggest barrier preventing Side Launch from conducting formal marketing research?

2. What is the "research problem" acknowledged by VP Sales and Marketing Chuck Galea that Side Launch would like to solve?

3. What are some of the secondary data sources that Side Launch can use in its marketing research? What are the limitations of such data in informing Side Launch?

Side Launch Brewing Company

6 Consumer Decision Making

LEARNING OUTCOMES

6-1 Explain why marketing managers should understand consumer behaviour

6-2 Analyze the components of the consumer decision-making process

6-3 Identify the types of consumer buying decisions and discuss the significance of consumer involvement

6-4 Identify and understand the cultural factors that affect consumer buying decisions

6-5 Identify and understand the social factors that affect consumer buying decisions

6-6 Identify and understand the individual factors that affect consumer buying decisions

6-7 Identify and understand the psychological factors that affect consumer buying decisions

"Human behaviour flows from three main sources: desire, emotion and knowledge."
—attributed to Plato

6-1 THE IMPORTANCE OF UNDERSTANDING CONSUMER BEHAVIOUR

To create a proper marketing mix for a well-defined market, marketing managers must have a thorough knowledge of consumer behaviour. The understanding of consumer behaviour is even more critical given that consumers' product preferences are constantly changing. **Consumer behaviour** describes how consumers make purchase decisions and how they use and dispose of the purchased products. The study of consumer behaviour also includes an analysis of factors that influence purchase decisions and product use.

Understanding how consumers make purchase decisions can help mar-

consumer behaviour how consumers make purchase decisions and how they use and dispose of purchased goods or services; also includes the factors that influence purchase decisions and product use

keters in several ways. For example, if they know through research that gas mileage is the most important attribute in an automobile for a certain target market, they can redesign the product to meet that criterion. If the firm cannot change the product design in the short run, they can use other marketing elements in an effort to change consumers' decision-making criteria. When Tesla realized that Gen-X and Gen-Y drivers loved the concept of Tesla's electric car, but simply couldn't afford it, Tesla developed a new model, bearing all the expected Tesla traits, but making it more affordable. The Tesla 3 joined the Model X and Model S and was available for pre-order in 2016. At a base price of $35,000, it was roughly half the price of the Model X, yet it maintained the environmentally friendly promise that came with the Tesla brand. An unprecedented 325,000 Model 3s were ordered within a week of launch in 2016.[1] But was it just price driving these purchase decisions? Maybe it was an altruistic sense of personal environmental responsibility. On the

Elizaveta Galitckaia/Shutterstock.com

other hand, it might have been that silent but provocative voice of the customers' ideal self—coaxing them to make a commitment not to a car they cared little about, but to a sense of the type of person they wanted to be. Elon Musk, founder of Tesla, knew that all three influencers, and others, would submit to the Tesla value proposition, because each of them—all 325,000 of them—interpreted value in their own unique way.

6-2 THE CONSUMER DECISION-MAKING PROCESS

When buying products, consumers generally follow a series of steps known as the **consumer decision-making process**, shown in Exhibit 6.1. The steps in the process are (1) need recognition, (2) information search, (3) evaluation of alternatives, (4) purchase, and (5) postpurchase behaviour. These five steps represent a general process that can be used as a guide for studying how consumers make decisions. This guideline does not assume that consumers' decisions will proceed in order through all the steps of the process. In fact, the consumer may end the process at any time or may not even make a purchase.

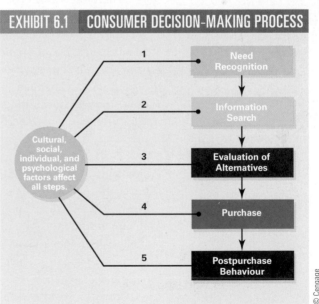

EXHIBIT 6.1 CONSUMER DECISION-MAKING PROCESS

Cultural, social, individual, and psychological factors affect all steps.

1. Need Recognition
2. Information Search
3. Evaluation of Alternatives
4. Purchase
5. Postpurchase Behaviour

© Cengage

The section on the types of consumer buying decisions later in the chapter discusses why a consumer's progression through these steps may vary. Before addressing this issue, however, we will describe each step in the process in detail.

consumer decision-making process a five-step process used by consumers when buying goods or services

6-2a Need Recognition

The first stage in the consumer decision-making process is need recognition. **Need recognition** occurs when consumers are faced with an imbalance between actual and desired states. This imbalance is triggered when a consumer is exposed to either an internal or an external **stimulus**. *Internal stimuli* are occurrences you experience, such as hunger or thirst. *External stimuli* are influences from an outside source, such as someone's recommendation of a new restaurant, the design of a package, or an advertisement on television or radio.

Marketers know, however, that in the world of marketing, wants and needs are the same thing, with some more basic and some more specific and psychological (which will be covered later in this chapter). Because of this, when one need is met, firms can create more needs on the part of the consumer—sort of an **engineered demand**. The **need** is for a particular product or service that the consumer perceives as being unfulfilled. It can be for a specific product, or it can be for a certain attribute or feature of a product. For example, if you lose your cellphone, you'll need to buy a replacement, but you'll also need to decide whether you need the new version, as it comes with the latest technology.

Therefore, a key objective for marketers is to get consumers to recognize an imbalance between their current status and their preferred state. Communications through advertising, sales promotion, and more frequently through digital devices, often provide this stimulus. By surveying buyer preferences, marketers gain information about consumer needs and wants, which they can then use to tailor their products and services.

Another way marketers create new products and services is by observing trends in the marketplace. IKEA, the home furnishing giant, realized that Generation-Y consumers prefer furniture that is stylish, easy to clean, multifunctional, and portable, so it created a line of products to meet those preferences. One item in the line is a space-saving multifunction desk that can be converted into a dining table—and it has wheels so that it can be easily moved.[2]

Consumers recognize unfulfilled needs in various ways. The two most common occur when a current product isn't performing properly and when the consumer is about to run out of something that is generally kept on hand. Consumers may also recognize unfulfilled wants if they become aware of a product that seems superior to the one they currently use. Such was the case with Apple's iPhone through its first 10 years. The computer giant made a point of introducing a new version of the phone just about every year, not because the previous version was unusable, but because the newer version would be positioned as much more advanced than its predecessor—thus engineering a need among smartphone consumers.

And as you read in Chapter 4, marketers selling their products in global markets must carefully observe the needs and wants of consumers in various regions.

6-2b Information Search

After recognizing a need, consumers search for information about the various alternatives available to satisfy it. An information search can occur internally, externally, or both. An **internal information search** is the process of recalling information stored in one's memory. This stored information stems largely from previous experience with a product—for example, recalling whether a hotel where you stayed earlier in the year had clean rooms and friendly service.

In contrast, an **external information search** is the process of seeking information in the outside environment. Historically, there have been two basic types of external information sources: nonmarketing-controlled and marketing-controlled. A **nonmarketing-controlled information source** is one that doesn't originate from the firm(s) making the product. These information sources include personal experiences (trying or observing a new product); personal sources (family, friends, acquaintances, and co-workers who may recommend a product or service); and public sources, such as *Consumer Reports* and other rating organizations that comment on products and services. For example, if you feel like streaming a movie, you may search your memory for past experiences with different service providers such as Shaw, Telus, or Netflix (personal experience). To choose which movie to see, you may rely on the recommendation of a friend or family member (personal sources), or you may read the critical reviews as contributed by others who've watched the

need recognition the result of an imbalance between actual and desired states

stimulus any unit of input affecting one or more of the five senses: sight, smell, taste, touch, hearing

engineered demand where firms, led by marketers, discover a marketable need not yet known by the consumer

need a state of being where we desire something that we do not possess but yearn to acquire

internal information search the process of recalling information stored in one's memory

external information search the process of seeking information in the outside environment

nonmarketing-controlled information source a product information source not associated with advertising or promotion

movie and have rated it through a third party such as Rotten Tomatoes (public sources).

On the other hand, a **marketing-controlled information source** originates with marketers promoting the product. Marketing-controlled information sources include mass-media advertising (out-of-home, radio, newspaper, television, digital and magazine advertising), sales promotions (contests, displays, and premiums), salespeople, public relations, and product labels and packaging. Many consumers, however, are wary of the information they receive from marketing-controlled sources, believing that most marketing campaigns stress the product's attributes and ignore its faults. These sentiments tend to be stronger among better-educated and higher-income consumers. Social media are being used extensively by consumers to seek product information from both marketer and nonmarketer sources.

The culmination of this trend has introduced a third form of external information source—**consumer-to-consumer (C2C) reviews.** The inundation of **platform**-based businesses, such as Uber, Airbnb, or Amazon, has introduced this additional, and perhaps most valuable, information source where past consumers of a product purchased through one of these platforms post reviews about their experience. The aggregated reviews are then made available to would-be purchasers. Unlike consumer reports in nonpartisan publications, C2C reviews are willingly and transparently posted directly through the vendors' sites. You have instant exposure to reviews of Uber drivers or Airbnb hosts (and guests) within the Web or the mobile apps of these firms. This trend is reshaping the business landscape because it is reshaping how customers make purchase decisions. In the meantime, marketers in turn are exposed to enormous new information sources to use to figure out and attract customers.

The extent to which an individual conducts an external search depends on his or her perceived risk, knowledge, prior experience, and level of interest in the good or service. Generally, as the perceived risk of the purchase increases, the consumer expands the search and considers alternative brands. For example, you would spend more time researching the purchase of a car than the purchase of an energy drink. A consumer's knowledge about the product or service will also affect the extent of an external information search. A consumer who is knowledgeable and well informed about a potential purchase is less likely to search for additional information and will conduct the search more efficiently, thereby requiring less time to search.

The extent of a consumer's external search is also affected by confidence in one's decision-making ability.

A confident consumer not only has sufficient stored information about the product but also feels self-assured about making the right decision. People lacking this confidence will continue an information search even when they know a great deal about the product. A third factor influencing the external information search is product experience. Consumers who have had a positive prior experience with a product are more likely to limit their search to items related to the positive experience. For example, when planning a trip, consumers are likely to choose airlines with which they have had positive experiences, such as consistent on-time arrivals, and will likely avoid airlines with which they had a negative experience, such as lost luggage.

Finally, the extent of the search is positively related to the amount of interest a consumer has in a product. A consumer who is more interested in a product will spend more time searching for information and alternatives. A dedicated runner searching for a new pair of running shoes may enjoy reading about the new brands available and, as a result, may spend more time and effort than other buyers in deciding on the next shoe purchase.

The buyer's **evoked set** (or **consideration set**) is a group of the most preferred alternatives resulting from an information search, which a buyer can further evaluate to make a final choice. Consumers do not consider all brands available in a product category, but they do seriously consider a much smaller set. The hardcore runner mentioned in the previous paragraph may be loyal to Nike, for instance, but may have been told by peers about the benefits of Asics or Saucony and thus includes these two additional brands as her evoked set. Having too many choices can, in fact, confuse consumers and cause them to delay the decision to buy or, in some instances, can cause them to not buy at all.

6-2c Evaluation of Alternatives and Purchase

After acquiring information and constructing a set of alternative products, the consumer is ready to make a decision. A consumer will use the information stored

---

marketing-controlled information source a product information source that originates with marketers promoting the product

consumer-to-consumer (C2C) reviews consumers' reviews of products on the vendors' sites where the products were purchased

platform a business model, usually digital, where producers and buyers exchange value

evoked set (consideration set) a group of the most preferred alternatives resulting from an information search, which a buyer can further evaluate to make a final choice

Itzf/Shutterstock.com

in memory and obtained from outside sources to develop a set of criteria. These standards help the consumer to evaluate and compare alternatives. One way to begin narrowing the number of choices in the consideration set is to pick a product attribute and then exclude all products in the set without that attribute. For example, if you are buying a car and live in the mountains, you will probably exclude all cars without four-wheel drive.

Another way to narrow the number of choices is to use cutoffs. Cutoffs are either minimum or maximum levels of an attribute that an alternative must pass to be considered. If your budget for that new car is $25,000, you will not consider any four-wheel drive vehicle above that price. A final way to narrow the choices is to rank the attributes under consideration in order of importance and evaluate the products on how well each performs on the most important attributes.

If new brands are added to a consideration set, the consumer's evaluation of the existing brands in that set changes. As a result, certain brands in the original set may become more desirable. If you discover that you can get the exact car you want, used, for $18,000 instead of spending $25,000 for a new model, you may revise your criteria and select the used car.

The goal of the marketing manager is to determine which attributes have the most influence on a consumer's choice. Several attributes may collectively affect a consumer's evaluation of products. A single attribute, such as price, may not adequately explain how consumers form their consideration set. Moreover, attributes the marketer thinks are important may not be very important to the consumer. A brand name can also have a significant impact on a consumer's ultimate choice. By providing consumers with a certain set of promises, brands in essence simplify the consumer decision-making process so consumers do not have to rethink their options every time they need something.[3] Following the evaluation of alternatives, the consumer decides which product to buy or decides not to buy a product at all. If he or she decides to make a purchase, the next step in the process is an evaluation of the product after the purchase.

6-2d Postpurchase Behaviour

When buying products, consumers expect certain outcomes from the purchase. How well these expectations are met determines whether the consumer is satisfied or dissatisfied with the purchase. For the marketer, an important element of any postpurchase marketing activity is reducing any lingering doubts that the decision was sound. Eliminating such doubts is particularly important to increase consumer satisfaction with their purchases. Marketers thus must provide **decision confirmation** support beginning at the evaluation of alternatives stage, through the purchase itself, and into postpurchase. The decision confirmation is the reaffirmation of the wisdom of the decision a consumer has made, and such a need is stronger among consumers after making an important purchase.

A failure to confirm one's decision may result in **cognitive dissonance**—also popularly known as buyer's remorse—induced by constant doubt about one's choice. Cognitive dissonance is defined as an inner tension that a consumer experiences after recognizing an inconsistency between behaviour and values or opinions. For example, suppose a consumer is looking to purchase a mountain bike that is light, yet durable, with disc brakes and priced under $1,000. In such a situation, no one of the alternatives he has in his evoked set is clearly offering all the key attributes he is seeking. Thus proceeding with the purchase is likely to result in cognitive dissonance.

Marketing managers can help reduce dissonance through effective communication with purchasers. Postpurchase communication by sellers and dissonance-reducing statements in instruction booklets may help customers to feel more at ease with their purchase. Advertising that displays the product's superiority over competing brands or guarantees can also help relieve the possible dissonance of someone who has already bought the product. Ultimately, the marketer's goal is to ensure that the outcome meets or exceeds the customer's expectations rather than being a disappointment.

decision confirmation the reaffirmation of the wisdom of the decision a consumer has made

cognitive dissonance the inner tension that a consumer experiences after recognizing an inconsistency between behaviour and values or opinions

TYPES OF CONSUMER BUYING DECISIONS AND CONSUMER INVOLVEMENT

All consumer buying decisions generally fall along a continuum of three broad categories: routine response behaviour, limited decision making, and extensive decision making (see Exhibit 6.2). Goods and services in these three categories can best be described in terms of five factors: level of consumer involvement, length of time to make a decision, cost of the good or service, degree of information search, and the number of alternatives considered. The level of consumer involvement is perhaps the most significant determinant in classifying buying decisions. **Involvement** is the amount of time and effort a buyer invests in the search, evaluation, and decision processes of consumer behaviour.

Frequently purchased, low-cost goods and services are generally associated with **routine response behaviour**. These goods and services can also be called low-involvement products because consumers spend little time on the search and decision before making the purchase. Usually, buyers are familiar with several different brands in the product category but stick with one brand. Consumers engaged in routine response behaviour normally don't experience need recognition until they are exposed to advertising or see the product displayed on a store shelf. These consumers buy first and evaluate later, whereas the reverse is true for consumers who engage in extensive decision making.

Limited decision making requires a moderate amount of time for gathering information and deliberating about an unfamiliar brand in a familiar product category. It typically occurs when a consumer has previous product experience but is unfamiliar with the current brands available. Limited decision making is also associated with lower levels of involvement (although higher

than routine decisions) because consumers expend only moderate effort in searching for information or in considering various alternatives. If a consumer's usual brand is sold out, he or she will likely evaluate several other brands before making a final decision.

Consumers practise **extensive decision making** when considering the purchase of an unfamiliar, expensive product or an infrequently purchased item. This process is the most complex type of consumer buying decision and is associated with high involvement on the part of the consumer. The process resembles the model outlined in Exhibit 6.1. Because these consumers want to make the right decision, they want to know as much as they can about the product category and the available brands. Buyers use several criteria for evaluating their options and spend much time seeking information. Buying a home or a car, for example, requires extensive decision making.

The type of decision making that consumers use to purchase a product does not necessarily remain constant. If a routinely purchased product no longer satisfies, consumers may practise limited or extensive decision making to switch to another brand. Consumers who first use extensive decision making may then use limited or routine decision making for future purchases. For example, a family may spend a lot of time figuring out that their new puppy prefers hard food to soft, but once they know, the purchase will become routine.

6-3a Factors Determining the Level of Consumer Involvement

The level of involvement in the purchase depends on the following five factors:

- **Previous experience:** When consumers have had previous experience with a good or service, the level of involvement typically decreases. After repeated product trials, consumers learn to make quick choices. Because consumers are familiar with the product and know whether it

involvement the amount of time and effort a buyer invests in the search, evaluation, and decision processes of consumer behaviour

routine response behaviour the type of decision making exhibited by consumers buying frequently purchased, low-cost goods and services; requires little search and decision time

limited decision making the type of decision making that requires a moderate amount of time for gathering information and deliberating about an unfamiliar brand in a familiar product category

extensive decision making the most complex type of consumer decision making, used when considering the purchase of an unfamiliar, expensive product or an infrequently purchased item; requires the use of several criteria for evaluating options and much time for seeking information

EXHIBIT 6.2	CONTINUUM OF CONSUMER BUYING DECISIONS		
	Routine	**Limited**	**Extensive**
Involvement	Low	Low to moderate	High
Time	Short	Short to moderate	Long
Cost	Low	Low to moderate	High
Information Search	Internal only	Mostly internal	Internal and external
Number of Alternatives	One	Few	Many

© Cengage

will satisfy their needs, they become less involved in the purchase.

- **Interest:** Involvement is directly related to consumer interests, as in cars, music, movies, bicycling, or electronics. Naturally, these areas of interest vary from one individual to another. A person highly involved in bike racing will be more interested in the type of bike she owns than someone who rides a bike only for recreation.

- **Perceived risk of negative consequences:** As the perceived risk in purchasing a product increases, so does a consumer's level of involvement. The types of risks that concern consumers include financial risk, social risk, and psychological risk. First, financial risk is exposure to loss of wealth or purchasing power. Because high risk is associated with high-priced purchases, consumers tend to become extremely involved. Therefore, price and involvement are usually directly related: as price increases, so does the level of involvement. Second, consumers take social risks when they buy products that can affect people's social opinions of them (for example, driving an old, beat-up car or wearing unstylish clothes). Third, buyers undergo psychological risk if they feel that making the wrong decision might cause some concern or anxiety. For example, some consumers feel guilty about eating foods that are not healthy, such as regular ice cream rather than fat-free frozen yogurt.

- **Situation:** The circumstances of a purchase may temporarily transform a low-involvement decision into a high-involvement one. High involvement comes into play when the consumer perceives risk in a specific situation. For example, an individual might routinely buy frozen fruit and vegetables, but for dinner parties shop for high-quality fresh produce.

- **Social visibility:** Involvement also increases as the social visibility of a product increases. Products that are often on social display include clothing (especially designer labels), jewellery, cars, and furniture. All these items make a statement about the purchaser and, therefore, carry a social risk.

6-3b Marketing Implications of Involvement

Marketing strategy varies according to the level of involvement associated with the product. For high-involvement product purchases, marketing managers have several responsibilities. First, promotion to the target market should be extensive and informative. A good ad

Tide uses bright, eye-catching packaging to draw customers to what is otherwise a low-involvement product.

gives consumers the information they need to make the purchase decision and specifies the benefits and unique advantages of owning the product.

For low-involvement product purchases, consumers may not recognize their wants until they are in the store. Therefore, marketers focus on package design so the product will be eye-catching and easily recognized on the shelf. In-store promotions and displays also stimulate sales of low-involvement products. A good display can explain the product's purpose and prompt recognition of a want. Coupons, cents-off deals, and two-for-one offers also effectively promote low-involvement items.

At the opposite end of the spectrum, marketers can draw from their knowledge of the marketing

environment to assist customers in their decision about extensive-involvement purchases. For instance, when buying a home, purchasers are forever weighing not only the immediate costs of a down payment but the future costs of monthly mortgage payments. During economic periods when the interest rates on loans are low, marketers can reinforce the importance of timing their purchase to would-be home buyers. This tactic not only compels buyers to act in a timely manner but also preempts or reduces cognitive dissonance.

6-3c Factors Influencing Consumer Buying Decisions

The consumer decision-making process does not occur in a vacuum. On the contrary, the decision process is strongly influenced by underlying cultural, social, individual, and psychological factors. These factors are central to the deeper concept of consumer behaviour and have an effect from the time a consumer perceives a stimulus through to the time of postpurchase behaviour. Cultural factors, which include culture and values, subculture, and social class, exert the broadest influence over consumer decision making. Social factors sum up the social interactions between a consumer and influential groups of people, such as reference groups, opinion leaders, and family members. Individual factors, which include gender, age, family life-cycle stage, personality, self-concept, and lifestyle, are unique to each individual

and play a major role in the type of products and services consumers want. Psychological factors determine how consumers perceive and interact with their environments and influence the ultimate decisions consumers make. They include perception, motivation, learning, beliefs, and attitudes. Exhibit 6.3 summarizes these influences.

6-4 CULTURAL INFLUENCES ON CONSUMER BUYING DECISIONS

Cultural factors exert a deep influence on consumer decision making. Marketers must understand the way people's culture and its accompanying values, as well as their subculture and social class, influence their buying behaviour.

6-4a Culture and Values

Culture comprises the set of values, norms, attitudes, and other meaningful symbols that shape human behaviour and the artifacts, or products, of that behaviour as they are transmitted from one generation to the next. Culture is the essential character of a society that distinguishes it from other cultural groups.

> **culture** the set of values, norms, attitudes, and other meaningful symbols that shape human behaviour and the artifacts, or products, of that behaviour as they are transmitted from one generation to the next

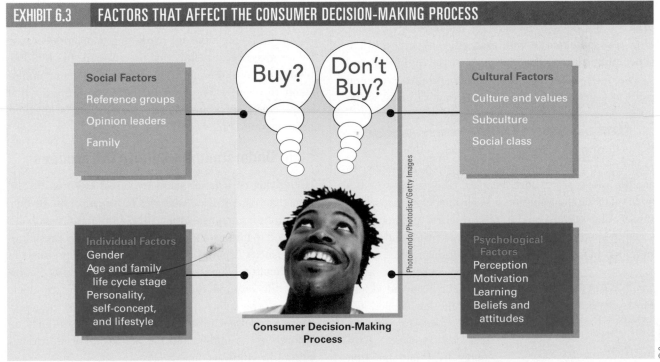

EXHIBIT 6.3   FACTORS THAT AFFECT THE CONSUMER DECISION-MAKING PROCESS

Social Factors
Reference groups
Opinion leaders
Family

Buy? Don't Buy?

Cultural Factors
Culture and values
Subculture
Social class

Individual Factors
Gender
Age and family life cycle stage
Personality, self-concept, and lifestyle

Consumer Decision-Making Process

Psychological Factors
Perception
Motivation
Learning
Beliefs and attitudes

Photomondo/Photodisc/Getty Images

© Cengage

Culture is pervasive. What people eat, how they dress, what they think and feel, and what language they speak are all dimensions of culture. Culture encompasses all the things consumers do without conscious choice because their culture's values, customs, and rituals are ingrained in their daily habits.

Culture is functional. Human interaction creates values and prescribes acceptable behaviour for each culture. By establishing common expectations, culture gives order to society. Sometimes these expectations are enacted into laws, such as the expectation that drivers will stop at red lights. Other times, these expectations are taken for granted: grocery stores and hospitals are open 24 hours, whereas banks are not.

Culture is learned. Consumers are not born knowing the values and norms of their society. Instead, they must learn what is acceptable from family and friends. Children learn the values that will govern their behaviour from parents, teachers, and peers.

Culture is dynamic. It adapts to changing needs and an evolving environment. The rapid growth of technology in today's world has accelerated the rate of cultural change. How we communicate with each other regardless of the geographical distance has changed with the use of WiFi and mobile devices. Another factor that contributes to cultural shifts in Canada is our rapidly increasing diversity, which influences our food, music, clothing, and entertainment.

The most defining element of a culture is its **values**— the enduring beliefs shared by a society that a specific mode of conduct is personally or socially preferable to another mode of conduct. People's value systems have a great effect on their consumer behaviour. Consumers with similar value systems tend to react similarly to various marketing-related inducements. Values also correspond to consumption patterns. For example, Canadians place a high value on convenience, as we are in a time-starved society. This value has created lucrative markets for products such as breakfast bars, energy bars, and nutrition

value the enduring belief shared by a society that a specific mode of conduct is personally or socially preferable to another mode of conduct

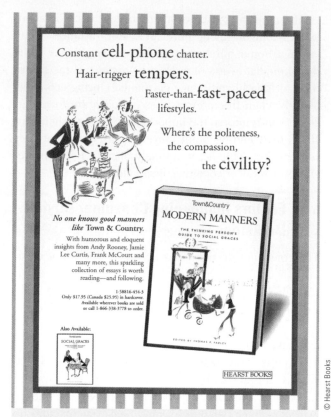

© Hearst Books

Modern Manners explores the ways in which new technologies, like cellphones, have changed North American culture.

bars that allow consumers to eat on the go.[4] Those values considered central to the Canadian way of life include success, freedom, materialism, capitalism, progress, and youth.

The personal values of target consumers have important implications for marketing managers because values give rise to beliefs that, in turn, are the building blocks of consumer attitude. When marketers understand the core values that underlie the attitudes that shape consumers' buying patterns, they can target their message more effectively.

6-4b Understanding Culture Differences

Underlying core values can vary across cultures. As the Canadian marketplace becomes more culturally diverse and more companies expand their operations globally, the need to understand different cultures becomes more important. A firm has little chance of selling products in a multicultural country like Canada if it does not understand the cultural differences. Like people, products have cultural values and rules that influence their perception and use. Culture, therefore, must be understood before we can understand the behaviour of individuals within the cultural context.

Language is another important aspect of culture that Canadian marketers must consider, although the influence of the French language on this assertion is decreasing as time goes on. According to *Maclean's*, "Outside of Quebec, the rate of bilingualism (French/English) is less than 10%."[5] However, it is significant to note that the number of Canadians proficient in English and one of the immigrant languages has increased in recent years.[6] This change in language usage has considerable implications for Canadian marketers.

6-4c Subculture

A culture can be divided into subcultures on the basis of demographic characteristics, geographic regions, national and ethnic background, political beliefs, and religious beliefs. A **subculture** is a homogeneous group of people who share elements of the overall culture and also have their own unique cultural elements. Within subcultures, people's attitudes, values, and purchase decisions are even more similar than they are within the broader culture. Subcultural differences may result in considerable variation within a culture with regard to how, when, and where people buy goods and services, and what they buy.

In Canada's multicultural society, French Canadians represent a dominant subculture. While this subculture is mainly based in Quebec, Canada is officially a bilingual nation, and marketers in all regions of the country must be knowledgeable about the language and lifestyle values of the French Canadian subculture. As previously mentioned, it is important to note that the nature of bilingualism in Canada is changing: an increasing proportion of the population is bilingual not in English and French but in English and one of the immigrant languages.

The broadcast team of Hockey Night in Canada Punjabi (from left to right): Harnarayan Singh, Amrit Gill, Harpreet Pandher, and Bhupinder Hundal.

Once marketers identify subcultures, they can design special marketing programs to serve their needs. In response to the growing Asian market, companies have been spending a larger percentage of their marketing budgets advertising to this group. Canadian banks, such as TD Canada Trust and CIBC, have developed marketing campaigns targeting the Asian market, particularly in Vancouver and Toronto. *Hockey Night in Canada*, an all-Canadian cultural brand if there ever was one, added *Hockey Night in Punjabi* in 2008. When Rogers acquired the broadcasting rights from the National Hockey League in 2014, it placed the broadcasts on its multi-ethnic affiliate, OMNI, where it has since become a fixture.[7]

6-4d Social Class

A **social class** is a group of people who are considered nearly equal in status or community esteem, who regularly socialize among themselves both formally and informally, and who share behavioural norms.

The majority of Canadians today define themselves as middle class, regardless of their actual income or educational attainment. This phenomenon most likely occurs because working-class Canadians tend to aspire to the middle-class lifestyle while some of those who achieve affluence may downwardly aspire to respectable middle-class status as a matter of principle.

Social class is typically measured as a combination of occupation, income, education, wealth, and other variables. For instance, affluent upper-class consumers are more likely to be salaried executives or self-employed professionals with at least an undergraduate degree. Working-class or middle-class consumers are more likely to be hourly service workers or blue-collar employees with only a high-school education. Educational attainment, however, seems to be the most reliable indicator of a person's social and economic status. Those with university or college degrees or graduate degrees are more likely to fall into the upper classes, while those people with some postsecondary experience fall closer to traditional concepts of the middle class.

Marketers are interested in social class as an integral part of segmentation and targeting, covered in Chapter 8. Segmentation is a process where marketers divide larger populations into groups based upon a number of variables, including demographics. Among many other descriptors, demographics can be represented by individual and household

subculture a homogeneous group of people who share elements of the overall culture and also have their own unique cultural elements

social class a group of people who are considered nearly equal in status or community esteem, who regularly socialize among themselves both formally and informally, and who share behavioural norms

Education is usually a reliable indicator of a person's social and economic status. Those with postsecondary degrees are more likely to fall into the upper classes, while those with some postsecondary experience tend to fall into the middle class.

income, a telltale sign as to how much money people have to spend on goods and services. Targeting is the directed pursuit of a given segment based on its attractiveness to a firm. Thus Lululemon, with its high-end yoga-lifestyle apparel, will target not just image- and fit-conscious consumers (mostly women), but only those with some discretionary income to spend on a relatively expensive item.

6-5 SOCIAL INFLUENCES ON CONSUMER BUYING DECISIONS

Most consumers are likely to seek out the opinions of others to reduce their search and evaluation effort or uncertainty, especially as the perceived risk of the decision increases. Consumers may also seek out others' opinions for guidance on new products or services, products with image-related attributes, expensive products, or products where attribute information is lacking or uninformative. Specifically, consumers interact socially with reference groups, opinion leaders, and family members to obtain product information and decision approval.

reference group a group in society that influences an individual's purchasing behaviour

primary membership groups groups with which individuals interact regularly in an informal, face-to-face manner

secondary membership groups groups with which individuals interact less consistently and more formally than with primary membership groups

aspirational reference groups groups that an individual would like to join

norms the values and attitudes deemed acceptable by a group

6-5a Reference Groups

All the formal and informal groups that influence the purchasing behaviour of an individual are that person's **reference groups.** Consumers may use products or brands to identify with or become a member of a group. Consumers observe how members of their reference groups consume, and they use the same criteria to make their own consumer decisions.

Reference groups can be broadly categorized as being either direct or indirect (see Exhibit 6.4). Direct reference groups are face-to-face membership groups that touch people's lives directly. They can be either primary or secondary. **Primary membership groups** include all groups with which people interact regularly in an informal, face-to-face manner, such as family, friends, and co-workers. In contrast, people associate with **secondary membership groups** less consistently and more formally. These groups might include clubs, professional associations, and people who share a religious affiliation.

Consumers are also influenced by many indirect, nonmembership reference groups they do not belong to. **Aspirational reference groups** are those groups that a person would like to join. To join an aspirational group, a person must conform to that group's **norms**—that is, the values and attitudes deemed acceptable by the group. Thus a person who wants to be elected to public office may begin to dress more conservatively, to match the attire of other politicians. Athletes are an aspirational group for several market segments. To appeal to the Ottawa-area automobile market, two very different businesses turned to two different players from the Ottawa Senators. Mark Motors Porsche secured all-star defenceman Erik Karlsson to be brand ambassador for one year, while drive-through garage service Oil Changers acquired

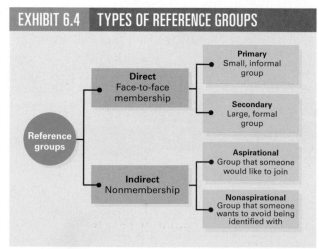

EXHIBIT 6.4   TYPES OF REFERENCE GROUPS

tough guy Chris Neil.[8] Neither athlete commands the endorsement premiums of global icons like LeBron James or Serena Williams, but then smaller local firms aren't trying to resonate with a global market.

Nonaspirational reference groups, or **dissociative groups**, influence our behaviour because we try to maintain distance from them. A consumer may avoid buying some types of clothing or cars, going to certain restaurants or stores, or even buying a home in a certain neighbourhood to avoid being associated with a particular group.

The activities, values, and goals of reference groups directly influence consumer behaviour. For marketers, reference groups have three important implications: (1) they serve as information sources and influence perceptions; (2) they affect an individual's aspiration levels; and (3) their norms either constrain or stimulate consumer behaviour. Understanding the effect of reference groups on a product is important for marketers as they track the life cycle of their products. Marketers continually face the challenge of identifying the trendsetters in a particular target market. For example, a snowboard manufacturer can determine what is considered cool in the snowboard market by seeking out the trendsetters on their favourite slopes. The unique ways in which these snowboarders personalize their equipment and clothing can be looked on as being desirable and thus may be modified by the influencers who are seeking to express their own individual character. Once the fad look is embraced by the influencers, it has the potential to be adopted by the others in that socio-geographic group. However, as the adoption of the latest trend becomes more common, that trend loses its appeal to the trendsetters, and they seek new ways to express their individualism. The effects of reference groups are especially important both for products that satisfy such visible, unique, socially desirable, high-involvement needs as wine, fashion, and the latest foods, and for personal services, such as spa treatments and vacation destinations and activities. Thus marketers must understand and track the effects of reference groups on the sales of a product as it moves through its life cycle.

6-5b Opinion Leaders

Reference groups frequently include individuals known as group leaders, or **opinion leaders**—those who influence others. Obviously, it is important for marketing

managers to persuade such people to purchase their goods or services.

Opinion leaders are often the first to try new products and services, usually as the result of pure curiosity. They are typically self-indulgent, making them more likely to explore unproven but intriguing products and services. Technology companies have found that teenagers, because of their willingness to experiment, are key opinion leaders for the success of new technologies. Texting became popular with teenagers before it gained widespread appeal. Today, Snapchat has become a major means of communication. As a result, many companies include Snapchat posts in their marketing programs targeted to teens. Recent studies on opinion leaders in the pharmaceutical industry have uncovered the key influencer to be the **sociometric leader**, typically a well-respected collaborative professional who is socially and professionally well connected. These lower-profile individuals have certainly had marketers reflecting on whom they should be marketing to and with.[9]

After identifying potential opinion leaders, marketers will often endeavour to engage these people to support their products. On a wider scale, large companies, groups, associations, and causes will seek out recognized organizations or individuals in sports, business, entertainment, religion, or politics to endorse or support the promotion of their product. The organization's or individual's familiarity, attractiveness, credibility, and relative association, can greatly influence a target group. Thus, while Alessia Cara and Shawn Mendes—two of Billboard's "Top 21 under 21" in 2016[10] (who both also happen to be Canadian)—can influence teens' fashion or desire to go to a summer music event, a promotion featuring Connor McDavid might influence an athlete or hockey fan, and a local company's support of a new charity fundraiser or disaster relief can influence other companies, communities, and individuals to also support the cause.

6-5c Family

The family is the most important social institution for many consumers, strongly influencing their values, attitudes, self-concepts—and buying

Kathy Hutchins/Shutterstock.com

nonaspirational reference groups (dissociative groups) groups that influence our behaviour because we try to maintain distance from them

opinion leader an individual who influences the opinions of others

sociometric leader a low-profile, well-respected collaborative professional who is socially and professionally well connected

behaviour. For example, a family that strongly values good health will have a grocery list distinctly different from that of a family that views every dinner as a gourmet event. Moreover, the family is responsible for the **socialization process**—the passing down of cultural values and norms to children. Because children learn by observing their parents' consumption patterns, they will tend to shop in a similar pattern.

Decision-making roles among family members tend to vary significantly, depending on the types of items purchased. Family members assume a variety of roles in the purchase process. *Initiators* suggest, initiate, or plant the seed for the purchase process. The initiator can be any member of the family. For example, a sister might initiate the product search by asking for a new bicycle as a birthday present. *Influencers* are those members of the family whose opinions are valued. In our example, Mom might function as a price-range watchdog, an influencer whose main role is to veto or approve price ranges. A brother may give his opinion on certain makes of bicycles. The *decision maker* is the family member who actually makes the decision to buy or not to buy. For example, a parent is likely to choose the final brand and model of bicycle to buy after seeking further information from the sister regarding cosmetic features, such as colour, and after imposing additional parental criteria, such as durability and safety. The *purchaser* (probably a parent) is the one who actually exchanges money for the product. Finally, the *consumer* is the actual user—the sister, in the case of the bicycle.

Marketers should consider family purchase situations along with the distribution of consumer and decision-maker roles among family members. Ordinary marketing views the individual as both decision maker and consumer. Family marketing adds several other possibilities: sometimes more than one family member or all family members are involved in the decision; sometimes only children are involved in the decision; sometimes more than one consumer is involved; and sometimes the decision maker and the consumer are different people.

6-6 INDIVIDUAL INFLUENCES ON CONSUMER BUYING DECISIONS

A person's buying decisions are also influenced by personal characteristics that are unique to each individual, such as gender; age and life-cycle stage; and personality, self-concept, and lifestyle. Individual characteristics are generally

socialization process the passing down of cultural values and norms to children

stable over the course of one's life. For instance, most people do not change their gender, and the act of changing personality or lifestyle requires a complete reorientation of one's life. In the case of age and life-cycle stage, these changes occur gradually over time.

6-6a Gender

Physiological differences between men and women result in different needs. Just as important are the distinct cultural, social, and economic roles played by men and women and the effects that these roles have on their decision-making processes. Most car manufacturers have realized that men and women tend to look at different features when purchasing a vehicle. Generally, men gravitate toward gadgets and performance-related items, while women prefer to focus on convenience features, such as ease of access, carrying capacity, cup holders, and heated/cooled seats.

Indeed, men and women do shop differently. Studies show that men and women share similar motivations about where to shop—that is, seeking reasonable prices, merchandise quality, and a friendly, low-pressure environment—but they don't necessarily feel the same about shopping in general. Most women enjoy shopping, while most men claim to dislike the experience and shop only out of necessity. Further, men desire simple shopping experiences, such as stores with less variety and more convenience.

Trends in gender marketing are influenced by the changing roles of men and women in society. Companies must develop new strategies that reflect the changing roles of men and women both at home and at work. As *Canadian Grocer* points out, in 60 percent of Canadian households, a male is either the primary or shared grocery shopper, due largely to the sharp increase of stay-at-home dads, which had risen to 12 percent of households by 2015.[11]

6-6b Age and Family Life-Cycle Stage

The age and family life-cycle stage of a consumer can have a significant impact on consumer behaviour. How old a consumer is generally indicates the products he or she may be interested in purchasing. Consumer tastes in food, clothing, technology, cars, furniture, and recreation are often age related. In a research study by Harris Interactive, the first Youth EquiTrend Study asked 8- to 24-year-olds to rate brands on familiarity, quality, and purchase consideration. The results showed marked differences in age groups. The 8- to 12-year-old tweens listed as their top preferences Nintendo, Doritos, Oreos,

Ian Dagnall/Alamy Stock Photo

and M&Ms. The teens (ages 13 to 17) shifted to Apple, Google, M&Ms, and Oreos. The young adults' (ages 18 to 24) choices were more tech-savvy products, namely Apple, Google, Facebook, and Gatorade.[12]

Related to a person's age is his or her place in the family life cycle. As Chapter 8 explains in more detail, the *family life cycle* is an orderly series of stages through which consumers' attitudes and behavioural tendencies evolve through maturity, experience, and changing income and status. Marketers often define their target markets in terms of family life cycle, such as "young singles," "young married with children," and "middle-aged married without children." As you can imagine, the spending habits of young singles, young parents, and empty nesters are very different. For instance, the presence of children in the home is the most significant determinant of the type of vehicle that's driven off the new-car lot. Parents are the ultimate need-driven car consumers, requiring larger cars and trucks to haul their children and all their belongings, which explains why sport utility vehicles (SUVs) and minivans were selling at a brisk pace before rising fuel costs became a major consideration when purchasing a vehicle.

Marketers should also be aware of the many nontraditional life-cycle paths that are common today and provide insights into the needs and wants of such consumers as divorced parents, lifelong singles, and childless couples.

6-6c Personality, Self-Concept, and Lifestyle

Each consumer has a unique personality. **Personality** is a broad concept that can be thought of as a way of organizing and grouping the consistency of an individual's reactions to situations. Thus personality combines psychological makeup and environmental forces. It also includes people's underlying dispositions, especially their most dominant characteristics. Some marketers believe that personality influences the types and brands of products purchased. For instance, the type of car, clothes, or jewellery a consumer buys may reflect one or more personality traits.

Self-concept, or self-perception, is how consumers perceive themselves in terms of attitudes, perceptions, beliefs, and self-evaluations. Although a self-concept may change, the change is often gradual. Through self-concept, people define their identity, which in turn provides for consistent and coherent behaviour.

Self-concept combines the **ideal self-image** (the way an individual would like to be) and the **real self-image** (the way an individual actually perceives himself or herself to be). Generally, we try to raise our real self-image toward our ideal (or at least narrow the gap). Consumers seldom buy products that jeopardize their self-image. For example, a woman who sees herself as a trendsetter wouldn't buy clothing that doesn't project a contemporary image.

Human behaviour depends largely on self-concept. Because consumers want to protect their identity as individuals, the products they buy, the stores they patronize, and the credit cards they carry support their self-image. By influencing the degree to which consumers perceive a good or service to be self-relevant, marketers can affect consumers' motivation to learn about, shop for, and buy a certain brand. Marketers also consider self-concept important because it helps explain the relationship between individuals' perceptions of themselves and their consumer behaviour.

An important component of self-concept is *body image*, the perception of the attractiveness of one's own physical features. For example, a person's perception of body image can be a stronger reason for weight loss than either good health or other social factors.[13] With the median age of Canadians rising, many companies are introducing products and services aimed at aging Baby Boomers who are concerned about their age and physical appearance. Marketers are also seeing Boomers respond to products aimed at younger audiences. For instance, several of the cars designed and targeted at Gen Y have attracted more buyers from the oldest of the Baby Boom cohort (ages 65 to 70).[14]

Personality and self-concept are reflected in lifestyle. A **lifestyle**

personality a way of organizing and grouping the consistency of an individual's reactions to situations

self-concept how consumers perceive themselves in terms of attitudes, perceptions, beliefs, and self-evaluations

ideal self-image the way an individual would like to be

real self-image the way an individual actually perceives himself or herself to be

lifestyle a mode of living as identified by a person's activities, interests, and opinions

is a mode of living, as identified by a person's activities, interests, and opinions. *Psychographics* is the analytical technique used to examine consumer lifestyles and to categorize consumers. Unlike personality characteristics, which can be difficult to describe and measure, lifestyle characteristics are useful in segmenting and targeting consumers. We, as consumers, are ever-changing in our affluence (income and spending focus), where we live (urban, suburban, or rural), and our relationships (family stage or life-stage groups). Lifestyle and psychographic analyses explicitly address the way consumers outwardly express their inner selves in their social and cultural environment. For example, to better understand their market segments, many Canadian companies now use psychographics such as PRIZM, which segments consumers into 66 different groups (e.g., Winner's Circle, a classification to which many of you aspire).[15] Psychographics and lifestyle segmentation are discussed in more detail in Chapter 8.

6-7 PSYCHOLOGICAL INFLUENCES ON CONSUMER BUYING DECISIONS

An individual's buying decisions are further influenced by **psychological factors**: perception, motivation, learning, beliefs, and attitudes. These factors are what consumers use to interact with their world, recognize their feelings, gather and analyze information, formulate thoughts and opinions, and take action. Unlike the other three influences on consumer behaviour, psychological influences can be affected by a person's environment because they are applied on specific occasions. For example, you will perceive different stimuli and process these stimuli in different ways depending on whether you are sitting in class concentrating on the instructor, sitting outside of class talking to friends, or sitting in your dorm room watching television.

psychological factors tools that consumers use to recognize, gather, analyze, and self-organize to aid in decision making

perception the process by which people select, organize, and interpret stimuli into a meaningful and coherent picture

selective exposure the process whereby a consumer decides which stimuli to notice and which to ignore

selective distortion a process whereby consumers change or distort information that conflicts with their feelings or beliefs

selective retention a process whereby consumers remember only information that supports their personal beliefs

6-7a Perception

The world is full of stimuli. A stimulus is any unit of input affecting one or more of the five senses: sight, smell, taste, touch, or hearing. The process by which we select, organize, and interpret these stimuli into a meaningful and coherent picture is called **perception**. In essence, perception is how we see the world around us and how we recognize that we need some help in making a purchasing decision.

People cannot perceive every stimulus in their environment. Therefore, they use **selective exposure**, a process whereby a consumer decides which stimuli to notice and which to ignore. The familiarity of an object, as well as its contrast, movement, intensity (such as increased volume), and smell, are cues that influence perception. Consumers use these cues to identify and define products and brands. The shape of a product's packaging, such as Coca-Cola's signature contour bottle, can influence perception. Colour is another cue, and it plays a key role in consumers' perceptions. Packaged food manufacturers use colour to trigger unconscious associations for grocery shoppers who typically make their shopping decisions in the blink of an eye. Food marketers use green to signal environmental well-being and healthy, low-fat foods, whereas black, brown, and gold are used to convey premium ingredients.[16] The shape and look of a product's packaging can also influence perception.

What is perceived by consumers may also depend on the vividness or shock value of the stimulus. Graphic warnings of the hazards associated with a product's use are perceived more readily and remembered more accurately than less vivid warnings or warnings that are written in text. Sexier ads excel at attracting the attention of younger consumers. Companies such as Calvin Klein and Guess use sensuous ads to "cut through the clutter" of competing ads and other stimuli to capture the attention of the target audience.

Two other concepts closely related to selective exposure are selective distortion and selective retention. **Selective distortion** occurs when consumers change or distort information that conflicts with their feelings or beliefs. For example, suppose you buy a new iPhone. After the purchase, if you receive new information about an alternative brand, such as the Google Pixel, you may distort the information to make it more consistent with the prior view that the iPhone is just as good as the Pixel, if not better. **Selective retention** is a process whereby consumers remember only information that supports their personal feelings or beliefs. The consumer forgets all information that may be inconsistent. Consumers may see a news report on suspected illegal practices by their favourite retail store but soon forget the reason the store was featured on the news.

Which stimuli will be perceived often depends on the individual. People can be exposed to the same stimuli under identical conditions but perceive them very differently. For example, two people viewing a TV commercial may have different interpretations of the advertising message. One person may be thoroughly engrossed by the message and become highly motivated to buy the product. Thirty seconds after the ad ends, the second person may not be able to recall the content of the message or even the product advertised.

MARKETING IMPLICATIONS OF PERCEPTION

Marketers must recognize the importance of cues, or signals, in consumers' perception of products. Marketing managers first identify the important attributes that the targeted consumers want in a product, such as price, social acceptance, or quantity, and then design signals to communicate these attributes. Gibson Guitar Corporation briefly cut prices on many of its guitars to compete with Japanese rivals Yamaha and Ibanez but found instead that it sold more guitars when it charged more. Consumers perceived the higher price as indicating a better-quality instrument.[17]

Marketing managers are also interested in the *threshold level of perception:* the minimum difference in a stimulus that the consumer will notice. This concept is sometimes referred to as the "just-noticeable difference." For example, how much would Apple have to drop the price of its watch before consumers recognized it as a bargain—$25? $50? or more? One study found that the just-noticeable difference in a stimulus is about a 20 percent change. That is, consumers will likely notice a 20 percent price decrease more quickly than a 15 percent decrease. This marketing principle can also be applied to other marketing variables, such as package size or loudness of a broadcast advertisement.[18]

Another study showed that the bargain-price threshold for a name brand is lower than that for a store brand. In other words, consumers perceive a bargain more readily when stores offer a small discount on a name-brand item than when they offer the same discount on a store brand; a larger discount is needed to achieve a similar effect for a store brand.[19] Researchers also found that for low-cost grocery items, consumers typically do not see past the second digit in the price. For instance, consumers do not perceive any real difference between two comparable cans of tuna, one priced at $1.52 and the other at $1.59, because they ignore the last digit.[20]

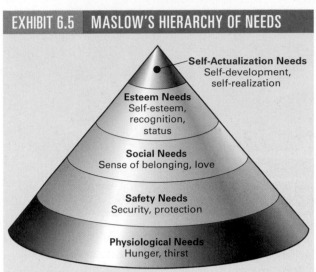

EXHIBIT 6.5 | MASLOW'S HIERARCHY OF NEEDS

Self-Actualization Needs
Self-development, self-realization

Esteem Needs
Self-esteem, recognition, status

Social Needs
Sense of belonging, love

Safety Needs
Security, protection

Physiological Needs
Hunger, thirst

© Cengage

Marketing managers who intend to do business in global markets should be aware of how foreign consumers perceive their products. For instance, in Japan, product labels are often written in English or French, even though they may not translate into anything meaningful. Many Japanese associate the foreign words with products that are exotic, expensive, and of high quality.

6-7b Motivation

By studying motivation, marketers can analyze the major forces influencing consumers to buy or not buy products. When you buy a product, you usually do so to fulfill some kind of need. These needs become motives when aroused sufficiently. For instance, you can be motivated by hunger to stop at McDonald's for, say, an Egg McMuffin before an early morning class. **Motives** are the driving forces that cause a person to take action to satisfy specific needs.

Why are people driven by particular needs at particular times? One popular theory is **Maslow's hierarchy of needs**, shown in Exhibit 6.5, which arranges needs in ascending order of importance: physiological, safety, social, esteem, and self-actualization. As a person learns how to satisfy a need at one level, a higher-level need becomes the next challenge.

The most basic human needs are *physiological*—that is, the needs for food, water, and shelter. Because these needs are essential

> **motives** driving forces that cause a person to take action to satisfy specific needs
>
> **Maslow's hierarchy of needs** a method of classifying human needs and motivations into five categories in ascending order of importance: physiological, safety, social, esteem, and self-actualization

More than one motive may drive a consumer's purchase. Consumers often look to products that satisfy multiple needs such as status and the value of family.

to survival, they must be satisfied first. *Safety* needs include security and freedom from pain, discomfort, and anxiety. Marketers sometimes appeal to consumers' fears about safety and their well-being in order to sell their products.

After physiological and safety needs have been fulfilled, *social needs*—especially love and a sense of belonging—become the focus. Love includes acceptance by one's peers, as well as sexual and romantic love. Over the latter part of the 20th century and into the 21st century, marketers have recognized our vulnerability at this level of need and have thus zeroed in on the abundant resulting marketing opportunities. The need to belong is also a favourite of marketers, especially those marketing products to teens. Shoes and clothing brands, such as Nike, Volcom, Hollister, and American Eagle Outfitters, score high with teenagers, who wear these labels to feel and look like they belong to the "in" crowd.

Self-esteem needs are the needs to feel good about ourselves, including self-respect and a sense of accomplishment. Esteem needs also include prestige, fame, and recognition of one's accomplishments. Indeed, marketers of luxury products, such as Dom Pérignon, Coach, Prada, and Mercedes-Benz, find that demand for their products is so strong among image-conscious consumers that their sales are generally unaffected by economic downturns. Beyond impressing others, self-esteem needs also motivate us to indulge in purchases that truly reflect who we are.

learning a process that creates changes in behaviour, immediate or expected, through experience and practice

The highest human need of Maslow's hierarchy—which we become aware of last—is *self-actualization*. It refers to realizing our true potential, or discovering our true purpose. Maslow felt that very few people ever attain this level. Even so, marketers churn out products and accompany them with messages focusing on this type of need by appealing to consumers' ambition, such as encouraging adults to go back to school, look for better career opportunities, or volunteer for charities that are consistent with their values and goals. Although self-actualization is not synonymous with self-help, the overlap is obvious, and the $10 billion market value of the self-help market in the United States alone should remind us why so many marketers pursue even a small portion of this pie.[21]

Maslow's hierarchy at a first glance seems to suggest rigid boundaries, and a linear sequential escalation between different levels, but this would be an oversimplification of the theory. Do we need to *fully* meet all our needs at one level before we move to the next higher level? Do we stop satisfying a need after moving on to the next? Can an individual try to meet needs at two different levels at the same time? In fact, we do not need to meet all our needs at one level before moving to the next. New university graduates, for example, tend to rent their first apartment (a physiological need) before buying a larger house at a later stage in life. At the same time, the new graduates spend money on clothing to meet their self-esteem needs and making friends and joining dating sites to look for potential mates. This pattern suggests that consumers must realize some level of achievement at one level before moving to the next higher level and effortlessly move between different levels at the same time.

6-7c Learning

Almost all consumer behaviour results from **learning**, which is the process that creates changes in behaviour, immediate or expected, through experience and practice. It is not possible to observe learning directly, but we can infer when it has occurred by a person's actions. For example, suppose you see an advertisement for a new and improved cold medicine. If you go to the store that day and buy that remedy, you have most likely learned something about the cold medicine.

There are two types of learning: experiential and conceptual. *Experiential learning* occurs when an experience changes your behaviour. For example, if the new cold medicine does not relieve your symptoms, you may not buy that brand again. *Conceptual learning*, which is not acquired through direct experience, is the second type of learning. Assume, for example, that you are a habitual bottled-water drinker and you see someone

WENN Ltd/Alamy Stock Photo

Learning theory is helpful for reminding marketers that concrete and timely actions are what reinforce desired consumer behaviour.

Repetition is a key strategy in promotional campaigns because it can lead to increased learning. Most marketers use repetitious advertising so that consumers will learn their unique advantage over the competition. Generally, to heighten learning, advertising messages should be spread over time rather than clustered together.

6-7d Beliefs and Attitudes

Beliefs and attitudes are closely linked to values. A **belief** is an organized pattern of knowledge that an individual holds as true about his or her world. A consumer may believe that GoPro makes the videos of his or her active lifestyle look exciting, that the camera is tough and durable, and that it's reasonably priced. These beliefs may be based on knowledge, faith, or hearsay. Consumers tend to develop a set of beliefs about a product's attributes and then, through these beliefs, form a *brand image*—a set of beliefs about a particular brand. In turn, the brand image shapes consumers' attitudes toward the product.

An **attitude** is a learned tendency to respond consistently toward a given object, such as a brand. Attitudes rest on an individual's value system, which represents personal standards of good and bad, right and wrong, and so forth; therefore, attitudes tend to be more enduring and complex than beliefs. For an example of the nature of attitudes, consider the differing attitudes of Millennial and Baby Boomer consumers toward the practice of purchasing on credit. Millennials don't think twice about charging goods and services and are willing to pay high interest rates for the privilege of postponing payment. To older Baby Boomer consumers, however, doing what amounts to taking out a loan, even a small one, to pay for anything seems absurd.

CHANGING BELIEFS If a good or service is meeting its profit goals, positive attitudes toward the product merely need to be reinforced. If the brand is not succeeding, however, the marketing manager must strive to change target consumers' attitudes toward it. This change can be accomplished in three ways: (1) changing beliefs about the brand's attributes, (2) changing the relative importance of these beliefs, or (3) adding new beliefs. The first technique is to turn neutral or negative beliefs about product attributes into positive beliefs.

from an aspirational reference group (discussed earlier in this chapter) drinking from a trendy S'well reusable bottle. You note that it looks good, and then your ideal self-image (also discussed earlier) kicks in, imploring you to stop using disposable bottles. This new learning motivates you to buy the S'well bottle and change your behaviour. You have learned a new behaviour without even trying out the S'well bottle first.

Reinforcement and repetition boost learning. Reinforcement can be positive or negative. For example, if you see a vendor selling frozen yogurt (a stimulus), and you buy it (your response), you may find the yogurt to be quite refreshing (your reward). In this example, your behaviour has been positively reinforced. On the other hand, if you buy a new flavour of yogurt and it does not taste good (negative reinforcement), you will not buy that flavour of yogurt again (your response). Without positive or negative reinforcement, a person will not be motivated to repeat the behaviour pattern or to avoid it. Thus, if a new brand evokes neutral feelings, some marketing activity, such as a price change or an increase in promotion, may be required to induce further consumption.

> **belief** an organized pattern of knowledge that an individual holds as true about his or her world
>
> **attitude** a learned tendency to respond consistently toward a given object

For example, many younger consumers believe that Harley-Davidson is a motorcycle brand targeted at their fathers, or even grandfathers. In 2016, however, Harley-Davidson introduced a completely different looking motorcycle, the Street series, featuring a sleeker, more youthful look, with a weight and price much more befitting a younger market that had been quickly disappearing.

Changing consumers' beliefs about a service can be more difficult because service attributes are intangible. Convincing consumers to switch hairstylists or lawyers or to go to a mall dental clinic can be much more difficult than getting them to change their brand of razor blades. Image, which is also largely intangible, significantly determines service patronage. Service marketing is explored in detail in Chapter 12.

The second approach to modifying attitudes is to change the relative importance of beliefs about an attribute. For example, milk has always been considered a healthy beverage for children and adults. Now, however, dairies are aware of milk's added benefits, primarily the importance of calcium for bone strength, which they now actively promote on their packaging. The third approach to transforming attitudes is to add new beliefs, such as that LinkedIn is not just for job-seekers and recruiters, but also a social medium for professionals to connect and exchange ideas.

6-7e Consumer Behaviour Elements— Working Together

As a result of their environment, individuals change, which, in turn, changes the nature of the goods and services they consume. By using the stages of the buying process to make the best choices, consumers become more experienced. This experience changes the parts of the buying process they use, the degree of effort and time they spend on each stage of buying, and the importance of each of the psychological influences in their final buying decision. Effective marketers will carefully study their target markets, noting these changes and the degrees of difference. Then, after understanding the consumers' needs, these marketers can adjust their approach to the various elements in the marketing mix to meet the consumers' needs and help them move through the buying process.

STUDY TOOLS

IN THE BOOK, YOU CAN:

✔ Rip out the Chapter in Review card at the back of the book.

ONLINE, YOU CAN:

✔ Stay organized and efficient with a single online destination with all the course material and study aids you need to succeed.

Go to nelson.com/student to access the digital resources.

SIDE LAUNCH
BREWING COMPANY
CONTINUING CASE

Looks Matter

"We used to joke," begins Dave Sands, VP Operations, "that marketing sells the first beer, and brewing sells every one after that." What goes through the mind of a craft beer consumer is starkly different from the decision process of a macro beer consumer. For one, the need is convenience. For the other, the need is adventure. And for those seeking adventure—the craft beer enthusiasts—the purchase decision often starts with the attention a brand can attract from the shelf of the liquor store. "You're going to get consumers that go into the craft section and make their decision based on the shelf space presence," reveals Chuck Galea, VP Sales and Marketing, proudly demonstrating the perforations of a Mountain Lager box, which, when "zipped" open, conveniently provide both a practicality and attractiveness retailers and consumers like.

"I think the branding is really important," remarks founding brewer Michael Hancock, somewhat surprisingly after passionately describing every intricate taste nuance that separates each of the four beers Side Launch produces year-round. Clearly driven by producing the highest quality and most flavourful beers, he appreciates that good looks are also important. "I had a very traditional label," he recalls of Denison's, one of Canada's first wheat beers he produced independently from the late 1980s through the early 2000s. "I could only produce so much—I was highly constrained by production. But this branding," he says, with a confident nod to the four bold and colourful cans stacked impressively in the company's front desk refrigerator, "is really good. It stands out from a mile and consumers love it."

However, because of craft beer's rapid growth as a category, cool, eye-catching brands are appearing all the time, so eventually other influencers must penetrate the decision process of the craft beer drinker. "It's amazing, but RateBeer," begins Chuck, referring to the online platform where craft enthusiasts provide numerical values of the beers they taste, "has become so influential in both the growth in popularity of craft, but also the decisions people make when buying craft." Side Launch, which enjoys extraordinarily high reviews across not only its four core brands but every limited release that has ever left the brewery, certainly benefits from sites like this that nudge would-be consumers in their direction. "If someone's in the Beer Store or LCBO and they see a beer on the shelf they know nothing about, they might take out their phone and look up the score," claims Chuck. "Same at a bar," adds founder Garnet Pratt. "If you're at a place that has 50 beers on tap and you're about to tuck into a pint, you don't want to take two sips and say 'blah,' so again you might look up the rating online . . . So in that respect these sites can hurt you as much as help you, but if your rating is above a certain threshold, people will usually give you a try."

Every consumer wants to make the right purchase decision, but arriving at what is "right" can be a deeply complicated and psychological process. Craft brewers, as much as any other consumer category, must seize upon every possible detail that might tip the scale in their favour. Side Launch, bolstered by an uncompromising commitment to quality and an eye-catching look, swizzled with the forces of social media and beer consuming trends, has evidently hit its stride, in parallel with craft beer consumer behaviour.

Questions

1. What is the "problem" a craft beer drinker has recognized by the time he or she arrives at a retailer to purchase beer?

2. When craft beer consumers use sources like Ratebeer, what stage(s) in the purchase decision process are they encountering?

3. Much of what is said in this case emphasizes the importance of labelling in the purchase decision process for a craft beer drinker. Discuss some of the ways in which this plays into individual, social, psychological, and even cultural influencers of the purchase decision process.

Side Launch Brewing Company

MINDTAP

MindTap empowers students.
Personalized content in an easy-to-use interface
helps you achieve better grades.

The new **MindTap Mobile App** allows
for learning anytime, anywhere with
flashcards, quizzes and notifications.

The **MindTap Reader** lets you highlight
and take notes online, right within the
pages, and easily reference them later.

nelson.com/mindtap

NELSON

7 | Business Marketing

LEARNING OUTCOMES

7-1 Describe business marketing

7-2 Explain the differences between business and consumer marketing

7-3 Summarize the network and relationships approach to business marketing

7-4 State the fundamental aspects of business marketing

7-5 Classify business customers

7-6 Identify aspects of business buying behaviour

7-7 Describe the ways in which business marketing has gone online

> *"Coming together is a beginning. Keeping together is progress. Working together is success."*
>
> —Henry Ford[1]

7-1 WHAT IS BUSINESS MARKETING?

Describing business marketing is not as simple as inserting the word "business" in front of marketing terms and concluding that this is how it is different from consumer marketing. Business marketing is not just differentiated because of the volume of transactions between businesses, nor is it different because there are unique jobs and career paths in business marketing.

Business marketing is marketing. But it is marketing done differently.

Business marketing is often referred to as **business-to-business (B2B) marketing**, and the hyphens between those bolded words are important. Those hyphens represent a connection between two entities, and it is that idea of a connection that is vital to understanding business marketing.

In Chapter 1, you encountered the concept of relationships and learned how successful marketers seek to build relationships with customers over time. The challenge in forming such relationships is to figure out how to create a system to keep track of all those customers (see Chapter 9 on customer relationship management). In business marketing, the number of customers is also the challenge in building relationships—not because there are so many, but the exact opposite: because there are so few.

With limited options to choose from, it becomes important to treat any relationship with care and attention.

Marketing to consumers is often described as creating a marketing mix (recall the four Ps) and delivering it to a consumer. There is a sense that marketing is an activity done separate from the consumer. In business marketing, there needs to be an active interaction

---

business-to-business (B2B) marketing the process of matching capabilities between two nonconsumer entities to create value for both organizations and the "customer's customer"; also referred to as *business marketing*

between businesses to ensure needs are met. There needs to be trust, mutual respect, and an understanding that even if both parties work together there is still the possibility of achieving one's own company goals.

7-2 BUSINESS VERSUS CONSUMER MARKETING

In trying to describe marketing of any kind, we'll use examples that you can relate to: a consumer (the buyer) goes into a store and purchases a widely distributed product from a store (the seller). Often the discussion surrounds what the seller can do to better understand the needs of this customer, to determine why the consumer is buying the product, and to figure out how to influence this and future purchases. But what this explanation implies is that the customer is passive, simply waiting to be researched, analyzed, and retained.

In business marketing, neither the seller nor the buyer can afford to be passive. Neither business interest can rely on the other party doing all the work—there needs to be effort and cooperation on both sides of the exchange. This level of cooperation is not yet seen in consumer marketing, but that may change.

Consumer marketing is now seeing a more engaged buyer. Aided by the information and options afforded by technology, specifically the Internet and social media, consumers are taking a more active role in the exchange process of marketing. For example, term life insurance policy premiums were reduced quite significantly with the emergence of online insurance quote websites. Once consumers were given access to choice and information, they became less passive and more willing to actively involve themselves in the role of buyer.[2] For example, KANETIX.ca, a Canadian online insurance comparison website, offers consumers multiple quotes from a variety of insurance providers in Canada. In addition to comparing insurance rates, consumers can also check rates for mortgages and credit cards with very little effort.

What then has to be created in business marketing is a sense of involved self-interest mixed with mutual benefit. The Canadian Marketing Association, a leading advocate for the marketing community in Canada, has taken on this approach of mutual benefit when describing business marketing:

> What makes B-to-B different than consumer marketing is the complex nature of *relationships* and *interactions* that form a buying process and customer lifecycle that lasts months or years. It involves

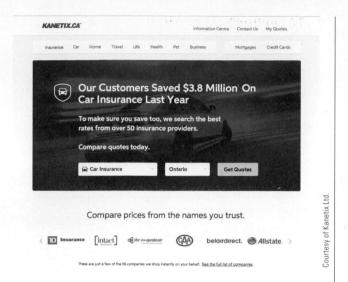

Compare prices from the names you trust.

These are just a few of the 56 companies we shop instantly on your behalf. See the full list of companies.

Courtesy of Kanetix Ltd.

a *network* of individuals from buyer, seller, and even third-party partners who have different needs and interests.[3]

The terms provided in this quotation—*relationships, interactions, networks*—are not always ones associated with marketing and need to be explained further. Let's now consider what these terms mean in the context of business marketing.

7-3 THE NETWORK AND RELATIONSHIPS APPROACH TO BUSINESS MARKETING

In looking at business marketing from a network and relationships perspective, one must understand how each of these terms is meant and applied.

7-3a Relationships in Business Marketing

Clearly, relationships are important in marketing, but they are usually the result of greater effort on one side (the seller). In business marketing, business relationships are more complex, as they involve greater commitment from both sides, and thus more company resources and effort. There are two particularly important aspects of such relationships: commitment and trust.

Relationship commitment is a firm's belief that an ongoing relationship with some other firm is so important that it warrants

relationship commitment
a firm's belief that an ongoing relationship with another firm is so important that the relationship warrants maximum efforts at maintaining it indefinitely

trust confidence in an exchange partner's reliability and integrity

maximum efforts at maintaining it indefinitely.[4] A perceived breakdown in commitment by one of the parties often leads to a reduction in the relationship.

Trust exists when one party has confidence in an exchange partner's reliability and integrity.[5] It has been noted extensively that power plays a large role in trust between two business entities in a relationship. However, there was never agreement on whether having a large or small difference in power between partners is a good thing. That is, until a study in 2015 showed that power in fact plays a much smaller role in building trust between B2B partners. So what is the most important factor to ensure trust if it's not power? Goal congruence. The study published in *Industrial Marketing Management* magazine found that it was most important that the strategies of the two businesses were compatible. If this was true, there was a better chance that a shared vision could be reached, thus allowing for trust to be built.[6]

The concepts of trust and commitment show the importance of collaboration between entities in a business-to-business relationship. To build and develop a relationship requires a level of cooperation that is not always comfortable for firms used to competing for market share and industry profits. North American firms often believe that laws and regulations are the most important components in maintaining business relationships. However, in many parts of the world, cooperation is a vital part of conducting business. In Japan, for example, exchange between firms is based on personal relationships that are developed through what is called *amae*, or indulgent dependency. *Amae* is the feeling of nurturing concern for, and dependence on, another. Reciprocity and personal relationships contribute to *amae*. Relationships between companies can develop into a *keiretsu*—a network of interlocking corporate affiliates.

7-3b Interaction in Business Marketing

To understand the concept of interaction, we need to go back to Kevin Roberts (recall his quotation from Chapter 1: "Marketing is dead"). In a speech, he mentioned that marketing needed to go from "interruption to interaction."[7] In his view, marketing was too often focused on getting attention through whatever means possible, trying essentially to interrupt consumers from whatever they were doing at the time.

What this interruption approach achieves are a series of one-off transactions, which generate short-term revenue and profits, but little in long-term gain. A long-term perspective is precisely what interaction is about. An interaction can be seen as the culmination of numerous transactions (sales) between two business entities that build over time. Interaction includes not only transactions but also negotiations, discussions, customizations—anything that is part of the relationship between the two organizations.

An example of transaction versus interaction can be seen with buying versus leasing an automobile. Car companies often prefer to lease vehicles, as evidenced by the many incentive programs offered for leasing vehicles. Through leasing programs, a car company can develop a relationship with the customer over time. If a customer buys a vehicle, on the other hand, the relationship may be limited to warranty issues and may end as soon as the customer drives off the lot.

The Industrial Marketing and Purchasing Group (IMP Group), a leading group of researchers in business marketing, developed an interaction model that provides a good explanation of interaction: "Business exchange cannot be understood as a series of disembedded and independent transactions of given resources—but rather as complex relationships between buying and selling organisations, where what is exchanged is created in interaction."[8]

7-3c Networks in Business Marketing

The Canadian Marketing Association's definition of business marketing describes a "network" of buyers, sellers, and other third parties. This network approach to business marketing takes the interactions and relationships and places them into a bigger context.

To understand the network approach, we must note how it differs from two other approaches to business marketing:

- **The sales approach:** If you look for "B2B marketing" on any search engine, most of the results will focus on sales and selling to companies. The sales approach is focused on generating leads and new business through various persuasion techniques. This approach focuses on what a company has to offer to other firms, but very little time is spent on understanding the problems facing potential customers.

- **The market management approach:** This approach looks at B2B marketing much like B2C (business-to-consumer) marketing. Develop a product, price it, place it, and promote it—all to a waiting set of customers. This approach focuses on that passive customer and assumes that all customers will have the same needs and will respond in a similar way. 4 P's

- **The network approach:** This approach looks at the factors and forces around a firm and the other firms that will have an impact on their business—suppliers, customers, and even competitors. Companies are encouraged to research the external marketplace and by doing so should develop an idea of the forces and challenges facing them and the rest of the companies in their network.

Companies in a network can then develop their relationships through interaction over time. Cooperation gets built into these networks, as it becomes evident that working together can achieve goals that might not have been possible if one firm had tried to work on its own or just on a transaction basis. See Exhibit 7.1 for an example of a representation of a business network.

The concept of business networks is not new. Cooperation and making a profit are not seen as two competing forces in places like Japan and China. As mentioned earlier, in Japan, the concept of *amae* is used in business interaction and denotes mutual dependence

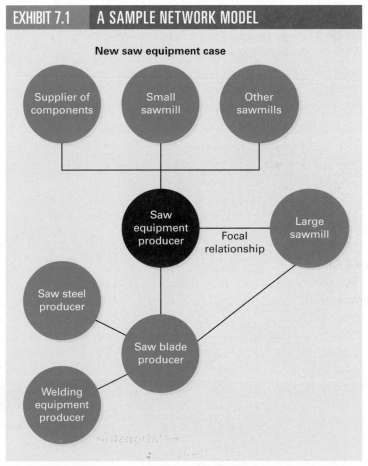

EXHIBIT 7.1   A SAMPLE NETWORK MODEL

New saw equipment case

Supplier of components

Small sawmill

Other sawmills

Saw equipment producer

Focal relationship

Large sawmill

Saw steel producer

Saw blade producer

Welding equipment producer

Source: Republished with permission of Amercian Marketing Association, from James C. Anderson, Håkan Håkansson and Jan Johanson, "Dyadic Business Relationships within a Business Network Context," *Journal of Marketing*, Vol. 58 No. 4, October 1994, pp. 1-15; permission conveyed through Copyright Clearance Center, Inc.

EXHIBIT 7.2   EVOLUTION OF A NETWORK SUPPLIER MODEL

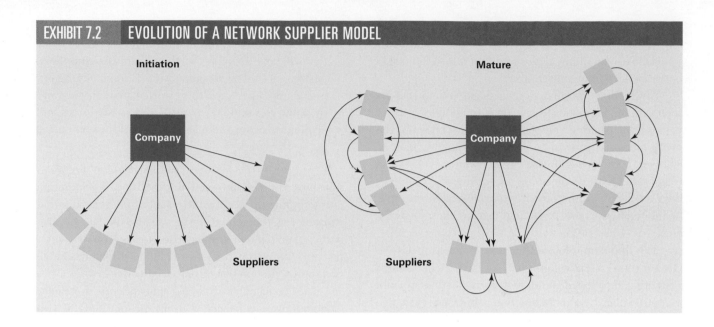

and respect, and a network called a *keiretsu* is developed based on *amae*. Within a *keiretsu*, executives may sit on the boards of their customers or their suppliers. Members of a *keiretsu* trade with each other whenever possible and often engage in joint product development, finance, and marketing activity. For example, the Toyota Group *keiretsu* includes 14 core companies and an additional 170 companies that receive preferential treatment. Toyota holds an equity position in many of these 170 member firms and is represented on many of their boards of directors. (See Exhibit 7.2.)

In China, *guanxi* is a term that loosely means "relationships" or "networking," and in business, *guanxi* refers to a network of firms tied together based not only on economic relationships but also on personal relationships. *Guanxi* networks help to distinguish collaborators from competitors and serve to build trust in business relationships.[9] There can be negative aspects to the *guanxi* network

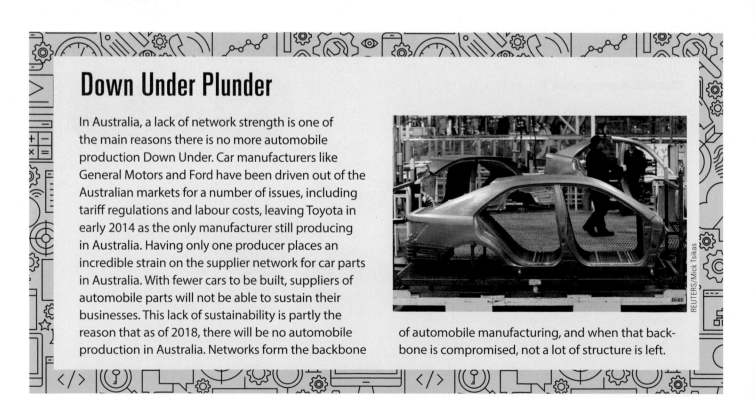

Down Under Plunder

In Australia, a lack of network strength is one of the main reasons there is no more automobile production Down Under. Car manufacturers like General Motors and Ford have been driven out of the Australian markets for a number of issues, including tariff regulations and labour costs, leaving Toyota in early 2014 as the only manufacturer still producing in Australia. Having only one producer places an incredible strain on the supplier network for car parts in Australia. With fewer cars to be built, suppliers of automobile parts will not be able to sustain their businesses. This lack of sustainability is partly the reason that as of 2018, there will be no automobile production in Australia. Networks form the backbone of automobile manufacturing, and when that backbone is compromised, not a lot of structure is left.

REUTERS/Mick Tsikas

Keeping Their "WITS" about the Network

PREVNet is an umbrella network of more than 120 leading Canadian researchers and 60 national youth-serving organizations in Canada. PREVNet's mission is to stop bullying in Canada and to promote safe and healthy relationships for all Canadian children and youth. This network was created through funding from the Government of Canada's Networks of Centres of Excellence (NCE) in 2006, and it has created numerous initiatives, resources, and assessment tools thanks to the cooperation of network members. Faced with the challenge of reducing the incidence of bullying in Canada (Canada ranks 25th out of 36 countries for bullying incidents according to the World Health Organization), PREVNet has connected two of its partner organizations, the Rock Solid Foundation and the Royal Canadian Mounted Police (RCMP), to further promote and disseminate WITS programs, which were first developed in the mid-1990s in Victoria, B.C.

WITS, which stands for "Walk away, Ignore, Talk it out, Seek help," is a program designed to provide skills to children from kindergarten to Grade 3 to deal with bullying and peer victimization. WITS LEADS stands for "Look and listen, Explore points of view, Act, Did it work?, and Seek help," which was created to provide developmentally appropriate strategies and resources to older elementary students so that they may become WITS Leaders in their schools.

Sources: PREVNet, "About Promoting Relationships and Eliminating Violence Network," 2014, www.prevnet.ca/about (accessed August 9, 2014); PREVNet, "WITS: Walk Away, Ignore, Talk It Out, Seek Help," www.prevnet.ca/projects/wits (accessed August 9, 2014); and WITS Program, "Using Your WITS," www.witsprogram.ca (accessed August 9, 2014).

---

model, as it can lead to a group of insiders unwilling to interact with external firms and creating internal rules and regulations that fall outside the law. Many Canadian firms have found that the best way to compete in Asian countries is to form relationships with Asian firms.

The Canadian government created the Networks of Centres of Excellence (NCE) in 1989, but the program has really taken off since a new technology strategy was introduced in 2007. The NCE program brings together government and industry funding to develop networks of organizations to tackle economic and social changes in Canada. Consider some interesting facts about the NCE program:

- There was a 160 percent rise in industry contributions to NCE from 2009 to 2012.

- In 2011–2012, NCEs created 145 new products and filed for 267 patents.

- In 2011–2012, there were 2483 new jobs created as a result of NCE activity.[10]

7-4 FUNDAMENTAL ASPECTS OF BUSINESS MARKETING

Now that we can appreciate the importance of relationships and networks, let's look at the fundamental aspects of business marketing. These aspects highlight the importance of the purchasing relationship between buyer and seller in a business interaction. Without knowledge of the types of buyers, buying situations, products, and services in business marketing, it would be virtually impossible to create a network of strong relationships.

7-4a Types of Demand

Because demand in business markets is driven by comparatively fewer buyers, there are aspects of demand that are important to consider. These include derived, inelastic, and joint demand.

DERIVED DEMAND The demand for business products is called **derived demand** because organizations buy products to be used in producing their customers' products. For example, the market for central processing units (CPUs), hard drives, and CD-ROMs is derived from the demand for personal computers (PCs). These items are valuable only as components of computers. Demand for these items rises and falls with the demand for PCs.

Because demand is derived, business marketers must carefully monitor demand patterns and changing preferences in final consumer markets, even though their customers are not in those markets. Moreover, business marketers must carefully monitor their customers' forecasts because derived demand is based on expectations of future demand for those customers' products.

Some business marketers not only monitor final consumer demand and customer forecasts but also try to influence final consumer demand. Aluminum producers use television and magazine advertisements to point out the convenience and recycling opportunities that aluminum offers to consumers who can choose to purchase juice and soft drinks in either aluminum or plastic containers.

INELASTIC DEMAND The demand for many business products is inelastic with regard to price. *Inelastic demand* means that an increase or a decrease in the price of the product will not significantly affect demand for the product.

© iStockphoto.com/Evgeny Terentyev

The price of a product used either in the production of another product or as part of another product is often a minor portion of the final product's total price. Therefore, demand for the final consumer product is not affected. If the price of automobile paint or spark plugs rises significantly—for example, 200 percent in one year—will the price increase affect the number of new automobiles sold that year? Probably not.

JOINT DEMAND **Joint demand** refers to the demand for two or more items used together in a final product. For example, a decline in the availability of memory chips will slow the production of microcomputers, which will in turn reduce the demand for disk drives. Likewise, the demand for Apple operating systems exists as long as there is demand for Apple devices. Sales of the two products are directly linked.

FLUCTUATING DEMAND The demand for business products, particularly for new plants and equipment, tends to be less stable than the demand for consumer products. A small increase or decrease in consumer demand can produce a much larger change in demand for the facilities and equipment needed to make the consumer product. Economists refer to this phenomenon as the **multiplier effect** (or **accelerator principle**).

7-4b Number of Customers

Business marketers usually have far fewer customers than consumer marketers. The advantage is that it is much easier to identify prospective buyers, monitor current customers' needs and levels of satisfaction, and personally attend to existing customers. The main disadvantage is that each customer becomes crucial—especially for those manufacturers that have only one customer. In many cases, this customer is the Canadian government. The success or failure of one bid can make the difference between prosperity and bankruptcy.

7-4c Location of Buyers

Business customers tend to be much more geographically concentrated than consumers. For instance, many of Canada's largest B2B buyers are located in or around the large urban centres of Canada: Toronto, Montréal, Calgary, and Vancouver. The oil and gas industry is centred in Alberta, the automotive industry in southwestern Ontario, and the wine industry primarily in British Columbia and southern Ontario.

7-4d Type of Negotiations

Consumers are used to negotiating prices on automobiles and real estate. In most cases, however, Canadian consumers expect sellers to set the price and other

derived demand demand in the business market that comes from demand in the consumer market

joint demand the demand for two or more items used together in a final product

multiplier effect (accelerator principle) the phenomenon in which a small increase or decrease in consumer demand can produce a much larger change in demand for the facilities and equipment needed to make the consumer product

Education Derivation

Here is a quick activity to help you understand derived demand better: Take the textbook you have in your hands (or on your laptop or mobile phone). First, think about all the companies that had to work together for this textbook to have been published. Done? Your list should have included pulp and paper companies, ink producers, binding companies (for the hard copy of the book), the publisher (Nelson's headquarters can be seen in the picture!), the companies with pictures in the textbook, and of course the postsecondary institutions (instructors, bookstore). The question that remains is, What is the consumer demand that the demand for a marketing textbook is derived from?

© Nelson Education Ltd.

conditions of sale, such as time of delivery and credit terms. In contrast, negotiating is common in business marketing. Buyers and sellers negotiate product specifications, delivery dates, payment terms, and other pricing matters. Sometimes these negotiations occur during many meetings over several months. Final contracts are often very long and detailed.

7-4e Use of Reciprocity

Business purchasers often choose to buy from their own customers, a practice known as **reciprocity**. Once trust is developed in a business network, reciprocity is a natural progression where companies will become each other's best customers. For example, General Motors (GM) buys engines for use in its automobiles and trucks from BorgWarner, which in turn buys many of the automobiles and trucks it needs from GM. This practice is neither unethical nor illegal unless one party coerces the other and the result is unfair competition. The Japanese *keiretsu* and Chinese *guanxi* are good examples of systems that encourage reciprocity.

7-4f Use of Leasing

Consumers normally buy products rather than lease them. But businesses commonly lease expensive equipment, such as computers, construction equipment and vehicles, and automobiles. Leasing allows firms to reduce their capital outflow, acquire a seller's latest products, receive better services, and gain tax advantages.

The lessor, the firm providing the product, may be either the manufacturer or an independent firm. The benefits to the lessor include greater total revenue from leasing compared with selling and an opportunity to do business with customers who cannot afford to buy.

The concept of leasing fits well into the relationships and network model. A lease provides the basis for a long-term interaction, where two firms are reliant on each other for either payment for or use of a leased product.

7-4g Types of Business Products

There are numerous types of business products, and there are different classification systems used for them. (See Exhibit 7.3.) Here are the main categories:

- **Major equipment:** large and expensive purchases that depreciate over time (e.g., buildings, machinery).

- **Accessory equipment:** smaller in size and expense than major equipment, this equipment is more standardized and often sold to consumers as well (e.g., power tools, printers).

- **Raw materials:** unprocessed or untapped materials that are extracted or harvested for consumption of further processing (e.g., oil, canola, potash).

- **Component parts and materials:** finished products ready for

> **reciprocity** a practice where business purchasers choose to buy from their own customers

EXHIBIT 7.3   TYPES OF BUSINESS PRODUCTS

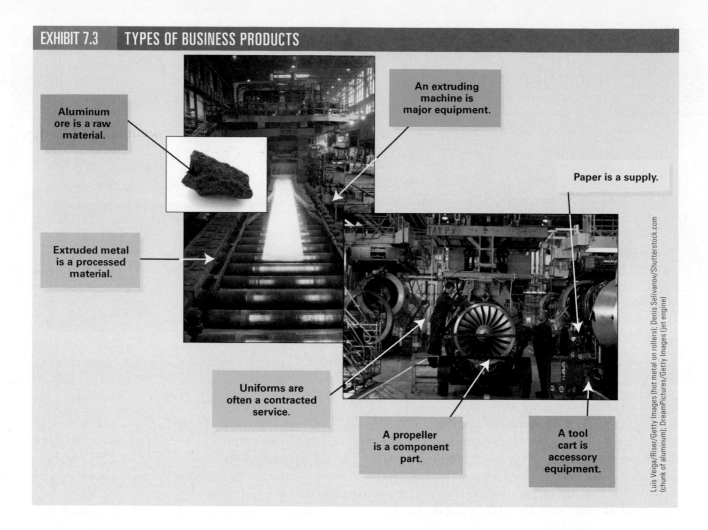

Aluminum ore is a raw material.

An extruding machine is major equipment.

Paper is a supply.

Extruded metal is a processed material.

Uniforms are often a contracted service.

A propeller is a component part.

A tool cart is accessory equipment.

Luis Veiga/Riser/Getty Images (hot metal on rollers); Denis Selivanov/Shutterstock.com (chunk of aluminum); DreamPictures/Getty Images (jet engine)

assembly or requiring very little in the way of further processing to become part of other products (e.g., engines, pulp paper, chemicals).

- **Supplies:** consumable items that are not part of the final product but provide some solution to a business's needs (pencils, paper, coffee).

BUSINESS SERVICES Business services include a number of actions that are not necessarily part of the final product but may have a direct impact on the customer's willingness to buy and maintain a relationship over time. While services can be as basic as hiring janitorial staff to clean an office on a weekend, there are important services that can be provided to customers.

Providing a support or help line for customers to help with or troubleshoot any challenges with a product is one example of an important business service. With the rising importance of leasing options for a number of industries, the product becomes only part of the interaction, as much

business services
complementary and ancillary actions that companies undertake to meet business customers' needs

of the focus is placed on the services that are needed during the leasing period.

7-5 CLASSIFYING BUSINESS CUSTOMERS

Now that the major components of business marketing have been identified, it is time to turn our attention to the business customer. While traditional means of segmentation are not as useful in business marketing because of the unique nature of the business customer, there are still means with which to organize and structure business customers.

7-5a Major Categories of Business Customers

The business market consists of four major categories of customers: producers, resellers, governments, and institutions.

IMPORTANCE OF BEING MALLEY-ABLE

Malley Industries is a New Brunswick–based company that provides specialty vehicles to organizations that carry equipment, cargo, or people. Malley specializes in ambulances, which it sells to customers as far away as Chile. Malley Industries also manufactures equipment for wheelchair-accessible conversions and law enforcement vehicles, and produces a broad variety of custom commercial vehicles. As well, it designs and manufactures plastic components, creating unique products that enhance special functionality for end users in the automotive sector and numerous other industries. This company has been successful by meeting clients' varying needs and ensuring that its products exceed customer expectations. Its growth has been a result of its ability to diversify and develop creative methods and products to solve problems for their expanding customer base.

Courtesy of Malley Industries Inc.

Sources: "Malley Industries," Canadian Business Journal, 2014, www.cbj.ca /business_in_action/manufacturing/it_took_20_years_for_malley_industries _to_become_an_overnight_su.html (accessed August 9, 2014); and "Malley: About Us," www.malleyindustries.com/about-us/ (accessed August 9, 2014).

PRODUCERS The producer segment of the business market includes profit-oriented individuals and organizations that use purchased goods and services to produce other products, to incorporate into other products, or to facilitate the daily operations of the organization. Examples of producers are construction, manufacturing, transportation, finance, real estate, and food service firms. In the early 2000s, Canada was a major exporter of cars, pulp and paper, and electronics. Today, all those areas of production have lower export numbers. These areas of production have been replaced by oil and gas, minerals, chemicals, and food products.[11] It is believed that some of the jobs lost from the car industry earlier in the century might return. However, it is likely these "jobs" will be taken by artificial intelligence of some kind—be it computer or robot.

Producers are often called **original equipment manufacturers (OEMs)**. This term includes all individuals and organizations that buy business goods and incorporate them into the products that they produce for eventual sale to other producers or to consumers. Companies such as General Motors that buy steel, paint, tires, and batteries are said to be OEMs.

RESELLERS The reseller market includes retail and wholesale businesses that buy finished goods and resell them for a profit. A retailer sells mainly to final consumers; wholesalers sell mostly to retailers and other organizational customers. Wholesalers are predominately smaller business (98 percent have fewer than 100 employees) that offer an average hourly wage of $23.17.[12]

Consumer product firms, such as Procter & Gamble, McCain Foods, and Canada Dry Motts, sell directly to large retailers and retail chains and through wholesalers to smaller retail units. Retailing is explored in detail in Chapter 15.

Business product distributors are wholesalers that buy business products and resell them to business customers. They often carry thousands of items in stock and employ sales forces to call on business customers. Businesses that want to buy a gross of pencils or a hundred kilograms of fertilizer typically purchase these items from local distributors rather than directly from manufacturers.

GOVERNMENTS A third major segment of the business market is government. Government organizations include thousands of federal, provincial or territorial, and municipal buying units. They make up what may be the largest single market for goods and services in Canada.

Contracts for government purchases are often put out for bid. Interested vendors submit bids (usually sealed) to provide specified products during a particular time. Sometimes the lowest bidder is awarded the contract. When the lowest bidder is not awarded the contract, strong evidence must be presented to justify the decision. Grounds

original equipment manufacturers (OEMs)
individuals and organizations that buy business goods and incorporate them into the products that they produce for eventual sale to other producers or to consumers

Zhong Chen/Shutterstock.com

for rejecting the lowest bid include lack of experience, inadequate financing, or poor past performance. Bidding allows all potential suppliers a fair chance at winning government contracts and helps ensure that public funds are spent wisely.

FEDERAL GOVERNMENT Name just about any good or service and chances are that someone in the federal government uses it. The federal government buys goods and services valued at approximately $18 billion per year, making it the country's largest customer.[13]

Although much of the federal government's buying is centralized, no single federal agency contracts for all the government's requirements, and no single buyer in any agency purchases all that the agency needs. We can view the federal government as a combination of several large companies with overlapping responsibilities and thousands of small independent units.

MUNICIPAL, ACADEMIC, SOCIAL, AND HOSPITALS (MASH) Many of the entities in this category are run by either provincial, territorial, or local governments. These are significant customers in their size and scope in the Canadian market: health and social services institutions employ 2.38 million people, while educational services employ over 1.2 million.[14]

In Canada, each province and territory sets its own regulations and buying procedures within this municipal, academic, social, and hospitals (MASH) sector. The potential for both large and small vendors is great, however, as more than six thousand municipal clients are spread across all the provinces and territories.

North American Industry Classification System (NAICS) an industry classification system developed by the United States, Canada, and Mexico to classify North American business establishments by their main production processes

INSTITUTIONS The fourth major segment of the business market consists of institutions that

seek to achieve goals other than the standard business goals of profit, market share, and return on investment. Excluding the MASH sector, this segment includes places of worship, labour unions, fraternal organizations, civic clubs, foundations, and other so-called nonbusiness organizations. Many firms have a separate sales force that calls on these customers.

7-5b Classification by Industry

If you are looking for more detail than a general classification of business customers provides, you can look to the NAICS system. The **North American Industry Classification System (NAICS)** is an industry classification system for North American business establishments. The system, developed jointly by the United States, Canada, and Mexico, provides a common industry classification system for the North American Free Trade Agreement (NAFTA) partners. Goods- or service-producing firms that use identical or similar production processes are grouped together. (See Exhibit 7.4.) This makes searching for, and finding, companies that provide products and services in hundreds of different industries across North America more efficient.

NAICS is an extremely valuable tool for business marketers engaged in analyzing, segmenting, and targeting markets. Each classification group is relatively homogeneous with regard to raw materials required, components used, manufacturing processes employed, and problems faced. The more digits in a code, the more homogeneous the group is. Therefore, if a supplier understands the needs and requirements of a few firms within a classification, requirements can be projected for all firms in that category. The number, size, and geographic dispersion of firms can also be identified. This information can be converted to market potential estimates, market share estimates, and sales forecasts. It can also be used for identifying potential new customers. NAICS codes can help identify firms that may be prospective users of a supplier's goods and

EXHIBIT 7.4	HOW NAICS WORKS	
NAICS Level	**NAICS Code**	**Description**
Sector	51	Information
Subsector	513	Broadcasting and telecommunications
Industry group	5133	Telecommunications
Industry	51332	Wireless telecommunications carriers, except satellite
Subdivision of industry	513321	Paging

services. For a complete listing of all NAICS codes, visit **www.naics.com**.

7-6 BUSINESS BUYING BEHAVIOUR

Once you are able to identify your customers, you still have to understand how they make purchase decisions. Learning about the makeup and motivation behind business buying provides excellent insights for marketers on how to create products and services that meet the needs of business customers.

7-6a Buying Centres

A **buying centre** includes all those people in an organization who become involved in the purchase decision. Membership and influence vary from company to company. For instance, in engineering-dominated firms, such as Bell Helicopter, the buying centre may consist almost entirely of engineers. In marketing-oriented firms, such as Toyota and IBM, marketing and engineering have almost equal authority. In consumer goods firms, such as Procter & Gamble, product managers and other marketing decision makers may dominate the buying centre. In a small manufacturing company, almost everyone may be a member.

The number of people involved in a buying centre varies with the complexity and importance of the purchase decision. The composition of the buying group will usually change from one purchase to another and sometimes even during various stages of the buying process. To make matters more complicated, buying centres do not appear on formal organization charts.

For example, although a formal committee may have been set up to choose a new plant site, such a committee is only part of the buying centre. Other people, such as the company president, often play informal yet powerful roles. In a lengthy decision-making process, such as finding a new plant location, some members may drop out of the buying centre when they can no longer play a useful role. Others whose talents are needed then become part of the centre. No formal announcement is ever made concerning "who is in" and "who is out."

NATURE OF BUYING Unlike consumers, business buyers usually approach purchasing rather formally. Businesses use professionally trained purchasing agents or buyers who spend their entire career purchasing a limited number of items. They get to know the items and the sellers well. Some professional purchasers earn the designation of Certified Purchasing Manager (CPM) after participating in a rigorous certification program.

NATURE OF BUYING INFLUENCE Typically, more people are involved in a single business purchase decision than in a consumer purchase. Experts from fields as varied as quality control, marketing, and finance, as well as professional buyers and users, may be grouped in a buying centre.

ROLES IN THE BUYING CENTRE As in family purchasing decisions, several people may play a role in the business purchase process.

IMPLICATIONS OF BUYING CENTRES FOR THE MARKETING MANAGER Successful vendors realize the importance of identifying who is in the decision-making unit, each member's relative influence in the buying decision, and each member's evaluative criteria. Successful selling strategies often focus on determining the most important buying influences and tailoring sales presentations to the evaluative criteria most important to these buying-centre members. For example, Loctite Corporation, the manufacturer of Super Glue and industrial adhesives and sealants, found that engineers were the most important influencers and deciders in adhesive and sealant purchase decisions. As a result, Loctite focused its marketing efforts on production and maintenance engineers.

7-6b Buying Situations

Business firms, especially manufacturers, must often decide whether to make something or buy it from an outside supplier. The decision is essentially one of economics. Can an item of similar quality be bought at a lower price elsewhere? If not, is manufacturing it in-house the best use of limited company resources? For example, Briggs & Stratton Corporation, a major manufacturer of four-cycle engines, might be able to save $150,000 annually on outside purchases by spending $500,000 on the equipment needed to produce gas throttles internally. Yet Briggs & Stratton could also use that $500,000 to upgrade its carburetor assembly line, which would save $225,000 annually. If a firm does decide to buy a product instead of making it, the purchase will either be a new task buy, a modified rebuy, or a straight rebuy.

NEW TASK BUY A **new task buy** is a situation requiring the purchase of a product for the first time. For example, suppose a manufacturing company needs a better way to page managers while they are

> **buying centre** all those people in an organization who become involved in the purchase decision
>
> **new task buy** a situation requiring the purchase of a product for the first time

BUSINESS PURCHASING ROLES

▸ **Initiator:** the person who first suggests making a purchase.

▸ **Influencers/Evaluators:** people who influence the buying decision. They often help define specifications and provide information for evaluating options. Technical personnel are especially important as influencers.

▸ **Gatekeepers:** group members who regulate the flow of information. Frequently, the purchasing agent views the gatekeeping role as a source of his or her power. An administrative assistant may also act as a gatekeeper by determining which vendors schedule an appointment with a buyer.

▸ **Decider:** the person who has the formal or informal power to choose or approve the selection of the supplier or brand. In complex situations, it is often difficult to determine who makes the final decision.

▸ **Purchaser:** the person who actually negotiates the purchase. It could be anyone from the president of the company to the purchasing agent, depending on the importance of the decision.

▸ **Users:** members of the organization who will actually use the product. Users often initiate the buying process and help define product specifications.

MODIFIED REBUY A **modified rebuy** is normally less critical and less time-consuming than a new buy. In a modified-rebuy situation, the purchaser wants some change in the original good or service. It may be a new colour, greater tensile strength in a component part, more respondents in a marketing research study, or additional services in a janitorial contract.

Because the two parties are familiar with each other and credibility has been established, buyer and seller can concentrate on the specifics of the modification. In some cases, though, modified rebuys are open to outside bidders. The purchaser uses this strategy to ensure that the new terms are competitive. An example is the manufacturing company buying radios with a vibrating feature for managers who have trouble hearing the ring over the factory noise. The firm may open the bidding to examine the price/quality offerings of several suppliers.

STRAIGHT REBUY A **straight rebuy** is the situation vendors prefer. The purchaser is not looking for new information or new suppliers. An order is placed and the product is provided as in previous orders. Usually, a straight rebuy is routine because the terms of the purchase have been agreed to in earlier negotiations. An example would be the previously cited manufacturing company purchasing, on a regular basis, additional radios from the same supplier.

One common instrument used in straight-rebuy situations is the purchasing contract. Purchasing contracts are used with high-volume products that are bought frequently. In essence, because of the purchasing contract, the buyer's decision making becomes routine and the salesperson is promised a sure sale. The advantage to the buyer is a quick, confident decision, and the advantage to the salesperson is reduced or eliminated competition.

Suppliers must remember not to take straight-rebuy

working on the shop floor. Currently, each of the several managers has a distinct ring—for example, two short and one long, which sounds over the plant intercom when a manager is being paged in the factory. The company decides to replace its buzzer system of paging with hand-held wireless radio technology that will allow managers to communicate immediately with the department initiating the page. This situation represents the greatest opportunity for new vendors. No long-term relationship has been established for this product, specifications may be somewhat fluid, and the buyers are generally more open to new vendors.

If the new item is a raw material or a critical component part, the buyer cannot afford to run out of supply. The seller must be able to convince the buyer that the seller's firm consistently delivers a high-quality product on time.

modified rebuy a situation where the purchaser wants some change in the original good or service

straight rebuy a situation in which the purchaser reorders the same goods or services without looking for new information or new suppliers

Eimantas Buzas/Shutterstock.com

relationships for granted. Retaining existing customers is much easier than attracting new ones.

7-6c Evaluative Criteria for Business Buyers

Business buyers evaluate products and suppliers against three important criteria: quality, service, and price—often in that order.

QUALITY In evaluative criteria, quality refers to technical suitability. A superior tool can do a better job in the production process, and superior packaging can increase dealer and consumer acceptance of a brand. Evaluation of quality also applies to the salesperson and the salesperson's firm. Business buyers want to deal with reputable salespeople and companies that are financially responsible. Quality improvement should be part of every organization's marketing strategy.

SERVICE Almost as much as business buyers want satisfactory products, they also want satisfactory service. A purchase offers several opportunities for service. Suppose a vendor is selling heavy equipment. Prepurchase service could include a survey of the buyer's needs. After thorough analysis of the survey findings, the vendor could prepare a report and recommendations in the form of a purchasing proposal. If a purchase results, postpurchase service might consist of installing the equipment and training those who will be using it. Postpurchase services may also include maintenance and repairs. Another service that business buyers seek is dependability of supply. They must be able to count on delivery of their order when it is scheduled to be delivered. Buyers also welcome services that help them to sell their finished products. Services of this sort are especially appropriate when the seller's product is an identifiable part of the buyer's end product.

PRICE Business buyers want to buy at low prices—at the lowest prices, in most circumstances. However, when a buyer pressures a supplier to cut prices to a point where the supplier loses money, the supplier is almost forced to take shortcuts on quality. The buyer also may, in effect, force the supplier to quit selling to him or her. The buyer will then need to find a new source of supply.

SUPPLIER–BUYER RELATIONSHIP The three buying situations described above provide a context to the changing nature of supplier–buyer relationships. While there can be some stability with a straight re-buy, often buyers are looking for the supplier to make adjustments and improvement to maintain the relationship over time. The supplier–buyer relationship has been called "the backbone of economic activities in the modern world." A recent study looked at the supplier–buyer relationship by examining 130 suppliers and the multinational firm with which they were conducting business. It was determined that the average number of years of a supplier–buyer relationship was slightly over six. The suppliers came from different industries and provided different products ranging from machinery and equipment to component parts and materials. The researchers in this study also noted that the more of an identity that suppliers create in their networks, the stronger and more sustainable the relationships become.[15]

7-7 BUSINESS MARKETING ONLINE

The online world presents a great opportunity for business marketing. Given the challenge of trying to find customers and suppliers to create a network of solid relationships, firms are looking online for help. While the possibilities for business marketing online are immense, the B2B world is still trying to find the best way to conduct business online.

The creation and growth of business marketing online followed a pattern similar to that of the Internet. As websites became more advanced and online security was improved, businesses began to conduct business online. The term *e-commerce* (electronic commerce) was attached to the business-to-business world and described the transactions that were taking place between firms via the Internet. Given the sheer volume of products and services exchanged between businesses around the world, the ability to complete transactions online created a buzz.

Huge sales numbers were published, touting an online e-commerce world with billions of dollars changing hands in transactions. Canadian consumers are becoming more comfortable purchasing online, with almost half of Canadians surveyed reporting that they purchased clothing (42 percent) and travel packages (40 percent) online. Canadian small business owners are getting in on the act as well, with even higher purchase numbers than consumers for clothing (50 percent) and travel (61 percent).[16]

With new technologies creating excellent online interfaces, it is perplexing why Canadian business-to-business companies do not invest more time and effort to create a stronger online presence. Almost all businesses reported using the Internet in 2016; however, only 60 percent reported having a website.[17] Companies that reported selling to consumers had a much higher likelihood of having a website than businesses focused on selling to other businesses.

These troubling statistics prompted the federal government to table a report titled "E-Commerce in Canada: Pursuing the Promise." The report highlights many of the statistical trends previously mentioned and attempts to find a way to get Canadian businesses more engaged in the world of online commerce. According to a study cited in the report, only 15 percent of Canadian companies surveyed used an online presence for marketing purposes.[18] (See Exhibit 7.5 for usage rates of specific B2B marketing tactics.)

The problem? There are several. Most notable is the cost of creating an online presence and the access to funding to make that happen. Other concerns include security issues and the fear of revealing company information online. The government report presented some solutions to the problem, with the focus on improving broadband Internet access and improving online payment systems.[19]

There are many roadblocks for business marketing online in Canada, but there are some trends in the marketplace that might make this move forward a little easier.

7-7a Trends in B2B Online Marketing

A number of new technologies and approaches can help businesses improve online presence and sales.

THE GROWTH OF MOBILE Oracle, a worldwide leader in technology and online services for businesses, published its well-known "B2B Commerce Study" based on discussions with world leaders in business marketing online. A main finding from the Oracle report: almost one-third of respondents in the survey stated an intention to invest in mobile technologies.[20] Business marketers are beginning to see the power of online applications that are built for phones and tablets, and how building their own application could greatly improve the chances of conducting business online.

IMPORTANCE OF CONTENT MARKETING Borrowing from the business-to-consumer (B2C) market is another solid trend for business marketers. An area of greater importance for B2B marketers online is getting the word out about their company—which is what content marketing is all about. Recently, the B2B Content Marketing Benchmarks Report was published, and it showed that 93 percent of B2B marketers are using content marketing.[21] Much of that content marketing is

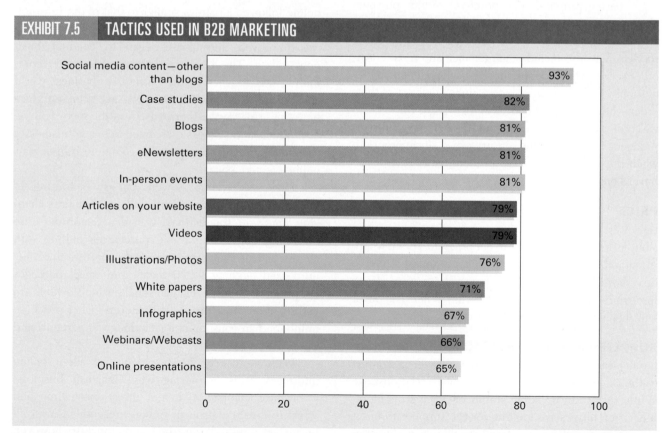

EXHIBIT 7.5 TACTICS USED IN B2B MARKETING

- Social media content—other than blogs: 93%
- Case studies: 82%
- Blogs: 81%
- eNewsletters: 81%
- In-person events: 81%
- Articles on your website: 79%
- Videos: 79%
- Illustrations/Photos: 76%
- White papers: 71%
- Infographics: 67%
- Webinars/Webcasts: 66%
- Online presentations: 65%

Source: Content Marketing Institute & MarketingProfs, "B2B Content Marketing: 2016 Benchmarks, Budgets, and Trends—North America," http://contentmarketinginstitute.com/wp-content/uploads/2015/09/2016_B2B_Report_Final.pdf, p. 15.

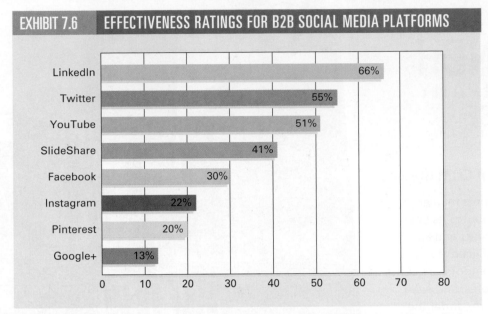

EXHIBIT 7.6   EFFECTIVENESS RATINGS FOR B2B SOCIAL MEDIA PLATFORMS

LinkedIn 66%
Twitter 55%
YouTube 51%
SlideShare 41%
Facebook 30%
Instagram 22%
Pinterest 20%
Google+ 13%

Source: Content Marketing Institute & MarketingProfs, "B2B Content Marketing: 2016 Benchmarks, Budgets, and Trends—North America," http://contentmarketinginstitute.com/wp-content/uploads/2015/09/2016_B2B_Report_Final.pdf, p. 18.

happening online with B2B online content marketing tools, such as blogs, articles on websites, e-newsletters, videos, and the most popular—social media.

SOCIAL MEDIA GROWTH While many view social media as a consumer-driven phenomenon, it is important to remember that some of the earliest adopters of social media were firms with a strong B2B component: IBM, Sun Microsystems, and Hewlett Packard. Given the importance of each relationship in business marketing, companies need to put a great deal of time and effort into making sure their social media presence is handled properly.

Recently, CEOs of B2B companies were polled and asked about the importance of social media in online business interactions. Almost eight out of ten CEOs identified the importance of social networks and social media as part of an online engagement strategy.[22]

However, it is becoming clearer that simply a presence in social media will not be good enough to create true engagement. Customers are beginning to use social media as a method of inquiry, be it for more information about a company or to voice concern over an issue with a company. Companies using social media send 20 times more promotional messages over social media than actual responses to customer queries. This can be quite problematic in a B2B environment where both the speed and nature of a response can have a significant impact on the relationship between two companies. Therefore it is vital that companies embarking in the social space for B2B have a clear policy for ensuring that any account representing a company will do so in a responsible and responsive manner. Via Rail Canada has had a clear social media policy for a number of years and even has a dedicated community manager who must be forewarned about any social media account created in the name of Via Rail Canada. This manager is tasked with ensuring that conduct in social media represents the values of the organization.[23]

With regard to social media effectiveness for B2B interactions, it is clear that LinkedIn still leads the way. As a social media platform, LinkedIn is considered a very strong environment for generating leads for salespeople and also a great resource for human resources looking for new talent. The LinkedIn environment can be a potential source for finding new vendors, partners, and other business interactions. Other social media platforms can also be of use. Twitter and YouTube provide channels for interacting with customers, but they are not as effective at getting the type of interaction that LinkedIn can provide. Other social media platforms that are more common for B2C interactions, such as Facebook, Instagram, and Pinterest, are noticeably less effective in a B2B setting where the focus is on achieving engagement and interaction for business purposes.

STUDY TOOLS

IN THE BOOK, YOU CAN:

✔ Rip out the Chapter in Review card at the back of the book.

ONLINE, YOU CAN:

✔ Stay organized and efficient with a single online destination with all the course material and study aids you need to succeed.

Go to nelson.com/student to access the digital resources.

SIDE LAUNCH
BREWING COMPANY
CONTINUING CASE

Side Launch Brewing Company

The Forbidden Fruit of Craft Brewers

Within its primary geographic market of Ontario, Side Launch distributes its beer through a finite set of retailers and an endlessly expanding list of licensees. The retailers, or off-premises vendors, are LCBO, The Beer Store, grocery stores, and even the Side Launch onsite store. Under the Ontario government's rules, there is no real way to differentiate in this space. Single or uniform pricing is in place, meaning that a Side Launch beer sold at a Loblaws store must be exactly the same price as the same beer sold by any other vendor. The real creativity, resourcefulness, and competitiveness come into play with on-premises licensees—the thousands of bars, pubs, restaurants, and hotels scattered around Ontario with a liquor licence. While Side Launch cans are sold at these places, the real battle is for taps—those logo-bearing levers the bartender tugs on to pour you a pint, extracted from a keg produced from a specific brewer.

As Side Launch continues to rapidly expand, its brand becomes more widely known, craft beer aficionados start asking for it, and in turn the licensees ratchet up their orders. It's an enviable position to be in, admits Chuck Galea, VP Sales and Marketing, but one fraught with a barrage of brand dilemmas. "We have to make sure that we remain humble. I've seen it happen at other breweries. You get really popular, the bigger accounts start to bring you on, and you forget about the little guys. You get a tap at one of these accounts, and you can sell as much there in one month as you would in a year at a smaller account. But you can't forget the little guy." As mentioned—it's an interesting predicament that in a way is a significant indicator of success.

On the other hand, craft beer and its brewers walk a line between profit and reputation so thin it is invisible. Remain small and obscure, and forgo selling opportunities. Grow big through intensive distribution, and you're no longer considered a craft brewer. You've just become another big beer company—the death knell, no doubt, for a craft brewer intent on remaining authentic. "Sometimes being in one or two of these big chain restaurants or bars can be bad perceptually. A bar that thinks of itself as

authentically craft will find out you're in a big chain restaurant and will say, 'You've just sold out. Screw you. Come pick up your tap handles.'"

Remaining true to its values, true to its brand, and true to itself and operating in a marketing environment that is so clearly tilting in its favour is like an entrepreneur's Garden of Eden. And excessive sales are the forbidden fruit. "We talk about it all the time," admits founder Garnet Pratt. "But I didn't get into this to monetize assets. I like this," she explains, raising a pint of Dark Lager and motioning it around the Huron Club, one of the first pubs in Collingwood to carry Side Launch. "I like having a beer at a place that shares our passion, then going back to the plant in which it is made, by passionate people who love making it."

Questions

1. What are the two different types of retailers through which Side Launch distributes its beer?

2. Describe how Side Launch demonstrates a relationship commitment with its retail partners.

3. Explain the concept of derived demand as it pertains to the craft beer industry.

Side Launch Brewing Company

8 | Segmenting, Targeting, and Positioning

LEARNING OUTCOMES

8-1 Describe the characteristics of markets and market segments

8-2 Explain the importance of market segmentation

8-3 Describe the bases commonly used to segment consumer markets

8-4 Discuss criteria for successful market segmentation

8-5 Describe the bases for segmenting business markets

8-6 List the steps involved in segmenting markets

8-7 Discuss alternative strategies for selecting target markets

8-8 Explain how and why firms implement positioning strategies and how product differentiation plays a role

Jirsak/Shutterstock.com

"In the business world, the rearview mirror is always clearer than the windshield."

—Warren Buffet

8-1 MARKET SEGMENTATION

The term **market** means different things to different people. We are all familiar with the supermarket, stock market, labour market, fish market, and flea market. All these types of markets share several characteristics. First, they are composed of people (consumer markets) or organizations (business markets). Second, these people or organizations have wants and needs that can be satisfied by particular product categories. Third, they have the ability to buy the products they seek. Fourth, they are willing to exchange their resources, usually money or credit, for desired products.

In sum, a market is (1) people or organizations with (2) needs or wants and with (3) the ability and (4) the willingness to buy. A group of people or an organization that lacks any one of these characteristics is not a market.

Within a market, a **market segment** is a subgroup of people or organizations sharing one or more characteristics that cause them to have similar product needs. At one extreme, we can define every person and every organization in the world as a market segment because each is unique. At the other extreme, we can define the entire consumer market as one large market segment and the business market as another large segment. All people have some similar characteristics and needs, as do all organizations.

From a marketing perspective, market segments can be described as being somewhere between the two extremes. The process of dividing a market into meaningful, relatively similar, and identifiable segments or groups is called **market segmentation**. The purpose of market segmentation is to enable the marketer to

market people or organizations with needs or wants and the ability and willingness to buy

market segment a subgroup of people or organizations sharing one or more characteristics that cause them to have similar product needs

market segmentation the process of dividing a market into meaningful, relatively similar, and identifiable segments or groups

tailor marketing mixes to meet the needs of one or more specific segments.

8-2 THE IMPORTANCE OF MARKET SEGMENTATION

Until the 1960s, few firms practised market segmentation. When they did, it was more likely a haphazard effort rather than a formal marketing strategy. Before 1960, for example, the Coca-Cola Company produced only one beverage and aimed it at the entire pop market. Today, Coca-Cola offers more than a dozen different products to market segments on the basis of diverse consumer preferences for flavours and for calorie and caffeine content. Coca-Cola offers traditional pop flavours, energy drinks (Powerade), organic bottled tea (Honest Tea), fruit drinks (Minute Maid, Simply Orange), and water (Dasani).

Market segmentation plays a key role in the marketing strategy of most successful organizations and is a powerful marketing tool. Market segmentation enables marketers to identify groups of customers with similar needs and to analyze the characteristics and buying behaviour of these groups. That information forms the basis

of marketing mixes designed specifically with the characteristics and desires of one or more segments. Because market segments differ in size and potential, segmentation helps decision makers to more accurately define marketing objectives and better allocate resources. In turn, performance can be better evaluated when objectives are more precise. Market segmentation is consistent with the marketing concept as discussed in Chapter 1. The 60-year-old company Canada Goose has stayed true to its roots and brand promise, creating luxury "Made in Canada" outdoor apparel for extreme weather conditions for consumers who are willing to pay a premium for the Canada Goose guarantee of warmth in extreme conditions.

8-3 BASES FOR SEGMENTING CONSUMER MARKETS

Marketers use **segmentation bases**, or **variables**, which are characteristics of individuals, groups, or organizations, to divide a total market into segments. The choice of segmentation bases is crucial because

segmentation bases (variables) characteristics of individuals, groups, or organizations

an inappropriate segmentation strategy may lead to lost sales and missed profit opportunities. The key is to identify bases that will produce substantial, measurable, and accessible segments that exhibit different response patterns to marketing mixes.

Markets can be segmented by using a single variable, such as age group, or by using several variables, such as age group, gender, and education. Although a single-variable segmentation is less precise, it has the advantage of being simpler and easier to use than multiple-variable segmentation. The disadvantages of multiple-variable segmentation are that it is often more difficult to use than single-variable segmentation; usable secondary data are less likely to be available; and as the number of segmentation bases increases, the size of the resulting segments decreases. Nevertheless, the current trend is toward using more rather than fewer variables to segment most markets. Multiple-variable segmentation is clearly more precise than single-variable segmentation.

To maximize the potential of multiple-variable segmentation, marketers often turn to data-driven consulting firms such as Environics Analytics. Environics Analytics utilizes data-driven research and an extensive suite of data-based products and services to help organizations better understand their customer segments to create marketing campaigns that maximize return on investment. As an example, Arc'teryx, an outdoor equipment and sports clothing manufacturer, headquartered in Vancouver, was looking to expand its branded stores beyond its single location in Montreal, but weren't sure which geographic areas would be most profitable. Environics analysts identified geographic concentrations of customers, collected sales data from bricks-and-mortar and e-commerce transactions of their distributors over a five-year period, and then used a proprietary database to create target groups of core customers based on demographics, lifestyles, and social values. In calculating where to open a branded store, Environics researchers completed an analysis that identified demographics and lifestyles that predicted sales. They then mapped the results to ensure that a new location would not compete with the current distributor network. The result was 12 prospective branded store locations in Canada and the United States described by sales potential, new and current customers, and competition.[1]

Consumer goods marketers commonly use one or more of the following characteristics to segment

Kevin Schafer/Moment Mobile/Getty Images

markets: geography, demographics, psychographics, benefits sought, and usage rate.

8-3a Geographic Segmentation

Geographic segmentation refers to segmenting markets by a region of a country or a region of the world, market size, market density, or climate. Market density means the number of people within a unit of land, such as a census tract. Climate is commonly used for geographic segmentation because of its dramatic impact on residents' needs and purchasing behaviour. Snow blowers, water and snow skis, clothing, and air-conditioning and heating systems are products with varying appeal, depending on climate.

A regional approach to marketing can ensure a more competitive marketing strategy. Data from organizations such as Environics (discussed above) and from retail store checkout stations with scanners provide marketers with information on what is selling best in various regions. Carlton Cards used Environics's proprietary software and sales by trading area to analyze sales to create the optimal merchandise mix for various store locations.[2]

8-3b Demographic Segmentation

Marketers often segment markets on the basis of demographic information because such information is widely available and often relates to consumers' buying and consuming behaviour. Some common bases of **demographic segmentation** are age, gender, income, ethnic background, and family life cycle.

geographic segmentation
segmenting markets by region of a country or the world, market size, market density, or climate

demographic segmentation
segmenting markets by age, gender, income, ethnic background, and family life cycle

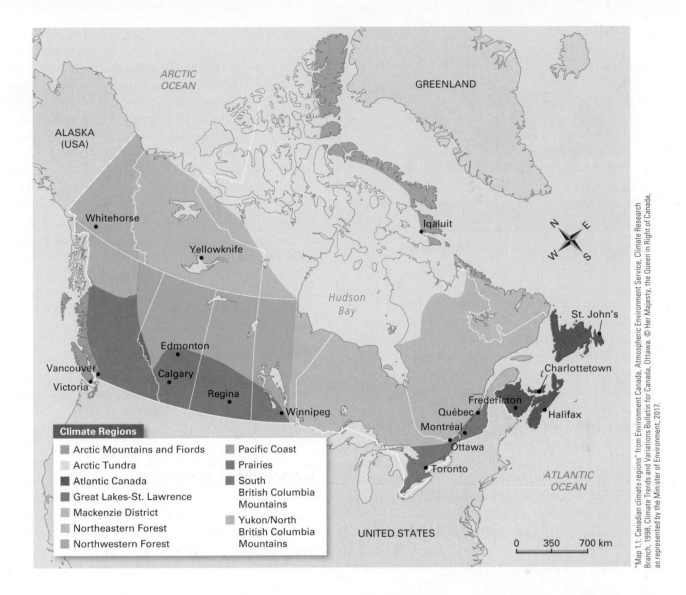

"Map 1.1: Canadian climate regions" from Environment Canada, Atmospheric Environment Service, Climate Research Branch, 1998, Climate Trends and Variations Bulletin for Canada, Ottawa. © Her Majesty, the Queen in Right of Canada, as represented by the Minister of Environment, 2017.

AGE SEGMENTATION Marketers use a variety of terms to refer to different age groups: newborns, infants, preschoolers, young children, tweens, teens, young adults, Baby Boomers, Millennials, Generation X, Generation Y, and seniors. Age segmentation can be an important tool identifying potential profitable market segments with unique needs and wants.

Many companies have long targeted parents of babies and young children with products such as disposable diapers, baby food, and toys. Recently, other companies that have not traditionally marketed to young children are developing products and services to attract this group. For example, the high-intensity fitness company CrossFit recently developed a program for kids. Good movement learned early in life translates to physical literacy and a lower incidence of sports injuries. In addition, research has indicated that physical activity has a cognitive benefit. Consistent participation in physical activity can therefore have a positive influence on academic achievement.[3]

As we learned in Chapter 2, through the spending of their allowances, earnings, and gifts, children account for and influence a great deal of consumption. Tweens (ages 9 to 14), who make up approximately 2.5 million of Canada's total population, have direct spending power of more than $2 billion and an influence over how their families spend another $20 billion.[4] The teenage market (ages 15 to 19) includes more than 2.1 million individuals,[5] and, like the tweens, this market accounts for substantial purchasing power. This segment is important to marketers because they tend to be early adopters without strongly defined brand preferences. They have grown up with rapid product obsolescence, so they tend to be loyal to best in class rather than a brand. They have grown up with digital technology; they are leading the way with mobile technology; social media is their chosen form of communication. Like tweens they are highly influential within the family, suggesting marketers need to pay attention to this group in creating marketing strategies.[6]

Crossfit Kids—making getting fit fun.

Generation Y—or as they are often called, the Millennials—are those born between 1980 and 2000. With about 9 million Canadians in this demographic group, Millennials are a significant segment to consider. Like tweens and teens, millennials are tech savvy, with a comfort in using digital media. Most of the media consumption of this group is online, including accessing news and watching television. This group is the most educated and most diverse. Millennials are ethical consumers who are willing to spend more on an ethically made product and are more likely to demonstrate loyalty to brands that have a social consciousness and are socially responsible.[7]

The Baby Boom generation, born between 1947 and 1965, represents approximately 27 percent of the entire Canadian population. This generation is quickly reaching retirement age, bringing a host of new challenges to the Canadian economy and marketers. Baby Boomers are often nostalgic and eager to continue their active lives, and many can now can afford to buy top-of-the-line models of products from their youth. Baby Boomers are leading the luxury real estate market and are driving demand for luxury holidays. About 19 percent of Baby Boomers are now considered seniors (those aged 65 and older) and this group is especially attracted to companies that build relationships by taking the time to get to know them and their preferences.[8] Canadian seniors are increasingly using technology to stay in touch with their extended families and to shop for products and services they need; however, the rate of adoption of new technological devices, such as a smartphone, still remains lower than the general population. Despite the lower rate of adoption, almost 60 percent of seniors claim to regularly go online.[9]

GENDER SEGMENTATION Women are powerful consumers. As women continue to serve as the primary caregivers for children and the elderly, they have a huge influence on consumer purchasing. Women buy on behalf of the people living in their home as well as for their extended family. Women today are more healthy, active, and wealthy than ever. Over the next 10 years two-thirds of women will control consumer wealth in the United States.[10] This affluent group should be paid attention to. As much as women need to be paid attention to in a different way than in the past, so should marketers look at men differently. Almost 40 percent of men are the primary grocery shopper, taking on larger

Real Heroes

Unilever's "real heroes" campaign is striving to break gender stereotypes. The ads are attempting to change the perspective on masculinity—the caring side of men is a sign of strength. The ads present everyday dads as heroes, such as the dad in the photo with a tattoo replicating his young daughter's cochlear implant to show his support. Research by Unilever revealed that only 7 percent of men could relate to the way media depicts masculinity, with nine out of ten agreeing that masculinity has evolved since their fathers' time.

and larger roles in household management. However, men shop differently, making fewer impulse purchases, are less price sensitive, and are focused on getting in and out of the store as quickly as possible. Given this, consumer goods marketers recognize that the strategy today in reaching men must be built around creating a strong brand image.[11] The blurring of once traditional lines in the family and the continued movement toward equality in the workplace is affecting how marketers build campaigns. Unilever is promoting an end to gender stereotyping in advertising. In 2016 Unilever changed the approach used for Axe. Traditionally marketed with a strong sexual appeal about masculinity, the new Axe ads move beyond this sex appeal to ads that promote individuality. The Dove Men's line is promoted with the line "Care Makes a Man Stronger," demonstrating through real father moments, that care is no longer the opposite of strong.[12]

INCOME SEGMENTATION

Income is a popular demographic variable for segmenting markets because income level influences consumers' wants and determines their buying power. Many markets are segmented by income, including the markets for housing, clothing, automobiles, and food. For example, in the auto industry, many car manufacturers have two different brands aimed at different income groups, such as Honda and Acura; Nissan and Infiniti; Toyota and Lexus.

ETHNIC SEGMENTATION

Canada is a very culturally diverse country, and Canadian marketers are strongly aware of the multicultural makeup of the market. When considering Canada's ethnic communities, marketers might first focus on French Canadian and English Canadian markets, which are the largest, but they will then consider the other ethnic populations. Many companies are segmenting their markets according to ethnicity, and some marketers are developing unique approaches to sizable ethnic segments.

Tracking ethnic communities is one of a multicultural marketer's most challenging and most important tasks. Some companies have found that segmenting according to the main ethnicities is not precise enough.

Regardless of the segment being targeted, marketers need to stay educated about the consumers they are pursuing, convey a message that is relevant to each particular market, use the Internet as a vehicle to educate ethnic markets about brands and products, and use integrated marketing techniques to reinforce the message in various ways.

Hurst Photo/Shutterstock.com

FAMILY LIFE-CYCLE SEGMENTATION

Consumer buying behaviour varies, and the variations are often not sufficiently explained by the demographic factors of gender, age, and income. The consumption patterns among people of the same age and gender frequently differ because they are in different stages of the family life cycle. The **family life cycle (FLC)** is a series of stages determined by a combination of age, marital status, and the presence or absence of children.

There are 9.4 million families in Canada. Out of this number, one-quarter are what are known as the "traditional" families, made up of a husband, a wife, and children.[13] The number of same-sex couples increased 42.4 percent between 2006 and 2011 to 64,575, with nearly one-third of them classified as same-sex married couples while others were in common-law relationships.[14]

Exhibit 8.1 illustrates numerous FLC patterns and shows how families' needs, incomes, resources, and expenditures differ at each stage. The horizontal flow shows the traditional family life cycle. The lower part of the exhibit lists some of the characteristics and purchase patterns of families in each stage of the traditional life cycle. The exhibit also acknowledges that about half of all first marriages end in divorce. When young married couples move into the young-divorced stage, their consumption patterns often revert to those of the young-single stage of the cycle. About four out of five divorced persons remarry by middle age and re-enter the traditional life cycle, as indicated in the exhibit by the recycled flow.

At certain points in the life cycle, consumers are especially receptive to marketing efforts. Soon-to-be-married couples are typically considered to be the most receptive because they are making brand decisions about products that could last longer than their marriages. Similarly, young parents are the target of companies promoting

> **family life cycle (FLC)** a series of stages determined by a combination of age, marital status, and the presence or absence of children

EXHIBIT 8.1 FAMILY LIFE CYCLE

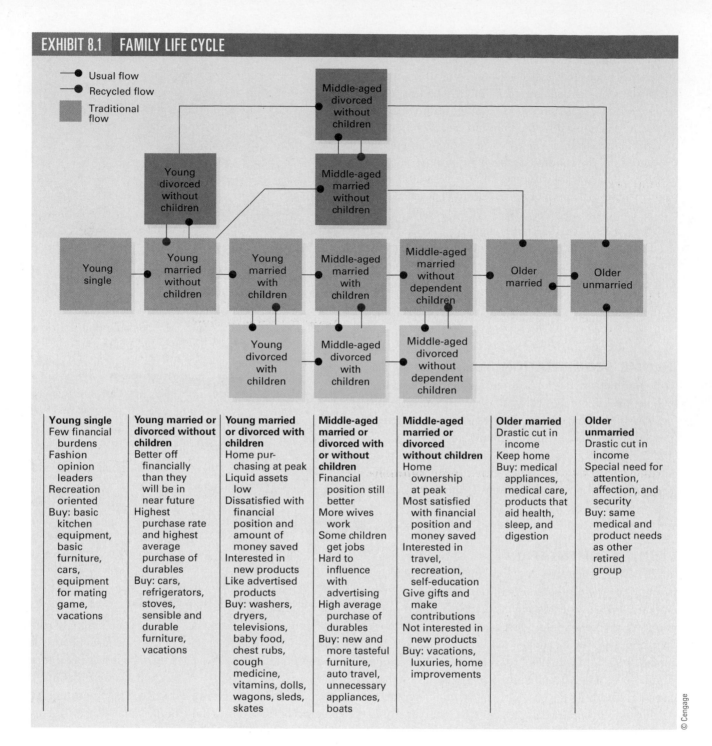

Young single	Young married or divorced without children	Young married or divorced with children	Middle-aged married or divorced with or without children	Middle-aged married or divorced without children	Older married	Older unmarried
Few financial burdens	Better off financially than they will be in near future	Home purchasing at peak	Financial position still better	Home ownership at peak	Drastic cut in income	Drastic cut in income
Fashion opinion leaders	Highest purchase rate and highest average purchase of durables	Liquid assets low	More wives work	Most satisfied with financial position and money saved	Keep home	Special need for attention, affection, and security
Recreation oriented	Buy: cars, refrigerators, stoves, sensible and durable furniture, vacations	Dissatisfied with financial position and amount of money saved	Some children get jobs	Interested in travel, recreation, self-education	Buy: medical appliances, medical care, products that aid health, sleep, and digestion	Buy: same medical and product needs as other retired group
Buy: basic kitchen equipment, basic furniture, cars, equipment for mating game, vacations		Interested in new products	Hard to influence with advertising	Give gifts and make contributions		
		Like advertised products	High average purchase of durables	Not interested in new products		
		Buy: washers, dryers, televisions, baby food, chest rubs, cough medicine, vitamins, dolls, wagons, sleds, skates	Buy: new and more tasteful furniture, auto travel, unnecessary appliances, boats	Buy: vacations, luxuries, home improvements		

© Cengage

baby products, as these parents expect to have higher expenses. A thorough understanding of the FLC can help marketers to design, develop, and successfully sell their products in the most competitive manner.

8-3c Psychographic Segmentation

Age, gender, income, ethnicity, family life-cycle stage, and other demographic variables are usually helpful in developing segmentation strategies, but often they don't paint the entire picture. Demographics provide the skeleton, but psychographics add meat to the bones. **Psychographic segmentation** is market segmentation on the basis of the following variables:

- **Personality:** Personality is a person's traits, attitudes, and habits. Clothing is the ultimate personality descriptor. Fashionistas wear high-end trendy clothes while hipsters enjoy jeans and T-shirts with tennis

psychographic segmentation market segmentation on the basis of personality, motives, lifestyles, and geodemographic categories

shoes. People buy clothes that they feel represent their personalities and give others an idea of who they are. Porsche Cars North America knew the demographics of their target, males with university education earning over high six-figure salaries. Further research revealed five distinct personality types that allowed Porsche to more effectively reach the target consumer. The company's sales rose by 48 percent.[15]

- **Motives:** Marketers of baby products and life insurance appeal to consumers' emotional motives—namely, to care for their loved ones. Using appeals to economy, reliability, and dependability, carmakers such as Subaru and Suzuki target customers by appealing to their rational motives.

- **Lifestyles:** Lifestyle segmentation divides people into groups according to the way they spend their time, the importance of the things around them, their beliefs, and socioeconomic characteristics such as income and education. For example, record stores specializing in vinyl are targeting young people who enjoy listening to independent labels and pride themselves on being independent of big business. LEED-certified appliances appeal to environmentally conscious "green" consumers.

- **Geodemographics:** **Geodemographic segmentation** clusters potential customers into neighbourhood lifestyle categories. It combines geographic, demographic, and lifestyle segmentations. Geomographic segmentation helps marketers develop marketing programs tailored to prospective buyers who live in small geographic regions, such as neighbourhoods, or who have very specific lifestyle and demographic characteristics. Canadian Blood Services were able to utilize geodemographics and social values to identify communities that had a high potential of blood donors and then open clinics in those areas. The data not only supported the opening of new clinics, but also assisted in evaluating performance of the clinic against realistic benchmarks, ensuring subsequent marketing strategies were appropriately created.[16]

Psychographic variables can be used individually to segment markets or can be combined with other variables to provide more detailed descriptions of market segments. As mentioned earlier in the chapter, Environics Analytics has created a statistical tool that divides the Canadian population into 68 different lifestyle types, each with catchy names. The clusters combine basic demographic data, such as age, ethnicity, and income, with lifestyle information, such as media and sports preferences, taken from consumer surveys. For example, the "Satellite Burbs" group comprises older, upscale, exurban couples and families with an average household income of $143,173 who enjoy spending time with tight-knit groups but have a global consciousness. Satellite burbs are family-centric, active in their religious community, and enthusiastic about purchasing products and services, seeing themselves as opinion leaders and influencers to their peers. They are more likely to drive a domestic sports vehicle, like the movie network, purchase books online, and frequent Pinterest. They prefer Canadian whisky and enjoy shopping at factory outlet stores.[17] This information, combined with other information, can be extremely helpful to marketers. What lifestyle type do you fit into?

8-3d Benefit Segmentation

Benefit segmentation is the process of grouping customers into market segments according to the benefits they seek from the product. Most types of market segmentation are based on the assumption that related subgroups of people or organizations share one or more characteristics that cause them to have similar product needs. Benefit segmentation is different because it groups potential customers on the basis of their needs or wants rather than some other characteristic, such as age or gender.

Customer profiles can be developed by examining demographic information associated with people seeking certain benefits. This information can be used to match marketing strategies to selected target markets. The many different types of performance energy bars with various combinations of nutrients are aimed at consumers looking for different benefits. For example, PowerBar is designed for athletes looking for long-lasting fuel, while PowerBar Protein Plus is aimed at those who want extra protein for replenishing their muscles after strength training. Carb Solutions High Protein Bars are for those on low-carb diets; Luna Bars are targeted to women who want a bar with soy protein, calcium, and fewer calories; and Clif Bars are for people who want a natural bar made from such ingredients as rolled oats, soybeans, and organic soy flour.[18]

8-3e Usage-Rate Segmentation

Usage-rate segmentation divides a market by the amount of product bought or consumed. Categories

geodemographic segmentation segmenting potential customers into neighbourhood lifestyle categories

benefit segmentation the process of grouping customers into market segments according to the benefits they seek from the product

usage-rate segmentation dividing a market by the amount of product bought or consumed

vary depending on the product, but they are likely to include some combination of the following: former users, potential users, first-time users, light or irregular users, medium users, and heavy users. Segmenting by usage rate enables marketers to focus their efforts on heavy users or to develop multiple marketing mixes aimed at different segments. Because heavy users often account for a sizable portion of all product sales, some marketers focus on the heavy-user segment. Developing customers into heavy users is the goal behind many frequency and loyalty programs.

The **Pareto Principle** holds that 20 percent of all customers generate 80 percent of the demand. Although the percentages usually are not exact, the general idea often holds true. For example, in the fast-food industry, heavy users account for only one of five fast-food patrons but represent 60 percent of all visits to fast-food restaurants. Thus, according to an Agriculture and Agri-Food Canada report, heavy users account for $9.36 billion of the $15.6 billion spent on fast food at Canada's 25,000 fast-food restaurants.[19]

8-4 CRITERIA FOR SUCCESSFUL SEGMENTATION

To be useful, a segmentation scheme must produce segments that meet four basic criteria:

1. **Substantiality:** A segment must be large enough to warrant developing and maintaining a special marketing mix. This criterion does not necessarily mean that a segment must have many potential customers. Marketers of custom-designed homes and business buildings, commercial airplanes, and large computer systems typically develop marketing programs tailored to each potential customer's needs. In most cases, however, a market segment needs many potential customers to make commercial sense.

2. **Identifiability and measurability:** Segments must be identifiable and their size measurable. Data on the population within geographic boundaries, the number of people in various age categories, and other social and demographic characteristics are often easy to get, and they provide fairly concrete measures of segment size.

3. **Accessibility:** The firm must be able to reach members of targeted segments with customized marketing mixes.

Some market segments are more difficult to reach—for example, senior citizens (especially those with reading or hearing disabilities), individuals who don't speak English, and people who are illiterate.

4. **Responsiveness:** Markets can be segmented by using any criteria that seem logical. Unless one market segment responds to a marketing mix differently from other segments, however, that segment need not be treated separately. For instance, if all customers are equally price-conscious about a product, marketers have no need to offer high-, medium-, and low-priced versions to different segments.

8-5 BASES FOR SEGMENTING BUSINESS MARKETS

The business market consists of four broad segments: producers, resellers, government, and institutions (for a detailed discussion of the characteristics of these segments, see Chapter 7). Whether marketers focus on only one or on all four of these segments, they are likely to find diversity among potential customers. Thus further market segmentation offers just as many benefits to business marketers as it does to consumer-product marketers.

8-5a Company Characteristics

Company characteristics, such as geographic location, type of company, company size, and product use, can be important segmentation variables. Some markets tend to be regional because buyers prefer to purchase from local suppliers, and distant suppliers may have difficulty competing in price and service. Therefore, firms that sell to geographically concentrated industries benefit by locating close to their markets.

Segmenting by customer type allows business marketers to tailor their marketing mixes to the unique needs of particular types of organizations or industries. Many companies are finding this form of segmentation to be quite effective. For example, Lowes, one of the largest do-it-yourself retailers in Canada, has targeted professional repair and remodelling contractors in addition to consumers.

A commonly used basis for business segmentation is volume of purchase (heavy, moderate, light). Another is the buying organization's size, which may affect its purchasing procedures, the types and quantities of products it needs, and its responses to different marketing mixes. Many products, especially raw materials, such as steel, wood, and petroleum, have diverse

Pareto Principle a principle holding that 20 percent of all customers generate 80 percent of the demand

applications. How customers use a product may influence the amount they buy, their buying criteria, and their selection of vendors.

8-5b Buying Processes

Many business marketers find it helpful to segment current and prospective customers on the basis of how they buy. For example, companies can segment some business markets by ranking key purchasing criteria, such as price, quality, technical support, and service. Atlas Corporation developed a commanding position in the industrial door market by providing customized products in just four weeks, which was much faster than the industry average of 12 to 15 weeks. Atlas's primary market is companies with an immediate need for customized doors.

The purchasing strategies of buyers may provide useful segments. Two purchasing profiles that have been identified are satisficers and optimizers. **Satisficers** are business customers who place their order with the first familiar supplier to satisfy their product and delivery requirements. **Optimizers**, on the other hand, are business customers who consider numerous suppliers (both familiar and unfamiliar), solicit bids, and study all proposals carefully before selecting one.

The personal characteristics of the buyers themselves (their demographic characteristics, decision styles, tolerance for risk, confidence levels, job responsibilities, etc.) influence their buying behaviour and thus offer a viable basis for segmenting some business markets.

8-6 STEPS IN SEGMENTING A MARKET

The purpose of market segmentation, in both consumer and business markets, is to identify marketing opportunities. Markets are dynamic, so it is important that companies proactively monitor their segmentation strategies over time. Often, once customers or prospects have been assigned to a segment, marketers think their task is done. After customers are assigned to an age segment, for example, they stay there until they reach the next age bracket or category, which could be 10 years in the future. Thus the segmentation classifications are static, but the customers and prospects are changing. Marketing managers typically follow these six steps to segment a market based on the criteria described in the previous sections:

1. **Select a market or product category for study.** Define the overall market or product category to be studied. It may be a market in which the firm already competes, a new but related market or product category, or a totally new market or category.

2. **Choose a basis or bases for segmenting the market.** This step requires managerial insight, creativity, and market knowledge. No scientific procedures guide the selection of segmentation variables. However, a successful segmentation scheme must produce segments that meet the four basic criteria discussed earlier in this chapter.

3. **Select segmentation descriptors.** After choosing one or more bases, the marketer must select the segmentation descriptors. Descriptors identify the specific segmentation variables to use. For example, a company that selects usage segmentation needs to decide whether to pursue heavy users, nonusers, or light users.

4. **Profile and analyze segments.** The profile should include the segments' sizes, expected growth, purchase frequency, current brand usage, brand loyalty, and long-term sales and profit potential. This information can then be used to rank potential market segments by profit opportunity, risk, consistency with organizational mission and objectives, and other factors important to the firm. Included in the profile is the creation of a target persona, which is a holistic description of the target group that creates a three-dimensional picture. It is a composite sketch that aids in the creation of strong and targeted communications strategies.

5. **Select target markets.** Selecting target markets is not a part of the segmentation process but is a natural outcome of the segmentation process. It is a major decision that influences and often directly determines the firm's marketing mix. This topic is examined in detail later in this chapter.

6. **Design, implement, and maintain appropriate marketing mixes.** The marketing mix has been described as product, place (distribution), promotion, and pricing strategies intended to bring about mutually satisfying exchange relationships with target markets. Chapters 10 through 18 explore these topics in detail.

Not all segments are stable over time and dynamic segmentation reflects real-time changes made to market segments based on a customer's

satisficers business customers who place their order with the first familiar supplier to satisfy their product and delivery requirements

optimizers business customers who consider numerous suppliers, both familiar and unfamiliar, solicit bids, and study all proposals carefully before selecting one

EXHIBIT 8.2 ADVANTAGES AND DISADVANTAGES OF TARGET MARKETING STRATEGIES

Targeting Strategy	Advantages	Disadvantages
Undifferentiated targeting	Potential savings on production/marketing costs	Unimaginative product offerings Company more susceptible to competition
Concentrated targeting	Concentrates resources Can better meet the needs of a narrowly defined segment Allows some small firms to better compete with larger firms Provides strong positioning	Segments too small or changing Large competitors may more effectively market to niche segment
Multisegment targeting	Greater financial success Economies of scale in producing/marketing	High costs Cannibalization
One-to-One targeting	Delivers highly customized service High customer engagement/retention Increasing revenue through loyalty	High costs

© Cengage

ongoing search and shopping behaviours. For example, the website of Chapters Indigo, the bookselling chain, suggests book titles based on a site visitor's browsing and purchase pattern. Similar segmentation techniques are also used by Netflix and many companies utilizing online marketing today. Dynamic segmentation uses advanced mathematical and computer programming techniques to offer highly customized solutions to customers.

 ## 8-7 STRATEGIES FOR SELECTING TARGET MARKETS

So far, this chapter has focused on the market segmentation process, which is only the first step in deciding whom to approach about buying a product. The next task is to choose one or more target markets. A **target market** is a group of people or organizations for which an organization designs, implements, and maintains a marketing mix intended to meet the needs of that group, resulting in mutually satisfying exchanges. Because most markets will include customers with different characteristics, lifestyles, backgrounds, and income levels, a single marketing mix is unlikely to attract all segments of the market. Thus, if a marketer wants to appeal to more than one segment of the market, it must develop different marketing mixes. Three general strategies are used for selecting target markets— undifferentiated, concentrated, and multisegment

target market a group of people or organizations for which an organization designs, implements, and maintains a marketing mix intended to meet the needs of that group, resulting in mutually satisfying exchanges

undifferentiated targeting strategy a marketing approach that views the market as one big market with no individual segments and thus uses a single marketing mix

targeting. Exhibit 8.2 illustrates the advantages and disadvantages of each targeting strategy.

8-7a Undifferentiated Targeting

A firm using an **undifferentiated targeting strategy** essentially adopts a mass-market philosophy, viewing the market as one big one with no individual segments. The firm uses one marketing mix for the entire market. A firm that adopts an undifferentiated targeting strategy assumes that individual customers have similar needs that can be met through a common marketing mix. Thus marketers of commodity products, such as flour and sugar, are likely to use an undifferentiated targeting strategy.

The first firm in an industry sometimes uses an undifferentiated targeting strategy. With no competition, the firm may not need to tailor marketing mixes to the preferences of market segments. At one time, Coca-Cola used this strategy with its single product offered in a single size in a familiar shaped bottle. Undifferentiated marketing allows companies to save on production and marketing and achieve economies of mass production. Also, marketing costs may be lower when a company has only one product to promote and a single channel of distribution.

Too often, however, an undifferentiated strategy emerges by default rather than by design, reflecting a failure to consider the advantages of a segmented approach. The result is often sterile, unimaginative product offerings that have little appeal to anyone. Another problem associated with undifferentiated targeting is the company's greater susceptibility to competitive inroads. Coca-Cola forfeited its position as the leading cola seller in supermarkets to Pepsi-Cola in the late 1950s, when Pepsi began offering its cola in several sizes.

Undifferentiated marketing can succeed. A grocery store in a small, isolated town may define all the people who live in the town as its target market. It may offer one marketing mix that generally satisfies everyone. This strategy is not likely to be as effective, however, when a community has three or four grocery stores.

8-7b Concentrated Targeting

Firms using a **concentrated targeting strategy** select a market **niche** (one segment of a market) to target its marketing efforts. Because the firm is appealing to a single segment, it can concentrate on understanding the needs, motives, and satisfactions of that segment's members and on developing and maintaining a highly specialized marketing mix. Some firms find that concentrating resources and meeting the needs of a narrowly defined market segment is more profitable than spreading resources over several different segments.

Small firms often adopt a concentrated targeting strategy to compete effectively with much larger firms. ChickenBurger, a fast-food restaurant in Halifax, describes itself as "destination for families and friends" and refers to itself as a historical destination, thus using a concentrated strategy to compete against the large fast-food chain restaurants.[20]

Small firms often adopt a concentrated strategy to compete effectively with larger firms. Picone's Fine Foods, a 100-year tradition in the town of Dundas, Ontario, has stayed a small, specialty retailer of unique, fresh, and rare foods, allowing it to compete quite effectively with for a share of the consumers' grocery dollars.

Concentrated targeting violates the old adage "Don't put all your eggs in one basket." If the chosen segment is too small or if it shrinks because of environmental changes, the firm may suffer negative consequences. For instance, OshKosh B'gosh was highly successful selling

Courtesy of The Chickenburger

children's clothing in the 1980s. It was so successful, however, that children's clothing came to define the company image to the extent that the company could not sell clothes to anyone else. Attempts to market clothing to other market segments were unsuccessful. Recognizing that it was in the children's wear business, the company expanded into products such as children's eyeglasses, shoes, and other accessories. A concentrated strategy can also be disastrous for a firm that is not successful in its narrowly defined target market. For example, before Procter & Gamble introduced Head & Shoulders shampoo, several small firms were already selling anti-dandruff shampoos. Head & Shoulders was introduced with a large promotional campaign, and the new brand immediately captured over half the market. Within a year, several of the firms that had been concentrating on this market segment went out of business.

8-7c Multisegment Targeting

A firm that chooses to serve two or more well-defined market segments and develops a distinct marketing mix for each has a **multisegment targeting strategy**. Maple Leaf Foods offers many different kinds of bacon, such as regular and salt-reduced bacon. For convenience-seeking consumers, the company has developed Ready Crisp microwaveable bacon. For health-conscious segments, it offers turkey and chicken bacons.

Multisegment targeting is used for stores and shopping formats, not just for brands. Gap Inc. uses multisegment targeting to reach more than one customer segment with different brands within the store portfolio. The Gap brand itself targets individuals interested in a casual style, Athleta targets the fitness-minded women, Banana Republic reaches a slightly more sophisticated and less price-conscious shopper, while Old Navy is targeting a shopper interested in style but concerned with price.

Multisegment targeting offers many potential benefits to firms, including greater sales volume, higher profits, larger market share, and economies of scale in manufacturing and marketing. Yet it may also involve greater product design, production, promotion, inventory, marketing research, and management costs. Before deciding to use this strategy, firms should compare the benefits and costs of multisegment targeting to those of undifferentiated and concentrated targeting.

concentrated targeting strategy a strategy used to select one segment of a market to target marketing efforts

niche one segment of a market

multisegment targeting strategy a strategy that chooses two or more well-defined market segments and develops a distinct marketing mix for each

Another potential cost of multisegment targeting is **cannibalization**, which occurs when sales of a new product cut into sales of a firm's existing products. In many cases, however, companies prefer to steal sales from their own brands rather than lose sales to a competitor. Marketers may also be willing to cannibalize existing business to build new business.

8-7d One-to-One Marketing

Most businesses today use a mass-marketing approach designed to increase *market share* by selling their products to the greatest number of people. For many businesses, however, a more efficient and profitable strategy is to use **one-to-one marketing** to increase their *share of customers*—in other words, to sell more products to each customer. One-to-one marketing is an individualized marketing method that uses data generated through interactions between carefully defined groups of customers and the company to build long-term, personalized, and profitable relationships with each customer. The goal is to reduce costs through customer retention while increasing revenue through customer loyalty. Infinit Nutrition Canada is an energy beverage company that recognizes that athletes compete at different levels in different sports. This variability requires an energy beverage designed for each athlete's calorie, electrolyte, and carbohydrate requirements, as well as flavour preferences and strength. Using an online tool or through one-on-one consultations, the right beverage is created. With a 100 percent guarantee, athletes can vary the formulation until one that suits their unique needs is created.[21]

As many firms have discovered, a detailed and segmented understanding of the customer can be advantageous. There are at least four trends that will lead to the continuing growth of one-to-one marketing:

- **Personalization:** The one-size-fits-all marketing of the past no longer fits. Consumers do not want to be treated like the masses. Instead, they want to be treated as the individuals they are, with their own unique sets of needs and wants. By its personalized nature, one-to-one marketing can fulfill this desire.

- **Time savings:** Consumers will have little or no time to spend shopping and making purchase decisions. Because of the personal and targeted nature of one-to-one marketing, consumers can spend less time making purchase decisions and more time doing the things that are important.

- **Loyalty:** Consumers will be loyal only to those companies and brands that have earned their loyalty and reinforced it at every purchase occasion. One-to-one marketing techniques focus on finding a firm's best customers, rewarding them for their loyalty, and thanking them for their business.

- **Technology:** Advances in marketing research and database technology will allow marketers to collect detailed information on their customers, not just the approximation offered by demographics but specific names and addresses. Mass-media approaches will decline in importance as new technology and new media offer one-to-one marketers a more cost-effective way to reach customers and enables businesses to personalize their messages to customers. With the help of database technology, one-to-one marketers can track their customers as individuals, even if they number in the millions.

Although mass marketing will probably continue to be used, especially to create brand awareness or to remind consumers of a product, the advantages of one-to-one marketing cannot be ignored.

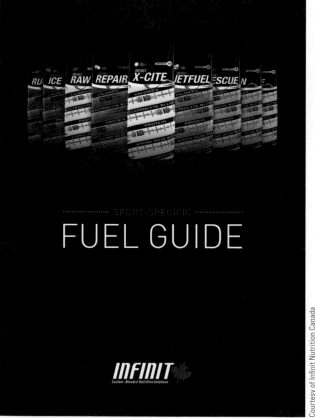

SPORT-SPECIFIC

FUEL GUIDE

INFINIT
Custom-Blended Nutrition Solutions

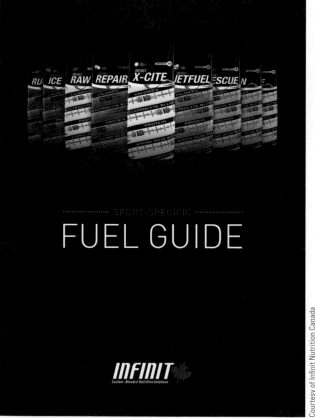
Courtesy of Infinit Nutrition Canada

cannibalization a situation that occurs when sales of a new product cut into sales of a firm's existing products

one-to-one marketing an individualized marketing method that uses customer information to build long-term, personalized, and profitable relationships with each customer

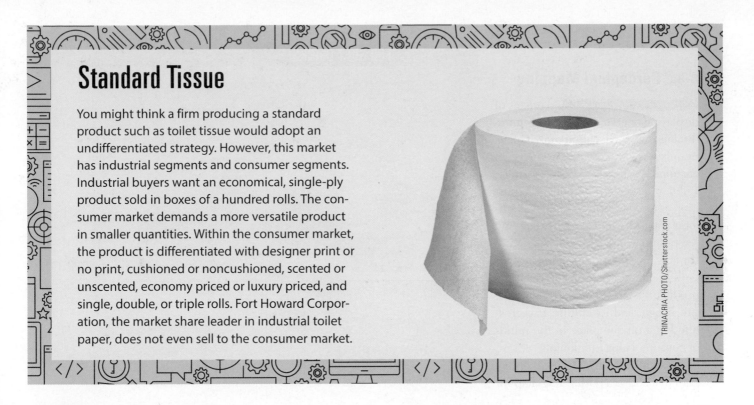

Standard Tissue

You might think a firm producing a standard product such as toilet tissue would adopt an undifferentiated strategy. However, this market has industrial segments and consumer segments. Industrial buyers want an economical, single-ply product sold in boxes of a hundred rolls. The consumer market demands a more versatile product in smaller quantities. Within the consumer market, the product is differentiated with designer print or no print, cushioned or noncushioned, scented or unscented, economy priced or luxury priced, and single, double, or triple rolls. Fort Howard Corporation, the market share leader in industrial toilet paper, does not even sell to the consumer market.

TRINACRIA PHOTO/Shutterstock.com

8-8 POSITIONING

The development of any marketing mix depends on **positioning**, a process that influences potential overall perception of a brand, a product line, or an organization in general. **Position** is the place a product, brand, or group of products occupies in consumers' minds relative to competing offerings. Consumer goods marketers are particularly concerned with positioning. Coca-Cola has multiple cola brands, each positioned to target a different segment of the market. Diet Coke is positioned as the same great taste without the calories, while Coca-Cola Zero is positioned as having a bolder taste and zero calories.

Positioning assumes that consumers compare products on the basis of important features. Marketing efforts that emphasize irrelevant features are therefore likely to misfire. Effective positioning requires assessing the positions occupied by competing products, determining the important dimensions underlying these positions, and choosing a position in the market where the organization's marketing efforts will have the greatest impact. For example, recent research by Toyota Canada revealed that safety was the number one feature desired in automobiles by Canadians of all ages. This led Toyota to place the safety message front and centre in its latest marketing campaign, focusing on the safety features, "Toyota Safety Sense," which come standard on most of their models, including base models. Recognizing that positioning on a safety benefit is not unique in the auto industry, Toyota has chosen to drive home the importance of safety by delivering a message that focuses on the importance (benefit) of a car designed with enhanced safety features: "… every safe arrival matters. Because we all deserve to arrive safely—Toyota Safety Sense."[22]

As the previous example illustrates, **product differentiation** is a positioning strategy that some firms use to distinguish their products from those of competitors. The distinctions can be either real or perceived. Companies can develop products that offer very real advantages for the target market. However, many everyday products, such as bleach, Aspirin, unleaded regular gasoline, and some soaps, are differentiated by such trivial means as brand names, packaging, colour, smell, or secret additives. The marketer attempts to convince consumers that a particular brand is distinctive and that they should demand it over competing brands.

Some firms, instead of using product differentiation, position their products as being similar to competing products or brands. For example, artificial sweeteners are advertised as tasting like sugar,

positioning a process that influences potential customers' overall perception of a brand, a product line, or an organization in general

position the place a product, brand, or group of products occupies in consumers' minds relative to competing offerings

product differentiation a positioning strategy that some firms use to distinguish their products from those of competitors

and margarine is touted as tasting like butter.

8-8a Perceptual Mapping

Perceptual mapping is a means of displaying or graphing, in two or more dimensions, the location of products, brands, or groups of products in customers' minds. For example, Lululemon has strengthened its position as a yoga-inspired technical athletic apparel company by expanding its product mix beyond yoga into running, cycling, and training and for both men and women. The resulting product mix, its retail stores, its website image, and its culture have resulted in a unique place in the minds of consumers for Lululemon.

Exhibit 8.3 presents a perceptual map that shows a positioning map for soft drinks.

8-8b Positioning Bases

Firms use a variety of bases for positioning, including the following:

- **Attribute:** A product is associated with an attribute, a product feature, or a customer benefit. The new General Mills Cereal "Tiny Toast" is positioned around its look, which resembles "micro pieces of sugary toast." In the highly competitive cereal market, General Mills believes this feature is something unique and of interest to the target consumer.

- **Price and quality:** This positioning base may stress high price as a signal of quality or emphasize low price as an indication of value. Denmark-based Lego uses a high-price strategy for its toy building blocks, whereas Montreal-based Mega Bloks uses a low-price strategy.[23] Similarly, Walmart has successfully followed the low-price and value strategy. By purchasing Saks Fifth Avenue, HBC has ventured into the high-price, high-quality retail market, for that is how Saks is positioned in consumers' minds.

- **Use or application:** A company can stress a product's uses or applications as an effective means of positioning it with buyers. Snapple

| EXHIBIT 8.3 | PERCEPTUAL MAP AND POSITIONING STRATEGY FOR SOFT DRINKS |

Source: Perceptual Maps for Marketing, http://www.perceptualmaps.com/example-maps/.

introduced a new drink called Snapple-a-Day that is intended for use as a meal replacement.

- **Product user:** This positioning base focuses on a personality or type of user. In the highly regulated mobile phone market, where everyone markets on the basis of the same features—service, price, products, and networks—it is extremely hard to differentiate a brand. To stand apart and establish uniqueness in consumers' minds, Fido (owned by Rogers) launched a campaign to create a difference by associating Fido with the things that matter to Millennials. The Fido campaign is designed to build deeper connections with Millennials by encouraging people to think about what they love to do and how Fido can enable them to do it.[24]

- **Product class:** The objective here is to position the product as being associated with a particular category of products—for example, positioning a margarine brand with butter. Alternatively, products can be disassociated from a category.

- **Competitor:** Positioning against competitors is part of any positioning strategy. Apple positions the iPhone

perceptual mapping a means of displaying or graphing, in two or more dimensions, the location of products, brands, or groups of products in customers' minds

as cooler and more up-to-date than Windows-based smartphones, and Samsung positions the Galaxy series as cooler and more up-to-date than the iPhone.

- **Emotion:** Positioning that uses emotion focuses on how the product makes customers feel. A number of companies use this approach. For example, Reebok Canada's latest campaign is designed to pump up women with an empowerment-powered message, "Express Your Strong." The ads are based on the concept of what it means for women to be strong—whether that be physical strength or the strength to take on the many demands placed on them in their lives.

It is not unusual for a marketer to use more than one of these bases. In a campaign launched by McDonald's—is a Big Mac with Bacon #NotABigMac or #StillABigMac?—McDonald's is using the following bases:

- **Product attribute/benefit:** The addition of bacon to a Big Mac is a benefit for those who love bacon.

- **Product user:** The spot is based on an argument suggesting that those involved in the argument are loyal Big Mac consumers.

- **Emotion:** Again because the ads are based on an argument, there is clearly a strong emotional connection with the brand.

8-8c Repositioning

Sometimes products or companies are repositioned to sustain growth in slow markets or to correct positioning mistakes. **Repositioning** refers to changing consumers' perceptions of a brand in relation to competing brands.

For example, in its early years, the Hyundai brand was synonymous with cheap, low-quality cars. To reposition its brand, Hyundai redesigned its cars to be more contemporary looking and started a supportive warranty program. Consumer perceptions changed because customers appreciated the new designs and were reassured of the cars' performance by the generous warranties. Today, Hyundai's brand reputation has vastly improved.[25]

8-8d Developing a Positioning Statement

Segmenting, targeting, and positioning are key managerial activities that go beyond simply understanding the process of how to complete each task. Marketing managers often fail to develop and communicate effective positioning statements for their products/brands even though they might have developed effective market segments; thus they fail to state how the business will compete in a given market segment. A positioning statement is also critical for consumers to understand what specific benefits will they

obtain from a product. Tybout and Sterthal[26] provide guidelines for crafting a positioning statement:

1. **Targeted consumers:** Develop a brief statement of the target market in terms of their segment description.

2. **Frame of reference:** Develop a statement of the goal for the target market about the product benefit, thus identifying the consumption situations in which the product/brand is to be used.

3. **Point of difference:** Develop a statement asserting why the product/brand being offered is superior.

4. **Reason to believe:** Provide evidence to support the claim provided in the frame of reference.

Following is an excellent positioning statement from Black & Decker for its DeWalt power tools: "To the tradesman who uses his power tools to make a living and cannot afford downtime on the job [target], DeWalt professional power tools [frame of reference] are more dependable than other brands of professional power tools [point of difference] because they are engineered to the brand's historic high-quality standards and are backed by Black & Decker's extensive service network and guarantee to repair or replace any tool within 48 hours [reasons to believe]."[27]

> **repositioning** changing consumers' perceptions of a brand in relation to competing brands

SIDE LAUNCH
BREWING COMPANY
CONTINUING CASE

Hipsterville Calling

"We put our beer, at the beginning, into the right places, hitting the right people, to drink our beer and they liked it," recalls VP Sales and Marketing Chuck Galea about the early days of Side Launch in 2014. "In Toronto, what they call 'hipsterville,' our beer was reaching to those people's hands. And when that beer gets into someone's hands, and someone across the room sees them holding our can, they're like 'I want that, I'll give that a try. That looks interesting.'"

Chuck has as good a compass on the Side Launch target market as anyone at the brewery. Having spent decades in sales, most of it in beer sales, he is an astute observer of human behaviour and a captive audience member of how it plays out from day to day. This knowledge has been strategically siphoned toward a fairly accurate depiction of the typical Side Launch drinker—its target market. This is not to be confused with the craft beer segment, an exponentially growing number of people switching from big beer to craft. Just as every craft brewery attempts to differentiate based on a unique value proposition, it targets that offering at a specific type of consumer, whose frequency of use is hopefully large enough to make a profitable product. How a brand is perceived by both current and prospective consumers depends on its position. But while segmenting, targeting, and positioning are designed by the producer, it is sometimes the target market that describes the position.

"This year [2017] we're getting approached to sponsor all these music and arts [events] and showcases. I'm being told 'Wow, we really want Side Launch at our event, because you are a hip brand,'" Chuck says with a laugh. "It's funny because I would never picture ourselves as that." And yet it would seem to some of its target market that Side Launch is "hip," which can't be a bad thing.

Despite the theory that segmentation has four dimensions (geographic, demographic, psychographic, and behavioural), the only one that really matters at the end of the day is the one that segments people based on what they want—which is the behavioural dimension. What is the benefit Side Launch drinkers seek? "Craft beer drinkers want better tasting beer," says Chuck of the craft beer segment. "Side Launch drinkers, those in Ontario, want not only craft, but only local. They want to be engaged through grassroots communication. They want to know the story of the brewery and each beer. They're interested in food pairings and beer dinners, right? They're not in it

for a piss-up. To them, it's like wine . . . to be savoured and enjoyed and appreciated for the quality that goes into it."

But there's another aspect to the Side Launch target market that is not obvious, given the stereotype of a beer drinker. "This [Collingwood/Blue Mountain] area is incredibly active," explains Chuck. "It's Blue Mountains skiing and mountain biking, and camping or vacationing in cottage country with your boat . . . you know, hiking and cycling, and we have associated ourselves with active people as well." In its growing product mix of merchandise, Chuck points to high-end cycling apparel bearing the Side Launch branding. "I think to myself, who's going to spend [$150] on a cycling jacket or tights?" he says with a self-effacing smirk, acknowledging his larger-than-average-cyclist structure. (Chuck is a big man.) "But you know what, we can't keep them on the shelves. So we have successfully identified ourselves with that fit, health-conscious, active psychographic as well."

Questions

1. Do some online research on Toronto's "Hipsterville" and create a description of the segment frequenting this district, along all four segmentation dimensions (geographic, demographic, psychographic, and behavioural).

2. What is one of the needs Toronto area craft beer drinkers seek to fill that benefits Side Launch?

3. List some of the psychographic descriptors of the Side Launch target market.

Side Launch Brewing Company

9 | Customer Relationship Management (CRM)

"How you gather, manage and use information will determine whether you win or lose."

—Bill Gates[1]

9-1 WHAT IS CUSTOMER RELATIONSHIP MANAGEMENT?

Customer relationship management (CRM) is the evolution of the importance of relationships to marketing success. Both academics and practitioners began to realize in the 1990s that being able to harness the immense potential of close customer relationships would be essential in truly grasping the relationship between company and customer. CRM is tasked with identifying those profitable customers, finding ways to interact with them, with the goal of maximizing the value that is attributed to that customer relationship. As the concept of CRM has evolved over the past two decades, it has become a vital part of most companies' marketing activities. Any organization

customer relationship management (CRM) a system that gathers information about customers that can help to build customer loyalty and retain those loyal customers

with customers should strive to know them better, and CRM has provided the tools to do that. This is why CRM is now often seen simultaneously as a process to help improve relationships, a system involving working with people in the firm (employees) and the external customer, and CRM incorporates technological systems to manage those people and processes. It is clear from Bill Gates's statement at the start of this chapter, there is much to be gained by putting in the heavy lifting to create a CRM system.

If we go back to Chapter 1, you will recall that marketing is about meeting the needs of customers. To do this, you must learn more about your customer by doing research, learning about customers' behaviours, segmenting them, and delivering something of value (the four Ps) to them. In Chapter 5, we discussed how to conduct research to learn more about the customer. What is next is to bring those tools together into one focused objective. And that objective is customer relationship management. CRM is about building customer

loyalty and retaining those valued customers. It is about delivering on the promises made and establishing a system that will continue to deliver over time. To return to another concept we've looked at in this book, CRM is about *interaction* with your customer over the long term, not just tracking transactions over the short term.

This leads us to an important statement: CRM is not just about tracking customer information. If you were to do an Internet search for "customer relationship management," you might get the impression that CRM is about building a computer system that captures information about your customers. In fact, in the 1990s and early 2000s, companies created information systems that were referred to as "CRM systems." These systems were costly, and most firms could not find the value in using IT systems to create better customer relationships. Faith in IT-based CRM solutions wavered as sales of CRM systems were drastically reduced in the early 2000s. Some saw CRM as just "another overhyped IT investment."[2]

While IT is part of the development of a strong CRM program, information about customers is useless without knowing how to attract and keep those customers over the long term. In the end, the value is not how much you can squeeze out of each customer through a computer program—the value is in developing a customer who

will be investing in maintaining a mutually beneficial interaction.

9-1a The Other CRM

As mentioned, there is an emphasis in customer relationship management on the hardware and software needed to gather consumer information. In fact, this focus on database creation is another CRM abbreviation—customer relationship *marketing*.

The two CRMs have seemingly been melded together by most companies; however, it is important to understand the difference between the two. Customer relationship marketing is more focused on acquiring the necessary hardware and software to create a database or system to gather and track customer information. It references relationship marketing, the term used since the 1920s to describe the importance of close customer relationships. Customer relationship management is an overall company strategy that a firm employs to understand the needs of customers, keep updated on their needs, and satisfy them over the long term. The heavy emphasis on technology in customer relationship management is understandable given the goals of trying to track customers down to an individual level, but it is still important to remember that this process has to be managed and assessed.

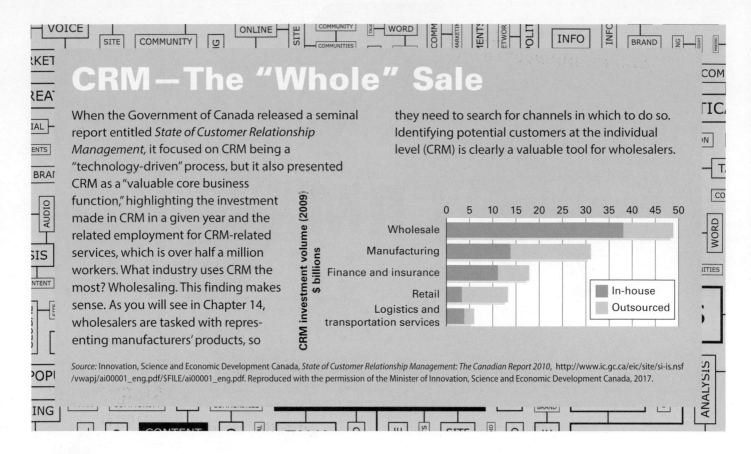

CRM—The "Whole" Sale

When the Government of Canada released a seminal report entitled *State of Customer Relationship Management,* it focused on CRM being a "technology-driven" process, but it also presented CRM as a "valuable core business function," highlighting the investment made in CRM in a given year and the related employment for CRM-related services, which is over half a million workers. What industry uses CRM the most? Wholesaling. This finding makes sense. As you will see in Chapter 14, wholesalers are tasked with representing manufacturers' products, so

they need to search for channels in which to do so. Identifying potential customers at the individual level (CRM) is clearly a valuable tool for wholesalers.

Source: Innovation, Science and Economic Development Canada, *State of Customer Relationship Management: The Canadian Report 2010,* http://www.ic.gc.ca/eic/site/si-is.nsf /vwapj/ai00001_eng.pdf/$FILE/ai00001_eng.pdf. Reproduced with the permission of the Minister of Innovation, Science and Economic Development Canada, 2017.

9-2 ## THE CRM CYCLE

In a report titled *State of Customer Relationship Management,* the Government of Canada presented a three-step CRM cycle: (1) marketing and market research, (2) business development, and (3) customer support (Exhibit 9.1). This comprehensive assessment of a CRM system was based on a seminal article in the Harvard Business Review on CRM, shortly after the downfall of IT-based CRM systems in the early 2000s.

CRM has often been described as a closed-loop system that builds relationships with customers. However, too often CRM has been reduced to a tool for selling software that promises to identify customers and provide information at a microscopic level. Little thought was given to using CRM as a tool to build long-term relationships with customers.

At its core, CRM is a relationship-building tool, and the sections that follow explain each stage of the CRM cycle. Stage 1 requires that companies understand what they have to offer to their customers and the marketing and market research tools that can help them use the four Ps. Stage 2 focuses on the use of technology to systematically identify customers, gather information on them, and store that information. Finally, in Stage 3 companies look at ways to use the information about customers to retain them in the long term by satisfying their needs.

Stage 2 of the CRM cycle includes many of the CRM tools and concepts a firm offering these types of solutions to companies would use. However, without an understanding of the context in Stage 1 and the ramifications of those CRM tools in Stage 3, CRM is a one-sided effort that lacks cooperation and inclusion of a most vital component—the customer.

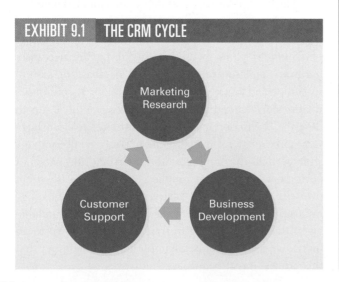

EXHIBIT 9.1 THE CRM CYCLE

9-3 THE CRM CYCLE—STAGE 1 (MARKETING RESEARCH)

During the first stage of creating a CRM system, companies must create an offering. This can be a product or service (or some combination of the two) that satisfies a customer need. Here is where marketing research can be helpful. As you recall from Chapter 5, conducting marketing research can help to identify customer needs, helping the marketer better understand the external marketplace where the company's offering will be sold.

Tools such as surveys, customer panels, and competitive intelligence are all helpful devices during this first stage for understanding the consumer and the marketplace. Product development and design (see Chapters 10 and 11) are also part of this initial stage, as companies develop ideas and concepts to prepare them for commercialization.

Companies should collect as much information as possible about the market and customer during this process. This will ensure that the offering supplied by the company reflects the current needs of customers. Companies can then make the right decisions about price (Chapter 13), place (Chapters 14 and 15), and promotion (Chapters 16 to 19) to provide an offering with the greatest opportunity for success in the marketplace.

Essentially, the first stage of developing a proper CRM system involves using the tools and techniques you have been learning about in the previous chapters. By creating an offering that reflects and satisfies customer needs, a company will develop a holistic CRM system. The data acquired through various IT methods (discussed in the section on Stage 2) will only be as useful as the marketing strategies created by a firm that truly understands what marketing is about.

An article in the *Journal of Marketing* identified the qualities necessary for an effective CRM program: "CRM provides enhanced opportunities to use data and information to both understand customers and co-create value with them. This requires a cross-functional integration of processes, people, operations, and marketing capabilities that is enabled through information, technology, and applications."[3] The article also provided a continuum of CRM programs similar to the one shown in Exhibit 9.2.

The continuum highlights the importance of developing a CRM system that not only is technology based but also considers strategy and marketing. By using what is known about marketing, from marketing research through to the four Ps, companies can establish the foundation for an effective CRM program. Once these foundations are created, the technology can be introduced. And that is what the second stage of the CRM cycle is all about.

9-4 THE CRM CYCLE—STAGE 2 (BUSINESS DEVELOPMENT)

Now that an offering has been developed that satisfies an identified customer need, the technology tools can be unleashed to seek out more detailed information on these customers. Exhibit 9.3 provides a flow model of the process of the technology stage of the CRM cycle.

To initiate Stage 2 of CRM cycle, a company must first *identify customer relationships with the organization.* This step may simply involve learning who the company's customers are or where they are located, or it may require more detailed information about the products and services these customers are using.

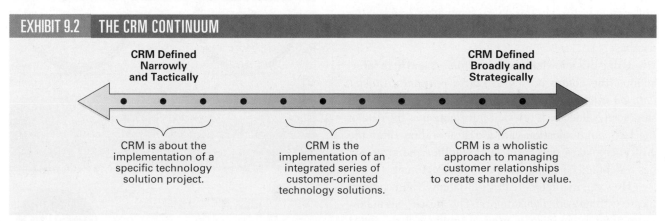

EXHIBIT 9.2 THE CRM CONTINUUM

CRM Defined Narrowly and Tactically ← → CRM Defined Broadly and Strategically

CRM is about the implementation of a specific technology solution project.

CRM is the implementation of an integrated series of customer-oriented technology solutions.

CRM is a wholistic approach to managing customer relationships to create shareholder value.

Source: Republished with permission of the American Marketing Association, from Adrian Payne, Pennie Frow (2005) A Strategic Framework for Customer Relationship Management. *Journal of Marketing*: October 2005, Vol. 69, No. 4, pp. 167–176; permission conveyed through Copyright Clearance Center, Inc.

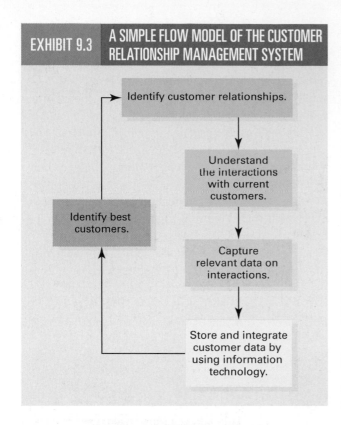

Bridgestone Canada Inc., a tire service company that produces Firestone tires, uses a CRM system called OnDemand5, which initially gathers data from a point-of-sale interaction.[4] The information includes basic demographic information, the frequency of consumers' purchases, how much they purchase, and how far they drive.

Next, the company must *understand its interactions with current customers*. Companies accomplish this task by collecting data on all types of communications a customer has with the company. Using its OnDemand5 system, Bridgestone Canada Inc. can add information that is based on additional interactions with the consumer, such as multiple visits to a physical store location and purchasing history. In this phase, companies build on the initial information collected and develop a more useful database.

Using this knowledge of its customers and their interactions, the company then *captures relevant customer data on interactions*. As an example, Bridgestone/Firestone can collect such relevant information as the date of the last communication with a customer, how often the customer makes purchases, and whether the customer has redeemed coupons sent through direct mail.

How can marketers realistically analyze and communicate with individual customers? The answer lies in how information technology is used to implement the CRM system. Fundamentally, a CRM approach is no more

than the relationship cultivated by a salesperson with the customer. A successful salesperson builds a relationship over time, constantly thinks about what the customer needs and wants, and is mindful of the trends and patterns in the customer's purchase history. The salesperson may also inform, educate, and instruct the customer about new products, technology, or applications in anticipation of the customer's future needs or requirements.

This kind of thoughtful attention is the basis of successful IT CRM flow systems. Information technology is used not only to enhance the collection of customer data but also to *store and integrate customer data* throughout the company and, ultimately, to get to know customers on a personal level. Customer data are the first-hand responses obtained from customers through investigation or by asking direct questions. These initial data, which might include individual answers to questionnaires, responses on warranty cards, or lists of purchases recorded by electronic cash registers, have not yet been analyzed or interpreted.

The value of customer data depends on the system that stores the data and the consistency and accuracy of the data captured. Obtaining high-quality, actionable data from various sources is a key element in any CRM system. Bridgestone Canada Inc. accomplishes this task by

managing all information in a central database accessible by marketers. Different kinds of database management software are available, from extremely high-tech, expensive, custom-designed databases to standardized programs.

Every customer wants to be a company's main priority, but not all customers are equally important in the eyes of a business. Consequently, the company must identify *its profitable and unprofitable customers*. The Pareto principle (mentioned in Chapter 8) indicates that 80 percent of a business's profit comes from 20 percent of its customers.

Data mining is an analytical process that compiles actionable data on the purchase habits of a firm's current and potential customers. Essentially, data mining transforms customer data into customer information that a company can use to make managerial decisions. Bridgestone Canada Inc. uses OnDemand5 to analyze its data to determine which customers qualify for the MasterCare Select program.

Once customer data are analyzed and transformed into usable information, the information must be *leveraged*. The CRM system sends the customer information to all areas of a business because the ultimate customer interacts with all aspects of the business. Essentially, the company is trying to enhance customer relationships by getting the right information to the right person in the right place at the right time.

Bridgestone Canada Inc. uses the information in its database to develop different marketing campaigns for each type of customer. Customers are also targeted with promotions aimed at increasing their store visits, upgrading their tires to higher-end models, and encouraging their purchases of additional services. Since the company customized its mailings to each type of customer, visits to stores have increased by more than 50 percent.[5]

9-4a Identify Customer Relationships

Companies that have a CRM system follow a customer-centric focus or model. Being **customer-centric** refers to an internal management philosophy similar to the marketing concept discussed in Chapter 1. Under this philosophy, the company customizes its product and service offerings based on data generated through interactions between the customer and the company. This philosophy transcends all functional areas of the business, producing an internal system where all of the company's decisions and actions are a direct result of customer information.

A customer-centric company builds long-lasting relationships by focusing on what satisfies and retains

charnsitr/Shutterstock.com

valuable customers. For example, Sony PlayStation's website (**www.playstation.ca**) focuses on learning, customer knowledge management, and empowerment to market its PlayStation gaming entertainment systems. The website offers online shopping, opportunities to try new games, customer support, and information on news, events, and promotions. The interactive features include online gaming and message boards.

The PlayStation site is designed to support Sony's CRM system. When PlayStation users want to access amenities on the site, they are required to log in and supply information, such as their name, email address, and birthdate. Users can opt to fill out a survey that asks questions about the types of computer entertainment systems they own, how many games are owned for each console, expected future game purchases, time spent playing games, types of games played, and level of Internet connectivity. Armed with this information, Sony marketers are then able to tailor the site, new games, and PlayStation hardware to the players' replies to the survey and their use of the website.[6]

Customer-centric companies continually learn ways to enhance their product and service offerings. **Learning** in a CRM environment involves the informal process of collecting customer information through comments and feedback on product and service performance.

Each unit of a business typically has its own way of recording what it learns and may even have its own customer information system. The departments' different interests make it difficult to pull all

data mining an analytical process that compiles actionable data on the purchase habits of a firm's current and potential customers

customer-centric a philosophy under which the company customizes its product and service offerings based on data generated through interactions between the customer and the company

learning (CRM) in a CRM environment, the informal process of collecting customer data through customer comments and feedback on product or service performance

the customer information together in one place using a common format. To overcome this problem, companies using CRM rely on **knowledge management**, a process by which learned information from customers is centralized and shared to enhance the relationship between customers and the organization. Information collected includes experiential observations, comments, customer actions, and qualitative facts about the customer.

Empowerment involves delegating authority to solve customers' problems quickly, usually by the first person who learns of the problem. In other words, **empowerment** is the latitude organizations give their representatives to negotiate mutually satisfying commitments with customers. Usually, organizational representatives are able to make changes during interactions with customers through email or by phone, or face to face.

An **interaction** occurs when a customer and a company representative exchange information and develop learning relationships. With CRM, the customer, and not the organization, defines the terms of the interaction, often by stating his or her preferences. The organization responds by designing products and services around customers' desired experiences. For example, students in Canada can purchase the Student Price Card, a loyalty card, for a nominal fee ($10) and use it to obtain discounts from affiliated retailers, such as Aldo, American Eagle Outfitters, Pink, and Forever 21.[7] Student Advantage tracks the cardholders' spending patterns and behaviours to gain a better understanding of what student customers want. Student Advantage then communicates this information to the affiliated retailers, who can tailor their discounts to meet students' needs.[8]

The success of CRM—building lasting and profitable relationships—can be directly measured by the effectiveness of the interaction between the customer and the organization. In fact, CRM is further differentiated from other strategic initiatives by the organization's ability to establish and manage interactions with its current customer base. The more latitude (empowerment) a company gives its representatives, the more likely the interaction will conclude in a way that satisfies the customer.

9-4b Understand Interactions of the Current Customer Base

The *interaction* between the customer and the organization is the foundation on which a CRM system is built. Only through effective interactions can organizations learn about the expectations of their customers, generate and manage knowledge about customers, negotiate mutually satisfying commitments, and build long-term relationships.

Exhibit 9.4 illustrates the customer-centric approach for managing customer interactions. Following a customer-centric approach, an interaction can occur through a formal or direct communication channel, such as a phone, the Internet, or a salesperson. Any activity or touch point a customer has with an organization, either directly or indirectly, constitutes an interaction.

knowledge management the process by which learned information from customers is centralized and shared for the purpose of enhancing the relationship between customers and the organization

empowerment delegation of authority to solve customers' problems quickly—usually by the first person who learns of the customer's problem

interaction the point at which a customer and a company representative exchange information and develop learning relationships

| EXHIBIT 9.4 | CUSTOMER-CENTRIC APPROACH FOR MANAGING CUSTOMER INTERACTIONS |

Current Transaction

Channel — Customer — Past Relationship

Requested Service

Image Source/Jupiterimages

© Cengage

Companies that effectively manage customer interactions recognize that customers provide data to the organization that affect a wide variety of touch points. In a CRM system, **touch points** are all possible areas of a business where customers have contact with that business and data might be gathered. Touch points might include a customer registering for a particular service; a customer communicating with customer service for product information; a customer making direct contact electronically via email or website visit; a customer completing and returning the warranty information card for a product; or a customer talking with salespeople, delivery personnel, and product installers. Data gathered at these touch points, once interpreted, provide information that affects touch points inside the company. Interpreted information may be redirected to marketing research to develop profiles of extended warranty purchasers; to production to analyze recurring problems and repair components; and to accounting to establish cost-control models for repair service calls.

Web-based interactions are an increasingly popular touch point for customers to communicate with companies on their own terms. Web users can evaluate and purchase products, make reservations, input preferential data, and provide customer feedback on services and products. Data from these Web-based interactions are then captured, compiled, and used to segment customers, refine marketing efforts, develop new products, and deliver a degree of individual customization to improve customer relationships.

Another touch point is **point-of-sale interactions,** communications between customers and organizations that occur at the point of sale, usually in a store but also at information kiosks. Many point-of-sale software packages enable customers to easily provide information about themselves without feeling violated. The information is then used in two ways: for marketing and merchandising activities, and for accurately identifying the store's best customers and the types of products they buy. Data collected at point-of-sale interactions are also used to increase customer satisfaction through the development of in-store services and customer recognition promotions.

9-4c Capture Customer Data

Vast amounts of data can be obtained from the interactions between an organization and its customers. Therefore, in a CRM system, the issue is not how much data can be obtained, but rather what types of data should be acquired and how the data can effectively be used for relationship enhancement.

The traditional approach for acquiring data from customers is through channel interactions. Channel interactions include store visits, conversations with salespeople, interactions via the Web, traditional phone conversations, and wireless communications. In a CRM system, channel interactions are viewed as prime information sources that are based on the channel selected to initiate the interaction rather than on the data acquired. For example, if a consumer logs on to the Sony website to find out why a Sony device is not functioning properly and the answer is not available online, the consumer is then referred to a page where he or she can describe the problem. The website then emails the problem description to a company representative, who will research the problem and reply via email. Sony continues to use the email mode of communication because the customer has established email as the preferred method of contact.[9]

Interactions between the company and the customer facilitate the collection of large amounts of data. Companies can obtain not only simple contact information (name, address, phone number) but also data pertaining to the customer's current relationship with the organization—past purchase history, quantity and frequency of purchases, average amount spent on purchases, sensitivity to promotional activities, and so forth.

In this manner, much information can be captured from one individual customer across several touch points. Multiply this information by the thousands of customers across

Point-of-sale interactions enable customers to provide information about themselves.

touch points all possible areas of a business where customers have contact with that business

point-of-sale interactions communications between customers and organizations that occur at the point of sale, usually in a store

all the touch points within an organization, and the volume of data that company personnel deal with can rapidly become unmanageable. The large volumes of data resulting from a CRM initiative can be managed effectively only through technology. Once customer data are collected, the question of who owns those data becomes extremely salient. In its privacy statement, Toysmart.com declared it would never sell information registered at its website, including children's names and birthdates, to a third party. However, when the company filed for bankruptcy protection in the United States, it said the information collected constituted a company asset that needed to be sold to pay creditors. Despite the outrage at this announcement, many companies closing their doors found they had little in the way of assets and followed Toysmart's lead. In Canada, the Personal Information Protection and Electronic Documents Act (PIPEDA), which deals with the protection of personal information, specifies only that disclosure must be made when third parties have access to personal information. PIPEDA does not address the selling of the information as a business asset (see the box for more information on PIPEDA).

PIPEDA—Perception of Privacy?

PIPEDA (the Personal Information Protection and Electronic Documents Act) is not a well-known acronym, but it is an important piece of legislation that affects all Canadians. Signed into law in 2001 with much fanfare, PIPEDA sets out the rules for companies on how they can use information customers supply when they buy something or enter a contest or other promotion. The act was brought in to deal with the ever-increasing volume of Canadians' personal information online. Through PIPEDA, you can request to see your personal information possessed by an organization with which you have had dealings, and even launch a complaint if a company violates the terms of PIPEDA. In 2013, the Office of the Privacy Commissioner (OPC) wrote a report that stated that most Canadian firms do not have the necessary tools to protect the personal information that falls under PIPEDA. The OPC noted that there is not enough enforcement and reporting of information breaches by companies, and it is pushing for legislation to strengthen PIPEDA. However, Parliament did not pass a bill in fall 2013 that would have required notification of a breach of personal information. In March 2016, yet another report from the Privacy Commissioner was published and noted in part, "We are left with 20th century tools to deal with 21st century problems. And in the meantime, 90 percent of Canadians feel

"OF COURSE I VALUE MY PRIVACY...THAT'S WHY I ONLY SHARE MY PERSONAL INFORMATION WITH 700 OF MY CLOSEST FRIENDS!"

they are losing control of their personal information and expect to be better protected."[10] Clearly, security of consumer information is a concern, however it seems that legislation is beginning to fall behind.

Sources: "A Guide for Individuals: Protecting Your Privacy: An Overview of the Office of the Privacy Commissioner of Canada and Federal Privacy Legislation," Office of the Privacy Commissioner of Canada, March 2014, www.priv.gc.ca/information/02_05_d_08_e.asp (accessed August 24, 2014); "The Case for Reforming the Personal Information Protection and Electronic Documents Act," Office of the Privacy Commissioner of Canada, May 2013, www.priv.gc.ca/parl/2013/pipeda_r_201305_e.asp (accessed August 24, 2014); Gonzalo S. Zeballos, James A. Sherer, and Alan M. Pate, "Canada: International Privacy—2013 Year in Review," Mondaq, January 6, 2014, www.mondaq.com/canada/x/284326/data+protection/International+Privacy+2013+Year+in+Review+Canada (accessed August 24, 2014); Office of the Privacy Commissioner of Canada, "2015–2016 Annual Report to Parliament on the Personal Information Protection and Electronic Documents Act and the Privacy Act," www.priv.gc.ca/en/opc-actions-and-decisions/reports-to-parliament/201516/ar_201516/ (accessed November 29, 2016).

9-4d Store and Integrate Customer Data

Customer data are only as valuable as the system in which they are stored and their consistency and accuracy. Gathering data is complicated because data needed by one unit of the organization, such as sales and marketing, are often generated by another area of the business or even a third-party supplier, such as an independent marketing research firm. Thus companies must use information technology to capture, store, and integrate strategically important customer information. This process of centralizing data in a CRM system is referred to as data warehousing.

A **data warehouse** is a central repository (*database*) of data collected by an organization. Essentially, it is a large computerized file of all information collected in the previous stage of the CRM process—for example, information collected in channel, transaction, and product or service touch points. The core of the data warehouse is the **database**, "a collection of data, especially one that can be accessed and manipulated by computer software."[11] The CRM database focuses on collecting vital statistics on consumers, their purchasing habits, transactions methods, and product usage in a centralized repository that is accessible by all functional areas of a company. By using a data warehouse, marketing managers can quickly access vast amounts of information to make decisions.

When a company builds its database, usually the first step is to develop a list. A **response list** is a customer list that includes the names and addresses of individuals who have responded to an offer of some kind, such as by mail, telephone, direct-response television, product rebates, contests or sweepstakes, or billing inserts. It can also be a compiled list, created by an outside company that has collected names and contact information for potential consumers. Response lists tend to be especially valuable because past behaviour is a strong predictor of future behaviour and because consumers who have indicated interest in the product or service are more likely to purchase in the future. **Compiled lists** usually are prepared by an outside company and are available for purchase. A compiled list is a customer list that was developed by gathering names and addresses gleaned from telephone directories or membership rosters, sometimes enhanced with information from public records, such as census data, auto registrations, birth announcements, business start-ups, or bankruptcies. Lists range from those owned by large list companies, such as Dun & Bradstreet, for business-to-business data, and Cornerstone Group of Companies, for consumer lists, to small groups or associations that are willing to sell their membership lists. Data compiled by large data-gathering companies are usually very accurate.

In this phase, companies are usually collecting channel, transaction, product, and service information, such as stores, salespersons, communication channels, contacts information, relationships, and brands.

A customer database becomes even more useful to marketing managers when it is enhanced to include more than simply a customer's or prospect's name, address, telephone number, and transaction history. Database enhancement involves purchasing information on customers or prospects to better describe their needs or to determine how responsive they might be to marketing programs. Enhancement data typically include demographic, lifestyle, or behavioural information.

Database enhancement can increase the effectiveness of marketing programs. By learning more about their best and most profitable customers, marketers can maximize the effectiveness of their marketing communications and cross-selling. Database enhancement also helps a company find new prospects.

Multinational companies building worldwide databases often face difficult problems when pulling together internal data about their customers. Differences in language, computer systems, and data-collection methods can be huge obstacles to overcome. In spite of the challenges, many global companies are committed to building databases. Bell Canada raised eyebrows in late 2013 with the announcement that Canada's largest telecommunications company would go mining for customer data. Specifically, Bell noted it would be tracking customer phone calls, app downloads, and television watching patterns. The reason? To create new profiles of customers that could then be used to entice advertisers with the opportunity to target specific Bell customers with promotional efforts. Then-privacy commissioner Jennifer Stoddart investigated Bell's move to see if it breached PIPEDA. In its defence, Bell noted it was following the lead of Google and

data warehouse a central repository of data from various functional areas of the organization that are stored and inventoried on a centralized computer system so that the information can be shared across all functional departments of the business

database an organized system of data collection that allows for assessment, usually by computer

response list a customer list that includes the names and addresses of individuals who have responded to an offer of some kind, such as by mail, telephone, direct-response television, product rebates, contests or sweepstakes, or billing inserts

compiled lists customer lists that are developed by gathering names and addresses gleaned from telephone directories and membership rosters, sometimes enhanced with information from public records, such as census data, auto registrations, birth announcements, business start-ups, or bankruptcies

iStock/Thinkstock

Facebook in gathering customer information and tailoring ads for those customers. The difference? Google and Facebook don't charge for their services. Bell did. Big data is a big sell to companies, but not respecting consumer privacy could lead to big trouble.[12]

9-4e Identifying the Best Customers

CRM manages interactions between a company and its customers. To be successful, companies need to identify those customers who yield high profits or high potential profits. To identify these customers, significant amounts of data must be gathered from customers, stored and integrated in the data warehouse, and then analyzed and interpreted for common patterns that can identify homogeneous customers who differ from other customer segments. Because not all customers are the same, organizations need to develop interactions that target the top 20 percent high-value customers' wants and needs. Therefore, the question becomes how to identify these customers. In a CRM system, the answer is data mining.

DATA MINING Data mining is used to find hidden patterns and relationships in the customer data stored in the data warehouse. A data analysis approach identifies patterns of characteristics that relate to particular customers or customer groups. Although businesses have been conducting such analyses for many years, the procedures typically were performed on small data sets containing as few as 300 to 400 customers. Today, with the development of sophisticated data warehouses, millions of customers' shopping patterns can be analyzed.

Using data mining, marketers can search the data warehouse, capture relevant data, categorize significant characteristics, and develop customer profiles. When using data mining, it is important to remember that the real value is in the company's ability to transform its data from operational bits and bytes into information marketers' need for successful marketing strategies.

Companies must analyze the data to identify and profile the best customers, calculate their lifetime value, and ultimately predict purchasing behaviour through statistical modelling. London Drugs uses data mining to identify commonly purchased items that should be displayed together on shelves and to learn what pop sells best in different parts of the country.

Before the information is leveraged, several types of analysis are often run on the data. These analyses include customer segmentation, recency-frequency-monetary (RFM) analysis, lifetime value (LTV) analysis, and predictive modelling.

Donating is uplifting.

centraide-mtl.org

Courtesy of Centraide of Greater Montreal

Much has been said about the privacy aspect of data mining and the potential impact on consumers and the security of their private information. But there are positive aspects of data mining, including helping nonprofit organizations. Manifold Data Mining, one of Canada's largest data-mining companies, has worked with nonprofit groups like the Red Cross and Centraide (United Way in Québec) to help them create more effective direct mail campaigns.

EXHIBIT 9.5 RFM ANALYSIS: ALL CUSTOMERS ARE NOT THE SAME

Best Customers	Average Customers	Poor Customers
High profit	Average profit	Low profit
Spent >$1500	Spent approximately $400	Spent <$100
Multiple purchases	Two purchases	One purchase
Purchase in past 6 months	Purchase in past 18 months	Purchase in past two years
Lifetime value = high	Lifetime value = average	Lifetime value = low
N = 2500 (18.5%)*	N = 4000 (29.6%)*	N = 7000 (51.9%)*
Total annual sales = $2.4 million	Total annual sales = $1.1 million	Total annual sales = $800,000

*N = number of customers in a category. The total number of customers is 13,500, and total annual sales are $4.3 million.

Source: From Lamb/Hair/McDaniel/Faria/Wellington. *Marketing*, 4E. © 2008 Nelson Education Ltd. Reproduced by permission. www.cengage.com/permissions.

CUSTOMER SEGMENTATION Recall that *customer segmentation* is the process of breaking large groups of customers into smaller, more homogeneous groups. This type of analysis generates a profile, or picture, of the customers' similar demographic, geographic, and psychographic traits, in addition to their previous purchase behaviour; it focuses particularly on the best customers. Profiles of the best customers can be compared and contrasted with other customer segments. For example, a bank can segment consumers on their frequency of usage, credit, age, and turnover.

Once a profile of the best customer is developed by using these criteria, this profile can be used to screen other potential consumers. Similarly, customer profiles can be used to introduce customers selectively to specific marketing actions. For example, young customers with an open mind can be introduced to online banking. See Chapter 8 for a detailed discussion of segmentation.

RECENCY-FREQUENCY-MONETARY(RFM)ANALYSIS
Recency-frequency-monetary (RFM) analysis allows firms to identify customers who have purchased recently and often and who have spent considerable money, because they are most likely to purchase again (see Exhibit 9.5). Firms develop equations to identify their best customers (often the top 20 percent of the customer base) by assigning a score to their customer records in the database based on how often, how recently, and how much customers have spent. Customers are then ranked to determine which will move to the top of the list and which will fall to the bottom. The ranking provides the basis for maximizing profits by enabling the firm to use the information to select those persons who have proved to be good sources of revenue.

LIFETIME VALUE (LTV) ANALYSIS Recency, frequency, and monetary data can also be used to create a lifetime value model on customers in the database. Whereas RFM looks at how valuable a customer currently is to a company, **lifetime value (LTV) analysis** projects the future value of the customer over a period of years. An example of LTV for a female 20 to 30 years old who has her hair done four times a year at an average cost of $120 per visit, given data-mined information of an average typical patronage life of five years, is $2400 ($120/visit × 4 visits/year × 5 years). One of the basic assumptions in any LTV calculation is that marketing to repeat customers is more profitable than marketing to first-time buyers. That is, it costs more to find a new customer, in terms of promotion and gaining trust, than to sell more to a customer who is already loyal.

Customer lifetime value has numerous benefits. It shows marketers how much they can spend to *acquire* new customers, it tells them the level of spending to *retain* customers, and it facilitates targeting new customers who are identified as likely to be profitable. While these are strong benefits, LTV can be problematic if companies treat customers like the numbers that appear on the screen. While keeping customers is a noble goal, the reasons should go beyond the numbers, and companies should remember that they need specific systems in place (e.g., customer satisfaction measurement) to maintain a relationship over time.

> **recency-frequency-monetary (RFM) analysis** the analysis of customer activity by recency, frequency, and monetary value
>
> **lifetime value (LTV) analysis** a data manipulation technique that projects the future value of the customer over a period of years by using the assumption that marketing to repeat customers is more profitable than marketing to first-time buyers

CHAPTER 9: Customer Relationship Management (CRM)

PREDICTIVE MODELLING The ability to reasonably predict future customer behaviour gives marketers a significant competitive advantage. Through **predictive modelling**, a data manipulation technique, marketers try to determine, using a past set of occurrences, the odds that some other occurrence, such as an inquiry or a purchase, will take place in the future. SPSS Predictive Marketing is one tool marketers can use to answer questions about their consumers. The software requires minimal knowledge of statistical analysis. Users operate from a prebuilt model, which generates profiles in three to four days. SPSS also has an online product that predicts website users' behaviour.

9-5 THE CRM CYCLE—STAGE 3 (CUSTOMER FEEDBACK)

As is clear from Stage 2 of the CRM cycle, technology is an important driver of a successful CRM system. However, an overreliance on technology and data down to the individual customer level can lead to companies losing sight of the real goal of customer relationship management—maintaining long-term relationships with those who buy the products and services.

As long as firms can see CRM as a means to build a relationship with customers, and not as a sales tool or technology solution, they will see the need to complete the cycle. This is done by implementing measures of customer satisfaction to establish whether what the firm is doing is meeting the needs of those customers.

In the *MIT Sloan Management Review*, an article entitled "Putting the 'Relationship' Back into CRM" highlighted some of the concerns over how firms use CRM. The authors came up with three ways the current practice of CRM is failing companies:[13]

1. CRM programs focus too much on transactions and not on other aspects of the customer's life.

2. Relationships cannot be solely about achieving loyalty, and companies need to find multiple ways to retain their customers.

3. A relationship is dynamic and two sided. It is not enough to get a list of customers and their spending habits. The relationship will evolve with each transaction, and CRM systems must as well.

This third concern is the most serious. If marketing is about understanding and meeting customer needs, it is important to appreciate that those needs and how to meet them will change over time. Any relationship (whether it's between a business and a consumer, a business and another business, or even between family members) involves a series of interactions. The relationship builds over time with more of these interactions. The needs of both parties change, and the other party has to be willing to adjust to those changes to be successful. Companies that ignore this do so at their own peril.

To create a two-sided relationship that focuses on more than just loyalty, companies must leverage the customer information they have gathered. While there is an adage that states keeping an existing customer is cheaper than finding a new customer, a CRM system has to have the ability to move beyond just finding those loyal customers. A company can undertake to best leverage the information gathered through the database and IT solutions from Stage 2. Some of the benefits that can be gained by gathering this information can be seen in Exhibit 9.6.

9-5a Leverage Customer Information

Data mining identifies the most profitable customers and prospects. Managers can then design tailored marketing strategies to best appeal to the identified segments. In CRM, this activity is commonly referred to as leveraging customer information to facilitate enhanced relationships with customers.

CAMPAIGN MANAGEMENT Through campaign management, all areas of the company participate in the development of programs targeted to customers. **Campaign management** refers to developing product or service offerings customized for the appropriate customer segment and then pricing and communicating these offerings to enhance customer relationships. It involves monitoring and leveraging customer interactions to sell a company's products and to improve customer service. Campaigns are based directly on data obtained from customers through various interactions. Campaign management includes monitoring the success of the communications on the basis of customer reactions, such as customer inquiries, sales, orders, callbacks to the company, and the like. If a campaign

---

predictive modelling a data manipulation technique in which marketers try to determine, based on some past set of occurrences, the odds that some other occurrence, such as an inquiry or a purchase, will take place in the future

campaign management developing product or service offerings customized for the appropriate customer segment and then pricing and communicating these offerings to enhance customer relationships

EXHIBIT 9.6 | COMMON CRM MARKETING DATABASE APPLICATIONS

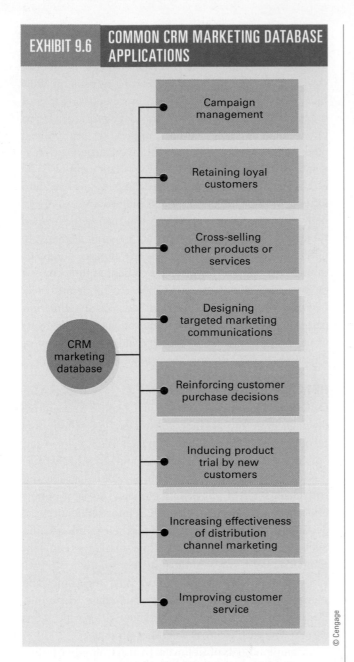

© Cengage

appears unsuccessful, it is evaluated and changed to better achieve the company's desired objective.

Campaign management involves customizing product and service offerings, which requires managing multiple interactions with customers and giving priority to those products and services that are viewed as most desirable for a specifically designated customer. Even within a highly defined market segment, individual customer differences will emerge. Therefore, interactions among customers must focus on individual experiences, expectations, and desires.

RETAINING LOYAL CUSTOMERS After a company has identified its best customers, it should make every effort to maintain and increase their loyalty. Loyalty programs reward loyal customers for making multiple purchases. The objective is to build long-term mutually beneficial relationships between a company and its key customers. Marriott, Hilton, and Starwood Hotels, for instance, reward their best customers with special perks not available to customers who stay less frequently. Travellers who spend a specified number of nights per year receive reservation guarantees, welcome gifts such as fruit baskets and wine in their rooms, and access to concierge lounges. Loyal members who sign up to collect points can use their accumulated points to receive discounts at hotels in exotic locations, free nights, free flights, and reduced rates on car rentals.

In addition to rewarding good customers, loyalty programs provide businesses with a wealth of information about their customers and shopping trends that can be used to make future business decisions. A yearly report released by Canadian-based Bond Brand Loyalty examines the most critical factors to success for loyalty programs. It asks for information from more than 19,000 North American consumers and assesses more than 280 programs in order to develop data on the success factors in the loyalty reward program business. The top drivers of loyalty program satisfaction are fit with the brand, meets customers' needs, enjoyment level of being part of the program, effort level needed to earn a redemption, and ease of redemption.[14] The report also highlights some concerning trends for loyalty programs among Canadians: only 22 percent of customers found the loyalty programs trustworthy.[15] And what made a trustworthy and strong loyalty program? It came down to personal interaction. Customers who felt there was an attempt to personalize their loyalty reward program were much more likely to be satisfied or very satisfied with the program.

The report also ranked the top (and bottom) loyalty programs in Canada. Before you look at the list in Exhibit 9.7, what would your experiences with loyalty programs tell you about good and bad loyalty programs? The categories are retail, grocery and drug store, quick service restaurants (QSR), coalition (multiple businesses), consumer packaged goods (CPG), and co-branded debit (two firms joining together).

CROSS-SELLING OTHER PRODUCTS AND SERVICES CRM provides many opportunities to cross-sell related products. Marketers can use the database to match product profiles with consumer profiles, enabling the cross-selling of products that match

EXHIBIT 9.7	THE TOP- AND BOTTOM-RANKED LOYALTY PROGRAMS IN CANADA

Top-Ranked Programs

Top Retail Loyalty Program: **Canadian Tire**

Top Grocery/Drug Store: **Shoppers Drug Mart**

Top Quick Service Restaurant: **Starbucks**

Top Coalition: **Air Miles**

Top Consumer Packaged Goods: **Johnson & Johnson Healthy Essentials**

Top Co-Branded Debit: **President's Choice's PC Financial Debit Card**

Bottom-Ranked Programs

Bottom Retail Loyalty Program: **TJX (Homesense, Winners)**

Bottom Grocery/Drug Store: **Longo's**

Bottom Quick Service Restaurant: **Pizza Pizza**

Bottom Coalition: **Aeroplan**

Bottom Consumer Packaged Goods: **Huggies Rewards**

Bottom Co-Branded Debit: **BMO Air Miles Debit Card**

Source: Megan Haynes, "Loyalty Cards: Where's the Love?", *Strategy*, June 8, 2016, http://strategyonline.ca/2016/06/08/loyalty-cards-wheres-the-love.

consumers' demographic, lifestyle, or behavioural characteristics. Ingersoll Rand, a global manufacturer of everything from air compressors to refrigeration units, saw the benefits of cross-selling. One of Ingersoll Rand's business units, Club Car, sells golf carts. The company soon found out that Club Car's customers were also potential customers in other areas, such as for excavators and loaders. Ingersoll Rand began to share information about customers across all of the more than 30 business units of the organization. In the first year of doing this, Ingersoll Rand brought in $6.2 million in incremental cross-selling revenue.[16]

Online firms use product and customer profiling to reveal cross-selling opportunities while a customer is surfing their site. Past purchases on a particular website and the website a surfer comes from provide online marketers with clues about the surfer's interests and what items to cross-sell. Similarly, profiles on customers enable sales representatives or customer service people to personalize their communications while the customer is shopping. Knowing a customer's past purchases and preferences can enable the employee to provide more advice or suggestions that fit with the customer's tastes.

DESIGNING TARGETED MARKETING COMMUNICATIONS By using transaction and purchase data, a database allows marketers to track customers' relationships to the company's products and services and to then modify their marketing message accordingly. By creating this database, companies can answer a question that would

seem at first to be an obvious one: "How many customers do we have?" But it is surprising how many companies focus on units sold or other metrics. Once the number of customers is determined, there can be a focus on "how much"—as in, how much are your customers worth to your brand? Transaction and purchase data provide insights into average purchase volume, purchase by location, and other factors. Once these records are organized in a clear database, a firm can get on to the important focus of "Who is our customer?" Customers can also be segmented into infrequent users, moderate users, and heavy users. A segmented communications strategy can then be developed to target the customer segment. Communications to infrequent users might encourage repeat purchases through a direct incentive, such as a limited-time coupon or price discount. Communications to moderate users may use fewer incentives and more reinforcement of their past purchase decisions. Communications to heavy users would be designed around loyalty and reinforcement of the purchase rather than price promotions.

REINFORCING CUSTOMER PURCHASE DECISIONS As you learned in Chapter 6, cognitive dissonance is the feeling consumers get when they recognize an inconsistency between their values and opinions and their purchase behaviour. In other words, they doubt the soundness of their purchase decision and feel anxious. CRM offers marketers an excellent opportunity to reach out to customers to reinforce the purchase decision. By thanking customers for their purchases and telling customers they are important, marketers can help cement a long-term, profitable relationship.

Updating customers periodically regarding the status of their order reinforces purchase decisions. Postsale emails also afford the chance to provide more customer service or cross-sell other products.

Campion Boats of Kelowna, British Columbia, builds custom pleasure and recreational sport fishing boats that can cost upward of $200,000 each. The company uses its website to monitor customer profiles, broadcast company information, and communicate with its dealers and customers worldwide. For example, it can post pictures of a purchaser's boat in progress, thus both reinforcing the buyer's decision and perception of the quality of the craftsmanship and reducing the customer's likelihood of having feelings of cognitive dissonance.[17]

INDUCING PRODUCT TRIAL BY NEW CUSTOMERS Although significant time and money are expended on encouraging repeat purchases by the best customers, a marketing database is also used to identify new customers. Because a firm using a marketing database already has a profile of its best customers, it can easily use the results of modelling to profile potential customers. Bell Canada uses modelling to identify prospective residential and commercial telephone customers and successfully attract their business.

Marketing managers generally use demographic and behavioural data overlaid on existing customer data to develop a detailed customer profile that is a powerful tool for evaluating lists of prospects. For instance, if a firm's best customers are 35 to 50 years of age, live in suburban areas, and enjoy mountain climbing, the company can match this profile to prospects already in its database or to customers currently identified as using a competitor's product.

INCREASING EFFECTIVENESS OF DISTRIBUTION CHANNEL MARKETING A marketing channel is a business structure of interdependent organizations, such as wholesalers and retailers, which move a product from the producer to the ultimate consumer (you will read more about this in Chapter 14). Most marketers rely on indirect channels to move their products to the end user. Thus marketers often lose touch with customers as individuals because the relationship is really between the retailer and the consumers. Marketers in this predicament often view their customers as aggregate statistics because specific customer information is difficult to gather.

Using CRM databases, manufacturers now have a tool to gain insight into who is buying their products. Instead of simply unloading products into the distribution channel and leaving marketing and relationship building to dealers, auto manufacturers today are using websites to keep in touch with customers and prospects, to learn about their lifestyles and hobbies, to understand their vehicle needs, and to develop relationships in hopes these consumers will reward them with brand loyalty in the future. BMW and other vehicle manufacturers have databases filled with contact information on the millions of consumers who have expressed an interest in their products.

With many bricks-and-mortar stores setting up shop online, companies are now challenged to monitor the purchases of customers who shop both in-store and online. This concept is referred to as multichannel marketing. After Lands' End determined that multichannel customers are the most valuable, the company targeted marketing campaigns toward retaining these customers and increased sales significantly.

Companies are also using radio-frequency identification (RFID) technology to improve distribution. This technology uses a microchip with an antenna that tracks anything from a pop can to a car. A computer can locate the product usually within two metres of a scanner but new technology and applications can, in

Olay, a brand of Procter & Gamble, invites customers to join Club Olay, which offers special discounts, free samples, and the opportunity to purchase products before they are available in stores. But members are also able to communicate with the company by sharing their beauty secrets and entering various sweepstakes.

some situations, enable detection up to 20 metres. The main implication of this technology is that companies will enjoy a reduction both in theft and in loss of merchandise shipments and will always know where merchandise is in the distribution channel. Moreover, as this technology is further developed, marketers will be able to gather essential information related to product usage and consumption.[18]

IMPROVING CUSTOMER SERVICE CRM marketing techniques are increasingly being used to improve customer service. Many companies are using information and training webinars for their product or service to make personal contact with interested customers. Those interested in a topic are asked to register and provide a bit of information about themselves and their company's needs. Before or immediately after the webinar, a representative will contact them to answer questions and provide further information. Other companies, such as Canadian Tire, follow up customers' visits to the store with a call and a short survey to determine each customer's level of service satisfaction and whether any additional service is needed.

9-6 PRIVACY CONCERNS AND CRM

Before rushing out to invest in a CRM system and build a database, marketers should consider consumers' reactions to the growing use of databases. Many customers are concerned about databases because of the potential for invasion of privacy. The sheer volume of information that is aggregated in databases makes this information vulnerable to unauthorized access and use. A fundamental aspect of marketing using CRM databases is providing valuable services to customers based on knowledge of what customers really value. It is critical, however, that marketers remember that these relationships should be built on trust. Although database technology enables marketers to compile ever-richer information about their customers that can be used to build and manage relationships, if these customers feel their privacy is being violated, then the relationship becomes a liability.

The popularity of the Internet for customer data collection and as a repository for sensitive customer data has alarmed privacy-minded customers. Online users complain loudly about being spammed, and Web surfers, including children, are routinely asked to divulge personal information to access certain screens or to purchase goods or services. Internet users are disturbed by the amount of information businesses collect on them as they visit various sites in cyberspace. Indeed, many users are unaware of how personal information is collected, used, and distributed. The government actively sells huge amounts of personal information to list companies. Consumer credit databases are often used by credit-card marketers to prescreen targets for solicitations. Online and off-line privacy concerns are growing and ultimately will have to be dealt with by businesses and regulators.

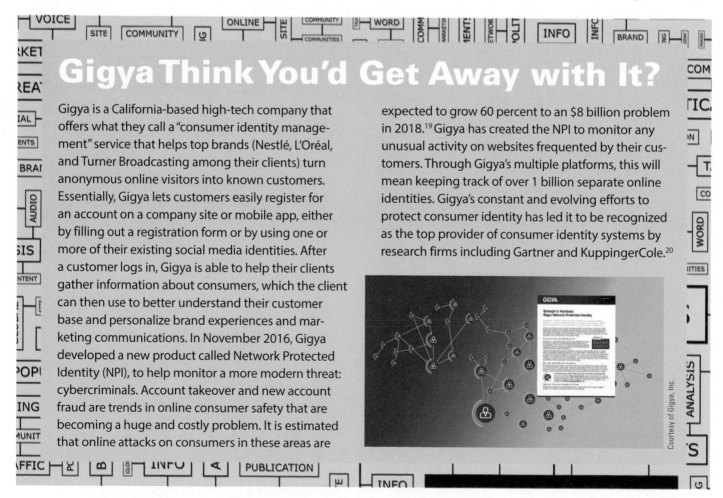

Gigya Think You'd Get Away with It?

Gigya is a California-based high-tech company that offers what they call a "consumer identity management" service that helps top brands (Nestlé, L'Oréal, and Turner Broadcasting among their clients) turn anonymous online visitors into known customers. Essentially, Gigya lets customers easily register for an account on a company site or mobile app, either by filling out a registration form or by using one or more of their existing social media identities. After a customer logs in, Gigya is able to help their clients gather information about consumers, which the client can then use to better understand their customer base and personalize brand experiences and marketing communications. In November 2016, Gigya developed a new product called Network Protected Identity (NPI), to help monitor a more modern threat: cybercriminals. Account takeover and new account fraud are trends in online consumer safety that are becoming a huge and costly problem. It is estimated that online attacks on consumers in these areas are expected to grow 60 percent to an $8 billion problem in 2018.[19] Gigya has created the NPI to monitor any unusual activity on websites frequented by their customers. Through Gigya's multiple platforms, this will mean keeping track of over 1 billion separate online identities. Gigya's constant and evolving efforts to protect consumer identity has led it to be recognized as the top provider of consumer identity systems by research firms including Gartner and KuppingerCole.[20]

Courtesy of Gigya, Inc.

NEL

As we have discussed, privacy policies for Canadian companies are regulated by PIPEDA and the Privacy Act. But collecting data on consumers outside Canada is a different matter. For database marketers venturing beyond our borders, success requires careful navigation of foreign privacy laws. For example, under the European Union's European Data Protection Directive, any business that trades with a European organization must comply with the EU's rules for handling information about individuals or risk prosecution. More than 50 nations have developed, or are developing, privacy legislation. The EU nations have the strictest legislation regarding the collection and use of customer data, and other countries look to that legislation when formulating their policies.

9-7 THE FUTURE OF CRM

Some think CRM as it exists now will soon be obsolete. A recent article in the *Harvard Business Review* stated, "CRM isn't dead (yet), but (users) will cease to use it unless it can get smart and save them time, rather than burden them with time-intensive data entry and lookup."[21] So while technology has been an important part of the growth and success of customer relationship management, continued use of the newest and best technologies will be vital to CRM maintaining its relevance. Other than the introduction of cloud storage systems to keep track of data (like customer loyalty information), technological innovations have escaped the CRM world.

While the CRM systems that have been described in this chapter do help to create efficiencies for organizations, there is greater concern as to the amount of time needed to input data into these systems and manage the information that comes out. Research shows that sales representatives are spending less time actually selling, and more time on what are deemed "administrative" tasks that often include the upkeep and management of the CRM systems.

And to solve this problem, it seems that more technology would not be the answer. However, there is a movement in CRM toward customer relationship automation, given the pressures of continuous improvement in organizations and the prevalence of predictive technologies and relational databases. This is best exemplified by Amazon's highly sophisticated technologies related to CRM. Anyone who has an Amazon account is often mystified by how well Amazon can track your preferences by your search history and previous purchases.

Although popular culture provides us with many cautionary tales, allowing machines to "take over" might

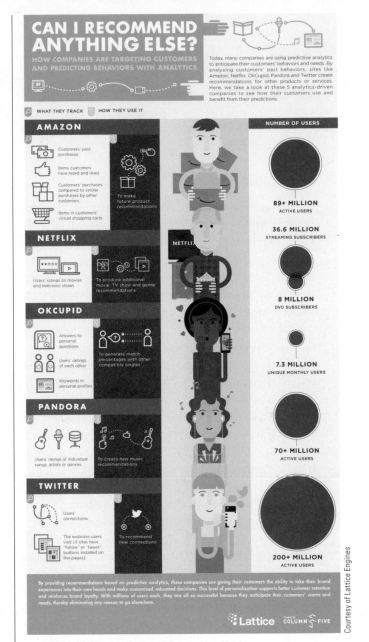

Courtesy of Lattice Engines

not be a bad idea when it comes to CRM. As interactions with customers become more focused in the digital world (e.g., social media, email, text), predictive data analytics similar to Amazon's could be used to offer insights to companies and their sales reps into not only what customers are doing, but what they are *thinking*. This is an attempt to get more personal in an increasingly impersonal world, but the future of CRM does not lie in simply tracking metrics like sales. It lies in the ability of companies to use technology and machines to help predict what consumers might do. The future of CRM rests on the ability of firms to reengineer what has been done in the past and take a more engaged approach at truly investing in the relationship with the customer.

SIDE LAUNCH
BREWING COMPANY
CONTINUING CASE

Side Launch Brewing Company

CSR in on Board

Breweries big and small, like so many other consumer goods companies, essentially have two target markets. Their business customers (B2B) and their product consumers (B2C). However, apart from its onsite retail store, offering up perfectly chilled cans of each of its beer products and an impressive array of branded merchandise, Side Launch must reach the consumer through its retail customers—its B2B partners. Conversely, those retailers rely on Side Launch and hundreds of other producers to stock their shelves and fill their keg taps. Despite this interdependency, the onus is usually on the producer, rather than the retailer, to initiate, cultivate, and manage the relationship. For Side Launch, a relatively large craft brewer by Canadian standards but dwarfed by macro brewers, "Our job one is to get our beer into people's hands," claims Chuck Galea, VP Sales and Marketing. A closely high-ranking priority, however, is to make sure those responsible for literally getting beer into consumers' hands, the retailers, are happy.

But Chuck has come up with an innovative sales/operations design to help accomplish both of these at once. "We don't call our delivery guys truck drivers." Chuck states. "They're customer service representatives, and they report to me rather than operations or distribution." Sure enough, the four truck drivers who depart from the loading dock in the back of 200 Mountain Road, Collingwood, all have bestowed upon them the title of CSR. But it's more than just a title. "Whenever there's a new product released, they (truck drivers, er, Customer Service Reps) get the same email as the account managers. They're part of the sales team and need to know the sales story. Who we're selling it to, how much we're selling it for, what it tastes like, what we're going to be doing to support it . . . they're all part of that culture."

The communication process works in the opposite direction as well. "If one of our guys is at a bar and they're in a keg fridge delivering a keg and a customer says, 'Hey by the way, do you know if you guys have any new seasonals?' our drivers can say, 'I do, as a matter of fact,' and they can start telling the story, then alert the sales rep of the opportunity."

It is easy to see the logic in this as Chuck contrasts the old way of thinking—drivers reporting to operations—to the Side Launch way. He recalls near fistfights between sales and truck drivers in a previous job with a different brewer and chalks it all up to a different culture. "Our drivers buy in

to the overall objective. They also know that this is a way for them to get in at the ground level and potentially grow into more of an actual sales role. Plus, we pay our drivers well—above what the industry average is for craft brewers."

The truck driver CSR is a most unconventional concept as part of a customer relationship management program, and yet the fluidity of communication between Side Launch and its customers is more efficient—and customers are more appreciative.

Questions

1. How does the Side Launch decision to make its truck drivers customer service reps demonstrate a customer-centric corporate philosophy?

2. How does including truck drivers in new product information fall into the first stage of the CRM cycle?

3. When bar managers ask a Side Launch truck driver to inform them of new seasonal beers, they are integrating themselves into the CRM loop by providing feedback. How do the truck drivers then leverage those inquiries into useful customer information?

Side Launch Brewing Company

Part 2 Case
Marketing Concept Review

Halfway There

You are about halfway through this book. It's not time to breathe, but rather to look back. This case is all about seeing how well you can apply the material you have learned so far. You have covered everything from the definition of marketing to the key elements of a customer relationship management program.

This is a do-it-yourself (DIY) case where you are asked to make decisions based on the material the textbook has covered so far. This is a case where you do some of the work while reading the case, and you build the pieces you will then use to help solve the case. This case should provide you with a good indication of how well you have understood the material so far. And since much about marketing is dependent on how well you can apply concepts, this case provides a good context for your understanding of marketing.

You will be given a scenario to follow. You will need to review the material from your text, along with undertaking some online research as well. You will look back at important concepts from each of the chapters so far (Chapters 1 through 9), and you will be tasked with applying the concepts you have read about.

Your first task is to choose one of your favourite products. It could be a device (e.g., Apple iPad) or a consumer good you use every day (e.g., Gillette razor). Refrain from using a service (e.g., Cineplex movie theatre) as the service concept will be taught to you in Chapter 12.

Write the name of the product here: _____
_____

CHAPTER 1 CONCEPT APPLICATION

Describe how the product you chose would be dealt with using each of the following Orientations of Marketing:

1. Production Orientation
2. Sales Orientation
3. Marketing Company Orientation
4. Societal Orientation

CHAPTER 2 CONCEPT APPLICATION

In order to better understand how your chosen product is dealing with the external environment, you are tasked with coming up with the top three trends you believe have the greatest impact on your chosen product. You will need to provide sources in order to support each of the trends. One source can be from the Internet; the other source has to come from a database at your school:

Trend 1: _____

_____

(Internet source: _____)

Trend 1: _____

_____

(Database source: _____)

Trend 2: _____

_____

(Internet source: _____)

Trend 2: _____

_____

(Database source: _____)

Trend 3: _____

_____

(Internet source: _____)

Trend 3: _____

_____

(Database source: _____ **)**

CHAPTER 3 CONCEPT APPLICATION

A vital tool for anyone interested in marketing is the SWOT analysis. In your Chapter 2 review, you would have found three external trends that had an impact on your chosen product. You have learned that in the opportunities and threats in a SWOT, that is exactly what you would need to use in order to fill out those parts of the model.

Conduct some research on your product in order to fill in the Strengths and Weaknesses. Be sure to look for sources that do not originate from the company behind your product or service. It is important to get a balanced assessment of where the company stands as part of your SWOT analysis.

Fill out the following SWOT matrix with two well-explained points under each heading:

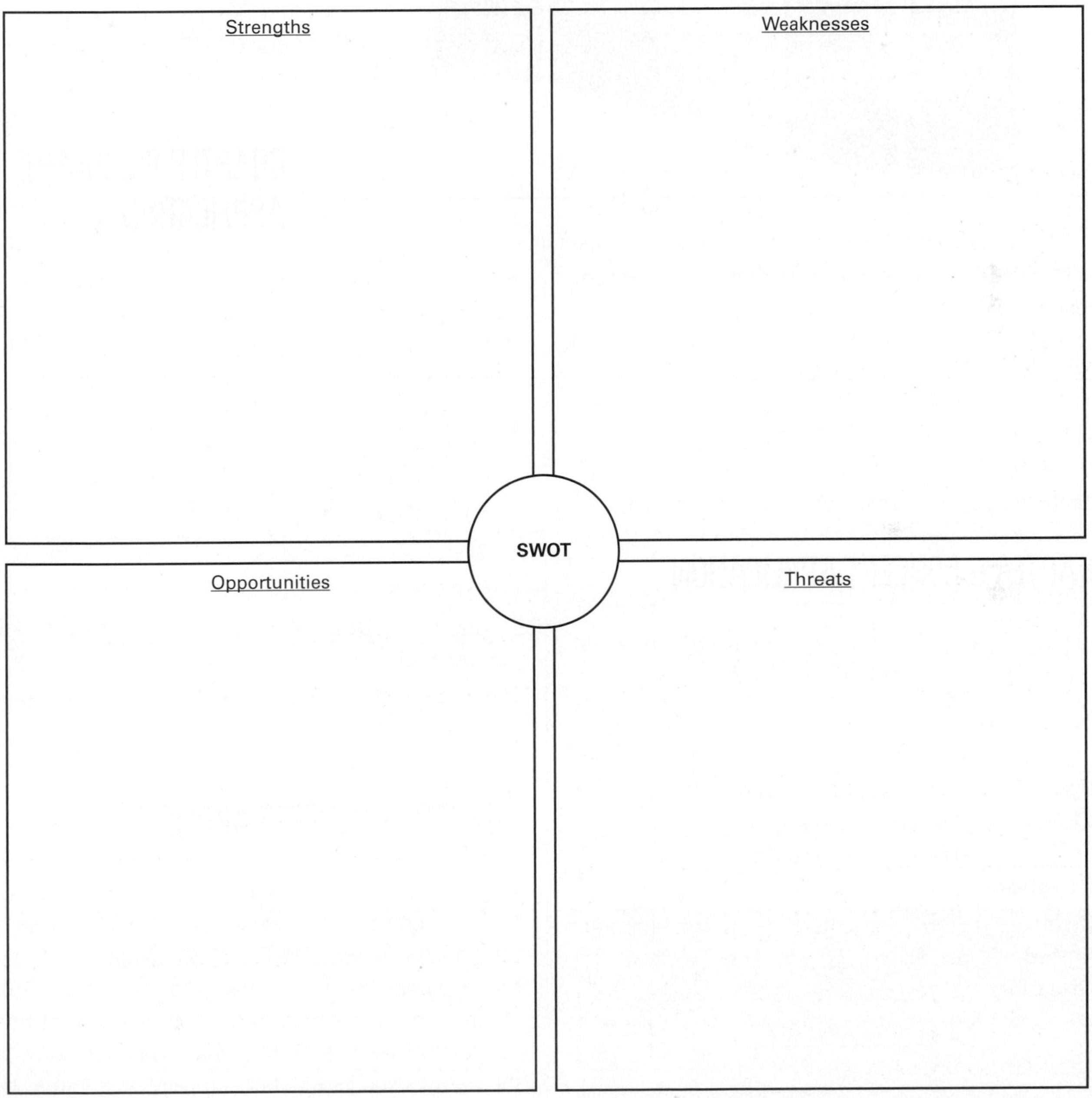

Strengths	Weaknesses

SWOT

Opportunities	Threats

CHAPTER 4 CONCEPT APPLICATION

Your external focus from the Opportunities and Threats from a SWOT become even broader when applying concepts from this chapter. Your chosen product is more than likely made available in more countries than just Canada.

Use Exhibit 4.4 from page 60 of your text:

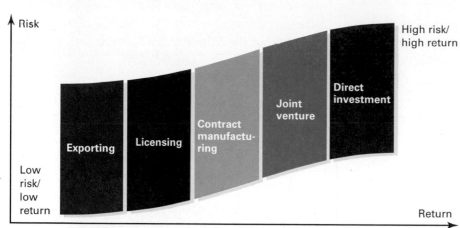

Choose two of the methods described above and write a brief memo on how you would recommend the company offering your chosen product could enter into a new market. Your new market would be one of the countries in the G20 (see Chapter 4) where your product is not available.

The memo should be brief and should be addressed to a member of the leadership team from your chosen company. You will need to conduct research online for your chosen country and on how to write a proper business memo.

CHAPTER 5 CONCEPT APPLICATION

You have likely noticed by now that you are being asked to conduct research for this case. So far you have been looking at secondary research, which already has been

	Reason For
Closed Ended Question	How would you rate Product X on …. (1= poor, 5= excellent) 1 2 3 4 5
Open Ended Question	When you remember the last time you bought a _____, describe how you…? _____ _____ _____ _____ _____

collected for another purpose and already exists in some format.

Your application of concepts in Chapter 5 is focused on primary research. Specifically, you are going to create a short survey for your chosen product. You will assume that you have been given the go-a-head from the leader you addressed the memo to in the previous section, and now you are being asked to create a questionnaire to see if there is indeed a market for your product in the new country you have chosen.

Create a four-question survey with two open-ended and two closed-ended questions.

CHAPTER 6 CONCEPT APPLICATION

You are now going to assess how consumers in the "new" country you are entering are going to react to your chosen product. Specifically you will look at the cultural influences on consumer decisions discussed in Chapter 6.

Complete the following tasks to better understand the cultural environment and how it will have an impact on the customer in this new market.

- Values—Identify two specific cultural values that relate to your product.

- Subculture—Describe a subculture that exists in your chosen country.

- Differences—Determine two cultural differences between Canada and your chosen country.

CHAPTER 7 CONCEPT APPLICATION

As part of entering a new market, it will be important for your company to leverage relationships in order to build a solid network. The B2B network model highlights the important business partners that exist in a market for any company. Based on your understanding of business-to-business relationships from Chapter 7, draw out the network model for your company, in a format like Exhibit P1.2:

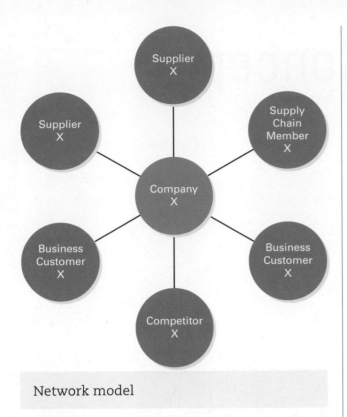

Network model

CHAPTER 8 CONCEPT APPLICATION

Now that you have a solid understanding of your product, the market you will enter into, and the impact on the consumer and business relationships, you can create a working market segment.

This market segment would be the target market for the new G20 country you are entering with your product of choice. You can complete all elements of a segment thanks to the material from Chapter 9.

Market Segment Variable	Description
Title	
Geographic	
Demographic	
Psychographic	
Behavioural	

CHAPTER 9 CONCEPT APPLICATION

The essence of customer relationship management is to bring together elements of customer service, marketing research and technology.

Using Exhibit 9.1, you are to develop the basic framework of a CRM system.

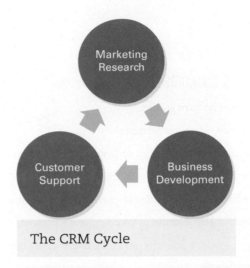

The CRM Cycle

Use your understanding of marketing research and consumer behaviour to come up with a basic system for a CRM. The only thing missing will be the technology aspect, and for this you will use your secondary research skills by looking at what CRM systems exist (e.g., Salesforce) and describe how that could be integrated into what you have done for this case on your chosen product.

10 | Product Concepts

Courtesy of Tylko

LEARNING OUTCOMES

10-1 Define the term *product*

10-2 Classify consumer products

10-3 Define the terms *product item, product line,* and *product mix*

10-4 Describe marketing uses of branding

10-5 Describe marketing uses of packaging and labelling

10-6 Discuss global issues in branding and packaging

10-7 Describe how and why product warranties are important marketing tools

"Great companies are built on great products."
—Elon Musk, CEO, Tesla Motors[1]

10-1 WHAT IS A PRODUCT?

The product offering, the heart of an organization's marketing program, is usually the starting point in creating a marketing mix. Many marketing mix decisions are made simultaneously; however, a marketing manager cannot determine a price, design a promotion strategy, or create a distribution channel until the firm has a product to sell. Moreover, an excellent distribution channel, a persuasive promotion campaign, and a fair price have no value when the product offering is poor or inadequate.

A **product** may be defined as anything, both favourable and unfavourable, received by a person in an exchange for possession, consumption, attention, or short-term use. It is important to note that not all products received by someone can be owned by them because a product may be a tangible good

product anything, both favourable and unfavourable, received by a person in an exchange for possession, consumption, attention, or short-term use

(a pair of shoes), a service (a haircut), an idea ("don't litter"), a person (a political candidate or a celebrity), a place (a tourism destination "Inspiring the world to explore Canada"), or any combination of these. Customers can own a tangible product, like a pair of shoes, but they only use a service, such as staying at a hotel (for more on services, please see Chapter 12). For a tangible good, packaging, style, colour, options, and size are some typical product features. Just as important are such intangibles as service, the seller's image, the manufacturer's reputation, and the way consumers believe others will view the product.

To most people, the term *product* means a tangible good, but product can also include services, ideas, persons, and places as these are all part of what companies offer to customers. (Chapter 12 focuses specifically on the unique aspects of marketing services.)

The concept of a product will continue to evolve with the inclusion of technology into the mix. One technology that is already seeping into the way products

will be defined, identified, and sold is augmented reality. Not to be confused with virtual reality, augmented reality is defined by business management consultants Accenture as "the overlaying of physical environments with digital content and images to provide users an enhanced (or augmented) experience of reality."[2] The popularity of augmented reality has been helped immensely by the popularity of Snapchat and Pokemon Go, which allow you to enhance photos by using elements of augmented reality. Augmented reality will affect the product by enhancing the information provided, usually via a smartphone.

In order to be effective, augmented reality should be used in real-world environments, like a retail store. Consumers would use an application on their phone and direct the phone's camera toward products in the retail environment. Their phone would reveal information about the products, such as nutritional information, coupons, features, and other attributes of the product. Some companies are even using augmented reality to allow customers to create products, as the furniture company Tylko has done with its augmented reality app. As the picture at the start of this chapter shows, consumers can use augmented reality and parametric design to create their own furniture products such as shelves. This is a great example of how technology is shaping the

marketing world and, in the case of augmented reality, possibly even changing how we define the concept of product.

10-2 TYPES OF CONSUMER PRODUCTS

Products can be broadly classified as either business or consumer products, depending on the buyer's intentions. The key distinction, as discussed earlier in the book, between the two types of products is their intended use. If the intended use is a business purpose, the product is classified as a business or industrial product. As explained in Chapter 7, a **business product** is used to manufacture other goods or provide services, to facilitate an organization's operations, or to resell to other customers. A **consumer product** is bought to satisfy an individual's personal wants. Sometimes the same item can be classified as either a business or a consumer product, depending on its intended use. Examples are light bulbs, pencils and paper, and computers.

> **business product**
> a product used to manufacture other goods or services, to facilitate an organization's operations, or to resell to other customers
>
> **consumer product** a product bought to satisfy an individual's personal wants

We need to know about product classifications because different products are marketed differently: They are marketed to different target markets, often using different distribution, promotion, and pricing strategies.

Chapter 7 examined seven categories of business products and services: major equipment, accessory equipment, component parts, processed materials, raw materials, supplies, and services. This chapter examines an effective way of categorizing consumer products. Although they can be classified in several ways, the most popular approach includes these four types: convenience products, shopping products, specialty products, and unsought products. This approach classifies products according to how much effort is normally used to shop for them.

10-2a Convenience Products

A **convenience product** is a relatively inexpensive item that merits little shopping effort—that is, a consumer is unwilling to shop extensively for such an item. Candy, pop, small hardware items, and many grocery items fall into the convenience product category.

Consumers buy convenience products regularly, usually without much planning. Nevertheless, consumers do know the brand names of popular convenience products, such as Coca-Cola, Colgate toothpaste, Right Guard deodorant, and Gillette razors like the Venus Breeze. Convenience products normally require wide distribution to be easily accessible to consumers. For example, Dentyne Ice gum is available everywhere, including at Walmart, Shoppers Drug Mart, Shell gas stations, newsstands, and vending machines.

Impulse products are a type of convenience products that consumers purchase without any planning and are usually stocked near the cash registers in stores. For example, candies, single servings of beverages, various fashion and gossip magazines, and unusual knick-knacks fall into this category and are placed near the cash registers for consumers to see and purchase at the last minute.

10-2b Shopping Products

A **shopping product** is a product that requires comparison shopping because it is usually more expensive than a convenience product and is found in fewer stores.

Consumers usually buy a shopping product only after comparing different brands' style, practicality, price, and lifestyle compatibility. Shoppers are typically willing to invest some effort in this process to get their desired benefits.

Gillette® Venus Breeze™ SPA

Shopping products can be divided into two types: homogeneous and heterogeneous. Consumers perceive *homogeneous* shopping products as being basically similar in their functions and features—for example, toasters, mixers, and other kitchen appliances tend to be similar. When shopping for homogeneous shopping products, consumers typically look for the lowest-priced brand that has the desired features. For example, consumers might compare Black & Decker, Betty Crocker, and Sunbeam toasters, perceive them to be similar, and select the one with the lowest price.

In contrast, consumers perceive *heterogeneous* shopping products as essentially different in their features, quality, and performance—for example, furniture, clothing, housing, and universities. Consumers often have trouble comparing heterogeneous shopping products because the prices, quality, and features vary so much. The benefit of comparing heterogeneous shopping products is that consumers can find the best product or brand for their needs, a decision that is often highly individual. For example, it can be difficult to compare a small, private university with a large, public university.

convenience product
a relatively inexpensive item that merits little shopping effort

shopping product a product that requires comparison shopping because it is usually more expensive than a convenience product and is found in fewer stores

10-2c Specialty Products

When consumers search extensively for a particular item with unique characteristics and are very reluctant to accept substitutes, that item is known as a **specialty product**. Specialty products don't have to be expensive; however, most expensive products, such as Patek Philippe watches, Rolls-Royce automobiles, Bose speakers, Ruth's Chris Steak House, and highly specialized forms of medical care are generally considered specialty products. An inexpensive product can also be considered a specialty item if it possesses a unique product or brand attribute; for example, people visiting several Canadian cities may want to try the pastry known as BeaverTails because of its unique taste, presentation, and limited availability.

Marketers of specialty products often use selective advertising to maintain their product's exclusive image. Distribution is often limited to one or a very few outlets in a geographic area. Brand names and quality of service are often very important.

10-2d Unsought Products

A product unknown to the potential buyer or a known product that the buyer does not actively seek is referred to as an **unsought product**. New products fall into this category until consumer awareness of them is increased through advertising and distribution.

Some goods are always marketed as unsought items, especially needed products that we do not like to think about or do not care to spend money on. Insurance, burial plots, and similar items require aggressive personal selling and highly persuasive advertising. Salespeople actively seek leads to potential buyers. Because consumers usually do not seek out this type of product, the company must approach customers directly through a salesperson, direct mail, or direct-response advertising.

10-3 PRODUCT ITEMS, LINES, AND MIXES

Rarely does a company sell a single product. More often, it sells a variety of products. Marketing managers make important decisions regarding the number and type of products a company should sell under a brand name in a given market. A **product item** is a specific version of a product that can be designated as a distinct offering among an organization's products. Campbell's Cream of Chicken Soup is an example of a product item (see Exhibit 10.1).

A group of closely related product items is a **product line**. For example, the column in Exhibit 10.1 titled "Soups" represents one of Campbell's product lines. Different container sizes and shapes also distinguish items in a product line. Diet Coke, for example, is available in cans and various plastic containers. Each size and each container is a separate product item.

An organization's **product mix** includes all the products it sells. All Campbell's products—soups, sauces, beverages, and biscuits—constitute its product mix. Each product item in the product mix may require a separate marketing strategy. In some cases, however, product lines and even entire product mixes share some marketing strategy components. LG consumer electronics promotes all its products with the same theme of "Life Is Good." Companies derive several benefits from organizing related items into product lines.

The product mix of a business organization can be described in terms of product mix width, product line length, depth, and consistency.

Product mix width (or breadth) refers to the number of product lines an organization offers. In Exhibit 10.1, for example, the width of Campbell's product mix is four product lines. **Product line length** is the number of product items in a product line. As shown in Exhibit 10.1, the sauces product line consists of four product items; while the line of soups has so many items it would take up at least two pages of this textbook. **Product line depth** refers to the number of types and sizes offered for each product in the line. For example, Campbell's soup offers different sizes of the tomato soups that also come in different flavours.

Firms increase the *width* of their product mix to diversify risk. To generate sales and boost profits, firms spread risk across many product lines rather than depending on only one or two. Firms also widen their product mix to capitalize on established

specialty product a particular item with unique characteristics for which consumers search extensively and for which they are very reluctant to accept substitutes.

unsought product a product unknown to the potential buyer or a known product that the buyer does not actively seek

product item a specific version of a product that can be designated as a distinct offering among an organization's products

product line a group of closely related product items

product mix all products that an organization sells

product mix width the number of product lines an organization offers

product line length the number of product items in a product line

product line depth the different versions of a product item in a product line

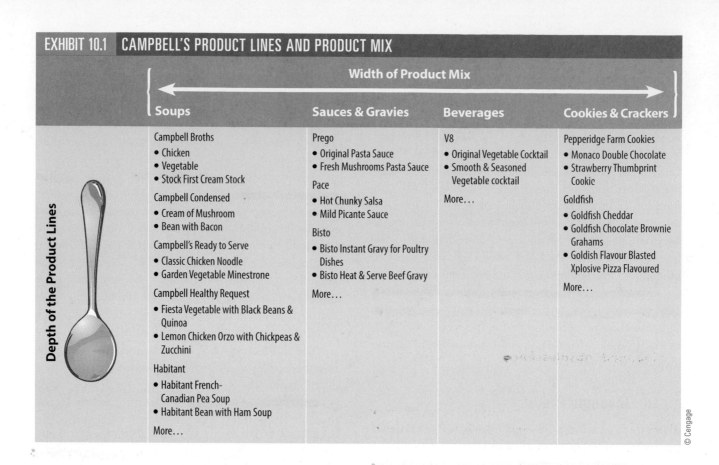

EXHIBIT 10.1 CAMPBELL'S PRODUCT LINES AND PRODUCT MIX

Width of Product Mix

Soups	Sauces & Gravies	Beverages	Cookies & Crackers
Campbell Broths • Chicken • Vegetable • Stock First Cream Stock Campbell Condensed • Cream of Mushroom • Bean with Bacon Campbell's Ready to Serve • Classic Chicken Noodle • Garden Vegetable Minestrone Campbell Healthy Request • Fiesta Vegetable with Black Beans & Quinoa • Lemon Chicken Orzo with Chickpeas & Zucchini Habitant • Habitant French-Canadian Pea Soup • Habitant Bean with Ham Soup More…	Prego • Original Pasta Sauce • Fresh Mushrooms Pasta Sauce Pace • Hot Chunky Salsa • Mild Picante Sauce Bisto • Bisto Instant Gravy for Poultry Dishes • Bisto Heat & Serve Beef Gravy More…	V8 • Original Vegetable Cocktail • Smooth & Seasoned Vegetable cocktail More…	Pepperidge Farm Cookies • Monaco Double Chocolate • Strawberry Thumbprint Cookie Goldfish • Goldfish Cheddar • Goldfish Chocolate Brownie Grahams • Goldish Flavour Blasted Xplosive Pizza Flavoured More…

Depth of the Product Lines

© Cengage

reputations. The Oreo Cookie brand has been extended to include items such as breakfast cereal, ice cream, Jell-O pudding, and cake mix.

Firms increase the *length* and *depth* of their product lines to attract buyers with different preferences, to increase sales and profits by further segmenting the market, to capitalize on economies of scale in production and marketing, and to even out seasonal sales patterns. P&G is adding some lower-priced versions of its namesake brands, including Bounty Basic and Charmin Basic. These brands are targeted to more price-sensitive customers, a segment that Procter & Gamble had not been serving with its more premium brands.[3]

10-3a Adjustments to Product Items, Lines, and Mixes

Over time, firms change product items, lines, and mixes to take advantage of new technical or product developments or to respond to changes in the environment. They may adjust by modifying products,

product modification
changing one or more of a product's characteristics

repositioning products, or extending or contracting product lines.

PRODUCT MODIFICATION Marketing managers must decide whether and when to modify existing products. **Product modification** changes one or more of a product's characteristics:

• **Quality modification:** a change in a product's dependability or durability. Reducing a product's quality may allow the manufacturer to lower the price, thereby appealing to target markets unable to afford the original product. Conversely, increasing quality can help the firm compete with rival firms. Increasing quality can also result in increased brand loyalty, greater ability to raise prices, or new opportunities for market segmentation. Inexpensive ink-jet printers have improved in quality to the point that they can now produce photo-quality images.

• **Functional modification:** a change in a product's versatility, effectiveness, convenience, or safety. Tide with Downy combines into one product the functions of both cleaning power and fabric softening.[4]

- **Style modification:** an aesthetic product change, rather than a quality or functional change. Clothing and auto manufacturers also commonly use style modifications to motivate customers to replace products before they are worn out.*

Companies often introduce changes that may focus on one of three types of modifications one at a time or sometimes modifications may include two or more dimensions at the same time. For example, Kleenex might introduce four-ply tissue paper that could be termed a quality modification only. However, suppose that Kleenex introduces a four-ply tissue paper in pink that also comes with or without moisturizer. In this case, the product introduction includes all three types of modifications. The key consideration here is that product modifications are periodically needed to meet changing consumer and competitive demands.

Planned obsolescence describes the practice of modifying products so that those products that have already been sold become obsolete before they actually need replacement. Some argue that planned obsolescence is wasteful; some claim it is unethical. Marketers respond that consumers favour planned obsolescence so that they can acquire products with the latest features and functions. Planned obsolescence is more frequent in some industries than in others. For example, computer and mobile phone manufacturers tend to introduce new models annually to entice consumers into replacing their older version of the products. Apple has created numerous public relations events where newer versions of its products (iPhone, iPad, Mac) are introduced and older versions are phased out, making them less compatible or completely incompatible with the newer operating systems and product accessories.

REPOSITIONING Repositioning, as Chapter 8 explained, involves changing consumers' perceptions of a brand. Recently, Listerine, known for its antibacterial mouthwash qualities, has introduced, among others, Listerine Whitening Plus Restoring, Listerine Total Care, and Listerine Zero to emphasize its new product positioning in the market. Similarly, Head & Shoulders has repositioned itself away from being a dandruff-only shampoo and introduced 14 different variations to suit different hair care needs. Changing demographics, declining sales, or changes in the social

*© Cengage

Courtesy of Dare Foods Limited

environment often motivate firms to reposition established brands.

PRODUCT LINE EXTENSIONS A **product line extension** occurs when a company's management decides to add products to an existing product line to compete more broadly in the industry. For example, Canadian food manufacturer Dare Foods has continually added to its line of very successful kids' snacks called Bear Paws. The product line is a soft cookie snack with flavours such as banana bread, baked apple, and brownie. Over time, Dare has added to this line with new flavours like birthday cake and molasses. The most recent addition to the Bear Paws product line was the "Dipped" line that added a layer of chocolate to the cookie. The Dipped line of Bear Paws received a Best New Product Award

planned obsolescence
the practice of modifying products so those that have already been sold become obsolete before they actually need replacement

product line extension
adding products to an existing product line to compete more broadly in the industry

in 2016 from Brandspark, which cited the whole grain ingredients and less than 10 grams of sugar as reasons for the award.[5]

PRODUCT LINE CONTRACTION Sometimes marketers can get carried away with product extensions (does the world really need 41 varieties of Crest toothpaste?), and some extensions are not embraced by the market, such as Vanilla Coke. Other times, contracting product lines is a strategic move. Heinz deleted a number of product lines, such as vegetables, poultry, frozen foods, and seafood, to concentrate instead on the products it sells best: ketchup, sauces, frozen snacks, and baby food.[6]

Three major benefits are likely when a firm contracts its overextended product lines. First, resources become concentrated on the most important products. Second, managers no longer waste resources trying to improve the sales and profits of poorly performing products. Third, new product items have a greater chance of being successful because

> **brand** a name, term, symbol, design, or combination thereof that identifies a seller's products and differentiates them from competitors' products

more financial and human resources are available to manage them.

10-4 BRANDING

The success of any business or consumer product depends in part on the target market's ability to distinguish one product from another. Branding is the main tool marketers use to distinguish their products from the competition's.

According to the American Marketing Association (AMA), a **brand** is a name, term, symbol, design, or combination thereof that identifies a seller's products and differentiates them from competitors' products.[7] However, in a broader sense a brand is much more than the name and symbols that a company can create: what a brand stands for also involves consumers and is the sum total of their expectations, feelings, thoughts, and actions that are associated with a brand. This deeper meaning of a brand is created by consumers over time when they hear, experience, and interact with a brand in various situations. Astute marketers strive to shape consumers' creation and interpretation of brand meaning through effective marketing programs and customer service.

Jeff Whyte/Shutterstock.com

Todd Korol/Toronto Star/Getty Images

kevin brine/Shutterstock.com

Richard Levine/Alamy Stock Photo

NAME

A **brand name** is that part of a brand that can be spoken, including letters (UPS, CML), words (Chevrolet), and numbers (WD-40, 7-Eleven). The elements of a brand that cannot be spoken are called the **brand mark**—for example, the well-known Mercedes-Benz and Air Canada symbols.

LOGO

10-4a Benefits of Branding

Branding has three main purposes: product identification, repeat sales, and new-product sales. The most important purpose is *product identification*. Branding allows marketers to distinguish their products from all others. Many brand names are familiar to consumers and indicate quality.

The term **brand equity** refers to the value of company and brand names. A brand that invokes strong and favourable thoughts, feelings, and actions and has high awareness, high perceived quality, and high brand loyalty among customers is said to have high brand equity. Canadian Tire, Scotiabank, and Tim Hortons are companies with high brand equity. A brand with strong brand equity is a valuable asset.

The term **global brand**, in general, refers to a brand that is available in many different countries at the same time. A company that is considering the development of a global brand should consider undertaking the following activities:

- Conduct research in the countries that are being considered for entry,

- Identify factors that would identify which markets are most attractive to enter,

- Determine if decisions will be made at the local level or centrally,

- Assess any aspects of a brand that might need to be altered or adjusted to foreign markets (e.g., colours, symbols, images, tag lines, etc.)[8]

Yum! Brands, which owns Pizza Hut, KFC, and Taco Bell, is a good example of a company that has developed strong global brands. Yum! believes in adapting its restaurants to local tastes and different cultural and political climates. For example, in Japan, KFC sells tempura crispy strips; in northern England, it offers gravy and potatoes; and in Thailand, it sells rice with soy or sweet chili sauce.

The best generator of *repeat sales* is satisfied customers. Branding helps consumers identify those products they want to buy again and avoid those they do not. **Brand loyalty**, a consistent preference for one brand over all others, is quite high in some product categories. More than half the users in product categories

such as mayonnaise, toothpaste, coffee, headache remedies, bath soap, and ketchup are loyal to one brand. Many students go to college or university and purchase the same brands they used at home rather than becoming price buyers. Brand identity is essential to developing brand loyalty.

The third main purpose of branding is to *facilitate new-product sales*. Having a well-known and respected company and brand name is extremely useful when introducing new products.

10-4b Branding Strategies

Firms face complex branding decisions, the first of which is whether to brand at all. Some firms actually use the lack of a brand name as a selling point. These unbranded products are called generic products. Firms that decide to brand their products may choose to follow a policy of using manufacturers' brands, private (distributor) brands, or both. In either case, they must then decide among a policy of individual branding (different brands for different products), family branding (common names for different products), or a combination of individual branding and family branding.

Examples?

GENERIC PRODUCTS VERSUS BRANDED PRODUCTS

A **generic product** is typically a no-frills, no-brand-name, low-cost product that is simply identified by its product category. (Note that a generic product is not the same as a brand name that becomes generic, such as cellophane.)

The main appeal of generics is their low price. Generic grocery products are usually 30 to 40 percent less expensive than manufacturers' brands in the same product category and 20 to 25 percent less expensive than retailer-owned brands. Pharmaceuticals are one example of a product category where generics have made large inroads. When patents on successful pharmaceutical products expire, low-cost generics rapidly appear on the market. For example, when the patent on Merck's popular anti-arthritis drug Clinoril expired, its sales declined by 50 percent almost immediately because of the introduction of generic drugs.

---

brand name that part of a brand that can be spoken, including letters, words, and numbers

brand mark the elements of a brand that cannot be spoken

brand equity the value of company and brand names

global brand a brand with at least 20 percent of the product sold outside its home country or region

brand loyalty a consistent preference for one brand over all others

generic product a no-frills, no-brand-name, low-cost product that is simply identified by its product category

Key Advantages of Carrying Manufacturers' Brands	Key Advantages of Carrying Private Brands
• Heavy advertising to the consumer by well-known manufacturers, such as Procter & Gamble, helps develop strong consumer loyalties.	• A wholesaler or retailer can usually earn higher profits on its own brands. In addition, because the private brand is exclusive, the retailer is under less pressure to mark the price down to meet competition.
• Well-known manufacturers' brands, such as Kodak and Fisher-Price, can attract new customers and enhance the dealer's (wholesaler's or retailer's) prestige.	• A manufacturer can decide to drop a brand or a reseller at any time or even to become a direct competitor to its dealers.
• Many manufacturers offer rapid delivery, enabling the dealer to carry less inventory.	• A private brand ties the customer to the wholesaler or retailer. A person who wants MotoMaster batteries must go to Canadian Tire.
• If a dealer happens to sell a manufacturer's brand of poor quality, the customer may simply switch brands and remain loyal to the dealer.	• Wholesalers and retailers have no control over the intensity of distribution of manufacturers' brands. Canadian Tire store managers don't have to worry about competing with other sellers of MotoMaster automotive products. They know that these brands are sold only at Canadian Tire.

MANUFACTURERS' BRANDS VERSUS PRIVATE BRANDS The brand name of a manufacturer—such as Samsung, La-Z-Boy, and Fruit of the Loom—is called a **manufacturer's brand**. Sometimes *national brand* is used as a synonym for *manufacturer's brand*; however, national brand is not always an accurate term because many manufacturers serve only regional markets. Using the term *manufacturer's brand* more precisely defines the brand's owner.

A **private brand**, also known as a private label or store brand, is a brand name owned by a wholesaler or a retailer. Private label brands are different from generic products in that generic products do not have any branding associated with them at all. Private-label products made exclusively by retailers account for one of every five items sold in Canada, representing a large part of sales in some retail sectors.[9] The image of private label brands as a low-cost alternative to manufacturers' brands has changed over the years. In a global study of consumer perception of brands, Ipsos marketing found that 80 percent of the customers found private label brands to be similar in quality to the national brands.[10] Some of the major private label brands in Canada are President's Choice from Loblaws, Life from Shoppers Drug Mart, Master Choice from Metro, and MasterCraft from Canadian Tire. Despite positive quality perception, however, Canadian consumers are beginning to see less value coming from private brands because of their lack of innovativeness and sustainability.[11]

manufacturer's brand the brand name of a manufacturer

private brand a brand name owned by a wholesaler or a retailer

Exhibit 10.2 illustrates key issues that wholesalers and retailers should consider in deciding whether to sell manufacturers' brands or private brands. Many firms offer a combination of both. Retailers love consumers' greater acceptance of private brands. Because their overhead is low and these products have no marketing costs, private label products bring 10 percent higher margins, on average, than manufacturers' brands. More than that, a trusted store brand can differentiate a chain from its competitors.

Brent Lewin/Bloomberg/Getty Images

TOP FIVE GLOBAL AND CANADIAN BRANDS

Top Five Global[a]	Canadian[b]
1. Apple	1. MEC
2. Google	2. Home Hardware
3. Coke	3. WestJet
4. Microsoft	4. Tim Hortons
5. Toyota	5. Cirque du Soleil

Sources: (a) http://interbrand.com/best-brands/best-global-brands/2016/ranking/, accessed March 2017; (b) http://www.canadianbusiness.com/lists-and-rankings/best-brands/canadas-best-brands-2017-the-top-25/, accessed March 2017.

Better Letters?

For decades, cars had comprehensible names: Lincoln called its top-of-the-line model the Town Car, and Cadillac models included the DeVille and Eldorado. Recently, however, luxury automakers have favoured alphanumeric combinations, like the BMW M5, the Audi A8, the Lexus LS 450, and the renowned Mercedes S-class. The idea behind alphanumeric branding is to build the image of a whole brand, not just one model. But some letters are more popular than others, leading to brand confusion. For example, car models include the Mercedes S-class, the Audi S series, and the Jaguar S type; in addition, there is an Acura MDX and a Lincoln MKX.

Shevel Artur/Shutterstock.com

Hot	Not	No Chance
X, S, and Z	O, P, U, Y	B (b-movie; second-class)
		F (failing; F-word)
		N (no; sounds like M)

Source: Gina Chon, "Henry Ford's Model A Would Be at Home in the Car-Name Game," *Wall Street Journal*, April 12, 2006, B1.

INDIVIDUAL BRANDS VERSUS FAMILY BRANDS Many companies use different brand names for different products, a practice referred to as **individual branding**. Companies use individual brands when their products vary greatly in use or performance. For instance, it would not make sense to use the same brand name for a pair of dress socks and a baseball bat. Procter & Gamble targets different segments of the laundry detergent market with Bold, Cheer, Dash, Dreft, Era, Gain, Ivory Snow, Oxydol, Solo, and Tide.

In contrast, a company that markets several different products under the same brand name is using a **family brand**. Sony's family brand includes radios, television sets, stereos, and other electronic products. A brand name can only be stretched so far, however. Do you know the differences between Holiday Inn, Holiday Inn Express, Holiday Inn Select, Holiday Inn Sunspree Resort, Holiday Inn Garden Court, and Holiday Inn Hotel & Suites? Neither do most travellers.

COBRANDING Cobranding involves placing two or more brand names on a product or its package. Three common types of cobranding are ingredient branding, cooperative branding, and complementary branding. *Ingredient branding* identifies the brand of a part that makes up the product—for example, an Intel microprocessor in a personal computer, such as Dell or Apple. *Cooperative branding* occurs when two brands receiving equal treatment (in the context of an advertisement) borrow on each other's brand equity. When Intel launched its Centrino wireless processor, it established cobranding relationships with Via Rail and hotel chains Marriott International and Westin Hotels & Resorts because of the mutual value in establishing these relationships. Via Rail was able to set up WiFi access to reach Intel's target market of mobile professionals, while the hotel chains enabled Intel to target business professionals.[12] Finally, with *complementary branding*, products are advertised or marketed together to suggest usage, such as a spirits brand (Seagram's) and a compatible mixer (7-Up).

Cobranding is a useful strategy when a combination

individual branding the use of different brand names for different products

family brand the marketing of several different products under the same brand name

cobranding placing two or more brand names on a product or its package

CHAPTER 10: Product Concepts

of brand names enhances the prestige or perceived value of a product or when it benefits brand owners and users. Cobranding may be used to increase a company's presence in markets where it has little or no market share. For example, Coach was able to build a presence in a whole new category when its leather upholstery with the company logo was used in Lexus automobiles.[13]

10-4c Trademarks

A **trademark** is the exclusive right to use a brand or part of a brand. Others are prohibited from using the brand without permission. A **service mark** performs the same function for services, such as H&R Block and Weight Watchers. Parts of a brand or other product identification may qualify for trademark protection. Some examples are

- shapes, such as the Jeep front grille and the Coca-Cola bottle

- ornamental colour or design, such as the decoration on Nike shoes, the black-and-copper colour combination of a Duracell battery, or the noticeable green colour of the Garnier Fructis bottles of hair and body care products.

- catchy phrases, such as Subway's "Eat Fresh," Nike's "Just do it," and Budweiser's "This Bud's for you"

- abbreviations, such as LG, H&M, or FedEx

- sounds, such as the MGM lion's roar

It is important to understand that trademark rights come from use rather than registration. In Canada, trademarks are registered under the Trade-marks Act and Regulations. When a company registers a trademark, it must have a genuine intention to use it and must actually use it within three years of the application being granted. Trademark protection typically lasts for 15 years. To renew the trademark, the company must prove it is using the mark. Rights to a trademark last as long as the mark is used. Normally, if the firm does not use a trademark for an extended period, it is considered abandoned, allowing a new user to claim exclusive ownership.

The Canadian Intellectual Property Office is responsible for registering trademarks and patents. Canada's Trade-marks Act and Regulations were updated in 2012 to include the trademarking of sounds like the MGM lion's roar.[14]

trademark the exclusive right to use a brand or part of a brand

service mark a trademark for a service

generic product name a term that identifies a product by class or type and cannot be trademarked

Companies that fail to protect their trademarks face the possibility that their product names will become generic. A **generic product name** identifies a product by class or type and cannot be trademarked. Former brand names that were not sufficiently protected by their owners and were subsequently declared to be generic product names by courts include cellophane, linoleum, thermos, kerosene, monopoly, cola, and shredded wheat.

Companies such as Rolls-Royce, Cross, Xerox, Levi Strauss, Frigidaire, and McDonald's aggressively enforce their trademarks. Rolls-Royce, Coca-Cola, and Xerox even run newspaper and magazine ads stating that their names are trademarks and should not be used as descriptive or generic terms. Some ads threaten lawsuits against competitors that violate trademarks.

Despite severe penalties for trademark violations, trademark infringement lawsuits are not uncommon. Some of the major battles involve brand names that closely resemble an established brand name. Donna Karan filed a lawsuit against Donnkenny, Inc., whose NASDAQ trading symbol—DNKY—was too close to Karan's DKNY trademark.

Companies must also contend with fake or unauthorized brands. Knockoffs of Burberry's trademarked tan, black, white, and red plaid are easy to find in cheap shops all over the world, and loose imitations are also found in some reputable department stores. One website sells a line of plaid bags, hats, and shoes that it says are "inspired by Burberry." Burberry says it spends

Brand Mark

TM

Registered Trademark

VIA Rail Canada

Courtesy of VIA Rail Canada

The Canadian Press/AP Photo/Nick Ut, File

a couple of million dollars a year running ads in trade publications and sending letters to trade groups, textile manufacturers, and retailers reminding them about its trademark rights. It also sues infringers, works with customs officials and local law enforcement to seize fakes, and scans the Internet to pick up online chatter about counterfeits.[15]

In Europe, you can sue counterfeiters only if your brand, logo, or trademark is formally registered. Until recently, formal registration was required in each country in which a company sought protection. Now, a company can use just one application to register its trademark in all European Union (EU) member countries.

10-5 PACKAGING

Packages have always served a practical function—that is, they hold contents together and protect goods as they move through the distribution channel. Today, however, packaging is also a container for promoting the product and making it easier and safer to use.

10-5a Packaging Functions

The three most important functions of packaging are to contain and protect products, to promote products, and to facilitate the storage, use, and convenience of products. A fourth function of packaging that is becoming increasingly important is to facilitate recycling and reduce environmental damage.

CONTAINING AND PROTECTING PRODUCTS The most obvious function of packaging is to contain products that are liquid, granular, or otherwise divisible. Packaging also enables manufacturers, wholesalers, and retailers to market products in specific quantities, such as kilograms.

Physical protection is another obvious function of packaging. Most products are handled several times between the time they are manufactured, harvested, or otherwise produced and the time they are consumed or used. Many products are shipped, stored, and inspected several times between production and consumption. Some products, such as milk, need to be refrigerated. Others,

such as beer, are sensitive to light. Still others, such as medicines and bandages, need to be kept sterile. Packages protect products from breakage, evaporation, spillage, spoilage, light, heat, cold, infestation, and many other conditions.

PROMOTING PRODUCTS Packaging does more than identify the brand, list the ingredients, specify features, and give directions. A package differentiates a product from competing products and may associate a new product with a family of other products from the same manufacturer. Welch's repackaged its line of grape juice–based jams, jellies, and juices to unify the line and get more impact on the shelf.

Packages use designs, colours, shapes, and materials to try to influence consumers' perceptions and buying behaviour. For example, marketing research shows that health-conscious consumers are likely to think that any food is probably good for them as long as it comes in green packaging. Packaging can also influence consumer perceptions of quality and prestige. And packaging has a measurable effect on sales. Quaker Oats revised the package for Rice-a-Roni without making any other changes in marketing strategy and experienced a 44 percent increase in sales in one year.

FACILITATING STORAGE, USE, AND CONVENIENCE Wholesalers and retailers prefer packages that are easy to ship, store, and stock on shelves. They also like packages that protect products, prevent spoilage or breakage, and extend the product's shelf life.

TEAR OFF CAP TO SQUEEZE

DIP & SQUEEZE™
MORE KETCHUP
THAN 9 GRAM PACKETS

HEINZ TOMATO KETCHUP

TO DIP   PEEL BACK

Kristoffer Tripplaar/Alamy Stock Photo

Consumers' requirements for storage, use, and convenience cover many dimensions. Consumers are constantly seeking items that are easy to handle, open, and reclose, and some consumers want packages that are tamperproof or childproof. Research indicates that hard-to-open packages are among consumers' top complaints.[16] Surveys conducted by *Sales & Marketing Management* magazine revealed that consumers dislike—and avoid buying—leaky ice cream boxes, overly heavy or fat vinegar bottles, immovable pry-up lids on glass bottles, key-opener sardine cans, and hard-to-pour cereal boxes. Such packaging innovations as zipper tear strips, hinged lids, tab slots, screw-on tops, and pour spouts were introduced to solve these and other problems. Easy openings are especially important for kids and older consumers.

MANY FUNCTIONS OF PACKAGING

Some firms use packaging to segment markets. Heinz creates small packages for use with meals on airplanes and in hotels and sells larger packages of their products to retail outlets that sell to consumers. Differently sized packages appeal to heavy, moderate, and light users. Campbell's soup is packaged in single-serving cans aimed at the seniors and singles market segments. Packaging convenience can increase a product's utility and, therefore, its market share and profits.

FACILITATING RECYCLING AND REDUCING ENVIRONMENTAL DAMAGE One of the most important packaging issues today is compatibility with the environment. Some firms use their packaging to target environmentally concerned market segments. Brocato International markets shampoo and hair conditioner in bottles that are biodegradable in landfills. Products as different as deodorant and furniture polish are packaged in eco-friendly, pump-spray packages that do not rely on aerosol propellants.

The concept of reducing and recycling has led to the "circular economy" movement. The concept has to do with companies focusing on the full life of their product packaging, which looks at the materials used to make the products and the proper disposal of the products to recycling or landfill facilities. In early 2017, Unilever announced that it had made a commitment to ensure that all of its plastic packaging would be fully recyclable, reusable, or compostable by 2025. A recent study showed that only 14 percent of all plastics packaging makes it to a recycling plant, with 40 percent ending up in a landfill and 33 percent in fragile ecosystems.[17] With Unilever selling its products in more than 190 countries worldwide and with 13 brands with more than $1 billion in sales, this type of promise from such a large consumer products company offers some hope that other companies will see the advantage of going in circles.

10-5b Labelling

An integral part of any package is its label. Labelling generally takes one of two forms: persuasive or informational. **Persuasive labelling** focuses on a promotional theme or logo,

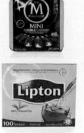

and consumer information is secondary. Note that the standard promotional claims—such as "new," "improved," and "super"—are no longer very persuasive. Consumers have been saturated with "newness" and thus discount these claims.

Informational labelling, in contrast, is designed to help consumers make proper product selections and to lower their cognitive dissonance after the purchase. Sears attaches a "label of confidence" to all its floor coverings. This label gives such product information as durability, colour, features, cleanability, care instructions, and construction standards. Most major furniture manufacturers affix labels to their wares that explain the products' construction features, such as type of frame, number of coils, and fabric characteristics. The Consumer Packaging and Labelling Act mandates detailed nutritional information on most food packages and standards for health claims on food packaging. An important outcome of this legislation has been guidelines from Health Canada for the use of such terms as *low fat, light, reduced cholesterol, low sodium, low calorie, low carb,* and *fresh*.

Another important section of the Act mandates the requirement that all information on a product label in Canada be in both French and English except for the dealer's name and address, which can be in either language. There are a few exceptions to this rule, including test market products that are exempt for up to one year, and products that require knowledge of either French or English for its proper use (e.g., books, greeting cards).[18] However, the requirement for both languages on products in Canada creates an extra step for companies first entering the Canadian market.

10-5c Universal Product Codes (UPCs)

The **universal product codes (UPCs)** that now appear on most items in supermarkets and other high-volume outlets were first introduced in 1974. Because the numerical codes appear as a series of thick and thin vertical lines, they are often called *bar codes*. The lines are read

persuasive labelling
package labelling that focuses on a promotional theme or logo; consumer information is secondary

informational labelling
package labelling designed to help consumers make proper product selections and to lower their cognitive dissonance after the purchase

universal product codes (UPCs) a series of thick and thin vertical lines (bar codes), readable by computerized optical scanners that match the codes to brand names, package sizes, and prices

The Canadian government assists companies entering the Canadian market by providing clear guidelines and pictures (like the one above) to provide specific details on packaging such as the requirement for bilingual labelling.

Source: Canadian Food Inspection Agency (2017). Retrieved from: http://www .inspection.gc.ca/food/labelling/food-labelling-for-industry/fish-and-fishproducts /eng/1393709636463/1393709677546?chap=14. Reproduced with the permission of the Canadian Food Inspection Agency, 2017.

by computerized optical scanners that match the codes to brand names, package sizes, and prices. They also print information on cash register tapes and help retailers rapidly and accurately prepare records of customer purchases, control inventories, and track sales.

10-6 GLOBAL ISSUES IN BRANDING AND PACKAGING

When planning to enter a foreign market with an existing product, a firm has three options for handling the brand name:

- **One brand name everywhere:** This strategy is useful when the company markets mainly one product and the brand name does not have negative connotations in any local market. The Coca-Cola Company uses a one-brand-name strategy in more than 200 countries around the world. The advantages of a one-brand-name strategy are greater identification of the product from market to market and ease of coordinating the promotion from market to market.

- **Adaptations and modifications:** A one-brand-name strategy is not possible when the name cannot be pronounced in the local language, when the brand name is owned by someone else, or when the brand name has a negative or vulgar connotation in the local language. The Iranian detergent "Barf," for example, might encounter some resistance in the Canadian market.

- **Different brand names in different markets:** Local brand names are often used when translation or pronunciation problems occur, when the marketer wants the brand to appear to be a local brand, or when regulations require localization. Henkel's Silkience hair conditioner is called Soyance in France and Sientel in Italy. The adaptations were deemed to be more appealing in the local markets. Coca-Cola's Sprite brand had to be renamed Kin in Korea to satisfy a government prohibition on the unnecessary use of foreign words.[*]

In addition to making global branding decisions, companies must consider global packaging needs. Three aspects of packaging especially important in international marketing are labelling, aesthetics, and climate considerations. The major concern is properly translating ingredient, promotional, and instructional information on labels. Care must also be employed in meeting all local labelling requirements. Several years ago, an Italian judge ordered that all bottles of Coca-Cola be removed from retail shelves because the ingredients were not properly labelled. In Canada, by law, labelling is required to be bilingual.

Package *aesthetics* may also require some attention. Even though simple visual elements of the brand, such as a symbol or logo, can be a standardizing element across products and countries, marketers must stay attuned to cultural traits in host countries. For example, colours may have different connotations. In some countries, red is associated with witchcraft, green may be a sign of danger, and white may be symbolic of death. Aesthetics also influence package sizes. Pop is not sold in six-packs in countries that lack refrigeration. In some countries, products such as detergent may be bought only in small quantities because of a lack of storage space. Other products, such as cigarettes, may be bought in small quantities, and even single units, because of the low purchasing power of buyers.

Extreme *climates* and long-distance shipping necessitate sturdier and more durable packages for goods sold overseas. Spillage, spoilage, and breakage are all more important concerns when products are shipped long distances or are frequently handled during shipping

[*] © Cengage

and storage. Packages may also have to ensure a longer product life if the time between production and consumption lengthens significantly.

10-7 PRODUCT WARRANTIES

Just as a package is designed to protect the product, a **warranty** protects the buyer and provides essential information about the product. A warranty confirms the quality or performance of a good or service. An **express warranty** is a written guarantee. Express warranties range from simple statements—such as "100 percent cotton" (a guarantee of quality) and "complete satisfaction guaranteed" (a statement of performance)—to extensive documents written in technical language.

In contrast, an **implied warranty** is an unwritten guarantee that the good or service is fit for the purpose for which it was sold.

Although court rulings might suggest that all products sold in Canada carry an implied warranty, actual warranties do vary depending on the province or territory. At the federal level, protection against misleading warranties is provided under the Competition Act. In general, products sold must be free from encumbrances (the seller must have clear title to ownership), the descriptions of the product on the package must be accurate, the product must be fit for its intended purpose, and the product must be of reasonable durability.

warranty a confirmation of the quality or performance of a good or service

express warranty a written guarantee

implied warranty an unwritten guarantee that the good or service is fit for the purpose for which it was sold

SIDE LAUNCH
BREWING COMPANY
CONTINUING CASE

The Art of Craft

To hear founding brewer Michael Hancock describe the care that goes into Side Launch beer is akin to hearing a violin maker describe, in impassioned detail, the difference between the acoustic nuances of spruce and maple. "The hops that we use here are very delicate and, as of yet, remain one of our best kept secrets—no one knows who supplies us." He continues, "The malt, however, which I brought in from Germany in 2007, is now the brand that most craft breweries use" for the lagers and the wheat beer. But his adamant stance on quality doesn't end merely with the basic ingredients. Achieving specific physical qualities of the wort boil, time periods of aging, even the temperatures maintained in the loading area, once the beer has been packaged and is ready for transport—all of these and dozens of other considerations are strictly monitored and enforced to achieve a flavour profile deserving of the Side Launch name.

It is clear that his steadfast commitment to quality is not merely tolerated by everyone in the brewery, but revered as perhaps the single most important aspect of the Side Launch success story. "It's true that every craft brewery is going to have quality as their calling card," reflects founder Garnet Pratt, "but how is quality really measured? You can look at high beer ratings scores and awards, but you also have to look at experience. Michael Hancock has been in the business for 30 years, and he's been brewing three of the four recipes in our year-round line-up for most of his career. So he's had a lot of time to get them right."

"It has to be authentic and true to style," emphasizes Michael. "But it also has to do with accessibility appealing to craft beer drinkers and aspiring craft beer drinkers. We stay away from heavily hopped IPAs, for example, that a certain number of people say they like, but when you really get down to the nitty gritty, in terms of a refreshing beverage, they'd gravitate toward something we produce on a regular basis." Those beers produced on a regular basis (at the time of this writing) were Pale Ale, Dark Lager, Wheat, and Mountain Lager. Each, according to Michael, a beer historian as much as a scientist, covers a significant and distinct category within a craft beer consumer's diverse palate. To maintain a level of innovation, seemingly another expectation of craft breweries, Side Launch produces quarterly seasonal beers through its "Ships of Collingwood" series. And for truly experimental styles, it makes the appropriately named line "Man Overboard."

But while "new" may be a differentiator in other industries, consistency is the anchor in craft, according to Michael. Copious, detailed, handwritten forms attached to clipboards hang from every fermentation tank in the brewery, documenting the precise life cycle of each specific batch of beer and thereby dictating when it's ready for canning and shipping. "People expect craft beers to be different with every brew and yeah, they might," explains Michael, "but if every brew you do is different, you're going to have a problem. Because no matter how much people say they don't mind variations in craft beer, they really do."

Questions

1. Based on the descriptions of convenience, shopping, and specialty products in this chapter, how would you categorize the Side Launch line of beers?

2. How would you organize the Side Launch product mix into product lines?

3. How is Side Launch beer both a business and consumer product simultaneously?

Side Launch Brewing Company

SIDE LAUNCH

Learning like never before.

4LTR PRESS

nelson.com/student

11 Developing and Managing Products

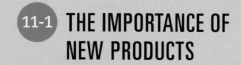

Joe Raedle/Getty Images

LEARNING OUTCOMES

11-1 Explain the importance of developing new products and describe the six categories of new products

11-2 Explain the steps in the new-product development process

11-3 Discuss global issues in new-product development

11-4 Explain the diffusion process through which new products are adopted

11-5 Explain the concept of product life cycles

> *"Innovation distinguishes between a leader and a follower."*
>
> —Steve Jobs[1]

11-1 THE IMPORTANCE OF NEW PRODUCTS

New products are important to sustain growth, increase revenues and profits, and replace obsolete items. New-product development and introduction are also important to meet ever-changing consumer wants and are compounded by the development of new technologies and shrinking product life cycles. In a large study of consumers from more than 60 countries by renowned global marketing data collection firm Neilsen, 63 percent responded that they like when manufacturers offer new products, with 57 percent of respondents indicating that they bought a new product the last time they were at a grocery store.[2] At the same time, the new-product development process is replete with failures and high introduction costs. Businesses must introduce new products to stay competitive or risk being pushed out of the market. It is no wonder. Despite spending huge sums on (R&D) and development, most companies have many more failures than successes; however, the companies that succeed in introducing new products reap substantial financial and market rewards. While there is no magic trick involved in launching a successful product, there are certain actions firms should take to be successful. The Nielsen report noted: "Success is not simply the result of luck or even genius. Rather, successful product launches are the culmination of organizational focus and commitment to product development, creative marketing, smart leadership and, above all else, an in-depth understanding of what drives consumer preferences."[3]

It is no surprise that Tesla Motors drove its way to the top ranking for Forbes' Most Innovative Companies list for both 2015 and 2016.[4] Tesla and its CEO, Elon Musk, have made selling electric cars cool and profitable. When Tesla's new more affordable car, Model 3, was to come out on the market in 2016, there were a staggering 400,000 reservations from consumer, totalling $16 billion in sales. In early 2017, Canadians were told that any reservations for a Model 3 would result in a new car being delivered to them by mid-2018 at the earliest. It is clear that Tesla has been able to test those consumer preferences, while at the same time testing their patience.

Other than patience, Canadians also have other qualities related to new products. Canada has been the home of a number of inventions over the years, many of which have had an impact on how people live their lives. Some truly Canadian inventions include these:

- Insulin
- Odometer
- Paint roller
- Electric wheelchair
- Egg carton
- Peanut butter

11-1a Categories of New Products

The term **new product** can be confusing because its meaning varies widely and has several correct definitions. A new product doesn't carry the same level of newness in different markets or companies: a product can be new to the market, new to the producer or seller, new to the world, or new to some combination of these (see Exhibit 11.1). The degree of newness even for the same product varies from one market to the other and from one company to the next. Based on the degree of newness, new products can be classified into six categories:

EXHIBIT 11.1 NEW PRODUCT CATEGORIES

New to the Company

- New Product Lines
- New to the World
- Improvements or Revisions of Existing Products
- Additions to Existing Product Lines
- Lower-priced Products
- Repositioned Products

New to the Market

new product a product new to the world, new to the market, new to the producer or seller, or new to some combination of these

- **New-to-the-world products (also called *discontinuous innovations*):** These products create an entirely new market. New-to-the-world products represent the smallest category of new products, since few products are seen as completely new by everyone.

- **New-product lines:** These products, which the firm has not previously offered, allow the firm to enter an established market. After Procter & Gamble purchased Iams pet food brand, its worldwide sales doubled and profits tripled. The brand moved from the fifth-best-selling pet food brand in the United States to the top spot in less than five years.[5]

- **Additions to existing product lines:** This category includes new products that supplement a firm's established line. Examples of product line additions are Huggies Pull-Ups, Pampers Kandoo baby wipes, and other personal care products for kids.

- **Improvements or revisions of existing products:** The new and improved product may be significantly or slightly changed. Gillette's Fusion and Fusion Proglide and Proshield razors are examples of product improvements. Another type of revision is package improvement. The Heinz EZ Squirt Ketchup bottle is short and made from easy-to-squeeze plastic; its needle-shaped nozzle lets small hands use it to decorate food. Most new products fit into the revision or improvement category.

- **Repositioned products:** These are existing products targeted at new markets or new market segments. In 2016, Danone-owned brand Activia repositioned its yogurt to target a younger demographic—women from ages 29 to 39. Instead of focusing on the probiotics ingredients in its yogurt, Danone Canada created the "Live InSync" campaign to target the Millennial female market by focusing on an overall emotional and mental health appeal to overcome one's internal critic.[6]

- **Lower-priced products:** This category refers to products that provide performance similar to that of competing brands at a lower price. The Canon Pixma MG7720 is a scanner, copier, printer, and fax machine combined. This relatively new category of all-in-one printers offers a pricing option much lower than conventional colour and laser copiers and much lower than the combined price of the four items purchased separately. The Canon Pixma line offers a greatly reduced price for all these products and does so for under $100. (Smart consumers should remember to take the price of ink replacements into consideration when buying any printer.)

NEW-TO-THE-WORLD PRODUCTS

The top 10 discontinuous innovations (new-to-the-world products) in the 20th century:

1. Penicillin
2. Transistor radio
3. Polio vaccine
4. Mosaic (the first graphic Web browser)
5. Microprocessor
6. Black-and-white television
7. Plain paper copier
8. Alto personal computer (prototype of today's PCs)
9. Microwave oven
10. Arpanet network (the groundwork for the Internet)

Discontinuous innovations in the 21st century are likely to derive from the bio-engineering, nano-technology, and robotics fields.

Source: "Changing the World," Entrepreneur, October 2003, 30.

 11-2

THE NEW-PRODUCT DEVELOPMENT PROCESS

The management consulting firm Booz Allen Hamilton has studied the new-product development process for more than 35 years. After analyzing five major studies undertaken during this period, the firm concluded that the companies most likely to succeed in developing and introducing new products are those that take the following actions:

- Make the long-term commitment needed to support innovation and new-product development.

- Use a company-specific approach, driven by corporate objectives and strategies, with a well-defined new-product strategy at its core.

- Capitalize on experience to achieve and maintain competitive advantage.

- Establish an environment—a management style, an organizational structure, and a degree of top-management support—conducive to achieving company-specific new-product and corporate objectives.

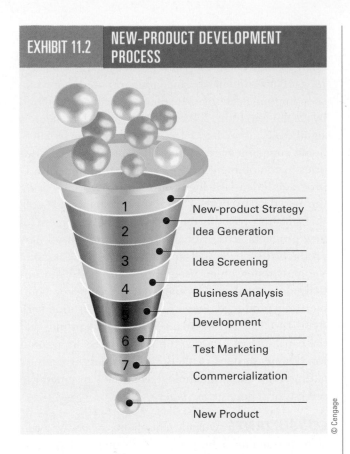

EXHIBIT 11.2 NEW-PRODUCT DEVELOPMENT PROCESS

1 New-product Strategy
2 Idea Generation
3 Idea Screening
4 Business Analysis
5 Development
6 Test Marketing
7 Commercialization

New Product

© Cengage

Most companies follow a formal new-product development process, usually starting with a new-product strategy. Exhibit 11.2 traces the seven-step process, which is discussed in this section. The exhibit is funnel-shaped to highlight the fact that each stage acts as a screen. The purpose is to filter out unworkable ideas.

11-2a New-Product Strategy

A **new-product strategy** links the new-product development process with the objectives of the marketing department, the business unit, and the corporation. A new-product strategy must be compatible with these objectives, and, in turn, all three objectives must be consistent with one another.

A new-product strategy is part of the organization's overall marketing strategy. It sharpens the focus and provides general guidelines for generating, screening, and evaluating new-product ideas. The new-product strategy specifies the roles that new products must play in the organization's overall plan and describes the characteristics of products the organization wants to offer and the markets it wants to serve. Some firms, like Apple, apply the new product strategy

to each of their existing lines, punctuating with public events to unveil new features and benefits of a new product.[7]

As discussed at the beginning of this chapter, companies with successful new-product introduction programs derive a substantial percentage of their total sales from new-product introductions. These companies tend to have numerous new-product ideas at various stages of development at the same time realizing that very few of their ideas will be successful in the market.

11-2b Idea Generation

New-product ideas come from many sources, including customers, employees, distributors, competitors, vendors, research and development (R&D), and consultants.

CUSTOMERS The marketing concept suggests that customers' wants and needs should be the springboard for developing new products. Many of today's most innovative and successful marketers have taken the approach of introducing fewer new products but taking steps to ensure these chosen few are truly unique, better, and, above all, really do address unmet consumer needs. How do they do that? They begin and end development with the customer.[8] The most common techniques for gathering new-product ideas from consumers are surveys, focus groups, observation, and the analysis of social media posts. Adobe has created the Kickbox for its employees, which is in fact a box that contains a $1000 prepaid credit card and some instructions on how to develop ideas for new products. At any time Adobe employees can open the box, follow the new product development process, and use the seed $1000 funding to investigate a potential idea. For good measure, the box also contains a Starbucks gift card and a chocolate bar—hoping that caffeine and sugar will help to fuel the new product development process.[9]

EMPLOYEES Marketing personnel—advertising and marketing research employees, as well as salespeople—often create new-product ideas because they analyze and are

bfk/Shutterstock.com

> **new-product strategy** a plan that links the new-product development process with the objectives of the marketing department, the business unit, and the corporation

involved in the marketplace. Encouraging employees from different divisions to exchange ideas is also a useful strategy. The developers of Mr. Clean AutoDry turned to scientists who worked on PUR water purification and Cascade dishwashing detergent to learn how to dry dishes without spotting.[10] Some firms reward employees for coming up with creative new ideas. At Google, employees can spend up to 20 percent of their time working on individual projects called Googlettes.[11]

DISTRIBUTORS A well-trained sales force routinely asks distributors about needs that are not being met. Because distributors are closer to end users, they are often more aware of customer needs than are manufacturers. The inspiration for Rubbermaid's Sidekick, a litter-free lunch box, came from a distributor's suggestion that the company place some of its plastic containers inside a lunch box and sell the set as an alternative to wrapping lunches in plastic wrap and paper bags.

COMPETITORS No firms rely solely on internally generated ideas for new products. A big part of any organization's marketing intelligence system should be monitoring the performance of competitors' products. One purpose of competitive monitoring is to determine which, if any, of the competitors' products should be copied. Many companies form alliances with competitors to market new and existing products. Procter & Gamble and Clorox combined the patented adhesive-film technology that P&G uses in its packaging to develop Glad Press'n Seal food storage wrap.[12]

VENDORS 7-Eleven regularly forges partnerships with vendors to create proprietary products, such as Candy Gulp (a plastic cup filled with Gummies) and Blue Vanilla Laffy Taffy Rope candy, developed by Nestlé's Wonka division exclusively for 7-Eleven.

RESEARCH AND DEVELOPMENT R&D is carried out in four distinct ways. You learned about basic research and applied research in Chapter 5. The other two ways are product development and product modification. **Product development** goes beyond applied research by converting applications into marketable products. Product modification makes cosmetic or functional changes to existing products. Many new-product breakthroughs come from R&D activities. Balancing the need to develop new products with pressure to lower costs creates a difficult dilemma for many managers. Although companies spend billions of dollars

product development a marketing strategy that entails the creation of new products for current customers

every year on research and development, as many as 40 percent of managers think their companies are not doing enough to develop new products.[13] In Canada, a recent Government of Canada report noted that while spending on R&D by Canadian companies increased by $2 billion from 2003 to 2013, there had been a significant cut in R&D from the recession in 2008. Some companies are establishing innovation laboratories to complement or even replace traditional R&D programs. Idea labs focus on substantially increasing the speed of innovation. Despite the important role that idea labs play in the systematic development of new products, it is critical to realize that not all new products are developed in this manner. For example, the glass touchscreen used on iPhones had been initially developed by Corning, but it was never commercially produced. Steve Jobs, in a conversation with the then-CEO of Corning, realized that Corning had the capability to produce the kind of glass he wanted for iPhone screens. Called Gorilla Glass, Corning's cutting-edge glass technology continues to grace the screens of iPhones everywhere.

CONSULTANTS Outside consultants are always available to examine a business and recommend product ideas. Examples are Booz Allen Hamilton and Management Decisions. Traditionally, consultants determine whether a company has a balanced portfolio of products and, if not, which new-product ideas are needed to offset the imbalance. These Canadian-based innovation consultants have developed a list of the most innovative companies in Canada. Booz Allen Hamilton can leverage the presentation of this list to discuss innovation and R&D issues in Canada, and raise the profile of companies on the list that are far from household names. Often it is lists of innovative companies that garner publicity and create a level of awareness that is often challenging for startups and new firms to achieve.

REUTERS/Steve Marcus

Creativity is the wellspring of new-product ideas, regardless of who comes up with them. A variety of approaches and techniques have been developed to stimulate creative thinking. The two considered most useful for generating new-product ideas are brainstorming and focus-group exercises. The goal of **brainstorming** is to get a group to think of unlimited ways to vary a product or solve a problem. Group members avoid criticism of an idea, no matter how ridiculous it may seem. Objective evaluation is postponed. The sheer quantity of ideas is what matters. As noted in Chapter 5, an objective of focus-group interviews is to stimulate insightful comments through group interaction. Focus groups usually consist of anywhere from 6 to 12 people. Sometimes consumer focus groups generate excellent new-product ideas. In the industrial market, focus groups have led to the evolution of machine tools, keyboard designs, aircraft interiors, and backhoe accessories.

11-2c Idea Screening

After new ideas have been generated, they pass through the first filter in the product development process. This stage, called **screening**, eliminates ideas that are inconsistent with the organization's new-product strategy or are inappropriate for some other reason. Managers screening new-product ideas must have a clear understanding of what their business is about. Some companies have a very broad definition of what is consistent with their business objectives. Google acquired smart thermostat manufacturer Nest for more than US$3.3 billion because Nest thermostats are high-tech and use wireless and the Internet for controlling house temperature, which Google considers to be one of its many domains of business.[14] In screening new-product ideas, companies need to have a certain degree of tolerance for risk and uncertainty.

Concept tests are often used at the screening stage to rate concept (or product) alternatives. A **concept test** is an evaluation of a new-product idea, usually before any prototype has been created. Typically, researchers survey consumer reactions to descriptions and visual representations of a proposed product.

Concept tests are considered fairly good predictors of success for line extensions. They have also been relatively precise predictors of success for new products that are not copycat items, are not easily classified into existing product categories, and do not require major changes in consumer behaviour—such as Planters Creamy peanut butter. Concept tests are usually inaccurate, however, in predicting the success of new products that create new consumption patterns and require major changes in consumer behaviour—such as microwave ovens, computers, and word processors.

11-2d Business Analysis

New-product ideas that survive the initial screening process move to the **business analysis** stage, the second stage of the screening process, where preliminary figures for demand, cost, sales, and profitability are calculated. For the first time, costs and revenues are estimated and compared. Depending on the nature of the product and the company, this process may be simple or complex.

The newness of the product, the size of the market, and the nature of the competition all affect the accuracy of revenue projections. In an established market, such as the pop business, industry estimates of total market size are available. Forecasting market share for a new entry is a bigger challenge.

Analyzing overall economic trends and their impact on estimated sales is especially important in product categories that are sensitive to fluctuations in the business cycle. If consumers view the economy as uncertain and risky, they will put off buying durable goods, such as major home appliances, automobiles, and homes. Likewise, business buyers postpone major equipment purchases if they expect a recession.

Answering questions during the business analysis stage may require studying the new product's markets, competition, costs, and technical capabilities. But at the end of this stage, management should have a good understanding of the product's market potential. This understanding is important because costs increase dramatically once a product idea enters the development stage.

11-2e Development

In the early stage of **development**, the R&D or engineering department may develop a prototype

---

brainstorming the process of getting a group to think of unlimited ways to vary a product or solve a problem

screening the first filter in the product development process, which eliminates ideas that are inconsistent with the organization's new-product strategy or are obviously inappropriate for some other reason

concept test evaluation of a new-product idea, usually before any prototype has been created

business analysis the second stage of the screening process, where preliminary figures for demand, cost, sales, and profitability are calculated

development the stage in the product development process in which a prototype is developed and a marketing strategy is outlined

of the product. During this stage, the firm should start sketching a marketing strategy. The marketing department should decide on the product's packaging, branding, labelling, and so forth. In addition, it should map out strategies for the product's preliminary promotion, price, and distribution. The feasibility of manufacturing the product at an acceptable cost should be thoroughly examined. The development stage can last a long time and thus be very expensive. It took 11 years to develop Crest toothpaste, 15 years to develop the Xerox copy machine, 18 years to develop Minute Rice, and 51 years to develop television. Gillette developed three shaving systems over a 27-year period (TracII, Atra, and Sensor) before introducing the Mach3 in 1998, Fusion in 2006, Fusion Pro Glide in 2011, and Fusion Pro Shield in 2015.[15] The Gillette Fusion line is the P&G product that reached the US$1 billion sales mark in the shortest time.[16]

Laboratory tests are often conducted on prototype models during the development stage. User safety is an important aspect of laboratory testing, which actually subjects products to much more severe treatment than is expected by end users. The Canada Consumer Product

REUTERS/Jason Reed

Apple introduced its Apple Watch in late 2014, with sales beginning in April 2015. Eighteen months later the Apple Watch Series 2 came out alongside the iPhone 7, and the Apple Watch Series 3 went on sale in September 2017.

Safety Act requires manufacturers to conduct a reasonable testing program to ensure that their products conform to established safety standards.

Crowdfunding and Product Development

The popularity of social media has affected many aspects of marketing, including product development. Crowdfunding is a way that companies can solicit investment from a large number of donors. With the advent of social networks like Facebook, it was inevitable that crowdfunding would have its own online networks. The top three crowdfunding sites are Gofundme, Kickstarter, and indiegogo. Not only are these sites a method to build a group of investors, but the online crowdfunding phenomenon has also raised an important connection with the product development process. *Entrepreneur* magazine highlighted these ways in which crowdfunding can help the development of new products:[17]

- Strong crowdfunding support can help make inferences about market readiness.
- The opportunity exists to use crowdfunding to help receive feedback on development and design.

Tashatuvango/Shutterstock.com

- It is a way to gather feedback, both good and bad, from potential customers.
- You can promote your product via online portals where customers will learn about the reason for developing your product and the benefits gained from its use.

London, Ontario—The Perfect Test Market

Nestled between Toronto and Detroit, London, Ontario, is the perfect test market: it's not too big and not too small. While large markets are attractive due to the sheer number of potential customers, a good test market needs to have a nice variety of characteristics. There needs to be a good mix of demographics, industries, and educational facilities. London has a rounded representation of ethnicity; manufacturing, health care, and technology industries; and the University of Western Ontario. These factors are very attractive for companies to test their products. The recent introduction of Tim Hortons dark roast coffee was tested in London.[18] And it not just London that is being pegged for test marketing efforts—recently the managing director

of Twitter admitted that Canada is being used for test marketing a variety of new product ideas and technologies.[19]

Many product prototypes that test well in the laboratory are also tried out in homes or businesses. Examples of product categories well suited for such tests include human and pet food products, household cleaning products, and industrial chemicals and supplies. These products are all relatively inexpensive, and their performance characteristics are apparent to users.

11-2f Test Marketing

After products and marketing programs have been developed, they are usually tested in the marketplace. **Test marketing** is the limited introduction of a product and associated marketing program to determine the reactions of potential customers in a market situation. Test marketing allows management to evaluate alternative strategies and to assess how well the various aspects of the marketing mix fit together. Even established products are test marketed to assess new marketing strategies.

It is important that the value of the test market be tempered by critically assessing the specific aspects of a company's offering. The locations chosen as test sites should reflect market conditions in the new product's projected market area as much as possible. Yet no test city exists that can universally represent actual market conditions, and a product's success or failure in one city doesn't guarantee its success or failure in the national market. When selecting test market cities, researchers should therefore find loca-

tions where the demographics and purchasing habits mirror the overall market. Some businesses can test market their products in their retail locations. For example, McDonald's is known to test-market new products in its own restaurants in select cities. Likewise, Starbucks conducted extensive test marketing before introducing various products in its stores, as the risk of its failing and thus damaging the parent brand, is always a serious concern.

THE HIGH COSTS OF TEST MARKETING Test marketing frequently takes one year or longer, and costs can exceed $1 million. Some products remain in test markets even longer. Despite the cost, many firms believe it is much better to fail in a test market than in a national introduction. Because test marketing is so expensive, some companies do not test line extensions of well-known brands. For example, because its Sara Lee brand is well known, Consolidated Foods Kitchen faced little risk in distributing its frozen croissants nationally. Other products introduced without being test marketed include General Foods' International Coffees and Quaker Oats' Chewy Granola Bars.

The high cost of test marketing is not just financial. One unavoidable problem is that test marketing exposes the new product and its marketing mix to competitors before

> **test marketing** the limited introduction of a product and a marketing program to determine the reactions of potential customers in a market situation

its introduction. Thus the element of surprise is lost. Competitors can also sabotage, or jam, a testing program by introducing their own sales promotion, pricing, or advertising campaign. The purpose is to hide or distort the normal conditions that the testing firm might expect in the market.

ALTERNATIVES TO TEST MARKETING Many firms are looking for cheaper, faster, safer alternatives to traditional test marketing. In the early 1980s, Information Resources, Inc., pioneered one alternative: single-source research using supermarket scanner data. Another alternative to traditional test marketing is **simulated (laboratory) market testing**, which involves the presentation of advertising and other promotional materials for several products, including the test product, to members of the product's target market. These people are then taken to shop at a mock or real store, where their purchases are recorded. Shopper behaviour, including repeat purchasing, is monitored to assess the product's likely performance under true market conditions. Computer simulation is also used extensively to test-market certain types of new products. For example, Google and Amazon extensively conduct test-market experiments to examine the effectiveness of various marketing programs.

Despite these alternatives, most firms still consider test marketing essential for most new products. The high price of failure simply prohibits the widespread introduction of most new products without testing. Many firms are finding that the Internet offers a fast, cost-effective way to conduct test marketing. Procter & Gamble is an avid proponent of using the Internet as a means of gauging customer demand for potential new products. Many products that are not available in grocery stores or drugstores can be sampled or purchased from P&G's corporate website, **www.pg.com**. Before launching Crest Whitestrips, management ran an eight-month campaign offering the strips exclusively on http://whitestrips.com at a test price of $44 per kit.

11-2g Commercialization

The final stage in the new-product development process is **commercialization**, the decision to market a product. This decision sets several tasks in motion: ordering production materials and equipment, starting production, building inventories, shipping the product to field distribution points, training the sales force, announcing the new product to the trade, and advertising to potential customers.

simulated (laboratory) market testing the presentation of advertising and other promotion materials for several products, including the test product, to members of the product's target market

commercialization the decision to market a product

The time from the initial commercialization decision to the product's actual introduction varies. It can range from a few weeks for simple products that use existing equipment to several years for technical products that require custom manufacturing equipment. And the total cost of development and initial introduction can be staggering. Gillette spent US$750 million developing Mach3, and the first-year marketing budget for the new three-bladed razor was US$300 million.

The most important factor in successful new-product introduction is a good match between the product and market needs—as the marketing concept would predict. Successful new products deliver a meaningful and perceivable benefit to a sizable number of people or organizations and are different in some significant way from their intended substitutes. Firms that routinely experience success in new-product introductions tend to share the following characteristics:

- A history of carefully listening to customers
- A vision of what the market will be like in the future
- Strong leadership
- A commitment to new-product development
- A project-based team approach to new-product development
- An insistence on getting every aspect of the product development process right

There are almost as many reasons why products fail, and often it comes down to the inaction or misguided

GILLETTE—PRODUCT DEVELOPMENT PROCESS

One company you have heard of continually in this chapter is Proctor & Gamble. This consumer products giant invests in over $2 billion worth of R&D every year. It has over eight thousand scientists working in global innovation centres around the world. Developing new products is not only a priority for P&G, but it is at the core of what makes the company successful. Given this investment of time, money, and resources, P&G provides a great example of what it takes to properly work through the new product development process and achieve success on the other end.

Using a recent new product, the Gillette Fusion ProGlide men's razor with FlexBall handle, we can see how the process of product development is undertaken in the real world. Here are some highlights of the P&G process to bring the FlexBall razor to market:[20]

- **Test subjects:** Fifty men come into a test facility for five days and shave. Each tester is of a different age, skin type, ethnicity, and profession. These men are videotaped during the use of razors and are photographed for any nicks and cuts, all while being watched for their overall behaviour while shaving.

- **Concept engineering:** Sketching and modelling of the human face is done to understand contours and other obstacles. Sketches are turned into cardboard prototypes and then a computer-aided design model. Next, 3D printing is used to produce a mock-up of the new razor. The razor is then tested, not only for the razor integrity and effectiveness, but also the pivoting angle of the new FlexBall technology.

- **Prototyping:** Once testing is done, a prototype is developed and tested. In the case of the FlexBall, the first prototype was developed in 2004, and after hundreds of new prototypes were tested and improved upon, the final design was developed in 2013.

- **Testing:** High-quality cameras are used to analyze the use of the final prototype in testing with human subjects. Statistics on blade use, usefulness, and efficiency are taken and assessed.

- **Inspection:** Final tests are completed, often outside of the R&D facility, in order to ensure all aspects of testing have been completed. Blade sharpness is of utmost importance at this stage.

- **Commercialization:** The Gillette Fusion ProGlide men's razor with FlexBall handle is released to market, behind the strength of a $200 million communications budget, with hopes for $188 million in sales in the first year. The product is to be sold at a price point of $11.49 or $12.59.[21]

Bborriss.67/Shutterstock.com

actions of a company. Some of the myriad of reasons why products fail are these:

- Incongruity between the product and the chosen target market

- Development process too long, leading to delayed market entry

- Company resources, from financial to human resources, ill-equipped to handle growth

- Poor initial product reviews, combined with few changes made based on customer feedback

- Poor execution of the marketing-mix activities necessary to execute strategy

11-3 GLOBAL ISSUES IN NEW-PRODUCT DEVELOPMENT

Increasing globalization of markets and of competition encourages multinational firms to consider new-product development from a worldwide perspective. A firm that starts with a global strategy is better able to develop products that are marketable worldwide. In many multinational corporations, every product is developed for potential worldwide distribution, and unique market requirements are built in whenever possible.

Some global marketers design their products to meet regulations in their major markets and then, if necessary, meet smaller markets' requirements country by country. Nissan develops lead-country car models that, with minor changes, can be sold in most markets. By using this approach, Nissan has been able to reduce the number of its basic models from 48 to 18. Some products, however, have little potential for global market penetration without modification. In other cases, companies cannot sell their product at affordable prices and still make a profit in many countries. We often hear about the popularity of American products in foreign countries. Recently, Canadian companies have been finding that products popular in foreign markets can become hits in Canada. For example, Häagen-Dazs introduced dulce de leche ice cream in Canada after successfully introducing in Argentina.

11-4 THE SPREAD OF NEW PRODUCTS

Managers have a better chance of successfully marketing new products if they understand how consumers learn about and adopt products. A person who buys a new product he or she has never before tried may ultimately become an **adopter**, a consumer who was happy enough with the trial experience with a product to use it again.

adopter a consumer who was satisfied enough with his or her trial experience with a product to use it again

innovation a product perceived as new by a potential adopter

diffusion the process by which the adoption of an innovation spreads

11-4a Diffusion of Innovation

An **innovation** is a product perceived as new by a potential adopter. It really doesn't matter whether the product is new to the world or belongs to some other category of new product. If the product is new to a potential adopter, in this context, it is considered an innovation. **Diffusion** is the process by which the adoption of an innovation spreads.

Five categories of adopters participate in the diffusion process:

- **Innovators:** The first 2.5 percent of all those who adopt the product. Innovators are eager to try new ideas and products, almost to the point of obsession. In addition to having higher incomes, innovators are typically more worldly and more active outside their communities than noninnovators. Innovators also rely less on group norms and are more self-confident. Because they tend to be well educated, they are more likely to get their information from scientific sources and experts. Innovators are characterized as being venturesome.

- **Early adopters:** The next 13.5 percent to adopt the product. Although early adopters are not the very first, they do adopt early in the product's life cycle. Compared with innovators, early adopters rely much more on group norms and values. They are also more oriented to the local community, in contrast to the innovators' worldly outlook. Early adopters are more likely than innovators to be opinion leaders because of their closer affiliation with groups. The respect of others is a dominant characteristic of early adopters.

- **Early majority:** The next 34 percent to adopt. The early majority weighs the pros and cons before adopting a new product. They are likely to collect more information and evaluate more brands than early adopters, thereby extending the adoption process. They rely on the group for information but are unlikely to be opinion leaders themselves. Instead, they tend to be opinion leaders' friends and neighbours. The early majority is an important link in the process of diffusing new ideas because they are positioned between earlier and later adopters. A dominant characteristic of the early majority is deliberateness. Most of the first residential broadband users were classic early adopters—white males, well educated, and wealthy, with a great deal of Internet experience.

- **Late majority:** The next 34 percent to adopt. The late majority adopts a new product because most of their friends have already adopted it. Because they also rely on group norms, their adoption stems from pressure to conform. This group tends to be older and below average in income and education. They depend mainly on word-of-mouth communication rather than on the mass media. The dominant characteristic of the late majority is skepticism.

- **Laggards:** The final 16 percent to adopt. Like innovators, laggards do not rely on group norms. Their independence is rooted in their ties to tradition. Thus, the past heavily influences their decisions. By the time laggards adopt an innovation, it has probably been outmoded and replaced by something else. For example, they may have bought their first digital camera once film cameras were no longer being produced. Laggards have the longest adoption time and the lowest socioeconomic status. They tend to be suspicious of new products and alienated from a rapidly advancing society. The dominant value of laggards is tradition. Marketers can benefit from laggards by introducing no-frills, low-cost products to this segment.

Note that some product categories may never be adopted by 100 percent of the population. The percentages noted in the adopter categories above refer to the percentage of all of those who will eventually adopt a product, not to percentages of the entire population. (See Exhibit 11.3.)

11-4b Product Characteristics and the Rate of Adoption

Five product characteristics can be used to predict and explain the rate of acceptance and diffusion of a new product:

- **Complexity:** The degree of difficulty involved in understanding and using a new product. The more complex the product, the slower is its diffusion.

According to the Business Development Bank of Canada, the early adopters in Canada vary based on city and type of offering.[22] Vancouver is known as the early adoption hub for electronics, Toronto is the focus for business, Ottawa for politics, and Montreal (in the picture above) is an early adoption centre for culture.

- **Compatibility:** The degree to which the new product is consistent with existing values and product knowledge, past experiences, and current needs. Incompatible products diffuse more slowly than compatible products.
- **Relative advantage:** The degree to which a product is perceived as superior to existing substitutes.

EXHIBIT 11.3 VARIABLE RATES OF ADOPTION FOR HOUSEHOLD DEVICES

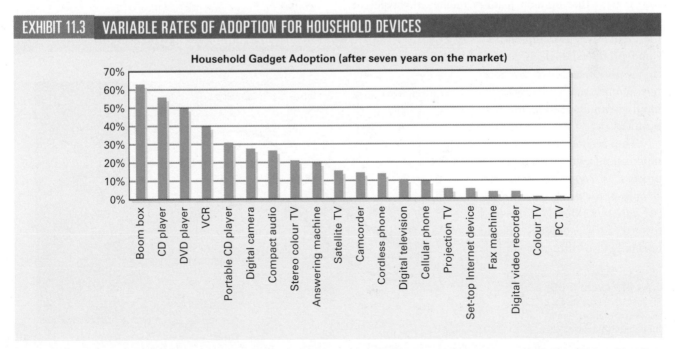

Source: Alexis C. Madrigal, "Guess What's the Fastest-Adopted Gadget of the Last 50 Years," *The Atlantic*, March 23, 2012. © 2012 The Atlantic Media Co., as first published in The Atlantic Magazine. All rights reserved. Distributed by Tribune Content Agency, LLC.

Because it can store and play back thousands of songs, the iPod has a clear relative advantage over a portable CD player.

- **Observability:** The degree to which the benefits or other results of using the product can be observed by others and communicated to target customers. For instance, fashion items and automobiles are highly visible and more observable than personal-care items.

- **Trialability:** The degree to which a product can be tried on a limited basis. Products that can be tried on a limited basis have a better chance of being adopted. It is much easier to try a new toothpaste or breakfast cereal than a new automobile or microcomputer. However, many products that are trying to enter into a crowded marketplace will often offer a free trial period to encourage trial. Apple Music has maintained a free three-month trial period throughout its existence, in hopes of getting users hooked on the product.

11-4c Marketing Implications of the Adoption Process

Two types of communication aid the diffusion process: *word-of-mouth communication,* both traditional and digital (also referred to as *word-of-mouse communication*), among consumers and communication from marketers to consumers. Word-of-mouth communication within and across groups speeds diffusion. Opinion leaders discuss new products with their followers and with other opinion leaders. Marketers must therefore ensure that opinion leaders receive the types of information that are desired in the media they use. Suppliers of some products, such as professional and healthcare services, rely almost solely on word-of-mouth communication for new business.

The second type of communication aiding the diffusion process is *communication directly from the marketer to potential adopters.* Messages directed toward early adopters should normally use different appeals than messages directed toward the early majority, the late majority, or the laggards. Early adopters are more important than innovators because they make up a larger group, are more socially active, and are usually opinion leaders.

As the focus of a promotional campaign shifts from early adopters to the early majority and the late majority, marketers should study these target markets' dominant characteristics, buying behaviour, and media characteristics. They should then revise their messages and media strategy to fit these target markets. The diffusion model helps guide marketers in developing and implementing promotion strategy.

11-5 PRODUCT LIFE CYCLES

The **product life cycle (PLC)**, one of the most familiar concepts in marketing, traces the stages of a product's acceptance, from its introduction (birth) to its decline (death). Few other general concepts have been so widely discussed. Although some researchers and consultants have challenged the theoretical basis and managerial value of the PLC, many believe it is a useful marketing management diagnostic tool and a general guide for marketing planning in various life-cycle stages.[23]

As Exhibit 11.4 shows, a product progresses through four major stages: introduction, growth, maturity, and decline.

product life cycle (PLC) a concept that traces the stages of a product's acceptance, from its introduction (birth) to its decline (death)

EXHIBIT 11.4 FOUR STAGES OF THE PRODUCT LIFE CYCLE

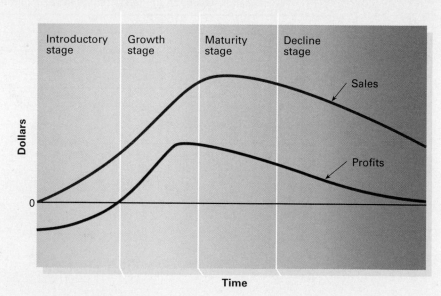

© Cengage

The PLC concept can be used to analyze a brand, a product form, or a product category. The PLC for a product form is usually longer than the PLC for any one brand. The exception would be a brand that was the first and last competitor in a product form market. In that situation, the brand and product form life cycles would be equal in length. Product categories have the longest life cycles. A **product category** includes all brands that satisfy a particular type of need, such as shaving products, passenger automobiles, or colas.

The time a product spends in any one stage of the life cycle may vary dramatically. Some products, such as trendy items, move through the entire cycle in weeks. Others, such as electric clothes washers and dryers, stay in the maturity stage for decades. Exhibit 11.4 illustrates the typical life cycle for a consumer durable good, such as a washer or dryer. In contrast, Exhibit 11.5 illustrates typical life cycles for styles (such as formal, business, or casual clothing), fashions (such as miniskirts or baggy jeans), and fads (such as leopard-print clothing). Changes in a product's uses, its image, or its positioning can extend that product's life cycle.

The PLC concept does not tell managers the length of a product's life cycle or its duration in any stage. It does not dictate marketing strategy. It is simply a tool to help marketers forecast future events and suggest appropriate strategies.

11-5a Introductory Stage

The **introductory stage** of the PLC represents the full-scale launch of a new product into the marketplace. Product categories that have recently entered the product life cycle include computer databases for personal use, room-deodorizing air-conditioning filters, and wind-powered home electric generators.

A high failure rate, little competition, frequent product modification, and limited distribution typify the introductory stage of the PLC.

Marketing costs in the introductory stage are normally high for several reasons. High dealer margins are often needed to obtain adequate distribution, and incentives are needed to convince consumers to try the new product. Advertising expenses are high because of the need to educate consumers about the new product's benefits. Production costs are also often high in this stage, as a result of product and manufacturing flaws being identified and then corrected and because of efforts undertaken to develop mass-production economies.

Sales normally increase slowly during the introductory stage. Moreover, profits are usually negative because of R&D costs, factory tooling, and high introduction costs. The length of the introductory phase is largely determined by product characteristics, such as the product's advantages over substitute products, the educational effort required to make the product known, and management's commitment of resources to the new item. A short introductory period is usually preferred to help reduce the impact of negative earnings and cash flows. As soon as the product gets off the ground, the financial burden should begin to diminish. Also, a short introduction helps dispel some of the uncertainty as to whether the new product will be successful.

Promotion strategy in the introductory stage focuses on developing product awareness and informing consumers about the product category's potential benefits. At this stage, the communication challenge is to stimulate primary demand—demand for the product in general rather than for a specific brand. Intensive personal selling is often required to gain acceptance for the product among wholesalers and retailers. Promotion of convenience products often requires heavy consumer sampling and couponing. Shopping and specialty products demand educational advertising and personal selling to the final consumer.

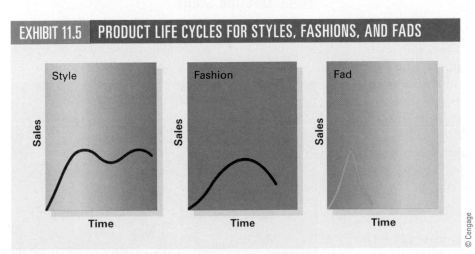

EXHIBIT 11.5 PRODUCT LIFE CYCLES FOR STYLES, FASHIONS, AND FADS

Style — Sales / Time

Fashion — Sales / Time

Fad — Sales / Time

© Cengage

product category all brands that satisfy a particular type of need

introductory stage the full-scale launch of a new product into the marketplace

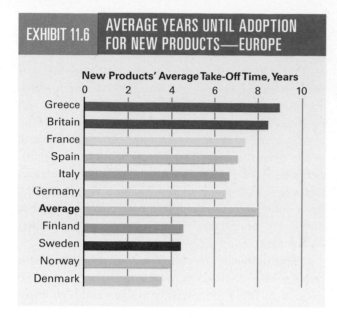

EXHIBIT 11.6 AVERAGE YEARS UNTIL ADOPTION FOR NEW PRODUCTS—EUROPE

New Products' Average Take-Off Time, Years

Country	Years
Greece	
Britain	
France	
Spain	
Italy	
Germany	
Average	
Finland	
Sweden	
Norway	
Denmark	

The PLC seems to vary among European countries, from just under four years in Denmark to about nine years in Greece. (See Exhibit 11.6.) Cultural factors seem to be largely responsible for these differences. Scandinavians are often more open to new ideas than people in other European countries.[24]

11-5b Growth Stage

If a product category survives the introductory stage, it advances to the **growth stage** of the life cycle. The growth stage is the second stage of the product life cycle, when sales typically grow at an increasing rate, many competitors enter the market, large companies may start to acquire small pioneering firms, and profits are healthy. Profits rise rapidly in the growth stage, reach their peak, and begin declining as competition intensifies. Emphasis switches from primary demand promotion (for example, promoting tablets) to aggressive brand advertising and communication of the differences between brands (for example, promoting the Apple iPad Pro and Google Pixel C).

Distribution becomes a major key to success during the growth stage and later stages. Manufacturers scramble to sign up dealers and distributors and to build long-term

growth stage the second stage of the product life cycle when sales typically grow at an increasing rate, many competitors enter the market, large companies may start to acquire small pioneering firms, and profits are healthy

maturity stage a period during which sales increase at a decreasing rate

decline stage a long-run drop in sales

relationships. Without adequate distribution, it is impossible to establish a strong market position.

11-5c Maturity Stage

A period during which sales increase at a decreasing rate signals the beginning of the **maturity stage** of the life cycle. New users cannot be added indefinitely, and, sooner or later, the market approaches saturation. Normally, the maturity stage is the longest stage of the product life cycle. Many major household appliances are in the maturity stage of their life cycles.

For shopping products, such as durable goods and electronics, and for many specialty products, annual models begin to appear during the maturity stage. Product lines are lengthened to appeal to additional market segments. Service and repair assume more important roles as manufacturers strive to distinguish their products from others. Product design changes tend to become stylistic (How can the product be made different?) rather than functional (How can the product be made better?).

As prices and profits continue to fall, marginal competitors start dropping out of the market. Dealer margins also shrink, resulting in less shelf space for mature items, lower dealer inventories, and a general reluctance to promote the product. Thus, promotion to dealers often intensifies during this stage to retain loyalty.

Heavy consumer promotion by the manufacturer is also required to maintain market share. Cutthroat competition during this stage can lead to price wars. Another characteristic of the maturity stage is the emergence of niche marketers that target narrow, well-defined, underserved segments of a market. Starbucks Coffee targets its gourmet line at the only segment of the coffee market that is growing: new, younger, more affluent coffee drinkers.

11-5d Decline Stage

A long-run drop in sales signals the beginning of the **decline stage**. The rate of decline is governed by how

Sorbis/Shutterstock.com

rapidly consumer tastes change or substitute products are adopted. Many convenience products and trendy items lose their market overnight, leaving large inventories of unsold items, such as designer jeans. Others die more slowly. Video rental stores like Blockbuster went out of business and were replaced by Netflix and other forms of digital entertainment.

Some firms have developed successful strategies for marketing products in the decline stage of the product life cycle. They eliminate all nonessential marketing expenses and let sales decline as more and more customers discontinue purchasing the products. Eventually, the product is withdrawn from the market.

Management sage Peter Drucker said that all companies should practise organized abandonment, which involves reviewing every product, service, and policy every two or three years and asking the critical question "If we didn't do this already, would we launch it now?" If the answer is no, it's time to begin the abandonment process.[25]

11-5e Implications for Marketing Management

The product life cycle concept encourages marketing managers to plan so that they can take the initiative instead of reacting to past events. The PLC is especially useful as a predicting, or forecasting, tool. Because products pass through distinctive stages, it is often possible to estimate a product's location on the curve by

Kodak's first consumer camera was introduced in 1888. With the rise of smartphone camera technology, this discontinuous innovation might be heading toward the end of its product life cycle.

using historical data. Profits, like sales, tend to follow a predictable path over a product's life cycle.

Exhibit 11.7 shows the relationship between the adopter categories and the stages of the PLC. Note that the various categories of adopters first buy products in different stages of the life cycle. Almost all sales in the maturity and decline stages represent repeat purchasing.

EXHIBIT 11.7 RELATIONSHIPS BETWEEN THE DIFFUSION PROCESS AND THE PRODUCT LIFE CYCLE

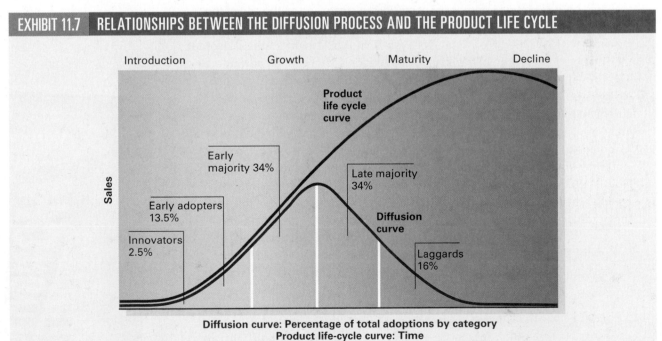

SIDE LAUNCH
BREWING COMPANY
CONTINUING CASE

Balancing a Beer Portfolio

"I think Coors Light is a very refreshing beverage." Not exactly the admission one might expect to hear from one of Canada's craft beer pioneers. But brewer Michael Hancock, who did his time in macro beer prior to launching his own Denison's brand of craft beer in the 1980s, has an instinct to see the upside of any kind of beer rather than possess a blind craft elitism often associated with craft beer producers. "People always think that's the kind of beer that no craft brewer would be seen dead with, but I don't fit that stereotype. Generally speaking though, for session drinking, as we call it, for people who know anything about beer, it just doesn't have enough substance," he concludes.

As discussed in Chapter 3, the Ansoff Growth Opportunity Matrix demonstrates four general growth strategies for firms, two of which—product development and diversification—involve creating new products to add to a firm's line-up. In the craft brewery space, there are always external pressures to refine existing beers or expand the product portfolio by offering something new, conforming to one beer trend or another. The Side Launch mindset, however, is a little bit different. "As craft brewers, admittedly we gravitate to trying new things for so many reasons," offers Dave Sands, VP Operations. "It's a great opportunity to learn about the infinite number of beers we can create and, at the end of the day, make something ourselves we're interested in tasting." The opportunity cost, he then concludes, is obvious. "The worst thing you can do, for the sake of making one brew's worth of new beer, is to upset or impact your breadwinners."

Those breadwinners, the ones that Side Launch is committed to producing year-round, the ones they base their entire operations on from procurement of raw materials to the preprinted packaging bearing that increasingly familiar Side Launch logo, are not merely "made" as much as they are "coddled" by Michael, Dave, and everyone involved in the operation. "So many craft breweries are cranking out minor variations on the same style, particularly IPAs," observes Michael, "but I think if we were to become obsessed with creating the next big thing, or following trends, then we would have missed the opportunity to make the best of these four. That's a very personal thing."

The conviction in his tone reflects a common mantra heard, seen, and felt from within the brewery itself as well as on the streets in the story told to customers by Side Launch sales reps: "True to style, honest, and authentic." Products aren't managed only at the production level. The way they are positioned and sold through the market requires patience and critical thinking as well, and constant open communication must occur between sales and production.

To VP Sales and Marketing Chuck Galea, overseeing the front end of the Side Launch operation, the understanding of the delicate balance of remaining true to style, even if it means marketing a product that may not perform as well as another, is vital to be seen as a complete craft beer brand. "The Dark Lager and the Pale haven't kept up to the pace of Wheat and Mountain in terms of rate of sale," he explains. "We have more distribution of our Dark Lager, with less volume, whereas we have lower distribution with Mountain Lager, but higher volume."

The easy business decision would be to crank up production of what's selling the best, while curtailing production of what's with selling less, and yet to do so would be to dismiss the importance of having strong representation across the four flavour profiles Side Launch produces year-round. Thus, from a brand perspective, the whole, as Side Launch sees it, is much greater than the sum of its parts.

Questions

1. As discussed in the previous chapter, Side Launch allocates a certain amount of resources toward innovating beyond its four core brands. In this chapter, we see how developing new products requires a rigorous process prior to commercialization. Does it appear to be Side Launch's goal to make money with its experimental beers? Explain.

2. VP Sales and Marketing Chuck Galea observes in this chapter that two of his core brands sell more, despite being less widely distributed than the other two. Does this automatically indicate that the two faster sellers are in the growth stage of the product life cycle and that the other two are in maturity?

3. With limited resources, brewing capacity and so on, the Side Launch focus on its four core brands might be seen as a compromise to innovation and commercialization of the "next big thing." How does Side Launch rationalize this particular part of its product strategy.

Side Launch Brewing Company

12 | Services and Nonprofit Organization Marketing

LEARNING OUTCOMES

12-1 Discuss the importance of services to the economy

12-2 Discuss the differences between services and goods

12-3 Describe the components of service quality and the gap model of service quality

12-4 Develop marketing mixes for services using the eight Ps of services marketing

12-5 Discuss relationship marketing in services

12-6 Explain internal marketing in services

12-7 Describe nonprofit organization marketing

"Great things in business are never done by one person, they're done by a team of people."

—Steve Jobs[1]

12-1 THE IMPORTANCE OF SERVICES

A **service** is the result of applying human or mechanical efforts to people or objects. Services involve a deed, a performance, or an effort that cannot be physically possessed. Today, the service sector substantially influences the Canadian economy. According to Statistics Canada, in 2016 the service sector accounted for 79 percent of all employment.[2] Canadian economic growth continues to be driven by growth in the service sector, with almost three-quarters of Canadian GDP coming from services.[3] The growing service sector is a key area for employment opportunities. In December 2016, 76 percent of all hours worked by Canadians were hours worked in the service producing sector.[4] While services continue to dominate the Canadian landscape at home, they also are dominating our export business. Although

traditional Canadian exports have struggled in the past few years, the export of Canadian services has grown. Today services account for over 40 percent of the value of Canadian exports.[5] As expected, our largest trading partner (both exports and imports) in services is the United States. Over the past decade, three out of the five fastest-growing exports were services, and as Canadian companies continue to invest in global strategies, service exports will continue to grow. Canadian services are of world-class quality, with financial services, management, and computer and information technology growing more than 50 percent in the past decade. Growth in the demand for services is expected to continue. To be successful in the global marketplace, service firms must first determine the nature of their core product, and the marketing mix elements should be designed to take into account each country's cultural, technological, and political environments. As business strategy continues to emphasize the integration of products and services, and as emerging markets and the rebounding U.S. economy

service the result of applying human or mechanical efforts to people or objects

blame

#NEVERBLAMETHEVICTIM

increase demand for Canadian natural resources and manufactured goods, service exports will grow alongside.[6]

Whether you are marketing a good or a service, the marketing process discussed in Chapter 1 is the same, although services have some unique characteristics that distinguish them from goods, and marketing strategies need to be adjusted for these characteristics.

12-2 HOW SERVICES DIFFER FROM GOODS

Services have four unique characteristics that distinguish them from goods. Services are intangible, they are inseparable, they run the risk of being inconsistent, and they cannot be inventoried.

12-2a Intangibility

The basic difference between services and goods is that services have no physical attributes. Because of their **intangibility**, they cannot be touched, seen, tasted, heard, or felt in the same manner that goods can be sensed.

Evaluating the quality of services before or even after making a purchase is harder than evaluating the quality of goods because, compared with goods,

services tend to exhibit fewer search qualities. A **search quality** is a characteristic that can be easily assessed before purchase—for instance, the colour of a car or the size of a smartphone. At the same time, services tend to exhibit more experience and credence qualities. An **experience quality** is a characteristic that can be assessed only after use, such as the quality of a meal in a restaurant. A **credence quality** is a characteristic that consumers may have difficulty assessing even after purchase because they do not have the necessary knowledge or experience. Medical and consulting services are examples of services that exhibit credence qualities.

These characteristics also make it more difficult for marketers to communicate the benefits of an intangible service than to communicate the benefits of tangible goods. Thus marketers often rely on tangible cues to communicate a service's nature and quality. For example, the amazon.ca

intangibility the inability of services to be touched, seen, tasted, heard, or felt in the same manner that goods can be sensed

search quality a characteristic that can be easily assessed before purchase

experience quality a characteristic that can be assessed only after use

credence quality a characteristic that consumers may have difficulty assessing even after purchase because they do not have the necessary knowledge or experience

Everything from "a" to "z" with a smile...

logo has an arrow from the "a" to the "z," communicating that Amazon has everything from a to z.

The facilities that customers visit, or from which services are delivered, are a critical tangible part of the total service offering. Messages about the organization are communicated to customers through such elements as the decor, the clutter or neatness of service areas, and the staff's manners and dress. Think of how you assess the service of a new hairdresser before your first appointment. Undoubtedly, you consider the appearance of both the salon and the hairdresser to get a sense of whether the salon's style suits your needs. This assessment, which is based on the physical surroundings, is critical in your decision to proceed with the appointment.

12-2b Inseparability

Goods are produced, sold, and then consumed. In contrast, services are often sold, and then produced and consumed at the same time. In other words, their production and consumption are inseparable activities. This **inseparability** means that because consumers must be present during the production of services, such as haircuts or surgery, they are actually involved in the production of the services they buy.

Simultaneous production and consumption also means that services normally cannot be produced in a centralized location and consumed in decentralized locations, as goods typically are. Services are also inseparable from the perspective of the service

inseparability the inability of the production and consumption of a service to be separated; consumers must be present during the production

inconsistency the inability of service quality to be consistent each time it is delivered because the service depends on the people who provide it

inventory the inability of services to be stored for future use

provider. Thus the quality of service that firms are able to deliver depends on the quality of their employees.

12-2c Inconsistency

One great strength of McDonald's is consistency. Whether customers order a Big Mac in Tokyo or Moscow, they know exactly what they will get. This is not the case with many service firms. Because services depend on a service provider, the quality of the service can reveal **inconsistency**. For example, physicians in a group practice or hairstylists in a salon differ in their technical and interpersonal skills. Because services tend to be labour intensive and production and consumption are inseparable, consistency and quality control can be difficult to achieve.

Standardization and training help increase consistency and reliability. In the competitive retail landscape, consistency of service quality is often key to building a competitive advantage. Saje Natural Wellness is a 25-year-old family-run Canadian business with 45 locations across North America and a 1017 percent growth over the past five years. The owners—a husband and wife team—are a perfect complement to one another to ensure continued growth and long-term success. Jean-Pierre LeBlanc has a background in corporate chemistry, which led to the launch of their initial products, still available at Saje today. Kate Ross, on the other hand, grew up in the retail industry and as she would tell you, "It is in my DNA to create outrageous customer experiences."[7] It is these customer experiences that ensure customers return. Saje's corporate philosophy is that all employees report to the customer. Sales staff listen and answer questions with honesty and sincerity, educating the customer to ensure the products purchased meet the customer's needs as discussed. At the same time Saje invests in the tangible product, ensuring that the product mix is composed of high-quality natural products.[8]

12-2d Inventory

The fourth characteristic of services is **inventory**. Services cannot be stored, warehoused, or inventoried. If a service is not consumed, it perishes. If the runs aren't busy at the Fernie Alpine Ski resort, they cannot be stored for the next day or the next busy day. The revenue from the lack of skiers is lost. Yet service organizations are often forced to turn away full-price customers during peak periods.

One of the most important challenges in many service industries is finding ways to synchronize supply and demand. The philosophy that some revenue is better than none has prompted many hotels to offer deep discounts on weekends and during the off-season. In some service sectors,

Roberto Machado Noa/LightRocket/Getty Images

compensation is based on a commission system in an attempt to not waste inventory cost on idle production capacity.

12-3 SERVICE QUALITY

Because of the four unique characteristics of services, service quality is more difficult to define and measure than the quality of tangible goods. Business executives rank the improvement of service quality as one of the most critical challenges facing them today.

Research has shown that customers evaluate service quality by the following five components:[9]

- **Reliability**: the ability to perform the service dependably, accurately, and consistently. Reliability refers to performing the service right the first time and every time. This component has been found to be the one most important to consumers. Reliability of delivery will create brand loyalty, which in the highly competitive service industry is coveted. Take, for example, the Calgary Philharmonic Orchestra (CPO). With a renowned conductor as music director and talented musicians offering a variety of consistently high-quality musical performances, it has come to be known as an orchestra of exceptional artistic excellence. This level of ongoing excellence has led to sold-out performances.

- **Responsiveness**: the ability to provide prompt service. Examples of responsiveness are returning customers' calls quickly, serving lunch fast to someone in a hurry, or ensuring that the consumer does not have to wait past the appointment time. The ultimate in responsiveness is offering service 24 hours a day, seven days a week.

- **Assurance**: the knowledge and courtesy of employees and their ability to convey trust. Skilled employees exemplify assurance when they treat customers with respect and when they make customers

feel that they can trust the firm. Hyatt Hotels have high employee retention and long tenure with their employees, which is unusual in an industry noted for high employee turnover. Hyatt Hotels has invested in its employees, empowering them to listen more closely to one another and to guests. By listening to each other and their guests, they are able to find individualized methods of solving customer concerns that better suit the customer and colleagues. All of Hyatt's 95,000 associates at their hotels around the globe have been trained in empathetic listening and changing the guest experience. In an industry heavily reliant on service, this approach is fostering loyalty with both employees and customers.[10]

- **Empathy**: caring, individualized attention paid to customers. Firms whose employees recognize customers and learn their specific requirements are providing empathy. Again, empowering employees to be partners provides the opportunity for Starbucks' baristas to be empathetic. The emphasis on creating connections is the stimulus for the barista–customer relationship that many Starbucks' baristas and customers have come to enjoy.

- **Tangibles**: the physical evidence of the service. The tangible parts of a service include the physical facilities, tools, and equipment used to provide the service, and the appearance of personnel. Starbucks' physical facility reinforces its desire to create and foster connections. Starbucks promotes socializing in the restaurants—they are neighbourhood gathering places offering comfortable seating, WiFi, and newspapers. The stores are a haven from the stresses of the day.

Overall service quality is measured by combining customers' evaluations for all five components.

12-3a The Gap Model of Service Quality

A model of service quality called the **gap model** identifies five gaps that can cause problems in service delivery and influence customer evaluations of service quality (see Exhibit 12.1):[11]

reliability the ability to perform a service dependably, accurately, and consistently

responsiveness the ability to provide prompt service

assurance the knowledge and courtesy of employees and their ability to convey trust

empathy caring, individualized attention paid to customers

tangibles the physical evidence of a service, including the physical facilities, tools, and equipment used to provide the service

gap model a model identifying five gaps that can cause problems in service delivery and influence customer evaluations of service quality

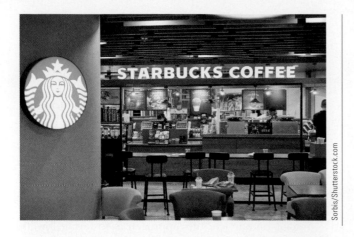

Sorbis/Shutterstock.com

- **GAP 1:** Knowledge gap—the gap between what customers want and what management thinks customers want. This gap results from a lack of understanding or a misinterpretation of the customers' needs, wants, or desires. A consumer's expectations may vary for a variety of reasons, including his or her past experiences and the type of situation. A firm that does little or no customer satisfaction research is likely to experience this gap. To close gap 1, firms must stay attuned to customer wants by researching customer needs and satisfaction. Because employees in a service setting are the

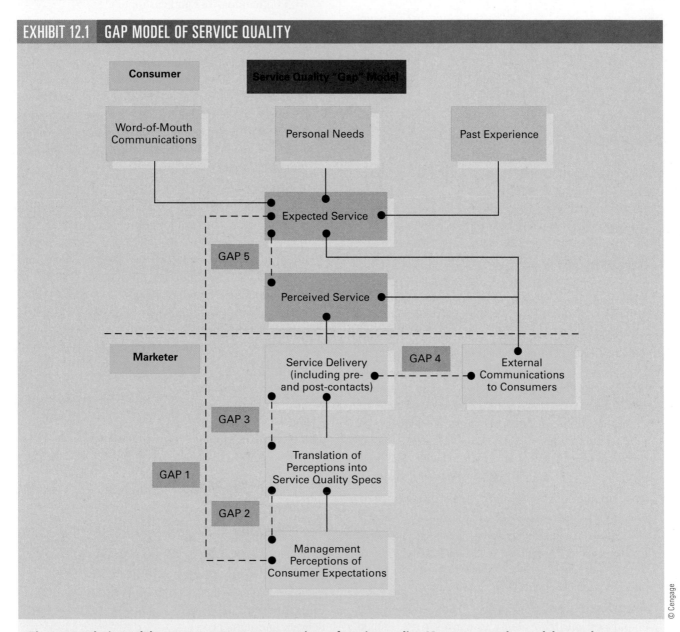

EXHIBIT 12.1   GAP MODEL OF SERVICE QUALITY

Service Quality "Gap" Model

Consumer

| Word-of-Mouth Communications | Personal Needs | Past Experience |

Expected Service

GAP 5

Perceived Service

Marketer

Service Delivery (including pre- and post-contacts)

GAP 4

External Communications to Consumers

GAP 3

Translation of Perceptions into Service Quality Specs

GAP 1

GAP 2

Management Perceptions of Consumer Expectations

© Cengage

The gap analysis model measures consumer perceptions of service quality. Managers use the model to analyze sources of quality problems and to understand how service quality can be improved.

service provider, gap 1 can be managed by increasing the interaction and communication between management and employees.

- **GAP 2:** Standards gap—the gap between what management think customers want and the quality specifications that management develops to provide the service. Essentially, this gap is the result of management's inability to translate customers' needs into delivery systems within the firm. In other words, the gap is a result of management not having provided the appropriate service designs and standards. The reduction in this gap is achieved through the creation of policies and procedures related to the delivery of the service, the establishment of metrics to measure performance on an ongoing basis, and the training and development of employees. As noted in the management of gap 1, employee involvement in the establishment of both the policies and procedures and the metrics is critical for success, as the employee is in constant contact with the customer in the delivery of the service and thus is extremely knowledgeable with respect to customer expectations.

- **GAP 3:** Delivery gap—the gap between the service quality specifications and the service that is actually provided. If both gaps 1 and 2 have been closed, then gap 3 results from the inability of management and employees to do what should be done. Management needs to ensure that employees have the skills and the proper tools to perform their jobs, including effective training programs and ongoing feedback. Hyatt Hotels invested in 95,000 associates with the necessary training to ensure they all had the required skills to interact with guests and the confidence to create unique solutions. New policies were created with new tools and new ways of working together demonstrated.[12]

- **GAP 4:** Communication gap—the gap between what the company provides and what the customer is told it provides. To close this gap, companies need to create realistic customer expectations through honest, accurate communication regarding what they can provide. Communication programs must be managed to ensure messaging reflects what the company can consistently deliver.

- **GAP 5:** Expectation gap—the gap between the service that customers expect they should receive and the perceived service after the service has been provided. This gap can be positive or negative and clearly influences consumers' perception of service

EXHIBIT 12.2	TOP 10 CUSTOMER SERVICE COMPANIES
Ranking	**Company**
1	Lexus
2	Napa AutoPro
3	Tangerine
4	RBC Royal Bank
5	ATB Financial
6	TD Canada Trust
7	Scotiabank
8	Intact Insurance
9	State Farm
10	The Cooperators

Source: Doug Murray, "19 Companies with the Best Customer Service in Canada," Slice.ca, June 15, 2016.

quality. Ongoing research is necessary to understand consumers' perceptions and to manage their expectations. In this age of social media, where peer-to-peer conversations are happening online in real time on a number of online forums, companies must be vigilant in their monitoring of these conversations to ensure timely responses.

When one or more of these gaps is large, service quality is perceived as being low. As the gaps shrink, service quality perception improves.

Forty-nine percent of Canadians have changed their minds about buying something or have gone to a competitor because of poor service quality. Once the consumer does go to a competitor, 68 percent say they will not return. It is absolutely imperative that companies get service quality right.[13]

12-4 MARKETING MIXES FOR SERVICES

Services' unique characteristics—intangibility, inseparability of production and consumption, inconsistency, and inventory—make the marketing of services more challenging. Elements of the marketing mix (product, place, promotion, and pricing) need to be adjusted to meet the special needs created by these characteristics. In addition, effective marketing of services requires the management of four additional Ps: people, process, productivity, and physical environment.

12-4a Product (Service) Strategy

A product, as defined in Chapter 10, is everything a person receives in an exchange. In the case of a service organization, the product offering is intangible and is part of a process or a series of processes. This definition suggests then that the service firm must attempt to make the intangible tangible by providing physical cues of the service quality and positioning. Logos, tag lines, and promotional materials attempt to create tangible evidence of the service offering.

SERVICE AS A PROCESS Two broad categories of things are processed in service organizations: people and objects. In some cases, the process is physical, or tangible; in other cases, the process is intangible. Using these characteristics, service processes can be placed into one of four categories:[14]

- *People processing* takes place when the service is directed at a customer. Examples are transportation services and healthcare.

- *Possession processing* occurs when the service is directed at customers' physical possessions. Examples are lawn care and veterinary services.

- *Mental stimulus processing* refers to services directed at people's minds. Examples are theatre performances and education.

- *Information processing* describes services that use technology or brainpower directed at a customer's assets. Examples are insurance and consulting.

Because customers' experiences and involvement differ for each of these types of services processes, marketing strategies may also differ. Take, for example, a season's pass to the games of a Canadian Football League (CFL) team. It is a mental stimulus–processing service where the quality of the product (the service) is very much dependent on the quality of the players and the coaching staff. The game outcome can never be controlled, but the individual clubs can control other aspects of the game to ensure the game attendee has a positive experience. The half-time shows, the game-day give-aways, the stadium itself, and the food and drink are elements of the product that can be controlled to enhance the service experience.

CORE AND SUPPLE-MENTARY SERVICE PRODUCTS The service offering can be viewed as a bundle of activities that includes the **core service**, which is the most basic benefit the customer is buying, and a group of **supplementary services** that support or enhance the core service. Exhibit 12.3 illustrates these concepts for a hotel like the Hyatt. The core service is providing bedrooms for rent, which involves people processing. The supplemental services might include food services, reservations, parking, WiFi, and television services. In many service industries, the core product becomes a commodity as competition increases. Thus firms usually emphasize supplemental services to create a competitive advantage. On the other hand, some firms are positioning themselves in the marketplace by greatly reducing supplemental services.

CUSTOMIZATION/STANDARDIZATION An important issue in developing the service offering is whether to customize or standardize it. Customized services are more flexible and respond to individual customers' needs. They also usually command a higher price. Standardized services are more efficient and cost less.

Instead of choosing to either standardize or customize a service, a firm may incorporate elements of both by adopting an emerging strategy called **mass customization**. Mass customization uses technology to deliver customized services on a mass basis, which results in giving each customer whatever she or he asks for.

THE SERVICE MIX Many service organizations market more than one service. For example, Vancouver City Savings Credit Union, more commonly known as

Fluke Transportation Group is an example of a possession-processing service. This service focuses less on the attractiveness of its physical environment than would a people-processing service, such as a massage therapist, but emphasis is still placed on the logo and the look of the physical cues that represent the company.

core service the most basic benefit the consumer is buying

supplementary services a group of services that support or enhance the core service

mass customization a strategy that uses technology to deliver customized services on a mass basis

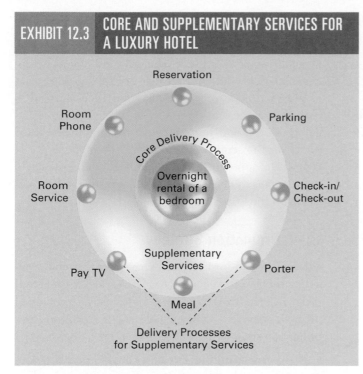

Source: Lovelock, Christopher H.; Wirtz, Jochen, *Services Marketing*, 7th, © 2011. Electronically reproduced by permission of Pearson Education, Inc., Upper Saddle River, New Jersey.

service positioning. To establish these processes, the knowledge gap must be reduced through market research that seeks to understand consumer expectations; a process protocol must then be established to ensure the service delivery meets customers' expectations. Process is fluid, which means that customer satisfaction should be evaluated on an ongoing basis and processes should be updated to ensure service delivery continues to meet expectations. The more standardized the delivery, the less likely the need for ongoing evaluation of process.

12-4c People Strategy

The standards gap and the delivery gap must be managed to improve the service. The service is provided by a service provider, but distinguishing between the two is often very difficult. Thus managing the employee who is the service provider is highly strategic. Strategies include providing incentives, training, and recognition programs that management consistently supports. Employees who are well trained, empowered, and rewarded will deliver on the service promise. Take Modo Yoga Studios as an example. Founded in Toronto in 2004 by two yoga practitioners, Modo Yoga (formerly known as Moksha Yoga) has grown into an international company offering a variety of yoga classes. Modo studios are independently owned and operated by individuals. To ensure the Modo brand's positioning is managed across all studios, Modo owner/operators must meet exacting specifications before being awarded a franchise. They must have taken the 11-month Modo teacher training program and demonstrate commitment to the Modo seven pillars. While each studio is unique to reflect the community it is in, the Modo seven pillars reflect, in part, a commitment to service excellence through lifelong learning, healthy living, community service and support, green living, and accessibility for all. These seven pillars form the foundation to ensure that each studio and each yoga class leader delivers on the Modo Yoga promise.[15]

Vancity, is a financial cooperative offering a wide range of banking and investment services to both individuals and organizations. Each service within the organization's service mix represents a set of opportunities, risks, and challenges. Each part of the service mix makes a different contribution to achieving the firm's overall goals. To succeed, each service may also need a different level of financial support. Designing a service strategy therefore means deciding what new services to introduce to which target market, what existing services to maintain, and what services to eliminate.

12-4b Process Strategy

Because services are delivered before or while being consumed, the marketing mix for services includes the strategic decisions surrounding the process. Here, *process* refers to the establishing of standards to ensure the service delivery is consistent and compatible with the

12-4d Place (Distribution) Strategy

Distribution strategies for service organizations must focus on such issues as convenience, number of outlets, direct versus indirect distribution, location, and scheduling. One of the key factors influencing the selection of a service provider is *convenience*. Hence, the place strategy is important to service firms.

goodfood

An interesting example of this is Goodfood, a weekly grocery service. Jonathan Ferrari, Neil Cuggy, and Raffi Krikorian co-founded Goodfood in 2014 with the goal of changing the way Canadians prepare and eat meals. Each week all the fresh ingredients you need to make delicious meals at home are delivered in a refrigerated box to your door free of charge. The convenience of having all the ingredients to prepare a wholesome meal delivered to your door is keeping families eating together at home. In an effort to further differentiate the brand, Goodfood supports local community charity initiatives that are dedicated to food-insecure children by providing a meal to a schoolchild in need for every box purchased. In 2017 Goodfood aims to provide 75,000 meals to children in need.[16]

An important distribution objective for many service firms is the *number of outlets* to use or the number of outlets to open during a certain time. Generally, the intensity of distribution should meet, but not exceed, the target market's needs and preferences. Having too few outlets may inconvenience customers; having too many outlets may boost costs unnecessarily. Intensity of distribution may also depend on the image desired. Having only a few outlets may make the service seem more exclusive or selective.

The next service distribution decision is whether to distribute services to end-users *directly* or *indirectly* through other firms. Because of the nature of services, many service firms choose to use direct distribution or franchising. Examples are legal, medical, accounting, and personal-care services. The Internet has given some service providers the opportunity to intensify their distribution and even to automate part of the service to better satisfy the customer. Most of the major airlines are now using online services to sell tickets directly to consumers, which results in lower distribution costs for the airline companies. Other firms with standardized service packages have developed indirect channels that place the service in more convenient locations for their customers. Bank ATMs located in gas stations and hotel lobbies are a good example of standardizing a service and intensifying distribution by relying on indirect channels.

The *location* of a service most clearly reveals the relationship between its target market strategy and its distribution strategy. For time-dependent service providers, such as airlines, physicians, and dentists, *scheduling* is often a more important factor.

12-4e Physical Evidence Strategy

Closely associated with managing place strategies to maintain service quality is managing the physical evidence surrounding the service delivery. All four categories of service processes can benefit from attention paid to both the physical environment in which the service is being offered and the quality of the equipment used to deliver the service. For example, when you arrive at your dental appointment, old equipment may lead you to question the ability of the dentist to provide the best oral care with the least amount of pain.

12-4f Promotion Strategy

Consumers and business users have more trouble evaluating services than goods because services are less tangible. In turn, marketers have more trouble promoting intangible services than tangible goods. Here are four promotion strategies for services:

- **Stressing tangible cues:** A tangible cue is a concrete symbol of the service offering. To make their services more tangible, hotels will turn down beds in the evening and leave a mint on the pillow, ensure concierge staff are attentive, and offer free newspapers outside the room door each morning.

- **Using personal information sources:** A personal information source is someone consumers are familiar with (such as a celebrity) or someone they know or can relate to personally. Service firms can set up blogs and stimulate customer interaction on the blogs to generate positive word of mouth. Facebook, Twitter, LinkedIn, and other social media sites are used by service firms in their promotion strategy to capitalize on the potential for consumer discussion around their service offerings. Of course, there is always the possibility of negative word of mouth, which requires a comprehensive and often swift crisis communication plan.

- **Creating a strong organizational image:** One way to create an image is to manage the evidence, including the physical environment of the service facility, the appearance of the service employees, and the tangible items associated with a service, such as the firm's website, stationery, and brochures. Canadian Tire employees all wear red uniforms, and the red logo and the colour red predominates in all communications.

- **Engaging in postpurchase communication:** Postpurchase communication refers to the follow-up activities that a service firm might engage in after a

Celebrity is a powerful promotional tool for services and nonprofits alike. Here Shawn Mendes takes selfies at We Day.

customer transaction. Emails, letters, and other types of follow-up are excellent ways to demonstrate to the customer that their feedback matters.

12-4g Price Strategy

Considerations in pricing a service are similar to the pricing considerations to be discussed in Chapter 13. However, the unique characteristics of services present special pricing challenges.

First, to price a service, it is important to define the unit of service consumption. For example, should pricing be based on the specific task (such as washing the car) or should it be time based (such as the amount of time it takes to wash the car)? Some services include the consumption of goods. Restaurants charge for the food and drink consumed, not for the table and chairs that have been used.

Second, for services that comprise multiple elements, the issue is whether pricing should be based on a bundle of elements or whether each element should be priced separately. Often a bundle price is used because consumers don't want to pay "extra" for every element in the service, and it is administratively easier for the service company.

Marketers should set performance objectives when pricing each service. Three categories of pricing objectives have been suggested:[17]

- Revenue-oriented pricing focuses on maximizing the surplus of income over costs. This is the same approach that many manufacturing firms use. A limitation of this approach is that determining costs can be difficult for many services.

- Operations-oriented pricing seeks to match supply and demand by varying prices. For example, matching hotel demand to the number of available rooms can be achieved by raising prices at peak times and decreasing them during slow times.

- Patronage-oriented pricing tries to maximize the number of customers using the service. Thus prices vary with different market segments' ability to pay, and methods of payment (such as credit) are offered to increase the likelihood of a purchase. Senior citizen and student discounts at movie theatres and restaurants are examples patronage-oriented pricing.

A firm may need to use more than one type of pricing objective. In fact, all three objectives may need to be included to some degree in a pricing strategy, although the importance of each type may vary depending on the type of service provided, the prices that competitors are charging, the differing ability of various customer segments to pay, or the opportunity to negotiate price. For customized services (such as construction services), customers may also have the ability to negotiate a price.

12-4h Productivity Strategy

Because services are often tied to a service provider and because the delivery of a service cannot be inventoried if supply exceeds demand, it is critical that the service firm work to manage the supply or the availability of the service without affecting service quality. Such a strategy is often referred to as capacity management. A trip to Florida during your February break is likely much more expensive than the same trip in September. Student demand for holidays to Florida is high in February, and hotels and airlines try to capitalize on the demand. In September, on the other hand, school has just started, and students and families are thus otherwise engaged, so hotels and airlines offer lower prices to stimulate demand. After all, the plane still has to fly despite empty seats, and the hotels are still open despite empty rooms. This method of capacity management is called *off-peak pricing*, and every day we see plenty of examples of it.

12-5 RELATIONSHIP MARKETING IN SERVICES

Many services involve ongoing interaction between the service organization and the customer. Thus these services can benefit from relationship marketing, the strategy described in Chapter 1, as a means of attracting, developing, and retaining customer relationships. The

racorn/Shutterstock.com

is designed to reward the consumer for repeat buying, the data gathered by the firm based on each purchase allows for targeted communication with the customer, which serves to further enhance the service–customer relationship. Relationship marketing can be practised at four levels:

- **Level 1: Financial.** Pricing incentives are used to encourage customers to continue doing business with a firm. Frequent flyer programs are an example of level 1 relationship marketing. This level of relationship marketing is the least effective in the long term because its price-based advantage is easily imitated by other firms.

- **Level 2: Social.** This level of relationship marketing also uses pricing incentives but seeks to build social bonds with customers. The firm stays in touch with its customers, learns about their needs, and designs services to meet those needs. Level 2 relationship marketing is often more effective than level 1 relationship marketing.

- **Level 3: Customization.** A customized approach encourages customer loyalty through intimate knowledge of individual customers (often referred to as customer intimacy) and the development of one-to-one solutions to fit customer needs.

- **Level 4: Structural.** At this level, the firm again uses financial and social bonds but adds structural bonds to the formula. Structural bonds are developed by offering value-added services that are not readily available from other firms. Many high-end hotels leave treats in repeat guests' hotel rooms when they celebrate special events, such as a bottle of wine for a couple celebrating an anniversary. Marketing programs like this one have the strongest potential for sustaining long-term relationships with customers.[18]

12-6 INTERNAL MARKETING IN SERVICE FIRMS

The service and the service provider are inseparable. Thus the quality of a firm's employees is crucial to delivering a consistently superior product and to building long-term relationships with customers. Employees who like their jobs and are satisfied with the firm they work for are more likely to deliver superior service to customers. Their superior service, in turn, increases the likelihood of retaining customers. Thus it is critical

idea is to develop strong loyalty by creating satisfied customers who will buy additional services from the firm and are unlikely to switch to a competitor. Satisfied customers are also likely to engage in positive word-of-mouth communication, thereby helping to bring in new customers.

Many businesses have found it more cost-effective to hang on to the customers they have than to focus only on attracting new customers.

Services that purchasers receive on a continuing basis (for example, prescriptions, banking, and insurance) can be considered membership services. This type of service naturally lends itself to relationship marketing. When services involve discrete transactions (for example, a movie screening, a restaurant meal, or public transportation), it may be more difficult to build membership-type relationships with customers. Nevertheless, services involving discrete transactions may be transformed into membership relationships by using marketing tools. For example, the service could be sold in bulk (for example, a subscription to a theatre season or a commuter pass on public transportation). Or a service firm could offer special benefits to customers who choose to register with the firm (for example, loyalty programs for hotels and airlines). While the registration process and subsequent use of the loyalty card at every purchase

Companies like Google have designed and instituted a wide variety of programs such as flextime, on-site daycare, and concierge service for their employees.

that service firms practise **internal marketing**, which means treating employees as customers and developing systems and benefits that satisfy their needs. While this strategy may also apply to goods manufacturers, it is even more critical in service firms. This is because in service industries, employees deliver the brand promise—their performance as a brand representative—directly to consumers. To satisfy employees, companies have designed and instituted a wide variety of programs, such as flextime, onsite daycare, investments in wellness, and compassionate-care top-up payments.

 ## 12-7 NONPROFIT ORGANIZATION MARKETING

A **nonprofit organization** is an organization that exists to achieve some goal other than the usual business goals of profit, market share, and return on investment. Both nonprofit organizations and private-sector service firms market intangible products, and both often require the customer to be present during the production process. Both for-profit and nonprofit services vary greatly from producer to producer and from day to day, even from the same producer.

Canada's nonprofit and voluntary sector is the second-largest in the world, behind the Netherlands. In Canada, more than two million people are employed in the nonprofit sector, representing 11.1 percent of the economically active population. The nonprofit sector represents $106 billion or 8.1 percent of Canada's gross

domestic product (GDP), which is larger than the manufacturing or automotive industries.[19]

The nonprofit sector includes many organizations that support those who are disadvantaged, as well as hospitals, colleges, and universities. If hospitals, colleges, and universities are removed from the picture, the remaining organizations are what Statistics Canada calls the core nonprofit sector. The core nonprofit sector accounts for about 2.4 percent of GDP, which is more than three times that accounted for by the motor vehicle industry. It is often assumed that the government funds charities and nonprofits. That is not the case, and in fact sale of goods and services account for 45 percent of the total income of the core nonprofit sector.[20]

12-7a What Is Nonprofit Organization Marketing?

Nonprofit organization marketing is the effort by nonprofit organizations to bring about mutually satisfying exchanges with target markets. Although these organizations vary substantially in size and purpose and operate in different environments, most perform the following marketing activities:

- Identifying the customers they want to serve or attract (although they usually use another term, such as clients, patients, members, or donors)

- Explicitly or implicitly specifying objectives

- Developing, managing, and maintaining programs and services

- Deciding on prices to charge (although they may use other terms, such as *fees, donations, tuition, fares, fines,* or *rates*)

- Scheduling events or programs, and determining where they will be held or where services will be offered

- Communicating their availability through both online and offline media vehicles; the nonprofit sector has embraced social media as fast and relatively inexpensive ways to build brand awareness and even to raise the much-needed donations. Nonprofit marketing companies must engage in marketing communication,

internal marketing treating employees as customers and developing systems and benefits that satisfy their needs

nonprofit organization an organization that exists to achieve some goal other than the usual business goals of profit, market share, or return on investment

nonprofit organization marketing the effort by nonprofit organizations to bring about mutually satisfying exchanges with target markets

and it needs to be recognized and valued as a means to build awareness of the nonprofits mission. As in for-profit marketing, marketing communications in the nonprofit sector can help to develop a better understanding of the target consumer thereby ensuring communication strategies that differentiate the nonprofit in the highly competitive market. Many nonprofits are involved in policy change, and marketing communications can play a large role in building awareness and understanding of the issues. For many nonprofits, fundraising is a key activity to support the ability to deliver their programs and services. Building awareness of the nonprofit's mission helps to build donor engagement for funding opportunities.

12-7b Unique Aspects of Nonprofit Organization Marketing Strategies

Like their counterparts in for-profit business organizations, nonprofit managers develop marketing strategies to bring about mutually satisfying exchanges with their target markets. However, marketing in nonprofit organizations is unique in many ways—including the setting of marketing objectives, the selection of target markets, and the development of appropriate marketing mixes.

OBJECTIVES In the private sector, the profit motive is both an objective for guiding decisions and a criterion for evaluating results. Nonprofit organizations do not seek to make a profit for redistribution to owners or shareholders. Rather, their focus is often on generating enough funds to deliver the service while covering expenses.

Most nonprofit organizations are expected to provide equitable, effective, and efficient services that respond to the wants and preferences of their multiple constituencies, which may include users, donors, politicians, appointed officials, the media, and the general public. Nonprofit organizations place great emphasis on building and maintaining relationships with a variety of constituent groups. Nonprofit organizations cannot measure their success or failure in strictly financial terms.

Managers in the nonprofit sector are challenged to demonstrate achievement of multiple, diverse, and often intangible objectives, which can make prioritizing objectives, making decisions, and performance evaluation difficult.

TARGET MARKETS Two issues relating to target markets are unique to nonprofit organizations:

- **Apathetic or strongly opposed targets:** Private-sector organizations usually give priority to developing those market segments that are most likely to respond to particular offerings. In contrast, some nonprofit organizations must, by nature of their service, target those who are apathetic about or strongly opposed to receiving their services, such as vaccinations or psychological counselling.

- **Pressure to adopt undifferentiated segmentation strategies:** Nonprofit organizations are sometimes forced to adopt undifferentiated strategies (see Chapter 8). Today however, as nonprofits become more sophisticated in their data management, they are recognizing the value of data mining to find like prospects to target with differentiated strategies. While the economies of scale often evident in an undifferentiated strategy may seem appealing, the higher returns (higher response rates, higher average donation) achieved by using a differentiated approach far outweigh the low-cost-per-person reach of an undifferentiated strategy.

POSITIONING DECISIONS Because of the unique issues relating to target markets, positioning decisions are critical to the nonprofit. The mission and vision of the nonprofit must be clearly articulated and communicated through the nonprofit's positioning statement, also referred to as the nonprofit's *value proposition*, which then drives all messaging. Because nonprofit organizations are in competition for donor dollars with many other nonprofits and are often in complementary roles with those offering similar services in the public sector, a single-minded positioning is key to maintaining an accurate perception of the nonprofit among all constituent groups. In addition to the single-minded positioning, the task of the nonprofit should be to identify underserved market segments and to develop marketing programs that match their needs, rather than target the niches that may be most profitable.

PRODUCT DECISIONS Three product-related characteristics distinguish business organizations from nonprofit organizations:

- **Benefit complexity:** Nonprofit organizations often market complex and emotional behaviours or ideas. Examples are the need to exercise or eat properly and the need to quit smoking. The benefits that a person receives are complex, long term, and intangible, and therefore are more difficult to communicate to consumers. Rosedale Hospice in Calgary is a seven-bed facility where cancer patients and their families can focus on quality of life at the end of life. This nonprofit offers 24-hour end-of-life care for adult cancer patients in a home-like setting, as well as supportive programs for family and friends. The benefit is enormous, but unless a family member has experienced the challenges of caring for a critically ill adult, how does Rosedale Hospice fully and accurately communicate its service?

- **Benefit strength:** The benefit strength of many nonprofit offerings is not immediate or is indirect. What are the direct, personal benefits to you of driving within the required speed limit or volunteering at your local hospice or putting out only one bag of garbage per week? In contrast, most private-sector service organizations can offer customers immediate and direct personal benefits.

- **Involvement:** The involvement level of the products offered by nonprofit organizations varies greatly by nature of the intangibility of the product and the perceived importance of the product to the target market ("I don't have an adult family member at end-of-life due to cancer, so why would I pay attention to or donate to Rosedale Hospice?"). Many nonprofit organizations market products that elicit very low involvement ("Prevent forest fires") or very high involvement ("Wear a helmet when cycling"). The typical range for private-sector goods is much narrower. Traditional promotional tools may be inadequate to motivate adoption of either low- or high-involvement products. As a means to make their product or service offering tangible, some nonprofits will make available tangible goods that are strong representations of the brand and can, over time, become iconic for the nonprofit. Take, for example, the pink ribbon pins that we all have come to associate with breast cancer.

In pursuit of new and sustainable funding and of ways and means to support their clients, some nonprofits have launched social enterprises. A social enterprise is a business operated by a charity or a nonprofit organization for the dual purpose of generating income and supporting improvements in the well-being of the nonprofit's clients. Social enterprises have grown significantly over the last few years—it is estimated that over 25,000 of them exist in Canada.[21] As an example, YWCA Hamilton runs a catering/wholesale/café initiative called At the Table. Revenue generated from At the Table sales is reinvested into the organization to support the many programs and services offered by YWCA Hamilton in support of women, girls, and their families. One of the programs offered is the Transitional Housing and Shelter program, where at any given time, 70 women are provided housing and support as they seek to turn their lives around from a past challenged by mental illness, addictions, violence, homelessness, food insecurity, and precarious employment. A key component of the At the Table social enterprise is offering the women in the program the opportunity to work in the At the Table kitchen, gaining employable skills in the food service sector.

Valeniker/Shutterstock.com

PLACE (DISTRIBUTION) DECISIONS

A nonprofit organization's capacity for distributing its service offerings to potential customer groups when and where they want them is typically a key variable in determining the success of those service offerings. For example, many universities and colleges have one or more satellite campus locations and offer online courses to provide easier access for students in other areas. Canadian Blood Services has placed a heavy emphasis on mobile donor sites that set up at the donor's place of business, in essence intensifying distribution.

The extent to which a service depends on fixed facilities has important implications for distribution decisions. Services such as those offered by a community food bank are limited by the space the food bank has to store the food.

PROMOTION DECISIONS Many nonprofit organizations are explicitly or implicitly prohibited from advertising, thus limiting their promotion options. Other nonprofit organizations simply do not have the resources to retain advertising agencies, promotion consultants, or marketing staff. However, nonprofit organizations have a few special promotion resources to call on:

- **Professional volunteers:** Nonprofit organizations often seek out marketing, sales, and advertising professionals to help them develop and implement promotion strategies. In some instances, an advertising agency donates its services in exchange for potential long-term benefits. Donated services create goodwill, personal contacts, and general awareness of the donor's organization, reputation, and competency.

- **Sales promotion activities:** Sales promotion activities that make use of existing services or other resources are increasingly being used to draw attention to the offerings of nonprofit organizations. Sometimes nonprofit charities even team up with other companies for promotional activities. Special events are a great way to reach many targets while partnering with both for-profit and nonprofit companies. A perfect example is the Running Room, which offers nonprofits the opportunity to associate with its sponsored runs. Runners can choose to run and raise money for the charity when registering for the run.

Courtesy of YWCA Hamilton

- **Public relations:** Public relations is a valuable tool for nonprofits. But organizations must ensure that their message is compelling and meaningful. One form of public relations used often by nonprofits is public service advertising. A **public service advertisement (PSA)** is an announcement that promotes a program of a nonprofit organization or of a federal, provincial or territorial, or local government. Unlike a commercial advertiser, the sponsor of the PSA does not pay for the time or space. Instead, these are donated by the medium as a public service. PSAs are used, for example, to help educate students about the dangers of misusing and abusing prescription drugs, as well as where to seek treatment for substance abuse problems.

- **Social media:** Nonprofits generally want to promote a message so that people will come together bound by a common goal. Social media can amplify the message by its ability to connect groups of people. Social media allow nonprofits to share their message to build community and to create action. Nonprofits are embracing podcasting, blogging, and social networking because, for very little money, they allow nonprofits to build relationships and engage with their stakeholders. As more and more social media tools are created to make the use of various social media sites

easier and increasingly more measureable, nonprofits' ability to maximize the potential of social media for engagement and relationship building will continue.

PRICING DECISIONS Five key characteristics distinguish the pricing decisions of nonprofit organizations from those of the profit sector:

- **Pricing objectives:** The main pricing objective in the profit sector is revenue or, more specifically, profit maximization, sales maximization, or target return on sales or investment. Many nonprofit organizations must also be concerned about revenue. Often, however, nonprofit organizations seek to either partially or fully defray costs rather than achieve a profit for distribution to stockholders. Nonprofit organizations also seek to redistribute income through the delivery of their service. Moreover, they strive to allocate resources fairly among individuals or households or across geographic or political boundaries.

- **Nonfinancial prices:** In many nonprofit situations, consumers are not charged a monetary price but instead must absorb nonmonetary costs. Nonmonetary costs include time and maybe even embarrassment, depending on the service being provided. Habitat for Humanity requires the recipients of a home to contribute sweat equity as part of the price of the building of their new home.

- **Indirect payment:** Indirect payment through taxes is common to marketers of free services, such as libraries, fire protection, and police protection. Indirect payment is not a common practice in the profit sector.

- **Separation between payers and users:** By design, the services of many charitable organizations are provided to those who are relatively poor and are largely paid for by those who are better off financially. Although examples of separation between payers and users can be found in the profit sector (such as insurance claims), the practice is much less prevalent.

- **Below-cost pricing:** An example of below-cost pricing is university tuition. Virtually all private and public colleges and universities price their services below their full costs.

public service advertisement (PSA) an announcement that promotes a program of a nonprofit organization or of a federal, provincial or territorial, or local government

SIDE LAUNCH
BREWING COMPANY
CONTINUING CASE

Take Care of Your Back Yard

Lily Findlay, Territory Manager, emerges from behind the bar at the Iron Skillet, beads of sweat on her brow but a glint in her eye and never-say-die look of optimism in her smile. Lily is the face of Side Launch Brewing Company to the Skillet and dozens of independently owned licensed restaurants and bars scattered across the pastoral Simcoe-Muskoka area of Ontario, which takes in the vast area around Georgian Bay in Lake Huron. She is a sales rep for Side Launch, but at this moment she is neither drinking beer nor selling beer to her client. She is instead trying to figure out how a beer line connecting a keg of Side Launch Dark Lager to its tap had suddenly acquired a "chemical" taste, despite no record of anyone actually cleaning the line that particular morning.

"A lot of people think being a beer rep is just drinking and socializing," she is quick to clarify. "There is some of that ... there needs to be, you need to be outgoing to succeed as a rep ... but there's a lot more stuff that takes up your time." With a smile Lily gestures toward herself as a way of demonstrating that hers is not a glamorous gig. While a gregarious personality and attitude are definitely integral to success in sales of just about anything, Side Launch has customer service baked into its culture. "We aim to be known as having the best customer service in craft beer—period," claims VP Sales and Marketing Chuck Galea. Any company in any industry can have that aspiration and make that lofty claim in its mission statement, but Side Launch is doing some pretty unconventional things to drive the point home.

In addition to making truck drivers its de facto customer service reps (discussed in Chapter 9), its succession plan involves promoting people like Lily into sales jobs if they demonstrate they have what it takes. "I actually started as the retail manager at the brewery when it opened. I did the in-house events and then became a sales rep two years later."

It goes without saying that any member of the Side Launch sales team must not only provide beer for its clients but also solve any problems that may become entangled in that process. As the local sales rep, stationed in Side Launch's hometown of Collingwood, Lily has some unique challenges, for which she becomes the problem solver and from which relationships are maintained. The mystery keg line episode discussed earlier is a prime example. As founder Garnet Pratt explains, "Suddenly we've got bad beer, so Lily gets the phone call. And regardless of what else is going on that day, the

CHAPTER 12: Services and Nonprofit Organization Marketing   227

Skillet's a good client. They're a few hundred yards from our brewery. We have to take care of our back yard."

This chapter distinguishes services from goods by identifying the unique challenges that go along with services. While Side Launch is clearly a consumer goods company, there is a distinct and important service function not only within the company but instilled within its culture. "It's not good enough to have the best beer," Chuck says as a reminder, "we need to have the best customer service too."

Questions

1. While Side Launch Brewing Company's beer is clearly good, the service provided by people like Lily is required to get the product to market, as well as to create and maintain positive relationships with clients. Which of the four "I's" of services is demonstrated in the examples noted above, where Lily must come to the aid of a client for beer to flow?

2. Which of the four "I's" of service do you think might be the most challenging for Side Launch to overcome, and why?

3. When Garnet states "We have to take care of our back yard," she is essentially referring to the expectation gap of services gap analysis. Explain.

Side Launch Brewing Company

Part 3 Case
Product Decisions

From Dragon's Den to Success

"The idea behind Velofix is simple but brilliant. It allows people to repair their bikes conveniently at their home or office saving them time and allowing them to get back on their bike and spend more time riding."—Jim Treliving, Dragon's Den Investor

Frustrated with trying to get their bikes to the shop for a tune-up before riding season began or in for a quick repair, avid cyclists Chris Guillemet and Davide Xausa teamed up with Boris Martin, a bike mechanic, to launch the mobile bike shop Velofix. "It was born out of the frustration of poor service and time constraints of having to take a bike to a bike shop to get serviced," said Chris. By visiting the Velofix website, a cyclist can choose the time of day and the day of week for the Velofix van to arrive at their home (or place of business) for a tune-up, repair, or accessory installation. The frustration of being without your bike and adhering to cycle shop retail hours are no longer issues and the success of Velofix suggests this clearly was an issue for many.

When they launched in 2013, not a single supplier in Canada would sell to them because they were not a bricks-and-mortar store. Today with close to 100 franchises in the United States and Canada; revenue growth of over 320 percent versus a year ago; Simon Whitfield, Olympic triathlon medallist, as an owner of two B.C. franchises and company strategic adviser; and the support of *Dragon's Den* investor Jim Treliving (who created the successful Boston Pizza franchise, is co-owner of Mr. Lube, and has an interest in 70 other businesses), Velofix is without question a successful disrupter in the bicycle repair market and is perfectly poised to continue to demonstrate growth.

Coincident with the launch of Velofix was the growth in sales in the bike market from a softening of sales in 2009 and 2010. The softening sales had indicated a mature category, but the growth was reflective of the continued interest in cycling as a form of transportation and increased interest in road racing, trail bike racing, and triathlons. Given the variable climate in most of Canada, bicycle riding is seasonal, making it difficult for a bicycle repair service to be a successful year-round business.

Since 2013, with the financial and business backing of Treliving, Velofix's product and service lines have grown. Today they consider themselves a complete mobile bike store, selling anything you need for your bike, as well as a source for new bikes. Capitalizing on the increase in online purchasing, Velofix inked deals with 26 bike manufacturers, launching Velofix DIRECT, which allows the customer to order online for shipping to a local Velofix franchisee for assembly, delivery, and fit. At-home or at-the-office bike repairs and tuning are still the company's bread and butter, with a tune-up taking about 60 to 90 minutes at a cost of about $70. The large decalled Mercedes diesel van that arrives to tune or repair is outfitted with a bike stand, tools and tool cases, trays of parts, and a fairly well-inventoried array of bike accessories, including glasses, gloves, and water bottles. In addition, the vehicles sport such customer luxuries as espresso machines, big screen TVs, and WiFi so if you have time, you can hang with the mechanic quite comfortably as they repair your bike.

Don't kid yourself, though; the more successful Velofix is, the more intense the competition is and will continue to be. Already bike shops are investing in vehicles to offer mobile repairs and at least one other mobile bike repair company has been launched with a similar business model.

The retail bike industry is highly fragmented. It has not seen the consolidation that many retail sectors have seen, so Velofix believes that quick growth is key to future success. But that growth must be managed so customer service remains high and franchisees remain strong with effective operational support. Velofix has invested in its website and a proprietary route-optimized booking service to maintain high levels of satisfaction with its bread-and-butter business, but franchisee training, marketing, human resources, and financial systems must be invested in to assist in managed growth.

The owners also know that they must stay ahead of competition with their product and service strategy. In addition to bike repairs and service and the complete bike sales program Velofix DIRECT, Velofix offers corporate services. It works with companies to promote active living and a healthy lifestyle for employees. Partner companies promote Velofix and encourage onsite repairs with discounts when five or more employees book service, or they can designate a portion of the cost of each service to be paid by the employee and the rest by the company or the company can pay all the service. Velofix already works with Microsoft, Snapchat, Facebook, Starbucks, and Google to maintain and fix bikes on their "campuses." Velofix also offers lunchtime learning sessions to provide employees the opportunity to learn about cycle safety, nutrition, and basic mechanics and hosts group rides for company employees.

Other product service offerings are a bike-boxing service and bike rentals.

Support to the riding community is key for Velofix to maintain awareness and credibility in the industry. Velofix sponsors and supports various clubs and helps host events in each of the cities it operates in. The local franchisee can be found offering pre- and post-race support at events, sponsorship and prizes for winners, and silent auctions. In 2016, the company was at more than 25,000 events—some franchise partners handle 40 to 50 events in the year. Participation at these events enhances Velofix's reputation and image among the target audience and if managed correctly builds a database for franchisees for future business development.

Franchises are owned by local market residents and are operated by certified mechanics. Owners pay $25,000 for a franchise and either lease the Mercedes Sprinter Van or buy them for $90,000. Franchisees pay an additional 8 percent in royalties and 2 percent for marketing. Some, like Simon Whitfield, hold the franchise and hire a mechanic; other franchisees are mechanics themselves.

"The fact these guys come to me is a home run," said a satisfied customer who spent time with the mechanic as he was fixing the customer's Trek mountain bike. He wanted the mechanic's opinion about a lighter, faster off-road bike he was contemplating buying to give him an advantage in a race.

With a goal to being the largest system of mobile bike shops in the world, Velofix seems to be well on its way.

SOURCES

- Guy Dixon. "Mobile Bike Shop Expands in High Gear," *Globe and Mail*, April 5, 2017, https://beta.theglobeandmail.com/report-on-business/small-business/sb-growth/the-challenge/mobile-bike-shop-expands-in-high-gear-across-n-america/article34576123/?ref=http://www.theglobeandmail.com&utm_source=twitter.com&utm_medium=Referrer:+Social+Network+/+Media&utm_campaign=Shared+Web+Article+Links&service=mobile (accessed May 9, 2017).

- Jim Rendon. "Innovations Threaten the Neighborhood Bike Shop," *New York Times*, January 27, 2017, https://www.nytimes.com/2017/01/27/business/innovations-bike-shop-bicycles.html?_r=1 (accessed May 9, 2017).

- Marc Sani. "Taiwan Manufacturers under Pressure Heading into Taipei Show," *Bicycle Retailer*, March 15, 2017, https://www.velofix.com/app/uploads/2017/03/brain-article-march-15.pdf (accessed May 9, 2017).

- "Velofix Closes 2016 with Record Growth," *PEZ Cycling News*, December 14, 2016, http://www.pezcyclingnews.com/newswire/velofix-closes-2016-with-record-growth/#.WRGl9FKZNTZ (accessed May 9, 2017).

QUESTIONS

1. **Go to Velofix's website, review its product/service line, and comment on the product mix, product lines, and product line depth.**

2. **What stage in the product life cycle is Velofix in? What marketing strategy recommendations would you make given the stage it is in?**

3. **Service is key to the success of Velofix. Discuss how services differ from physical goods. Explain the concept of the gap model of service quality in relation to Velofix franchisees.**

4. **Given the stage in the product life cycle you mention in question 2 and in recognition of the importance of service quality, create a marketing mix for Velofix. Be cognizant of the fact that this is a new company with limited financial resources.**

Education has changed,

nelson.com/student

13 | Setting the Right Price

LEARNING OUTCOMES

13-1 Explain the importance of price

13-2 Describe the four-step pricing process

13-3 Recognize the legalities and ethics of setting a price

DIPP
S'N

156 g

Torontonian/Alamy Stock Photo

"Price is what you pay, value is what you get."

—Warren Buffett[1]

13-1 THE IMPORTANCE OF PRICE

Price means one thing to the consumer and something else to the seller. To the consumer, price is the cost of something. To the seller, price is revenue, the primary source of profits. In the broadest sense, price allocates resources in a free-market economy.

But price goes beyond the supposed rationality of economics. Price is something that is debated between buyer and seller. Marketing has a large role to play in the determination of price—this is one area where marketing is directly responsible for revenue generation. But there are two aspects of pricing that must be considered: the internal pricing (determined by financial and accounting formulas) and the external pricing determinants (determined by an understanding of marketing, demand, and the external environment). Keeping both in mind will help ensure that companies establish a price that satisfies not only the bottom line but also the customer.

price that which is given up in an exchange to acquire a good or service

revenue the price per unit charged to customers multiplied by the number of units sold

costs the combined financial value of all inputs that go into the production of a company's products, both directly and indirectly

profit revenue minus expenses

13-1a What Is Price?

Price is that which is given up in an exchange to acquire a good or service. It is typically the money exchanged for the good or service, but it may also include the time lost while waiting to acquire the good or service.

Consumers are interested in obtaining a reasonable price, which refers to the perceived value at the time of the transaction. The price paid is based on the satisfaction consumers *expect* to receive from a product and not necessarily the satisfaction they *actually* receive. Price can relate to anything with perceived value, not just money. When goods and services are exchanged, the trade is called *barter*.

13-1b The Importance of Price to Marketing Managers

Prices are the key to revenues, which in turn are the key to profits for an organization. **Revenue** is the price per unit charged to customers multiplied by the number of units sold. Revenue is what pays for every activity—for all the **costs** the company incurs for production, finance, sales, distribution, overhead, and so on. What's left over (if anything) is **profit**. Managers usually strive to charge a price that will earn a fair profit.

Revenue = Price per unit × units sold

Profit = Revenue − Costs (fixed + variable)

Moreover, price invariably creates a perception of quality to customers. While customers are more savvy than ever, they still usually associate a high price with high quality and vice versa—especially when comparing similar products. This puts the onus on the firm to ensure that the price befits the value, as suggested in the Warren Buffett quote that opens this chapter.

To earn a profit, managers must choose a price that is neither too high nor too low, a price that equals the perceived value to target consumers. If, in consumers' minds, a price is set too high, the perceived value will be less than the cost, and sale opportunities will be lost. Conversely, if a price is too low, the consumer may perceive it as a great value, but the firm loses revenue it could have earned by charging a higher, but acceptable, price.

Trying to set the right price is one of the most stressful and pressure-filled tasks of the marketing manager, as attested to by the following trends in the consumer market:

- Potential buyers carefully evaluate the price of each product against the value of existing products.
- Increased availability of bargain-priced private and generic brands puts downward pressure on overall prices.

- Firms try to maintain or regain their market share by cutting prices.
- Internet and mobile access makes comparison shopping seamless and in many cases results in downward pressure on price.

In the business market, buyers are also becoming more price sensitive and better informed. Marketing information systems enable organizational buyers to compare price and performance with great ease and accuracy. Improved communication and the increased use of direct marketing and computer-aided selling have also opened up many markets to new competitors. Finally, competition in general is increasing, so some installations, accessories, and component parts are being marketed as indistinguishable commodities.

13-2 THE FOUR-STEP PRICING PROCESS

Now that we know what pricing is and why it is important, we need to look at the process of setting the right price. There is no easy formula here; while there are numbers, there are also considerations that go into setting a price that go beyond numbers.

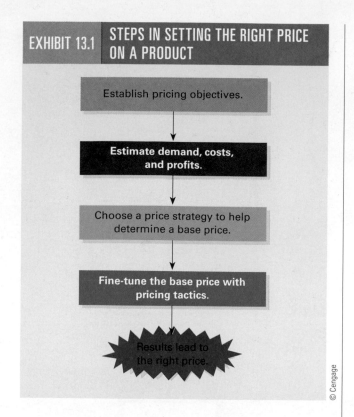

EXHIBIT 13.1 STEPS IN SETTING THE RIGHT PRICE ON A PRODUCT

Establish pricing objectives.

Estimate demand, costs, and profits.

Choose a price strategy to help determine a base price.

Fine-tune the base price with pricing tactics.

Results lead to the right price.

Setting the right price on a product is a four-step process (see Exhibit 13.1):

1. Establish pricing objectives.
2. Estimate demand, costs, and profits.
3. Choose a price strategy to help determine a base price.
4. Fine-tune the base price by using pricing tactics.

13-2a Step 1—Establish Pricing Objectives

The first step in setting the right price is to establish pricing objectives. Those objectives fall into three categories: profit oriented, sales oriented, and status quo. These objectives are derived from the firm's overall objectives. With a good understanding of the marketplace and of the consumer, a manager can sometimes tell very quickly whether an objective is realistic.

All pricing objectives have trade-offs that managers must weigh. A profit-maximization objective may require a bigger initial investment than the firm can commit or wants to commit. A sales-oriented objective, such as reaching the desired market share, often means sacrificing short-term profit, because without careful management, long-term profit objectives may not be met. Meeting the competition, a status quo objective, is the easiest pricing objective to implement, but it can also be short-sighted and costly.

In all situations, when managers set about establishing pricing objectives, they must consider the product's demand, costs, profits, and so forth, as it progresses through its life cycle. This process usually means trade-offs occur in meeting the target customer's needs, being competitive, having considerations for changing economic conditions, and meeting the company's corporate objectives. What follows is an explanation of the three main pricing objectives and their potential impact on overall corporate objectives.

PROFIT-ORIENTED PRICING OBJECTIVES

Profit-oriented objectives are profit maximization, satisfactory profits, and target return on investment.

- **Profit maximization:** Profit maximization means setting prices so that total revenue is as large as possible relative to total costs. Profit maximization does not always signify unreasonably high prices, however. Both price and profits depend on the type of competitive environment a firm faces, such as whether it is in a monopoly position (i.e., the firm is the only seller) or in a much more competitive situation. Although this goal may sound impressive to the firm's owners, it is not good enough for planning.

  When attempting to maximize profits, managers can try to expand revenue by increasing customer satisfaction, or they can attempt to reduce costs by operating more efficiently. A third possibility is to attempt to do both. Research has shown that striving to enhance customer satisfaction leads to greater profitability (and further customer satisfaction) than following a cost-reduction strategy or attempting to do both. While it is not always easy to focus on improving both customer satisfaction and productivity, firms such as WestJet have found a way to be successful.

- **Satisfactory profits:** Satisfactory profits are a reasonable level of profits. Rather than maximizing profits, many organizations strive for profits that are satisfactory to the shareholders and management—in other words, a level of profits consistent with the level of risk an organization faces. In a risky industry, a satisfactory profit may be 35 percent. In a low-risk industry, it might be 7 percent. Satisfactory profits are often connected to corporate social responsibility (CSR), where companies may forgo a blind pursuit of profits to focus on the environment, a safe work environment, and other CSR initiatives. Tentree is a Canadian apparel brand named for its value proposition—to plant ten trees for each item sold. This is a profit-eating proposition to begin with, and

further eroding the bottom line is Tentree's pledge to operate its manufacturing in a transparent and responsible manner.

- **Target return on investment:** The most common profit objective is a target **return on investment (ROI)**, sometimes called the firm's return on total assets. ROI measures management's overall effectiveness in generating profits with the company's assets that have come from its investors. The higher the firm's ROI, the better off the firm is. Many companies use a target ROI as their main pricing goal. ROI is a percentage that puts a firm's profits into perspective by showing profits relative to investment.

Generally, firms seek ROIs in the 10 to 30 percent range. In some industries, such as the grocery industry, however, a return of less than 5 percent is common and acceptable. A company with a target ROI can predetermine its desired level of profitability. The marketing manager can use the standard, such as 10 percent ROI, to determine whether a particular price and marketing mix are feasible. In addition, however, the manager must weigh the risk of a given strategy even if the return is in the acceptable range.

SALES-ORIENTED PRICING OBJECTIVES
Sales-oriented pricing objectives are often based on market share or total sales maximization.

- **Market share:** Market share is a company's product sales as a percentage of total sales for that industry. Sales can be reported in dollars or in units of product. However, market share is usually expressed in terms of revenue and not units.

Many companies believe that maintaining or increasing market share is an indicator of the effectiveness of their marketing mix. Larger market shares have indeed often meant higher profits, thanks to greater economies of scale, market power, and the ability to recruit and compensate top-quality management. Conventional wisdom also says that market share and return on investment are strongly related. For the most part they are; however, many companies with low market share survive and even prosper. To succeed with a low market share, companies need to compete in industries with slow growth and few product changes. Ferrari, the Italian sports car manufacturer, is one example of such a company. Otherwise, companies must compete in an industry that makes frequently purchased items, such as consumer convenience goods.

The conventional wisdom regarding market share and profitability isn't always reliable, however. Because of extreme competition in some industries, many market share leaders either do not reach their target ROI or actually lose money. Procter & Gamble switched from market share to ROI objectives after realizing that profits don't automatically follow as a result of a large market share. Still, for some companies, the struggle for market share can be all-consuming.

Exhibit 13.2 shows the market share of sales in the Canadian beer industry in 2016. Note the dominance of global conglomerates Anheuser-Busch InBev (owners of Budweiser, Labatt, and others) and Molson-Coors Brewing Company, together owning over 50 percent of all beer sales in Canada. Despite this dominance, the proliferation of new entrants into the craft beer market in Canada continues unabated. However, they enter the market not in pursuit of market share but rather a modest profit that allows them to build a brand in a growing lifestyle category. Some are choosing very unorthodox approaches in a market long associated exclusively with adult social activity. Town Square Brewing Co. of Edmonton, for instance, aspires to be a cozy hangout for families as well as traditional beer drinkers.[2] Meanwhile, Ottawa's Broadhead Brewing Company acknowledges the financial toils just to open its doors and wears its meagre profits as a badge of honour. In one of its many tongue-in-cheek infographics, it lists over 35,000 unpaid hours and 0 filthy-rich financial backers.[3] However, the growth in craft beer sales in Canada provides would-be start-ups with a built-in excuse for profit-based pricing. Craft beer consumers expect a different kind of

return on investment (ROI) net profits divided by the investment

market share a company's product sales as a percentage of total sales for that industry

EXHIBIT 13.2 TWO WAYS TO MEASURE MARKET SHARE

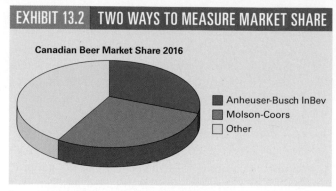

Canadian Beer Market Share 2016

- Anheuser-Busch InBev
- Molson-Coors
- Other

Source: Statistica, "Market share of companies within the Canadian brewing industry as of June 2017" https://www.statista.com/statistics/339828/market-share-of-the-canadian-brewing-industry/.

beer, produced from higher-quality ingredients and therefore automatically expect a higher price. They see value in the product more than the price. The challenge for craft brewers is finding that balance where perceived benefit is not outweighed by price.

Research organizations such as Nielsen and Information Resources, Inc., provide excellent market share reports for many different industries. These reports enable companies to track their performance in various product categories over time.

- **Sales maximization:** Rather than strive for market share, companies sometimes try to maximize sales. A firm with the objective of maximizing sales will ignore profits, competition, and the marketing environment as long as sales are rising.

If a company is strapped for funds or faces an uncertain future, it may try to generate a maximum amount of cash in the short run. Management's task when using this objective is to calculate which price–quantity relationship generates the greatest cash revenue. Sales maximization can also be effectively used on a temporary basis to sell off excess inventory.

Maximization of cash should never be a long-run objective because cash maximization may mean little or no profitability.

status quo pricing a pricing objective that maintains existing prices or meets the competition's prices

price sensitivity consumers' varying levels of desire to buy a given product at different price levels

price elasticity of demand a measurement of change in consumer demand for a product relative to the changes in its price

STATUS QUO PRICING OBJECTIVES Status quo pricing seeks to maintain existing prices or to meet the competition's prices. This third category of pricing objectives has the major advantage of requiring little planning. It is essentially a passive policy.

Often, firms competing in an industry with an established price leader simply meet the competition's prices. These industries typically have fewer price wars than those with direct price competition. In other cases, managers regularly shop competitors' stores to ensure that their prices are comparable.

13-2b Step 2—Estimate Demand, Costs, and Profits

After establishing pricing objectives, managers must estimate demand, costs, and profit. Estimating costs is relatively simple as it consists of adding up the separate costs of each input that goes into a finished product. These are called *variable costs* as they will vary based upon the number of products produced. However, there are other costs of running a business that the price of each product must also help to cover. These *fixed costs* stay the same over time, regardless of production. The craft breweries that we discussed earlier would count what they spend on water, hops, barley, bottles, labelling, and packaging as variable costs; property tax on their brewery and payroll of administrative staff would be examples of fixed costs.

Estimating demand is trickier, especially for a new product that hasn't yet been tested in the market. There are methods of getting some general idea of demand, such as researching historical sales data on similar products. Firms can use that information as a basis of estimating demand through the product's life cycle, which asserts that demand will change as a product goes through four distinct phases. (This concept is discussed more deeply in Chapter 11.) However, estimating demand requires a little more of a scientific approach in order to get closer to the truth.

The estimation of demand must begin with some broad assumptions associated with the fundamentals of economics—namely, **price sensitivity** and **price elasticity of demand**. Price sensitivity refers to consumers' varying levels of desire to buy a given product at different price levels. Price elasticity of demand measures the change of consumer demand for a product relative to the changes in its price.

There are mathematical calculations used to find precise answers to the questions posed by the concepts of sensitivity and elasticity (see the online appendix), but for now we examine these concepts at a high level by using one proven economic tool to demonstrate price sensitivity and a set of categories to help us understand elasticity.

Price sensitivity is commonly demonstrated using the demand curve, which shows the often-inverted

DEMAND THROUGH THE PRODUCT LIFE CYCLE

As a product moves through its life cycle, the demand for the product and the competitive conditions tend to change:

- **Introductory stage:** Management usually sets prices high during the introductory stage of a product. One reason is that the company hopes to recover its development costs quickly. In addition, demand originates in the core of the market (the customers whose needs ideally match the product's attributes) and thus is relatively inelastic. On the other hand, if the target market is highly price sensitive, management often finds it better to price the product at or below the market level.

- **Growth stage:** As the product enters the growth stage, prices generally begin to stabilize for several reasons. First, competitors have entered the market, increasing the available supply. Second, the product has begun to appeal to a broader market, often lower-income groups. Finally, economies of scale are lowering costs, and the savings can be passed on to the consumer in the form of lower prices.

- **Maturity stage:** Maturity usually brings further price decreases as competition increases and inefficient, high-cost firms are eliminated. Distribution channels become a significant cost factor, however, because of the need to offer wide product lines for highly segmented markets, extensive service requirements, and the sheer number of dealers necessary to absorb high-volume production. The manufacturers that remain in the market toward the end of the maturity stage typically offer similar prices. At this stage, price increases are usually cost initiated, not demand initiated. Nor do price reductions in the late phase of maturity stimulate much demand. Because demand is limited and producers have similar cost structures, the remaining competitors will probably match price reductions.

- **Decline stage:** The final stage of the life cycle may see further price decreases as the few remaining competitors try to salvage the last vestiges of demand. When only one firm is left in the market, prices begin to stabilize. In fact, prices may eventually rise dramatically if the product survives and moves into the specialty goods category, as have horse-drawn carriages and vinyl records.

relationship between demand and price. That is, it demonstrates a common behavioural truth in the market that you, as a consumer, have exhibited since you first started making purchase decisions: You are more willing to buy a product as its price lowers. Marketers, of course, realize this common truth as well, but plotting it on a graph demonstrates it with greater accuracy. Suppose, for instance, a craft brewer is grappling over the average price for a pint of its beer at the brewery's onsite pub. The firm has done enough research to see that other pubs are selling pints of beer for anywhere between $5 and $10. Curious as to how price increases of $1 might affect demand, they conduct an experiment that shows the following:

The table below is reasonably self-explanatory, but when applied to a line graph (see Exhibit 13.3), the story becomes clearer, showing the relationship between price and demand. All things being equal, the lower the price, the greater the demand. Conversely, the higher the price, the lower the demand. This rule of thumb, like

Price	Units Sold
$10	10
$9	12
$8	14
$7	16
$6	18
$5	20

most things in life, has its exceptions, but those are better explained in the context of economics and behavioural science.

The demand curve is helpful, but really only in showing us what we already know. Price changes will invariably result in changes of quantity demanded. But even this general assertion will depend on the type of product and the prevailing market environment. And this is where the concept of price elasticity of demand comes in handy.

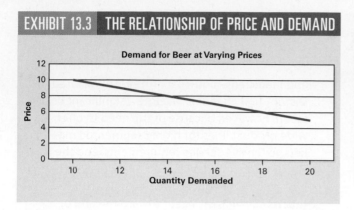

EXHIBIT 13.3 THE RELATIONSHIP OF PRICE AND DEMAND

Demand for Beer at Varying Prices

EXHIBIT 13.4	ELASTICITY OF DEMAND	
	Characteristics	**Product Examples**
Elastic	• Non-essential • Many alternatives • Maslow's Social, Esteem Needs	• Smartphones • Fashion • Automobiles
Inelastic	• Essential • Few alternatives • Maslow's Physiological Needs	• Home heating and electricity • Basic food staples • Winter boots

As discussed, price elasticity of demand refers to the degree of change in demand relative to changes in price. Mathematical calculations can be used to demonstrate this concept with great precision, but for the purposes of this discussion, we can divide price elasticity of demand into two categories: elastic demand and inelastic demand. *Elastic demand* occurs when changes in price greatly change levels of demand, whereas *inelastic demand* exists when changes in price have little or no impact on demand. Therefore, we can classify different types of products as either elastic or inelastic (see Exhibit 13.4).

While useful, the demand curve and elasticity only serve to tell us what we already know. Alone, they don't really help marketers decide exactly where to set the price. One more essential tool is needed here to help bring together the concepts of demand, costs, and profit. That tool is break-even analysis.

As discussed, the two biggest questions marketers must answer when pricing their product are these:

1. How much does it cost to bring the product to market?

2. How much is the market willing to pay for the product?

As all for-profit firms go into business to generate a profit, the desirable goal is to have a number for question 2 that is greater than the number for question 1. Break-even analysis helps us get partway there.

Break-even analysis calculates the threshold of either units sold or total revenue required that a firm must meet to cover its costs. Moreover, it demonstrates that beyond this threshold profit will occur.

Like the demand curve, break-even analysis is based on a foundation of mathematics and represented with a line graph. Here is the formula for calculating the break-even point (BEP):

break-even analysis the calculation of number of units sold, or total revenue required, a firm must meet to cover its costs, beyond which profit occurs

BEP = Fixed costs / (Variable price per unit − Variable cost per unit)

The denominator in this equation represents the margin earned on each sale of each product. In other words, using our craft brewery example, it accounts for the variable costs of producing each pint of beer (beer ingredients, beer-making labour, etc.). However, as discussed previously, the goal of the price is not just to cover these variable costs but also to cover fixed costs, which is why we place those in the numerator of the formula. Using our craft brewery's pub operation, let's demonstrate this concept. Suppose the owners have used their demand curve and decided that they want to sell each pint of beer for $8. Suppose further that they have calculated the variable costs of each pint to be $2. Referring to their monthly budget, they have determined that the fixed costs of running their brewery pub each month are $6000. Using our formula above, the owners of the brew pub would calculate their break-even point (BEP) as follows:

BEP = $6000/($8−$2)

BEP = $6000/$6

BEP = 1000

The break-even point in this example is 1000, meaning that the brew pub must sell 1000 pints to cover the costs of making and serving the beer, as well as contribute to the monthly costs of running the pub. However, two caveats need to be mentioned here. First, the pub is naturally going to be selling other products besides pints of beer, such as other beverages and food menu items. Second, the 1000 units sold represents the break-even point only, meaning that is the number of units sold required to cover costs. Every pint sold beyond 1000 represents profit, which is the ultimate goal of the brewery and all other for-profit businesses. The online appendix for this chapter goes into more detail on the theory and mathematics involved in break-even

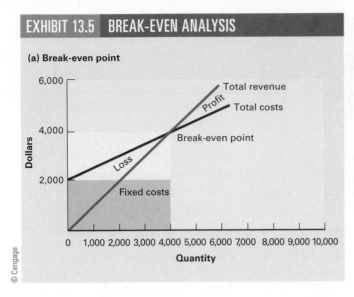

EXHIBIT 13.5 BREAK-EVEN ANALYSIS

(a) Break-even point

© Cengage

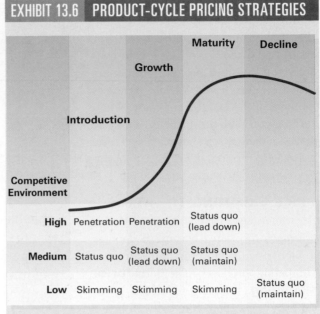

EXHIBIT 13.6 PRODUCT-CYCLE PRICING STRATEGIES

Competitive Environment	Introduction	Growth	Maturity	Decline
High	Penetration	Penetration	Status quo (lead down)	
Medium	Status quo	Status quo (lead down)	Status quo (maintain)	
Low	Skimming	Skimming	Skimming	Status quo (maintain)

analysis, including examples of both break-even volume (as demonstrated above) and break-even price.

Exhibit 13.5 illustrates the concept of break-even analysis. Note that fixed costs remain the same regardless of units sold, and total costs increase with each unit produced. The total revenue line in turn begins at zero, but as it grows it eventually catches up to the total costs. The point at which it does so is the exact break-even point. Everything beyond this point is profit. See the online appendix for this chapter for a more thorough look at the mathematics of break-even analysis.

Despite the rigour of demand curve and break-even calculations, the marketer is still left with a fundamental question when it comes to setting the actual price: What will the market bear? Let's look at one of our key challenges of price setting—estimating demand. In practice, the marketer will not know for sure until the product is offered for sale at a given price and the market responds accordingly. If the firm has a hard time keeping the product in stock, there's a good chance that the price is too low. Conversely, if the product isn't moving at all, a likely cause is that the market is reacting to a price it feels is too high for the value offered.

Now that this section has brought us closer to setting that optimal price, let's proceed to choosing a price strategy.

13-2c Step 3—Choose a Price Strategy

The basic, long-term pricing framework for a good or service should be a logical extension of the pricing goals, while working within estimates of costs and demand. The marketing manager's chosen **price strategy** defines the initial price and the intended direction for price movements over the product life cycle (see Exhibit 13.6).

The price strategy sets a competitive price in a specific market segment that is based on a well-defined positioning strategy (see Chapters 6 and 7). Changing a price level from medium to high may require a change in the product itself, the target customers served, the promotional strategy, or the distribution channels.

A company's freedom in pricing a new product and devising a price strategy depends on the market conditions and the other elements of the marketing mix. If a firm launches a new item resembling several others already on the market, its pricing freedom will be restricted. To succeed, the company will probably need to charge a price close to the average market price of similar competitors' products. In contrast, a firm that introduces a new product with no close substitutes will have considerable pricing freedom.

Strategic pricing decisions tend to be made without an understanding of the likely response from either buyers or the competition. Managers often make tactical pricing decisions without reviewing how they may fit into the firm's overall pricing or marketing strategy. Many companies make pricing decisions and changes without an existing process for managing the pricing activity. As a result, many of them do not have a serious pricing strategy and do not conduct pricing research to develop their strategy.[4]

On the other hand, those companies that conduct both research and serious planning for

> **price strategy** a basic, long-term pricing framework that establishes the initial price for a product and the intended direction for price movements over the product life cycle

creating a pricing strategy are endeavouring to understand the environment that their product has entered or is currently in. These companies first consider their current product positioning (see Chapters 6 and 7), the product's demand and costs, the company's long-term goals, and the product life-cycle stage, and then select from three basic approaches: price skimming, penetration pricing, and status quo pricing.

PRICE SKIMMING Price skimming is sometimes called a *market-plus approach to pricing* because it denotes a high price relative to the prices of competing products. The term **price skimming**, referring to a high introductory price, often coupled with heavy promotion, is derived from the phrase "skimming the cream off the top." Companies often use this strategy for new products when the product is perceived by the target market as having unique customer benefits. Often, companies will use skimming and then lower prices over time, known as *sliding down the demand curve*. We saw this happening with products such as flat-screen televisions and hybrid motorized vehicles. Other manufacturers maintain skimming prices throughout a product's life cycle.

Price skimming works best when the market is willing to buy the product even though it carries an above-average price. Firms can also effectively use price skimming when a product is well protected legally, when it represents a technological breakthrough, or when it has in some other way blocked the entry of competitors. Managers may follow a skimming strategy when production cannot be expanded rapidly because of technological difficulties, shortages, or constraints imposed by the skill and time required to produce a product. As long as demand is greater than supply, skimming is an attainable strategy.

A successful skimming strategy enables management to recover its product development costs quickly.

Hadrian/Shutterstock.com

Apple has added a twist to the skimming strategy. Rather than introducing their products at a high price and then lowering their prices over time, Apple stakes out a price and then maintains and defends that price by significantly increasing the value of their products in future iterations. The new version is released at a higher price than its predecessor, but the predecessor units that remain in inventory are often sold off through price reductions.

Even if the market perceives an introductory price as being too high, managers can lower the price. Firms often feel it is better to test the market at a high price and then lower the price if sales are too slow. Successful skimming strategies are not limited to products. Well-known athletes, lawyers, and hairstylists are experts at price skimming. Naturally, a skimming strategy will encourage competitors to enter the market.

PENETRATION PRICING Penetration pricing is at the opposite end of the spectrum from skimming. **Penetration pricing** means charging a relatively low price for a product initially as a way to reach the mass market. The low price is designed to capture a large share of a substantial market, resulting in lower production costs. If a marketing manager has decided that the firm's pricing object is to obtain a large market share, then penetration pricing is a logical choice.

Penetration pricing does mean lower profit per unit. Therefore, to reach the break-even point, the company requires a higher volume of sales than needed under a skimming policy. The recovery of product development costs may be slow. As you might expect, penetration pricing tends to discourage competition.

A penetration strategy tends to be effective in a price-sensitive market. As discussed previously, price should decline more rapidly when demand is elastic (i.e., demand for a product is price sensitive) because the market can be increased in response to a lower price. Also, price sensitivity and greater competitive pressure should lead either to a stable low price or to a lower initial price and then a later, relatively slow decline in the price.

Although Walmart is typically associated with penetration pricing, other chains have also done an excellent job of following this strategy. Dollar stores, those bare-bones, strip-mall chains that sell staples at cut-rate prices, are now the fastest-growing retailers in North America. Dollar chains can locate their small stores right in inner-city neighbourhoods or suburbs, where their shoppers

price skimming a high introductory price, often coupled with heavy promotion

penetration pricing a relatively low price for a product initially as a way to reach the mass market

Dollar Stores are Profitable

Great Canadian Dollar Store started in British Columbia in 1993 and by 2017 had grown to over 100 locations across Canada. Claiming to have found a niche by selling products for between $1 and $3, the Great Canadian Dollar Store offers those low prices while also providing good customer service.

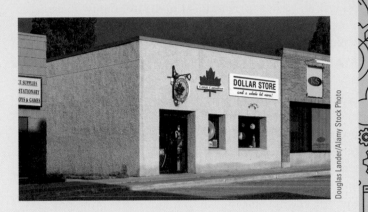

Douglas Lander/Alamy Stock Photo

live. Parking is readily available, and shoppers can be in and out in less time than it takes to hike across a jumbo Walmart parking lot.[5]

If a firm has a low fixed-cost structure and each sale provides a large contribution to those fixed costs, penetration pricing can boost sales and provide large increases in profits—but only if the market size grows or if competitors choose not to respond. Low prices can attract additional buyers to the market. The increased sales can justify production expansion or the adoption of new technologies, both of which can reduce costs. And, if firms have excess capacity, even low-priced business can provide incremental dollars toward fixed costs.

Penetration pricing can also be effective if an **experience curve** will cause costs per unit to drop significantly. The experience curve proposes that per-unit costs will decrease as a firm's production experience increases. Manufacturers that fail to take advantage of these effects will find themselves at a competitive cost disadvantage relative to others that are further along the curve.

One of the advantages of penetration pricing is that it can make it difficult for the competition to compete. However, penetration pricing also means gearing up to sell a large volume at a low price. If the volume or demand fails to materialize, the company will face losses.

Penetration pricing can also prove disastrous for a prestige brand that adopts the strategy in an effort to gain market share and fails. When Omega—once a more prestigious brand than Rolex—was trying to improve the market share of its watches, it adopted a penetration pricing strategy that destroyed the watch's brand image by flooding the market with lower-priced products. Omega never gained sufficient share on its lower-priced and lower-image competitors to justify destroying its brand image and high-priced position with upscale buyers.

STATUS QUO PRICING The third basic price strategy a firm may choose is status quo pricing, also *called meeting the competition* or *going-rate pricing*. It means charging a price identical to or very close to the competition's price.

Although status quo pricing has the advantage of simplicity, its disadvantage is that the strategy may ignore demand or cost, or both. If the firm is comparatively small, however, meeting the competition may be the safest route to long-term survival.

13-2d Step 4—Use a Price Tactic

After managers have set pricing goals; estimated demand, costs, and profits; and chosen a pricing strategy, they should set a base price. A **base price** is the general price level at which the company expects to sell the good or service. The general price level is correlated with the actions taken in the first three steps of the price-setting process. Once a base price has been determined, a series of price tactics are offered to help fine-tune the base price to make sure it satisfies the company and customer.

Fine-tuning techniques are short-run approaches that do not change the general price level. They do, however,

> **experience curves** curves that show costs declining at a predictable rate as experience with a product increases

> **base price** the general price level at which the company expects to sell the good or service

result in changes within a general price level. These pricing tactics allow the firm to adjust for competition in certain markets, meet ever-changing government regulations, take advantage of unique demand situations, and meet promotional and positioning goals. Fine-tuning pricing tactics include various sorts of discounts, geographic pricing, and other pricing tactics.

MARKUP Before proceeding with a long, and still non-exhaustive list of pricing tactics, it is important to point out that all for-profit firms enter into a business endeavour with the intention of earning a profit. Thus no matter what tactic or fine-tuning approach a business takes in setting its price, it must first attend to profit, which results from some form of markup. Markup, in fact, pervades all three pricing strategies discussed in the previous section as well. Markup is the profit-producing device of price and thus must be a component of each pricing tactic. Because there are several different markup methods, ranging from the nonmathematical to the mathematical, you are encouraged to review the Markup Pricing section in the online appendix for this chapter.

DISCOUNTS AND ALLOWANCES

A base price can be lowered through discounts and allowances. Managers use the various forms of discounts to encourage customers to do what they would not ordinarily do, such as paying cash rather than using credit, taking delivery out of season, or performing certain functions within a distribution channel.[6] The following are the most common tactics:

- **Quantity discounts:** When buyers are charged a lower unit price when buying either in multiple units or at more than a specified dollar amount, they are receiving a **quantity discount**. A **cumulative quantity discount** is a deduction from list price that applies to the buyer's total purchases made during a specific period; it is intended to encourage customer loyalty. In contrast, a **noncumulative quantity discount** is a deduction from list price that applies to a single order rather than to the total volume of orders placed during a certain period. It is intended to encourage orders in large quantities.

- **Cash discounts:** A **cash discount** is a price reduction offered to a consumer, an industrial user, or a marketing intermediary in return for prompt payment of a bill (for example, 2/10, net 30). Prompt payment saves the seller carrying charges and billing expenses and allows the seller to avoid bad debt.

- **Functional discounts:** When distribution channel intermediaries, such as wholesalers or retailers, perform a service or function for the manufacturer (for example, setting up retail displays or extending credit), they must be compensated. This compensation, typically a percentage discount from the base price, is called a **functional discount** (or **trade discount**). Functional discounts vary greatly from channel to channel, depending on the tasks performed by the intermediary.

- **Seasonal discounts:** A **seasonal discount** is a price reduction for buying merchandise out of season (for example, buying new ski equipment in March and accepting delivery in July). It shifts the storage function to the purchaser. Seasonal discounts also enable manufacturers to maintain a steady production schedule year-round.

VALUE-BASED PRICING

Value-based pricing, also called *value pricing*, is a pricing strategy that has grown out of the quality movement. Instead of determining prices on the basis of costs or competitors' prices, value-based pricing starts with the customer, considers the competition, and then determines the appropriate price. The basic assumption is that the firm is customer driven, seeking to understand the attributes customers want in the goods and services they buy and the value of that bundle of attributes to customers. Because very few firms operate in a pure monopoly, however, a marketer using value-based pricing must also determine the value of competitive offerings to customers. Customers determine the value of a product (not just its price) relative to the value of alternatives. In value-based pricing, therefore, the price of the product is set at a level that seems to the customer to be a good price compared with the prices of other options.

---

quantity discount a unit price reduction offered to buyers buying either in multiple units or at more than a specified dollar amount

cumulative quantity discount a deduction from list price that applies to the buyer's total purchases made during a specific period

noncumulative quantity discount a deduction from list price that applies to a single order rather than to the total volume of orders placed during a certain period

cash discount a price reduction offered to a consumer, an industrial user, or a marketing intermediary in return for prompt payment of a bill

functional discount (trade discount) a discount to wholesalers and retailers for performing channel functions

seasonal discount a price reduction for buying merchandise out of season

value-based pricing setting the price at a level that seems to the customer to be a good price compared with the prices of other options

Because of Walmart's strong market entry into groceries, rival supermarkets are adopting value-based pricing as a defensive move. Shoppers in competitive markets are seeing prices fall as Walmart pushes rivals to match its value prices. Numerous regional grocery chains have switched to value pricing. In the past, they offered weekly specials to attract shoppers and then made up the lost profit by keeping nonsale prices substantially higher. Now, Costco and Walmart have conditioned consumers to expect inexpensive goods every day.[7]

GEOGRAPHIC PRICING Because many sellers ship their wares to a nationwide or even a worldwide market, the cost of freight can greatly affect the total cost of a product. Sellers may use several different geographic pricing tactics to moderate the impact of freight costs on distant customers. The following methods of geographic pricing are the most common:

- **FOB origin pricing: FOB origin pricing**, also called FOB factory or FOB shipping point, is a price tactic that requires the buyer to absorb the freight costs from the shipping point ("free on board"). The farther buyers are from sellers, the more they pay, because transportation costs generally increase with the distance merchandise is shipped.

- **Uniform delivered pricing:** If the marketing manager wants total costs, including freight, to be equal for all purchasers of identical products, the firm will adopt **uniform delivered pricing**, or postage stamp pricing. With uniform delivered pricing, the seller pays the actual freight charges and bills every purchaser an identical, flat freight charge.

- **Zone pricing:** A marketing manager who wants to equalize total costs among buyers within large geographic areas—but not necessarily in all of the seller's market area—may modify the base price with a zone-pricing tactic. **Zone pricing** is a modification of uniform delivered pricing. Rather than using a uniform freight rate for its total market, the firm divides it into segments or zones and charges a flat freight rate to all customers in a given zone. Honda, for example, has standardized freight charges on its vehicles, which are based on costs from the point of origin to a specific region.

- **Freight absorption pricing:** In **freight absorption pricing**, the seller pays all or part of the actual

freight charges and does not pass them on to the buyer. The manager may use this tactic in intensely competitive areas or as a way to break into new market areas.

- **Basing-point pricing:** With **basing-point pricing**, the seller designates a location as a basing point and charges all buyers the freight cost from that point, regardless of the city from which the goods are shipped. Thanks to several adverse court rulings, basing-point pricing has waned in popularity. Freight fees charged when none were actually incurred, called phantom freight, have been declared illegal.

OTHER PRICING TACTICS Unlike geographic pricing, other pricing tactics are unique and defy neat categorization. Managers use these tactics for various reasons—for example, to stimulate demand for specific products, to increase store patronage, and to offer a wider variety of merchandise at a specific price point. Other pricing tactics include a single-price tactic, flexible pricing, professional services pricing, price lining, leader pricing, bait pricing, odd–even pricing, price bundling, and two-part pricing.

- **Single-price tactic:** A merchant using a **single-price tactic** offers all goods and services at the same price (or perhaps two or three prices). Netflix is an example of a single-price tactic where for a nominal amount per month, members can watch unlimited movies and TV episodes on their TVs and computers. Dollar stores are another example of retailers using the single-price tactic.

Single-price selling removes price comparisons from the buyer's decision-making process. The retailer enjoys the benefits of a simplified pricing system and minimal clerical errors. However, continually

Zone pricing
Shipped to Kelowna: $10
Shipped to Toronto: $20

khz/Shutterstock.com

FOB origin pricing the buyer absorbs the freight costs from the shipping point ("free on board")

uniform delivered pricing the seller pays the actual freight charges and bills every purchaser an identical, flat freight charge

zone pricing a modification of uniform delivered pricing that divides the total market into segments or zones and charges a flat freight rate to all customers in a given zone

freight absorption pricing the seller pays all or part of the actual freight charges and does not pass them on to the buyer

basing-point pricing charging freight from a given (basing) point, regardless of the city from which the goods are shipped

single-price tactic offering all goods and services at the same price (or perhaps two or three prices)

rising costs are a headache for retailers that follow this strategy. In times of inflation, they must frequently raise the selling price.

- **Flexible pricing:** **Flexible pricing** (or **variable pricing**) means that different customers pay different prices for essentially the same merchandise bought in equal quantities. This tactic is often found in the sale of shopping goods, specialty merchandise, and most industrial goods except supply items. Car dealers and many appliance retailers commonly follow the practice. It allows the seller to adjust for competition by meeting another seller's price. Thus a marketing manager with a status quo pricing objective might readily adopt the tactic. Flexible pricing also enables the seller to close a sale with price-conscious consumers.

The obvious disadvantages of flexible pricing are the lack of consistent profit margins, the potential ill will of high-paying purchasers, the tendency for salespeople to automatically lower the price to make a sale, and the possibility of a price war among sellers.

- **Professional services pricing: Professional services pricing** is used by people with lengthy experience, training, and often certification by a licensing board—for example, lawyers, dentists, and family counsellors. Professionals typically charge customers at an hourly rate, but sometimes fees are based on the solution of a problem or performance of an act (such as an eye examination) rather than on the actual time involved.

Those who use professional pricing have an ethical responsibility not to overcharge a customer. Because demand is sometimes highly inelastic (demand for a product will not change when there is a rise or a reduction in price), there may be a temptation to charge what the market will bear.[8]

- **Price lining:** When a seller establishes a series of prices for a type of merchandise, it creates a price line. **Price lining** is the practice of offering a product line with several items at specific price points. The Limited may offer women's dresses at \$40, \$70, and \$100, with no merchandise marked at prices between those figures. Instead of a normal demand curve (a curve that represents the relationship between price and quantity demanded) running from \$40 to \$100, The Limited has three demand points (prices). Theoretically, the curve exists only because people would buy goods at the in-between prices if it were possible to do so.

Price lining reduces confusion for both the salesperson and the consumer. The buyer may be offered a wider variety of merchandise at each established price. Price lines may also enable a seller to reach several market segments. For buyers, the question of price may be quite simple: all they have to do is find a suitable product at the predetermined price. Moreover, price lining is a valuable tactic for the marketing manager because the firm may be able to carry a smaller total inventory than it could without price lines. The results may include fewer markdowns, simplified purchasing, and lower inventory-carrying charges.

Price lines also present drawbacks, especially if costs are continually rising. Sellers can offset rising costs in three ways. First, they can begin stocking lower-quality merchandise at each price point. Second, sellers can change the prices, although frequent price line changes may confuse buyers. Third, sellers can accept lower profit margins and hold quality and prices constant. This third alternative has short-run benefits, but its long-run handicaps may drive sellers out of business.

- **Loss leader pricing: Loss leader pricing** is selling a product near or even below cost in the hope that shoppers will buy other items once they are in the store. This type of pricing appears weekly in the newspaper advertising of supermarkets. Leader

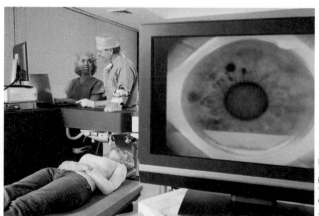

Professional services pricing

---

flexible pricing (variable pricing) different customers pay different prices for essentially the same merchandise bought in equal quantities

professional services pricing used by people with experience, training, and often certification, fees are typically charged at an hourly rate, but may be based on the solution of a problem or performance of an act

price lining offering a product line with several items at specific price points

loss-leader pricing a product is sold near or even below cost in the hope that shoppers will buy other items once they are in the store

Penny For Your Tactic?

While it is a very common pricing tactic, odd–even pricing might be running into a problem—the death of the penny. In early 2013, the Royal Canadian Mint officially stopped producing the Canadian one-cent coin. This means that retailers have had to make changes to their prices, at a cost of more than $100,000 for some large organizations (that's a lot of pennies!). Rounding has also become an issue, as prices that were using odd pricing of 99 cents may be rounded up if customers are not paying with credit, debit, or cheque. The Royal Canadian Mint has put out information on these changes, but it is still something that both companies and consumers will have to get used to. Odd pricing might become even odder as the penny-less reality takes hold.

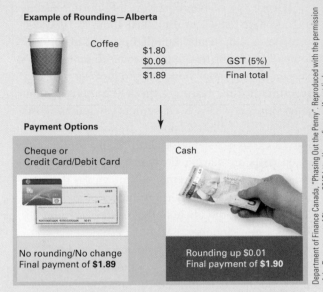

Example of Rounding—Alberta

Coffee	$1.80	
	$0.09	GST (5%)
	$1.89	Final total

Payment Options

| Cheque or Credit Card/Debit Card | Cash |
| No rounding/No change Final payment of **$1.89** | Rounding up $0.01 Final payment of **$1.90** |

Department of Finance Canada, "Phasing Out the Penny". Reproduced with the permission of the Department of Finance, 2015 http://www.fin.gc.ca/1cent/index-eng.asp

Sources: John Rieti, "5 Odd Questions about the Death of the Penny," CBC News, February 1, 2013, www.cbc.ca/news/canada/5-odd-questions-about-the-death-of-the-penny-1.1353684 (accessed August 11, 2014); and Royal Canadian Mint, "Phasing Out the Penny," www.mint.ca/store/mint/learn/phasing-out-the-penny-6900002#.UtQ7oRZ23ww (accessed August 11, 2014).

---

pricing is normally used on well-known items that consumers can easily recognize as bargains. The goal is not necessarily to sell large quantities of leader items but to try to appeal to customers who might shop elsewhere.[9]

Leader pricing is not limited to products. Health and fitness clubs often offer a one-month free trial as a loss leader.

- **Odd–even pricing:** **Odd–even pricing** (or **psychological pricing**) means using odd-numbered prices to connote a bargain and even-numbered prices to imply quality. For years, many retailers have priced their products in odd numbers—for example, $99.95—to make consumers feel they are paying a lower price for the product.

- **Price bundling:** **Price bundling** is marketing two or more products in a single package for a special price. For example, Microsoft offers suites of software that bundle spreadsheets, word processing, graphics, electronic mail, Internet access, and groupware for networks of microcomputers. Price bundling can stimulate demand for the bundled

items if the target market perceives the price as a good value.

Hotels and airlines sell a perishable commodity (hotel rooms and airline seats) with relatively constant fixed costs. Bundling can be an important income stream for these businesses because the variable cost tends to be low—for instance, the cost of cleaning a hotel room. Therefore, most of the revenue can help cover fixed costs and generate profits.

Bundling has also been used in the telecommunications industry. Companies offer local service, long-distance service, DSL Internet service, wireless, and even cable TV in various menus of bundling. Telecom companies use bundling as a way to protect their market share and fight off competition by locking customers into a group of services. For consumers, comparison shopping may be difficult since they may not be able to determine how much they are really paying for

odd–even pricing (psychological pricing) odd-numbered prices connote bargains, and even-numbered prices imply quality

price bundling marketing two or more products in a single package for a special price

each component of the bundle. A related price tactic is **unbundling**, or reducing the bundle of services that comes with the basic product. To help hold the line on costs, some stores require customers to pay for gift wrapping.

Clearly, price bundling can influence consumers' purchase behaviour. But what about the decision to consume a particular bundled product or service? Some of the latest research has focused on how people consume certain bundled products or services. According to this research, the key to consumption behaviour is how closely consumers can link the costs and benefits of the exchange.[10] In complex transactions, such as a holiday package, it may be unclear which costs are paying for which benefits. In such cases, consumers tend to mentally downplay their upfront costs for the bundled product, so they may be more likely to forgo a benefit that's part of the bundle, such as a free dinner.

Similarly, when people buy season's tickets to a concert series, sporting event, or other activity, the sunk costs (price of the bundle) and the pending benefit (going to see the events) become decoupled. The result is a reduced likelihood of consumption of all the events over time. Researchers found that theatregoers who purchased tickets to four plays were only 84 percent likely to use their first-play tickets and only 78 percent likely to use any given ticket across the four plays.[11]

If one of the plays in the bundle is *Wicked*, however, that might change things. Although the production eventually grossed $1.3 million a week in New York and broke box office records in Toronto, *Wicked* was not an instant success. Despite the show's initially low consumer awareness, producer Marc Platt was convinced that if he could just get people in the door, they would find the performance completely captivating. So he cut ticket prices by 30 percent and watched as patrons began to make repeat ticket purchases during intermission.

Theatregoers who purchase tickets to a single play are almost certain to use those tickets. This behaviour is consistent with the idea that in a one-to-one transaction (i.e., one payment, one benefit), the costs and benefits of that transaction are tightly coupled, resulting in strong sunk cost pressure to consume the pending benefit.

A theatre manager might expect a no-show rate of 20 percent when the percentage of season's ticket holders is high, but a no-show rate of only 5 percent when the percentage of season's ticket holders is low. When a theatre has a high number of season's ticket holders, a manager can oversell performances and maximize the revenue for the theatre.

The physical format of the transaction also figures in. A ski lift pass in the form of a booklet of tickets strengthens the cost–benefit link for consumers, whereas a single pass for multiple ski lifts weakens that link.

Although the price bundling of services can result in a lower rate of total consumption of that service, the same is not necessarily true for products. Consider the purchase of an expensive bottle of wine. When the wine is purchased as a single unit, its cost and eventual benefit are tightly coupled. As a result, the cost of the wine will be significant, and a person will likely reserve that wine for a special occasion. When the wine is purchased as part of a bundle (e.g., as part of a case of wine), however, the cost and benefit of that individual bottle of wine will likely become decoupled, reducing the impact of the cost on eventual consumption. Thus, in contrast to the price bundling of services, the price bundling of physical goods could lead to an increase in product consumption.

unbundling reducing the bundle of services that comes with the basic product

- **Two-part pricing: Two-part pricing** means charging two separate amounts to consume a single good or service. Health and fitness clubs charge a membership fee and then a flat fee each time a person uses certain equipment or facilities.

Consumers sometimes prefer two-part pricing because they are uncertain about the number and the types of activities they might use, such as at an amusement park. Also, the people who use a service most often pay a higher total price. Two-part pricing can increase a seller's revenue by attracting consumers who would not pay a high fee even for unlimited use.

Lance Bellers/Shutterstock.com

13-3 THE LEGALITY AND ETHICS OF SETTING A PRICE

As we mentioned in Chapter 2, some pricing decisions are subject to government regulation. Companies and marketers need to be aware of the laws within the Competition Act before establishing any strategy. The Act covers legal and ethical issues relating to deceptive pricing, price fixing, predatory pricing, resale price maintenance, and price discrimination. Both alleged and proven unethical pricing practices can have serious consequences for the companies and the marketing managers involved.

13-3a Bait Pricing

In contrast to loss leader pricing, which is a genuine attempt to give the consumer a reduced price, bait pricing is deceptive. **Bait pricing** is a price tactic that tries to get the consumer into a store through false or misleading price advertising and then uses high-pressure selling to persuade the consumer to buy more expensive merchandise instead.

The Competition Bureau considers bait pricing a deceptive act and has banned its use, but sometimes enforcement is lax.

13-3b Deceptive Pricing

Deceptive pricing refers to promoting a price or price saving that is not actually available. It occurs when the seller leads the purchaser to believe that he or she can receive or is receiving the good or service at the promoted or reduced price. Sellers who use deceptive pricing typically promote a low price on a product for which they have very little stock, or no stock at all, with the intent of selling the customer another, higher-priced product as a substitute. This tactic is called a *bait and switch*. To avoid the perception of using this tactic, marketers must ensure that they have adequate stock on hand or that they clearly indicate the limited quantities available at the reduced price; if the stock quickly sells out, they should offer rain checks.

A second form of deceptive pricing occurs when a seller promotes a discount from a regular price that, in fact, has not been the regular price for a significant time.

Other deceptive pricing practices include selling a product at a price above the advertised price (a civil court issue) and double ticketing, in which a product is sold for more than the lowest of two or more prices tagged on it (a criminal offence). Any company and its employees need to ensure that such deceptive pricing practices are not happening in their retail operations.

13-3c Price Fixing

Price fixing occurs when two or more companies conspire to set the prices for their products or services. It can be done by establishing a floor, or lowest price, in a bidding situation or by simply setting the market price that the consumer will pay. Proving an allegation of price fixing is often a very difficult and lengthy process. In a recent case, the Quebec gasoline cartel case, 10 people and 11 companies were found guilty of conspiring to fix the gasoline prices paid by customers at the pump.[12] (A one-cent increase in

two-part pricing charging two separate amounts to consume a single good or service

bait pricing a price tactic that tries to get consumers into a store through false or misleading price advertising and then uses high-pressure selling to persuade consumers to buy more expensive merchandise instead

deceptive pricing promoting a price or price saving that is not actually available

price fixing an agreement between two or more firms on the price they will charge for a product

gas prices over one year would have cost consumers an estimated $2 million.) The companies and some individuals in this case faced fines; other consequences of the charges could include lost consumer confidence, lost jobs, jail sentences, and potential loss of franchise rights.

13-3d Predatory Pricing

Although a normal business strategy might be to set prices low to lure business away from the competition and gain market share, such action must be done within reason. **Predatory pricing** occurs when a company sets its prices very low with the intention of driving its competition out of either the market or the business. To do this, the company lowers its price below its average variable cost for an extended time—more time than is typical of any short-term loss leader that might be used to attract business or move excess inventory. Once the very low price has eliminated the competitor who cannot afford to operate at that price, the company will raise its prices. Predatory pricing situations are difficult to prove as evidence must show a willful intent to destroy the competition.

13-3e Resale Price Maintenance

Producers usually take the time to research where they want their products to be positioned with regard to price and quality, and in relation to their competitors, so that they achieve their desired profit goals. They cannot, however, dictate the retailer's selling price or determine a floor price. They may give their channel members a manufacturer's suggested retail price (MSRP) and even indicate the MSRP by way of a label on the product, but they cannot discriminate against any retailers that do not follow their recommendations. In Canada, **resale price maintenance**, producers' attempts to control the price of their products in retail stores, is illegal. However, companies operating both in Canada and in the United States will find that resale price maintenance is legal south of the border, and, thus, such firms may need two separate pricing policies.

13-3f Price Discrimination

Price discrimination is the practice of charging different prices to different buyers for goods of like grade and quality within relatively the same period to substantially reduce the competition. This type of price discrimination does not apply to services, end-users, or consumers; thus movie theatres and dry cleaners, for example, can charge different prices for students and seniors or charge different prices on various days of the week.

Producers can legally offer promotional (push) incentives to channel members, but they must do so on a proportional basis; that is, sale prices and any savings can be in relation to and proportional to transactional or logistical costs. Sellers may also lower their prices to buyers in their efforts to meet competitive challenges. Note that the Competition Act also makes it illegal for buyers to use their influence of purchasing power to force discriminatory prices or services.

Six elements are necessary for price discrimination to occur:

1. Two or three instances of discrimination must have occurred over time.
2. The sales in question must have occurred within a relatively short time.
3. The products sold must be commodities or tangible goods.
4. The seller must charge different prices to two or more buyers for the same product.
5. The products sold must be of the same quality and grade.
6. The buyers of the goods must be competitors.

predatory pricing the practice of charging a very low price for a product with the intent of driving competitors out of business or out of a market

resale price maintenance attempts by a producer to control a store's retail price for the product

SIDE LAUNCH
BREWING COMPANY
CONTINUING CASE

An Accessible Price

Beverage alcohol is just about the most heavily regulated consumer industry in Canada, with specifications on how products are priced at every stage between a producer like Side Launch and its ultimate consumers—craft beer lovers across a growing segment of Canada. But while it has unique constraints with regard to pricing its product going out the door, Side Launch, as well as all other Ontario-based brewers, must determine that sweet spot in pricing that manages to consider costs, demand, perceived value, brand consistency, and last but not least—profit.

When it comes to finding that sweet spot, even within this regulated environment, founder Garnet Pratt claims, "Frankly we have all the latitude we want, but there is a minimum." This means that neither Side Launch nor its competitors can enter into a price war with one another for shelf space at the retailers, below a given minimum. And because those retailers are composed mostly of the government's Liquor Control Board of Ontario, suppliers must operate their entire marketing mix (not the least of which is price) within the Liquor Control Act's tight pricing policy. Aside from the minimum price policy, the government also dictates a uniform pricing policy, which means, explains VP Sales and Marketing Chuck Galea, "each of our four brands, packaged in the same sized cans that you'll see in LCBO, TBS [The Beer Store], and grocery, will all be $2.90 a can." The same dictum applies to licensee sales as well. No one brewer can sell a keg to a pub for one price, then turn around and sell to another pub for a different price. "What happens though," sounds off Garnet, "is that big beer will find out a way to keep other brands and craft beer out of a given pub. Which is technically illegal, but is rampant, and continues to be one of our biggest challenges."

Of course, pricing involves more than simply meeting a minimum and maintaining a uniform price. If only it were that easy. Pricing is deeply psychological, as most of us automatically, consciously or unconsciously, evaluate the quality of the product largely by its price. "We have very expensive inputs," asserts Garnet, her financial brain taking over with expert precision, "so our price must first reflect our costs, and costs rise year over year. But we can't make huge jumps in our prices without negative reaction from our customers." Thus landing in a sweet spot where buyers and sellers are happy is for Side Launch, like any other business, the desired goal of pricing. But in an environment like craft, where customers are cognizant of costly ingredients and processes, and prices can vary wildly based on positions desired by brewers, landing on that sweet spot without turning off fans is a delicate balance. "We would like to be a place where we are in the middle of the pack," says Garnet. "We are priced well among our craft brethren," agrees Chuck, referring to recently conducted industry analysis.

In a space where the beer, by virtue of being craft, is already expected to be higher quality and thus somewhat justified in higher price, Side Launch has kept an even keel. "We're priced accessibly," reasons VP Operations Dave Sands, "but we're priced at a discount to a high percentage of the craft market." As he leans into the philosophical discussion on price with brewer Michael Hancock, Dave continues, "The question is what's the volume sensitivity to price. We have a loyal consumer following and repeat customers, and what would be their tolerance to a price increase?" "Not very high," answers Michael, perhaps lamenting the unknown opportunity cost in pricing decisions. And yet, in the same breath, he is aware of a basic truth in marketing. "Even though a price increase may be a deterrent to sales, I don't need to tell you that a higher price is usually perceived by the public as higher quality." And so, like many other marketing decisions, pricing is part calculation and part prediction.

Questions

1. Beyond mere profit, what are some of the pricing goals held by Side Launch?

2. When Dave and Garnet refer to reaction from their customers to changes in price, they are referring to what fundamental tenet of pricing and economics?

3. Which of the three main pricing strategies described in this chapter do you feel Side Launch is more likely to use?

Side Launch Brewing Company

Part 4 Case
Pricing Decisions

Price Cent-sitive Travellers

For WestJetters (WestJet employees) or Canadian travellers old enough to remember WestJet's fabled launch in 1996, there had to be a sense of déjà vu when the Calgary-based airline announced it was creating a new business serving the "ultra low cost carrier" (ULCC) category. This no frills/low-priced model, after all, is how WestJet first made a dent in Canadian air travel on its way to carving off half of Air Canada's market share. By 2017, however, competitive and consumer behaviour trends had evolved in one direction, while WestJet had grown in another, giving the company reason to figure out how to retrench itself in the price-sensitive space, while also competing as an international company.

While other value-priced airlines had emerged between the time of WestJet's launch and the mid-2010s—who could forget Greyhound's ill-fated attempt to take its long-distance passenger bus model to the sky—no one had given WestJet a serious run for its money. However, when it began adding trans-Atlantic flights in 2015, purchasing Boeing Dreamliner airplanes in 2017, and announcing new international destinations on a fairly regular basis, it was clear that WestJet had outgrown the "little airline that could" persona and was now squarely focused on competing with its arch-rival Air Canada in international travel.

But while it was competing for that space, it became necessary to ratchet up services and add back the frills that appeal to international travellers. The movement in that direction left WestJet vulnerable in the low-cost travel category, and would-be heirs to that position eventually began moving in. Winnipeg-based NewLeaf, at time of this writing, appeared to be the Canada's first clear entrant into this category, joining international players Ryanair, from Ireland, and Florida-based Spirit.

Much like WestJet in 1996 and WestJet's unofficial mentor, Southwest Airlines years prior, the new ULCC players have an irreverent, "us against them" attitude, and a cost-structure sheared down to the bone. NewLeaf, borrowing a page from the Uber playbook, didn't even own any planes as of 2017. They were more of a retailer for planes owned by Flair Airlines. Ryanair, for its part, was still growing fleet and adding destinations in 2017, but doing so while still claiming to offer the lowest fares. Spirit was making the most audacious claims. That same year it was boasting unabashedly on its website the following:

> We add more seats to our planes because when we fly with more people, the cost per person goes down. Our seats are simple: they don't recline, so you don't wind up with someone's head in your lap. And we don't have Wi-Fi or video, so be sure to download a movie to your phone or tablet. A little cozier seating and fewer expensive extras mean lower fares for you.

Imagine, bragging about creating a tighter squeeze in the air travel experience and making it sound like a badge of honour. These and moves by other airlines the world over prompted Jimmy Kimmel to remark, in the wake of the United Airlines "passenger removal" debacle in April 2017, "It doesn't matter if it's United or Delta, if one of those flights is one dollar less than the others —that's the one we'll pick." It's also what expedited WestJet's decision to jump back into the ring of low-priced air travel.

This WestJet example shows the theory of price sensitivity in the preceding chapter playing itself out in real life. It also demonstrates one of the most important concepts not only of marketing, but also of economics: price elasticity of demand and the demand curve. These concepts assert that for many products that are not necessary to meet our physical needs (like air travel), the lower the price, the greater the quantity we'll demand.

Most of us are price sensitive. All things being equal, we'll choose the lower-priced option on just about any purchase aside from that for which we have a specific brand preference. More and more, air travel is one such category where, whether we prefer WestJet or Air Canada, in this country we'll choose the lowest fare. This is NewLeaf's market assumption, and the reason WestJet is launching a ULCC.

The specifics regarding the WestJet launch are unknown at the time of this writing; however, it seems likely that a new brand name will be created, along with more seats per plane and a reduction in costs, spurred by a total unbundling of services. In the ULCC space, passengers are rewarded for their minimalism in packing, carry-ons, on-flight consumption, and yes, even personal space. Like the ULCCs before them, WestJet's new down-market brand will no doubt charge a fee for everything from a coffee (no more freebies there) to printing your boarding pass. Every microgram of weight prevented from coming on board (aside from humans, of course) will mean lighter loads, greater fuel efficiency, and presumed ongoing low-cost travel.

All of which leads to the question "Why doesn't WestJet just cut costs and lower its prices once again?" It's a reasonable question but one with many complexities, not the least of which is the intersecting point where pricing and positioning meet. Pricing isn't just a part of the marketing mix because it performs the mathematical task of covering costs and generating profit. It also encodes to customers something intangible about the quality of product experience. It suggests something about a brand and helps secure position—subjects discussed in previous chapters. WestJet held the low-cost position in Canada for over a decade, before essentially outgrowing it and needing to expand into a larger, more profitable category. Once in that category, there was no turning back.

However, the position of WestJet the airline doesn't preclude WestJet the company from creating a ULCC product. In fact, as president/CEO Gregg Saretsky stated when the company announced its ULCC plans, "Our new airline will provide Canadians a pro-competitive, cheap and cheerful flying experience from a company with a proven track record." His statement was likely an indicator that, somehow, the DNA responsible for the positioning and subsequent repositioning of WestJet would be at play once again as it entered into the growing ultra-competitive, ultra-low-cost-carrier air space.

SOURCES

- "About Us." Ryanair, https://www.ryanair.com/us/en/useful-info/about-ryanair/about_us (accessed May 12, 2017).
- Canadian Press. "WestJet Announces Plans for Ultra Low Cost Carrier," Global News, April 20, 2017, http://globalnews.ca/news/3391329/westjet-ultra-low-cost-carrier-cheap-airline/ (accessed May 12, 2017).
- *Jimmy Kimmel Live.* ABC Television Network, Episode Airing April 10, 2017.
- "The Why Behind How We Fly," Spirit Airlines, 2017, http://marketing.spirit.com/how-to-fly-spirit-airlines/en/ (accessed May 12, 2017).

QUESTIONS

1. Go to WestJet's website and third-party online travel sites such as Expedia, and identify and differentiate between the pricing strategies used by WestJet and its ULCC brand.

2. At the time of this writing, NewLeaf was adamant that it would not sell tickets through a third-party retailer such as Expedia. Again, this was communicated as a cost-cutting tactic. It is possible, though, that NewLeaf is now selling through travel services such as Expedia, Hotwire, and the like. Why, or why not, did NewLeaf make this strategic decision?

3. What other ULCC brands have emerged since 2017, when WestJet announced its plans to launch later that same year? Conduct a thorough competitive analysis of both Canadian-based ULCCs, such as the WestJet-owned affiliate and NewLeaf, as well as those from any other countries (like Ryanair and Spirit) that fly into Canada.

4. What other products, goods, or services can you identify that have created an ultra-low-cost business model? Why or why not are they successful?

14 | Marketing Channels and Supply Chain Management

LEARNING OUTCOMES

14-1 Explain the nature of marketing channels

14-2 Identify different channel intermediaries and their functions

14-3 Describe the types of marketing channels

14-4 Summarize how to make channel strategy decisions

14-5 Recognize how to handle channel relationships

14-6 Learn about supply chain management

14-7 List channel and distribution challenges in global markets

> *"Having a great idea for a product is important, but having a great idea for product distribution is even more important."*
>
> —Reid Hoffman, founder of LinkedIn[1]

14-1 THE NATURE OF MARKETING CHANNELS

14-1a A Plea for Place—The Forgotten P

Now that the market has been segmented, the product or service has been created, and the price has been determined, what's left? We need to promote the product to the customer. But there's still another significant element missing—one that is often forgotten—distribution. Sometimes referred to as the forgotten P, place is an element of the marketing mix that focuses on getting a finished product to the end customer.

Why is place often forgotten? Perhaps because the activities involved in distribution do not seem to coincide with what most people think constitutes marketing. When we create a product, find a price, and promote it, these are activities normally associated with marketing. In addition, as consumers we see the products, look at the prices, and are exposed to the promotions—but we rarely see anything to do with distribution.

Aside from a retail employee stocking a shelf or a transportation truck with a large company logo passing by, people are not often exposed to what distribution can provide. And what it can provide is significant—a source of competitive advantage that is unrivalled by any of the other three Ps of the marketing mix. It is becoming increasingly difficult to gain a competitive advantage based on product, price, or promotion. Because of constant innovation and technology transfer, products have a hard time standing out from each other and have become commoditized. Thanks to globalization, firms can find cheap means of production for their product, thus keeping prices within a competitive range. Oversaturation of the marketplace with constant communication with and promotion to customers has left many customers seeking a way to distance themselves from the promotional noise.

Therefore, distributing a product from the manufacturer to the end customer is a vital exercise. As Reid Hoffman noted in the quote to start the chapter, you can have a great product idea, but if you don't have the means to get the idea to the customer, there is not much chance of success.

Place can work in concert with the other three Ps, helping determine the price or provide insights into the best packaging. There are many ways in which place can help with the other elements of the marketing mix. But it is important to first understand what makes the P of place work.

Channels of distribution can achieve competitive advantage through a thoughtful strategy that takes advantage of several trends:

- Continual push for growth in most companies

- Increased power of retailers

- Greater role of information technology

Ultimately, the main reason that place can be a source of competitive advantage is that if done right, a well-operated channel of distribution is very difficult and expensive to emulate.

This fact is evidenced by the one company that is known more for its distribution than any other aspect of its business: Amazon. The Seattle-based company is well known for its service and delivery promises, and it has used the investment made in getting products to consumers in a timely manner as a means to grow its business into other areas. Consumers are aware that if

they are looking for almost any type of consumer product (except for fresh or frozen food) in a hurry, then a visit to Amazon.ca is an essential part of fulfilling their needs. With services that take anywhere from days to hours to fulfill, Amazon is changing the expectations that customers have to get products in a timely and efficient manner. And if you become a member of Amazon's Prime Service, for one yearly fee you can get all your deliveries free of charge.

But what is not free is the cost to create and maintain such a system. In one quarter in 2016, Amazon spent $3.88 billion on its distribution network—a 35 percent jump from the same time in 2015. Of the total operating expenses in 2015, the company spent 14 percent on distribution, or what Amazon calls "fulfillment." The fulfillment centres developed by Amazon are almost unfathomable, with a labyrinth of chutes, conveyor belts, and machinery working at a constant pace.

The number of packages being moved in this type of facility is staggering, and Amazon continues to look for innovative ways to deliver their products—such as drones. There is no doubting that Amazon is the world leader in distribution, or fulfillment, due to its willingness to put its money where the competitive advantage is.

Martin Divisek/Bloomberg/Getty Images

14-1b The Marketing Channel and Intermediaries Defined

A **marketing channel** (also called a **channel of distribution**) is a business structure of interdependent organizations that reach from the point of product origin to the customer, whose purpose is to move products to their final consumption destination. In other words, a marketing channel is a set of interdependent organizations that ease the transfer of ownership as products move from producer to business user or consumer. Marketing channels represent the *place* or *distribution* function in the marketing mix (product, price, promotion, and place). The marketing channel is all about getting the right product to the right place at the right time.

Many different types of organizations participate in marketing channels. **Channel members** (also called *intermediaries and resellers*) comprise all parties in the marketing channel that negotiate with one another, buy and sell products, and facilitate the change of ownership between buyer and seller as they move products from the manufacturer into the hands of the final consumer. An important aspect of marketing channels is the joint effort of all channel members to create a continuous and seamless supply chain. The **supply chain** is the connected chain of all the business entities, both internal and external to the company, that perform or support the marketing channel functions.

14-1c How Intermediaries Help the Supply Chain

As products move through the supply chain, channel members facilitate the distribution process through three key actions: providing specialization and division of labour, overcoming discrepancies, and providing contact efficiency.

PROVIDING SPECIALIZATION AND DIVISION OF LABOUR According to the concept of specialization and division of labour, breaking down a complex task into smaller, simpler tasks and then allocating them to specialists will both create greater efficiency and lower average production costs. Manufacturers achieve economies of scale through producing large quantities of a single product.

Marketing channels can also attain economies of scale through specialization and division of labour by aiding producers who lack the motivation, financing, or expertise to market directly to end-users or consumers. In some cases, as with most consumer convenience goods, such as pop, the cost of marketing directly to millions of consumers—taking and shipping individual orders—makes no sense.

For this reason, producers hire channel members, such as wholesalers and retailers, to do what the producers are not equipped to do or what channel members are better prepared to do. Channel members can do some things more efficiently than producers because they have built good relationships with their customers. Therefore, their specialized expertise enhances the overall performance of the channel.

OVERCOMING DISCREPANCIES Marketing channels also aid in overcoming discrepancies of quantity, assortment, time, and space created by economies of scale in production. For example, assume that Quaker Oats can efficiently produce its Aunt Jemima instant pancake mix at a rate of 5000 units in a typical day. Not even the most ardent pancake fan could consume that amount in a year, much less in a day. The quantity produced to achieve low unit costs has created a **discrepancy of quantity**, which is the difference between the amount of product produced and the amount an end-user wants to buy. By storing the product and distributing it in the appropriate amounts, marketing channels overcome quantity discrepancies by making products available in the quantities that consumers desire.

---

marketing channel (channel of distribution) a set of interdependent organizations that ease the transfer of ownership as products move from producer to business user or consumer

channel members all parties in the marketing channel that negotiate with one another, buy and sell products, and facilitate the change of ownership between buyer and seller as they move the product from the manufacturer into the hands of the final consumer

supply chain the connected chain of all the business entities, both internal and external to the company, that perform or support the marketing channel functions

discrepancy of quantity the difference between the amount of product produced and the amount an end-user wants to buy

Mass production creates not only discrepancies of quantity but also discrepancies of assortment. A **discrepancy of assortment** occurs when a consumer does not have all the items needed to receive full satisfaction from a product. For pancakes to provide maximum satisfaction, several other products are required to complete the assortment. At the very least, most people want a knife, a fork, a plate, butter, and syrup. Even though Quaker is a large consumer-products company, it does not come close to providing the optimal assortment to go with its Aunt Jemima pancakes. To overcome discrepancies of assortment, marketing channels assemble in one place many of the products necessary to complete a consumer's needed assortment.

A **temporal discrepancy** is created when a product is produced but a consumer is not ready to buy it. Marketing channels overcome temporal discrepancies by maintaining inventories in anticipation of demand. For example, manufacturers of seasonal merchandise, such as Christmas or Halloween decorations, operate year-round, despite consumer demand being concentrated only during certain months of the year. Channel intermediaries will make the product available whenever it is needed, even taking into consideration the extra hours needed to produce for a special order or unique circumstances.

Furthermore, because mass production requires many potential buyers, markets are usually scattered over large geographic regions, creating a **spatial discrepancy**. Often global, or at least nationwide, markets are needed to absorb the outputs of mass producers. Marketing channels overcome spatial discrepancies by making products

> **discrepancy of assortment** the lack of all the items a customer needs to receive full satisfaction from a product or products
>
> **temporal discrepancy** a product is produced but a customer is not ready to buy it
>
> **spatial discrepancy** the difference between the location of a producer and the location of widely scattered markets

CANADIAN SUPPLY CHAIN—MUST-SEE TV

Canada's immense size and low population density are causes for concern for any company setting up a distribution channel. Because of this spatial discrepancy, the economies of scale so coveted in marketing channels become very difficult to achieve with so much ground to cover. Add to this Canada's unpredictable climate and you have a very challenging market in which to create a successful marketing channel and supply chain system. However, these challenges are not bad news to everyone. Discovery Canada has a popular show called *Highway Thru Hell* that chronicles the work of a heavy-vehicle towing company in Hope, British Columbia. The show revolves around the rescue of large transport trucks carrying out channel and supply chain functions on treacherous roads in bad weather on highways in British Columbia. The show's premiere in 2012 attracted the largest audience in Discovery Canada's history. It would seem that people are in fact interested in channels and supply chains after all!

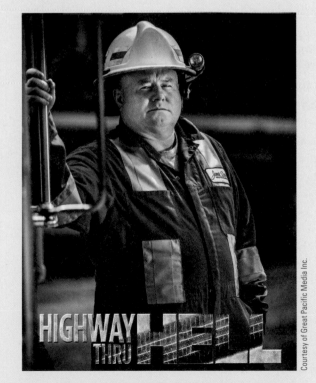

Courtesy of Great Pacific Media Inc.

Sources: *Highway Thru Hell*, Discovery Canada, http://highwaythruhell.discovery.ca (accessed February 2017); and "Big Wrecks and Big Guys Fill Screen in TV's *Highway Thru Hell*," *The Province*, August 28, 2014, http://blogs.theprovince.com/2014/08/28/big-wrecks-and-big-guys-fill-screen-in-tvs-highway-thru-hell/ (accessed February 2017).

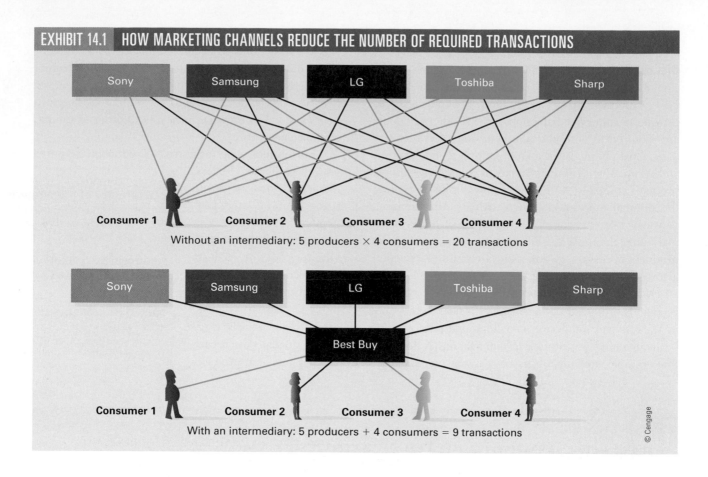

Without an intermediary: 5 producers × 4 consumers = 20 transactions

With an intermediary: 5 producers + 4 consumers = 9 transactions

available in locations convenient to consumers. For example, if all the Aunt Jemima pancake mix is produced in Peterborough, Ontario, then the Quaker Oats Company must use an intermediary to distribute the product to other regions of Canada.

PROVIDING CONTACT EFFICIENCY The third need fulfilled by marketing channels is the contact efficiency provided by reducing the number of stores customers must shop in to complete their purchases. Suppose you had to buy your milk at a dairy and your meat at a stockyard. You would spend a great deal of time, money, and energy shopping for just a few groceries. Supply chains simplify distribution by cutting the number of transactions required to move products from manufacturers to consumers and by making an assortment of goods available in one location.

Consider the example illustrated in Exhibit 14.1. Four consumers each want to buy a new LED television. Without a retail intermediary, such as Best Buy, television manufacturers Sony, Samsung, LG, Toshiba, and Sharp would each have to make four contacts to reach the four buyers who are in the target market, for a total of 20 transactions. However, when Best Buy acts as an intermediary between the producer and customers, each producer makes only one contact, reducing the

number of transactions to nine. Each producer sells to one retailer rather than to four customers. In turn, customers buy from one retailer instead of from five producers. Information technology has enhanced contact efficiency by making information on products and services easily available online. Shoppers can find the best bargains without physically searching for them and can also search for ratings and feedback on products without having to visit the store.

14-2 CHANNEL INTERMEDIARIES AND THEIR FUNCTIONS

Channel intermediaries must find a way to work together while simultaneously achieving their business goals and objectives. Intermediaries in a channel will have to negotiate with one another, decide on terms of ownership transfer between buyers and sellers, and coordinate the physical movement of finished products from the manufacturer to the final consumer.

What separates intermediaries is the fundamental idea of ownership or title. *Taking title* means that an intermediary made the decision to own the merchandise and control the terms of the sale—for example, price and delivery date. Retailers and merchant wholesalers are examples of intermediaries that take title to products in the marketing channel and resell them. **Retailers** are firms that sell mainly to consumers and business customers. Retailers will be discussed in more detail in Chapter 15.

The main characteristics that determine what type of intermediary should be used by a manufacturer (producer) are as follows:

- *Product characteristics*, which may require a certain type of wholesaling intermediary, include whether the product is standardized or customized, the complexity of the product, and the gross margin of the product. For example, a customized product, such as insurance, is sold through an insurance agent or broker who may represent one or multiple companies. In contrast, a standardized product, such as a chocolate bar, is sold through a merchant wholesaler that takes possession of the product and reships it to the appropriate retailers.

- *Buyer considerations* that affect the wholesaler choice include how often the product is purchased and how long the buyer is willing to wait to receive the product. For example, at the beginning of the school term, a student may be willing to wait a few days for a textbook if it means paying a lower price by ordering online. Thus this type of product can be distributed directly. But if the student waits to buy the book until right before an exam and needs the book immediately, the student will need to purchase it for full price at the school bookstore or pay even more by adding on high shipping charges to have it delivered immediately from an online site.

- *Market characteristics* that determine the wholesaler type include the number of buyers in the market and whether they are concentrated in a general location or are widely dispersed. Chocolate bars and textbooks, for example, are produced in one location and consumed in many other locations. Therefore, a merchant wholesaler is needed to distribute the products. In contrast, in a home sale, the buyer and seller are localized in one area, which facilitates the use of an agent or a broker relationship.

14-2a Channel Functions Performed by Intermediaries

Retailing and wholesaling intermediaries in marketing channels perform several essential functions that enable the flow of goods between producer and buyer. The three basic functions that intermediaries perform are summarized in Exhibit 14.2.

> **retailer** a channel intermediary that sells mainly to consumers and business customers

EXHIBIT 14.2 MARKETING CHANNEL FUNCTIONS PERFORMED BY INTERMEDIARIES

Type of Function	Description
Transactional functions	*Contacting and promoting:* Contacting potential customers, promoting products, and soliciting orders
	Negotiating: Determining how many goods or services to buy and sell, type of transportation to use, when to deliver, and method and timing of payment
	Risk taking: Assuming the risk of owning inventory
Logistical functions	*Physically distributing:* Transporting and sorting goods to overcome temporal and spatial discrepancies
	Storing: Maintaining inventories and protecting goods
	Sorting: Overcoming discrepancies of quantity and assortment
	Sorting out: Breaking down a heterogeneous supply into separate homogeneous stocks
	Accumulating: Combining similar stocks into a larger homogeneous supply
	Allocating: Breaking a homogeneous supply into smaller and smaller lots ("breaking bulk"; see example in the upcoming "Breaking Bulk" box)
	Assorting: Combining products into collections or assortments that buyers want available at one place
Facilitating functions	*Researching:* Gathering information about other channel members and customers
	Financing: Extending credit and other financial services to facilitate the flow of goods through the channel to the final consumer

EXHIBIT 14.3 MARKETING CHANNELS FOR CONSUMER PRODUCTS

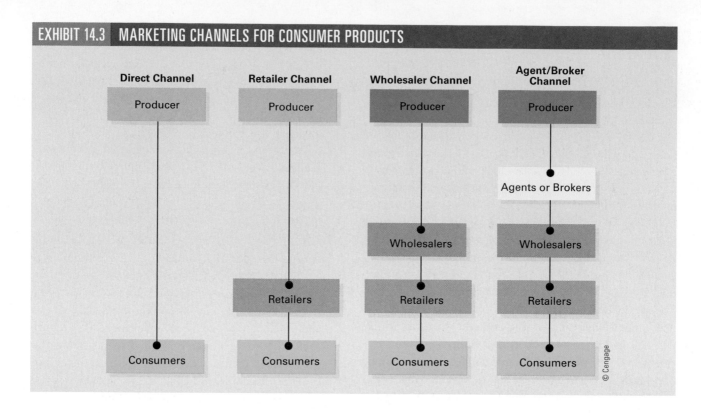

Although individual members can be added to or deleted from a channel, someone must still perform these essential functions. They can be performed by producers, end-users or consumers, channel intermediaries such as wholesalers and retailers, and sometimes by nonmember channel participants. For example, if a manufacturer decides to eliminate its private fleet of trucks, it must still move the goods to the wholesaler. This task may be accomplished by the wholesaler, which may have its own fleet of trucks, or by a nonmember channel participant, such as an independent trucking firm. Nonmembers also provide many other essential functions that may at one time have been provided by a channel member. For example, research firms may perform the research function; advertising agencies may provide the promotion function; transportation and storage firms, the physical distribution function; and banks, the financing function.

14-3 TYPES OF MARKETING CHANNELS

A product can take many routes to reach its final customer. Marketers search for the most efficient channel from the many alternatives available. Marketing a consumer convenience good, such as gum or candy,

direct channel a distribution channel in which producers sell directly to customers

differs from marketing a specialty good, such as a Coach handbag. The next sections discuss the structures of typical and alternative marketing channels for consumer and business-to-business products.

14-3a Channels for Consumer Products

Exhibit 14.3 illustrates the four ways manufacturers can route products to consumers. Producers use the **direct channel** to sell directly to customers. Direct-marketing activities—including telemarketing, mail-order and catalogue shopping, and online shopping—are a good example of this type of channel structure. Direct channels have no intermediaries. Producer-owned stores and factory outlet stores—such as Danier Leather and Rocky Mountain Chocolate Factory—are examples of direct channels. Direct marketing and factory outlets are discussed in more detail in Chapter 15.

By contrast, an *agent/broker channel* is fairly complicated and is typically used in markets characterized by many small manufacturers and many retailers that lack the resources to find each other. Agents or brokers bring manufacturers and wholesalers together for negotiations, but they do not take title to merchandise. Ownership passes directly to one or more wholesalers and then to retailers. Finally, retailers sell to the ultimate consumer of the product. For example, a food broker represents buyers and sellers of grocery products. Canadian-based Marsham International is a food broker specializing in

Breaking Bulk

The term *breaking bulk* (see Exhibit 14.2) came from shipping, where it referred to the extraction of some part of the cargo on a ship. Cargo could be in the form of barrels, crates, and boxes on a ship, and when the ship reached a port, breaking bulk involved pulling off a certain amount of that cargo for distribution. This would have been an arduous and back-breaking task. Today, a marketing channel intermediary (usually a wholesaler) buys a large amount of a product and breaks the bulk of its purchase in preparation for resale to its own customers. However, intermediaries have access to machinery and technology that the tea bulk breakers would have marvelled at.

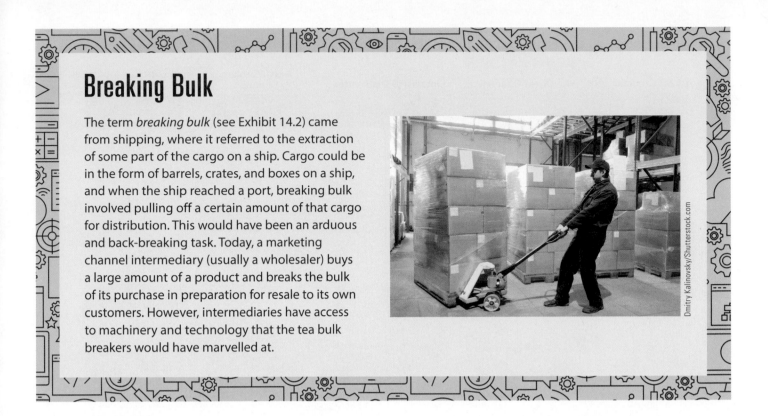

Dmitry Kalinovsky/Shutterstock.com

natural and organic foods. The company promises to work with food manufacturers to get their natural food products on the shelves of retailers. They do this by employing retail professionals who have multiple years of experience getting product on the very competitive shelves of food retailers.[2]

Most consumer products are sold through distribution channels similar to the other two alternatives: the retailer channel and the wholesaler channel. A *retailer channel* is most common when the retailer is large and can buy in large quantities directly from the manufacturer. Chapters Indigo is an example of retailers that often bypass a wholesaler. Online entities like eBay claim to be a "wholesaler's marketplace," where the majority of products are sold at a wholesaler's price. A *wholesaler channel* is commonly used for low-cost and low-involvement items that are frequently purchased, such as candy, gum, and magazines.

14-3b Channels for Business and Industrial Products

As Exhibit 14.4 illustrates, five channel structures are common in business and industrial markets. First, direct channels are typical in business and industrial markets. For example, manufacturers buy large quantities of raw materials, major equipment, processed materials, and supplies directly from other manufacturers.

Manufacturers that require suppliers to meet detailed technical specifications often prefer direct channels. The direct communication required between Chrysler Canada and its suppliers, for example, along with the tremendous size of the orders, makes anything but a direct channel impractical. The channel from producer to government buyers is also a direct channel. Since much government buying is done through bidding, a direct channel is attractive.

Companies selling standardized items of moderate or low value often rely on *industrial distributors*. In many ways, an industrial distributor is like a supermarket for organizations. Industrial distributors are wholesalers and channel members that buy and take title to products. Moreover, they usually keep inventories of their products and sell and service them. Often, small manufacturers cannot afford to employ their own sales force. Instead, they rely on manufacturers' representatives or selling agents to sell to either industrial distributors or users, such as Sysco.

The Internet has enabled virtual distributors to emerge and thereby has forced traditional industrial distributors to expand their business model. Many manufacturers and customers are bypassing distributors and going direct, often online. Companies looking to drop the intermediary from the supply chain have created exchanges. Retailers use the Worldwide Retail Exchange to make purchases (that in the past would have required

EXHIBIT 14.4   CHANNELS FOR BUSINESS AND INDUSTRIAL PRODUCTS

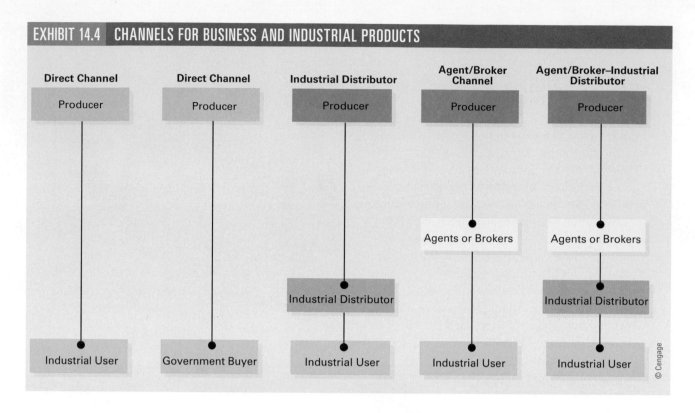

Direct Channel	Direct Channel	Industrial Distributor	Agent/Broker Channel	Agent/Broker–Industrial Distributor
Producer	Producer	Producer	Producer	Producer
			Agents or Brokers	Agents or Brokers
		Industrial Distributor		Industrial Distributor
Industrial User	Government Buyer	Industrial User	Industrial User	Industrial User

© Cengage

telephone, fax, or face-to-face sales calls) and, in so doing, save approximately 15 percent in their purchasing costs. Finally, a third type of Internet marketplace is a private exchange. Private exchanges allow companies to automate their supply chains while sharing information only with select suppliers. Dell, IBM, and Hewlett-Packard, for example, use private exchanges to manage their inventory supplies and save on distribution and freight costs.[3]

14-3c Alternative Channel Arrangements

Rarely does a producer use just one type of channel to move its product. It usually employs several different or alternative channels, which include multiple channels, nontraditional channels, and strategic channel alliances.

dual distribution (multiple distribution) the use of two or more channels to distribute the same product to target markets

MULTIPLE CHANNELS

When a producer selects two or more channels to distribute the same product to target markets, this arrangement is called **dual distribution** (or **multiple distribution**). As more people have access to the Internet and embrace online shopping, an increasing number of retailers are choosing to use multiple distribution channels. For example, companies such as Roots, which includes Roots Home Design, Roots Business to Business, and Roots Yoga, sell in-store, online, and through catalogues.

NONTRADITIONAL CHANNELS

Often nontraditional channel arrangements help differentiate a firm's product from the competition. Nontraditional channels include the Internet, mail-order channels, and infomercials. Although nontraditional channels may limit a brand's coverage, for a producer serving a niche market, they provide a way to gain market access and customer attention without having to establish channel intermediaries.

Nontraditional channels can also provide another avenue of sales for larger firms. For example, vending machines, which are often associated with dispensing pop, snacks, or cash, are taking on new roles. A British publisher sells short stories through vending machines in the London Underground. Instead of the traditional book format, the stories are printed like folded maps,

Tyler McKay/Shutterstock.com

making them an easy-to-read alternative for commuters. A California company called Medbox recently signed an agreement with a lab in Canada licensed by Health Canada to provide marijuana via vending machines. However, Canadian law would prohibit anyone wanting to purchase marijuana for medical reasons to access the vending machines directly. Only licensed sellers of marijuana could access the Medbox vending machines, and they would then ship the product to the customer. Medbox vending machines are already being used at doctors' offices and hospitals in California. The company believes that the Canadian market provides a significant growth opportunity for the firm.[4]

STRATEGIC CHANNEL ALLIANCES Companies often form **strategic channel alliances**, which are cooperative agreements between business firms to use one of the manufacturer's already established channels. Alliances are used most often when the creation of marketing channel relationships may be too expensive and time-consuming. Starbucks contracted with Pepsi to develop and bottle a Starbucks brand of ready-to-drink (RTD) coffee. The resulting Frappuccino and Doubleshot were an immediate success. Today, the Pepsi Bottling Group is still the sole distributor for Starbucks RTD beverages, and Starbucks has continued access to the thousands of outlets where Pepsi is sold.[5] Strategic channel alliances are proving to be more successful for growing businesses than for mergers and acquisitions. This success is especially true in global markets where cultural differences, distance, and other barriers can prove challenging.

 ## 14-4 MAKING CHANNEL STRATEGY DECISIONS

Devising a marketing channel strategy requires several critical decisions. Supply chain managers must decide what role distribution will play in the overall marketing strategy. In addition, they must be sure that the channel strategy chosen is consistent with product, promotion, and pricing strategies. In making these decisions, marketing managers must determine which factors will influence the choice of channel and the appropriate level of distribution intensity.

14-4a Factors Affecting Channel Choice

Supply chain managers must answer many questions before choosing a marketing channel. The final choice depends on their desired distribution channel object-

ives with regard to coverage, costs, and control of their products. To determine the final choice means first analyzing several factors that often interact with each other. These factors can be grouped as market factors, product factors, and producer factors.

MARKET FACTORS Among the most important market factors affecting the choice of distribution channel are target customer considerations. Specifically, supply chain managers should answer the following questions: Who are the potential customers? What do they buy? Where do they buy? When do they buy? How do they buy? Additionally, the choice of channel depends on whether the producer is selling to consumers or to industrial customers. Industrial customers tend to buy in larger quantities and often require more customer service than consumers. For example, Toyota Industrial Equipment manufactures the leading lift truck used to move materials in and out of warehouses and other industrial facilities. Its business customers buy large numbers of trucks at one time and require additional services, such as data tracking on how the lift truck is used.[6] In contrast, consumers usually buy in very small quantities and sometimes do not mind if they receive little or no service, such as when shopping in discount stores like Walmart and Target.

The geographic location and the size of the market are also important in channel selection. As a rule, if the target market is concentrated in one or more specific areas, then direct selling through a sales force is appropriate. When markets are more widely dispersed, intermediaries would be less expensive. The size of the market also influences channel choice. Generally, larger markets require more intermediaries. For instance,

strategic channel alliances cooperative agreements between business firms to use one of the manufacturer's already established distribution channels

Procter & Gamble has to reach millions of consumers with its many brands of household goods. As a result, it needs many intermediaries, including wholesalers and retailers.

PRODUCT FACTORS Products that are more complex, customized, and expensive tend to benefit from shorter and more direct marketing channels. These types of products sell better through a direct sales force. Examples are pharmaceuticals, scientific instruments, airplanes, and mainframe computer systems. On the other hand, the more standardized a product is, the longer its distribution channel can be and the greater the number of intermediaries that can be involved. For example, with the exception of flavour and shape, the formula for chewing gum is about the same from producer to producer. Chewing gum is also very inexpensive, so the distribution channel for gum tends to involve many wholesalers and retailers.

The product's life cycle is also an important factor in choosing a marketing channel. In fact, the choice of channel may change over the life of the product. As products become more common and less intimidating to potential users, producers tend to look for alternative channels. Brokerhouse Distributors, a leading wholesale supplier in Canada, started out selling vending machines, but now offers customers an array of products. Instead of just selling machines that dispense chocolate bars or cans of pop, Brokerhouse provides the hospitality industry in Canada with everything from professional milk frothers to water coolers.[7]

Another factor is the delicacy of the product. Perishable products, such as vegetables and milk, have a relatively short lifespan. Therefore, they require fairly short marketing channels. Today, consumers' desire for fresh (often organic) produce and other farm products has led to a renewed growth across Canada in farmers' markets and in businesses delivering these products from the farm directly to consumers' homes.

PRODUCER FACTORS Several factors pertaining to the producer itself are important to the selection of a marketing channel. In general, producers with large financial, managerial, and marketing resources are better able to use more direct channels. These producers have the ability to hire and train their own sales force, warehouse their own goods, and extend credit to their customers. Smaller or weaker

ZoomSystems provides in-store retail solutions (otherwise known as vending machines) that dispense everything from headphones to espresso.

firms, on the other hand, must rely on intermediaries to provide these services. Compared with producers that have only one or two product lines, producers that sell several products in a related area are able to choose channels that are more direct. Their sales expenses then can be spread over more products.

A producer's desire to control pricing, positioning, brand image, and customer support also tends to influence channel selection. For instance, firms that sell products with exclusive brand images, such as designer perfumes and clothing, usually avoid channels in which discount retailers are present, preferring instead to sell their wares only in expensive stores to maintain an image of exclusivity. Many producers have opted to risk their image, however, and test sales in discount channels. Well-recognized brands will work directly with discount retailers like Dollarama to get overstock and discontinued items on to a Dollarama shelf.[8]

14-4b Levels of Distribution Intensity

Organizations have three options for intensity of distribution: intensive distribution, selective distribution, or exclusive distribution.

INTENSIVE DISTRIBUTION Intensive distribution is a form of distribution aimed at maximum market coverage. **Coverage** refers to ensuring product availability in every outlet where potential customers might want to buy it. If buyers are unwilling to search for a product (as is true of convenience goods and operating supplies), then the product must be very accessible to buyers.

Most manufacturers pursuing an intensive distribution strategy sell to a large percentage of the wholesalers

intensive distribution a form of distribution aimed at having a product available in every outlet where target customers might want to buy it

coverage ensuring product availability in every outlet where potential customers might want to buy it

willing to stock their products. Retailers' willingness (or unwillingness) to handle items tends to control the manufacturer's ability to achieve intensive distribution. For products like soft drinks it is important that manufacturers get the product out to as many different retailers as possible. Whether it is at a five-star restaurant or a remote gas station, soft drink providers should try to be in as many places as consumers would expect them to be when looking for a soft drink.

SELECTIVE DISTRIBUTION **Selective distribution** is achieved by screening dealers and retailers to eliminate all but a few in any single area. Because only a few are chosen, the consumer must seek out the product. For example, when Heeling Sports Ltd. launched Heelys, thick-soled sneakers with a wheel embedded in each heel, the company needed to create demand. It hired a group of 40 teens to perform Heelys exhibitions in targeted malls, skate parks, and college and university campuses across the country. The company then made the decision to avoid large stores, such as Sears, preferring instead to distribute the shoes only through selected mall retailers and skate and surf shops, where the Heelys could be positioned as "cool and kind of irreverent." [9] Heelys are available only in bricks-and-mortar retail stores in Ontario but can be purchased online via Amazon.ca.

Selective distribution strategies often hinge on a manufacturer's desire to maintain a superior product image so as to be able to charge a premium price.

EXCLUSIVE DISTRIBUTION The most restrictive form of market coverage is **exclusive distribution**, which is a form of distribution that involves only one or a few dealers within a given area. Because buyers may have to search or travel extensively to buy the product, exclusive distribution is usually confined to consumer specialty goods, a few shopping goods, and major industrial equipment. Sometimes, exclusive territories are granted by new companies (such as franchisers) to obtain market coverage in a particular area. Limited distribution may also serve to project an exclusive image for the product.

Retailers and wholesalers may be unwilling to commit the time and money necessary to promote and service a product unless the manufacturer guarantees them an exclusive territory. This arrangement shields the dealer from direct competition and enables it to be the main beneficiary of the manufacturer's promotion efforts in that geographic area. In an exclusive distribution, channels of communication are usually well established because the manufacturer works with a limited number of dealers rather than many accounts.

Exclusive distribution also takes place within a retailer's store rather than a geographic area—for example, when a retailer does not sell competing brands. Mark's partners with manufacturers to produce its Dakota and WindRiver lines, brands sold only in its stores.

14-5 HANDLING CHANNEL RELATIONSHIPS

A marketing channel is more than a set of institutions linked by economic ties. Social relationships play an important role in building unity among channel members. A critical aspect of supply chain management, therefore, is managing the social relationships among channel members to achieve synergy. The basic social dimensions of channels are power, control, leadership, conflict, and partnering.

14-5a Channel Power, Control, and Leadership

Channel power is a channel member's capacity to control or influence the behaviour of other channel members. **Channel control** occurs when one channel member intentionally affects another member's behaviour. To achieve control, a channel member assumes channel leadership and exercises authority and power. This member is termed the **channel leader**, or **channel captain**. In one marketing channel, a manufacturer may be the leader because it controls new-product designs and product availability. In another marketing channel, a retailer may be the channel leader because it wields power and control over the retail price, inventory levels, and postsale service.

The exercise of channel power is a routine element of many business activities in which the outcome is often greater control over a company's brands. Apple started its line of retail stores because management was dissatisfied with how distributors were selling the company's

selective distribution a form of distribution achieved by screening dealers to eliminate all but a few in any single area

exclusive distribution a form of distribution that involves only one or a few dealers within a given area

channel power a marketing channel member's capacity to control or influence the behaviour of other channel members

channel control one marketing channel member intentionally affects another member's behaviour

channel leader (channel captain) a member of a marketing channel who exercises authority and power over the activities of other channel members

computers (i.e., with its lack of control). Their products were often buried inside other major retail stores, surrounded by personal computers running Microsoft's more popular Windows operating systems. To regain channel power, Apple hired a retail executive to develop a retail strategy that relied heavily on company-owned stores that reflect Apple's design sensibilities.[10]

14-5b Channel Conflict

Inequitable channel relationships often lead to **channel conflict,** which is a clash of goals and methods among distribution channel members. In a broad context, conflict may not be bad. Often it arises because staid, traditional channel members refuse to keep pace with the times. Removing an outdated intermediary may result in reduced costs for the entire supply chain. The Internet has forced many intermediaries to offer online services, such as merchandise tracking and inventory availability.

Conflicts among channel members can be due to many different situations and factors. Often, conflict arises because channel members have conflicting goals, as was the case with Apple and its distributors. Conflict can also arise when channel members fail to fulfill expectations of other channel members—for example, when a franchisee does not follow the rules set down by the franchiser or when communications channels break down between channel members. Further, ideological differences and different perceptions of reality can also cause conflict among channel members. For instance, some retailers, believing the customer is always right, may offer a very liberal return policy. Conversely, some wholesalers and manufacturers may feel that people often try to get something for nothing or don't follow product instructions carefully. These differing views of allowable returns will undoubtedly conflict with those of retailers.

Conflict within a channel can be either horizontal or vertical. **Horizontal conflict** is a channel conflict that occurs among channel members on the same level, such as two or more different wholesalers or two or more different retailers that handle the same manufacturer's brands. This type of channel conflict is found most often when manufacturers practise dual or multiple distributions. Horizontal conflict can also occur when channel members feel that other members on the same level are being treated differently by the manufacturer, such as only some channel members receiving substantial discounts. An example of a horizontal conflict is a turf war, where a manufacturer does not clearly stipulate the geographical ranges and restrictions for its distributors. This leads to conflict between the two distributors, who are both at the same level in the distribution channel system.

Many regard horizontal conflict as healthy competition. Much more serious is **vertical conflict**, which occurs between different levels in a marketing channel, most typically between the manufacturer and wholesaler or the manufacturer and retailer. Producer-versus-wholesaler conflict occurs when the producer chooses to bypass the wholesaler and deal directly with the consumer or retailer.

Dual distribution strategies can also cause vertical conflict in the channel, such as when high-end fashion designers sell their goods through their own boutiques and luxury department stores. Similarly, manufacturers experimenting with selling to customers directly over the Internet create conflict with their traditional retailing intermediaries. Producers and retailers may also disagree over the terms of the sale or other aspects of the business relationship.

14-5c Channel Partnering

Regardless of the locus of power, channel members rely heavily on one another. Even the most powerful manufacturers depend on dealers to sell their products; and even the most powerful retailers require the products provided by suppliers. In sharp contrast to the adversarial relationships of the past between buyers and sellers, contemporary management emphasizes the development of close working partnerships among channel members. **Channel partnering**, or **channel cooperation**, is the joint effort of all channel members to create a supply chain that serves customers and creates a competitive advantage. Channel partnering is vital if each member is to gain something from other members. By cooperating, retailers, wholesalers, manufacturers, and suppliers can speed up inventory replenishment, improve customer service, and reduce the total costs of the marketing channel.

Channel alliances and partnerships help supply chain managers create the parallel flow of materials and information required to leverage the supply chain's

---

channel conflict a clash of goals and methods among distribution channel members

horizontal conflict a channel conflict that occurs among channel members on the same level

vertical conflict a channel conflict that occurs between different levels in a marketing channel, most typically between the manufacturer and wholesaler or between the manufacturer and retailer

channel partnering (channel cooperation) the joint effort of all channel members to create a supply chain that serves customers and creates a competitive advantage

intellectual, material, and marketing resources. The rapid growth in channel partnering is due to new technology and the need to lower costs. Collaborating channel partners meet the needs of customers more effectively, thus boosting sales and profits. Forced to become more efficient, many companies are turning formerly adversarial relationships into partnerships.

An example of a well-established channel partnership is the more than decade-long cooperation between Apple and AT&T. The two parties began discussions in 2005 on working together on Apple's new revolutionary product offering: the iPhone. After two years of negotiations, a deal was struck. To show the level of distrust often present with channel members, Apple refused to show AT&T officials an actual iPhone until the deal was signed. The deal involved AT&T being the exclusive distributor for the first iteration of the iPhone by providing a reliable voice and data network. As the relationship grew, the two channel partners worked on the development of App Store and have continued to work together on the new iterations of the iPhone product line.[11] Apple recently showed interest in buying Time Warner Cable to assist in producing content for their various platforms—that is, until AT&T got involved and signed an agreement to merge with Time Warner.[12]

14-6 MANAGING THE SUPPLY CHAIN

A supply chain consists of a group of companies working together to produce, handle, and distribute products to an end customer. Many modern companies are turning to **supply chain management** to gain a competitive advantage. The goal of supply chain management is to coordinate and integrate all the activities performed by supply chain members into a seamless process, from the source to the point of consumption, ultimately giving supply chain managers total visualization of the supply chain, both inside and outside the firm. The philosophy behind supply chain management is that by visualizing the entire supply chain, supply chain managers can maximize strengths and efficiencies at each level of the process to create a highly competitive, customer-driven supply system that is able to respond immediately to changes in supply and demand.

Supply chain management is mostly customer driven. In the mass-production era, manufacturers produced standardized products that were pushed down through the supply channel to the consumer. In today's marketplace, however, products are being driven by customers, who expect to receive product configurations

and services matched to their unique needs. The focus is on pulling products into the marketplace and partnering with members of the supply chain to enhance customer value. Customizing an automobile is now possible because of new supply chain relationships between the automobile manufacturers and the after-market auto-parts industry.[13]

This reversal of the flow of demand from a push to a pull has resulted in a radical reformulation of market expectations and traditional marketing, production, and distribution functions. Integrated channel partnerships allow companies to respond with the unique product configuration and mix of services demanded by the customer. Today, supply chain management is both a *communicator* of customer demand that extends from the point of sale all the way back to the supplier, and a *physical flow* process that engineers the timely and cost-effective movement of goods through the entire supply pipeline.

14-6a Benefits of Supply Chain Management

Supply chain management is both a key means of differentiation for a firm and a critical component in marketing and corporate strategy. Companies that focus on supply chain management commonly report lower costs of inventory, transportation, warehousing, and packaging; greater supply chain flexibility; improved customer service; and higher revenues. Research has shown a clear relationship between supply chain performance and profitability.

A company that has benefited greatly from the use of supply chain is the fashion retailer Zara. In order to stay ahead in the fashion game, Zara uses sourcing, logistics, and turnaround time just as much as it uses fabric, zippers, and stitching. Zara takes great pride in vertically integrating the intermediary activities, and thus controlling what gets made and how long it takes to get from the runway to the store. Zara commits to no more than 25 percent of a season's line of clothing before a season, and only about half of its line is determined before the start of a season. This leaves Zara with up to half of any season's clothing line to be determined by the outside world—be it fashion designers, bloggers, or simply people on the street.[14]

This flexibility in and control of a supply chain has translated into business

> **supply chain management**
> a management system that coordinates and integrates all the activities performed by supply chain members into a seamless process, from the source to the point of consumption, resulting in enhanced customer and economic value

REUTERS/Miguel Vidal

success for Zara. It has more than 7000 stores worldwide, more than 150,000 employees, and sales and profit increases of more than 15 percent from 2014 to 2015.[15]

14-6b Managing Logistics in the Supply Chain

Critical to any supply chain is orchestrating the physical means through which products move through it. **Logistics** is the process of strategically managing the efficient flow and storage of raw materials, in-process inventory, and finished goods from point of origin to point of consumption. As mentioned earlier, supply chain management coordinates and integrates all the activities performed by supply chain members into a seamless process. The supply chain consists of several interrelated and integrated logistical components: (1) sourcing and procurement of raw materials and supplies, (2) production scheduling, (3) order processing, and (4) inventory control.

The **logistics information system** is the link connecting all the logistics components of the supply chain. The components of the system include, for example, software for materials acquisition and handling, warehouse management and enterprise-wide solutions, data storage and integration in data warehouses, mobile communications, electronic data interchange, radio-frequency identification (RFID) chips, and the Internet. Working together, the components of the logistics information system are the fundamental enablers of successful supply chain management.

The **supply chain team**, in concert with the logistics information system, orchestrates the movement of goods, services, and information from the source to the consumer. Supply chain teams typically cut across organizational boundaries, embracing all parties that participate in moving the product to market. The best supply chain teams also move beyond the organization to include the external participants in the chain, such as suppliers, transportation carriers, and third-party logistics suppliers. Members of the supply chain communicate, coordinate, and cooperate extensively.

14-6c Sourcing and Procurement

One of the most important links in the supply chain occurs between the manufacturer and the supplier. Purchasing professionals are on the front lines of supply chain management. Purchasing departments plan purchasing strategies, develop specifications, select suppliers, and negotiate price and service levels.

The goal of most sourcing and **procurement** activities is to reduce the costs of raw materials and supplies. Purchasing professionals have traditionally relied on tough negotiations to get the lowest price possible from suppliers of raw materials, supplies, and components.

Perhaps the biggest contribution purchasing can make to supply chain management, however, is in the area of vendor relations. Companies can use the purchasing function to strategically manage suppliers to reduce the total cost of materials and services. Through enhanced vendor relations, buyers and sellers can develop cooperative relationships that reduce costs and improve efficiency with the aim of lowering prices and enhancing profits. By integrating suppliers into their companies' businesses, purchasing managers have become better able to streamline purchasing processes, manage inventory levels, and reduce overall costs of the sourcing and procurement operations.

14-6d Production Scheduling

In traditional mass-market manufacturing, production begins when forecasts call for additional products to be made or when inventory control systems signal low inventory levels. The firm then makes a product and transports the finished goods to its own warehouses or those of intermediaries, where the goods wait to be ordered by retailers or customers. For example,

logistics the process of strategically managing the efficient flow and storage of raw materials, in-process inventory, and finished goods from point of origin to point of consumption

logistics information system the link that connects all the logistics functions of the supply chain

supply chain team an entire group of individuals who orchestrate the movement of goods, services, and information from the source to the consumer

procurement the process of buying goods and services for use in the operations of an organization

many types of convenience goods, such as toothpaste, deodorant, and detergent, are manufactured on the basis of past sales and demand and then sent to retailers to resell. Production scheduling that is based on pushing a product down to the consumer obviously has its disadvantages, the most notable being that companies risk making products that may become obsolete or that consumers don't want in the first place.

In a customer "pull" manufacturing environment, which is growing in popularity, production of goods or services is not scheduled until an order is placed by the customer specifying the desired configuration. This process, known as **mass customization**, or **build-to-order**, uniquely tailors mass-market goods and services to the needs of the individuals who buy them. Companies as diverse as BMW, Dell, Levi Strauss, Mattel, and a host of online businesses are adopting mass customization to maintain or obtain a competitive edge.

As more companies move toward mass customization—and away from mass marketing—of goods, the need to stay on top of consumer demand is forcing manufacturers to make their supply chains more flexible. Flexibility is critical to a manufacturer's success when responding to dramatic swings in demand. To meet consumers' demand for customized products, companies must adapt their manufacturing approach or even create a completely new process. For years, Nike sold its shoes through specialty retailers to hard-core runners who cared little what the shoes looked like. Over time, however, runners began to demand more stylish designs and more technologically advanced footwear. To keep pace with rapidly changing fashions and trends, Nike launched NIKEiD, a set of specialty stores and a website through which consumers can design and order athletic shoes.[16]

JUST-IN-TIME MANUFACTURING An important manufacturing process common today among manufacturers is just-in-time manufacturing. Borrowed from the Japanese, **just-in-time production (JIT)**, sometimes called *lean production*, requires manufacturers to work closely with suppliers and transportation providers to get necessary items to the assembly line or factory floor at the precise time they are needed for production. For the manufacturer, JIT means that raw materials arrive at the assembly line in guaranteed working order "just in time" to be installed, and finished products are generally shipped to the customer immediately after completion. For the supplier, JIT means supplying customers with products in just a few days, or even a few hours, rather than weeks. For the ultimate end-user, JIT means lower costs, shorter lead times, and products that more closely meet the consumer's needs. Companies that have taken the leap to JIT have found substantial impacts on their business operations. Harley Davidson introduced JIT and saw inventory levels go down by 75 percent while productivity actually increased.[17]

14-6e Order Processing

The order is often the catalyst that sets the supply chain in motion, especially in build-to-order environments. The **order processing system** processes the requirements of the customer and sends the information into the supply chain via the logistics information system. The order goes to the manufacturer's warehouse. If the product is in stock, the order is filled and arrangements are made to ship it. If the product is not in stock, it triggers a replenishment request that finds its way to the factory floor.

Proper order processing is critical to good service. As an order enters the system, management must monitor two flows: the flow of goods and the flow of information. Good communication among sales representatives, office personnel, and warehouse and shipping personnel is essential to accurate order processing. Shipping incorrect merchandise or partially filled orders can create just as much dissatisfaction as stockouts or slow deliveries. The flow of goods and information must be continually monitored so that mistakes can be corrected before an invoice is prepared and the merchandise shipped.

Getty Images/Getty Images for Nike

> **mass customization (build-to-order)** a production method whereby products are not made until an order is placed by the customer; products are made according to customer specifications
>
> **just-in-time production (JIT)** a process that redefines and simplifies manufacturing by reducing inventory levels and delivering raw materials just when they are needed on the production line
>
> **order processing system** a system whereby orders are entered into the supply chain and filled

CHAPTER 14: Marketing Channels and Supply Chain Management

Today's companies rely on sophisticated software to help them control inventories.

Order processing is becoming more automated through the use of computer technology known as **electronic data interchange (EDI)**. The basic idea of EDI is to replace the paper documents that usually accompany business transactions, such as purchase orders and invoices, with electronic transmission of the needed information. A typical EDI message includes all the information that would traditionally be included on a paper invoice, such as product code, quantity, and transportation details. The information is usually sent via private networks, which are more secure and reliable than the networks used for standard email messages. Most importantly, the information can be read and processed by computers, significantly reducing costs and increasing efficiency. Companies that use EDI can reduce inventory levels, improve cash flow, streamline operations, and increase the speed and accuracy of information transmission. EDI also creates a closer relationship between buyers and sellers.

EDI works hand in hand with retailers' *efficient consumer response* programs to ensure the right products are on the shelf, in the right styles and colours, at the right time, through improved techniques for tracking inventory, ordering, and distribution. Canada's oldest retailer, the Hudson's Bay Company, is proudly EDI compliant and has taken

electronic data interchange (EDI)
information technology that replaces the paper documents that usually accompany business transactions, such as purchase orders and invoices, with electronic transmission of the needed information to reduce inventory levels, improve cash flow, streamline operations, and increase the speed and accuracy of information transmission

inventory control system a method of developing and maintaining an adequate assortment of materials or products to meet a manufacturer's or a customer's demand

steps to ensure that smaller businesses can interact with the large retailer. The Bay offers web-based EDI systems to small businesses so there is no need to purchase costly software, and the Bay offers short-term contracts to firms to test out the EDI system.[18]

14-6f Inventory Control

The **inventory control system** develops and maintains an adequate assortment of materials or products to meet a manufacturer's or a customer's demands. Inventory decisions, for both raw materials and finished goods, have a big impact on supply chain costs and the level of service provided. If too many products are kept in inventory, costs increase—as do risks of obsolescence, theft, and damage shrinkage. If too few products are kept on hand, then the company risks product shortages, angry customers, and ultimately lost sales. The goal of inventory management, therefore, is to keep inventory levels as low as possible while maintaining an adequate supply of goods to meet customer demand.

As you would expect, JIT has a significant impact on reducing inventory levels. Because supplies are delivered exactly when they are needed on the factory floor, little inventory of any kind is needed, and companies can order materials in smaller quantities. Those lower inventory levels can give firms a competitive edge through the flexibility to halt production of existing products in favour of those gaining popularity with consumers. Savings also come from having less capital tied up in inventory and from the reduced need for storage facilities. At the retail level, the reduced need for storage space allows for more extensive use of the retail store's area (its real estate space) for the display of more products to their customers.

 14-7 # DISTRIBUTION CHALLENGES IN WORLD MARKETS

With the spread of free-trade agreements and treaties, global marketing channels and management of the supply chain have become increasingly important to corporations that export their products or manufacture abroad.

14-7a Developing Global Marketing Channels

Manufacturers introducing products in global markets must decide which type of channel structure to use. Using company salespeople generally provides more control and is less risky than using foreign intermediaries. However, setting up a sales force in a foreign country also involves a greater commitment, both financially and organizationally.

Channel structures and types abroad may differ from those in North America. For instance, the more highly developed a nation is economically, the more specialized its channel types. Therefore, a marketer wanting to sell in Germany or Japan will have several channel types to choose from. Conversely, developing countries, such as India, Ethiopia, and Venezuela, have limited channel types available: typically, these countries have few mail-order channels, vending machines, or specialized retailers and wholesalers.

14-7b Global Logistics and Supply Chain Management

One of the most critical global logistical issues for importers of any size is coping with the legalities of trade in other countries. Shippers and distributors must be aware of the permits, licences, and registrations they may need to acquire and, depending on the type of product they are importing, the tariffs, quotas, and other regulations that apply in each country. This multitude of different rules is why multinational companies are committed to working through the World Trade Organization to develop a global set of rules and to encourage countries to participate.

Transportation can also be a major issue for companies dealing with global supply chains. Uncertainty regarding shipping usually tops the list of reasons that companies, especially smaller ones, resist international markets. In some instances, poor infrastructure makes transportation dangerous and unreliable. And the process of moving goods across the borders of even the most industrialized nations can still be complicated by government regulations. To make the process easier, Wide Range Transportation Services operates a 3700-square-metre (40,000-square-foot) facility in Grimsby, Ontario, between Hamilton and Buffalo, New York. It offers brokerage, warehousing, fleet, and logistics services to help its clients reduce costs and save time shipping goods across the border.[19] The company uses technology similar to E-ZPass (an electronic toll collection system used extensively in the eastern United States) to automate border crossings. The new system sends short-range radio signals containing information on the load to tollbooths, weigh stations, and border crossings. If the cargo meets requirements, the truck or train receives a green light to go ahead. Questionable cargo is set aside for further inspection. Transportation industry experts say the system can reduce delivery times by more than three hours.[20]

SIDE LAUNCH
BREWING COMPANY
CONTINUING CASE

Getting Beer into Hands

One step through the front door of Side Launch Brewing company, located on Mountain Road, just east of Blue Mountain resort in Collingwood, Ontario, will bring an assault to the senses. Immediately you are struck by the towering, shiny, metallic fermentation tanks in plain sight from the reception area and the din of the filling, canning, and packaging station, over the nonstop drone of a forklift relocating pallets of packaged beer. And then there's the nose—perhaps the strongest indicator that you are now in a brewery. "It's the wort boiling," assures brewer Michael Hancock, as if to say, "What you're smelling right now is normal." For him and fellow beer aficionados, the sharp aroma is pure joy; to others it might be most diplomatically described as "a little strong."

When building the brewery, Michael and founder Garnet Pratt wanted, among other things, to create a total integration of operations and administration into an open, living, breathing, exposed, and natural environment. In doing so, they reveal the central exchange area of the Side Launch supply chain. "Those two white pipes up there," says Michael, pointing almost to the full height of the 26-foot ceiling of the facility, "are where the barley malt comes into the brewhouse." His pointed finger then traces the extensive fixture across the ceiling until it reaches an elbow joint that directs the grains downward into one of four cavernous steel tanks from which the brewing process begins. Toward the end of Michael's brewery tour, you find yourself in a 5 degree Celsius loading room where the meticulously crafted and packaged beer awaits its departure to any number of retailers scattered around Ontario and beyond, as far east as New Brunswick and as far west as British Columbia.

Several cans are pulled off each production run and steered to the tasting room and lab, where they undergo quality assurance testing. Several others are directed right to the front of the building, only metres from where their journey began, to a glass-faced refrigerator where they await purchase by locals, some of whom go out of their way to experience the brewery while picking up a supply of their favourite Side Launch flavour. To witness the meticulously sourced raw materials being converted into award-winning beer through state-of-the art-equipment—all envisioned by Michael—is to see engineering, machinery, entrepreneurship, and processes performing in a symphony of industrial precision. It is a supply chain within a supply chain.

An invisible, complex layer of regulations and taxation is placed overtop of the elegant process that brings grains, hops, yeast, and water, along with the packaging components, into the brewery, producing glossy, attractive

cans containing the award-winning brew that is Side Launch. This layer, far too complicated to get into in any detail here, is there to ensure that every drop going out the door not only adheres to health and safety standards and legal guidelines but is also part of a physical accounting process from which tax revenue can be generated for provincial and federal coffers.

Side Launch Brewing Company, over the course of its first few years, has been the maker of its own largest challenge—keeping up with demand. "LCBO [Liquor Control Board of Ontario] is the main [off-premises] retailer of alcohol in Ontario," explains VP Sales and Marketing Chuck Galea, "and you deal with them and their limited locations and limited shelf space in a fairly predictable manner. Our on-premises partners—bars, pubs, and restaurants—are different. They provide us with more opportunities to get our beer into customers' hands due to the sheer number of them in the province." That intensifying distribution, it turns out, continues to create a growing appetite for what comes out of the little craft brewery that could, on Mountain Road, Collingwood.

Questions

1. How would you classify the types of intermediaries identified by Chuck for the Side Launch Brewing Company?

2. Given that provincial governments will place taxes on alcohol before it gets to the consumer, they become part of the marketing channel. Therefore, the alcohol marketing channel takes on more of an agency structure. Explain how governments would be considered agents in this structure.

3. What are some of the inputs to production that Michael must manage within his supply chain?

Side Launch Brewing Company

15 | Retailing

LEARNING OUTCOMES

15-1 Discuss the importance of retailing in the Canadian economy

15-2 Explain the dimensions by which retailers can be classified

15-3 Describe the major types of retail operations

15-4 Discuss nonstore retailing techniques

15-5 Define franchising and describe its two basic forms

15-6 List the major tasks involved in developing a retail marketing strategy

15-7 Discuss retail product and service failures and means to improve

15-8 Discuss retailer and retail consumer trends that will affect retailing in the future

"You can't get away with retail being just a transactional space any more. Customers want an experience. Retailers need to make their experience memorable—even before it starts and after it ends."

—Anne Forkutza, Creative Strategist, iQmetrix[1]

15-1 THE ROLE OF RETAILING

Retailing—all the activities directly related to the sale of goods and services to the ultimate consumer for personal, nonbusiness use—has enhanced the quality of our daily lives. When we shop, whether that be online or in store, for a variety of products and services, we are involved in retailing. The millions of goods and services provided by retailers mirror the needs and styles of Canadian society.

Retailing affects all of us directly or indirectly. The retailing industry is one of the largest employers in Canada and is an industry being pushed to innovate. **Retailers** ring up over $513 billion in sales annually, contributing $76.9 billion to Canada's GDP.[2] The retail sector is the largest industry in Canada, employing over 2 million people. Global retailers are successfully entering the Canadian market, challenging domestic retailers. Canadian consumers are changing quickly and expect retailers to anticipate their changing needs and offer personalized shopping experiences. They are driving the omni-channel approach to retailing. When the Canadian dollar is as soft as it has been of late, it presents a problem for retailers as it results in higher costs of goods sold and uncompetitive labour costs. Technology is the game changer as consumers continue to shop online from every device and invest a significant amount of their time in social media. The Canadian economy is heavily dependent on retailing, and although many of the jobs are casual and young workers dominate the industry, it does serve as a key driver to our economy.[3]

retailing all the activities directly related to the sale of goods and services to the ultimate consumer for personal, nonbusiness use

retailer the market intermediary that sells goods and services to the final consumer

The retailing landscape in Canada is dotted with small independents surrounded by large chains. Successful retailers are those that have built trusted relationships with their shoppers. The market research firm BrandSpark International conducted a study of 7500 Canadians to identify their most trusted retailers. The most trusted retailer across Canada in the Auto Parts and Accessories category is the iconic Canadian retailer Canadian Tire, while the most trusted in the clothing/fashion category is the Hudson's Bay Company.[4]

 15-2 ## CLASSIFICATION OF RETAIL OPERATIONS

A retail establishment can be classified according to its ownership, level of service, product assortment, and price. Specifically, retailers use the last three variables to position themselves in the competitive marketplace. (As noted in Chapter 8, positioning is the strategy used to influence how consumers perceive one product in relation to all competing products.) These three variables can be combined in several ways to create distinctly different retail operations.

EXHIBIT 15.1	CANADA'S MOST TRUSTED RETAILERS
Retail Category	**National Most Trusted Retailers**
Auto Parts and Accessories	Canadian Tire
Baby/Children's Clothing	Carter's/WalMart (tie)
Beauty & Personal Care	Shoppers Drug Mart
Clothing/Fashion	Hudson's Bay Company
Department Store	Walmart
Electronics	Best Buy
Footwear	Payless
Furniture	Leon's
Health/Pharmacy	Shoppers Drug Mart
Home Décor	HomeSense
Home Improvement/Hardware	Home Depot
Housewares/Kitchenware	Walmart
Mass Merchant	Walmart
Sporting Goods	Sport Chek/Sports Experts
Supermarket/Grocery	Real Canadian Superstore
Toys & Games	Toys R Us

Source: "BrandSpark International, Canadian Shopper Study, 2016. http://www.retail-insider.com/retail-insider/2016/4/survey".

15-2a Ownership

Retailers can be broadly classified by form of ownership: independent, part of a chain, or franchise outlet. Retailers owned by a single person or partnership and not operated as part of a larger retail institution are **independent retailers**. Around the world, most retailers are independent, operating one or a few stores in their community. In many communities there is a resurgence of local independent retail, particularly in specialty gift shops.

Chain stores are owned and operated as a group by a single organization. Under this form of ownership, the home office for the entire chain handles many administrative tasks. The home office also buys most of the merchandise sold in the stores. Gap and Starbucks are examples of chains.

Franchises, such as Subway and Tim Hortons, are owned and operated by individuals but are licensed by a larger supporting organization. The franchising approach combines the advantages of independent ownership with those of the chain store organization.

15-2b Level of Service

The level of service that retailers provide can be classified along a continuum, from full service to self-service. Some retailers, such as exclusive clothing stores, offer high levels of service. They provide alterations, credit, delivery, consulting, liberal return policies, layaway, gift wrapping, and personal shopping. Other retailers, such as factory outlets and warehouse clubs, offer virtually no services.

15-2c Product Assortment

The third basis for positioning or classifying stores is by the breadth and depth of their product line. Specialty stores—for example, Maison Birks—have the most concentrated product assortments, usually carrying single or narrow product lines but in considerable depth. On the other end of the spectrum, full-line discounters typically carry broad assortments of merchandise with limited depth. For example, Costco carries automotive supplies, household cleaning products, furniture, and appliances. Typically, though, it carries a very limited selection of

Courtesy of Goemans Appliances

appliances. In contrast, a specialty appliance store such as Goemans Appliances, a family-owned and -operated retailer with eight locations in southwestern Ontario, carries a seemingly endless number of makes and models of every appliance imaginable.

Other retailers, such as factory outlet stores, may carry only part of a single line. Nike stores sell only certain items of its own brand. Discount specialty stores, such as Best Buy and Toys "R" Us, carry a broad assortment in concentrated product lines, such as electronics and toys.

15-2d Price

Price is a fourth way to position retail stores. Traditional department stores and specialty stores typically charge the full suggested retail price. In contrast, discounters, factory outlets, and off-price retailers use low prices as a major lure for shoppers.

Gross margin—the amount of money the retailer makes as a percentage of sales after the cost of goods sold is subtracted and the price level of a retailer generally match. For example, a traditional jewellery store (specialty store) has high prices and high gross margins of approximately 50 percent. Gross margins can decline as a result of markdowns on merchandise during sale periods and price wars among competitors, when stores lower their prices on certain items in an effort to win customers.

15-3 MAJOR TYPES OF RETAIL OPERATIONS

Traditionally, retail stores have been of several distinct types, with each offering a different product assortment, type of service, and price level, according to its customers' shopping preferences. A recent trend, however,

---

independent retailers retailers owned by a single person or partnership and not operated as part of a larger retail institution

chain stores stores owned and operated as a group by a single organization

gross margin the amount of money the retailer makes as a percentage of sales after the cost of goods sold is subtracted

has retailers experimenting with alternative formats that make it difficult to categorize them by using the traditional classifications. For instance, supermarkets are expanding their nonfood items and services. Loblaw Companies Limited has been highly successful with the launch of the Joe Fresh brand. Discounters like Walmart have added groceries; drugstores like Shoppers Drug Mart, which is now owned by Loblaws Companies Inc., are becoming more like convenience stores; and department stores, and even some discounters, are experimenting with smaller stores. Nevertheless, many stores still fall into one of the basic types.

- **Department stores** such as the Bay house several departments under one roof, carrying a wide variety of shopping and specialty goods, including apparel, cosmetics, housewares, electronics, and sometimes furniture. Purchases are generally made within each department rather than at one central checkout area. Each department is treated as a separate buying centre but central management sets broad policies about the types of merchandise carried and price ranges. Central management is also responsible for the overall advertising program, credit policies, store expansion, customer service, and so on. While large independent department stores are not as common as in the past, there appears to be a renaissance. Simons, the Quebec based, family-run department store is expanding across Canada with stores in Edmonton, Vancouver, and Toronto. The Bay, which operates 90 Hudson's Bay department stores across Canada, Saks Fifth Avenue and Lord & Taylor in the United States, and 69 home specialty superstores under the banner Home Outfitters, is expanding the Saks Fifth Avenue presence with launches in Toronto, Calgary, and Montreal.

- **Specialty stores** allow retailers to refine their segmentation strategies and tailor their merchandise to specific target markets. A typical specialty store carries a deeper but narrower assortment of merchandise within a single category of interest. The specialized knowledge of their sales clerks allows for more attentive customer service. The Children's Place and Running Room are well-known specialty retailers.

- **Supermarkets** are large, departmentalized, self-service retailers that specialize in food and some nonfood items. Some conventional supermarkets are being replaced by much larger *superstores*. Superstores meet the needs of today's customers for convenience, variety, and service by offering one-stop shopping for many food and nonfood needs, as well as services such as pharmacists, florists, on-site prepared meals for take away, sit-down restaurants, photo processing kiosks, and banking centres. Some even offer family dentistry and optical shops, and many now have gas stations. This tendency to offer a wide variety of nontraditional goods and services under one roof is called **scrambled merchandising**.

  To stand out in an increasingly competitive marketplace, supermarkets are tailoring their marketing strategies to appeal to specific consumer segments and individual consumers by utilizing the data captured through their *loyalty marketing programs*.

- **Drugstores** stock pharmacy-related products and services as their main draw, but they also carry an extensive selection of over-the-counter (OTC) medications, cosmetics, health and beauty aids, seasonal merchandise, specialty items such as greeting cards and a limited selection of toys, and even refrigerated convenience foods. As competition has increased from mass merchandisers and supermarkets that have their own pharmacies, drugstores have added such services as 24-hour drive-through pharmacies and low-cost health clinics staffed by nurse practitioners. Drugstores are also selling more food products, including perishables.

- **Convenience stores** can be defined as miniature supermarkets, carrying a limited line of high-turnover convenience goods. There are almost 27,000 convenience stores in Canada, generating over $51 billion in sales each year.[5] These self-service stores, such as Quickie Convenience,

department store a store housing several departments under one roof

specialty store a retail store specializing in a given type of merchandise

supermarkets large, departmentalized, self-service retailers that specialize in food and some nonfood items

scrambled merchandising the tendency to offer a wide variety of nontraditional goods and services under one roof

drugstores retail stores that stock pharmacy-related products and services as their main draw

convenience store a miniature supermarket, carrying only a limited line of high-turnover convenience goods

Courtesy of Running Room Canada Inc.

Going Back to Its Roots

Costco has announced that it is launching a new store format that is taking it back to its beginnings. The new (old) store format has been designed to target small businesses such as doctors, lawyers, restaurateurs, and a variety of small specialty shops, with the hope that the changes will also be preferred by some of its regular nonbusiness customers as well.

So what is the difference? The redesigned stores will be smaller and the product line will offer more depth. There will be no ancillary services. At these new-format stores you won't find an optician, a bakery, a butcher. Nor will you be able to buy your next new watch or diamond earrings. But if you are a small spa and want to buy water in larger quantities to have onsite for your customers, you will be able to choose from a variety of brands. The novelty of Costco offering depth in product lines will attract its regular customers, as well as the small business owner. In addition to depth within the product line, this new format will offer enhanced service; hours of operation will be geared to the small business owner—opening for business at 7:00 a.m. Monday to Saturday, and same-day and next-day delivery will be provided. Online shopping will be available with the launch of this new format. With over 1.2 million employer businesses in Canada and over 90 percent of them defined as micro-enterprises (one to four employees), it appears that Costco is onto something!

stillbeyou/Alamy Stock Photo

Sources: Francine Kopun, "Costco to Launch New Store Format in GTA," The Star, December 14, 2016. www.thestar.com/business/2016/12/14/costco-to-launch-new-store-format-in-gta.html; Innovation, Science and Economic Development Canada, *Key Small Business Statistics – June 2016* (http://www.ic.gc.ca/eic/site/061.nsf/eng/h_03018.html).

---

discount store a retailer that competes on the basis of low prices, high turnover, and high volume

full-line discount stores retailers that offer consumers very limited service and carry a broad assortment of well-known, nationally branded hard goods

mass merchandising a retailing strategy using moderate to low prices on large quantities of merchandise and lower levels of service to stimulate high turnover of products

supercentres retail stores that combine groceries and general merchandise goods with a wide range of services

Circle K, Alimentation Couche-Tard, and Mac's Convenience, are typically located near residential areas, and many are open 24 hours, seven days a week.

- **Discount stores** compete on the basis of low prices, high turnover, and high volume. Discounters can be classified into five major categories: full-line discount stores, specialty discount stores, warehouse clubs, and off-price discount retailers.

- **Full-line discount stores** offer consumers very limited service and carry a much broader assortment of well-known, nationally branded hard goods, including housewares, toys, automotive parts, hardware, sporting goods, and garden items, in addition to clothing, bedding, and linens. Full-line discounters use the retailing strategy of **mass merchandising**: the use of moderate to low prices on large quantities of merchandise and lower levels of service to stimulate high turnover of products.

- **Supercentres** extend the full-line concept to include groceries and general merchandise with a wide range of services, such as pharmacy, dry cleaning, portrait studios, photo finishing, hair salons, optical shops, and restaurants—all in one location. Walmart stores have evolved to supercentres where customers are drawn in by food, but

EXHIBIT 15.2   TYPES OF STORES AND THEIR CHARACTERISTICS

Type of Retailer	Level of Service	Product Assortment	Price	Gross Margin
Department store	Moderately high to high	Broad	Moderate to high	Moderately high
Specialty store	High	Narrow	Moderate to high	High
Supermarket	Low	Broad	Moderate	Low
Convenience store	Low	Medium to narrow	Moderately high	Moderately high
Drugstore	Low to moderate	Medium	Moderate	Low
Full-line discount store	Moderate to low	Medium to broad	Moderately low	Moderately low
Discount specialty store	Moderate to low	Medium to broad	Moderately low to low	Moderately low
Warehouse clubs	Low	Broad	Low to very low	Low
Off-price retailer	Low	Medium to narrow	Low	Low
Restaurant	Low to high	Narrow	Low to high	Low to high

end up purchasing other items from the full-line discount inventory.

- Single-line **specialty discount stores** offer a nearly complete selection of merchandise within a single category and use self-service, discount prices, high volume, and high turnover to their advantage. A **category killer** such as Home Depot is a specialty discount store that heavily dominates its narrow merchandise segment.

- **Warehouse membership clubs** sell grocery products and merchandise items. The product mix is generally quite wide and the items are often sold in bulk at discounted prices in exchange for a membership fee. Merchandise is displayed without any frills and inventory turns over quickly. Currently, the leading store in this category is Costco, with over 89 stores in nine provinces in Canada.

- An **off-price retailer** such as Winners and Marshall's sells brand-name merchandise at considerable discounts. Off-price retailers buy manufacturers'

Douglas Carr/Alamy Stock Photo

overruns, closeouts on lines, or orders from manufacturers that department stores may have cancelled at below cost. Off-price retailers have done very well as their strong value proposition has resonated with the consumer.

- A **factory outlet** is an off-price retailer that is owned and operated by a single manufacturer and carries one line of merchandise—its own. By operating factory outlets, manufacturers can regulate where their surplus merchandise is sold and realize higher profit margins than if they disposed of the goods through independent wholesalers and retailers.

- **Restaurants** straddle the line between retailing establishments and service establishments. Restaurants do sell tangible products—food and drink—but they also provide a valuable service for consumers in the form of food preparation and food service. Most restaurants could even be defined as specialty retailers, given that most concentrate their menu offerings on a distinctive type of cuisine—for example, Swiss Chalet and Starbucks coffee shops.

specialty discount stores retail stores that offer a nearly complete selection of single-line merchandise and use self-service, discount prices, high volume, and high turnover

category killers specialty discount stores that heavily dominate their narrow merchandise segment

warehouse membership clubs limited-service merchant wholesalers that sell a limited selection of brand-name appliances, household items, and groceries to members, small businesses, and groups

off-price retailer a retailer that sells brand-name merchandise at considerable discounts

factory outlet an off-price retailer that is owned and operated by a manufacturer

THE RISE OF NONSTORE RETAILING

The retailing formats discussed so far entail physical stores where merchandise is displayed and to which customers must travel in order to shop. In contrast, **nonstore retailing** provides shopping without visiting a physical location. Nonstore retailing adds a level of convenience for customers who wish to shop from their current locations. Due to broader changes in culture and society, nonstore retailing is currently growing faster than in-store retailing. The major forms of nonstore retailing are automatic vending, direct retailing, direct marketing, and Internet retailing (or *e-tailing*). In response to the recent successes seen by nonstore retailers, traditional bricks-and-mortar retailers have begun seeking a presence in limited nonstore formats.

- **Automatic vending** entails the use of machines to offer goods for sale—for example, the vending machines dispensing pop, candy, and snacks typically found in cafeterias and office buildings. Food and beverages account for about 85 percent of all sales from vending machines. Retailers constantly seek new opportunities to sell via vending machines. As a result, modern vending machines today sell merchandise such as videos, toys, sports cards, office supplies, and even Apple products and other electronics. A key aspect of their continuing success is the proliferation of cashless payment systems in response to consumers' diminishing preference for carrying cash. They are becoming increasingly more interactive with digital screens and video cameras. These "smart" machines can prompt consumers to buy additional products, run advertisements, and track users' purchases to offer frequency discounts.

- **Self-service technologies (SST)** comprise a form of automatic vending where services are the primary focus. Automatic teller machines, pay-at-the-pump gas stations, and movie ticket kiosks allow customers to make purchases that once required assistance from a company employee. However, as with any sort of self-service technology, automatic vending comes with failure risks due to human or technological error. Unless customers expect that they can easily recover from such errors, they may end up shopping elsewhere.

- In **direct retailing**, representatives sell products door-to-door, office-to-office, or in at-home sales parties. In Canada alone more than 2800 permanent employees and more than 882,000 direct sellers are involved in direct retailing.[6] Companies such as Avon and The Pampered Chef have used this approach for years. Although most direct sellers, like Thirty-one (thirtyonegifts.ca), still encourage the "party" method, the realities of the marketplace have forced them to be more creative in reaching their target customer. Direct sales representatives now hold sales opportunities in offices, parks, libraries, and other common locations. Many direct retailers are also turning to direct mail, the telephone, and social media to reach their target customer.

- **Direct marketing** (DM) includes techniques used to encourage consumers to make a purchase from their home, office, or other convenient locations. Common techniques are direct mail, catalogues and mail order, and telemarketing. Shoppers using these methods are less bound by traditional shopping situations. Time-strapped consumers and those who live in rural or suburban areas are most likely to be direct-response shoppers because they value the convenience

nonstore retailing
provides shopping without visiting a store

automatic vending the use of machines to offer goods for sale

self-service technologies (SST) technological interfaces that allow customers to provide themselves with products and/or services without the intervention of a service employee

direct retailing the selling of products by representatives who work door-to-door, office-to-office, or at in-home parties

direct marketing (direct-response marketing) techniques used to get consumers to make a purchase from their home, office, or another non-retail setting

Kyodo News/Getty Images

Vending machines are now equipped to accept mobile payments.

and flexibility provided by direct marketing. DM occurs in several forms:

- **Direct mail** can be the most efficient or the least efficient retailing method, depending on the quality of the mailing list and the effectiveness of the mailing piece. By using direct mail, marketers can precisely target their customers according to demographics, geography, and even psychographics. Good mailing lists come from an internal database or are available from list brokers.

    More and more retailers are investing in the direct-to-consumer channel that direct mail offers, but are doing so by investing in digital and mobile technologies that are driving the growth of online retailing. As a result, traditional direct mail as a form of nonstore retailing will decline in importance.

- **Catalogues and mail order** offer the opportunity for consumers to buy just about anything from the mundane to the outlandish through the mail. Successful catalogues are usually created and designed for highly segmented markets. The print catalogue industry in Canada is nowhere near as developed as in the United States, and the Internet has certainly made the catalogue less necessary. The IKEA print catalogue is the world's most widely distributed commercial publication with over 200 million copies printed in 29 different languages each year. Canadians use the catalogue as a way to gather information about the vast number of items carried in an IKEA store before a store visit. Those not located near an IKEA store use the catalogue in combination with the IKEA website to place their orders. Again, as consumers are increasingly using websites as information sources and are increasing their comfort with purchasing online, the need for printed catalogues will be eliminated.

- **Telemarketing** is the use of the telephone to sell directly to consumers. It consists of outbound sales calls, usually unsolicited, and inbound calls, which are usually customer orders made through toll-free 800 numbers or fee-based 900 numbers.

    Rising postage rates and decreasing long-distance phone rates have made *outbound* telemarketing an attractive direct-marketing technique. *Inbound* telemarketing programs, which use 800 and 900 numbers, are mainly used to take orders, generate leads, and provide customer service. Inbound 800 telemarketing has successfully supplemented direct-response TV, radio, and print advertising for more than 25 years.

- **Shop-at-home television networks** such as The Shopping Channel (TSC) produce television shows that display merchandise to home viewers and use inbound telemarketing to place orders directly using credit cards for payment. As part of Rogers Broadcasting Limited, this form of retailing has grown significantly in Canada in the recent years, as innovative and quality products in a variety of areas are offered to consumers for viewing and purchase via online, tablets, and mobile apps.

- **Online retailing** or **e-tailing** enables a customer to shop over the Internet and have items delivered directly to their door or to a bricks-and-mortar location for pick-up. Today global online retailing accounts for more than $1.3 trillion in sales and is expected to reach $2.5 trillion by 2018.[7] It is estimated that by 2019, online retail spending by Canadians will rise to $39 billion, just under 10 percent of all retail purchases in Canada.[8] The popularity of online retailing is leading traditional bricks-and-mortar retailers to set up dedicated Canadian websites and encouraging U.S. retailer websites to offer shipping to Canada.[9] Interactive shopping tools and live chats substitute for the in-store interactions with salespeople and product trials that customers traditionally use to make purchase decisions. Shoppers can look at a much wider variety of products online because there are no physical space

Ken Wolter/Shutterstock.com

restrictions. While the majority of online purchases are made using a desktop or laptop computer, an increasing number of purchases are being made via mobile devices. Canadians are using their smartphones as a digital shopping tool for shopping both online and in-store. They compare prices and utilize digital loyalty programs. A recent study by software developer SOTI Inc. reported that 92 percent of consumers want to shop in a store that is equipped with mobile opportunities.[10] Shopify, the e-commerce platform used by many Canadian businesses, reported that in 2014 more than half of the sales on the Shopify platform came from mobile devices.[11] A KPMG study reported that 87 percent of Millennials use more than two tech devices a day, and 54 percent said they prefer to pay for goods and services using a smartphone or mobile wallet. Over 40 percent of Canadians compare prices while in stores on their mobile device, and even more use their mobile device while shopping in-store to collect loyalty points and find promotional offers.

The consumer is demanding a seamless, mobile-enhanced, multi-channel shopping experience.[12] This form of retailing, referred to as **omni channel retailing**, is the key to success for today's retailers. The Hudson's Bay Company (HBC) has embraced omni channel retailing and it has paid off, as both foot traffic and online sales have continued to grow. HBC has complemented the traditional retail experience with digital technology, empowering the consumer to use the HBC website, via their digital platform of choice, to research their purchases and identify savings before completing the purchase either online or in-store. While Canadians are increasingly shopping online, they still enjoy the bricks-and-mortar experience, as a recent research study found that Canadian consumers were more likely (47 percent) to research online and make the purchase in-store than browse in-store

omni channel retailing an approach that combines the advantages of the physical store experience with the information-rich experience of online shipping, providing the consumer with a seamless experience through all available shopping channels

webrooming researching a product online and then going to a store to buy it

showrooming searching for a product in a store and then going online to try to find it at a better price

franchise a relationship in which the business rights to operate and sell a product are granted by the franchisor to the franchisee

franchiser the originator of a trade name, product, methods of operation, and so on, that grants operating rights to another party to sell its product

Source: Demac Media, Ecommerce Benchmark Report, Q1, 2016, p. 12. http://cdn2.hubspot.net/hubfs/174347/Demac_Media_Q1_2016_eCommerce_Benchmark_Report.pdf.

first (19 percent) and then purchase online.[13] The practice of researching online and buying in-store is referred to as **webrooming** while the opposite, seeing something in-store and then going online to buy it, is called **showrooming**.

Busy Canadians appreciate the convenience of e-tailing. More than 75 percent of Canadian consumers believe that online shopping offers the best selection when making purchases and is the fastest, most efficient way to shop. Online shopping makes it easy to compare prices and find a variety of options, and delivery to the door is convenient.[14]

In addition to visiting retailer websites for information, consumers are increasingly using social media applications as both shopping platforms and sources of information. In fact, a recent study found that almost 40 percent of Canadian shoppers say that the opinions of family and friends, bloggers, and other influencers found on social media sites influence their shopping behaviour. For Millennials this number increases to 55 percent.[15] This information has led many retailers to reach out to key influencers and to build strategy on ways to use social media to engage their consumers.

15-5 FRANCHISING

A **franchise** is a continuing relationship in which a franchiser grants to a franchisee the right to operate a business or to sell a product. The **franchiser** originates the trade name, product, methods of operation, and so on. The **franchisee**, in return, pays the franchiser for the right to use its name, product, or business methods. In Canada approximately one in fourteen working Canadians is directly or indirectly employed in the franchise industry. There are over 78,000 franchise units in Canada and over 60 percent of these are in the nonfood sectors and industries.[16]

To be granted the rights to a franchise, a franchisee usually pays an initial, one-time franchise fee. The amount of this fee depends solely on the individual franchiser. In addition to this initial franchise fee, the franchisee is expected to pay royalty fees, usually in the range of 3 to 7 percent of gross revenues. The franchisee may also be expected to pay advertising fees, which usually cover the cost of promotional materials and, if the franchise organization is large enough, regional or national advertising. Crock A Doodle is a Canadian paint-your-own-pottery franchise. It is a fun and family-friendly franchise that has a fairly typical franchising agreement. The total investment is between $75,000 and $120,000. That initial investment includes a franchise fee of $20,000 plus start-up costs. Start-up costs include rent deposit, store retrofit, training, inventory, and equipment. The franchise term is a ten-year renewable term and offers market exclusivity. Contrary to many franchises, franchisees pay no royalties and pay only 2 percent of sales to cover marketing costs. Crock A Doodle provides training, tools, and support to franchisees to help build a successful pottery-painting franchise. The margins are attractive to franchisees, who also appreciate Crock A Doodle's strong brand and supportive head office marketing.

Two basic forms of franchises are used today: product and trade name franchising and business format franchising. In *product and trade name franchising*, a dealer agrees to sell certain products provided by a manufacturer or a wholesaler. This approach has been used most widely in the auto and truck, pop bottling, tire, and gasoline service industries—for example,

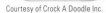

Courtesy of Crock A Doodle Inc.

a local tire retailer may hold a franchise to sell Michelin tires.

Business format franchising is an ongoing business relationship between a franchiser and a franchisee. Typically, a franchiser sells a franchisee the rights to use the franchiser's format or approach to doing business. This form of franchising has rapidly expanded since the 1950s through retailing, restaurant, food-service, hotel and motel, printing, and real estate franchises.

15-6 RETAIL MARKETING STRATEGY

Retail managers develop marketing strategies based on the goals established by stakeholders and the overall strategic plans developed by company leadership. Strategic retailing goals typically focus on increasing total sales, reducing cost of goods sold, and improving financial ratios such as return on assets or equity. At the store level, more tactical retailing goals include increased store traffic, higher sales of a specific item, developing a more upscale image, and creating heightened public awareness of the retail operation and its products or services. The tactical strategies that retailers use to obtain their goals include having a sale, updating decor, and launching a new advertising campaign. The key strategic tasks that precede these tactical decisions are defining and selecting a target market and developing the retailing mix to successfully meet the needs of the chosen target market.

15-6a Defining a Target Market

The first task in developing a retail strategy is to define the target market. This process begins with market segmentation, one of the topics of Chapter 8. Successful retailing has always been based on knowing the customer.

Determining a target market is a prerequisite to creating the retailing mix.

> **franchisee** an individual or a business that is granted the right to sell a franchiser's product

Donato Sardella/Getty Images

Target markets in retailing are often defined by demographics, geography, and psychographics. For instance, Hudson's Bay Co. (HBC) believes that luxury shoppers—particularly high-income-earning, middle-aged women—are leaving Canada to shop. In an effort to keep luxury shoppers' retail spending in Canada, HBC purchased Saks, the American luxury goods retailer. Since the acquisition, HBC has opened two Saks stores, with a third planned for Calgary. In addition, recognizing the increasing role of online retailing, as well as the importance of off-price retailing, HBC acquired Gilt in February 2016. Gilt.com is a member-based online retailer offering 70 percent off the retail price on top designer labels.[17]

retailing mix a combination of the six Ps—product, place, promotion, price, presentation, and personnel—to sell goods and services to the ultimate consumer

product offering the mix of products offered to the consumer by the retailer; also called the product assortment or merchandise mix

15-6b Choosing the Retailing Mix

Retailers combine the elements of the retailing mix to come up with a single retailing method to attract the target market. The **retailing mix** consists of six Ps: the four Ps of the marketing mix (product, place, promotion, and price) plus presentation and personnel (see Exhibit 15.4).

The combination of the six Ps projects a store's (or website's) image, which influences consumers' perceptions. Using these impressions of stores, shoppers position one store against another. A retail marketing manager must ensure that the store's positioning is compatible with the target customers' expectations. As discussed at the beginning of the chapter, retail stores can be positioned on three broad dimensions: service provided by store personnel, product assortment, and price. Management should use everything else—place, presentation, and promotion—to fine-tune the basic positioning of the store.

THE PRODUCT OFFERING The first element in the retailing mix is the **product offering**, also called the *product assortment* or *merchandise mix*. Developing a product offering is essentially a question of the width and depth of the product assortment. *Width* refers to the assortment of products offered; *depth* refers to the number of different brands offered within each assortment. Price, store design, displays, and service are important to consumers in determining where to shop, but the most critical factor is merchandise selection. This reasoning also holds true for online retailers. Amazon.ca, for instance, offers considerable width in its product assortment with millions of different items, including books, music, toys, videos, tools and hardware, health and beauty aids, electronics, and software. Conversely, online specialty retailers—such as Clearly, which sells optical products—focus on a single category of merchandise,

EXHIBIT 15.4 THE RETAILING MIX

Product — Width and depth of product assortment

Place (distribution) — Location and hours

Promotion — Advertising, publicity, and public relations

Price

Presentation — Layout and atmosphere

Personnel — Customer service and personal selling

Target Market

© Cengage

hoping to attract loyal customers with their larger depth of products at lower prices and better customer service. Many online retailers purposely focus on single-product-line niches that could never garner enough foot traffic to support a traditional bricks-and-mortar store.

clearly ™

Retailers decide the product offering on the basis of what their target market wants to buy. Using data mining techniques, retailers analyze past sales, fashion trends, customer requests, competition, and other data sources to determine what the target will most likely buy. The data they collect in CRM (customer relationship management) databases allows them to gain better insight into who is buying their products and how to build relationships to be rewarded with customer loyalty. Shoppers Drug Mart's successful points program is a brilliant tool that collects shopping data that is mined to enhance Shoppers Drug Mart's ability to build relationships and improve the consumer's shopping experience. Chapters Indigo's Plum rewards works in the same fashion. The shopping habits of a consumer not only assist the retailer to determine the merchandise selection but also to develop ongoing consumer engagement strategies as past purchase data can be used to build targeted online messaging to the consumer.

PROMOTION Retail promotion strategy includes advertising, public relations and publicity, and sales promotion. The goal is to help position the store in consumers' minds. Retailers design intriguing ads, stage special events, engage in social media conversations, and develop specific promotions for their target markets. Today's grand openings are a carefully orchestrated blend of advertising, merchandising, goodwill, and glitter. All the elements of an opening—press coverage, social media activity, special events, media advertising, and store displays—are carefully planned. Other promotions that are often used successfully are sales events, coupons, and discounts for certain products or customer groups. Retailers must exercise caution with store promotions that brand cannibalization doesn't occur. **Brand cannibalization** is a situation whereby the promotion intended to draw in new customers simply shifts current customer from buying one brand to another, versus increasing overall sales. In addition, retailers need to be cognizant of training customers to buy only when sales are offered.

Retailers' advertising is carried out mostly at the local level. Local advertising by retailers usually provides specific information about their stores, such as location, merchandise, hours, prices, and special sales. In contrast, national retail advertising generally focuses on image. Hudson's Bay Co. emphasizes product mix and pricing in newspaper advertisements, inserts, and flyers on a weekly basis. Advertising campaigns also take advantage of cooperative advertising, another popular retail advertising practice. Traditionally, marketers paid retailers to feature their products in store mailers, or a marketer developed a TV campaign for the product and simply tacked on several retailers' names at the end. Another common form of cooperative advertising involves the promotion of exclusive products. Hudson's Bay Co. teamed up with designer Brian Gluckstein, offering signature products under the Gluckstein label, sold exclusively at The Bay and thebay.com.

PLACE The retailing axiom "location, location, location" has long emphasized the importance of place to the retail mix. The physical location decision is important first because the retailer is making a large, semi-permanent commitment of resources that may reduce its future flexibility. Second, the physical location will affect the store's growth and profitability.

Physical site location begins by choosing a community. Important factors to consider are the area's economic growth potential, the amount of competition, and geography. For instance, Walmart will build in a new community, or an area of a community, that is still under development. Fast-food restaurants tend to place a priority on locations with other fast-food restaurants, because being located in clusters helps to draw customers for each restaurant. Starbucks seeks densely populated urban communities for its stores.

After settling on a geographic region or community, retailers must choose a specific site. In addition to growth potential, the important factors are neighbourhood socioeconomic characteristics, traffic flows, land costs, zoning regulations, and public transportation. A particular site's visibility, parking, entrance and exit locations, accessibility, and safety and security issues are also considered. Additionally, a retailer should consider how its store would fit into the surrounding environment—for example, the Hudson's Bay Co. would be unlikely to locate one of its new Saks stores next to a Dollarama.

In addition, retailers face the decision as to

brand cannibalization the reduction of sales for one brand as the result of the introduction of a new product or promotion of a current product or brand

whether to have a freestanding unit or to become a tenant in a shopping centre or mall.

FREESTANDING STORES An isolated, freestanding location is often used by large retailers of shopping goods such as furniture, cars, or electronics. Best Buy and HomeSense tend to utilize a freestanding store location, which likely offers the advantage of low site cost or rent and no nearby competitors. On the other hand, it may be difficult to attract customers to a freestanding location, and no neighbouring retailers are around to share costs. To be successful, stores in isolated locations must become destination stores. **Destination stores** are stores consumers seek out and purposely plan to visit.

Websites can also be destinations for shoppers. Well.ca is a destination website for a variety of health, wellness, and baby and beauty products, and trivago.ca is a destination for travellers looking for the best price for a hotel room.

Freestanding units are increasing in popularity as bricks-and-mortar retailers strive to make their stores more convenient to access, more enticing to shop in, and more profitable. Perhaps the greatest reason for developing a freestanding site is greater visibility. Retailers often feel they get lost in huge shopping centres and malls, but freestanding units can help stores develop an identity with shoppers. Also, an aggressive expansion plan may not allow time to wait for the shopping centre to be built. Drugstore chains, such as Shoppers Drug Mart, have been determinedly relocating their existing shopping centre stores to freestanding sites, especially street corner sites for drive-through accessibility.

SHOPPING CENTRES Shopping centres began in the 1950s when Canadians started migrating to the suburbs. The first shopping centres were *strip malls,* typically located along busy streets. They usually included a supermarket, a variety store, and perhaps a few specialty stores. Next, *community shopping centres* emerged, with one or two small department stores, more specialty stores, a couple of restaurants, and several apparel stores. These community shopping centres provided off-street parking and a broader variety of merchandise.

Regional malls offering a much wider variety of merchandise started appearing in the mid-1970s. Regional malls are either entirely enclosed or roofed to allow shopping in any weather. Most are landscaped with trees, fountains, sculptures, and the like to enhance the shopping environment. They have hectares of free parking. The *anchor stores*

or *generator stores* (often major department stores) are usually located at opposite ends of the mall to create heavy foot traffic.

According to shopping centre developers, *lifestyle centres* are emerging as the newest generation of shopping centres. Lifestyle centres typically combine outdoor shopping areas that comprise upscale retailers and restaurants, plazas, fountains, and pedestrian streets. The Shops at Don Mills in Toronto is a good example of such a lifestyle mall bringing together fine restaurants, theatre, and condo living with a park, public spaces, and retail stores all in one location. They appeal to retail developers looking for an alternative to the traditional shopping mall, a concept rapidly losing favour among shoppers.

Many smaller specialty lines are opening shops inside larger stores to expand their retail opportunities without risking investment in a separate store. This strategy reflects a popular trend of **pop-up shops**—tiny, temporary stores that stay in one location for only a few months. Pop-up shops help retailers reach a wide market while avoiding high rent at retail locations. They have become a marketing tool for large retailers who desire to target a new consumer. Jelly Modern Doughnuts, a gourmet doughnut bakery café, uses pop-ups to build brand awareness and sales by opening up pop-ups in stores that align with the brand. Jelly Modern Doughnuts has opened pop-ups in Holt Renfrew, Williams-Sonoma, Crate and Barrel, and Pottery Barn. For Jelly Modern Doughnuts, revenue in a pop-up is upwards of $800 per day.[18]

In addition to the above considerations, retailers must also learn about the legal implications of the arrangement they are entering, whether that be a lease or a purchase contact. Consideration such as leasehold improvements, length of the lease, rent increases, and stipulations regarding sub-leasing are key to understand and are likely worth legal advice. The same holds for entering into a purchase contract.

destination stores stores that consumers purposely plan to visit

pop-up shop temporary retail space that sells merchandise of any kind

Courtesy of Jelly Modern Doughnuts

PRICE Another important element in the retailing mix is price. Retailing's ultimate goal is to sell products to consumers, and the right price is critical in ensuring sales. Because retail prices are usually based on the cost of the merchandise, an essential part of pricing is efficient and timely buying.

Price is also a key element in a retail store's positioning strategy. Higher prices often indicate a level of quality and help reinforce the prestigious image of retailers, as they do for Harry Rosen and Maison Birks. On the other hand, discounters and off-price retailers, such as TJ Maxx and Winners, offer good value for the money spent.

PRESENTATION The presentation of a retail store helps determine the store's image and positions the retail store in consumers' minds. For instance, a retailer that wants to position itself as an upscale store would use a lavish or sophisticated presentation.

The main element of a store's presentation is its **atmosphere**, the overall impression conveyed by a store's physical layout, decor, and surroundings. The atmosphere might create a relaxed or busy feeling, a sense of luxury or of efficiency, a friendly or cold attitude, a sense of organization or of clutter, or a fun or serious mood. Mountain Equipment Co-op (MEC) uses a rustic, unfinished wood, casual look to convey an outdoorsy feel.

The layout of retail stores is a key factor in their success. The goal is to use all of the store's space effectively, including aisles, fixtures, merchandise displays, and nonselling areas. In addition to making shopping easy and convenient for the customer, an effective layout has a powerful influence on traffic patterns and purchasing behaviour. IKEA uses a unique circular store layout, which encourages customers to pass all the store's departments to reach the checkout lanes. The shopper thus is exposed to all of IKEA's merchandise assortment.

Layout also includes the placement of products in the store. Many technologically advanced retailers are using a technique called *market-basket analysis* to analyze the huge amounts of data collected through their point-of-purchase scanning equipment. The analysis looks for products that are commonly purchased together to help retailers find ideal locations for each product. Wal-mart uses market-basket analysis to determine where in the store to stock products for customer convenience. Kleenex tissues, for example, are in the paper-goods aisle and beside the cold medicines.

The following factors are the most influential in creating a store's atmosphere:

- *Employee type and density:* Employee type refers to an employee's general characteristics—for instance, being neat, friendly, knowledgeable, or service oriented. Density is the number of employees per thousand square feet of selling space. Whereas low employee density creates a do-it-yourself, casual atmosphere, high employee density denotes readiness to serve the customer's every whim.

- *Merchandise type and density:* A prestigious retailer, such as Harry Rosen, carries the best brand names and displays them in a neat, uncluttered arrangement. Discounters and off-price retailers often carry seconds or out-of-season goods crowded into small spaces and hung on long racks by category—tops, pants, skirts, etc.—creating the impression that "We've got so much stuff, we're practically giving it away."

- *Fixture type and density:* Fixtures can be elegant (rich woods), trendy (chrome and smoked glass), or consist of old, beat-up tables, as in an antiques store. The fixtures should be consistent with the general atmosphere the store is trying to create.

- *Sound:* Sound can be pleasant or unpleasant for a customer. Music can entice customers to stay in the store longer and buy more or eat quickly and leave a table for others. It can also control the pace of the store traffic, create an image, and attract or direct the shopper's attention.

- *Odours:* Smell can either stimulate or detract from sales. Research suggests that people evaluate merchandise more positively, spend more time shopping, and are generally in a better mood when an agreeable

The atmosphere of MEC helps to position the store.

The Canadian Press/Deborah Baic/The Globe and Mail

> **atmosphere** the overall impression conveyed by a store's physical layout, decor, and surroundings

odour is present. Retailers use fragrances as an extension of their retail strategy.

- *Visual factors:* Colours can create a mood or focus attention and therefore are an important factor in atmosphere. Red, yellow, and orange are considered warm colours and are used when a feeling of warmth and closeness is desired. Cool colours, such as blue, green, and violet, are used to open up closed-in places and create an air of elegance and cleanliness. Many retailers have found that natural lighting, either from windows or skylights, can lead to increased sales. Outdoor lighting can also affect consumer patronage.

PERSONNEL People are a unique aspect of retailing. Most retail sales involve a customer–salesperson relationship, if only briefly. Sales personnel provide their customers with the amount of service prescribed in the retail strategy of the store.

Retail salespeople serve another important selling function: they persuade shoppers to buy. They must therefore be able to persuade customers that what they are selling is what the customer needs. Salespeople are trained in two common selling techniques: trading up and suggestion selling. *Trading up* means persuading customers to buy a higher-priced item than they originally intended to buy. To avoid selling customers something they do not need or want, however, salespeople should take care when practising trading-up techniques. *Suggestion selling*, a common practice among most retailers, seeks to broaden customers' original purchases with related items. For example, if you buy a new printer at Staples, the sales representative will ask whether you want to purchase paper, a USB cable, or extra ink cartridges. Suggestion selling and trading up should always help shoppers recognize true needs rather than sell them unwanted merchandise.

Providing great customer service is one of the most challenging elements in the retail mix because customer expectations for service are so varied. What customers expect in a department store is very different from their expectations for a discount store. Customer expectations also change. Ten years ago, shoppers wanted personal one-on-one attention. Today, most customers are happy to help themselves as long as they can easily find what they need.

Customer service is also critical for online retailers. Online shoppers expect a retailer's website to be easy to use, products to be available, and returns to be simple. Online retailers need to design their sites to give their customers the information they need, such as what's new and what's on sale, and consider using suggestive selling. On the women's clothing site, loft.ca, when a purchase choice is made, complementary items are recommended to upsell the shopper.

 15-7 ADDRESSING RETAIL PRODUCT/ SERVICE FAILURES

In spite of retailers' best intentions and efforts to satisfy each and every customer, consumer dissatisfaction can occur. No retailer can be everything to every customer. A product may be located where customers cannot easily find it, an employee may provide mistaken information about a product's features or benefits, a promotional item may be out of stock by the time the customer attempts to purchase, or the item may go on sale shortly after the customer makes the purchase. Customers are generally indifferent to the reasons for retailer errors, and their reactions to mistakes can range widely. In this era of instantaneous and widespread communications via social media, an upset customer can have far-reaching effects.

The best retailers have plans in place not only to recover from inevitable lapses in service but also perhaps to even benefit from them. For these top-performing stores, service recovery is handled proactively as part of an overarching plan to maximize the customer experience. These are some actions that might be taken:

- notifying customers in advance of stockouts and explaining the reasons why certain products are not available

- implementing liberal return policies designed to ensure that the customer can bring back any item for any reason (if the product fails to work as planned, or even if the customer simply doesn't like it)

- issuing product recalls in conjunction with promotional offers that provide future incentives to repurchase

In short, the best retailers treat customer disappointments as opportunities to interact with and improve relations with their customers. Evidence indicates that successful handling of such failures can sometimes yield even higher levels of customer loyalty than if the failure had never occurred at all.

 15-8 RETAILER AND RETAIL CONSUMER TRENDS AND ADVANCEMENTS

Though retailing has been around for thousands of years, it continues to change every day. Retailers are constantly innovating. They are always looking for new products and services (or ways to offer them) that will attract new customers or inspire current ones to buy in greater quantities or more frequently. Many of the most interesting and effective retail innovations are related to the use of technology to help find new and better ways to entice customers into a store or to a website—and then to spend more money once there.

Consumers are shopping online and offline. They are integrating online behaviour with offline behaviour—they are researching online and making purchases offline and vice versa. Given such customer shopping behaviour, retailers are investing in **shopper marketing**. Shopper marketing focuses on understanding how a brand's target consumers behave as shoppers in different channels and formats and then uses this information in business-based strategies and initiatives that are carefully designed to deliver balanced benefits to all stakeholders—brands, channel members, and customers. It may sound simple, but it is anything but. Both manufacturers and retailers now think about consumers specifically while they are in shopping mode. They use **shopper analytics** to dig deeply into customers' shopping attitudes, perceptions, emotions, and behaviours, both online and offline, to learn how their individual shopping experience shapes their behaviour. More and more companies are conducting or participating in big data analytics projects to better understand how shoppers think when they shop at a store or on a website and what factors influence their thinking.

Retailers such as Walmart, Loblaws, and Shoppers Drug Mart collect data at the point of sale and throughout the store, which provides invaluable customer insights. Through the use of **big data analytics**, a process whereby retailers use complex mathematical models to make better retail mix decisions, stores like these can determine which products to stock and at what prices, how to manage markdowns, and how to advertise to draw target customers and keep them loyal. Big data analytics will allow for loyalty programs to be improved. Consumers are looking for personalization. They want personalized rewards and personalized offers pushed to their mobiles, as well as great products and convenience—big data analytics can take loyalty programs to that level.

A retailing advancement with great growth potential is the leveraging of technology to increase touchpoints with customers, enhance the shopping convenience, and generate greater profitability. The use of mobile devices and social media while browsing and comparison-shopping is becoming extremely pervasive, leading retailers to rethink how they should appeal to shoppers in the decision-making mode.

BestStockFoto/Shutterstock.com

As consumers are increasingly willing to use their mobile devices to pay for their purchases, strategic retailers should consider the opportunity this presents. This behaviour provides the retailer with the ability to offer the consumer a perfect synergy between ordering, payment, loyalty marketing, and advertising.[19] Starbucks' investment in mobile has done just that. The Starbucks customer can place an order, pay for it, and identify where they want to pick it up, all with a couple of clicks. The Starbucks mobile app stores your favourite beverage for next-time purchases, stores your favourite location for pick-up so you needn't search a second time, shares with you products that are on special that day, and lets you know how many Starbucks stars you have collected.

Even in the grocery industry, where online ordering represents only about 1 percent of sales, mobile is creating competitive advantages. Loblaws expanded the **click-and-collect** strategy to over 100 stores in 2016. Click-and-collect enables customers to make their purchases online. Rather than waiting for orders to arrive at their homes, customers drive to physical stores to pick their orders up.[20]

In addition to offering the online shopper convenience, an investment in mobile technology can improve in-store convenience. The use of iPads as point-of-sale (POS) devices means the POS location can come to the customer, and when the store is busy more iPads can be used to ensure no one waits to pay for their purchases.

shopper marketing understanding how one's target consumers behave as shoppers, in different channels and formats, and leveraging this intelligence to generate sales or other positive outcomes

shopper analytics searching for and discovering meaningful patterns in shopper data for the purpose of fine-tuning, developing, or changing market offerings

big data analytics the process of discovering patterns in large data sets for the purposes of extracting knowledge and understanding human behaviour

click-and-collect the practice of buying something online and then travelling to a physical store location to take delivery of the merchandise

Amazon Go—Is It Here to Stay?

Amazon, the online giant, has entered the offline retail industry. Amazon Go is an 1800-square-foot retail convenience store located in the company's hometown of Seattle, Washington. Offering a product mix of convenience goods, the store provides the unique benefit of never waiting in line to pay. You simply shop and leave! When you enter the store, you scan an app, which combined with computer vision and sensors throughout the store, identifies what you have put in your cart. As you leave, your Amazon account is charged for your "purchases." One can imagine the data that are being collected as you shop! What you pick up and put back on the shelf, what aisles you spend more time in, what you pause to consider are all noted.

This information can be used, and likely will be used, by Amazon to enhance your online shopping experience by selecting, organizing, and presenting products that you are likely to be interested in.[21]

Jack Young–Places/Alamy Stock Photo

Consumers shopping online are easily frustrated with computer glitches. As more consumers move to online shopping (driven to such, through events such as Black Friday and Cyber Monday), retailers must invest in ensuring the technology doesn't go down.

In addition to customers' being easily frustrated, instant gratification is important, so if retailers want to keep the consumer shopping online, same-day shipping will become more important.[22]

Investments in strategies to enhance convenience for the online shopper are leading retailers to reconsider their physical location and their product mix. Retailers are downsizing, IKEA and Best Buy are both investing in smaller format stores, and they are being more strategic in the product mix being offered the consumer. When today's shoppers can research, purchase, and have their purchase shipped immediately to their door, they don't have to wander around large stores with endless variety. They want smaller, well-laid-out stores with well-curated product offerings.[23]

For offline shoppers, the in-store experience continues to be important. Offering shopping experience enhancements, such as on-site specialty coffee shops or pop-up doughnut shops, as mentioned earlier in this chapter, will keep the customer coming back.

Lastly with regard to trends and advancements, social media continue to reign. Social media will continue to be used to enhance engagement with the consumer, but more and more retailers will utilize social media for e-commerce.

STUDY TOOLS

IN THE BOOK, YOU CAN:

✔ Rip out the Chapter in Review card at the back of the book.

ONLINE, YOU CAN:

✔ Stay organized and efficient with a single online destination with all the course material and study aids you need to succeed.

Go to nelson.com/student to access the digital resources.

SIDE LAUNCH
BREWING COMPANY
CONTINUING CASE

Dealing in a Duopoly

A smartly dressed young Collingwood professional exits his Subaru, having pulled into the parking lot at Side Launch Brewing Company. All signs indicate an active type of individual. The mud-encrusted tires of both his car and the mountain bike perched on its rooftop, and a variety of active brand stickers adorning the rear window, would suggest he's more than just a weekend warrior. Upon entry to the brewery, he waves familiarly to Laura, who's hosting the retail outlet in the building, and Laura waves back like a good neighbour would. The young man makes a beeline to the well-stocked Side Launch refrigerator and pulls out a box of the bright yellow Wheat beer cans. Laura and the man exchange pleasantries as the transaction is carried out, and he's on his way out the door in moments. If all Side Launch sales could be so easy, so frictionless … so autonomous. But, alas, neither Side Launch nor any brewery can have total control of every sale of its product and still reach any level of scale.

Alcoholic beverage producers have two distinct retail channels—on-premises, the sale of product through bars, pubs, restaurants, and the like; and off-premises, the sale of product through liquor stores and vendors. As mentioned in the previous chapter, the thousands of licensees (bars, restaurants, and pubs) scattered around its geographical reach provide Side Launch with enormous opportunity to sell cans and kegs where people gather to enjoy a cold one outside of the home (on-premises). But for the other segment of the market (off-premises), Side Launch and all other brewers in Ontario have minimal choice. "It's a duopoly," states Chuck Galea, VP Sales and Marketing. "You have LCBO [Liquor Control Board of Ontario] primarily, and the Beer Store." The irony is that the Ontario government regulates the production and distribution of beer and operates the 660-plus LCBO stores in the province, but The Beer Store is a privately owned retailer that operates 450-plus stores *and* serves as distributor to LCBO and 20,000 licensees in the province.

The relationship between a small private craft brewer like Side Launch and a massively powerful entity that is both the regulator and retailer, LCBO, is predictably complicated. "The LCBO, on the one hand, is great for craft in that they do promote us, and they are the major retailer in the province, but they have a bit of hard row to hoe in that craft beer is their fastest-growing segment but it is their lowest margin," explains Garnet Pratt, CEO. "So when it comes to allocating shelf space they've got a bit of a battle: their customers want more craft, but every inch of shelf space they give to craft, they have to take away from something that is more profitable."

Recently grocery stores have been allowed to enter the beer-selling picture, and the government has mandated 450 licences can be granted in Ontario by 2018. "Loblaws will get some of those licences and yes, we'll have three of our styles of beer in every single Loblaws store with a licence," claims Garnet confidently. However, in defence of her craft beer brethren (she sits on the board of Ontario Craft Brewers), she says, "A lot of the small breweries, they could never supply all Loblaws stores, they just don't have enough beer."

For Side Launch, the relationship with retail is bittersweet as it finds itself benefiting from a standardized and consistent retail channel for its growing brand but is still somewhat encumbered by the regulator, which ultimately plays a role in influencing that demand.

Questions

1. Using retail classification terms discussed in the chapter, describe the difference between LCBO stores and Loblaws stores now selling beer in Ontario.

2. Bars, restaurants, pubs, and hotels are also retailers for Side Launch products. How do they differ from specialty stores and supermarkets?

3. Does the increase in number of retail categories where beer can be sold help or hinder Side Launch?

Side Launch Brewing Company

Part 5 Case
Distribution Decisions
Do What Simons Says

Simons

Picture this: a retail experience where the merchandise is presented with pride, the staff is present and knowledgeable, and the prices are neither dirt cheap nor exorbitant. Does such a place really exist?

This scenario is the express goal of Quebec-based retailer La Maison Simons Inc., better known to Canadians as Simons. But this is no upstart retailer looking to disrupt the Canadian retailer industry. The company began with a presence in Quebec City in 1840, and it took more than 150 years for Simons to expand beyond the cobbled streets of Quebec's capital. However, its unique approach to retail and the supply chain do make it a breath of fresh air in the often-stagnating retail environment in Canada.

The story of the Canadian retail industry is often told through its failures, rather than its successes. By far the most well-known Canadian retailer, the Hudson's Bay Company, in its close to 350-year existence has rarely faced as great a challenge as recent economic and societal changes, which have affected other retailers too. U.S.-based retailer Target has been successful in almost every market south of the 49th parallel, but its Canadian experiment failed spectacularly. Other Canadian retailers like Jacob and Mexx announced their demise to the world with barely a whimper or outcry. Sears Canada has been on life support for years, and could have gone out of business by the time you are reading these words in a book or online.

It would seem that online is the answer for retailers. With the immense success seen by Amazon, many retailers are looking toward the digital world for their loyal shoppers. An expected growth in e-commerce sales in Canada could be worth $39 billion by 2019. This would make online sales account for about 10 percent of all retail sales.

When you think of these numbers in the context of the number of vacant shops in malls across Canada, it's easy to see why retail's failures have become so prevalent.

It seems that even the most popular malls (called "A" malls) are struggling to keep tenants, as consumers continue to seek online options. Consumers still visit malls, but many do so to comparison shop with what they have found online. And the online option is often the cheapest, creating a huge challenge for the retail world that relies so heavily on bricks-and-mortar stores.

It is precisely the bricks and mortar that Simons is using that is making a difference, or more precisely how it uses building materials that forms one part of a unique retail strategy in the Canadian market. When Simons builds a store, it looks for a unique location in a city. However, the company won't overpay for real estate and will take its time to find the right location.

It won't just slap the Simons green logo on top of crumbling infrastructure. The retailer takes the time to create a welcome and inviting retail environment. In Calgary, Simons opened a store in the CORE shopping centre in the downtown area. The store occupies the Lancaster Building, a heritage building on Calgary's popular pedestrian street, Stephen Avenue Mall. The Lancaster received a modern facelift, and Simons worked with a local architectural firm to keep the traditional elements from its original 1919 design, but with a clear indication of Simons's new entry in the retail environment.

CALGARY'S SIMONS LOCATION

The interior of Simons stores are designed individually, and local artists are offered opportunities to create art installations alongside more famous contributors like Douglas Coupland.

The Calgary location is one of a handful of new stores for Simons, a bold foray into new markets that lack much of the brand awareness that is present in its home province of Quebec. The first store outside of Quebec was, surprisingly, at the cavernous West Edmonton Mall. Since then,

Calgary's Simons Location

a Simons has opened up in each of Vancouver, Calgary, Mississauga, and Ottawa.

Many people outside of Quebec have never heard of Simons until a store takes root in their community. In fact, many people assume that the name is pronounced using the French pronunciation of the name Simon (see-mon), when in fact the Simons name comes from the Scottish immigrant John Simons, who started a dry goods store in Quebec in 1840, and it's pronounced "sye-munz."

No matter how you pronounce it, the Simons family has had a lasting impact in Quebec and is now trying to translate its successful formula to the rest of Canada. The recipe for that formula includes a basic contradiction: quality and competitive pricing. Simons has prided itself on finding little-known fashion brands and mixing them in with more popular and often higher- end brands.

This challenge is highlighted by Peter Simons, the current CEO and fifth-generation Simons family member to be head of the Simons *maison:*

> We're going to build a world-class company in Canada. We're going to try to make some really good long-term choices. The world can't have boiled

down to everyone just wanting the lowest price at Wal-Mart. I am sensing a much more responsible-consumption purchasing pattern developing. People are finding a new equilibrium between quality and value, and it's just not disposable fashion and I think we're really well-positioned to do that.

However, to keep prices competitive Simons has to make sure it can achieve the economies of scale to be found in running a large-scale operation. The challenge is that Simons often works with smaller fashion companies, and getting volume can be difficult at times. And in a country the size of Canada, distribution and supply chains cannot be ignored (just ask Target—https://hbr.org/2015/01/why-targets-canadian-expansion-failed).

In 2016, Simons received the Excellence in Retailing Award from the Retail Council of Canada for Innovation in Supply Chain. The award was given to recognize the work that Simons has done to coordinate an ever-growing supply chain with the introduction of so many new stores across the vast expanse of the Canadian market. The Retail Council acknowledged the integration of logistics, planning, warehouse management, replenishment, and forecasting.

This award was the feather in the cap for a retailer looking to expand in an environment that often is contracting. But Simons is not alone in the market. It has lost out on prime retail real estate to U.S.-based Nordstrom's. And given the wide assortment of offerings that it provides, Simons must look to companies like Zara, Victoria's Secret, Forever 21, and myriad other retailers as their competitors.

But Simons tries to listen to its partners in order to stay humble and meet the needs of customers. La Maison de Simons receives plenty of mail from customers, online and in-store. CEO Peter Simons personally responds to letters addressed to him. As well, even suppliers can provide feedback—and often report a positive relationship with this growing fashion giant.

And it is this kind of feedback that is needed from you, the reader. Your task is to help Simons enter a new market in Canada. You will need to focus on a large enough urban area. You will need to include the success factors that Simons has been using in its successful expansion, but try not to get caught doing only as Simons says.

SOURCES

Sophie Cousineau. "Retailer Simons Crashes Canada, One Door at a Time," *Globe and Mail,* September 5, 2013, http://www.theglobeandmail.com/report-on-business/simons-crashes-canada-one-door-at-a-time/article14148615/.

Jennifer Friesen. "Douglas Coupland Invites Calgary to Be a Part of His 3D Art Installation," *Metro,* March 30, 2017, http://www.metronews.ca/news/calgary/2017/03/30/douglas-coupland-invites-calgary-join-3d-art-installation.html.

Francine Kopun. "Simons Looks to Grow a Canadian Retail Empire," *Toronto Star,* February 22, 2016, https://www.thestar.com/business/2016/02/22/simons-looks-to-grow-a-canadian-retail-empire.html.

"La Maison Simons Wins Supply Chain Innovation Award," Retalon, http://retalon.com/news-updates/la-maison-simons-wins-supply-chain-innovation-award.

Simons, http://www.simons.com.

Matt Smith. "Are We Witnessing the Death of Retail?" *The Motley Fool,* April 13, 2017, http://www.fool.ca/2017/04/13/are-we-witnessing-the-death-of-retail/.

QUESTIONS

1. Create a proper SWOT for Simons, with a focus on a Canadian CMA that does not currently have a Simons location (visit the Simons website, www.simons.ca, to get the most up-to-date list of current stores).

2. Once you have determined a geographic market, create a proper market segment for a consumer market you believe would be an important focus for Simons.

3. Go to the Simons website and determine the online options for purchasing and the overall e-commerce options for Simons. Write a brief report to CEO Peter Simons describing the benefits of e-commerce for a retailer like Simons for this new market.

16 | Marketing Communications

LEARNING OUTCOMES

16-1 Discuss the role of promotion in the marketing mix

16-2 Describe the communication process

16-3 Outline the goals and tasks of promotion

16-4 Discuss the elements of the promotional mix

16-5 Discuss the AIDA concept and its relationship to the promotional mix

16-6 Discuss the concept of integrated marketing communications

16-7 Know the factors that affect the promotional mix

Lightspring/Shutterstock.com

"Think like a wise man but communicate in the language of the people."
—W.B. Yeats[1]

16-1 THE ROLE OF PROMOTION IN THE MARKETING MIX

Few goods or services, no matter how well developed, priced, or distributed, can survive in the marketplace without effective **promotion**—communication by marketers that informs, persuades, reminds, and connects potential buyers to a product or service for the purpose of influencing their opinion or eliciting a response.

Promotional strategy is a plan for the optimal use of the elements of promotion (the promotional mix elements): advertising, public relations, sales promotion, personal selling, direct-response communication, and social media. As Exhibit 16.1 shows, the marketing manager determines the goals of the company's promotional strategy in light of the firm's overall goals for the marketing mix—product, place (distribution), promotion, and price. Using these overall goals, marketers combine the elements of the promotional strategy (the promotional mix) to form a coordinated plan. The promotion plan then becomes another integral part of the marketing strategy for reaching the target market.

The main function of a marketer's promotional strategy is to convince target customers that the goods and services offered provide a competitive advantage over the competition. A **competitive advantage** is the set of unique features of a company, and its products that are perceived by the target market as significant and superior to those of the competition. Such features can include high product quality, rapid delivery, low prices, excellent service, or any feature not offered by the competition. In the highly competitive cellphone market Koodo is attempting to add new customers, and retain

> **promotion** communication by marketers that informs, persuades, reminds, and connects potential buyers to a product for the purpose of influencing an opinion or eliciting a response
>
> **promotional strategy** a plan for the use of the elements of promotion: advertising, public relations, personal selling, sales promotion, direct-response communication, and social media

current, by promoting what it has coined as "shock-free data." Shock-free data puts consumers in control of their own data usage by sending a text when they are at 50 percent, 90 percent, and 100 percent of data used. If the consumer reaches the data limit, Koodo will pause data access, at which time the Koodo customer can top up data directly from their cellphone. While the CRTC Wireless Code mandates that service providers must pause data if consumers reach $50 within a single billing month, this unique service by Koodo puts the consumer in charge, ensuring cellphone bills are "shock-free"![2] Koodo has created a competitive advantage in an attempt to differentiate itself in the highly competitive cellphone provider market.

Promotion is a vital component of the marketing mix, informing consumers of a product's benefits and thereby positioning the product in the marketplace.

16-2 MARKETING COMMUNICATION

Promotional strategy is closely related to the process of communication. **Communication** is the process by which we exchange or share meanings through a common set of symbols. When a company develops a new product,

EXHIBIT 16.1 ROLE OF PROMOTION IN THE MARKETING MIX

Overall Marketing Objectives

Marketing Mix
- Product
- Place (distribution)
- Promotion
- Price

Target Market

Promotional Mix
- Advertising
- Direct marketing
- Public relations
- Sales promotion
- Personal selling
- Online marketing

Promotion Plan

© Cengage

competitive advantage the set of unique features of a company and its products that are perceived by the target market as significant and superior to the competition

communication the process by which we exchange or share meanings through a common set of symbols

EXHIBIT 16.2 COMMUNICATION PROCESS

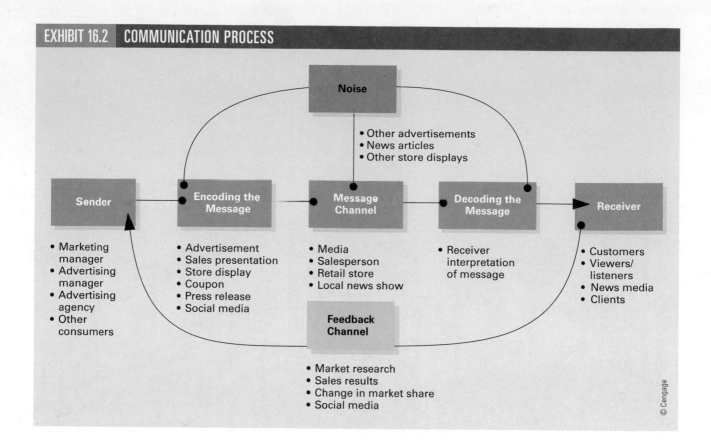

changes an old one, or simply tries to increase sales of an existing good or service, marketers use promotion programs to communicate information about the firm and its products to potential customers and various publics.

Communication can be divided into two major categories: interpersonal communication and mass communication. **Interpersonal communication** is direct, face-to-face communication between two or more people. When communicating face to face, each person can see the other's reaction and can respond almost immediately. A salesperson speaking directly with a client is an example of an interpersonal marketing communication.

Mass communication involves communicating a concept or message to large audiences. A great deal of marketing communication is directed to consumers as a whole, usually through a mass medium, such as television or magazines. When a company uses mass communication, it generally does not personally know the people with whom it is trying to communicate. Furthermore, the company is unable to respond immediately to consumers'

reactions to its message. Any clutter from competitors' messages or other distractions in the environment can reduce the effectiveness of the mass-communication effort. While Starbucks continues to use mass communication to build brand value, loyalty, and market share, it places great emphasis on creating a memorable in-store experience, which begins with training all staff to treat each customer in an engaging and friendly manner. This interpersonal communication adds to the consumer's coffee experience, creating loyalty in the highly competitive coffee market.

16-2a The Communication Process

Marketers are both senders and receivers of messages. As *senders,* marketers attempt to inform, persuade, remind, and connect with the target market to adopt a particular course of action. As *receivers,* marketers listen to the target market so they can develop the appropriate messages, adapt existing messages, spot new communication opportunities, and connect with the target audience. In this way, marketing communication is a two-way, rather than one-way, process. The two-way nature of the communication process is shown in Exhibit 16.2.

THE SENDER AND ENCODING The **sender** is the originator of the message in the communication process.

interpersonal communication direct, fact-to-face communication between two or more people

mass communication the communication of a concept or message to large audiences

sender the originator of the message in the communication process

In an interpersonal conversation, the sender may be a parent, a friend, or a salesperson. For an advertisement, press release, or social media campaign, the sender is the company or organization. It can sometimes be difficult to tell who the sender of a promotional message is, as the advertiser may intentionally obscure its identities in the hopes of building buzz around the message. Katy Perry launched a unique campaign in advance of the release of her single "Chained to the Rhythm." On the Wednesday prior to the Friday release of the single, disco balls could be found in cities around the world. The balls were chained to posts, poles, and benches. When they were found, the consumer could plug headphones into the balls to hear a portion of the song "Chained to the Rhythm." Not surprisingly #chainedtotherhythm trended on Twitter and fans enthusiastically and quickly shared their experience of locating and listening.

Encoding is the conversion of the sender's ideas and thoughts into a message, usually in the form of words or signs. A basic principle of encoding is that what is important is not what the sender says, but rather what the receiver hears. To convey messages that the receiver will hear properly, marketers use concrete words and visual images. Newfoundland and Labrador's tourism campaign, "Find Yourself Here," which was launched in 2006, has resulted in consistent year-over-year increases in visits to the province, generating over $1.1 billion in visitor spending each year.[3] Each execution in the campaign utilizes imagery that showcases the unique houses, landscapes, and nature of the province, generating a desire to experience a province and a people uniquely different from all others in Canada. The message is being decoded appropriately!

MESSAGE TRANSMISSION Transmission of a message requires a **channel**—a voice, radio, newspaper, or other communication medium. A facial expression or gesture can also serve as a channel. The Newfoundland and Labrador's "Find Yourself" campaign has consistently utilized television and in-flight advertising to communicate the message, as well as online display ads, Web video sites, and national newspapers.

Reception occurs when the message is detected by the receiver and enters his or her frame of reference. In a two-way conversation, such as a sales pitch given by a sales representative to a potential client, reception is normally high. In contrast, the desired receivers may or may not detect the message when it is mass communicated because most media are cluttered by **noise**—anything that interferes with, distorts, or slows down the transmission of information. Transmission can also be hindered by situational factors in the physical surroundings, such as light, sound, location, and weather; the presence of other people; or the temporary moods consumers might bring to the situation. The combination of media used by Newfoundland and Labrador Tourism to reach the target consumer is a strategy to help achieve reception among the greatest number of target consumers.

THE RECEIVER AND DECODING Marketers communicate their message through a channel to customers, or **receivers**, who will decode the message. It is important to note that there can be multiple receivers as consumers share their experiences and their recommendations online through social networks and other types of social media, as happened with the campaign used by Katy Perry to help launch the single "Chained to the Rhythm." These online conversations are highly influential and they reach many people quickly and exponentially. Thus the empowered consumer (receiver) in this new level of engagement is transforming marketing and promotion as marketers (senders) constantly try to create, follow, and connect with these conversations.

Decoding is the interpretation of the language and symbols sent by the source through a channel. Effective communication requires a common understanding or common frame of reference between two communicators. Therefore, marketing managers must ensure a proper match between the message to be conveyed and the target market's attitudes and ideas.

Even if a message has been received, it will not

> **encoding** the conversion of the sender's ideas and thoughts into a message, usually in the form of words or signs
>
> **channel** a medium of communication—such as a voice, radio, or newspaper—used for transmitting a message
>
> **noise** anything that interferes with, distorts, or slows down the transmission of information
>
> **receivers** the people who decode a message
>
> **decoding** interpretation of the language and symbols sent by the source through a channel

necessarily be properly decoded because of selective exposure, selective perception, and selective retention. When people receive a message, they tend to manipulate, alter, and modify it to reflect their own biases, needs, knowledge, and culture. Differences in age, social class, education, culture, and ethnicity can lead to miscommunication. Further, because people don't always listen or read carefully, they can easily misinterpret what is said or written. In fact, researchers have found that consumers misunderstand a large proportion of both printed and televised communications. Global marketers have an even greater challenge as they try to decide if the product's or service's message should be standardized or customized. Standardized messaging makes sense, given the impact that the Internet has had on connecting consumers globally, but cultural differences do exist, and a standardized message runs the risk of miscommunication.

FEEDBACK In interpersonal communication, the receiver's response to a message is direct **feedback** to the source. Feedback may be verbal, as in saying, "Yes, I will buy," or nonverbal, as in nodding, smiling, frowning, or gesturing. Feedback can also occur digitally as in the Katy Perry campaign, which generated millions of likes and tremendous chatter in both the digital and traditional media landscapes.

Because mass communicators are often cut off from direct feedback, they must rely on market research, social media, or an analysis of viewer responses for indirect feedback. They might use such measurements as the percentage of television viewers who recognized, recalled, or stated that they were exposed to the company's message. Indirect feedback provides the analytics necessary to determine if the message is meeting the communication objectives.

The increasing use of online advertising has changed the nature of feedback as it provides for feedback that is interactive, two-way, and often in real time. Marketers can use Web analytics to measure the length of time a consumer stays on a particular page within their website, how often they visit the site, or how many pages they view. These analytics are available instantly, providing the opportunity to make immediate adjustments.

Social media also enables instant feedback by allowing companies to respond immediately to online posts, whether they are on the companies' blogs, hosted on their websites, or social media sites. In traditional communication, a marketer can see the results of consumer behaviour (for example, a rise or drop in sales) but they must rely on their judgement to explain the

feedback the receiver's response to a message

behaviour. Today, consumers use social media platforms to comment publicly on marketing efforts. This opens the door for a marketer to engage in a personal, two-way conversation with the consumer. However, because social media conversations occur in real time, and are public, any negative posts or complaints are highly visible. Thus many companies have crisis communication strategies to deal with negative information and promote good brand reputations.

Social media has changed the role of the consumer in communications. A consumer who provides a comment on Facebook or Yelp is essentially a sender, meaning the communication model today is much more complicated than in the past.

16-3 THE GOALS OF PROMOTION

People communicate with one another for many reasons. They seek amusement, ask for help, give assistance or instructions, provide information, and express ideas and thoughts. Promotion, on the other hand, seeks to modify behaviour and thoughts in some way. For example, General Mills is trying to persuade consumers to change their breakfast cereal to Honey Nut Cheerios by promoting an issue—the very real threat that bees are on the edge of extinction. Cheerios pulled the mascot Buzz the Bee off

the Honey Nut Cheerios cereal box, claiming that Buzz is missing because the bee population, including honey bees like Buzz, is declining at an alarming rate. Families were encouraged to visit bringbackthebees.ca to get their free package of wildflower seeds to plant, to help provide a source of nutrition for the bees. Honey Nut Cheerios' goal was to plant over 200 million wildflower seeds across North America, providing bees with pollen and nectar to stay healthy and happy.[4] The brand ended up giving away over 1.5 billion seeds in the effort to bring back the bees.

Promotion also strives to reinforce existing behaviour—for instance, encouraging consumers to complement their summer barbecues with local craft beers versus a national brand. The source (the seller) hopes to project a favourable image or to motivate a purchase of the company's goods and services.

Promotion can perform one or more of four tasks: *inform* the target audience, *persuade* the target audience, *remind* the target audience, or *connect* the target audience. (See Exhibit 16.3.) Connecting the target audience is a new task made possible by the increasing acceptance of social media. Often a marketer will try to accomplish two or more of these tasks at the same time.

16-3a Informing

Informative promotion seeks to convert an existing need into a want or to stimulate interest in a new product. This type of promotion is generally more prevalent during the

Nadezda Murmakova/Shutterstock.com

early stages of the product life cycle. People typically will not buy a product or service or support a nonprofit organization until they understand its purpose and its benefits to them. Complex and technical products, such as automobiles, computers, and investment services, often continue to use informative promotion well after the product or service has moved beyond the introductory stage of the product life cycle. This continued promotion is due to the nature of the purchase decision and the risk involved in the purchase. Informative promotion is also important when a new brand is being introduced into an old product class. The new product cannot establish itself against more mature products unless potential buyers are aware of it, value its benefits, and understand its positioning in the marketplace. For example, Tesla, a California-based auto company that manufactures electric cars only, focuses its advertising messages on the gas savings that consumers will experience from driving an electric car.

16-3b Persuading

Persuasive promotion is designed to stimulate a purchase or an action. Persuasion normally becomes the main promotion goal when the product enters the growth stage of its life cycle. By this time, those in the target market should have general awareness of the product category and some knowledge of how the category can fulfill their wants. Therefore, the company's promotional task switches from informing consumers about the product category to persuading them to buy its brand rather than the competitor's. The promotional message thus emphasizes the product's real and perceived competitive advantages, often appealing to emotional needs, such as love, belonging, self-esteem, and ego satisfaction.

Persuasion can also be an important goal for very competitive, mature product categories, such as many

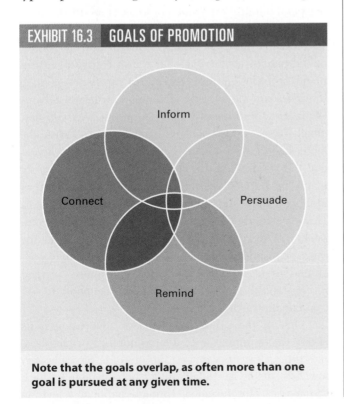

EXHIBIT 16.3 GOALS OF PROMOTION

Inform

Connect

Persuade

Remind

Note that the goals overlap, as often more than one goal is pursued at any given time.

household items and consumer consumables. In a marketplace characterized by many competitors, the promotional message often encourages brand switching and aims to convert some buyers into loyal users. For example, in the case of the Riviera brand, the packaging is the promotional message. In a category where dairy products line the shelves in plastic packages, Riviera stands out by packaging in reusable glass containers that are being repurposed by consumers into small flowerpots, Christmas ornaments, and candleholders.

Critics believe that some promotional messages and techniques can be too persuasive, causing consumers to buy products and services they really don't need.

16-3c Reminding

Reminder promotion is used to keep the product and brand name in the public's mind. This type of promotion prevails during the maturity stage of the life cycle. A reminder promotion assumes that the target market has already been persuaded of the merits of the good or service. Its purpose is simply to trigger a memory. Crest toothpaste and other consumer products often use reminder promotion.

16-3d Connecting

The increasing acceptance and use of social media are beneficial in helping companies develop relationships with their customers. These relationships, if nurtured properly, can result in increased consumer loyalty, which is highly coveted in the later stages of the product life cycle.

promotional mix the combination of promotional tools—including advertising, publicity, sales promotion, personal selling, direct-response communication, and social media—used to reach the target market and fulfill the organization's overall goals

advertising impersonal, one-way mass communication about a product or an organization that is paid for by a marketer

Not only does social media allow companies to connect with customers, but it also allows customers to connect with each other. The resulting heightened consumer loyalty and connection can create product advocates that promote brands to others through their social networks.

16-4 THE PROMOTIONAL MIX

Most promotional strategies use several ingredients—which may include advertising, publicity, sales promotion, personal selling, direct-response communication, and social media—to reach a target market. That combination is called the **promotional mix**. The proper promotional mix is the one that management believes will meet the needs of the target market and will fulfill the organization's overall goals. Data play a very important role in how marketers distribute funding among their promotional mix tactics. The more funds allocated to each promotional tool and the more managerial emphasis placed on each tool, the more important that element is thought to be in the overall mix.

16-4a Advertising

Almost all companies selling a product or service use advertising, whether in the form of a multimillion-dollar campaign or a poster placed on the side of a delivery vehicle. **Advertising** is any form of impersonal, one-way mass communication about a product or an organization that is paid for by a marketer. Traditional media—such as television, radio, newspapers, magazines, billboards, online banner advertising, and transit cards (advertisements on buses and taxis and at bus stops)—are among the most commonly used mediums to transmit advertisements to consumers. Other options include websites, email, blogs, videos, and interactive games. With the increasing fragmentation of traditional media choices and the accelerated use of social media by consumers, marketing budgets are shifting toward buying advertisements on these digital options, including social media. However, as the Internet becomes a more vital component of many companies' promotion and marketing mixes, consumers and lawmakers are increasingly concerned about possible violations of consumers' privacy, forcing social media sites such as Facebook to re-examine their privacy policies.

One of the primary benefits of advertising is its ability to communicate to a large number of people at one time. Cost per contact, therefore, is typically very low. Advertising has the advantage of being able to reach the masses (for instance, through national television networks), but it can also be used to microtarget smaller groups of potential customers by placing ads in special-interest sections of local newspapers. Although the cost per contact in advertising is very low, the total cost to advertise is typically very high. This hurdle tends to restrict advertising on a national basis. Chapter 17 examines advertising in greater detail.

16-4b Publicity

Organizations that are concerned with how they are perceived by their target markets often spend large sums to build a positive public image. Publicity is a mass communication tool that is not paid for by marketers but can be used to earn public understanding and acceptance. Publicity is often achieved by the execution of **public relations** strategies. Public relations is a communications tool that evaluates public attitudes, identifies areas within the organization the public may be interested in, and executes a program of action. Publicity helps an organization communicate with its customers, suppliers, shareholders, government officials, employees, and the community in which it operates. Marketers use publicity not only to maintain a positive image but also to educate the public about the company's goals and objectives, introduce new products, reinforce a product's positioning, achieve a competitive advantage, and help support the sales effort.

Heinz capitalized on some great publicity with a short-lived but long-in-the-making advertising campaign for Heinz ketchup. During an episode in season six of the series *Mad Men*, Don Draper, the creative director with the fictional advertising agency Stirling, Cooper, Draper, Pryce, pitched an unconventional ad campaign entitled "Pass the Heinz." The campaign featured mouth-watering images of food that were missing a key ingredient—ketchup. In the episode, Heinz executives turned down the campaign, stating, "I want to see the bottle. I want to see the product." Today Heinz executives think Don Draper was completely correct on positioning, and so, with the direction of their current advertising agency David, they recreated the three ads exactly as presented in season six. The campaign ran in the *New York Post* and *Variety* and on outdoor billboards in New York City in early spring 2017. The back story to this campaign was so interesting and unique that it was talked about in the media, creating significant publicity for Heinz and generating greater awareness than that which would have been achieved with the campaign's limited media buy.[5]

As demonstrated with Heinz, a public relations program can generate favourable **publicity**—public

An unconventional approach to creating publicity.

information about a company, a product, a service, or an issue appearing in the mass media as a news item. Social media sites such as Twitter can provide large amounts of publicity quickly. Organizations generally do not pay for the publicity and are not identified as the source of the information, but they can benefit from it.

Although organizations do not directly pay for publicity, it should not be viewed as "free." Preparing news releases, staging special events, and persuading media personnel to broadcast or print publicity messages costs money. Public relations and publicity are examined further in Chapter 17.

16-4c Sales Promotion

Sales promotion consists of all marketing activities—other than personal selling, advertising, direct-response marketing, and public relations—that stimulate consumer purchasing, dealer effectiveness, and sales force enthusiasm. Sales promotion is generally a short-run tool used to stimulate immediate increases in demand. Sales promotion can be aimed at end consumers, trade customers, or a company's employees. Sales promotions include free samples, contests and sweepstakes, premiums, trade shows, and coupons. Increasingly, companies such as Groupon and WagJag have combined social networks and sales promotion. Facebook is also a growing platform for sales promotion activities—companies

> **public relations** the marketing function that evaluates public attitudes, identifies areas within the organization the public may be interested in, and executes a program of action to earn public understanding and acceptance

> **publicity** public information about a company, a product, a service, or an issue appearing in the mass media as a news item

> **sales promotion** marketing activities—other than personal selling, advertising, direct-response marketing, and public relations—that stimulate consumer buying and dealer effectiveness

can give away coupons, run contests or sweepstakes, or even execute a well-targeted sampling program. For example, on Valentine's Day, KFC Canada ran a Facebook contest called KFC ChickenGram. Lovesick chicken lovers could enter by submitting their love story for a chance to have a heart-shaped box of KFC delivered free of charge to their door.[6] Just what you have always wanted for your Valentine's Day dinner!

Marketers often use sales promotion to improve the effectiveness of other ingredients in the promotional mix, especially advertising and personal selling. Adding value to the brand is the main intent of sales promotion, which makes it a particularly valuable activity for promoting new brands or brands in highly competitive marketplaces. Research shows that sales promotion complements advertising by yielding faster short-term sales responses. In many instances, more money is spent on sales promotion than on advertising. Sales promotion is discussed in more detail in Chapter 18.

16-4d Personal Selling

Personal selling is a purchase situation involving a personal, paid-for communication between two people in an attempt to influence each other. Here, both the buyer and the seller have specific objectives they want to accomplish. The buyer may need to minimize cost or ensure a quality product, whereas the salesperson may need to maximize revenue and profits.

A traditional method of personal selling is a planned presentation to one or more prospective buyers for the purpose of making a sale. Whether the personal selling takes place face to face or over the phone, it attempts to persuade the buyer to accept a point of view. Frequently, in this traditional view of personal selling, the objectives of the salesperson are at the expense of the buyer, creating a win–lose situation. Currently, Canada's large banks are under fire for establishing unrealistic sales targets for their front-line staff, resulting in aggressive sales tactics that are often not in the best interest of the consumer.

Today, personal selling is characterized by the relationship that develops between a salesperson and a buyer. Initially, this concept was more typical in business-to-business selling situations, involving the sale of such products as heavy machinery and computer systems, which tend to take a long time to close and often result in modifications to the product to meet the unique needs of the buyer. More recently, both business-to-business and business-to-consumer selling have tended to focus on building long-term relationships rather than on making a one-time sale.

Relationship selling emphasizes a win–win outcome and the accomplishment of mutual objectives that benefit both buyer and salesperson in the long term. Rather than focusing on a quick sale, relationship selling attempts to create a long-term, committed relationship that is based on trust, increased customer loyalty, and a continuation of the relationship between the salesperson and the customer. Personal selling, like other promotional mix elements, is increasingly dependent on the Internet. Most companies use their websites to attract potential buyers seeking information on products and services and to drive customers to their physical locations, where personal selling can close the sale. Personal selling is discussed further in Chapter 18.

16-4e Direct-Response Communication

Direct-response communication, often referred to as *direct marketing*, is the communication of a message directly from a marketing company and directly to an intended individual target audience. The objective is to generate profitable business results through targeted communications to a specific audience. Direct-response communication uses a combination of relevant messaging and offers that can be tracked, measured, analyzed, stored, and leveraged to drive future marketing initiatives.

Direct-response communication has grown in importance in integrated marketing communication programs for many reasons, but two factors have played key roles: (1) the results of the communication program can be measured and, hence, immediately altered (if necessary) to improve performance; and (2) the use of the Internet as a communication tool provides one-to-one communication to the intended target, which is the foundation of direct-marketing communication.

Direct-marketing communication uses a variety of media to deliver the personalized message, including television and radio, referred to as *direct-response broadcast*; newspaper and magazines, referred to as *direct-response print*; the telephone, referred to as *telemarketing*; the Internet, both email and websites; and postal mail, referred to as *direct mail*. The most common form of direct-response communication is direct mail.

Direct-response communication can be highly successful because the consumer often finds the targeted

personal selling a purchase situation involving a personal, paid-for communication between two people in an attempt to influence each other

direct-response communication communication of a message directly from a marketing company and directly to an intended individual target audience

communication to be more appealing as it is more personal. Direct marketing is designed to meet consumers' unique needs. Potential buyers can learn about the product and make a purchase at the same time. Direct response is discussed further in Chapter 17.

16-4f Online Marketing, Content Marketing, and Social Media

Online marketing is communication delivered through the Internet. The rapid growth of consumers' use of the Internet and its pervasive impact on consumers' daily lives have led to new communication opportunities for marketers. The Internet creates real-time, two-way communication with consumers. This allows the marketer to alter the message to better suit the consumer. Not only can consumers immediately respond to the marketer's message with further inquiries or even a purchase, but as a result of email and social media, they can also share it instantly with their friends and family. The penetration of Internet usage has also created the opportunity for marketers to become publishers of content that is easily accessible to consumers through marketers' email marketing, search engine optimization, paid search, and display advertising strategies that pull the consumer to the company's website or social media channels, to engage them with the content and thus the brand. Content created by marketers adds value to a brand and can help to reinforce a brand's positioning in the marketplace relative to competition. In 2015 Nike launched a campaign targeting women entitled "Better for It." The campaign was a global effort to encourage women to push themselves to see how far they could go, no matter how far that was. The launch of the campaign relied heavily on traditional media, including print and digital ads. A year after the launch, Nike created an eight-episode YouTube series in support of the message, which they believed was highly authentic and relatable and would thus create conversation and connection among the intended target.[7] Content created by marketers for their brands is typically distributed through social media.

Social media are promotion tools used to facilitate conversations and other interactions among people. Consumers can hold intimate conversations with companies that can be shared through "likes" on Facebook and Instagram and retweets on Twitter. In the same way, social media allow consumers to speak to one another often in a public forum, such as on Facebook, providing instantaneous and wide-reaching word of mouth. **Social media** include blogs; microblogs, like Twitter; video platforms, such as YouTube and Vine; podcasts; vodcasts; and social networks, such as Facebook, Pinterest, Snapchat, and LinkedIn. The consumer who uses social media is in control of the message, the medium, and the response. This increased consumer empowerment can be frightening for companies, but they have come to see that when used properly, social media have value. Indeed, social media have become a "layer" in promotional strategies. Social media are ubiquitous—it just depends on how deep that layer goes for each brand. The various social media tools have created a completely new way for marketers to manage their image, connect with consumers, and generate interest in and desire for their products. If the marketer can listen and learn, he or she can engage more successfully. Marketers are using social media as an integral aspect of their campaigns and as a way to extend the benefits of traditional media. Social media are discussed in more detail in Chapters 18 and 19.

16-4g The Communication Process and the Promotional Mix

The elements of the promotional mix differ in their ability to affect the target audience. Exhibit 16.4 outlines differences among the promotional mix elements with respect to mode of communication, marketer's control over the communication process, amount and speed of feedback, direction of message flow, marketer's control over the message, identification of the sender, speed in reaching large audiences, and message flexibility.

From Exhibit 16.4, you can see that most elements of the promotional mix are indirect and impersonal when used to communicate with a target market, providing only one direction of message flow. For example, advertising, public relations, and sales promotion are generally impersonal, one-way means of mass communication controlled by the marketer. Because these elements of the promotional mix provide no opportunity for direct feedback, altering the promotional message and adapting to changing consumer preferences, individual differences, and personal goals is difficult to do quickly.

Personal selling, on the other hand, is personal, two-way communication offering the opportunity to adjust the message as required. Personal selling, however, is very slow in dispersing the marketer's message to large audiences. Direct-response communication is meant to be targeted, two-way communication but the extent of the personalization is dependent on the medium used to reach the intended target.

online marketing two-way communication of a message delivered through the Internet to the consumer

social media a collection of online communication tools that facilitate conversations online; when used by marketers, social media tools encourage consumer empowerment

EXHIBIT 16.4

CHARACTERISTICS OF THE ELEMENTS IN THE PROMOTIONAL MIX (INCLUDING DIRECT-RESPONSE COMMUNICATION)

	Advertising	Public Relations	Sales Promotion	Personal Selling	Direct-Response Communication	Social Media
Mode of Communication	Indirect and impersonal	Usually indirect and impersonal	Usually indirect and impersonal	Direct and face-to-face	Direct but often impersonal	Indirect but instant
Communicator Control over the Situation	Low	Moderate to low	Moderate to low	High	Some, depending on medium used	Some, depending on medium used
Amount of Feedback	Little	Little	Little to moderate	Much	High	High
Speed of Feedback	Delayed	Delayed	Varies	Immediate	Varies	Immediate
Direction of Message	Flow one-way	One-way	Mostly one-way	Two-way	Mostly two-way	Two-way/multiple ways
Control over Message Content	Yes	No	Yes	Yes	Some	Varies
Identification of Sponsor	Yes	No	Yes	Yes	Yes	Yes
Speed in Reaching Large Audience	Fast	Usually fast	Fast	Slow	Slow	Fast
Message Flexibility	Same message to all audiences	Usually no direct control over message audiences	Same message to varied target	Tailored to prospective buyer	Tailored to prospective target	Tailored to prospective target—the most targeted

© Cengage

The Internet has changed the landscape tremendously. Both the marketer and the consumer, with the consumer often in control, are now sharing the communication space. Consumers can pass judgment on a brand or the brand's message in a public forum, through online posts (whether they're asked to do so or not), and they can alter the communication message immediately or create their own. This is referred to as **consumer-generated content**.

Astute marketers, recognizing that consumers trust each other more than they trust brands, have created campaigns that encourage the consumer to create consumer-generated content. Many new products have been successfully launched, and established products have continued to remain relevant, on the basis of consumer-generated content. Take Lucky Charms as an example. General Mills wanted to reconnect the brand with Millennials. Research indicated that Millennials relied on consumer-generated content in making purchase decisions. In addition, research identified that to build credibility with Millennials, you needed to be where they are, talking to them through influencers they know and trust, in a language they perceive as

consumer-generated content any form of publicly available online content created by consumers; also referred to as user-generated content

Used with permission of General Mills Marketing, Inc.

authentic. To that end General Mills created branded content using a personality Millennials could relate to, brought Lucky Charms to events that Millennials were already at, and engaged in unique social media that allowed Millennials to create fun, customizable, and shareable content that included Lucky Charms.

As a result of the impact of social media, as well as the proliferation of new platforms, tools, and ideas, promotional tactics can also be categorized according to media types—paid, earned, or owned (see Exhibit 16.5). **Paid media** are based on the traditional advertising model, where a brand pays for media space. Traditionally, paid media have included television, magazine, outdoor, radio, or newspaper advertising. Increasingly, paid media come in the form of display advertising on websites or pay-per-click advertising on search engines, such as Google. Paid media are quite important, especially as they migrate to the Web. **Earned media** are based on the traditional publicity model. The idea is to get people talking about the brand—whether through media coverage (as in traditional public relations) or through word of mouth (through sharing on social media sites). Search engine optimization (SEO), where companies embed key words into content to increase their positioning on search results, can also be considered earned media. **Owned media** are those where brands become publishers of their own content to maximize brand value to the customer. Owned media are often referred to as **branded content**. Owned media include a company's own website and its official presence on Facebook, Twitter, YouTube channels, blogs, and other platforms. These media are controlled by the brand but continually keep the consumer in mind. This type of media can be highly engaging by encouraging consumer conversation and can be very cost-effective if consumer engagement leads to online sharing.

16-5 PROMOTIONAL GOALS AND THE AIDA CONCEPT

The ultimate goal of any promotion is to have someone buy a good or service or, in the case of nonprofit organizations, to take some action (such as donate online). A classic model for achieving promotional goals is called the **AIDA concept**.[8] The acronym stands for *attention, interest, desire,* and *action*—the stages of consumer involvement with a promotional message.

This model proposes that consumers respond to marketing messages in a cognitive (thinking), affective (feeling), and conative (doing) sequence. First, a promotion manager may focus on attracting a consumer's *attention* by training a salesperson to use a friendly greeting and approach, by using music that is relevant to the target, or by using bold headlines, movement, bright colours, and other similar creative devices in an advertisement. Next, a good sales presentation, demonstration, or advertisement creates *interest* in the product and then, by illustrating how the product's features will satisfy the consumer's needs, arouses desire. Finally, a special offer or a strong closing sales pitch may be used to obtain purchase action.

The AIDA concept assumes that promotion propels consumers along the following four steps in the purchase-decision process:

1. **Attention:** The advertiser must first gain the attention of the target market. A firm cannot sell its product if the market does not know that the good or service exists. In an attempt to regain relevance in the

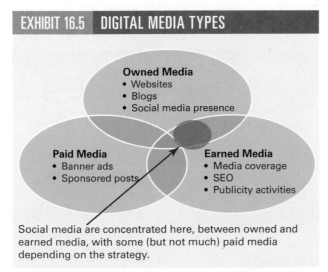

EXHIBIT 16.5 DIGITAL MEDIA TYPES

Owned Media
• Websites
• Blogs
• Social media presence

Paid Media
• Banner ads
• Sponsored posts

Earned Media
• Media coverage
• SEO
• Publicity activities

Social media are concentrated here, between owned and earned media, with some (but not much) paid media depending on the strategy.

Source: Adapted from Dave Fleet, "Why Paying Bloggers for Posts Changes the Game," DaveFleet.com, December 12, 2010, http://davefleet.com/2010/12/bloggers-money=posts-game (Accessed May 17, 2017).

paid media a category of promotional tactic based on the traditional advertising model whereby a brand pays for advertising space

earned media a category of promotional tactic based on a public relations model that gets customers talking about products or services

owned media a category of promotional tactic based on brands becoming publishers of their own content to maximize the brands' value to consumers

branded content creation of engaging bespoke content as a way to promote a particular brand that attracts and builds relationships with consumers

AIDA concept a model that outlines the process for achieving promotional goals in terms of stages of consumer involvement with the message; the acronym stands for *attention, interest, desire,* and *action*

Canadian market at a time when its U.S. counterpart is struggling with declining sales and the threat of closure, Sears Canada tried reaching out to a younger demographic with an investment in fast fashion. Sears Canada created the S label, a brand that targets women in their teens to early twenties. Recognizing the intensity of competition in this segment (H&M, Forever 21), Sears acted quickly and brought the brand to market in less than six months. To build awareness of the label, Sears opened a pop-up in Toronto and launched a marketing campaign heavily dependent on social media. The campaign utilized the hashtag #wehavechanged, and Sears built relationships with key influencers, encouraging online conversations. In addition to the social media campaign, some traditional advertising was used, including streetcar wraps and a coffee partnership with local cafés. Knowing that the life cycle of fashion is short, Sears recognized that it needed to build awareness quickly and effectively.

2. **Interest:** Simple awareness of a brand seldom leads to a sale. The next step is to create interest in the product. In the case of the S brand by Sears, the pop-up in Toronto allowed the consumer to touch and try on the item, heightening understanding in relation to the key competition. The hashtag encouraged sharing on social media, allowing Sears to engage in the conversations with the audience and for the audience to share with their contacts.

3. **Desire:** The S brand was Sears' first entry into the highly competitive fast-fashion market, to a target consumer that did not perceive Sears favourably. To be successful Sears needed to build on its knowledge of the target consumer, bring fresh looks to the line quickly, and engage in strong communication opportunities to convince the target consumers that the S brand was relevant to them and their lifestyle.

4. **Action:** While some consumers may have visited the pop-up store and viewed social media mentions of the S brand, many did not make a purchase. Sears tried to motivate purchase by offering innovative fashion within the line and promoting the brand in ways that were engaging with the target consumer.[9]

Unfortunately the above strategy and others employed by Sears to rebuild the business appears to have failed, for in June 2107 Sears applied for and was granted protection from its creditors under the Companies' Creditors Arrangement Act, when it announced the closing of 59 stores and the layoff of almost 3000 employees.

Most buyers involved in high-involvement purchase situations pass through the four stages of the AIDA

model on their way to making a purchase, but a repeat purchase or a low-risk purchase may not require the consumer to pass through all four stages. The promoter's task is to first determine where on the purchase ladder most of the target consumers are located and to then design a promotion plan to meet their needs. The AIDA concept does not explain how all promotions influence purchase decisions. The model suggests that promotional effectiveness can be measured by consumers progressing from one stage to the next. However, much debate surrounds the order of the stages and whether consumers go through all steps. A purchase can occur without interest or desire, such as when a low-involvement product is bought on impulse. Regardless of the order of the stages or consumers' progression through these stages, the AIDA concept helps marketers by suggesting which promotional strategy will be most effective.[10]

The AIDA model, if taken too literally, has its limitations. Action as the end goal suggests a purchase (or a donation, in the case of a charity), but a single purchase or donation is not the end goal. Marketers are concerned about loyalty—continual purchase behaviour. Hence marketers develop integrated marketing communication programs that turn the action into loyalty. A brand-loyal consumer can become a brand advocate.

16-5a AIDA and the Promotional Mix

Exhibit 16.6 depicts the relationship between the promotional mix and the AIDA model. It shows that, although advertising does have an impact in the later stages, it is most useful in gaining attention for goods or services. In contrast, personal selling reaches fewer people at first. Salespeople are more effective at creating customer interest for merchandise or a service and at creating desire. For example, advertising may help a potential

EXHIBIT 16.6 THE PROMOTIONAL MIX AND THE AIDA MODEL				
	Attention	**Interest**	**Desire**	**Action**
Advertising	●	●	◑	○
Public Relations	●	●	●	○
Sales Promotion	◑	◑	●	◑
Personal Selling	◑	●	●	●
Direct Marketing	◑	●	●	●
Social Media	◑	●	●	●

● Very effective ◑ Somewhat effective ○ Not effective

© Cengage

computer purchaser to gain knowledge about competing brands, but the salesperson may be the one who actually encourages the buyer to decide that a particular brand is the best choice. The salesperson also has the advantage of having the product, such as a computer, physically there to demonstrate its capabilities to the buyer.

Public relations' greatest impact is gaining attention for a company, good, or service. Many companies can attract attention and build goodwill by sponsoring community events that benefit a worthy cause. Such sponsorships project a positive image of the firm and its products into the minds of consumers and potential consumers. Book publishers push to get their titles on the bestseller lists of major publications such as *The Globe and Mail*, to be included in the yearly CBC Canada Reads series, and to get their authors included in literary events throughout the country.

Sales promotion's greatest strength is in creating strong desire and purchase intent. Frequent-buyer sales promotion programs, popular among retailers, allow consumers to accumulate points or dollars that can later be redeemed for goods. Frequent-buyer programs tend to increase purchase intent and loyalty and encourage repeat purchases.

Social media are a strong way to gain attention and interest in a brand, particularly if content goes viral. It can then reach a massive audience. Social media are also effective at engaging with customers and enabling companies to maintain interest in a brand if properly managed.

16-6 INTEGRATED MARKETING COMMUNICATIONS

Ideally, marketing communications from each promotional mix element (advertising, public relations, sales promotion, personal selling, direct-response communication, and social media) should be integrated—that is, the message reaching the consumer should be the same regardless of whether it is from an advertisement, a salesperson in the field, a magazine article, a Facebook page, or a coupon in a newspaper insert.

Consumers do not think in terms of the six elements of promotion. Instead, everything is an "ad." The only people who recognize the distinctions among these communications elements are the marketers themselves. So, unfortunately, when planning promotional messages, some marketers treat each of the promotion elements separately, failing to integrate the communications efforts from one element to the next.

To prevent this disjointed communication from happening, companies today have adopted the concept of **integrated marketing communications (IMC)**. IMC is the careful coordination of all promotional

integrated marketing communications (IMC)
the careful coordination of all promotional messages for a product or a service to ensure the consistency of messages at every contact point where a company meets the consumer

A Fine Balance

Tea is the second-most-consumed beverage next to water, and consumption is growing. Tea drinkers have on average 11 types of tea in their cupboard.[11] Tetley is the leading tea brand in the category in Canada, but as Canadians increase their consumption of tea, competition within the category has intensified, providing consumers much in the way of variety. Such a competitive landscape requires innovation to stay relevant to the consumer. Tetley's latest launch is a line of Ayurvedic teas. The Ayurvedic Balance teas were inspired by Ayuveda, an alternative medicine with roots in India, which is based on the idea of balancing the mind, body, and spirit. Such balance is believed to be essential for holistic well-being. While consumers weren't necessarily aware of Ayurveda, research indicated that they were very interested in the concept of balance in their lives. To launch the brand, Tetley utilized print ads, sampling at health and wellness-focused events, and a strong social media campaign. To reinforce the new line's positioning, Tetley created branded content by hosting Tea Talk—a TED Talk-like event with health and wellness speakers that was open to 200 people and live-streamed over Facebook to many more. The fully integrated campaign was designed to drive awareness of the new line of teas as well as the concept that the line was positioned around.[12]

messages—traditional advertising, public relations, sales promotion, personal selling, direct-response communication, and social media—for a product or service to ensure the consistency of messages at every contact point where a company meets the consumer. Following the concept of IMC, marketing managers carefully work out the roles that various promotional mix tools will play in the communications strategy. The timing of promotional activities is coordinated, and the results of each campaign are carefully monitored to improve future use of the promotional mix tools.

The IMC concept continues to grow in popularity for several reasons. First, the proliferation of thousands of media choices and the continued use of social media by all age groups has made communication a more complicated task. Instead of promoting a product through only mass-media options, such as television and magazines, promotional messages today can appear in a variety of sources.

Further, the mass market is highly fragmented. The traditional broad market groups that marketers promoted to in years past have been replaced by selectively segmented markets requiring niche marketing strategies that rely on well-integrated communication campaigns. Finally, marketers have slashed their advertising spending in favour of promotional techniques that generate immediate sales responses, those that are more easily measured, and those that offer heightened consumer engagement. Online advertising has thus earned a bigger share of the budget because of its measurability, the immediacy of feedback, and its success at engaging the individual consumer. The interest in IMC is largely a reaction to the scrutiny that marketing communications has come under and, particularly, to suggestions that uncoordinated promotional activity leads to a strategy that is wasteful and inefficient.

16-7 FACTORS AFFECTING THE PROMOTIONAL MIX

Promotional mixes vary a great deal from one product and one industry to the next. Normally, advertising and personal selling are used to promote goods and services supported and supplemented by sales promotion. Public relations helps to develop a positive image for the organization and the product line. Social media have been used more for consumer goods, but business-to-business marketers are increasingly using them as well. A firm may choose not to use all six promotional elements in its promotional mix, or it may choose to use them only

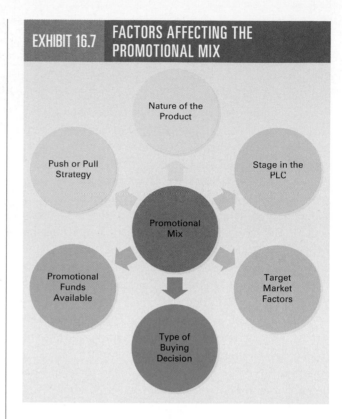

EXHIBIT 16.7 FACTORS AFFECTING THE PROMOTIONAL MIX

in varying degrees. The particular promotional mix chosen by a firm for a product or service depends on several factors: the nature of the product, the stage in the product life cycle, target market characteristics, the type of buying decision, funds available for promotion, and whether a push or a pull strategy will be used.

16-7a Nature of the Product

Characteristics of the product itself can influence the promotional mix. For instance, a product can be classified as either a business product or a consumer product (refer to Chapters 7 and 10). As business products are often custom-tailored to the buyer's exact specifications, they are typically not well suited to mass promotion. Therefore, producers of most business goods, such as computer systems or industrial machinery, rely more heavily on personal selling than on advertising. However, advertising can still serve a purpose in promoting business goods as a strategic campaign in a trade publication can help locate potential customers for the sales force.

In contrast, because consumer products generally are not custom made, they do not require the selling efforts of a company representative to tailor them to the user's needs. Thus consumer goods are promoted mainly through advertising or social media to create brand familiarity. Sales promotion, the brand name, and the product's packaging are about twice as important for consumer goods as for business products.

The costs and risks associated with a product also influence the promotional mix. As a general rule, when the costs or risks of buying and using a product increase, persuasive personal selling becomes more important. The more expensive the item is, whether it be a consumer or business good, the more important it is that a salesperson be available to assure buyers that they are spending their money wisely and not taking an undue financial risk. Social risk is also an issue. When a consumer is purchasing specialty products such as jewellery or clothing, a salesperson can be useful to guide the decision.

16-7b Stage in the Product Life Cycle

The product's stage in its life cycle is a factor in designing a promotional mix (see Exhibit 16.8). During the *introduction stage*, the basic goal of promotion is to inform the target audience that the product is available. Initially, the emphasis is on the general product class—for example, electric cars. This emphasis gradually changes to gaining attention for a particular brand, such as the Nissan Leaf or the Tesla. Typically, both extensive advertising and public relations inform the target audience of the product class or brand and heighten awareness levels. Companies use owned media here to manage the message and to provide consumers with the information they seek to become knowledgeable about the product class and the brand. Sales promotion encourages early trial of the product, and personal selling gets retailers to carry the product.

When the product reaches the *growth stage* of the life cycle, the promotion blend may shift. Often a change is necessary because different types of potential buyers

EXHIBIT 16.8 PRODUCT LIFE CYCLE AND THE PROMOTIONAL MIX

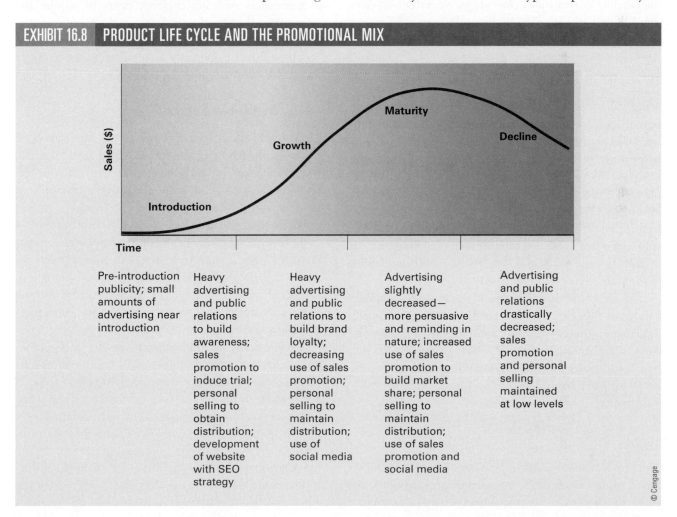

| Pre-introduction publicity; small amounts of advertising near introduction | Heavy advertising and public relations to build awareness; sales promotion to induce trial; personal selling to obtain distribution; development of website with SEO strategy | Heavy advertising and public relations to build brand loyalty; decreasing use of sales promotion; personal selling to maintain distribution; use of social media | Advertising slightly decreased— more persuasive and reminding in nature; increased use of sales promotion to build market share; personal selling to maintain distribution; use of sales promotion and social media | Advertising and public relations drastically decreased; sales promotion and personal selling maintained at low levels |

are targeted. Although advertising and public relations continue to be major elements of the promotional mix, sales promotion can be reduced because consumers need fewer incentives to purchase. The promotional strategy is to emphasize the product's differential advantage over the competition. Persuasive promotion is used to build and maintain brand loyalty during the growth stage. Social media can be quite effective here as they can be used to heighten consumer engagement, create online conversations about the brand, and establish peer-to-peer advice, resulting in brand preference. By this stage, personal selling has usually succeeded in achieving adequate distribution for the product.

As the product reaches the *maturity stage* of its life cycle, competition becomes fiercer and thus persuasive; reminder advertising is more strongly emphasized. Sales promotion comes back into focus as product sellers try to increase their market share. Social media, in particular the innovative use of social media, such as the encouragement of consumer-generated content, can keep the brand top of mind with consumers.

All promotion, especially advertising, is reduced as the product enters the *decline stage*. Nevertheless, personal selling and sales promotion efforts may be maintained, particularly at the retail level.

16-7c Target Market Characteristics

A target market that is characterized by widely scattered potential customers, highly informed buyers, and brand-loyal repeat purchasers generally requires a promotional mix with more advertising, social media, and sales promotion, and less personal selling. Sometimes, however, personal selling is required even when buyers are well informed and geographically dispersed. Although industrial installations may be sold to well-educated people with extensive work experience, salespeople must be present to explain the product and work out the details of the purchase agreement.

Firms often sell goods and services in markets where potential customers are difficult to locate. Social media and direct-response print advertising can be used to find these customers. The consumer is invited to call for more information, mail in a reply card for a detailed brochure, or visit a website to receive more information.

16-7d Type of Buying Decision

The promotional mix also depends on the type of buying. For routine consumer decisions, such as buying toothpaste, the most effective promotion calls attention to the brand or reminds the consumer about the brand and its distinguishing characteristics. Advertising, social media, and sales promotion are the most productive promotion tools to use for routine decisions.

If the decision is neither routine nor complex, advertising, social media, in particular branded content, and public relations help establish awareness for the good or service. Take for example the purchase of hiking shoes. Although the consumer may have never bought hiking shoes before, his or her need for a pair has heightened his or her awareness of options. An advertisement, a blog post by a hiker, a review on a website will help to establish the brand preference in the purchase decision.

In contrast, consumers who make complex buying decisions are more extensively involved. They rely on large amounts of information to help them reach a purchase decision. Personal selling is effective in helping these consumers decide. For example, consumers thinking about buying a car often depend on a salesperson to provide the information they need to reach a decision. Again, social media are playing an important role here as purchasers seek advice from peers to acquire the information they need to make the right brand decision. Print advertising may also be used for high-involvement purchase decisions because it can often provide a large amount of information to the consumer.

16-7e Available Funds

Money, or the lack of it, may easily be the most important factor in determining the promotional mix. A small, undercapitalized manufacturer may rely heavily on social media for a good online SEO strategy that places the company's website in the top few results as well as publicity to create demand. If the situation warrants a sales force, a financially strained firm may turn to manufacturers' agents, who work on a commission basis with no advances or expense accounts. Even well-capitalized organizations may not be able to afford the advertising rates of highly rated television programs or printed publications with strong circulation.

When funds are available to permit a mix of promotional elements, a firm will generally try to optimize its return on promotion dollars while minimizing the *cost per contact*, or the cost of reaching one member of the target market. In general, the cost per contact is very high for personal selling, public relations, and sales promotions, such as samplings and demonstrations. On the other hand, given the number of people national advertising and social media reach, they have very low cost per contact. Usually, a trade-off is made among the funds

EXHIBIT 16.9 PUSH STRATEGY VERSUS PULL STRATEGY

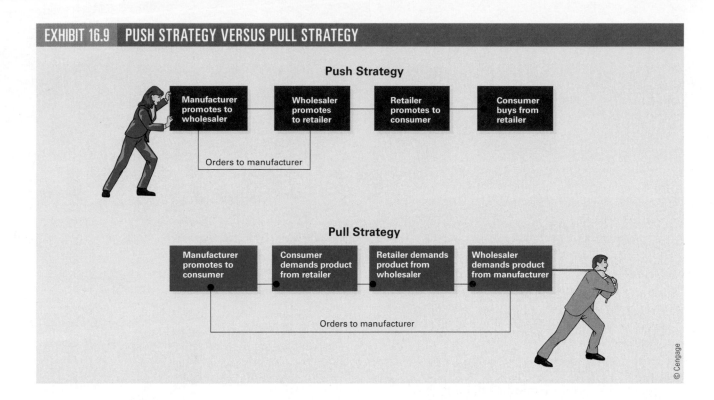

Push Strategy

Manufacturer promotes to wholesaler → Wholesaler promotes to retailer → Retailer promotes to consumer → Consumer buys from retailer

Orders to manufacturer

Pull Strategy

Manufacturer promotes to consumer · Consumer demands product from retailer · Retailer demands product from wholesaler · Wholesaler demands product from manufacturer

Orders to manufacturer

© Cengage

available, the number of people in the target market, the quality of communication needed, and the relative costs of the promotional elements. There are plenty of low-cost options available to companies without a huge budget. Many of these include online strategies and public relations efforts, in which the company relies on free publicity.

16-7f Push and Pull Strategies

The last factor that affects the promotional mix is whether a push or a pull promotional strategy will be used. Manufacturers may use aggressive personal selling and trade advertising to convince a wholesaler or a retailer to carry and sell their merchandise. This approach is known as a **push strategy** (see Exhibit 16.9). The wholesaler, in turn, must often push the merchandise forward by persuading the retailer to handle the goods. The retailer then uses advertising, displays, and other forms of promotion to convince the consumer to buy the pushed products. This concept also applies to services.

At the other extreme is a **pull strategy**, which stimulates consumer demand to obtain product distribution. Rather than trying to sell to the wholesaler, the manufacturer using a pull strategy focuses its promotional efforts on end consumers or opinion leaders. Social media and content or branded marketing are the most recent (and best) example of a pull strategy. The idea is that social media content does not interrupt a consumer's experience with media (like a television commercial interrupts the viewing of a show). Instead the content invites customers to experience it on social media or a website. This encourages more engaged behaviour between consumers and a brand, thereby heightening brand knowledge and encouraging a desire to seek out the brand to purchase. Heavy sampling, introductory consumer advertising, cents-off campaigns, and couponing are also all part of a pull strategy.

Rarely does a company use a pull or a push strategy exclusively. Instead, the mix will usually emphasize one of these strategies. For example, pharmaceutical companies generally use a push strategy, through personal selling and trade advertising, to promote their drugs and therapies to physicians. Sales presentations and advertisements in medical journals give physicians the detailed information they need to prescribe medication to their patients. Most pharmaceutical companies supplement their push promotional strategy with a pull strategy targeted directly to potential patients through advertisements in consumer magazines and on television.

push strategy a marketing strategy that uses aggressive personal selling and trade advertising to convince a wholesaler or a retailer to carry and sell particular merchandise

pull strategy a marketing strategy that stimulates consumer demand to obtain product distribution

SIDE LAUNCH
BREWING COMPANY
CONTINUING CASE

Side Launch Brewing Company

On-Message Is More Than Words

In the increasingly competitive space of craft beer, there is often little means of differentiation besides the story told by its players. This story, a combination of what physically makes one brand different from the next and an actual personality attached to it, becomes crucial as a company attempts to first hook a prospective customer. The remaining chapters of this book are devoted to how that story is told from the Side Launch playbook. This chapter, however, implores marketers to coordinate a singular message through the growing number of tools that are used to tell the story.

Marketing communications, or integrated marketing communications (IMC), is a concept that borrows from the political campaign lesson of being on-message. No matter where the story is told, no matter how it may be viewed or heard, no matter who is telling the story—everything must be on-message. What is the Side Launch message?

"Quality," proclaims Chuck Galea, VP Sales and Marketing.

"Approachable and drinkable," states Garnet Pratt, founder.

"Accessible and consistent," asserts Michael Hancock, brewer.

"Passion," concludes Lily Findlay, Territory Manager.

"Authentic," states Dave Sands, VP Operations.

While no two Side Launch people might use the same words to describe the value proposition that must be communicated, it comes through in something less tangible—a feeling or attitude that is somehow released when the tab is popped on top of a can, or a tap handle is pulled by a bartender. "When we decided that we were going to start a brewery in Collingwood, the name 'Side Launch' just seemed perfect," recalls Garnet. The name comes from a legendary practice of how the shipbuilders of Collingwood, sadly removed from the economy years ago, would launch newly christened ships into the waters of Georgian Bay in Lake Huron—sideways. The massive and sudden displacement of water caused by the mammoth ships plunging sideways into the lake became a spectacle attracting visitors from far and near. "We were all enamoured with the celebratory nature of the side launch," Michael recalls. "It spoke of workmanship, people, gathering, and community—all values we wanted to come from each pour," added Garnet.

In the Side Launch Brewing Company world, integrated marketing communications is not even a conscious strategy. It breathes through

every pore of the operation. The front desk, reception area, and retail area are literally part of the brewery. You see, smell, hear the experience of beer being made whether you come for a meeting, for a job interview, or to pick up a few cans of your favourite brew. The actual "desk" itself is a bar built of beautifully restored 40-foot Douglas fir logs reclaimed from the shipyards from which the brewery got its name. The logo is on all the packaging, carefully thought through to convey the emotion. The bold and empowered Canadian-made ship icon, of course, also graces every piece of swag (proudly worn by every employee and clearly visible to the world that visits). Its attitude bleeds through all advertising, social media post, sales calls, or any of the multiple events in which Side Launch participates. It is presented iconically *everywhere,* communicating the values, the promise, the celebration of Side Launch.

Questions

1. Besides a commitment to making high-quality beer, what other words could be used in an IMC campaign for Side Launch?

2. Go online and identify IMC tools currently being used by Side Launch.

3. Given the young age of Side Launch as a brewery, and some of its beer products specifically, what is the most logical strategy for it to use in its marketing communications?

Side Launch Brewing Company

17 | Advertising, Public Relations, and Direct Response

LEARNING OUTCOMES

17-1 Define advertising and understand the effect of advertising

17-2 Identify the major types of advertising

17-3 Discuss the creative decisions in developing an advertising campaign

17-4 Describe media evaluation and selection techniques and how media are purchased

17-5 Discuss the role of public relations in the promotional mix

17-6 Discuss the role of direct-response communication in the promotional mix

"Many a small thing has been made large by the right kind of advertising."

—Mark Twain

17-1 WHAT IS ADVERTISING?

In Chapter 1, we learned that marketing is about understanding the needs of the customer. It helps to shape a business's products and services, based on an understanding of what the customer is looking for. We learned that marketing is about engaging in a *conversation* with that customer and guiding the delivery of what is required to satisfy those needs. *Advertising can help to start the conversation.*

In Chapter 16, we defined *advertising* as any form of impersonal, paid communication in which the sponsor or company is identified. It is a popular form of promotion, especially for consumer packaged goods and services, for both its entertainment value and persuasiveness. Increasingly, as more and more marketers consolidate their operations, advertising is seen as an international endeavour.

There are a number of advertising media or media types that marketers can use to help start the conversation. In Canada the disrupter in the industry continues to be digital or online media. In 2016 digital accounted for just over 40 percent of advertising spending. While television

placed second in spending, it represents about half of what is spent on digital, and television-spending growth is anticipated to be flat into the next decade.[1] This is despite the high entertainment value of television advertising, as evidenced by the anticipation surrounding the television commercials featured during the Super Bowl. Companies have come to see the Super Bowl as one of the biggest media events that bring people together; thus they are willing to pay over US$5 million for a 30-second spot. Consumers eagerly anticipate seeing these commercials, which receive almost as much prior promotion as the Super Bowl itself. Viewership of the game on traditional network television is still the norm; however in 2017, 16 percent of fans watched the game via live-streaming video apps or the Web. This migration away from network television has led advertisers to create Super Bowl commercials for airing during the digital live-stream of the game.[2] Such as strategy offers a less costly approach to gaining airtime during the most watched program (the television audience for the 2017 Super Bowl was 111.9 million), and the dynamic insertion of local ads offers improved relevance to the viewer.[3] As digital live streaming continues, the media buy for the Super Bowl

is likely to see continued migration to this medium. To see some of the commercials featured during the Super Bowl, go to www.superbowlcommercials.co/.

17-1a Advertising and Market Share

On the global stage the most valuable brand is Google at $109.5 billion followed by Apple at $107.1 billion. In Canada, Tim Hortons remains in the top ten most valuable brands along with the top four banks (RBC, TD, Scotiabank, and BMO). Interestingly, all these brands have been built over many years using strong advertising and marketing communications investments. Scotiabank's strong cultural sponsorship and relationship with Cineplex and the joint Scene loyalty program have no doubt helped to increase its brand value, while Tim Hortons' iconic Canadian advertising and product innovations are solid investments.[4] In 2017 Apple's global value declined in the face of intense competition, while Google experienced 24 percent growth, largely on the use of digital platforms versus traditional advertising and marketing investments.[5] Today's advertising dollars for successful brands are spent on maintaining brand awareness and market share. The challenge for marketers has always been to determine the most appropriate advertising budget. As a percentage of sales, established

brands like Tim Hortons generally spend proportionally less on advertising than new brands, but whether you are marketing an established product or a new product, marketers must be aware of the phenomenon of the **advertising response function**. The advertising response function helps marketers establish the most effective dollar amount to spend on advertising. The advertising response function demonstrates that there exists a diminishing return from advertising spending. That is, sales or market share tend to level off or begin to decrease no matter how much is spent on advertising. Marketers need to measure the incremental value of spending additional money on advertising versus sales increase to ensure the greatest return on investment.

17-1b The Effects of Advertising on Consumers

Advertising affects consumers' daily lives, informing them about products and services and influencing their attitudes, beliefs, and ultimately their purchases. Advertising affects the TV programs people watch, the content of the newspapers they read,

> **advertising response function** a phenomenon in which spending for advertising and sales promotion increases sales or market share up to a certain level but then produces diminishing returns

Wishes Do Come True

To reinforce its positioning, "We're here to help," and in celebration of its 200th anniversary, BMO launched an emotional campaign centred on the idea of making wishes come true. In early 2017 BMO installed a 17-foot wish fountain in Toronto and extended the fountain nationally through social media, creating a "wish it forward" initiative and encouraging Canadians to make a wish. One wish per month was granted in combination with local branch initiatives. In support of this campaign, advertisements for television, YouTube, and Facebook were created. The first ad, "Weightless," featured a man flying in a zero-gravity chamber. As the spot unfolds, the viewer becomes aware that the man uses a wheelchair and that his wife had made the wish. The emotional spot and the emotionally based campaign were designed to increased consumers' perception of BMO as the bank that is there to help.

Courtesy of BMO Financial Group

---

the politicians they elect, the medicines they take, and the toys their children play with. Consequently, the influence of advertising on the Canadian socioeconomic system has been the subject of extensive debate in nearly all corners of society.

Though advertising cannot change consumers' deeply rooted values and attitudes, it may succeed in transforming a person's negative attitude toward a product into a positive one. For instance, serious or dramatic advertisements are more effective at changing consumers' negative attitudes. Humorous ads have been found to increase the viewer's involvement in the ad, thereby increasing the impact of the advertisement's message.[6] Advertising also reinforces positive attitudes toward brands. When consumers have a neutral or favourable frame of reference for a product or brand, advertising often positively influences them. When consumers are already highly loyal to a brand, they may buy more of it when advertising and promotion for that brand increase.[7]

Advertising can also affect the way consumers rank a brand's attributes. In past years, car ads emphasized such brand attributes as speed and fuel efficiency. Today, car man-ufacturers have added safety, technology, customization, and environmental considerations, to the list.

institutional advertising a form of advertising designed to enhance a company's image rather than promote a particular product

product advertising a form of advertising that promotes the benefits of a specific good or service

17-2 MAJOR TYPES OF ADVERTISING

The firm's promotional objectives determine the type of advertising it uses. If the goal of the promotion plan is to improve the image of the company or the industry, **institutional advertising** may be used. In contrast, if the advertiser wants to enhance the sales of a specific good or service, **product advertising**, which promotes the benefits of a specific good or service, is used.

17-2a Institutional Advertising

Historically, advertising in Canada has been product oriented. Today, many companies market multiple products and need a different type of advertising. Institutional advertising, or corporate advertising, promotes the corporation as a whole and is designed to establish, change, or maintain the corporation's identity. It usually does not ask the audience to do anything but maintain a favourable attitude toward the advertiser and its goods and services. Ideally, this favourable attitude will transfer to the products being marketed by the company, thereby creating a competitive advantage over other companies. Roots Canada launched a campaign in 2017 in support of Canada's 150th birthday by playing off Canadians' image of "being nice." The campaign not only celebrated what Canada has done that is nice, but also highlighted things that Canadians hadn't done well enough. The video, played in cinemas across Canada, included "funny *nice*" with John Candy and Dan Aykroyd, Greenpeace's "disruptive *nice,*" Romeo Dallaire's "kind of *nice* that takes guts," and reconciliation with indigenous Canadians, "*Nice* is knowing when sorry just isn't enough." As part of an integrated campaign in celebration of Canada's sesquicentennial, Roots was reinforcing its image as #RootsisCanada.

Advocacy advertising is a form of institutional advertising in which an organization expresses its views on a particular issue or cause. Companies have increased their investment in advocacy advertising, as the benefits of publicly supporting social issues and causes that their target consumer is committed to has proven valuable.

17-2b Product Advertising

Unlike institutional advertising, product advertising promotes the benefits of a specific good or service. The product's stage in its life cycle often determines whether the product advertising used is pioneering advertising, competitive advertising, or comparative advertising.

PIONEERING ADVERTISING Pioneering advertising is intended to stimulate primary demand for a new product or product category. Heavily used during the introductory stage of the product life cycle, pioneering advertising offers consumers in-depth information about the benefits of the product class. Pioneering advertising also seeks to create interest. Pharmaceutical companies often use pioneering advertising.

COMPETITIVE ADVERTISING Firms use competitive or brand advertising when a product enters the growth phase of the product life cycle and other companies begin to enter the marketplace. Instead of building demand for the product category, the goal of **competitive advertising** is to influence demand for a specific brand. During this phase, promotion often becomes less informative and, instead, appeals more to emotions. Advertisements may begin to stress subtle differences between brands, with heavy emphasis on building recall of a brand name and creating a favourable attitude toward the brand. Automobile advertising has long used very competitive messages, drawing distinctions on the basis of such factors as quality, performance, and image.

Supporting the launch of a new flavour with an integrated campaign that includes social and mobile ads, online video, and couponing, Kellogg Canada hopes to reach Millennials and "those who embrace new things" with this new flavour in the highly competitive snack market.[8]

COMPARATIVE ADVERTISING Comparative advertising directly or indirectly compares two or more competing brands on one or more specific attributes. Some advertisers even use comparative advertising against their own brands. Products experiencing sluggish growth or those entering the marketplace against strong competitors are more likely to employ comparative claims in their advertising.

Before the 1970s, comparative advertising was allowed only if the competing brand was veiled and unidentified. In 1971, the Federal Trade Commission (FTC) in the United States fostered the growth of comparative advertising, claiming it provided consumers with useful information. In Canada advertisers should air with caution when using comparative advertising. There are a number of key restrictions, including creating a false impression (make sure what is being said is true and the visuals

advocacy advertising a form of advertising in which an organization expresses its views on a particular issue or cause

pioneering advertising a form of advertising designed to stimulate primary demand for a new product or product category

competitive advertising a form of advertising designed to influence demand for a specific brand

do not distort the message), ensuring that the advertisement is not misleading, and that all that is said in the ad is accurate. Claims can be made to an appropriate regulatory body, should a named competitor feel that the ad is misrepresenting its product, as well as with the Advertising Standards Council.[9] Nabob coffee continues to reinforce its positioning of quality coffee by communicating in its advertising the absurdity of the current coffee culture of lattes with no foam and creamy macchiatos—comparative positioning that makes honest claims.

 ## 17-3 CREATIVE DECISIONS IN ADVERTISING

Advertising strategies are typically organized around an advertising campaign. An **advertising campaign** is a series of related advertisements focusing on a common theme, slogan, and set of advertising appeals. It is a specific advertising effort for a particular product that extends for a defined period of time.

Before any creative work can begin on an advertising campaign, it is important to determine what goals or objectives the advertising should achieve. An **advertising objective** is the specific communication task that a campaign should accomplish for a specified target audience during a specified period. The objectives of a specific advertising campaign often depend on the overall corporate objectives, the product being advertised, and, according to research, where the consumer is with respect to product adoption. Where the consumer is in the AIDA process (see Chapter 16) helps to determine whether the advertising objective is to create awareness, arouse interest, stimulate desire, or create a purchase.

The DAGMAR approach (Defining Advertising Goals for Measured Advertising Results) establishes a protocol for writing advertising objectives. According to this method, all advertising objectives should precisely define the target audience, the desired percentage change in a specified measure of effectiveness, and the time frame during which that change is to occur.

advertising campaign a series of related advertisements focusing on a common theme, slogan, and set of advertising appeals

advertising objective a specific communication task that a campaign should accomplish for a specified target audience during a specified period

advertising appeal a reason for a person to buy a product

unique selling proposition a desirable, exclusive, and believable advertising appeal selected as the theme for a campaign

Once the advertising objectives are defined, creative work can begin on the advertising campaign. Specifically, creative decisions include identifying product benefits, developing and evaluating advertising appeals, executing the message, and evaluating the effectiveness of the campaign.

17-3a Identifying Product Benefits

A well-known rule of thumb in the advertising industry is "Sell the sizzle, not the steak." In other words, the advertising goal is to sell the benefits of the product, not its attributes. Customers do not buy attributes, they buy benefits. An attribute is simply a feature of the product, such as in the case of Nabob coffee, where the quality of the coffee bean in the can is the attribute. The benefit is what the consumer will receive or achieve by using the product. With Nabob, the resulting benefit is an authentic, simple, good-tasting cup of black coffee.

Marketing research and intuition are usually used to unearth the perceived benefits of a product and to rank consumers' preferences for these benefits.

17-3b Developing and Evaluating Advertising Appeals

An **advertising appeal** identifies a reason for a person to buy a product. Developing advertising appeals, a challenging task, is generally the responsibility of the creative people in the advertising agency. Advertising appeals typically play off consumers' emotions or address consumers' needs or wants.

Advertising campaigns can focus on one or more advertising appeals. Often the appeals are quite general, thereby allowing the firm to develop a number of subthemes or mini-campaigns using both advertising and sales promotion. Several possible advertising appeals are listed in Exhibit 17.1.

Choosing the most appropriate appeal normally requires market research. Criteria for evaluation include desirability, exclusiveness, and believability. The appeal first must make a positive impression on and be desirable to the target market. It must also be exclusive or unique; consumers must be able to distinguish the advertiser's message from competitors' messages. Most important, the appeal should be believable. An appeal that makes extravagant claims not only wastes promotional dollars but also creates ill will toward the advertiser.

The advertising appeal selected for the campaign becomes what advertisers call its **unique selling proposition**. The unique selling proposition often becomes all or part of the campaign's slogan. The BMO campaign mentioned earlier in this chapter is built on

EXHIBIT 17.1 COMMON ADVERTISING APPEALS

Profit	Informs consumers whether the product will save them money, make them money, or keep them from losing money
Health	Appeals to those who are body conscious or who want to be healthy
Love or Romance	Appeals to the consumer, setting the product apart in a competitive category, often used to sell cosmetics and perfume, it appeals to emotions
Fear	Effectively encourages engagement, but as a powerful appeal technique, advertisers need to exercise care when using this type of appeal
Admiration	Often leads to the use of celebrity spokespeople in advertising
Convenience	Communicates how the product or service will save time or money, is easier or simpler to use
Fun and Pleasure	Are often the key to advertising vacations, beer, amusement parks, and more
Environmental Consciousness	Centres on protecting the environment and being considerate of others in the community
Emotion	The use of feelings to engage people to pay attention and ultimately to buy
Vanity and Egotism	Are used most often for expensive or conspicuous items such as cars and clothing

© Cengage

its positioning of "We're here to help," and the unique selling proposition in the campaign is "Helping you to give back—that is the BMO effect" by granting wishes made by individuals through the BMO wishing fountain.

17-3c Executing the Message

Message execution is the way an advertisement portrays its information. Again, the AIDA plan (see Chapter 16) is a good blueprint for executing an advertising message. Any ad should immediately draw the attention of the reader, viewer, or listener. The advertiser must then use the message to hold interest, create desire for the good or service, and ultimately motivate a purchase.

The style in which the message is executed is one of the most creative elements of an advertisement.

Exhibit 17.2 lists examples of executional styles used by advertisers. Executional styles often dictate what type of media is used to convey the message. Scientific executional styles lend themselves well to print advertising, where more information can be conveyed. Testimonials by athletes are one of the more popular executional styles.

Injecting humour into an advertisement is a popular and effective executional style. Humorous executional styles are more often used in radio and television advertising than in print or magazine advertising where humour is less easily communicated. Humorous ads are typically used for lower-risk, low-involvement, routine purchases. Advertisers must exercise caution, however, when using humour. They must ensure that it is the brand that is remembered, not the humour itself.

EXHIBIT 17.2 TEN COMMON EXECUTIONAL STYLES FOR ADVERTISING

Slice of Life	Depicts people in settings where the product would normally be used.
Lifestyle	Shows how well the product will fit in or enhance the consumer's lifestyle.
Spokesperson/Testimonial	Can feature a celebrity, a company official, or a typical consumer making a testimonial or endorsing a product. Galen Weston appears in television ads with regular consumers, promoting the launch of the new PC Plus program.
Fantasy	Creates a fantasy for the viewer built around use of the product. Car makers often use this style to let viewers fantasize about how they would feel speeding around tight corners or down long country roads in their cars.
Humorous	Advertisers often use humour in their ads to break through the clutter and be memorable.
Real/Animated Product Symbols	Creates a character that represents the product in advertisements. The Telus animals have become product symbols.
Mood or Image	Builds a mood or an image around the product, such as peace, love, or beauty. J'adore by Dior perfume ads present the iconic fragrance as the ultimate expression of femininity, luxury, and sexuality through the use of beautiful actresses and images.
Demonstration	Shows consumers the expected benefit. Many consumer products use this technique. Tide laundry detergent is famous for demonstrating how their product will clean clothes whiter and brighter.
Musical	Conveys the message of the advertisement through song.
Scientific	Uses research or scientific evidence to depict a brand's superiority over competitors.

© Cengage

NAME THAT BRAND

Memorable tag lines are often a hallmark of a strong brand. Can you identify the brands advertised with each tag line?

1. Outwit, outlast, outplay

2. Impossible is nothing

3. The Ultimate Driving Machine

4. Just do it

5. Buy It, Sell It, Love It

6. It Gives You Wings

7. Owners Care

(1) Survivor, (2) Adidas, (3) BMW, (4) Nike, (5) eBay, (6) Red Bull, (7) WestJet

LunaseeStudios/Shutterstock.com

Sometimes a company will modify its executional styles to make its advertising more relevant or to make it stand out among competitive advertisements. Canadian Tire advertisements that include the Canadian Tire "guy" have evolved over the past few years to include a good deal of humour as a tool to ensure we remember Canadian Tire as the store for all our needs. In addition to the humour used with the Canadian Tire guy, Canadian Tire has utilized emotional appeals. During the 2017 Olympics, two of their "We All Play for Canada" ads received more than 40 million views on Facebook, without any paid support, simply because of the emotionally charged beauty of the message.[10] View the spots here. www.youtube.com/watch?v=pFuwUiHo-WI www.youtube.com/watch?v=_ml3ZCyEs0c

17-3d Postcampaign Evaluation

Evaluating an advertising campaign can be a demanding task. How can one be sure that the change in product awareness, sales, or market share is solely the result of the advertising campaign? Many advertising campaigns are designed to create an image. How does one measure whether the intended image has been created? So many variables shape whether a product or service has achieved its objectives that determining the true impact of the advertising campaign is often impossible. Nonetheless,

programmatic buying
using an automated system to make media buying decisions in real time

marketers spend considerable time studying advertising effectiveness and its probable impact on sales, market share, or awareness.

Testing ad effectiveness can be done either before or after the campaign. Before a campaign is released, marketing managers use pretests to determine the best advertising appeal, layout, and media vehicle. After advertisers implement a campaign, they use several monitoring techniques to determine whether the campaign has met its original goals. Even if a campaign has been highly successful, advertisers still typically do a postcampaign analysis to identify how the campaign might have been more efficient and which factors contributed to its success.

Automated media buying, or **programmatic buying** as it is referred to, is improving the effectiveness of media buying by providing for more efficient and effective buying creating real-time evaluation. At the moment, programmatic buying is accounting for a large component of digital media buying. However, technology advances are making the practice possible for traditional media as well. While programmatic buying doesn't assess the impact of the creative on the achievement of objectives, it does allow for instantaneous media placement evaluation and subsequent media placement alterations to improve achievement of objectives.[11] It is anticipated that in the not-too-distant future we will see more brands experimenting with programmatic buying, thereby creating individualized messages and media selection.

17-4 MEDIA DECISIONS IN ADVERTISING

A major decision for advertisers is the choice of **medium**—the channel used to convey a message to a target market. **Media planning**, therefore, is the series of decisions advertisers make regarding the selection and use of media, allowing the marketer to optimally and cost-effectively communicate the message to the target audience. Specifically, advertisers must determine which types of media will best communicate the benefits of their product or service to the target audience and when and for how long the advertisement will run.

Media selection is affected by the target market and the promotional objectives, as well as by the advertising appeal and execution decisions. Both creative and media decisions are made at the same time. Creative work cannot be completed without knowing which medium will be used to convey the message to the target market. In many cases, the advertising objectives dictate the medium and the creative approach to be used. For example, if the objective is to demonstrate how fast a product operates, the best medium to show this action is likely a video that is shown on television, in theatres, on social media, or all of these.

In 2016, Canadian advertising expenditures totalled just under $11.6 billion, an increase of 1.4 percent. Television and newspapers accounted for just under $4.0 billion of the total, with digital spending accounting for more than television and newspapers combined, at $4.1 billion. Canadian advertising expenditures are expected to demonstrate continued slow growth in the coming years due to anticipated decreases in ad spending in all media with the exception of out of home and digital. Most of the growth in digital spending will be fuelled by advertising on mobile devices such as smart phones and tablets. mobile.[12] Mobile's share of total digital ad spending is close to 50 percent, and the share of digital spending accounted for by mobile is anticipated to reach over 70 percent by 2020.[13]

17-4a Media Types

Advertising media are channels that advertisers use in mass communication. The traditional advertising media of newspapers, magazines, radio, television, outdoor media, and direct response are being challenged by digital media. Digital media are evolving to meet new consumer trends and to respond to the proliferation of data made possible by technology. Exhibit 17.4 summarizes the advantages and disadvantages of these channels.

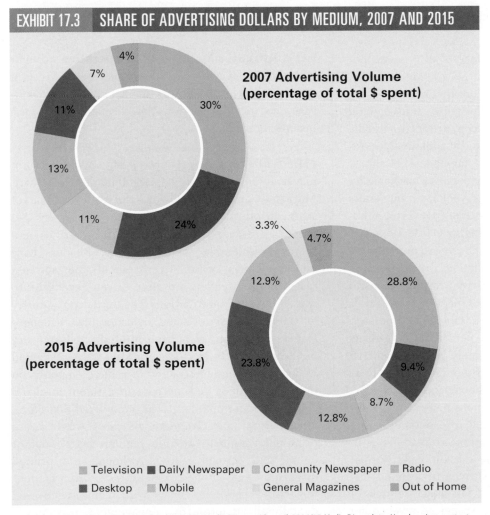

EXHIBIT 17.3 SHARE OF ADVERTISING DOLLARS BY MEDIUM, 2007 AND 2015

2007 Advertising Volume (percentage of total $ spent)
- 30%
- 24%
- 11%
- 13%
- 11%
- 7%
- 4%

2015 Advertising Volume (percentage of total $ spent)
- 28.8%
- 9.4%
- 8.7%
- 12.8%
- 23.8%
- 12.9%
- 3.3%
- 4.7%

Legend: ■ Television ■ Daily Newspaper ■ Community Newspaper ■ Radio ■ Desktop ■ Mobile ■ General Magazines ■ Out of Home

Source: Reproduced by permission of the Canadian Media Directors' Council, 2016/17 *Media Digest*, http://cmdc.ca/wp-content/uploads/2017/01/CMDC-MEDIA-DIGEST-2017.pdf, p. 23.

medium the channel used to convey a message to a target market

media planning the series of decisions advertisers make regarding the selection and use of media, allowing the marketer to optimally and cost-effectively communicate the message to the target audience

EXHIBIT 17.4 ADVANTAGES AND DISADVANTAGES OF MAJOR ADVERTISING MEDIA

Medium	Advantages	Disadvantages
Newspapers	Geographic selectivity and flexibility; short-term advertiser commitments; news value and immediacy; year-round readership; high individual market coverage; co-op and local tie-in availability; short lead time; highly credible	Little demographic selectivity; limited colour capabilities; low pass-along rate; may be expensive
Magazines	Good reproduction, especially for colour; demographic selectivity; regional selectivity; local market selectivity; relatively long advertising life; high pass-along rate	Long-term advertiser commitments; slow audience buildup; limited demonstration capabilities; lack of urgency; long lead time
Radio	Low cost; immediacy of message; can be scheduled on short notice; relatively no seasonal change in audience; highly portable; short-term advertiser commitments; entertainment carryover	No visual treatment; short advertising life of message; high frequency required to generate comprehension and retention; distractions from background sound; commercial clutter
Television	Ability to reach a wide, diverse audience; low cost per thousand; creative opportunities for demonstration; immediacy of messages; entertainment carryover; demographic selectivity with cable specialty stations; emotional medium	Short life of message; some consumer skepticism about claims; high campaign cost; little demographic selectivity with network stations; long-term advertiser commitments; long lead times required for production; commercial clutter
Outdoor Media	Repetition; moderate cost; flexibility; geographic selectivity; high creativity	Short message; lack of demographic selectivity; high "noise" level distracting audience
Direct Response	Geographic selectivity; one-to-one direct contact with audience; like a personal sales call; can be personalized; can contain multiple messages and offers	Low response rates; high cost per person reached; poor image, especially for direct mail and telemarketing
Digital and Mobile	Fastest-growing medium; ability to reach a narrow target audience; relatively short lead time required for creating Web-based advertising; moderate cost; ability to engage consumers as video content grows	Ad exposure relies on "click-through" from banner ads; measurement for social media needs much improvement; 80% of adults access the Internet; not all consumers use social media

© Cengage

NEWSPAPERS The advantages of newspaper advertising include engagement, geographic flexibility, and timeliness. Newspaper readers are highly engaged, as professional journalists, editorialists, and opinion leaders create content. Because copywriters can usually prepare newspaper ads quickly and at a reasonable cost, local merchants can reach their target market almost daily. Because newspapers are generally a mass-market medium, they may not be the best vehicle for marketers trying to reach a very narrow market; however, newspapers have innovated by creating special sections that target specific market segments. Newspaper advertising also encounters many distractions from competing ads and news stories. In response to consumer demand for real-time information, newspapers' content is now distributed to smartphones, tablets, and desktop computers with more than 25 percent of Canadians reading news across all four channels. Newspapers have embraced social media, with writers establishing their own Twitter accounts and Facebook pages that readers can follow to get up-to-the-minute news. Newspaper advertising spending is expected to experience more erosion as readership in the traditional format continues to decline.[14]

The main sources of newspaper ad revenue are local retailers, classified ads, and cooperative advertising. In **cooperative advertising**, the manufacturer and the retailer split the costs of advertising the manufacturer's brand. Cooperative advertising encourages retailers to devote more effort to the manufacturer's lines.

MAGAZINES One of the main advantages of magazine advertising is its target market selectivity. Magazines are published for virtually every market segment, offering meaningful target market engagement. Consumers choose to read magazines and spend considerable time doing so. Readers have high acceptance of the advertisements they see in a magazine, and readers are often driven to websites to seek additional information. The magazine industry in Canada is experiencing considerable challenges as readers migrate away from printed publications to online reading. In fact, Rogers Media has revamped its magazine content strategy to reduce emphasis on print publications and increase investment in digital content. As an example, it was announced that *Flare*, *MoneySense*, and *Canadian Business* would cease print publication to provide regular digital content online and through apps.[15] Although the printed magazine is threatened, magazines deliver content that readers choose to engage with. Content delivered digitally allows interactive engagement, providing a highly attractive advertising medium.

cooperative advertising
an arrangement in which the manufacturer and the retailer split the costs of advertising the manufacturer's brand

© Pixellover RM 4/Alamy

RADIO As an advertising medium, radio offers selectivity and audience segmentation, a large out-of-home audience, low unit and production costs, timeliness, and geographic flexibility. Local advertisers are the most frequent users of radio advertising. Like newspapers, radio lends itself well to cooperative advertising.

The ability to target specific demographic groups is a major selling point for radio stations. Radio listeners tend to listen habitually and at predictable times. However, radio is losing ground with Millennials as they are shifting their audio listening to other options such as Spotify, Google Play, or podcasts. Radio is responding by offering online streaming and mobile apps such as IHeartRadio.

Radio is still a highly effective medium for retailers, automobiles, and impulse products. Radio often enhances a media plan that combines other media because of the ability to inexpensively increase reach and frequency, particularly among commuters.

TELEVISION Television broadcasters are made up of national, regional, and specialty and digital networks, independent stations, and pay-television services. As a result, the television audience is highly fragmented.

In today's digital world and with Canadians' high consumption of online video, some are questioning the role of television. Yet Canadians continue to spend more time with television than any other medium. Canadians still prefer watching television on their larger television screens rather than their computer screens because they offer the best overall sound and visual experience, making it a highly engaging and influential medium. While Canadians' online video consumption is high relative to other countries, live traditional television viewing still continues to be the norm.

Canadians multitask while watching television. They are just as likely to be on their mobile device, laptop, or tablet while the television is on. Given this viewing behaviour, television advertisers are using the television commercial to drive the viewer to a website for further brand engagement.

PVRs—personal video recorders—are found in over half of all Canadian homes but their penetration has slowed as Canadians engage in alternative ways to access video, such as streaming and video on demand (VOD). For cable companies a real threat is "**cord cutting**"—discontinuing or never committing to a TV cable or satellite provider. With the increase in penetration of Netflix and its quality programming, more and more Canadians may choose to "unplug."

Advertising time on television can be very expensive, especially for network and popular cable channels. Specials events and first-run prime-time shows for top-ranked TV programs command the highest rates for a typical 30-second spot. **Infomercials** continue to be a successful television format as they are relatively inexpensive to produce and air. Advertisers use infomercials when the information to be presented to the consumer is relatively complicated.

OUT-OF-HOME MEDIA Outdoor, or out-of-home, advertising is a flexible, low-cost medium that may take a variety of forms. Examples are billboards, skywriting, giant inflatables, transit shelters, street columns, interior and exterior bus and subway signs, signs in sports arenas and airports, and ads painted on cars, trucks, water towers, manhole covers, and even people. Out-of-home is showing modest growth in advertising spending, as marketers incorporate a digital element in the campaign whether that be through the use of technology innovations with out-of-home properties, or integrated campaigns that include a digital component. Transit shelters offer interactivity, entire bus shelters can be interactive 3D advertisements, and increasingly marketers are using transit for visual domination by covering entire buses with ads or dominating interior buses and subway cars with their message. A recent technology innovation with out-of-home advertising generating excitement in the industry is the use of beacons. Beacons are small devices that enable content-related interactions with someone near the out-of-home property. As an example, a beacon-enabled billboard can send a notification to a mobile device of a person standing in the area of the beacon. The billboard may be advertising a new yogurt, and the notification to the person's mobile device could be for a discount on the yogurt at a store in the vicinity.[16]

cord cutting discontinuing or never committing to a TV cable or satellite provider

infomercial a 30-minute or longer advertisement that looks more like a TV talk show than a sales pitch

CASHMERE LENDS A HAND

Cashmere bathroom tissue knows that public bathrooms are too quiet, and for many people, a "shy bladder" creates an uncomfortable problem. Bathroom tissue is largely bought on price with little brand loyalty. In an effort to drive consumer decision making past price, Cashmere created a cheeky campaign using out-of-home advertising. The company inserted a device in 400 washroom stalls that, when activated, streams classical music. The stall user can control the volume, ensuring that a person's "shy bladder syndrome" is effectively managed.

TOO SHY TO GO?

Live stream our playlist to cover the sound of your stream at
NowStreaming.ca

Cashmere
BATHROOM TISSUE

Courtesy of Kruger Products L.P. — makers of Cashmere Bathroom Tissue

Another type of out-of-home media is place-based media. Place-based media communicate to consumers where they live, work, and play. Their content is created to be personalized and relevant. A variety of place-based media allows marketers to reach the right consumer at the right place at the right time,

mobile advertising
advertising that displays text, images, and animated ads via mobile phones or other mobile devices that are data enabled

such as washroom ads in bars, restaurants, schools, and fitness facilities. The Cashmere bathroom tissue ad is an example of place-based out-of-home advertising, and when you consider that approximately 70 percent of all brand decisions are made at the point of purchase, place-based media can be critical to include in the media mix.

Outdoor advertising reaches a broad and diverse market, making it ideal both for promoting convenience products and services and for directing consumers to local businesses. One of the main advantages of outdoor media over other media is its very high exposure frequency and very low clutter from competing ads. Outdoor advertising can also be customized to local marketing needs, which is why local businesses are often the leading outdoor advertisers in any given region.

THE INTERNET Internet advertising revenue continues to grow. Mobile advertising is fuelling the growth with an increase of over 75 percent in advertising dollar volume compared to 2014. As noted in Exhibit 17.5, in 2015 Internet dollar volume accounted for 36.7 percent of the total advertising dollar volume, far outpacing television, which fell to 26.6 percent. Internet advertising provides an interactive, versatile medium that is able to target specific groups and that offers rich data on consumer usage and measurable results.

Canadians are highly engaged online, spending more hours online than anyone else in the world. Online activity is still most often undertaken via a desktop computer, but increasingly (particularly among the 18-to-34-year-old group) a mobile device is used. Over 60 percent of Canadians own a mobile device and spend on average 2.5 hours on their phones per day. Mobile phones are intensely personal devices, with the owners at all times. Email is the number one reason why Canadians are online, followed by accessing social media sites. Canadians are more likely to access social media sites on their smartphones than their desktop and are more likely to spend more time on social media sites when they visit them via their smartphones. Facebook has over 25 million users in Canada. With such penetration, creative marketers are building social media into their integrated marketing communication plans.

As consumers use the Internet more and more, marketers are increasingly investing in digital campaigns that include search engine marketing, display advertising (banner ads), social media advertising (such as Facebook ads), email marketing, and mobile marketing.

Including advertising messages in Web-based, mobile, console, or handheld video games to advertise or promote a product, service, or idea, referred to as

EXHIBIT 17.5 NET ADVERTISING VOLUME BY MAJOR MEDIA IN CANADA, 2014–2015

Rank		2014 $ Millions	% of Total	2015 $ millions	% of Total
1	Television	3,361	27.8	3,342	26.6
	Internet—Desktop	2,890	23.9	2,984	23.8
	Internet—Mobile	903	7.5	1,620	12.9
2	Total Internet*	3,793	31.4	4,604	36.7
	Daily Newspapers	1,392	11.5	1,181	9.4
	Community Newspaper	925	7.7	841	6.7
	Online Newspapers	273	2.3	283	2.3
3	Total Newspaper	2,590	21.4	2,305	18.4
4	Radio	1,589	13.1	1,576	12.6
5	Magazines	472	3.9	412	3.3
6	Out of home	569	4.6	586	4.7
	Total	12,091	100%	12,543	100.00

Source: Media Digest, Canadian Media Directors Council, 2017 (http://cmdc.ca/wp-content/uploads/2017/01/CMDC-MEDIA-DIGEST-2017.pdf), page 21.

advergaming, is still popular. Some games amount to virtual commercials; others encourage players to buy in-game items and power-ups to advance; and still others allow advertisers to sponsor games or buy ad space for product placements. Many of these are social games played on Facebook or mobile networks, where players can interact with each other. **Social gaming** sites, which allow for social interaction between players, are also popular locations for digital ads, particularly campaigns targeting a younger population.

17-4b Media Selection Considerations

An important element in any advertising campaign is the **media mix**, the combination of media to be used. Media mix decisions are typically based on several factors: cost per contact, reach, frequency, target audience considerations, flexibility of the medium, noise level, and the lifespan of the medium.

Cost per contact is the cost of reaching one member of the target market. Naturally, as the size of the audience increases, so does the total cost. Cost per contact enables an advertiser to compare media vehicles, such as television versus radio, magazine versus newspaper, or one website versus another. The advertiser might then pick the vehicle with the lowest cost per contact to maximize advertising punch for the money spent. **Cost per click** is the cost associated with a consumer clicking on a display or banner ad. Although there are several variations, this option enables the marketer to pay only for "engaged" consumers—those who clicked on an ad.

Reach is the number of different target consumers who are exposed to a message at least once during a specific period, usually four weeks. Media plans for product introductions and attempts at increasing brand awareness usually emphasize reach. For example, an advertiser might try to reach 70 percent of the target audience during the first three months of the campaign. Reach is related to a medium's ratings, generally referred to in the industry as *gross ratings points*, or GRP. A television program with a higher GRP means that more people are tuning in to the show and the reach is higher. Accordingly, as GRP increases for a particular medium, so does cost per contact.

Because the typical ad is short-lived and because often only a small portion of an ad may be perceived at one time, advertisers repeat their ads so that consumers will remember the message. **Frequency** is the number of times an individual is exposed to a message during a specific period. Advertisers use average frequency to

advergaming placing advertising messages in Web-based or video games to advertise or promote a product, a service, an organization, or an issue

social gaming playing an online game that allows for social interaction between players on a social media platform

media mix the combination of media to be used for a promotional campaign

cost per contact the cost of reaching one member of the target market

cost per click the cost associated with a consumer clicking on a display or banner ad

reach the number of target consumers exposed to a commercial at least once during a specific period, usually four weeks

frequency the number of times an individual is exposed to a given message during a specific period

measure the intensity of a specific medium's coverage. For example, Red Bull GmbH, the Austrian company selling the energy drink Red Bull, might want an average exposure frequency of five for its Red Bull television ads to ensure the Red Bull company slogan, "Red Bull gives you wings," is well entrenched in the target consumers' minds. In other words, Red Bull wants each television viewer to see the ad an average of five times.

Media selection is also a matter of matching the advertising medium with the product's target market. If marketers are trying to reach teenage females, they might select advertising on the retailer Sephora's website. A medium's ability to reach a precisely defined market is its **audience selectivity**. Some media vehicles, such as general newspapers and network television, appeal to a wide cross-section of the population. Others—such as Zoomer, Runners World, HGTV, and Christian radio stations—appeal to very specific groups.

The *flexibility* of a medium can be extremely important to an advertiser. For example, because of layouts and design, the lead time for magazine advertising is considerably longer than for other media types and so is less flexible. By contrast, radio and Internet advertising provide maximum flexibility. If necessary, an advertiser can change a radio ad on the day it is to air.

Noise level is the level of distraction of the target audience in a medium. Noise can be created by competing ads, as when a street is lined with billboards or when a television program is cluttered with competing ads. Whereas newspapers and magazines have a high noise level, direct mail is a private medium with a low noise level. Typically, no other advertising media or news stories compete for direct-mail readers' attention.

Media have either a short or a long *lifespan,* which means that messages can either quickly fade or persist as tangible copy to be carefully studied. A radio commercial may last less than a minute, but advertisers can overcome this short lifespan by repeating radio ads often. In contrast, a magazine has a relatively long lifespan, which is further increased by a high pass-along rate.

Media planners have traditionally relied on the factors we've just discussed for selecting an effective media mix, with reach, frequency, and cost often being the overriding criteria. Well-established brands with familiar messages probably need fewer exposures to be effective, whereas newer or unfamiliar brands likely need more exposures to

This Molson commercial sings the praises of multiculturalism. With the climate created by the U.S. immigration and refugee ban announced by President Donald Trump in early 2017, this advertisement, which was originally created and aired before Canada Day 2016, resurfaced on social media. In less than a week, the ad received more than 10 million views. And it all happened without Molson or its advertising agency doing anything, but rather by consumers using it to speak to the political climate of the time.[17]

become familiar. In addition, today's media planners have more media options than ever before.

The proliferation of media channels is causing *media fragmentation* and forcing media planners to pay as much attention to where they place their advertising as to how often the advertisement is repeated. That is, marketers should evaluate reach *and* frequency when assessing the effectiveness of advertising. In certain situations, it may be important to reach potential consumers through as many media vehicles as possible. When this approach is considered, however, the budget must be large enough to achieve sufficient levels of frequency to have an impact. In evaluating reach versus frequency, therefore, the media planner ultimately must select an approach that is most likely to result in the ad being understood and remembered when a purchase decision is being made.

Advertisers also evaluate the qualitative factors involved in media selection, including attention to the commercial and the program, involvement, program liking, lack of distractions, and other audience behaviours that affect the likelihood that a commercial message is being seen and, ideally, absorbed. While advertisers can advertise their product in as many media as possible and repeat the ad as many times as they like, the ad still may

audience selectivity the ability of an advertising medium to reach a precisely defined market

There are many ways for viewers to avoid watching commercials, including the use of a PVR.

not be effective if the audience is not paying attention. Research on audience attentiveness for television, for example, shows that the longer viewers stay tuned to a particular program, the more memorable they find the commercials. With the strong penetration of the Internet, accessed from mobiles and tablets, consumers are more and more often multitasking while engaging in any particular medium. Hence the challenge exists to build media plans that utilize multiple mediums with a message that is consistent across the mediums.

17-4c Media Scheduling

After choosing the media for the advertising campaign, advertisers must schedule the ads. A **media schedule** designates the media to be used (such as magazines, television, or radio), the specific vehicles (such as Home Depot website, the TV show *The Blacklist* or *Kim's Convenience,* or the Saturday edition of the *Globe and Mail*) and the insertion dates of the advertising.

Media schedules are divided into three basic types:

- Products in the later stages of the product life cycle, which are advertised on a reminder basis, use a **continuous media schedule**. A continuous schedule allows the advertising to run steadily throughout the advertising period. Examples are Boston Pizza, which may have a television commercial on Global every Wednesday at 7:30 and billboards in 14 major cities across Canada over a 12-week period.

- With a **flighted media schedule**, the advertiser may schedule the ads heavily every other month or every two weeks to achieve a greater impact with an increased frequency and reach at those times. Movie studios might schedule television advertising on Wednesday and Thursday nights, when moviegoers are deciding which films to see that weekend.

- A **pulsing media schedule** combines continuous scheduling with a flighted media schedule. Continuous

advertising is simply heavier during the best sale periods. A retail department store may advertise year-round but place more advertising during certain sale periods, such as Thanksgiving, Christmas, and back to school.

- Certain times of the year call for a **seasonal media schedule**. Modo Yoga (formerly Moksha Yoga) and other fitness facilities tend to follow a seasonal strategy, placing greater emphasis on January as New Year's resolutions are being made.

Research comparing continuous media schedules versus flighted ones found that continuous schedules for television advertisements are more effective in driving sales than flighted schedules. The research suggests that it may be more important to get exposure as close as possible to the time when a consumer makes a purchase. Therefore, the advertiser should maintain a continuous schedule over as long a period as possible. Often called *recency planning,* this theory of scheduling is now commonly used for scheduling television advertising for frequently purchased products, such as Coca-Cola or Tide detergent. Recency planning's main premise is that advertising works by influencing the brand choice of people who are ready to buy. Mobile advertising is one of the more promising tactics for contacting consumers when they are thinking about a specific product, as demonstrated throughout the chapter.

17-4d Media Buying

Media buyers in advertising agencies purchase media. Media are bought through a negotiation process, although rate

media schedule designation of the media, the specific publications or programs, and the insertion dates of advertising

continuous media schedule a media scheduling strategy in which advertising is run steadily throughout the advertising period; used for products in the later stages of the product life cycle

flighted media schedule a media scheduling strategy in which ads are run heavily every other month or every two weeks, to achieve a greater impact with an increased frequency and reach at those times

pulsing media schedule a media scheduling strategy that uses continuous scheduling throughout the year coupled with a flighted schedule during the best sales periods

seasonal media schedule a media scheduling strategy that runs advertising only during times of the year when the product is most likely to be purchased

EXHIBIT 17.6   MEDIA SCHEDULING

Continuous Media Schedule	Advertising is run steadily throughout the advertising period
Flighted Media Schedule	Advertising is run heavily every other month or every two weeks
Pulsing Media Schedule	Advertising combines continuous scheduling through the year, with a flighted schedule during the best sales periods
Seasonal Media Schedule	Advertising is run only during times when the product is most likely to be purchased

cards do exist for most media. Advertising agencies are compensated on a percentage basis for the media they buy. The commission earned on media purchased generally runs between 12 and 15 percent. All media to be purchased is negotiable, despite published rate cards, and media rates really are a result of supply and demand. TV rates for a highly rated program that everyone wants to buy air time on, the Super Bowl for example, will be higher than the rates for another program that has much lower reach. With the proliferation of media choices today, advertisers, no matter the size of the budget, should be able to create impactful media buys. Media buyers need to be challenged to build media plans that achieve the clients' objectives at the lowest possible cost. When agency compensation for media is commission based, this can be a challenge.

17-5 PUBLIC RELATIONS

Public relations is the element in the promotional mix that evaluates public attitudes, identifies issues that may elicit public concern, and executes programs to gain public understanding and acceptance. Public relations is a vital link in a progressive company's marketing communication mix. Marketing managers plan solid public relations campaigns that fit into overall marketing plans and focus on targeted audiences. These campaigns strive to maintain a positive image of the corporation in the eyes of the public. Thus they should capitalize on the factors that enhance the firm's image and minimize the factors that could generate a negative image. In Canada, public relations practitioners can become members of the Canadian Public Relations Society (CPRS, **www.cprs.ca/aboutus**), which oversees the practice of public relations for the benefit and protection of public interest.

Publicity is the effort to capture media attention—for example, through articles or editorials in publications

or through human-interest stories on radio or television programs. Corporations usually initiate publicity by issuing a media release that furthers their public relations plans. A company that is about to introduce a new product or open a new store may send out media releases in the hope that the story will be published or broadcast. Savvy publicity can often create overnight sensations or build up a reserve of goodwill with consumers. Corporate donations and sponsorships can also create favourable publicity.

Public relations departments may perform any or all of the following functions:

- *Media relations:* placing positive, newsworthy information in the news media to attract attention to a product, a service, or a person associated with the firm or institution

- *Product publicity:* publicizing specific products or services

- *Corporate communication:* creating internal and external messages to promote a positive image of the firm or institution

- *Public affairs:* building and maintaining national or local community relations

- *Lobbying:* influencing legislators and government officials to promote or defeat legislation and regulation

- *Employee and investor relations:* maintaining positive relationships with employees, shareholders, and others in the financial community

- *Crisis management:* responding to unfavourable publicity or a negative event

17-5a Major Public Relations Tools

Public relations professionals commonly use several tools, many of which require an active role on the part of the public relations professional, such as writing media releases and engaging in proactive media relations. Sometimes, however, these techniques create their own publicity.

PRODUCT PUBLICITY Publicity is instrumental in introducing new products and services. Publicity can help advertisers explain the special features of their new product by prompting free news stories or positive word of mouth. During the introductory period, an especially innovative new product often needs more exposure than conventional paid advertising affords. Public relations

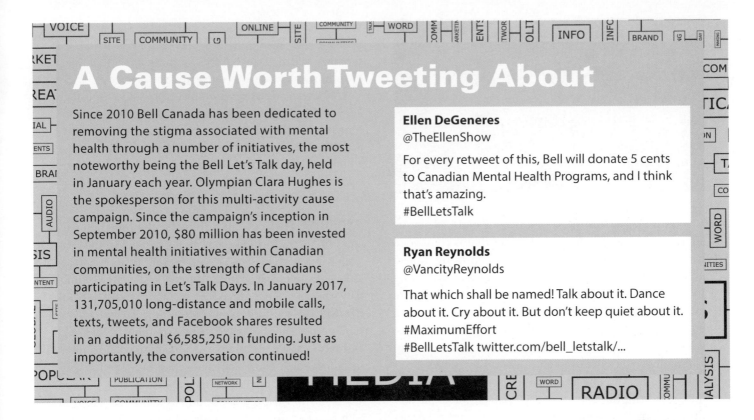

professionals write media releases, develop videos, post messages and videos on social media sites, in an effort to generate news about their new product. They also jockey for exposure of their product or service at major events, on popular television and news shows, or in the hands of influential people. The Dairy Farmers of Canada, in an effort to reinforce the positioning "take charge with milk" and build consumption among athletes as a restorative beverage after a workout, are often found offering samples of chocolate milk at major races and triathlon events.

PRODUCT PLACEMENT Marketers are increasingly using product placement to reinforce brand awareness and create favourable attitudes. **Product placement** is a strategy that involves getting a product, service, or company name to appear in a movie, television show, radio program, magazine, newspaper, video game, video or audio clip, book, or commercial for another product; on the Internet; or at special events. Good product placement— that is, product placement that reinforces brand personality and positioning—is placement whereby the brand is used in an appropriate context and by those that represent the brand's target group. Good product placement can also add a sense of realism to a movie, television show, video game book, or similar vehicle. More than two-thirds of all product placements are in movies and television shows, but placements in alternative media are growing,

particularly on the Internet and in video games. Digital technology now enables companies to "virtually" place their products in any audio or video production. Virtual placement not only reduces the cost of product placement for new productions but also enables companies to place their products in previously produced programs such as reruns of television shows. Overall, companies obtain valuable product exposure, brand reinforcement, and increased sales through product placement. *The Amazing Race Canada* is a prime example of a television program full of product placement— air carriers, credit card companies, automobiles and retailers, entertainment venues, and gas stations.

SPONSORSHIP Sponsorships are increasing both in number and as a proportion of companies' marketing budgets, with worldwide sponsorship spending reached over US$62 billion. North American sponsorship spending in 2016 was $22.3 billion, increasing over 4 percent from 2015.[18] Probably the biggest reason for the increasing use of sponsorships is the difficulty of reaching audiences and differentiating a product from competing brands in today's highly fragmented media environment.

> **product placement** a public relations strategy that involves getting a product, service, or company name to appear in a movie, television show, radio program, magazine, newspaper, video game, video or audio clip, book, or commercial for another product; on the Internet; or at special events

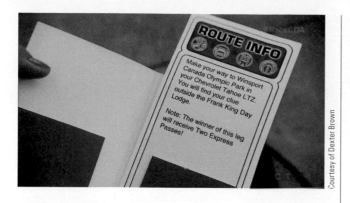

Courtesy of Dexter Brown

With **sponsorship**, a company spends money to support an issue, a cause, or an event that is consistent with corporate objectives, such as improving brand awareness or enhancing corporate image. Most commonly, companies sponsor events, such as festivals and fairs, conventions, expositions, sporting events, arts and entertainment spectaculars, and charity benefits. Sports and entertainment sponsorship are the top two areas where dollars are being spent, followed by causes. Scotiabank is heavily involved in a number of sponsorship initiatives with the objective of 70 percent of its philanthropic spending being directed to youth and children. Scotiabank sponsors hockey at all levels across Canada, including the NHL and over 8000 youth hockey teams. Scotiabank is also heavily involved in cultural sponsorships, most notably the Scotiabank Giller Prize.

A special type of sponsorship, **cause-related marketing**, involves the association of a for-profit company with a nonprofit organization. Through the sponsorship, the company's product or service is promoted, and money is raised for the nonprofit. In a common type of cause-related sponsorship, a company agrees to donate a percentage of the purchase price for a particular item to a charity, but some arrangements are more complex. Bell Canada Let's Talk campaign is an example of sponsorship referred to as cause marketing, whereby the investment of funds by a for-profit company is

to increase awareness of a social cause. A strategically planned and well-executed ongoing cause-marketing program will engage both consumers and employees, giving an organization a competitive advantage.

When an advertiser attempts to position itself with an event but has not been sanctioned as an official sponsor, the advertiser is participating in **ambush marketing**. There are plenty of examples of ambush marketing surrounding the Olympics because of the strong reach of the Olympic games coverage, yet the high cost of being an official Olympic sponsor.

EXPERIENTIAL People are an effective form of media and can deliver key messages about a brand to the consumer in a personal way. When trained people (ambassadors) communicate with consumers in a natural setting, they can offer deeper brand engagement. **Experiential marketing** is a form of marketing that helps the consumer experience the brand. When combined with brand ambassadors, the resulting experience can create a more memorable and emotional connection between the consumer and the brand. Adidas Sporting Goods hired an agency to train a team of ambassadors that engaged with running groups at a variety of retail partners across Canada. The purpose was to undertake wear-testing and receive feedback of Adidas running apparel.

COMPANY WEBSITES Company websites are wonderful public relations tools as they are used to introduce new products; promote existing products; provide information to the media, including through social media news releases; obtain consumer feedback; communicate legislative and regulatory information; showcase upcoming events; provide links to related sites (including

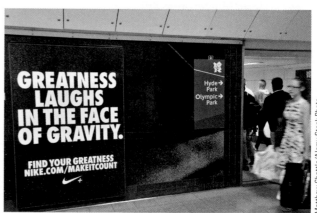

Matthew Chattle/Alamy Stock Photo

Nike have historically capitalized on the Olympic Games by creatively associating themselves with the games without paying the significant sponsorship dollars.

sponsorship a public relations strategy in which a company spends money to support an issue, a cause, or an event that is consistent with corporate objectives, such as improving brand awareness or enhancing corporate image

cause-related marketing a type of sponsorship involving the association of a for-profit company with a nonprofit organization; through the sponsorship, the company's product or service is promoted, and money is raised for the nonprofit

ambush marketing when an advertiser attempts to position itself with an event but is not sanctioned as an official sponsor

experiential marketing a form of advertising that focuses on helping consumers experience a brand such that a memorable and emotional connection is formed between the consumer and the brand

corporate and noncorporate blogs, Facebook, Twitter, LinkedIn, and Instagram); release financial information; interact with customers and potential customers; and perform many more marketing activities. Social media are playing a larger role in how companies interact with customers online. Indeed, online reviews (good and bad) from opinion leaders and other consumers help marketers sway purchasing decisions in their favour.

17-5b Managing Unfavourable Publicity

Although marketers try to avoid unpleasant situations, crises do happen. In our free-press environment, with extremely social media-savvy consumers, publicity is not easily controlled, especially in a crisis. **Crisis management** is the coordinated effort to handle the effects of unfavourable publicity or an unexpected unfavourable event, ensuring fast and accurate communication in times of emergency.

In 2015 WestJet faced four bomb threats within a five-day period, all of which fortunately turned out to be hoaxes. Rather than trying to keep a lid on the crisis, WestJet used social media to share information on the threats with the public, to reiterate their safety policies, and to thank local emergency crews who responded to the threats. Such transparency demonstrated proactiveness and a respect for all stakeholders. In addition, the response reinforced West-Jet's highest regard for safety and its commitment to honest and open communication with its customers. Importantly, the proactive nature of handling the crisis put WestJet in place as the source for the news and allowed for realistic and real-time handling of concerns by the public.[19]

17-6 DIRECT-RESPONSE COMMUNICATION

Direct-response communication is often referred to as *direct marketing*. It involves generating profitable business results through targeted communications to a specific audience. Direct-response communication uses a combination of relevant messaging and offers that can be tracked, measured, analyzed, stored, and leveraged to drive future marketing initiatives.

Direct-response communication provides the opportunity for one-to-one communication resulting in more targeted messaging and relationship building. Not-for-profits, whose objective is to raise awareness and generate donations, rely heavily on this form of communication because it can be tailored, its effectiveness is measurable, and it builds relationships that are key to effective stewardship.

Direct-response communication can be successful because the targeted communication is often more appealing to the consumer than mass-market communication. It is designed to meet consumers' unique needs, and they can learn about the product and make a purchase all at one time.

When creating a direct-response marketing campaign, keep in mind the following five key elements:

- *The offer:* The offer is the catalyst that stimulates the consumer to respond to the sales proposition in the message. The more time-sensitive the offer, the more immediate the need for a response.

- *The creative:* Special considerations are needed when developing a direct-response campaign; industry experts exist to assist marketers in this task.

- *The media:* To deliver a personalized message, direct response communication can use television, radio, newspapers, magazines, telephone, the Internet, mail, or any combination of these media.

- *Response and tracking mechanism:* The strength of direct-response communication is the ability to track results and report progress relative to the communication objective. Such metrics must be in place.

- *Customer call service:* Because direct response is built around an immediate consumer response, a call centre should exist to handle the calls.

17-6a The Tools of Direct-Response Communication

DIRECT-RESPONSE BROADCAST Direct-response broadcast uses television and radio. **Direct-response television (DRTV)** refers to television commercials that end with a call to action. DRTV can vary in length: short-form DRTVs can be 15, 30, 60, 90, or 120 seconds. Long-form DRTVs typically run for 30 to 60 minutes and are often referred to as *infomercials*. Because the return on investment with direct response is measured and is a critical key success factor, marketers don't want to pay regular rates for the spots. Thus stations offer discounts on inventory not sold, which explains why much DRTV is seen at odd hours in the day. Direct-response radio

crisis management a coordinated effort to handle all the effects of either unfavourable publicity or an unexpected unfavourable event

direct-response broadcast advertising that uses television or radio and includes a direct call to action asking the consumer to respond immediately

direct-response television (DRTV) advertising that appears on television and encourages viewers to respond immediately

isn't as widely used as direct-response television because of the nature of radio as a medium (portable and no visuals), but some advertisers will create messaging around the call-to-action tool (the phone number) to enhance the success of radio as a direct-response medium.

DIRECT-RESPONSE PRINT Direct-response print includes newspapers, magazines, and inserts. Often marketers will want to capitalize on the subscriber base of the magazine or newspaper to reach a certain demographic or psychographic. The decline in subscribers to these types of publications is affecting this tool. The ad is a direct-response print ad if it includes a direct call to action.

TELEMARKETING Telemarketing refers to outbound (a company calling the customer) and inbound (a customer calling the company) sales calls to secure an order. Inbound telemarketing is what we do each time we call a number to place an order. Outbound telemarketing is what we often are annoyed with. In Canada consumers can voluntarily register on a **Do Not Call List (DNCL)**. Companies that use telemarketing must update their database every 30 days to ensure that those registered on the DCNL are not contacted. Companies will be fined if they are found in violation of the DNCL.

DIRECT MAIL Direct mail refers to printed communications distributed to the consumer via Canada Post or independent contractors. The key is that the material is delivered directly to the consumer. Direct mail has two forms—addressed and unaddressed—and addressed direct mail generally receives higher response rates. A successful campaign must obviously reach the right person, be read by that person, and be persuasive enough to lead to a response. A critical element in a direct-mail campaign is the mailing list. Mailing lists can be internal (such as a company-created database) or can be rented or purchased from companies that specialize in lists. Another critical element is the creative—the envelope must be interesting and intriguing enough to be opened, and the enclosed letter must be persuasive enough to prompt a response. The dramatic rise in postage rates puts the success of direct mail as a communications tool in question.

DIRECT RESPONSE USING THE INTERNET The nature of the Internet suggests it can be a valuable direct-response tool, as it easily provides targeted communication that can be measured and analyzed. A common form of direct response using the Internet is email. When used with the intent to acquire new customers or convince customers to purchase something immediately, email communication can be a cost-effective direct-response tool. Email communication is targeted communication that provides the recipient with the opportunity to seek additional information or to place an order with the click of a mouse.

Michael D Brown/Shutterstock.com

direct-response print advertising in a print medium that includes a direct call to action

telemarketing the use of telecommunications to sell a product or service; involves both outbound and inbound calls

Do Not Call List (DNCL) a free service whereby Canadians register their telephone number to reduce or eliminate phone calls from telemarketers

direct mail a printed form of direct-response communication that is delivered directly to consumers' homes

STUDY TOOLS

IN THE BOOK, YOU CAN:

✔ Rip out the Chapter in Review card at the back of the book.

ONLINE, YOU CAN:

✔ Stay organized and efficient with a single online destination with all the course material and study aids you need to succeed.

Go to nelson.com/student to access the digital resources.

Reaching the Right Audience

One of the characteristics craft beer drinkers love most about craft beer is what it is not. It is not about one colour, one flavour, one label, and most certainly isn't about one loud, obnoxious (and often demeaning) ad campaign driven by big beer (see Molson, Coors, Budweiser, and Labatt). And yet the story cannot be told in a vacuum. It must come out. The question is, by what storytelling strategies and channels will that message be heard most effectively? Advertising is an obvious place to begin looking at communications alternatives, but it's not necessarily the most effective channel for craft beer, if only because "beer ads" have that big beer stigma attached to them.

"Advertising options have changed parallel with the digital age," explains Chuck Galea, VP Sales and Marketing. "Digital advertising allows for finer targeting and more easily produced metrics, so we want to be in those spaces online that we should be. At the same time, there are still traditional ad buys out there that we can select to tell our story." In the quaint, hyper-health-conscious, and active town of Collingwood, two local glossy magazines adorn trendy shops, cafés, and watering holes. *Mountain Living* and *Escarpment*, targeted at men and women readers respectively, "are super effective for us," Chuck says, "as they not only spread our message but show us as active members of the community."

Side Launch's current campaign reads, "It's not just a side launch, it's a celebration"—a message that is consistent with the brewery's landing page as well. "There is a crazy mountain bike community here, and our print ads tie into that, parallel with our landing page message. It's also important to be seen in local publications like that because part of the growth of craft comes from the buy local movement as well," Chuck continues.

At the time of writing, Side Launch was doing radio advertising as well, but not in the traditional sense. "I just signed a 12-week deal to be the 'beer of summer' on the Humble and Fred Show [Sirius XM show], and we're already seeing email traffic from people hearing us on that show. It's usually hard to measure radio, but this at least lets us see something tangible."

Of course, Side Launch came into being at a time when smartphones, social media, and inbound marketing were making both advertising and direct response infinitely easier for brands to tell their story at much lower costs. Small but ambitious young craft breweries do not have limitless ad buy budgets and wouldn't be able to compete with a macro beer ad buy, even if they wanted to. So targeted traditional media placement, mixed with a plethora of messaging options afforded by social media, helps increase reach that would have been unheard of 10 years ago. "But," cautions founder Garnet

Pratt, "all of those things make sense only if you're physically, visibly out there. It makes no sense for someone to see or hear the Side Launch name, be it in a magazine ad or a shared Facebook post, then not see us in the liquor retailers or on-premises establishments."

All of these considerations make a strong case for the concept of integrated marketing communications. Whatever the channels—social streams, satellite radio, digital or traditional advertising, or public relations events—the story must be frequent, consistent, and on-message.

Questions

1. The Side Launch message "It's not just a Side Launch, it's a celebration" appears in a print ad featuring a photograph of a cyclist in full gear preparing for a ride—not a single image of a beer in sight. Is this product advertising or institutional advertising? Explain.

2. Describe and justify Side Launch's choice of media for its advertising of the campaign mentioned in question 1.

3. What sorts of public relations tactics would have been suitably integrated with the "It's not just a Side Launch, it's a celebration" campaign?

Side Launch Brewing Company

Learning like never before.

nelson.com/student

18 | Sales Promotion and Personal Selling

LEARNING OUTCOMES

18-1 Define and state the objectives of sales promotion

18-2 Discuss the most common forms of consumer sales promotion

18-3 Discuss the most common forms of trade sales promotion

18-4 Describe personal selling

18-5 Discuss the key differences between relationship selling and traditional selling

18-6 List the steps in the selling process and discuss key issues

"You have to be odd to be number one."

—Dr. Seuss

18-1 WHAT IS SALES PROMOTION?

You don't have to be odd to be number one, maybe a little different, probably a little better, and certainly better known. Advertising, publicity, and direct response, as we learned in Chapter 17, can help create and maintain knowledge of a brand's positioning, improving the likelihood that the consumer will choose that brand over others. But with today's plethora of products and services, how can marketers increase the likelihood that the consumer will continue to see their brand as number one and buy it repeatedly? Equally important, how can they increase the likelihood that the consumer will even buy the brand for the first time? Marketing managers use the tools discussed in Chapter 17 with the inclusion of sales promotion tactics.

Sales promotion is a communications tool that provides a short-term incentive to the consumer or members of the distribution channel as a motivation to try or purchase a good or service immediately. Sales promotion is used because it can have more effect on behaviour than on attitudes.

Sales promotion is a key element in an integrated marketing communications program because, as with the McDonald's example just presented, when used strategically, it can enhance the success of a product or service. Sales promotion, in contrast to advertising, is easy to measure. Marketers know the precise number of samples handed out, the number of clicks through to a website, or the number of contest entries received. The Internet is providing even greater opportunities as blogs, Facebook, Twitter, and other social media sites are being used to deliver sales promotion offers, providing instant two-way communication. Sales promotion strategies are playing a greater role in communication plans as a result of increased competition, changing consumer media habits, the increasing use of online marketing tools and social media, consumers and retailers demanding more deals from manufacturers, and the continued reliance on accountable and measurable marketing strategies.

18-1a The Sales Promotion Target

Sales promotion is usually targeted toward either of two distinctly different markets. Sales promotion targeted to the final consumer is referred to as **consumer sales promotion**. **Trade sales promotion** is directed to members of the marketing channel, such as wholesalers and retailers.

18-1b The Objectives of Sales Promotion

Sales promotion usually has more effect on behaviour than on attitudes. Immediate purchase is the goal of sales promotion, regardless of the form it takes. The objectives of a promotion depend on the general behaviour of target consumers (see Exhibit 18.1) and the stage in the product life cycle. In the introductory stage of the product life cycle, sales promotion techniques are used to gain channel member support, as the firm works to build distribution and to achieve trial by the final consumer. As the product moves through the product life cycle, the firm's objectives change, as does the behaviour of the target consumer. For example, marketers who are targeting loyal users of their product in the late growth and maturity stages of the product life cycle need to reinforce existing behaviour or increase product usage.

In this situation, loyalty programs work well. With over 70 percent of purchase decisions made in-store, and with the increasing use of digital technologies by the shopper (more often than not the female head of household), loyalty programs that are accessed by mobile devices are increasing in effectiveness. London Drugs launched a loyalty program in 2016 that is easily accessed online or on a mobile device. Called LDExtras, the program offers enrolled consumers tailor-made rewards based on every $10 spent. Consumers can track their rewards level online or through a mobile app. The rewards offered are based on the purchases made by the consumer. So, for example, if the consumer purchases a digital camera at a London Drugs retailer or online at www.londondrugs.com, the reward offered would be such things as tripods or flashes or even a one-on-one session with an expert photographer. This loyalty program goes beyond offering the consumer savings for continued loyalty. It strives to enhance the relationship between the retailer and the consumer by offering experiences that complement products

consumer sales promotion sales promotion activities targeting the ultimate consumer

trade sales promotion sales promotion activities targeting a marketing channel member, such as a wholesaler or retailer

MCDONALD'S AND TIFF

McDonald's has been a sponsor of the Toronto International Film Festival (TIFF) for the past few years and their coffee is the "official coffee" of TIFF. TIFF runs for only ten days in Toronto, and during those ten days McDonald's wants a strong connection with the TIFF audience. It wants the TIFF audience to view McCafé coffee as number one. In 2015, to achieve a connection with TIFF film lovers, McDonald's created low-budget, indie-type films that were parodies of classic films, using coffee beans as the stars. During all ten days of the film festival, the McCafé coffee truck handed out free samples to attendees, and while the audience waited in line to see a film they could scan the coffee sleeve of the free sample to go directly to a website that all five videos were playing on. The branded content and sales promotion technique of sampling worked. There were over 450,000 views of the movies and over 2.2 million people were reached via Twitter.[1]

Niloo/Shutterstock.com

ton koene/Alamy Stock Photo

purchased. LDExtras capitalizes on digital marketing trends and consumers' growing use of mobile technology when making purchases and avoids the "sameness" of many loyalty programs that are based on points for redemption. These redemption programs have received a bad reputation lately due to points devaluation.[2]

Once marketers understand the dynamics occurring within their product category and have determined the particular consumers and consumer behaviours they want to influence, they can then select the appropriate promotional tools to achieve these goals.

18-2 TOOLS FOR CONSUMER SALES PROMOTION

Marketing managers must decide which consumer sales promotion devices to use in a specific campaign. The methods chosen must suit the objectives to ensure success of the overall promotion plan.

EXHIBIT 18.1 TYPES OF CONSUMERS AND SALES PROMOTION GOALS

Type of Buyer	Desired Results	Sales Promotion Examples
Loyal customers People who buy a particular brand most of the time or all of the time	Reinforce behaviour, increase consumption, change purchase timing	• Loyalty marketing programs, such as frequent-buyer cards or frequent-shopper clubs • Bonus packs that give loyal consumers an incentive to stock up or offer premiums in return for proof of purchase
Competitor's customers People who buy a competitor's product most of the time or all of the time	Break loyalty, persuade to switch to another brand	• Sampling to introduce another brand's superior qualities compared with competing brands • Sweepstakes, contests, or premiums that create interest in the product
Brand switchers People who buy a variety of products in the category	Persuade to buy one brand more often	• Any promotion that lowers the price of the product, such as coupons, price-off packages, and bonus packs. A promotion that adds value to a product such as a contest. • Trade deals that help make the product more readily available than competing products
Price buyers People who consistently buy the least expensive brand	Appeal with low prices or supply added value that makes price less important	• Coupons, price-off packages, refunds, or trade deals that reduce the price of the brand to match or undercut the price of the brand that would have otherwise been purchased

Source: Adapted from *Sales Promotion Essentials*, 3rd ed., by Don E. Schulz, William A. Robinson, and Lisa A. Petrison. © McGraw-Hill Education.

18-2a Coupons

A **coupon** is a certificate that entitles consumers to an immediate price reduction when they buy the product. Coupons are a particularly good way to encourage product trial and repurchase. They are also likely to increase the amount of a product bought. Coupons can be distributed in a variety of ways, such as directly on the package, on the shelf in store, at the cash register or on a coupon wall as you enter the store, in weekly flyers, in a free-standing insert (FSI), and through various Internet daily deal sites that can be accessed via a computer or the consumer's tablet or smartphone. In-store coupons are still popular because they directly influence customers' buying decisions. Instant coupons on product packages and electronic coupons issued at the counter now achieve much higher redemption rates because consumers are making more in-store purchase decisions.

Canadians continue to use their mobile devices to research and shop, creating yet another coupon distribution method for companies. A variety of cellphone mobile apps exist for coupons, saving the consumer from clipping coupons and remembering to redeem them at the checkout. Canadians, particularly those aged 18 to 34, are interested in receiving coupons on their mobile devices, either via email or text message, which they then conveniently use a point of purchase for savings.[3] As the use of smartphones as mobile wallets grows, so will the use of mobile couponing. Digital coupons can have up to ten times higher redemption than paper coupons, so they do work.[4] Social media are also increasingly being used as a couponing distribution method. Facebook introduced Offers a few years ago, which allows businesses to post an offer, such as a coupon on their Facebook page. Consumers can click on the Offer and have it sent to their email address for redemption at point of purchase. Over 53 percent of Canadians "like" pages on Facebook to receive deals or coupons, and over 40 percent follow brands or retailers on Twitter to receive immediate information on deals and coupons.

vectorfusionart/Shutterstock.com

SUPPORT FROM COAST TO COAST

Subaru Canada, Inc. is proud to be a strong supporter of triathlon and running races in Canada, with events now held coast to coast. Last year, these ultra-competitive events attracted some 25,000 athletes from across the country and around the world. We are thrilled to have helped ignite the competitive spirit here in Canada and we are equally excited about supporting elite and recreational athletes as they get out and experience the world firsthand.

$750 ATHLETE REBATE* ON YOUR PURCHASE OR LEASE OF A NEW SUBARU VEHICLE

To show our appreciation to those athletes competing in any of Subaru Canada, Inc.'s sponsored triathlon or running events, we are offering a $750 CASH BACK rebate on the purchase or lease of a new Subaru vehicle in Canada. Just see a Subaru dealer to make your purchase or lease arrangements. Fill out the application, gather the required documentation and send it to Subaru Canada, Inc. for processing. Visit www.subaru.ca > buying a subaru > current promotions > rebates for eligibility and to download an application.

SUBARU
Confidence in Motion

Courtesy of Subaru Canada, Inc.

18-2b Rebates

Rebates are cash refunds given for the purchase of a product during a specific period. They are similar to coupons in that they offer the purchaser a price reduction; however, because the purchaser must usually mail in a rebate form and some proof of purchase, the reward is not immediate. Manufacturers prefer rebates for several reasons. Rebates allow manufacturers to offer price cuts to consumers directly. Manufacturers have more control over rebate promotions because they can be rolled out and shut off quickly. Further, because buyers must fill out forms with their names, addresses, and other data, manufacturers use rebate programs to build customer databases. Perhaps the best reason of all to offer rebates is that although rebates are particularly good at enticing a purchase, most consumers never bother to redeem them.

18-2c Premiums

A **premium** is an extra item offered to the consumer, usually in exchange for some proof that the

> **coupon** a certificate that entitles consumers to an immediate price reduction when they buy the product
>
> **rebates** cash refunds given for the purchase of a product during a specific period
>
> **premium** an extra item offered to the consumer, usually in exchange for some proof of purchase of the promoted product

promoted product has been purchased. Premiums reinforce the consumer's purchase decision, increase consumption, and persuade nonusers to switch brands. Premiums that are developed as collectibles can encourage brand loyalty. A classic example of a long-standing premium program is the McDonald's Happy Meal. A premium mentioned earlier that meets all the criteria of a good premium strategy is the General Mills Honey Nut Cheerios "Bring Back the Bees" campaign. The fully integrated campaign was built around the long-term environmental impact of the disappearance of the honey bee. As a response to this environmental concern, General Mills offered packages of wildflower seeds free on the campaign website in hopes that, with more wildflowers planted, the honey bee population would have an improved environment for pollination. Not only does this campaign offer the consumer something for engaging with the brand, but it is also a socially conscious campaign tapping into the environmental consciousness of the cereal consumer, creating a very positive reason for purchasing Honey Nut Cheerios over the many cereal alternatives consumers can choose from.

Premiums can also include more product for the regular price, such as two-for-the-price-of-one bonus packs or packages that include more of the product. Another possibility is to attach a premium to the product's package.

18-2d Loyalty Marketing Programs

Loyalty marketing programs, or **frequent-buyer programs**, reward loyal consumers for making multiple purchases (see Exhibit 18.2). Loyalty marketing programs are designed to build long-term, mutually beneficial relationships between a company and its key customers.

A recent study by Bain & Company, a consulting firm, reported that increasing consumer retention by 5 percent could boost a company's profits by 25 to 95 percent![5] In highly competitive marketplaces, loyalty programs can enhance profitability by discouraging brand switching. A recent study conducted of North American consumers found that on a per-person basis, members were actively engaged in only about 7 of the 13.4 loyalty programs that they belonged to. Not being able to participate in the program on their mobile device and dissatisfaction with the loyalty

loyalty marketing program a promotional program designed to build long-term, mutually beneficial relationships between a company and its key customers

frequent-buyer program a loyalty program in which loyal consumers are rewarded for making multiple purchases of a particular good or service

EXHIBIT 18.2	TOP 10 LOYALTY PROGRAMS IN CANADA BY MEMBERSHIP SIZE
Number	**Program**
1	Air Miles
2	Shoppers Optimum
3	Canadian Tire Rewards/Money
4	Aeroplan
5	HBC Rewards/Hudson's Bay Rewards
6	Petro Points
7	Scene
8	Club Sobeys
9	CAA
10	PC Points/PC Plus

Source: Abacus Data (accessed from www.greedyrates.ca/blog/the-top-15-canadian-loyalty-rewards-programs/#.WPkIIIKZNTY).

program website are two key reasons that members do not engage with programs they have signed on to. A good loyalty program should support the brand promise, be personalized to the member, encourage redemption through an easy-to-navigate website and be accessed on a smartphone. If loyalty programs can improve personalization, satisfaction levels increase significantly. Members who redeem their points for relevant rewards (personalization) and instantly in-store are far more likely to be satisfied with the loyalty program. The more satisfied members are with the loyalty program experience, the more likely they are to become a brand ambassador and for the program to meet the promotion objectives.[6]

Well-established loyalty programs can provide marketers with data on consumer purchases, including what they buy, when they buy, and even sometimes why they buy. Such data can be used to create more personalized and sophisticated marketing programs. In the 90s Loblaws started the consumer loyalty program PC Points, which has evolved to the current PCPlus program. PCPlus uses points as currency for purchases made in store. The program is personalized. With each swipe of the loyalty card, consumer purchase data are recorded and weekly customized "offers" are provided to the member via their mobile device or online. The customized offers are based on purchase history and often encourage consumers to buy more products by offering bonus points on items. By simply swiping the loyalty card at the checkout, the member can redeem accumulated points for free groceries. As a product enhancement, the loyalty program is linked to PC Financial Cards. If the consumer uses a PC credit or debit card for purchases, additional points are collected.[7] With Canadians

exhibiting limited loyalty to grocery retailers, Loblaws hopes this program will keep them coming back.

Cobranded credit cards are an increasingly popular loyalty marketing tool. Royal Bank, Scotiabank, Canadian Tire, Costco, Holt Renfrew, and Aeroplan are only a few of the companies sponsoring cobranded Visa, MasterCard, or American Express cards.

18-2e Contests and Sweepstakes

Contests and sweepstakes are generally designed to create interest in a good or service and, thereby, to encourage brand switching. *Contests* are promotions in which participants use some skill or ability to compete for prizes. A consumer contest usually requires entrants to submit a proof of purchase and answer questions, complete sentences, or write a paragraph about the product. Winning a *sweepstakes*, on the other hand, depends on chance, and participation is free. Sweepstakes usually draw about ten times as many entries as contests do.

While contests and sweepstakes may draw considerable interest and publicity, they are generally not effective tools for generating long-term sales. To increase their effectiveness, sales promotion managers must make certain the award will appeal to the target market. Offering several smaller prizes to many winners instead of one huge prize to just one person can often increase the effectiveness of the promotion, but there's no denying the attractiveness of a jackpot-type prize. Tim Hortons' classic Roll Up the Rim to Win is an example of a sweepstakes that combines both large and small prizes to ensure many winners.

18-2f Sampling

Sampling allows the customer to try a product or service for free. Sampling has been proven to increase sales, so it's no surprise that new consumer products often rely on sampling to build the business.

Samples can be mailed directly to the customer, delivered door to door, packaged with another product, or demonstrated and distributed at a retail store or service outlet. Sampling at special events is a popular, effective, and high-profile distribution method that permits marketers to piggyback onto fun-based consumer activities—including sporting events, college and university fests, fairs and festivals, beach events, and chili cook-offs.

With the growth of social media, online sampling has become popular. Branded products run contests through social media sites, connect with fans, show commercials and offer samples of new products in exchange for "liking" the brand. Recognizing the role of influencers in purchase decisions, marketers engage with bloggers as a way to create widespread influence. Bloggers are offered products to try, and good blogs will differentiate between products that have been offered by companies and products that they have purchased themselves. Such a level of transparency increases trust and the value of the reviews to the reader of the blog. Minute Rice launched an influencer marketing campaign, #WeekdayWin. A number of food bloggers were engaged to share recipes that could be made in 15 minutes and addressed the daily challenges young families face in feeding children: picky eaters and a lack of time. All the bloggers (influencers) were parents, with the intention of creating conversations about dinnertime challenges, positioning Minute Rice as an easy, affordable, and healthy third ingredient in a balanced meal of one protein, one vegetable, and Minute Rice.[8]

18-2g Shopper Marketing

Shopper marketing used to be referred to as point-of-purchase (P-O-P) promotion. As part of an integrated marketing communications program, shopper marketing focuses on the consumer from the point at which the need is stimulated through to selection and purchase of the item. Shopper marketing strategy leverages that knowledge to create effective point-of-purchase opportunities in the store to engage and influence the shopper. It includes promotions such as *shelf talkers* (signs attached to store shelves), shelf extenders (attachments that extend shelves so products stand out), ads on grocery carts and bags, end-of-aisle and floor-stand displays, television monitors at supermarket checkout counters, in-store audio messages, and audio-visual displays. One big

sampling a promotional program that allows the consumer the opportunity to try a product or service for free

shopper marketing promotion set up at the retailer's location to build traffic, advertise the product, or induce impulse buying

advantage of shopper marketing is that it offers manufacturers a captive audience in retail stores. With the majority of brand decisions made in-store, point of purchase is a critical tool in the promotion mix.

18-3 TOOLS FOR TRADE SALES PROMOTION

Whereas consumer promotions *pull* a product through the channel by creating demand, trade promotions *push* a product through the distribution channel (see Chapter 16). When selling to members of the distribution channel, manufacturers use many of the same sales promotion tools used in consumer promotions—such as sales contests, premiums, and point-of-purchase displays. Several tools, however, are unique to manufacturers and intermediaries.

- **Trade allowances:** A **trade allowance** is a price reduction offered by manufacturers to intermediaries, such as wholesalers and retailers. The price reduction or rebate is given in exchange for a specific activity, such as allocating space for a new product or buying a product during a promotional period. For example, a local Best Buy could receive a special discount for running its own promotion on a Bose Bluetooth speaker.

- **Push money:** Intermediaries receive **push money** as a bonus for pushing the manufacturer's brand through the distribution channel. Often the push money is directed toward a retailer's salespeople.

- **Training:** Sometimes a manufacturer will train an intermediary's personnel if the product is rather complex—as frequently occurs in the computer and telecommunications industries. Running shoe retail salespeople in specialty running retailers are trained by manufacturers to ensure they can sell the right shoe for the right runner.

- **Free merchandise:** Often a manufacturer offers retailers free merchandise in lieu of quantity discounts—"Buy 10 cases and get 11." Occasionally, free merchandise is used as payment for trade allowances normally provided through other sales promotions.

- **Store demonstrations:** Manufacturers can also arrange with retailers to perform an in-store demonstration. In the wine industry, the sommelier is often invited to a restaurant for an evening to demonstrate the winery's wines and provide suggestions to guests of the restaurant that evening.

- **Co-op advertising:** Co-op advertising is a partnership between channel members with the intent of sharing in the cost of advertising directed at the final consumer to improve sales. More often than not, the partnership is between the manufacturer (who is named in the advertisement) and the retailer. The manufacturer repays the retailer for all or some of the cost of the advertisement.

- **Business meetings, conventions, and trade shows:** Trade association meetings, conferences, and conventions are important aspects of sales promotion and a growing, multibillion-dollar market. At these shows, manufacturers, distributors, and other vendors can display their goods and describe their services to customers and potential customers. Trade shows have been uniquely effective in introducing new products; they can establish products in the marketplace more quickly than advertising, direct marketing, or sales calls. Companies participate in trade shows to attract and identify new prospects, serve current customers, introduce new products, increase corporate image, test the market response to new products, enhance corporate morale, and gather competitive product information.*

Trade promotions are popular among manufacturers for many reasons. Trade sales promotion tools help manufacturers gain new distributors for their products, obtain wholesaler and retailer support for consumer sales promotions, build or reduce dealer inventories, and improve trade relations. Car manufacturers annually sponsor dozens of auto shows for consumers. The shows attract millions of consumers, providing dealers with both increased store traffic and good leads.

18-4 PERSONAL SELLING

Personal selling is direct communication between a sales representative and one or more prospective buyers in an attempt to influence each other in a purchase situation. In a sense, all business people are

trade allowance a price reduction offered by manufacturers to intermediaries, such as wholesalers and retailers

push money money offered to channel intermediaries to encourage them to push products—that is, to encourage other members of the channel to sell the products

*© Cengage

ADVANTAGES OF PERSONAL SELLING

▸ Personal selling provides a detailed explanation or demonstration of the product. This capability is especially needed for goods and services that are complex or new.

▸ The sales message can be varied according to the motivations and interests of each prospective customer. Moreover, when the prospect has questions or raises objections, the salesperson is there to provide explanations. In contrast, advertising and sales promotion can respond only to the objections the copywriter thinks are important to customers.

▸ Personal selling can be directed only to qualified prospects. Other forms of promotion include some unavoidable waste because many people in the audience are not prospective customers.

▸ Personal selling costs can be controlled by adjusting the size of the sales force (and resulting expenses) in one-person increments. On the other hand, advertising and sales promotion must often be purchased in fairly large amounts.

▸ Perhaps the most important advantage is that personal selling is considerably more effective than other forms of promotion in obtaining a sale and gaining a satisfied customer.

EXHIBIT 18.3	COMPARISON OF PERSONAL SELLING AND ADVERTISING/SALES PROMOTION	
Personal selling is more important when…	**Advertising and sales promotion are more important when…**
The product has a high value.	The product has a low value.
It is a custom-made product.	It is a standardized product.
There are few customers.	There are many customers.
The product is technically complex.	The product is easy to understand.
Customers are concentrated.	Customers are geographically dispersed.
Examples: insurance policies, custom windows, airplane engines	**Examples:** soap, magazine subscriptions, cotton T-shirts

© Cengage

18-5 RELATIONSHIP SELLING

Until recently, marketing theory and practice concerning personal selling focused almost entirely on a planned presentation to prospective customers for the sole purpose of making the sale. Today, personal selling emphasizes the relationship that develops between a salesperson and a buyer. The traditional sales process emphasized persuasion; today, the sales process is a multistage process that involves building, maintaining, and enhancing interactions with customers to develop long-term satisfaction through mutually beneficial partnerships. The sales process today is often referred to as **relationship selling** or **consultative selling**. With relationship selling, the objective is to build long-term branded relationships with consumers and buyers. Thus the focus is on building mutual trust between the buyer and seller through the delivery of anticipated, long-term, value-added benefits to the buyer.

Relationship or consultative salespeople, therefore, need to become consultants, partners, and problem solvers for their customers. They strive to build long-term relationships with key accounts by developing trust over time. The emphasis shifts from a one-time sale to a long-term relationship in which the salesperson works with the customer to develop solutions for enhancing the customer's bottom line. Research has shown that positive customer–salesperson relationships contribute to trust, increased customer loyalty, and the intent to continue the relationship with the salesperson.[9] Thus relationship selling promotes a win–win situation for buyer and seller.

> **relationship selling (consultative selling)** a multistage sales process that involves building, maintaining, and enhancing interactions with customers for the purpose of developing long-term satisfaction through mutually beneficial partnerships

salespeople. An individual may be a plant manager, a chemist, an engineer, or a member of any profession and yet still have to sell. During a job search, applicants must sell themselves to prospective employers in the interview.

Personal selling offers several advantages over other forms of promotion.

Personal selling may also work better than other forms of promotion given certain customer and product characteristics. Generally speaking, personal selling becomes more important as the number of potential customers decreases, as the complexity of the product increases, and as the value of the product grows (see Exhibit 18.3). For highly complex goods, such as business jets or private communication systems, a salesperson is needed to determine the prospective customer's needs, explain the product's basic advantages, propose the exact features and accessories that will meet the client's needs, and establish a support plan for installation or use.

EXHIBIT 18.4	KEY DIFFERENCES BETWEEN TRADITIONAL SELLING AND RELATIONSHIP SELLING	
Traditional Personal Selling	**Relationship or Consultative Selling**	
Sell products (goods and services)	Sell advice, assistance, and counsel	
Focus on closing sales	Focus on improving the customer's bottom line	
Limited sales planning	Consider sales planning as top priority	
Spend most contact time telling customers about product	Spend most contact time attempting to build a problem-solving environment with the customer	
Conduct product-specific needs assessment	Conduct discovery in the full scope of the customer's operations	
"Lone wolf" approach to the account	Team approach to the account	
Proposals and presentations are based on pricing and product features	Proposals and presentations are based on profit impact and strategic benefits to the customer	
Sales follow-up is short term, focused on product delivery	Sales follow-up is long term, focused on long-term relationship enhancement	

Source: Robert M. Peterson, Patric L. Schul, and George H. Lucas, Jr., "Consultative Selling: Walking the Walk in the New Selling Environment", *National Conference on Sales Management Proceedings*, 140–41, March 1996.

The immediacy of communication provided by email and mobile messaging allows the relationship between buyer and seller to develop more quickly and strengthen sooner.

The result of relationship selling tends to be loyal customers who purchase from the company time after time. A relationship-selling strategy focused on retaining customers costs a company less than constantly prospecting and selling to new customers.

Relationship selling provides many advantages over traditional selling in the consumer goods market. Still relationship selling is more often used in selling situations for installation goods, such as heavy machinery or computer systems, and services, such as airlines and insurance, than for consumer goods. Exhibit 18.4 lists the key differences between traditional personal selling and relationship or consultative selling. These differences will become more apparent as we explore the personal selling process later in the chapter.

18-6 THE SELLING PROCESS

sales process (sales cycle) the set of steps a salesperson goes through to sell a particular product or service

Completing a sale actually requires several steps. The **sales process**, or **sales cycle**, is simply the set of steps a salesperson goes through to sell a particular product or service. The sales process or cycle can be unique for each product or service, depending on the features of the product or service, the characteristics of customer segments, and the internal processes in place within the firm, such as how leads are gathered.

Some sales take only a few minutes, but others may take much longer to complete. Sales of technical products, such as a Bombardier rail vehicle and customized goods and services typically take many months, perhaps even years, to complete. On the other end of the spectrum, sales of less technical products, such as office supplies, are generally more routine and may take only a few days. Whether a salesperson spends a few minutes or a few years on a sale, seven basic steps make up the personal selling process:

1. Generating leads
2. Qualifying leads
3. Approaching the customer and probing needs
4. Developing and proposing solutions
5. Handling objections
6. Closing the sale
7. Following up

Like other forms of promotion, these steps of selling follow the AIDA (attention, interest, desire, action) concept discussed in Chapter 16. Once a salesperson has located a prospect with the authority to buy, he or she tries to get the prospect's attention. The salesperson can generate interest through an effective sales proposal and presentation that have been developed after a thorough needs assessment. After developing the customer's initial desire (preferably during the presentation of the sales proposal), the salesperson closes by trying to get an agreement to buy. Follow-up after the sale, the final step in the selling process, not only lowers cognitive dissonance (refer to Chapter 6) but also may open up opportunities to discuss future sales. Effective follow-up can also lead to repeat business in which the process may start all over again at the needs assessment step.

Exhibit 18.5 outlines the objectives of each step in the selling process and some key activities that occur at each step.

Traditional selling and relationship selling follow the same basic steps. They differ in the relative importance placed on key steps in the process. Traditional selling efforts are transaction oriented, focusing on generating as many leads as possible, making as many presentations as possible, and closing as many sales as possible. In contrast, the salesperson practising relationship selling

EXHIBIT 18.5 STEPS IN THE SELLING PROCESS

Step	Objective	Comments
1. Generating leads	Identification of those firms and people most likely to buy	Leads can be generated through advertising, websites, trade shows, direct mail, and telemarketing. Networking is a great tool for generating leads. Referrals from current clients are strong leads.
2. Qualifying leads	To determine if the lead has a recognized need, the buying power, and the receptivity and accessibility to meet and discuss the potential deal	It can be more cost effective to use a sales support person or a prequalification system to complete the qualification process. Company websites are useful here.
3. Approaching the customer and probing needs	To gather information and decide how best to approach the prospect	Information sources include websites, directories, colleagues who may know the prospect, as well as current company salespeople. The ultimate goal is to conduct a *needs assessment* of the prospect to build a client profile.
4. Developing and proposing solutions	To create the solution and prepare the presentation that will effectively deliver the solution	To present successfully, the salesperson must be well prepared. Engaging the customer in the presentation is critical, and the presentation should be explicitly tied to the prospect's expressed interest.
5. Handling objections	To be prepared to engage in *negotiation*-type discussions with the customer	The ability to handle objections must be rehearsed so that they are handled flawlessly in the presentation. If the salesperson is not confident in handling an objection, it is best to be honest, acknowledge the objection, and communicate that an answer will be forthcoming.
6. Closing the sale	To obtain a commitment	The most difficult part of the presentation is often the close. A good salesperson will know, as the presentation evolves, how to close by observing signals provided by the client. This point in the selling process involves negotiation to ensure all parties' needs are met.
7. Following up	To ensure that the customer is satisfied	The salesperson must ensure that the promises made during the presentation are all met. To ensure repeat sales, the customer must not feel abandoned.

emphasizes an upfront investment in the time and effort needed to uncover each customer's specific needs and wants and meet them with the product or service offering. By doing the homework upfront, the salesperson creates the conditions necessary for a relatively straightforward close. Then a salesperson with strong relationship selling skills will follow up regularly to build and maintain a long-term relationship, as it is far more expensive to gain a new customer than it is to retain a current one. Relationship-selling theorists suggest that in addition to knowing the client well, salespeople should develop mutual trust with their prospect at the outset. Salespeople must sell themselves before they can sell the product. The goal from the outset is to ensure that the customer trusts that the salesperson is committed to continually meeting his or her needs in the most efficient and effective way possible.

18-6a Some Key Issues in Each Step of the Selling Process

Lead generation or **prospecting** is the lifeblood of an effective sales team as it ensures new customers are constantly being sought. Before the advent of more sophisticated methods of lead generation, most prospecting was done through **cold calling**—a form of lead generation in which the salesperson approaches potential buyers without any prior knowledge of the prospects' needs or financial status. Although this method is still used, many sales managers have realized the inefficiencies of having their top salespeople use their valuable selling time cold calling, and today this form of prospecting is often left to an internal sales support person.

A highly effective tool for gaining new clients or **referrals** is **networking**. Networking is using friends, business contacts, co-workers, acquaintances, and fellow members in professional and civic organizations to identify potential clients. Indeed, some national networking clubs have been started for the sole purpose of generating leads and providing valuable business advice.

Social media are also providing an opportunity for networking. LinkedIn is one such example. LinkedIn, a member-based social media tool with demonstrated effectiveness for creating connections and online networking, offers Sales Navigator, an online

lead generation (prospecting) identification of those firms and people most likely to buy the seller's offerings

cold calling a form of lead generation in which the salesperson approaches potential buyers without any prior knowledge of the prospects' needs or financial status

referrals recommendations to a salesperson from a customer or business associate

networking the use of friends, business contacts, co-workers, acquaintances, and fellow members in professional and civic organizations to identify potential clients

tool that helps sales professionals easily find and engage with the right prospects through social selling.

Social selling is about leveraging your social network to find the right prospects, build trusted relationships, and through such activities achieve sales targets. Social selling techniques can lead to better leads, enhancing the sales prospecting process and eliminating the need for cold calling. With social selling and tools such as LinkedIn's Sales Navigator, the salesperson can build and maintain relationships within a much larger network far more efficiently. To enhance the success of social selling, salespeople should ensure that they have created a professional brand for themselves. With the breadth of contacts that can be acquired through social selling, buyers can be selective, choosing only to work with salespeople whom they trust. A salesperson who demonstrates knowledge of the industry and is an active participant in the industry through a LinkedIn profile and other social media is more likely to be trusted.

Leads generated through any method do not necessarily warrant a sales call. **Lead qualification** involves determining the sales prospect's (1) recognized need, (2) buying power, and (3) receptivity and accessibility. Companies must be diligent in ensuring that the lead offers potential. Companies are using social media to drive prospects to their websites and are then using Web analytics to determine potential or to qualify leads. Website analytics offer the opportunity to measure the length of time people stay on a website, what they pay attention to on the website, and how often they return. Companies set up their websites so that visitors are encouraged to register, indicate the products and services they are interested in, and provide information on their time frame and resources. Leads from the website can then be prioritized and transferred to salespeople.

Before the actual sales call, a salesperson needs to conduct as much research as possible on all leads. This process is called the **preapproach** and ensures that the salesperson has enough prospect knowledge to engage them and keep them engaged throughout the actual presentation. A thorough preapproach will ensure

Sales professionals are increasingly using online networking sites, such as LinkedIn, to connect with targeted leads and clients around the world. LinkedIn is a business-oriented social networking site with more than 360 million registered users that allows its members to exchange knowledge, ideas, and opportunities in an online forum, 24 hours a day, seven days a week.

a consultative approach to selling. The salesperson's ultimate goal is to conduct a **needs assessment**, a determination of the customer's specific needs and wants and the range of options the customer has for satisfying them. In other words, the salesperson needs to find out as much as possible about the prospect's situation. The salesperson should determine how to maximize the fit between what the firm can offer and what the prospective customer wants. As part of the needs assessment, the consultative salesperson must know everything there is to know about the following:

- *The product or service:* The consultative salesperson must be an expert on his or her product or service, including performance comparisons with the competition, other customers' experiences with the product, and current advertising and promotional campaign messages
- *Customers and their needs:* The salesperson should know more about customers than they know about themselves. The goal of such knowledge is to become a trusted consultant and adviser.

social selling leveraging social networks to find the right prospects and build trusted relationships to achieve sales goals

lead qualification determination of a sales prospect's (1) recognized need, (2) buying power, and (3) receptivity and accessibility

preapproach a process that describes the research a salesperson must do before contacting a prospect

needs assessment a determination of the customer's specific needs and wants and the range of options the customer has for satisfying them

"You never get a second chance to make a good first impression" is a saying that all salespeople should remember. In today's competitive marketplace, the first impression can make or break the sale, and the handshake is a simple gesture that speaks volumes.

- *The competition:* The salesperson must know as much about competitor companies and products as he or she knows about his or her own company. Competitive intelligence ensures that the salesperson can handle objections well.

- *The industry:* The salesperson must know the impact of economic and financial conditions on the industry, as well as current legislation and regulations.

The result of the research is the creation of a *customer profile* that helps salespeople optimize their time and resources. This profile is then used to develop an intelligent analysis of the prospect's needs in preparation for the development of the presentation.

Once the salesperson has gathered the appropriate information about the client's needs and wants, the next step is to determine whether his or her company's products or services match the needs of the prospective customer. The salesperson then develops a solution, or possibly several solutions, in which the salesperson's product or service solves the client's problems or meets a specific need.

These solutions are typically presented to the client in the form of a sales proposal presented at a sales presentation. A **sales proposal** is a written document or professional presentation that outlines how the company's product or service will meet or exceed the client's needs. The **sales presentation** is the formal meeting in which the salesperson presents the sales proposal to a prospective buyer. The presentation should be explicitly tied to the prospect's expressed needs and should as much as possible include the customer in the discussion.

Because the salesperson often has only one opportunity to present solutions, the quality of both the sales proposal and presentation can make or break the sale. Salespeople must be able to present the proposal with confidence and professionalism and be prepared to knowledgeably handle any objections.

At the end of the presentation, the salesperson should ask the customer how he or she would like to proceed. If the customer exhibits signs of being ready to purchase, and all questions have been answered and objections have been met, then the salesperson can try to close the sale. Closing requires courage and skill. If the salesperson has developed a strong relationship with the customer, and the proposal and presentation are well prepared, only minimal efforts are needed to close a sale. However, in all likelihood some negotiation will play a role in closing the sale. **Negotiation** is the process during which both the salesperson and the prospect offer concessions in an attempt to arrive at a sales agreement. Effective negotiators avoid using price as a negotiation tool. Instead, salespeople should emphasize the value to the customer, rendering price a nonissue. Salespeople should also be prepared to ask for trade-offs and should try to avoid giving unilateral concessions.

Once the sale is closed, it is not complete. A basic goal of relationship selling is to motivate customers to come back, again and again, by developing and nurturing long-term relationships. Most businesses depend on repeat sales, and repeat sales depend on thorough and continued **follow-up** by the salesperson. When customers feel abandoned, cognitive dissonance arises, and repeat sales decline. Today, this issue is more pertinent than ever because customers are far less loyal to brands and vendors. Buyers are more inclined to look for the best deal, especially in the case of poor after-the-sale follow-up (see Exhibit 18.6).

sales proposal a formal written document or professional presentation that outlines how the salesperson's product or service will meet or exceed the prospect's needs

sales presentation a formal meeting in which the salesperson presents a sales proposal to a prospective buyer

negotiation the process during which both the salesperson and the prospect offer concessions in an attempt to arrive at a sales agreement

follow-up the final step of the selling process, in which the salesperson ensures that delivery schedules are met, that the goods or services perform as promised, and that the buyer's employees are properly trained to use the products

18-6b Personal Selling in a Global Marketplace

More and more Canadian companies are expanding their marketing and selling efforts into global markets. As discussed in Chapter 4, salespeople selling in foreign markets should tailor their presentation and closing styles to each market. Different personalities and skills will be successful in some countries and absolute failures in others. For instance, if a salesperson is an excellent closer and always focuses on the next sale, doing business in Latin America might be difficult because Latin Americans typically want to take a long time building a personal relationship with their suppliers. With Canada's continued low economic growth, companies need to develop business outside Canada. While there has been a focus on the countries of Brazil, Russia, India, and China (BRIC) of late, companies also need to recognize the opportunities in Middle Eastern countries. The cultural, language, and religious differences in doing business in different countries can be learned and hence should not be a barrier to effective business development. A growing number of business schools, recognizing the importance of doing business abroad, are working to expose graduates to these markets and the cultural nuances that will increase the success of business relationships.[10]

THE CANADIAN PROFESSIONAL SALES ASSOCIATION (CPSA)

The Canadian Professional Sales Association (CPSA) is the only organization in Canada to offer the Certified Sales Professional (CSP) designation, which carries with it a recognized standard of excellence. The CSP designation is a sign of a committed, honest, and knowledgeable sales expert with training in the consultative selling method. The CSP designation is well recognized in industry today and validates an individual's sales expertise. Individuals with the CSP designation report that it provides them with a competitive advantage, and 95 percent of them experience an increase in sales after training. The CPSA offers a course called Essential Sales Training with an emphasis on professional selling and selling online. Advanced selling courses are offered, as are programs in sales management. Members who have gone through the training programs find themselves equipped with new ideas and techniques that, combined with their already well-honed tools, ensure continued success.

Source: "Learn How Top-Tier Sales Professionals Get Great Results, Canadian Professional Sales Asociation, 2017, https://www.cpsa.com/learning -development/sales-training (accessed May 2017).

EXHIBIT 18.6   RELATIVE AMOUNT OF TIME SPENT IN THE KEY STEPS OF THE SELLING PROCESS

Source: Data from Robert M. Peterson, Patrick L. Schul, and George H. Lucas Jr., "Consultative Selling: Walking the Walk in the New Selling Environment," *National Conference on Sales Management Proceedings*, March 1996; and Mark Ellwood, How Sales Reps Spend Their Time, http://paceproductivity.com/files/How_Sales_Reps_Spend_Their_Time.pdf (accessed March 2015).

18-6c The Impact of Technology on Personal Selling

E-commerce, or buying, selling, marketing, collaborating with partners, and servicing customers electronically using the Internet, has had a significant impact on personal selling. Virtually all companies are involved in e-commerce and consider it to be necessary to compete in today's marketplace. For customers, the Web has become a powerful tool, providing accurate and up-to-date information on products, pricing, and order status. The Internet also cost-effectively processes orders and services requests. Although on the surface the Internet might look like a threat to the job security of salespeople, it actually releases sales reps from tedious administrative tasks, resulting in more time to focus on the needs of their clients.

Experts agree that a relationship between the salesperson and customer will always be necessary. Technology, when used appropriately, can improve the effectiveness and efficiency of the salesperson and can and does improve customer relationships. Information readily available to salespeople through Internet research helps the salesperson to work from a strong knowledge base when meeting customers for the first time. Smartphones, iPads, laptops, and email ensure that customers and salespeople can be connected all day, every day. This 24/7 connectedness can result in customer needs being handled in a timely and efficient manner, reinforcing the customer–salesperson relationship. As mentioned earlier, trust is a key component of the relationship, and technology can help to build and maintain that trust.

STUDY TOOLS

IN THE BOOK, YOU CAN:

✔ Rip out the Chapter in Review card at the back of the book.

ONLINE, YOU CAN:

✔ Stay organized and efficient with a single online destination with all the course material and study aids you need to succeed.

Go to nelson.com/student to access the digital resources.

SIDE LAUNCH
BREWING COMPANY
CONTINUING CASE

Side Launch Brewing Company

From Hard Work Come Good Things

Lily Findlay, Territory Manager, breezes into one of Collingwood's many friendly watering holes and takes a seat at a table. A conversation begins, not dissimilar to one between any two friends sitting down to get caught up. They inquire authentically about one another's life and comment flatteringly about hair and shoes. The disclaimer here is that Lily is at work, and the person she's chatting with is one of her clients. That they look, sound, and act like friends is not a façade. As the Side Launch rep covering the brewery's home turf of Collingwood, Simcoe County (including Owen Sound, Stayner, and the Muskoka area), and all of Northern Ontario, which is massive, Lily tends to make a lot of friends. For someone who began her short tenure with the brewery running the merchandise retail area and giving tours, managing over 50 retail clients and 60 licensee accounts might seem like a leap, but Lily seems perfectly suited. She loves her job, and her clients love her for it.

Still, not even love comes without challenge. "My biggest challenge is getting the Side Launch story heard by clients, over the competition," she begins, "but if you can get them to hear the honesty, truth, and passion that you bring regarding your product, they tend to hear your story better, and remember you next time you come calling." Hard work, also a Side Launch credo, is carried out by everyone from the truck drivers and packaging crew to the leadership team and across the sales force. One day Lily is setting up tables and tents to host an event in Stayner, the next day she is manually cleaning the tap line for a restaurateur who carries her beer but can't figure out why there seems to be a "funny" taste coming out of the keg.

"Most people think, Oh, you're a beer rep, you just sit around all day with bar owners, drinking Side Launch. The fact is, that is probably the activity I spend the least amount of time on," she laughs. "I probably spend most of my time driving and problem solving." Founder Garnet Pratt adds with a grin, "Bar owners are not always the lowest maintenance people in the world." "And yet," explains Lily, "you must overlook or manage their emotions, even if you know they made a mistake, with missed orders for example, and scramble to get them their beer when they need it."

Professional sales is one of the most common and, honestly, one of the most valuable entry-level gigs a marketing student could ever acquire on

graduation from business school. Particularly with a small company, your role is more than just taking orders and delivering product, it's about representing a brand as its ambassador. All the advertising, public relations, social media posts, and sales promotions mean nothing without strong personal encounters between buyers and sellers. "We began and will always be based on grassroots communication with our customers and our consumers," claims VP Sales and Marketing Chuck Galea, who obviously looks for that grassroots character in all his salespeople.

Although Lily will admit that "selling is a grind, and it's a lot of driving and many extra hours problem solving," she also asserts, "But it's not [just] working—it's a passion that we all bring to our work at Side Launch." The back of her business card says it all: "From hard work comes good things."

Questions

1. How would you describe the approach to personal selling used by Side Launch, as demonstrated by Lily in the examples given?

2. What are some of the challenges faced by Lily and the other Side Launch sales reps as they go about their business of getting their beer into the hands of craft beer drinkers?

3. How does the hiring of sales people with "grassroots character" tie in with Side Launch's integrated marketing communications?

Side Launch Brewing Company

264

256

19 | Social Media Strategies

LEARNING OUTCOMES

19-1 Describe social media's role in an integrated marketing communication plan

19-2 Explain how to create a social media campaign

19-3 Evaluate the various methods of measurement for social media

19-4 Explain consumer behaviour on social media

19-5 Describe the social media tools in a marketer's toolbox, and explain how they are useful

19-6 Describe the impact of mobile technology on social media

19-7 Understand the aspects of developing a social media plan

Rawpixel.com/Shutterstock.com

"Social media is more about sociology and psychology than it is about technology."

—Brian Solis, digital analyst[1]

19-1 WHAT IS SOCIAL MEDIA'S ROLE IN INTEGRATED MARKETING COMMUNICATIONS?

Social media came crashing into our society first with turbulence, then disruption, and finally, complete transformation. While the Worldwide Web quickly made Internet use pervasive in the late 1990s, social media made the Web use absolutely ubiquitous ten years later. Now as we near 2020, it is unfathomable to imagine a time without Facebook, Twitter, Snapchat, LinkedIn, Instagram, YouTube, Pinterest, and many other attention-grabbing platforms. But commercializing that attention—suddenly mass produced on social media—took longer than expected, and even now stakeholders of social media are con-

social media collection of online communication tools that facilitate conversations online; when used by marketers, social media tools encourage consumer empowerment

stantly striving to gain maximum efficiency from its overall reach and its complex roster of different players. Indeed, as a tool within the marketer's promotional toolkit, or integrated marketing communications (IMC), it has been a boon perhaps not seen since television reached its diffusion state in the 1950s and 60s. The eyeballs have just moved from one large screen to multiple smaller ones.

This massive global attention was not lost on the 2016 U.S. presidential campaign. For better or worse, the campaign was rife with off-hand tweets from all candidates, but none more prolific than eventual winner Donald Trump. "He has this direct pipeline to the American people, where he can talk back and forth," former White House Press Secretary Sean Spicer explained after Trump swept to victory.[2] While opponents and pundits had hoped the president-elect would curb his tweeting, it continued unabated, allowing him, as Spicer put it, to "put his thoughts out and hear what they're thinking in a way that no one's ever been able to do before."[3]

Social media have also changed the way that marketers communicate—from mass messages locally to intimate conversations globally. As marketers continue to delve into social media, they must remember that social media is meant to be a social experience, not a marketing experience. That is, it has reshaped the natural instinct of promoters from one-way content production to two-way conversations and, ultimately, community-building. Marketers must remember, however, that the social and interactive nature of social media means that messages are shared across these communities and must be permitted to flow openly and freely. This means taking the good with the bad—companies must accept the fact that what appears on their Facebook page, for example, will not always be flattering.

Marketers who understand the power of social media are vigilant in observing consumer behaviour online and respond immediately to negative situations, mitigating the adverse influence on the brand. Moreover, brands that possess a great deal of brand equity do not have to respond to potentially harmful content on their social media sites—they simply let their online community handle the dirty work for them.

Social media as communication tools provide marketers with the opportunity not only to respond immediately but also to listen. Marketers who listen can tap into co-marketing—capitalizing on consumer input to create message content. Co-marketing relies on a continual dialogue with the consumer, who is empowered to vocalize likes and dislikes. Astute marketers use this information for continual improvement, as a source for message content, and to get ideas for mass-market campaigns.[4] Indeed, the culture of participation offered by social media may well prove to be the fifth P for marketing.

Social media offer more sophisticated methods of measuring the impact and effectiveness of the conversations, which is critical for the creation of new and innovative marketing communication campaigns. Facebook likes and shares can be measured, and the number of tweets and retweets on Twitter can be easily determined. It is necessary, however, as with traditional communication tools, that objectives be set at the start of the campaign. Marketers need to conduct research to determine the influence of social media activity on revenue, market share, and other marketing goals.

Currently, social media include tools and platforms like social networks, blogs, microblogs, and media-sharing sites, which can be accessed through a growing number of devices, such as computers, smartphones, ereaders, tablets, and netbooks. This technology changes daily, offering consumers new ways to experience social media platforms, which must constantly innovate to keep up with consumer demands.

Canadians are online addicts, ranking first in time spent online at 36.3 hours per month—one full hour longer than our American counterparts, who place second.[6]

19-1a How Canadians Use Social Media

If Canadians are online addicts, social media are our drugs of choice. According to Statista, 63 percent of Canadians had at least one social network account in 2017, and 75 percent of those had used either Facebook or YouTube.[7] Gen Z users are the most prolific users of social media, clocking in an average of 48 minutes per day, most of it through a smartphone rather than any other device.[8] Smartphone penetration in Canada is close to 75 percent, and it is clearly the most popular way to access social media sites. Smartphones have become an indispensable part of day-to-day living. Many people will not leave home without their smartphones, using them frequently throughout the day for many activities beyond phone conversation, thus transforming behaviour. While viewing traditional media, consumers are doing other things, such as watching a Twitter feed on their smartphones. Over 50 percent of television viewers claim to use their smartphones to access additional information on a product or service immediately after seeing the product or service advertised on TV. And they don't just search for the product—many people often make purchases using their smartphones. Smartphone research influences buyer decisions and purchases, with 50 percent of smartphone users making a purchase on their phone after having used it to research a product or service.[9]

The unprecedented penetration of smartphones and the continual advances in digital devices and social media tools have resulted in consumers who are willing to use a variety of media platforms. Today's consumer may have started watching a program on TV, continued watching it on a smartphone on the way home from school, and finished watching it in bed on a tablet. Therefore, marketers must create campaigns that deliver content on many platforms. For example, Netflix, the DVD video rental company turned video streaming company turned original content production company, leverages some of that very content to populate its many social media platforms. It then sits back and actively participates in the conversations it starts. In March 2017, Netflix posted a trailer for its original series *Death Note* on Twitter, using the message "Shall We Begin? #DeathNote," quoting the show's ominous voiceover. Within one week the post had been retweeted over 33,000 times and had

Shall we begin? #DeathNote

4zevar/Shutterstock.com

received over 55,000 likes.[10] Not to be outdone, the very same message on Netflix's Facebook page generated 1.5 million views in two weeks.[11]

With online spending by marketers outpacing TV spending in 2015,[12] one can see that marketers today are embracing online and social media alongside traditional media. The resulting shift from one-to-many communication to many-to-many communication provides tremendous opportunity but also tremendous risk. Social media transfer control to the audience. Thus the audience can be in control of the message, the medium, or the response—or all three. This distribution of control is difficult for some companies to adjust to, but for those that do and for those that listen, influence and consumer engagement can be significantly more successful.

Embracing this redistribution of control and using consumers to develop and market products is called crowdsourcing. **Crowdsourcing** describes how the input of many people can be leveraged to make decisions that used to be based on the input of only a few people.[13] Asking consumers to provide feedback on marketing campaigns and products and responding to the feedback increases the chances of success and also creates brand advocates. Crowdsourcing is the foundation of co-branding.

SOCIAL COMMERCE As mentioned earlier, consumers are not just seeking product and service information on their digital platforms, but they are increasingly making online purchases. **Social commerce** is a subset of e-commerce that involves the interaction and user contribution aspects of social media to assist in the online buying and selling of products and services.[14] Basically, social commerce relies on user-generated content on websites to help consumers with purchases. Pinterest quickly grabbed the position of market leader in the social commerce space as it basically defined the category of social commerce. Users collect ideas and products from all over the Web and pin favourite items to individually curated pinboards. Other users browse boards by theme, keyword, or product; click on what they like; and are then either taken to the original site or are able to re-pin the item on their own pinboard. Another social commerce site gaining in popularity is Etsy, a marketplace where people around the world connect to buy and sell unique goods. Etsy gives users the opportunity to share on Facebook, Twitter, and Pinterest boards. Social commerce sites often include ratings and recommendations (like Amazon.ca) and social shopping tools (like Groupon). In general, social commerce sites are designed to help consumers make more informed decisions on purchases.

Courtesy of Etsy, Inc.

However, like so many other battlefronts in social media, the overall category kind, Facebook, seems to have the final say. According to a 2016 study, Facebook had squashed all competitors with a dominating 64 percent of total social revenue, versus Pinterest's meagre second-place showing of 16 percent.[15]

19-2 CREATING AND LEVERAGING A SOCIAL MEDIA CAMPAIGN

Though still underutilized, social media's potential for expanding a brand's impact is enormous. Because social media's costs are often minimal and its learning curve is relatively low, some organizations are tempted to dive headfirst into it. However, as with any marketing campaign, it is always important to start with objectives. In keeping with the concept of integrated marketing communications (IMC) discussed in Chapter 16, this means ensuring that the social media objectives are consistent with the overarching objectives governing advertising, public relations, sales promotions, and personal selling. It is important to link IMC objectives (e.g., increase awareness of new product at product launch) to the most effective social media tools (e.g., Facebook, Twitter, and Instagram) and to be able to measure the results to determine whether the objectives were met. This, of course, can be accomplished only by creating SMART objectives, as discussed in Chapter 3. It is also important to understand the various types of media involved.

The new communication paradigm created by a shift to social media marketing raises questions about categorization. In light of the convergence of traditional and digital media, researchers have explored different ways that interactive marketers can categorize media types, typically arriving at three distinct classifications: inbound, earned, and paid media

> **crowdsourcing** the use of consumers to develop and market products
>
> **social commerce** a subset of e-commerce that involves the interaction and user contribution aspects of social media to assist in the online buying and selling of products and services

(discussed in Chapter 15; see Exhibit 19.1) to include digital media types. *Inbound media* are online content that an organization creates and controls. This includes a brand's websites, blogs, and all social media channels. The purpose of inbound media is to develop deeper relationships with customers. *Earned media* is a public relations term connoting free media, such as mainstream media coverage. In an interactive space, media are earned through word of mouth or online buzz about something the brand is doing. Earned media include viral videos, retweets, comments on blogs, and other forms of customer feedback resulting from a social media presence. When consumers pass along brand information in the form of retweets, blog comments, or ratings and recommendations, this is an example of earned media. In other words, the word of mouth is spread online rather than face to face. *Paid media* are content paid for by the company to be placed online. Paid media are similar to advertising efforts that use traditional media, such as newspapers, magazines, and television. In an interactive space, paid media include display advertising, paid search words, and other types of either direct online advertising or search engine optimization (SEO).

As a result, social media can really be thought of as an additional layer that many brands decide to develop. Some layers are quite deep—Doritos, Old Spice, and Nike have deep layers of social media since these are brands that people are talking about. Other brands may have more a more shallow social media layer and provide access on only one or two social media platforms. Ultimately, the depth really depends on the type of product being sold and the customer's propensity to participate in social media.

To leverage all three types of media, marketers must follow a few key guidelines. First, they must maximize inbound media by reaching out beyond their existing websites to create portfolios of digital touchpoints. This approach is especially helpful for brands with tight budgets, as the organization may not be able to afford much paid media. Second, marketers must recognize that aptitude at public and media relations no longer translates into earned media. Instead, marketers must learn how to listen and respond to stakeholders. This will stimulate word of mouth. Finally, marketers must understand that paid media are not dead but should serve as a catalyst to drive customer engagement.[16] If balanced correctly, all three types of media can be powerful tools for interactive marketers.

Moreover, marketers must embrace their social media followers as their most empowered brand ambassadors—and leverage their reach. In this way, individuals become not only spokespersons, but also media outlets. According to Social Media Examiner, Sour Patch Kids, one of international packaged foods company Mon-

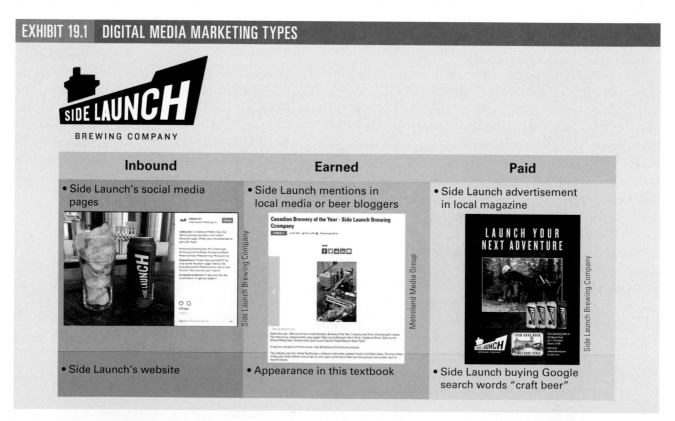

EXHIBIT 19.1 DIGITAL MEDIA MARKETING TYPES

Inbound	Earned	Paid
• Side Launch's social media pages	• Side Launch mentions in local media or beer bloggers	• Side Launch advertisement in local magazine
• Side Launch's website	• Appearance in this textbook	• Side Launch buying Google search words "craft beer"

dolez's brands, targeted teens by using one of teens' favourite social platforms, Snapchat, and one of its most popular users, Logan Paul, to pull an enormously successful social media campaign. Paul pulled off pranks on people labelled either "sweet" or "sour"—a nod to Sour Patch Kids flavours. The campaign then compelled followers to promote the next story across their network, accumulating over 120,000 new Snapchat followers.[17]

19-2a The Listening System

After determining how to integrate the social strategy into the greater IMC strategy, the next action a marketing team should take when initiating a social media campaign is simple—it should just listen. Developing an effective listening system is necessary to both understanding and engaging an online audience. Marketers must not only hear what is being said about the brand, the industry, the competition, and the customer—they must also pay attention to who is saying what. The specific ways that customers and noncustomers rate, rank, critique, praise, deride, recommend, snub, and generally discuss brands are all important. Negative comments and complaints are of particular importance, both because they can illuminate unknown brand flaws and because they are the comments that tend to go viral. Thus social media have created a new method of market research: customers telling marketers what they want and need (and don't want and need). Online tools, such as Google Alerts, Google Blog Search, Twitter Search, and others, are helpful in the development of efficient, effective listening. But there are probably none more trusted, more established, nor more ubiquitous in the space than Canadian-based Hootsuite. Created by Vernon, B.C.-born Ryan Holmes in 2008, Hootsuite has over 15 million users in 175 countries.[18] Its multiple uses and customizable interface help users deploy messages across all social channels efficiently, and it also tracks mentions, user habits, and patterns to assist companies in the daunting task of nonstop surveillance. In Exhibit 19.2, social media strategist Jeremiah Owyang outlines eight stages of effective listening. Listening to customers communicate about one's own brand can be very revealing, but using social media is also a great way to monitor competitors' online presences, fans, and followers. Paying attention to the ways that competing brands

EXHIBIT 19.2 EIGHT STAGES OF EFFECTIVE LISTENING

Stage	Description	Resources Required	Purpose
Stage 1: Being without an objective	The organization has established a listening system but has no goals.	Social media notification tools (Google Alerts)	To keep up with brand and competitor information
Stage 2: Tracking brand mentions	The organization tracks mentions in social space but has no guidance on next steps.	A listening platform with key word report capabilities (Radian6)	To track discussions, understand sentiment, and identify influencers to improve overall marketing strategy
Stage 3: Identifying market risks and opportunities	The organization seeks discussions online that may result in identification of problems and opportunities.	A listening platform with a large staff dedicated to the client (Converseon)	To seek out discussions and report to other teams, such as product development and sales; these teams then engage the customers directly or conduct further research.
Stage 4: Improving campaign efficiency	The organization uses tools to acquire real-time data on marketing efficiency.	Web analytics software (Google Analytics)	To gather a wealth of information about consumers' behaviour on their websites (and social media)
Stage 5: Measuring customer satisfaction	The organization collects information about satisfaction, including measures of sentiment.	Insight platforms that offer online focus group solutions	To measure the impact of satisfaction or frustration during interaction
Stage 6: Responding to customer inquiry	The organization identifies customers where they are (e.g., Twitter).	A customer service team is allowed to make real-time responses	To generate a high sense of satisfaction for customers
Stage 7: Understanding customers better	The organization adds social information to demographics and psychographics to gain better consumer profiles.	Social customer relationship management (CRM) systems to sync data	To create a powerful analytical tool by marrying the organization's database and social media. (See Chapter 9 for more on CRM.)
Stage 8: Being proactive and anticipating customer demands	The organization examines previous patterns of data and social behaviour to anticipate needs.	Advanced customer database with predictive application (yet to be created)	To modify the social media strategy to pre-empt consumer behaviour modifications on the basis of trends

Sources: Jeremiah Owyang, "Web Strategy Matrix: The Eight Stages of Listening", *Web Strategy*, November 10, 2009; and Jim Sterne, *Social Media Metrics* (Hoboken, NJ: John Wiley & Sons, 2010).

attract and engage with their customers can be particularly enlightening for both small businesses and global brands.

19-2b Social Media Strategies

As we have been stating over the last few pages, consistency between the social media plan and the overall IMC plan is key. This begins with having common SMART objectives shared across the IMC components. After that, and listening to the social media environment, discussed previously, the organization should develop strategies for its social media team to carry out in pursuit of stated objectives. These strategies must be developed with a clear understanding of how social media change the communication dynamic with and for customers. Remember—attempting to reach a mass audience with a static message will never be as successful as influencing people through conversation. Marketing managers must create strategies that reflect this reality. Here are some practical ideas that marketing managers should consider in the creation of strategies:

- **Listen, learn, respond, repeat:** Monitor what is being said about the brand and competitors, and glean insights about audiences. Use online tools and do research to implement the best social media practices. Establishing a listening strategy will assist with integrating a social message within the framework of the overarching IMC strategy.

- **Build relationships and trust:** Cultivate trust through meaningful dialogue with stakeholders by giving them compelling content across a variety of social media. Engage in conversations and answer customers' questions candidly, which will both increase Web traffic and boost your search engine ranking.

- **Promote products and services:** The clearest path to increasing the bottom line by using social media is to get customers talking about products and services, which ultimately translates into sales. Do this using the rich media afforded by the social media channels discussed in this chapter. Sticking to text only is so 2004. Share audio, video, and photos of people interacting with your brand.

- **Manage your reputation:** Develop and improve the brand's reputation by responding to comments and criticism that appear on blogs and in forums. Additionally, organizations can position themselves as helpful and benevolent by participating in other forums and discussions.

- **Improve customer service:** Customer comments about products and services will not always be positive.

Use social media to search out displeased customers and engage them directly to solve their service issues.

- **Champion those who champion you:** In the era of social media, anyone can be a rock star, news anchor, coach, mentor, advocate, and brand champion. When people fall in love with your brand or products and are compelled to share their love story publicly through social media—follow them, like them, repost them. Their influence can go farther than you can imagine.

19-3 EVALUATION AND MEASUREMENT OF SOCIAL MEDIA

Social media are revolutionizing the way organizations communicate with stakeholders. Given the relative ease and efficiency with which organizations can use social media, a positive return on investment (ROI) is likely, but as for anything else, the greater your investment in time, money, and human resources, the greater return you can expect. Hootsuite, the global leader in social media management software, provides a relatively simple equation for calculating social media ROI:

$$\text{ROI} = (\text{Profit}/\text{Social Media investment}) \times 100$$

Put simply, if you can attribute $1000 in sales directly to a social campaign that costs $500 (salaries, search engine optimization, etc.), you could easily calculate the profit as $500 ($1000 − $500). Entering these into the equation above, you would arrive at an ROI of 100%.

$$\text{ROI} = (\$500/\$500) \times 100$$

But as the Hootsuite blogger Sarah Dawley points out, the equation has its limits because, like any other tool within the integrated marketing communications (IMC) portfolio, not all revenue can be attributed to the message. In the same way, not all "return" should be measured by sheer revenue—but it's a start.[19]

Some marketers accept that this unknown variable and focus on social media are less about ROI than about deepening relationships with customers; others work tirelessly to better understand the measurement of social media's effectiveness. While literally hundreds of metrics have been developed to measure social media's value, these metrics are meaningless unless they are tied to key performance indicators.[20] For example, a local coffee shop manager may measure the success of her social media presence by her accumulated number of friends on Facebook and followers on Twitter. But these numbers depend entirely on context. The rate of accumulation, investment per fan and follower, and comparison to similarly sized coffee shops are all important variables to consider. Without context, measurements are meaningless.

Some social media metrics to consider are the following:

1. **Buzz:** Volume of consumer-related buzz for a brand based on posts and impression, by social channel, by stage in the purchase channel, by season, and by time of day

2. **Interest:** Number of likes, fans, followers, and friends; growth rates; rate of going viral or pass-along; and change in pass-along over time

3. **Participation:** Number of comments, ratings, social bookmarks, subscriptions, page views, uploads, downloads, embeds, retweets, Facebook posts, pins, and time spent with social media platforms

4. **Search engine ranks and results:** Increases and decreases on searches and changes in key words

5. **Influence:** Media mentions, influences of bloggers reached, influences of customers reached, and second-degree reach based on social graphs

6. **Sentiment analysis:** Positive, neutral, and negative sentiment; trends of sentiment; and volume of sentiment

7. **Website metrics:** Clicks, click-through rates, and percentage of traffic. The main issue is to start with good measurable objectives, determine what needs to be measured, and figure it out.

Even with this list, marketers and budget decision makers are still left with a raft of uncertainty. Only items 4 and 7 produce legitimate measurable data, from which some degree of change (positive or negative) can be linked to investment in social media tactics. Like advertising or any other component of the IMC tool kit, save personal selling and sales promotions, it is impossible to quantify with certainty the financial ROI associated with social media.

19-4 CONSUMER BEHAVIOUR ON SOCIAL MEDIA

Online activity has changed the way people learn and the way they interact with companies and with each other in their daily lives. Consumers seek news online from a variety of sources as the news is happening. They are online building relationships and interacting with each other and with companies through social media. They are online banking, investing, and purchasing. Social media have reinvented politics and civic engagement.

But who is using social media? How often are they online? How much time do they spend online? What types of social media do they use? How do they use social media? Do Twitter users retweet viral videos? How often do they post online? Are they just reading content or are they actually creating it? Does Facebook attract younger users? Why do consumers read blogs? These types of questions must be considered because they determine not only which tools will be most effective but also, more importantly, whether launching a social media campaign even makes sense for a particular organization.

Understanding an audience necessitates understanding how that audience uses social media. In *Groundswell*, Charlene Li and Josh Bernoff of Forrester Research identify six categories of social media users:

1. **Creators:** Those who produce and share online content, such as blogs, websites, articles, and videos

2. **Critics:** Those who post comments, ratings, and reviews of products and services on blogs and forums

3. **Collectors:** Those who use RSS feeds to collect information and vote for websites online

4. **Joiners:** Those who maintain a social networking profile and visit other sites

5. **Spectators:** Those who read blogs, listen to podcasts, watch videos, and generally consume media

6. **Inactives:** Those who do none of these things[21]

A more recent study by Aimia identified six segments as well:

1. **No Shows:** Those who haven't logged on to a social network in 30 days. They exhibit low degrees of trust and have no interest in sharing their world online with others.

2. **Newcomers:** Typically passive users of a single social media network who use it simply to enhance their offline relationships.

3. **Onlookers:** Lurkers who post infrequently and are online to keep up to date on others. They limit their own postings as they want control of their online information.

4. **Cliquers:** These are active, single-network users who primarily use Facebook for the purpose of posting photos, comments, and status updates. They are influential in their small network of close friends.

5. **Mix-n-Minglers:** They participate actively on multiple platforms. They follow brands to receive offers and stay ahead of the curve. Within their network of friends they're influential—and they meet many of these friends online.

EXHIBIT 19.3 | SOCIAL MEDIA USAGE FRAMEWORK

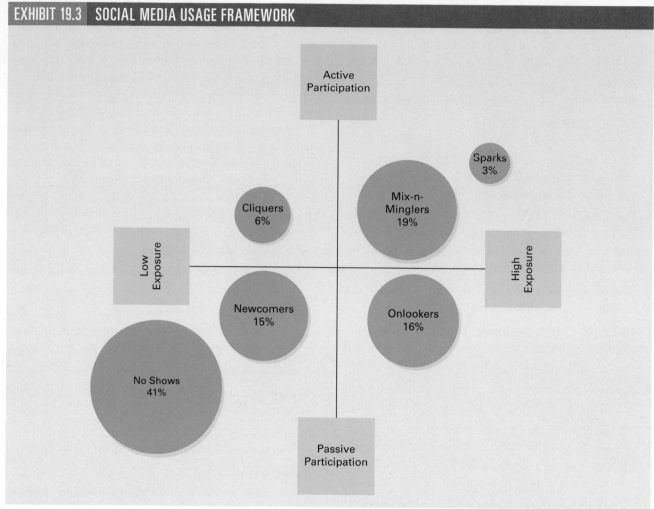

Source: Courtesy of Aimia, Inc.

6. Sparks: This group is the most active online. Social media are a way for them to express themselves, and they are active on a number of sites. They have the most open social networks, and they often actively support their favourite brands.*

Exhibit 19.3 illustrates where each of these segments fits on measures of exposure and participation.

As marketers come to understand how consumers engage with social media to the same extent that they understand consumer engagement with traditional media, they will be able to create integrative marketing communication campaigns that combine traditional and online tools more effectively with greater chances for success.

---

*Adapted with permission from Rozen, Doug, Mona Askalani, and Tom Senn, "Staring at the Sun: Identifying, Understanding and Influencing Social Media Users," Research Brief, Aimia, Inc., 2012, http://www.pamorama.net/wpcontent/uploads/2012/06/Aimia-Social-Media-White-Paper-6-types-of-social-media-users.pdf, p. 8. No Shows, Newcomers, Onlookers, Cliquers, Mix-n-Minglers, and Sparks are all trademarks of Aimia Canada Inc."

19-5 SOCIAL MEDIA TOOLS: CONSUMER- AND CORPORATE-GENERATED CONTENT

It is important for marketers to engage with customers on social media for the reasons mentioned throughout this chapter, and a number of tools and platforms can be employed as part of an organization's social media strategy. Blogs, microblogs, social networks, media creation and sharing sites, social news sites, location-based social networking sites, review sites, and virtual worlds and online gaming all have their place in a company's social marketing plan. These are all tools in a marketing manager's toolbox, available when applicable to the marketing plan but not necessarily to be used all at once. Because of the breakneck pace at which technology changes, this list of resources will surely look markedly different five years from now. More tools emerge every day, and branding strategies must keep up with the ever-changing world of technology. For now, the resources highlighted in this section remain a marketer's strongest set of platforms for conversing and strengthening relationships with customers.

19-5a Blogs

Blogs have become staples in many social media strategies and are often a brand's social media centrepiece. Blogs allow marketers to create content in the form of posts, which ideally build trust and a sense of authenticity in customers. Once posts are made, audience members can provide feedback through comments. Because the comments section of a blog post opens a dialogue and gives customers a voice, it is one of the most important avenues of conversation between brands and consumers.

Blogs can be divided into two broad categories: **corporate or professional blogs** and **noncorporate blogs**, such as personal blogs. Corporate blogs are sponsored by a company and have become a critical element in reinforcing corporate image, for communicating with customers, and for adding value. Whole Foods Market Inc. has a blog that does all of that. It features recipes, product information, how-to articles, and much more. The blog features a number of different writers, as well as the CEO. The blog allows the company to communicate Whole Foods Market Inc.'s image. In contrast, noncorporate blogs are independent and not associated with the marketing efforts of any particular company or brand. Because these blogs contain information not controlled by marketers, they are perceived to be more authentic than corporate blogs. Noncorporate blogs are really the birthplace of blogging—a space where anybody can be an expert on anything. The credibility of the noncorporate blogger is in the hands of the online community. People may follow, congregate, and accumulate around the blogger due to the blogger's expertise and/or unique blog product, or they will reject or ignore the blogger due to the lack of an interesting or credible offering. Whether blogs are about beer, fashion, or funerals, the ones that generate the widest reach are the ones that marketers should pay attention to and communicate with—as they would with traditional media channels. This is part of media relations in the era of social media. Whether bloggers are reviewing a product they have sourced themselves or are sampling a product, the review can be a critical influencer to purchase for those reading the blog.

A case can also be made for posting blogs on existing social media platforms, as opposed to burying them somewhere in a corporate website, never to be seen. LinkedIn, the professionals' social media hub, has become the perfect setting for such communication. With a built-in audience of corporate leaders, networkers, thinkers, and, yes, job seekers, LinkedIn's platform encourages individual account holders and employees of companies to post blogs of any size. They can be microblogs, along the same lines as Twitter, or they can be much longer—a deep dive into an issue or event relevant to the company or its industry. WestJet is prolific in this space, utilizing LinkedIn not only as a simultaneous repository for news releases, but also as an open canvas for leadership to opine, advocate, and champion the WestJet brand, its people, and its customers.

19-5b Microblogs

Microblogs are blogs with strict limits on the length of posts. Twitter, the most popular microblogging platform, requires that posts be no more than 140 characters (increased to 280 characters as of September 2017). Other microblogging platforms are Tumblr, Google Buzz, and Qaiku.

While Tumblr continues to grow, Twitter is already wildly popular. Having become a social messaging tool, Twitter is effective for disseminating breaking news, promoting longer blog posts and campaigns, sharing links, keeping in touch, announcing events, and promoting sales. When a company follows, retweets, responds to potential customers' tweets, and tweets content that inspires customers to engage with the brand or the company, Twitter users will quickly and efficiently lay a foundation for meaningful two-way conversation. Research has found that when operated correctly, corporate Twitter accounts are well respected and well received. Twitter can be used to build communities; aid in customer service; gain prospects; increase awareness; and, in the case of nonprofits, raise funds.

Twitter Amplify is a Twitter ad unit that allows advertisers to share content, such as sports replays or interviews with TV actors, at the same time as a TV broadcast.

Continuing the strategy that was started with the 2010 Vancouver Olympics, the Canadian

Olympic Committee employed Twitter as its "exclusive social media partner" to help Canadians feel connected to the athletes competing for Canada. Canadian Olympic partners were given the opportunity to promote Canadian Olympic tweets from approved athletes' handles and the official team handles.[22]

19-5c Social Networks

Social networking sites allow individuals to connect—or network—with friends, peers, and business associates. Connections may be made on the basis of shared interests, shared environments, or personal relationships. Depending on the site, connected individuals may be able to send each other messages, track each other's activity, see each other's personal information, share multimedia, or comment on each other's blog and microblog posts. Depending on its goals, a marketing team might engage several social networks as part of its social media strategy: Facebook is the largest social network; LinkedIn is geared toward professionals and businesses; Google+ has unique features such as Hangouts and Communities; and niche networks like MapMyRide and Match.com cater to specialized markets. Given the right strategy, increasing awareness, targeting audiences, promoting products, forging relationships, highlighting expertise and leadership, attracting event participants, performing research, and generating new business are attainable marketing goals on any social network.

Facebook has over 1.8 billion users, making it the most popular social networking site.[23] While individual Facebook users create profiles, brands, organizations, and nonprofit causes operate as pages. As opposed to individual profiles, all pages are public and are thus subject to search engine indexing. By maintaining a popular Facebook page, a brand not only increases its social media presence but also helps to optimize search engine results. Pages often include photo and video albums, brand information, and links to external sites. The most useful page feature, however, is the Timeline. The Timeline allows a brand to communicate directly with followers and customers via status updates, which enables marketers to build databases of interested stakeholders. When an individual becomes a follower of your organization or posts on your Timeline, that information is shared with the individual's friends, creating a mini-viral marketing campaign. Facebook is an extremely important platform for marketers and is becoming an integral part of marketing campaigns. Facebook is constantly upgrading its user interface, largely due to user input but sometimes in reaction (or pre-emption) of competitor revisions. Therefore, it is difficult to post a current list of Facebook terminology here. Still, it is vital for users, particularly business users, to get a handle on Facebook jargon. It is always advisable, when in doubt, to locate and open Facebook's online help centre, which exists to answer all questions from the obvious to the obscure.

LinkedIn is used primarily by professionals who want to build their personal brand online and by businesses as a tool to assist in recruitment and selection. LinkedIn features many of the same services as Facebook (profiles, status updates, private messages, company pages, and groups) but is oriented toward business and professional connections—it is designed to be information-rich rather than multimedia-rich.

19-5d Media-Sharing Sites

Media-sharing sites allow users to upload and distribute multimedia content, such as videos and photos. Sites such as Snapchat, YouTube, Flickr, Pinterest, and Periscope are particularly useful to brands' social marketing strategies because they add an interactive channel on which to distribute content. Today, organizations can tell compelling brand stories through videos, photos, and audio.

Photo sharing sites allow users to archive and share photos. Snapchat, Flickr, and Instagram—and even Facebook—all offer free photo hosting services that can be used by individuals and businesses alike.

Video creation and distribution have also gained popularity among marketers because of video's rich ability to tell stories. YouTube, the high-traffic video-based website, allows users to upload and stream their videos. YouTube dominates business video sharing, with over 90 percent of marketers who share videos saying they do so through YouTube. Creative marketers wanting to increase consumer engagement develop campaigns that encourage consumers to create product usage videos. Such user-generated content, if used strategically, can be a powerful tool for brands.

In one of the great social media campaigns in Canadian business history, if social media metrics are any indication, WestJet emotionally engaged viewers during Christmas 2013 with a holiday YouTube video showing WestJet employees making the wishes of travellers come true. After passengers checked in at Toronto Pearson

social networking sites
websites that allow individuals to connect—or network—with friends, peers, and business associates

media-sharing sites
websites that allow users to upload and distribute multimedia content, such as videos and photos

and Hamilton airports for flights to Calgary, they were asked by a virtual Santa what they wanted for Christmas, after scanning their boarding passes at kiosks. Responses were as varied as computers, socks, a flight home to see family and a big-screen TV. What passengers didn't know was that during their five-hour flight to Calgary, a team of more than 150 WestJet staff went shopping, wrapped presents, and delivered the gifts to the Calgary airport. When the passengers went to collect their baggage, wrapped presents addressed to them came down the carousel. The action by WestJet and its employees was wonderful, in the truest sense of the Christmas spirit, and the resulting video was gripping and emotional. The video hit 1 million viewers the first day it was posted, and within two days attracted over 7.5 million views. Three years later, the video was still generating views at 45 million and counting. The problem, or challenge, for WestJet was that it had now set a standard for itself that was going to be impossible to meet consistently. Undeterred, WestJet has made its Christmas Wish video a major strategy in its annual social media offering. With these videos, WestJet creates growing brand engagement that would have been hard to achieve with a traditional television ad—and it would have been unaffordable.[24]

Not to be outdone, in the winter of 2016–17 Tim Hortons, the quintessential Canadian brand, already top of mind with its annual winter sales promotion "Roll Up the Rim to Win," capitalized on the social trends of both altruism (doing the right thing) and narcissism (posting one's own thoughts and photos to social media platforms). Its #WarmWishes campaign invited participants to share stories of how others they know deserved a pick-me-up. "#WarmWishes" were to be posted to Tim Hortons' Twitter and Instagram communities. At the end of the campaign, an army of Tim Hortons owners and employees from across the country (along with film crews) set out to create a little warmth and cheer for targeted individuals. In true IMC form, the campaign was coupled with advertisements, public relations, personal selling, and sales promotions. While similar to social media campaigns conducted by other brands, including WestJet, Tim

Hortons further entrenched itself as one of the country's most beloved brands.[25]

A podcast, another type of user-generated media, is a digital audio or video file that is distributed serially for other people to listen to or watch. Podcasts can be streamed online, played on a computer, uploaded to a portable media player (like an iPod), or downloaded onto a smartphone. Podcasts are like radio shows that are distributed through various means and not linked to a scheduled time slot. One of the more significant players to enter the space is Periscope, a live video streaming app, launched in 2014 and quickly acquired by Twitter in 2015. A dizzying, somewhat surreal combination of Twitter, instant messaging, GPS, and video-blogging, Periscope puts a map of the world in the palm of your hand with indicators of live streaming "broadcasts" as they occur 24/7. At any moment you can join a stream as a passive viewer or an active participant, giving "broadcasters" instant feedback on the fly. Broadcasters, for their part, can be doing or talking about anything and can respond to comments as they pop up on the screen. With a rapidly rising user base in 2017, Twitter decided it was time to monetize its investment and began selling ad space in front of broadcasts.[26]

19-5e Social News Sites

Social news sites allow users to post news stories and multimedia on a platform, such as Reddit or Digg, for readers to then vote on. The more interest from readers, the more votes the post gets, and thus the higher it is ranked. Marketers have found that these sites are great for promoting campaigns. If marketing content posted to a social news site is voted up, discussed, and shared enough to be listed among the most popular topics of the day, it can go viral. Social bookmarking sites, such as StumbleUpon and Reddit, are similar to social news sites but the objective of their users is to collect, save, and share interesting and valuable links. The result is the creation of peer networks that are linked by a common interest.

19-5f Location-Based Social Networking Sites

Location-based social networking sites combine the fun of social networking with the utility of location-based GPS

Make this a season of #WarmWishes

Courtesy of Tim Hortons

social news sites websites that allow users to decide which content is promoted on a given website by voting that content up or down

location-based social networking sites websites that combine the fun of social networking with the utility of location-based GPS technology

Gil C/Shutterstock.com

technology. Foursquare, one of the most popular location sites, treats location-based micro networking as a game: users earn badges and special statuses that are based on the number of visits they make to particular locations. Users can write and read short reviews and tips about businesses, organize meet-ups, and see which Foursquare-using friends are nearby. Foursquare updates can also be posted to linked Twitter and Facebook accounts for followers and friends to see. In a recent survey, less than 20 percent of people claimed to use the location-based social platforms, while almost all of them use other social channels like Facebook. The added value offered by location-based sites like Foursquare just isn't there. Facebook provides the ability to share your location with your network, and Facebook, Twitter, Instagram, Pinterest, and other more robust sites provide all that Foursquare offers and more.

19-5g Review Sites

Individuals tend to trust other people's opinions when it comes to purchasing. According to Nielsen Media Research, more than 70 percent of consumers said that they trusted online consumer opinions. This percentage is much higher than that of consumers who trust traditional advertising. Based on the early work of Amazon and eBay to integrate user opinions into product and seller pages, countless websites have sprung up that allow users to voice their opinions across every segment of the Internet market. Some of the more popular general business review sites are Google My Business, Yelp, Foursquare, Facebook, Amazon, and Tripadvisor. However, the proliferation of review sites dives deeply and endlessly into specific industries and social issues. **Review sites** allow consumers to post, read, rate, and comment on opinions regarding all kinds of

> **review sites** websites that allow consumers to post, read, rate, and comment on opinions regarding all kinds of products and services

products and services. Review sites can enhance consumer engagement opportunities for those marketers who follow and respond to consumer posts about their products or services.

19-5h Virtual Worlds and Online Gaming

Virtual worlds and online gaming present additional opportunities for marketers to engage with consumers. These include massive multiplayer online games (MMOGs), such as World of Warcraft and The Sims Online, as well as online communities. Consultancy firm KZero Worldwide reported that almost 800 million people have participated in some sort of virtual world experience, and the sector's annual revenue is approaching $1 billion. Growth is expected to continue in this area as consumer devices, such as virtual reality headsets, start to become more mainstream. While unfamiliar to and even intimidating for many traditional marketers, the field of virtual worlds is an important, viable, and growing consideration for social media marketing.

One area of growth is social gaming. An increasing number of people are playing games within social networking sites like Facebook or on their mobile devices by downloading game apps. Some of the more popular games available for download on smartphones include Candy Crush, Minecraft, and Roblox. Such games are attractive because they can be played in just five minutes, perhaps while commuting home from school or work. A growing trend among mobile games is to use mobile ads to generate revenue for the game-makers. But the biggest splash in this space during the mid-2010s was Pokémon GO, a free, location-based reality game in which Pokémon characters are made to appear on players' phones (using their GPS systems) as if they were standing (or crouching) right around the corner, behind a tree, or on the other side of a house. The object is to capture and/or battle the Pokémon.

19-6 SOCIAL MEDIA AND MOBILE TECHNOLOGY

While much of the excitement in social media has been based on websites and new technology uses, much of the growth lies in new platforms. These platforms have grown beyond smartphones and tablets and into wearable technology, such as the Apple Watch and the Samsung Gear VR. The major implication of this development is that consumers now have a multitude of access points for websites.

19-6a Mobile and Smartphone Technology

By 2016, three out of every four Canadians owned a smartphone, and the usage figures suggest that they have become a necessary tool for everyday living.[27] Sixty-six percent of Canadians access the Internet every day from their smartphone, and very few smartphone users ever leave their home without them. Canadians use their smartphones to search for information, to watch videos, for social networking, and for traditional communication. Canadians download and use apps on their smartphones for a multitude of reasons, and they often multimedia-task; almost 50 percent of Canadians claim to use their phone while doing other things, such as watching television.[28]

In 2012, mobile advertising revenue in Canada was $160 million, representing a 1.3 percent share of reported media, and in 2013 it more than doubled to $290 million. Fast-forward to 2016, when mobile advertising revenue had topped $1 billion and was expected to rise to $4 billion by 2020.[29]

Tablet penetration was spurred in 2015 by the launch of "phablets"—portable enough to be a phone but large enough to be a tablet. Apple's iPhone 6+ ushered in this trend in full, although some of its competitors had been manufacturing larger mobile phones for some time. The most likely type of advertising winner as a result of tablet/phablet penetration was video, and Canadians lead the way in online video viewership growth, offering marketers a highly engaging communication opportunity.

The low barriers to entry that have been created by the standardization of mobile platforms, the seemingly reduced concerns over the once-worrisome privacy issues (especially among the younger population, who are the largest mobile users), and the portability of the smartphones are all reasons for the popularity and growth of mobile marketing. In addition, mobile marketing is measurable; metrics and usage statistics make it an effective tool for gaining insight into consumer behaviour, and mobile marketing's response rate is higher than that of traditional media types, further fuelling its popularity and growth.

One use for bar-code scanning apps is the reading and processing of Quick Response (QR) codes. When scanned by a smartphone's QR reader app, a QR code takes the user to a specific site with content about or a discount for products or services.

The smartphone trend called near *field communication* (NFC) uses small chips hidden in or behind products that, when touched by compatible devices, will transfer the information on the chip to the device. In Canada, NFC offers the opportunity for mobile payments via your smartphone.

COMMON MOBILE MARKETING TOOLS

▸ **SMS (Short Message Service):** 160-character text messages sent to and from cellphones. SMS is typically integrated with other tools.

▸ **MMS (Multimedia Messaging Service):** Similar to SMS but allows for the attachment of images, video, ringtones, and other multimedia to text messages.

▸ **Mobile Websites (MOBI and WAP Websites):** Websites designed specifically for viewing and navigation on mobile devices.

▸ **Mobile Ads:** Visual advertisements integrated into text messages, applications, and mobile websites. Mobile ads are often sold on a cost-per-click basis.

▸ **Bluetooth Marketing:** A signal is sent to Bluetooth-enabled devices that allows marketers to send targeted messages to users based on their geographic locations.

▸ **Smartphone Applications (Apps):** Software designed specifically for mobile and tablet devices. Theses apps include software to turn phones into scanners for various types of bar codes.

19-6b Applications and Widgets

Millions of applications or **apps** have been developed for the mobile market. These apps allow you to listen to music, track your calorie intake, play games, book a hotel, practise yoga, or find your way home. The CBC Olympic app, created for the 2014 Sochi Winter Olympic Games, drew 380 million views over the course of the games. Still more downloads occurred for the 2016 Rio games, after which the CBC converted it to the CBC Sports App, covering all things relevant and interesting to Canadian sports fans. Whether offering new or existing content, when an app is well branded and integrated into a company's overall marketing strategy, it can create buzz and generate customer engagement.

While some marketers focus their apps on connectivity, Nike created Nike+ to provide both utility and connectivity. Using an iPhone's GPS capabilities, users can track their jogging and cycling routes and examine mapping and details of their pace and calories burned. Information on treadmill runs and other exercise details can be entered manually as well, so as a training tool this app can provide powerful

> **apps** short for applications; free or purchased software programs that are downloaded to run on smartphones, tablet computers, and other mobile devices

information to the user. In addition, activities can be shared online with other runners and joggers.

Web widgets, also known as gadgets and badges, are software applications that run entirely within existing online platforms. Essentially, a Web widget allows a developer to embed a simple application, such as a weather forecast, horoscope, or stock market ticker, into a website, even if the developer did not write (or does not understand) the application's source code. From a marketing perspective, widgets allow customers to display company information (such as current promotions, coupons, news, or countdown clocks) on their own websites.

19-7 THE SOCIAL MEDIA PLAN

To effectively use the tools in the social media toolbox, marketers need a clearly outlined social media plan. The social media plan is linked to larger plans, such as a promotional plan or marketing plan, and should fit appropriately into the objectives and steps in those plans (for more information, review Chapters 3 and 16). It is important to research throughout the development of the social media plan to keep abreast of the rapidly changing social media world. Creating an effective social media plan has six stages:

1. **Set social media objectives:** Set objectives that can be specifically accomplished through social media, with special attention to how to measure the results. Numerous metrics are available, some of which are mentioned throughout the chapter.

2. **The listening stage:** This stage is covered in the discussion in section 19-2a, "The Listening System," earlier in the chapter.

3. **Identify the target audience:** This should line up with the target market defined in the marketing plan, but in the social media plan, pay special attention to how that audience participates and behaves online.

4. **Develop strategies, citing results from the listening phase, set out to support the objectives.** The strategies answer the question, How can we best reach and engage our target audience? In addition, your strategies should include the identification of your unique selling proposition (USP). It is with an understanding of your USP that you can create a list of key phrases around which you can build the content for your social media strategies.

5. **Select the tools and platforms:** Based on the result of step 4, choose the social media tools and platforms that will be most relevant. These choices are based on the knowledge of where the target audience participates on social media.

6. **Implement and monitor the strategy:** Social media campaigns can be fluid, so it is important to keep a close eye on what is successful and what isn't. Based on the observations, make changes as needed. It becomes important, therefore, to go back to the listening stage to interpret how consumers are perceiving the social media campaign.

Listening to customers and industry trends and continually revising the social media plan to meet the needs of the changing social media market are keys to successful social media marketing. Numerous industry leaders are sharing some of their best practices, and sources such as *Marketing Magazine* and the *Globe and Mail* report regularly on how large and small companies are successfully using social media to gain market share and sales. A good example of using social media strategies is HubSpot, which is a company that practises what it preaches, namely the benefits of building valuable content online and then using social media to pull customers to its website. Social engine profiles have increased HubSpot's website traffic, which has made its lead-generation program much more effective.

19-7a The Changing World of Social Media

As you read through the chapter, some of the trends that are noted may already seem ancient to you. The rate of change in social media is astounding—usage statistics change daily for sites like Facebook and Twitter. Snapchat, the upstart teen-targeted social media platform, was still, in 2017, eighth in usage among Canadians, and yet that same year, its parent company, Snap, issued its initial public offering, which saw the firm's market capitalization soar to nearly $30 billion overnight.[30] It was, at the time, the largest IPO, in terms of valuation, in history. Things softened significantly in subsequent weeks, but not enough to take all the shine off what was

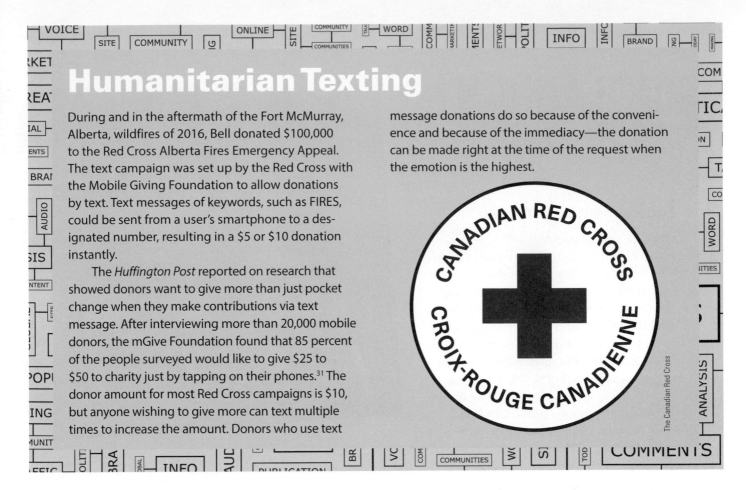

Humanitarian Texting

During and in the aftermath of the Fort McMurray, Alberta, wildfires of 2016, Bell donated $100,000 to the Red Cross Alberta Fires Emergency Appeal. The text campaign was set up by the Red Cross with the Mobile Giving Foundation to allow donations by text. Text messages of keywords, such as FIRES, could be sent from a user's smartphone to a designated number, resulting in a $5 or $10 donation instantly.

The *Huffington Post* reported on research that showed donors want to give more than just pocket change when they make contributions via text message. After interviewing more than 20,000 mobile donors, the mGive Foundation found that 85 percent of the people surveyed would like to give $25 to $50 to charity just by tapping on their phones.[31] The donor amount for most Red Cross campaigns is $10, but anyone wishing to give more can text multiple times to increase the amount. Donors who use text message donations do so because of the convenience and because of the immediacy—the donation can be made right at the time of the request when the emotion is the highest.

The Canadian Red Cross

a spectacular valuation of a social media company with little more than a few years' existence and a comparatively small community (relative to Facebook). By the time you read this book, Snap will likely have completed one of its goals, to become one of the world's largest video content companies, through the launch of its hardware platform—Spectacles, a sunglasses product that uses the click of a button to record what the user sees, then uploads the content to the user's Snapchat account. Where will Snap be in 2020? How will it fare against its current rivals Facebook, Twitter, Instagram, and YouTube? And where will each of those and the dozen or so other ubiquitous social media channels be?

Some things that are in the rumour mill as we write this may have exploded in popularity; others may have fizzled out without even appearing on your radar. Given the speed at which social media changes, marketers are obliged to stay on top of current tools and keep tabs on rumoured new entrants. Doing so may result in a competitive advantage because of the ability to understand and invest in the next big social media site or tool.

STUDY TOOLS

IN THE BOOK, YOU CAN:

✔ Rip out the Chapter in Review card at the back of the book.

ONLINE, YOU CAN:

✔ Stay organized and efficient with a single online destination with all the course material and study aids you need to succeed.

Go to nelson.com/student to access the digital resources.

SIDE LAUNCH
BREWING COMPANY
CONTINUING CASE

Engagement by Listening

While millions of people claim to be social media experts, in truth the number of people who might be accurately described as "expert" in the field may be zero. "I agree with that," claims Garnet Pratt, founder of Side Launch craft brewery. "It's too hard, if not impossible, to keep up with trends and be active, much less master the art of social media." And yet every consumer-facing business must be socially active. Perhaps there is no more consumer-facing business than craft beer.

"The demographic that's coming into this category is getting younger and younger," claims VP Sales and Marketing Chuck Galea, "and they are proportionately more and more involved socially." It is therefore imperative that a business like Side Launch be present, relevant, and authentic in telling its story digitally. "We have a few rules as to what we put out as content," he continues. "We cannot be political, because if we as a brand sit on one side of the fence, then we're going to alienate valued customers who sit on the other side of the fence."

Aside from "playing Switzerland," as Chuck likes to describe staying neutral on any controversial issues, he and the entire leadership team believe that social media, like every other communications tool, are just another great channel through which to tell the Side Launch story. "What's more important is to focus on the messages that we're trying to convey, and that's telling our story, including the history, the making of the beer, the different brands, and the process and care that goes into every can." Interestingly, Side Launch also likes to share the content on their social platforms with their customers. "We like to showcase our customers. Every sales rep has to showcase a bar every week. So, for instance, one of our people in Toronto will have an account that he or she wants to feature, so they'll be responsible for getting some photos and telling a story not only about us, but about that bar."

Of course, social media are a ubiquitous part of the business environment as well. Ratings sites and bloggers have a significant and growing influence on a brand's recognition, and can become a major influencer in the consumer purchase process as well. Ratebeer and Untappd are the go-to beer ratings sites of the day, with beer scores from the former's site even being used in point-of-purchase displays by U.S. retailers. But some of the more respected bloggers have great pull as well. One of the country's most respected beer bloggers, for instance, absolutely loved the Mountain Lager, calling it his

Side Launch Brewing Company

favourite beer. "But he gave this whole story as to why," recalls Chuck. "He talked about the beer and how it brought back memories, and how well made it is. And then we almost automatically started seeing his impact as people tried the beer, liked the beer, and mentioned it on their social media pages."

"It's also an absolute must to communicate things that are of really deep importance to us," adds Garnet, referring to the tainted Wheat beer crisis of 2016 (discussed in greater detail in Chapter 2). "We not only had our actions—to recall the beer and to be transparent about it—reaffirmed by our consumers, but we also earned a deeper level of respect by being able to leverage the reach of social media to communicate a bad news story and turn it into a positive outcome for our brand." News of the tainted beer had eventually hit traditional media, but by that time, Side Launch had gotten well ahead of the story, thanks in part to activating the Side Launch faithful through social media.

Questions

1. What role did social media serve when Side Launch encountered potentially damaging public relations resulting from its Wheat beer recall of 2016 (documented in Chapter 2)?

2. What are some of the ways that Side Launch "listens" through the use of social media?

3. Being neutral, or "playing Switzerland," as Chuck describes it, on politically charged subjects may be wise in most cases, but would there be an example of a social issue or concern where it would be in Side Launch's interest to take sides in social media?

Side Launch Brewing Company

Part 6 Case
Promotion Decisions

A Good Cup of Tea Is Always Better When Shared with Others

Who would have thought that in 10 years, a chance cup of tea would turn into a multi-million-dollar, North American–wide company. That is exactly the case with Steeped Tea. Steeped Tea is located in Ancaster, Ontario, a small town just west of Toronto. With grit, determination, and vision, Tonia Jahshan and her husband, Hatem, have turned a cup of tea into a "direct selling company that empowers people to start a business of their own and become passionate entrepreneurs, all while sharing a cup of tea."

In 2016 Steeped Tea had annual sales of more than $20 million, with over 9000 salespeople selling loose-leaf tea and accessories throughout North America, earning Tonia ranking as one of the top female entrepreneurs in Canada.

Tea is the second most consumed beverage in the world next to water. Canadians on average drink just over 6 cups of tea a week and have an average of 11 different varieties of tea in their cupboard. With representation in Canada from inherently strong tea-drinking cultures such as China, the Middle East, and India, the popularity of tea in this country should come as no surprise. In 2015 tea sales grew 23 percent over the previous year, reaching $1.3 billion, and in 2015 *Foodservice and Hospitality* named tea as one of the top five food trends for that year. It is expected that by 2020 tea consumption will grow by 40 percent, faster than the growth in consumption of coffee, soft drinks, and alcohol. Growth in consumption is coming not simply because of the mix of the Canadian population but also because of product innovations in the varieties of tea offered and the formats it is offered in. While tea bags remain the most popular format, loose tea is growing in popularity. Loose tea offers the opportunity for literally hundreds of variety options, as well as value. Loose tea can be steeped more than once, while tea bags are one-time uses. In addition to the variety offered with loose tea, the quality of the tea is better, particularly when the tea drinker is aware of how to steep tea properly. Today's tea drinker has been referred to as "conscious drinkers"—they want to know where the tea is grown, how it is harvested, its various tasting notes, and how to maximize the flavours. The image of tea is changing—it can also be used as an ingredient in cocktails, and *Forbes* noted that tea-infused cocktails were a top trend for 2017.

Where once you were considered old fashioned and dated when ordering tea, today many, including the highly influential Millennial segment, are not afraid to order a "cuppa," and they love the culture.

Interestingly, in contrast to coffee and other beverages, research indicates that 80 percent of Canadians drink tea at home rather than in food service establishments. Although there has been an increase in the consumption of tea over the years in food service establishments, and although it is always on the menu, it is not ordered as often as other beverages because tea lovers claim the quality and preparation of the tea just aren't good enough. It is more complicated to make a good cup of tea than other beverages, and food service staff either aren't trained or don't have the time to ensure each cup served is a quality cup of tea.

Like coffee, tea can be bought at your local grocery store and is considered a staple on the grocery lists of Canadian families. President's Choice has sought to capitalize on the growing consumption of tea and the sophistication of consumers' tea palates by launching specialty loose-leaf tea under the PC Black Label. Specialty tea retailers are also entering the market. Teavana, owned by Starbucks, has a number of locations in Canada offering hundreds of tea blends and tea accessories. As to be expected, retail staff spend time with customers, providing samples and instruction on how to steep tea; to enhance customer convenience, online ordering is possible.

David's Tea is a Canadian specialty tea and tea accessory retailer. David's Tea opened in 2008 and today boasts over 200 stores across Canada and the United States. David's Tea offers over 150 varieties of tea, including exclusive blends as well as tea accessories. Like Teavana, David's Tea retail staff is trained to educate and teach customers how to steep the best possible cup of tea.

As evidence of a growing love for tea, TWG Tea opened in late 2016 in Vancouver. TWG Tea was launched in Singapore, and the Vancouver location is the Canadian introduction of this luxury tea brand. TWG Tea is positioned as the finest in luxury tea. It is sold through branded retail locations that are a tea boutique, tasting salon, and restaurant. At TWG Tea in Vancouver, the prices range from $17 for 100 grams of tea to $2723 for 100 grams. Yes, that is over $2000 for 1000 grams! TWG Tea hopes to be the leader in educating today's tea drinkers that, like wine, taste is very much influenced by the quality of ingredients, and the higher the quality, the higher the price. Like both Teavana and David's Tea, staff at TWG Tea spend time with customers not just explaining the differences between teas, but also how the tea should be prepared. In TWG Tea's case, the staff even go so far as to explain what foods should be paired with various teas!

So back to Steeped Tea. How did they do it? What is the secret to their success? Can they continue this unbelievable trajectory of growth in the face of stiffer retail competition?

To begin with, they will tell you they aren't a tea company, they are a tea party company and that is one key to their success. They have hundreds of tea blends and tea accessories, but they also sell jams and baked goods—things that make for a good tea party. The other key to their success is their sales model.

Steeped Tea uses the direct sales model. According to the Direct Sellers Association of Canada, 91 percent of those involved in direct selling are women, 75 percent are married, and almost 60 percent have postsecondary education. A survey of direct sellers by the association revealed that the nature of direct selling enhances the quality of life of those in it. Direct sellers cite product savings, work schedule flexibility, and the social nature of the career as key benefits. The direct sales model provided Steeped Tea with the opportunity to sell tea via tea parties. The party setting gave the perfect opportunity to educate the purchaser, sample the tea (in proper tea accessories), and have fun. The consumable nature of the product ensured repeat sales. In addition, no one else was selling tea this way.

Steeped Tea quickly grew, and within two years Tonia knew she needed help. While brand awareness was strong and consultants were coming on board quickly, day-to-day finances and operations were chaotic and stressful. In stepped Tonia's husband, Hatem, and with changes to supplier agreements and the hiring of a bookkeeper, things perfected like a lovely cup of rooibos tea.

Steeped Tea was now at a tipping point. Continued growth meant expansion into the United States, but that required an influx of cash that Steeped Tea didn't have. In 2012 the company was profiled on *Dragon's Den*. The result was a deal with David Chilton and Jim Treliving for $250,000 for 20 percent of the company. With the expertise of these "dragons," Steeped Tea successfully entered the United States, and today the two investors remain committed to the company. Not only did Steeped Tea's appearance on *Dragon's Den* provide an influx of cash, it also increased company awareness. Within months of their appearance, the number of consultants grew from 500 to over 3000 and the company has not looked back. Today the company has over 50 staff in a 30,000-square-foot facility.

The increase in use of social media has been a bonus for Steeped Tea and its direct sales method of selling. The "mompreneurs" that have gravitated to Steeped Tea as consultants, or small business owners as they really are, are social media savvy. They use social media as ways to connect with one another and with their customers for new sales and repeat sales. Social media offer consultants a valuable tool to reach new customers and build brand ambassadors.

With tea continuing to be trendy to drink, competition to be the consumer's tea beverage company of choice will become tougher. Can Steeped Tea keep up this phenomenal growth? Can Steeped Tea keep consultants engaged? Can consultants continue to meet the needs of tea-consuming consumers? Tonia and Hatem believe so, but they say you won't see Steeped Tea on grocery store shelves. Can they keep the brand strong without that presence?

SOURCES

Lawrence Herzog. "Tea's Time Is Now!" Food Biz, http://foodbiz.ca/growing-profits-with-tea.

"The Industry." Direct Sales Association, http://dsa.ca/the-industry/industry-stats.

Mai Nguyen. "The Secret of Steeped Tea's Phenomenal Growth," Profitguide.com, May 16, 2016, http://www.profitguide.com/manage-grow/success-stories/w100-tonia-jahshan-steeped-tea-growth-103020.

Steeped Tea. http://www.steepedtea.com.

Robin Summerfield. "Are Canadians Trading Their Double-Doubles for Tea?" CBC News, September 29, 2015, http://www.cbc.ca/news/canada/are-canadians-trading-their-double-doubles-for-tea-1.3246849.

Maryam Siddiqi. "Something's Brewing," *Globe and Mail*, February 14, 2017, http://www.theglobeandmail.com/life/food-and-wine/food-trends/somethings-brewing-canada-warms-up-to-luxury-teamarket/article34016227.

Tea and Herbal Association of Canada. http://www.tea.ca/wp-content/uploads/2016/08/2015-Tea-Fact-Sheet.pdf.

QUESTIONS

1. Complete a SWOT analysis for Steeped Tea.

2. Complete some research on your own to understand the tea beverage segment of the market and the direct selling method of sales.

3. Given your research, develop an integrated marketing communications campaign for Steeped Tea to build brand awareness with the objective of increasing the number of consultants in Canada and hence overall sales.

4. Tea accessories are a big business. Branded accessories can increase awareness of Steeped Tea, as they remain in the home and are used by the tea-drinking consumer regularly. Should Steep Tea consider expanding this line to retail locations? Why or why not?

5. Assuming the company does decide to go retail with the accessories, build an integrated communications campaign that builds distribution and generates sales to the final consumer.

adopter a consumer who was happy enough with his or her trial experience with a product to use it again. p. 204

advergaming placing advertising messages in Web-based or video games to advertise or promote a product, a service, an organization, or an issue. p. 327

advertising impersonal, one-way mass communication about a product or an organization that is paid for by a marketer. p. 302

advertising appeal a reason for a person to buy a product. p. 320

advertising campaign a series of related advertisements focusing on a common theme, slogan, and set of advertising appeals. p. 320

advertising objective a specific communication task that a campaign should accomplish for a specified target audience during a specified period. p. 320

advertising response function a phenomenon in which spending for advertising and sales promotion increases sales or market share up to a certain level but then produces diminishing returns. p. 317

advocacy advertising a form of advertising in which an organization expresses its views on a particular issue or cause. p. 319

AIDA concept a model that outlines the process for achieving promotional goals in terms of stages of consumer involvement with the message; the acronym stands for *attention, interest, desire,* and *action.* p. 307

ambush marketing when an advertiser attempts to position itself with an event but is not sanctioned as an official sponsor. p. 332

applied research an attempt by marketers to use research to develop new or improved products. p. 26

apps short for applications; free or purchased software programs that are downloaded to run on smartphones, tablet computers, and other mobile devices. p. 367

aspirational reference groups groups that an individual would like to join. p. 104

assurance the knowledge and courtesy of employees and their ability to convey trust. p. 215

atmosphere the overall impression conveyed by a store's physical layout, decor, and surroundings. p. 287

attitude a learned tendency to respond consistently toward a given object. p. 111

audience selectivity the ability of an advertising medium to reach a precisely defined market. p. 328

automatic vending the use of machines to offer goods for sale. p. 280

baby boomers people born between 1947 and 1965. p. 24

bait pricing a price tactic that tries to get consumers into a store through false or misleading price advertising and then uses high-pressure selling to persuade consumers to buy more expensive merchandise instead. p. 247

base price the general price level at which the company expects to sell the good or service. p. 241

basic research pure research that aims to confirm an existing theory or to learn more about a concept or phenomenon. p. 26

basing-point pricing charging freight from a given (basing) point, regardless of the city from which the goods are shipped. p. 243

belief an organized pattern of knowledge that an individual holds as true about his or her world. p. 111

benefit segmentation the process of grouping customers into market segments according to the benefits they seek from the product. p. 141

big data large amounts of data collected from interactions with customers that reveal trends and patterns. p. 89

big data analytics the process of discovering patterns in large data sets for the purposes of extracting knowledge and understanding human behaviour. p. 289

blogs publicly accessible Web pages that function as interactive journals, whereby readers can post comments on the authors' entries. p. 363

brainstorming the process of getting a group to think of unlimited ways to vary a product or solve a problem. p. 199

brand a name, term, symbol, design, or combination thereof that identifies a seller's products and differentiates them from competitors' products. p. 182

brand cannibalization the reduction of sales for one brand as the result of the introduction of a new product or promotion of a current product or brand. p. 285

brand equity the value of company and brand names. p. 183

brand loyalty a consistent preference for one brand over all others. p. 183

brand mark the elements of a brand that cannot be spoken. p. 183

brand name that part of a brand that can be spoken, including letters, words, and numbers. p. 183

branded content creation of engaging bespoke content as a way to promote a particular brand that attracts and builds relationships with consumers. p. 307

break-even analysis the calculation of number of units sold, or total revenue required, a firm must meet to cover its costs, beyond which profit occurs. p. 238

business analysis the second stage of the screening process, where preliminary figures for demand, cost, sales, and profitability are calculated. p. 199

business product a product used to manufacture other goods or services, to facilitate an organization's operations, or to resell to other customers. p. 177

business services complementary and ancillary actions that companies undertake to meet business customers' needs. p. 124

business-to-business (B2B) marketing the process of matching capabilities between two nonconsumer entities to create value for both organizations and the "customer's customer"; also referred to as *business marketing*. p. 116

buyer for export an intermediary in the global market that assumes all ownership risks and sells globally for its own account. p. 60

buying centre all those people in an organization who become involved in the purchase decision. p. 127

campaign management developing product or service offerings customized for the appropriate customer segment and then pricing and communicating these offerings to enhance customer relationships. p. 164

Canadian-European Union Comprehensive Economic and Trade Agreement (CETA) a progressive free trade agreement, which covers almost all sectors, and aspects of Canada-EU trade in order to eliminate or reduce barriers. p. 56

cannibalization a situation that occurs when sales of a new product cut into sales of a firm's existing products. p. 146

capital intensive using more capital than labour in the production process. p. 51

cash discount a price reduction offered to a consumer, an industrial user, or a marketing intermediary in return for prompt payment of a bill. p. 242

category killers specialty discount stores that heavily dominate their narrow merchandise segment. p. 279

causal research a type of conclusive research that focuses on the cause and effect of two variables and attempts to find some correlation between them. p. 75

cause-related marketing a type of sponsorship involving the association of a for-profit company with a nonprofit organization; through the sponsorship, the company's product or service is promoted, and money is raised for the nonprofit. p. 332

central-location telephone (CLT) facility a specially designed phone room used to conduct telephone interviewing. p. 80

chain stores stores owned and operated as a group by a single organization. p. 276

channel a medium of communication—such as a voice, radio, or newspaper—used for transmitting a message. p. 299

channel conflict a clash of goals and methods among distribution channel members. p. 266

channel control one marketing channel member intentionally affects another member's behaviour. p. 265

channel leader (channel captain) a member of a marketing channel who exercises authority and power over the activities of other channel members. p. 265

channel members all parties in the marketing channel that negotiate with one another, buy and sell products, and facilitate the change of ownership between buyer and seller as they move the product from the manufacturer into the hands of the final consumer. p. 256

channel partnering (channel cooperation) the joint effort of all channel members to create a supply chain that serves customers and creates a competitive advantage. p. 266

channel power a marketing channel member's capacity to control or influence the behaviour of other channel members. p. 265

click-and-collect the practice of buying something online and then travelling to a physical store location to take delivery of the merchandise. p. 289

closed-ended question an interview question that asks the respondent to make a selection from a limited list of responses. p. 81

cobranding placing two or more brand names on a product or its package. p. 185

code of ethics a guideline to help marketing managers and other employees make better decisions. p. 30

cognitive dissonance the inner tension that a consumer experiences after recognizing an inconsistency between behaviour and values or opinions. p. 98

cold calling a form of lead generation in which the salesperson approaches potential buyers without any prior knowledge of the prospects' needs or financial status. p. 347

commercialization the decision to market a product. p. 202

communication the process by which we exchange or share meanings through a common set of symbols. p. 297

Competition Bureau the federal department charged with administering most marketplace laws. p. 17

competitive advantage the set of unique features of a company and its products that are perceived by the target market as significant and superior to the competition. pp. 39, 296

competitive advertising a form of advertising designed to influence demand for a specific brand. p. 319

competitive intelligence (CI) an intelligence system that helps managers assess their competition and vendors in order to become more efficient and effective competitors. p. 90

compiled lists customer lists that are developed by gathering names and addresses gleaned from telephone directories and membership rosters, sometimes enhanced with information from public records, such as census data, auto registrations, birth announcements, business start-ups, or bankruptcies. p. 161

component lifestyles modes of living that involve choosing goods and services that meet one's diverse needs and interests rather than conforming to a single, traditional lifestyle. p. 20

computer-assisted personal interviewing technique in which the interviewer reads the questions from a computer screen and enters the respondent's data directly into a computer. p. 80

computer-assisted self-interviewing technique in which the respondent reads questions on a computer screen and directly keys his or her answers into a computer. p. 80

concentrated targeting strategy a strategy used to select one segment of a market to target marketing efforts. p. 145

concept test evaluation of a new-product idea, usually before any prototype has been created. p. 199

conclusive research a more specific type of research that attempts to provide clarity to a decision maker by identifying specific courses of action. p. 75

consumer behaviour how consumers make purchase decisions and how they use and dispose of purchased goods or services; also includes the factors that influence purchase decisions and product use. p. 94

consumer decision-making process a five-step process used by consumers when buying goods or services. p. 95

consumer product a product bought to satisfy an individual's personal wants. p. 177

consumer sales promotion sales promotion activities targeting the ultimate consumer. p. 339

consumer-generated content any form of publicly available online content created by consumers; also referred to as user-generated content. p. 306

consumer-to-consumer (C2C) reviews consumers' reviews of products on the vendors' sites where the products were purchased. p. 97

continuous media schedule a media scheduling strategy in which advertising is run steadily throughout the advertising period; used for products in the later stages of the product life cycle. p. 329

contract manufacturing private-label manufacturing by a foreign company. p. 61

control provides the mechanisms both for evaluating marketing results in light of the plan's objectives and for correcting actions that do not help the organization reach those objectives within budget guidelines. p. 45

convenience product a relatively inexpensive item that merits little shopping effort. p. 178

convenience sample a form of nonprobability sample using respondents who are convenient, or readily accessible, to the researcher—for example, employees, friends, or relatives. p. 84

convenience store a miniature supermarket, carrying only a limited line of high-turnover convenience goods. p. 277

cooperative advertising an arrangement in which the manufacturer and the retailer split the costs of advertising the manufacturer's brand. p. 324

cord cutting discontinuing or never committing to a TV cable or satellite provider. p. 325

core competencies key unique strengths that are hard to imitate and underlie the functioning of an organization. p. 39

core service the most basic benefit the consumer is buying. p. 218

corporate or professional blogs blogs that are sponsored by a company or one of its brands and maintained by one or more of the company's employees. p. 363

corporate social responsibility a business's concern for society's welfare. p. 26

cost competitive advantage being the low-cost competitor in an industry while maintaining satisfactory profit margins. p. 39

cost per contact the cost of reaching one member of the target market. p. 327

cost per click the cost associated with a consumer clicking on a display or banner ad. p. 327

costs the combined financial value of all inputs that go into the production of a company's products, both directly and indirectly. p. 232

countertrade a form of trade in which all or part of the payment for goods or services is in the form of other goods or services. p. 65

coupon a certificate that entitles consumers to an immediate price reduction when they buy the product. p. 341

coverage ensuring product availability in every outlet where potential customers might want to buy it. p. 264

credence quality a characteristic that consumers may have difficulty assessing even after purchase because they do not have the necessary knowledge or experience. p. 213

crisis management a coordinated effort to handle all the effects of either unfavourable publicity or an unexpected unfavourable event. p. 333

cross-tabulation a method of analyzing data that shows the analyst the responses to one question in relation to the responses to one or more other questions. p. 85

crowdsourcing the use of consumers to develop and market products. p. 357

culture the set of values, norms, attitudes, and other meaningful symbols that shape human behaviour and the artifacts, or products, of that behaviour as they are transmitted from one generation to the next. p. 101

cumulative quantity discount a deduction from list price that applies to the buyer's total purchases made during a specific period. p. 242

customer relationship management (CRM) a system that gathers information about customers that can help to build customer loyalty and retain those loyal customers. p. 152

customer satisfaction customers' evaluation of a good or service in terms of whether it has met their needs and expectations. p. 6

customer value the relationship between benefits and the sacrifice necessary to obtain those benefits. p. 7

customer-centric a philosophy under which the company customizes its product and service offering based on data generated through interactions between the customer and the company. p. 157

data mining an analytical process that compiles actionable data on the purchase habits of a firm's current and potential customers. p. 157

data warehouse a central repository of data from various functional areas of the organization that are stored and inventoried on a centralized computer system so that the information can be shared across all functional departments of the business. p. 161

database an organized system of data collection that allows for assessment, usually by computer. p. 161

deceptive pricing promoting a price or price saving that is not actually available. p. 247

decision confirmation the reaffirmation of the wisdom of the decision a consumer has made. p. 98

decline stage a long-run drop in sales. p. 208

decoding interpretation of the language and symbols sent by the source through a channel. p. 299

demographic segmentation segmenting markets by age, gender, income, ethnic background, and family life cycle. p. 136

demography the study of people's vital statistics, such as their age, race and ethnicity, and location. p. 21

department store a store housing several departments under one roof. p. 277

depth interview an interview that involves a discussion between a well-trained researcher and a respondent who is asked about attitudes and perspectives on a topic. p. 78

derived demand demand in the business market that comes from demand in the consumer market. p. 122

descriptive research a type of conclusive research that attempts to describe marketing phenomena and characteristics. p. 75

destination stores stores that consumers purposely plan to visit. p. 286

development the stage in the product development process in which a prototype is developed and a marketing strategy is outlined. p. 199

diffusion the process by which the adoption of an innovation spreads. p. 204

direct channel a distribution channel in which producers sell directly to customers. p. 260

direct foreign investment active ownership of a foreign company or of overseas manufacturing or marketing facilities. p. 62

direct mail a printed form of direct-response communication that is delivered directly to consumers' homes. pp. 281, 334

direct marketing (direct-response marketing) techniques used to get consumers to make a purchase from their home, office, or another nonretail setting. p. 280

direct retailing the selling of products by representatives who work door-to-door, office-to-office, or at-home parties. p. 280

direct-response broadcast advertising that uses television or radio and includes a direct call to action asking the consumer to respond immediately. p. 333

direct-response communication communication of a message directly from a marketing company and directly to an intended individual target audience. p. 304

direct-response print advertising in a print medium that includes a direct call to action. p. 334

direct-response television (DRTV) advertising that appears on television and encourages viewers to respond immediately. p. 333

discount store a retailer that competes on the basis of low prices, high turnover, and high volume. p. 278

discrepancy of assortment the lack of all the items a customer needs to receive full satisfaction from a product or products. p. 257

discrepancy of quantity the difference between the amount of product produced and the amount an end-user wants to buy. p. 256

discretionary income the amount of money people have to spend on nonessential items. p. 19

diversification a strategy of increasing sales by introducing new products into new markets. p. 38

Do Not Call List (DNCL) a free service whereby Canadians register their telephone number to reduce or eliminate phone calls from telemarketers. p. 334

drugstores retail stores that stock pharmacy-related products and services as their main draw. p. 277

dual distribution (multiple distribution) the use of two or more channels to distribute the same product to target markets. p. 262

dumping the sale of an exported product at a price lower than that charged for the same or a like product in the home market of the exporter. p. 65

earned media a category of promotional tactic based on a public relations model that gets customers talking about products or services. p. 307

electronic data interchange (EDI) information technology that replaces the paper documents that usually accompany business transactions, such as purchase orders and invoices, with electronic transmission of the needed information to reduce inventory levels, improve cash flow, streamline operations, and increase the speed and accuracy of information transmission. p. 270

empathy caring, individualized attention paid to customers. p. 215

empowerment delegation of authority to solve customers' problems quickly—usually by the first person who learns of the customer's problem. p. 158

encoding the conversion of the sender's ideas and thoughts into a message, usually in the form of words or signs. p. 299

engineered demand where firms, led by marketers, discover a marketable need not yet known by the consumer. p. 96

environmental factors non-controllable factors caused by natural disasters, which negatively or positively affect organizations. p. 20

environmental scanning the collection and interpretation of information about forces, events, and relationships in the external environment that may affect the future of the organization or the implementation of the marketing plan. p. 37

ethics the moral principles or values that generally govern the conduct of an individual or a group. p. 28

ethnographic research the study of human behaviour in its natural context; involves observation of behaviour and physical setting. p. 82

European Union (EU) a free trade zone encompassing 28 European countries. p. 57

evaluation gauging the extent to which the marketing objectives have been achieved during the specified period. p. 45

evoked set (consideration set) a group of the most preferred alternatives resulting from an information search, which a buyer can further evaluate to make a final choice. p. 97

exchange people giving up one thing to receive another thing they would rather have. p. 7

exclusive distribution a form of distribution that involves only one or a few dealers within a given area. p. 265

experience curves curves that show costs declining at a predictable rate as experience with a product increases. pp. 39, 241

experience quality a characteristic that can be assessed only after use. p. 213

experiential marketing a form of advertising that focuses on helping consumers experience a brand such that a memorable and emotional connection is formed between the consumer and the brand. p. 332

experiment a method a researcher uses to gather primary data to determine cause and effect. p. 82

exploratory research an informal discovery process that attempts to gain insights and a better understanding of the management and research problems. p. 74

export agents intermediaries who act like manufacturers' agents for exporters; the export agents live in the foreign market. p. 60

export broker an intermediary who plays the traditional broker's role by bringing buyer and seller together. p. 60

exporting selling domestically produced products to buyers in another country. p. 60

express warranty a written guarantee. p. 190

extensive decision making the most complex type of consumer decision making, used when considering the purchase of an unfamiliar, expensive product or an infrequently purchased item; requires the use of several criteria for evaluating options and much time for seeking information. p. 99

external information search the process of seeking information in the outside environment. p. 96

factory outlet an off-price retailer that is owned and operated by a manufacturer. p. 279

family brand the marketing of several different products under the same brand name. p. 185

family life cycle (FLC) a series of stages determined by a combination of age, marital status, and the presence or absence of children. p. 139

feedback the receiver's response to a message. p. 300

flexible pricing (variable pricing) different customers pay different prices for essentially the same merchandise bought in equal quantities. p. 244

flighted media schedule a media scheduling strategy in which ads are run heavily every other month or every two weeks, to achieve a greater impact with an increased frequency and reach at those times. p. 329

floating exchange rates prices of different currencies move up and down based on the demand for and the supply of each currency. p. 65

FOB origin pricing the buyer absorbs the freight costs from the shipping point ("free on board"). p. 243

focus group a small group of recruited participants engaged in a nonstructured discussion in a casual environment. p. 78

follow-up the final step of the selling process, in which the salesperson ensures that delivery schedules are met, that the goods or services perform as promised, and that the buyers' employees are properly trained to use the products. p. 349

four Ps product, place, promotion, and price, which together make up the marketing mix. p. 43

frame error a sample drawn from a population that differs from the target population. p. 84

franchisee an individual or a business that is granted the right to sell a franchiser's product. p. 283

franchiser the originator of a trade name, product, methods of operation, and so on, that grants operating rights to another party to sell its product. p. 282

franchise relationships in which the business rights to operate and sell a product or service are granted by the franchiser to the franchisee. p. 282

freight absorption pricing the seller pays all or part of the actual freight charges and does not pass them on to the buyer. p. 243

frequency the number of times an individual is exposed to a given message during a specific period. p. 327

frequent-buyer program a loyalty program in which loyal consumers are rewarded for making multiple purchases of a particular good or service. p. 342

full-line discount stores retailers that offer consumers very limited service and carries a broad assortment of well-known, nationally branded hard goods. p. 278

functional discount (trade discount) a discount to wholesalers and retailers for performing channel functions. p. 242

gap model a model identifying five gaps that can cause problems in service delivery and influence customer evaluations of service quality. p. 215

General Agreement on Tariffs and Trade (GATT) a trade agreement that contained loopholes that enabled countries to avoid trade-barrier reduction agreements. p. 55

Generation X people born between 1966 and 1978. p. 23

Generation Y people born between 1979 and 2000. p. 22

Generation Z people born between 1995 and 2009. p. 21

generic product a no-frills, no-brand-name, low-cost product that is simply identified by its product category. p. 183

generic product name a term that identifies a product by class or type and cannot be trademarked. p. 186

geodemographic segmentation segmenting potential customers into neighbourhood lifestyle categories. p. 141

geographic segmentation segmenting markets by region of a country or the world, market size, market density, or climate. p. 136

global brand a brand where at least 20 percent of the product is sold outside its home country or region. p. 183

global marketing marketing that targets markets throughout the world. p. 48

global marketing standardization production of uniform products that can be sold the same way all over the world. p. 52

global vision a recognition of and reaction to international marketing opportunities using effective global marketing strategies and being aware of threats from foreign competitors in all markets. p. 48

green marketing the development and marketing of products designed to minimize negative effects on the physical environment. p. 28

gross domestic product (GDP) the total market value of all goods and services produced in a country for a given period. p. 50

gross margin the amount of money the retailer makes as a percentage of sales after the cost of goods sold is subtracted. p. 276

gross national income (GNI) per capita one measure of the ability of a country's citizens to buy various goods and services. p. 53

Group of Twenty (G20) a forum for international economic development that promotes discussion between industrial and emerging-market countries on key issues related to global economic stability. p. 58

growth stage the second stage of the product life cycle when sales typically grow at an increasing rate, many competitors enter the market, large companies may start to acquire small pioneering firms, and profits are healthy. p. 208

high-net-worth individuals (HNWI) individuals who have $1 million in liquid financial assets. p. 59

horizontal conflict a channel conflict that occurs among channel members on the same level. p. 266

ideal self-image the way an individual would like to be. p. 107

implementation the process that turns a marketing plan into action assignments and ensures that these assignments are executed in a way that accomplishes the plan's objectives. p. 44

implied warranty an unwritten guarantee that the good or service is fit for the purpose for which it was sold. p. 190

inconsistency the inability of service quality to be consistent each time it is delivered because the service depends on the people that provide it. p. 214

independent retailers retailers owned by a single person or partnership and not operated as part of a larger retail institution. p. 276

individual branding the use of different brand names for different products. p. 185

inflation a measure of the decrease in the value of money, expressed as the percentage reduction in value since the previous year. p. 19

infomercial a 30-minute or longer advertisement that looks more like a TV talk show than a sales pitch. p. 325

informational labelling package labelling designed to help consumers make proper product selections and to lower their cognitive dissonance after the purchase. p. 188

innovation a product perceived as new by a potential adopter. p. 204

inseparability the inability of the production and consumption of a service to be separated; consumers must be present during the production. p. 214

inshoring returning jobs to Canada. p. 50

institutional advertising a form of advertising designed to enhance a company's image rather than promote a particular product. p. 318

intangibility the inability of services to be touched, seen, tasted, heard, or felt in the same manner that goods can be sensed. p. 213

integrated marketing communications (IMC) the careful coordination of all promotional messages for a product or a service to ensure the consistency of messages at every contact point where a company meets the consumer. p. 309

intensive distribution a form of distribution aimed at having a product available in every outlet where target customers might want to buy it. p. 264

interaction the point at which a customer and a company representative exchange information and develop learning relationships. p. 158

internal information search the process of recalling information stored in one's memory. p. 96

internal marketing treating employees as customers and developing systems and benefits that satisfy their needs. p. 223

International Monetary Fund (IMF) an international organization that acts as a lender of last resort, providing loans to

troubled nations, and also works to promote trade through financial cooperation. p. 58

interpersonal communication direct, face-to-face communication between two or more people. p. 298

introductory stage the full-scale launch of a new product into the marketplace. p. 207

inventory the inability of services to be stored for future use. p. 214

inventory control system a method of developing and maintaining an adequate assortment of materials or products to meet a manufacturer's or a customer's demand. p. 270

involvement the amount of time and effort a buyer invests in the search, evaluation, and decision processes of consumer behaviour. p. 99

joint demand the demand for two or more items used together in a final product. p. 122

joint venture a domestic firm's purchase of part of a foreign company or a domestic firm joining with a foreign company to create a new entity. p. 61

just-in-time production (JIT) a process that redefines and simplifies manufacturing by reducing inventory levels and delivering raw materials just when they are needed on the production line. p. 269

knowledge management the process by which learned information from customers is centralized and shared for the purpose of enhancing the relationship between customers and the organization. p. 158

lead generation (prospecting) identification of those firms and people most likely to buy the seller's offerings. p. 347

lead qualification determination of a sales prospect's (1) recognized need, (2) buying power, and (3) receptivity and accessibility. p. 348

learning a process that creates changes in behaviour, immediate or expected, through experience and practice. p. 110

learning (CRM) in a CRM environment, the informal process of collecting customer data through customer comments and feedback on product or service performance. p. 157

licensing the legal process whereby a licensor agrees to let another firm use its manufacturing process, trademarks, patents, trade secrets, or other proprietary knowledge. p. 61

lifestyle a mode of living as identified by a person's activities, interests, and opinions. p. 107

lifetime value (LTV) analysis a data manipulation technique that projects the future value of the customer over a period of years by using the assumption that marketing to repeat customers is more profitable than marketing to first-time buyers. p. 163

limited decision making the type of decision making that requires a moderate amount of time for gathering information and deliberating about an unfamiliar brand in a familiar product category. p. 99

location-based social networking sites websites that combine the fun of social networking with the utility of location-based GPS technology. p. 365

logistics the process of strategically managing the efficient flow and storage of raw materials, in-process inventory, and finished goods from point of origin to point of consumption. p. 268

logistics information system the link that connects all the logistics functions of the supply chain. p. 268

loss-leader pricing a product is sold near or even below cost in the hope that shoppers will buy other items once they are in the store. p. 244

loyalty marketing program a promotional program designed to build long-term, mutually beneficial relationships between a company and its key customers. p. 342

mall intercept interview interviewing people in the common areas of shopping malls. p. 79

manufacturer's brand the brand name of a manufacturer. p. 184

market people or organizations with needs or wants and the ability and willingness to buy. p. 134

market development a marketing strategy that involves attracting new customers to existing products. p. 38

market opportunity analysis (MOA) the description and estimation of the size and sales potential of market segments that are of interest to the firm and the assessment of key competitors in these market segments. p. 43

market penetration a marketing strategy that tries to increase market share among existing customers, using existing products. p. 38

market segment a subgroup of people or organizations sharing one or more characteristics that cause them to have similar product needs. p. 134

market segmentation the process of dividing a market into meaningful, relatively similar, and identifiable segments or groups. p. 134

market share a company's product sales as a percentage of total sales for that industry. p. 235

marketing the activities that develop an offering in order to satisfy a customer need. p. 2

marketing audit a thorough, systematic, periodic evaluation of the objectives, strategies, structure, and performance of the marketing organization. p. 45

marketing channel (channel of distribution) a set of interdependent organizations that ease the transfer of ownership as products move from producer to business user or consumer. p. 256

marketing company orientation a strong emphasis on the marketing concept and development of a more comprehensive approach to understanding the customer. p. 5

marketing environment the entire set of situational conditions, both internal (strengths and weaknesses) and external (opportunities and threats), within which a business operates. p. 34

marketing mix a unique blend of product, place, promotion, and pricing strategies designed to produce mutually satisfying exchanges with a target market. p. 43

marketing objective a statement of what is to be accomplished through marketing activities. p. 42

marketing research the process of planning, collecting, and analyzing data relevant to a marketing decision. p. 72

marketing research objective specific statement about the information needed to solve the research question. p. 74

marketing strategy the activities of selecting and describing one or more target markets and developing and maintaining a marketing mix that will produce mutually satisfying exchanges with target markets. p. 42

marketing-controlled information source a product information source that originates with marketers promoting the product. p. 97

Maslow's hierarchy of needs a method of classifying human needs and motivations into five categories in ascending order of importance: physiological, safety, social, esteem, and self-actualization. p. 109

mass communication the communication of a concept or message to large audiences. p. 298

mass customization a strategy that uses technology to deliver customized services on a mass basis. p. 218

mass customization (build-to-order) a production method whereby products are not made until an order is placed by the customer; products are made according to customer specifications. p. 269

mass merchandising a retailing strategy using moderate to low prices on large quantities of merchandise and lower levels of service to stimulate high turnover of products. p. 278

maturity stage a period during which sales increase at a decreasing rate. p. 208

measurement error an error that occurs when the information desired by the researcher differs from the information provided by the measurement process. p. 84

media mix the combination of media to be used for a promotional campaign. p. 327

media planning the series of decisions advertisers make regarding the selection and use of media, allowing the marketer to optimally and cost-effectively communicate the message to the target audience. p. 323

media schedule designation of the media, the specific publications or programs, and the insertion dates of advertising. p. 329

media-sharing sites websites that allow users to upload and distribute multimedia content, such as videos and photos. p. 364

medium the channel used to convey a message to a target market. p. 323

Mercosur the largest Latin American trade agreement, made up of Argentina, Bolivia, Brazil, Chile, Colombia, Ecuador, Paraguay, Peru, Uruguay, and Venezuela. p. 55

microblogs blogs with strict post-length limits. p. 363

mission statement a statement of the firm's business based on a careful analysis of benefits sought by present and potential customers and an analysis of existing and anticipated environmental conditions. p. 36

mobile advertising advertising that displays text, images, and animated ads via mobile phones or other mobile devices that are data enabled. p. 326

modified rebuy a situation where the purchaser wants some change in the original good or service. p. 128

morals the rules people develop as a result of cultural values and norms. p. 29

motives driving forces that cause a person to take action to satisfy specific needs. p. 109

multiculturalism peaceful and equitable coexistence of different cultures, rather than one national culture, in a country. p. 25

multinational corporations companies that are heavily engaged in international trade, beyond exporting and importing. p. 51

multiplier effect (accelerator principle) the phenomenon in which a small increase or decrease in consumer demand can produce a much larger change in demand for the facilities and equipment needed to make the consumer product. p. 122

multisegment targeting strategy a strategy that chooses two or more well-defined market segments and develops a distinct marketing mix for each. p. 145

mystery shoppers researchers posing as customers who gather observational data about a store. p. 82

need a state of being where we desire something that we do not possess but yearn to acquire. pp. 2, 96

need recognition the result of an imbalance between actual and desired states. p. 96

needs assessment a determination of the customer's specific needs and wants and the range of options the customer has for satisfying them. p. 348

negotiation the process during which both the salesperson and the prospect offer concessions in an attempt to arrive at a sales agreement. p. 349

networking the use of friends, business contacts, co-workers, acquaintances, and fellow members in professional and civic organizations to identify potential clients. p. 347

new product a product new to the world, new to the market, new to the producer or seller, or new to some combination of these. p. 195

new task buy a situation requiring the purchase of a product for the first time. p. 127

new-product strategy a plan that links the new-product development process with the objectives of the marketing department, the business unit, and the corporation. p. 197

niche one segment of a market. p. 145

niche competitive advantage the advantage achieved when a firm seeks to target and effectively serve a single segment of the market. p. 41

noise anything that interferes with, distorts, or slows down the transmission of information. p. 299

nonaspirational reference groups (dissociative groups) groups that influence our behaviour because we try to maintain distance from them. p. 105

noncorporate blogs independent blogs that are not associated with the marketing efforts of any particular company or brand. p. 363

noncumulative quantity discount a deduction from list price that applies to a single order rather than to the total volume of orders placed during a certain period. p. 242

nonmarketing-controlled information source a product information source not associated with advertising or promotion. p. 96

nonprobability sample any sample in which little or no attempt is made to have a representative cross-section of the population. p. 83

nonprofit organization an organization that exists to achieve some goal other than the usual business goals of profit, market share, or return on investment. p. 223

nonprofit organization marketing the effort by nonprofit organizations to bring about mutually satisfying exchanges with target markets. p. 223

nonstore retailing provides shopping without visiting a store. p. 280

norms the values and attitudes deemed acceptable by a group. p. 104

North American Free Trade Agreement (NAFTA) an agreement among Canada, the United States, and Mexico that created the world's largest free trade zone at that time. p. 56

North American Industry Classification System (NAICS) an industry classification system developed by the United States, Canada, and Mexico to classify North American business establishments by their main production processes. p. 126

observation research a research method that relies on four types of observation: people watching people, people watching an activity, machines watching people, and machines watching an activity. p. 81

odd–even pricing (psychological pricing) odd-numbered prices connote bargains, and even-numbered prices imply quality. p. 245

off-price retailer a retailer that sells brand-name merchandise at considerable discounts. p. 279

omni channel retailing an approach that combines the advantages of the physical store experience with the information-rich experience of online shopping, providing the consumer with a seamless experience through all available shopping channels. p. 282

one-to-one marketing an individualized marketing method that uses customer information to build long-term, personalized, and profitable relationships with each customer. p. 146

online marketing two-way communication of a message delivered through the Internet to the consumer. p. 305

online retailing (e-tailing) a type of shopping available to consumers with personal computers and access to the Internet. p. 281

open-ended question an interview question that encourages an answer phrased in the respondent's own words. p. 80

opinion leader an individual who influences the opinions of others. p. 105

optimizers business customers who consider numerous suppliers, both familiar and unfamiliar, solicit bids, and study all proposals carefully before selecting one. p. 143

order processing system a system whereby orders are entered into the supply chain and filled. p. 269

original equipment manufacturers (OEMs) individuals and organizations that buy business goods and incorporate them into the products that they produce for eventual sale to other producers or to consumers. p. 125

outsourcing the practice of using an outside supplier, generally where the productions costs are lower, to complete the work. p. 50

owned media a category of promotional tactic based on brands becoming publishers of their own content to maximize the brands' value to consumers. p. 307

paid media a category of promotional tactic based on the traditional advertising model whereby a brand pays for advertising space. p. 307

Pareto Principle a principle holding that 20 percent of all customers generate 80 percent of the demand. p. 142

penetration pricing a relatively low price for a product initially as a way to reach the mass market. p. 240

perception the process by which people select, organize, and interpret stimuli into a meaningful and coherent picture. p. 108

perceptual mapping a means of displaying or graphing, in two or more dimensions, the location of products, brands, or groups of products in customers' minds. p. 148

personal selling a purchase situation involving a personal, paid-for communication between two people in an attempt to influence each other. p. 304

personality a way of organizing and grouping the consistency of an individual's reactions to situations. p. 107

persuasive labelling package labelling that focuses on a promotional theme or logo; consumer information is secondary. p. 188

pioneering advertising a form of advertising designed to stimulate primary demand for a new product or product category. p. 319

planned obsolescence the practice of modifying products so those that have already been sold become obsolete before they actually need replacement. p. 181

planning the process of anticipating future events and determining strategies to achieve organizational objectives in the future. p. 34

platform a business model, usually digital, where producers and buyers exchange value. p. 97

point-of-sale interactions communications between customers and organizations that occur at the point of sale, usually in a store. p. 159

pop-up shop temporary retail space that sells merchandise of any kind. p. 286

position the place a product, brand, or group of products occupies in consumers' minds relative to competing offerings. p. 147

positioning a process that influences potential customers' overall perception of a brand, a product line, or an organization in general. p. 147

preapproach a process that describes the research a salesperson must do before contacting a prospect. p. 348

predatory pricing the practice of charging a very low price for a product with the intent of driving competitors out of business or out of a market. p. 248

predictive modelling a data manipulation technique in which marketers try to determine, based on some past set of occurrences, the odds that some other occurrence, such as an inquiry or a purchase, will take place in the future. p. 164

premium an extra item offered to the consumer, usually in exchange for some proof of purchase of the promoted product. p. 341

price that which is given up in an exchange to acquire a good or service. p. 232

price bundling marketing two or more products in a single package for a special price. p. 245

price elasticity of demand a measurement of change in consumer demand for a product relative to the changes in its price. p. 236

price fixing an agreement between two or more firms on the price they will charge for a product. p. 247

price lining offering a product line with several items at specific price points. p. 244

price sensitivity consumers' varying levels of desire to buy a given product at different price levels. p. 236

price skimming a high introductory price, often coupled with heavy promotion. p. 240

price strategy a basic, long-term pricing framework that establishes the initial price for a product and the intended direction for price movements over the product life cycle. p. 239

primary data information that is collected for the first time and is used for solving the particular problem under investigation. p. 77

primary membership groups groups with which individuals interact regularly in an informal, face-to-face manner. p. 104

private brand a brand name owned by a wholesaler or a retailer. p. 184

probability sample a sample in which every element in the population has a known statistical likelihood of being selected. p. 83

procurement the process of buying goods and services for use in the operations of an organization. p. 268

product anything, both favourable and unfavourable, received by a person in an exchange for possession, consumption, attention, or short-term use. p. 176

product advertising a form of advertising that promotes the benefits of a specific good or service. p. 318

product category all brands that satisfy a particular type of need. p. 207

product development a marketing strategy that entails the creation of new products for current customers. pp. 38, 198

product differentiation a positioning strategy that some firms use to distinguish their products from those of competitors. p. 147

product item a specific version of a product that can be designated as a distinct offering among an organization's products. p. 179

product life cycle (PLC) a concept that traces the stages of a product's acceptance, from its introduction (birth) to its decline (death). p. 206

product line a group of closely related product items. p. 179

product line depth the different version of a product item in a product line. p. 179

product line extension adding products to an existing product line to compete more broadly in the industry. p. 181

product line length the number of product items in a product line. p. 179

product mix all products that an organization sells. p. 179

product mix width the number of product lines an organization offers. p. 179

product modification changing one or more of a product's characteristics. p. 180

product offering the mix of products offered to the consumer by the retailer; also called the product assortment or merchandise mix. p. 284

product placement a public relations strategy that involves getting a product, service, or company name to appear in a movie, television show, radio program, magazine, newspaper, video game, video or audio clip, book, or commercial for another product; on the Internet; or at special events. p. 331

product/service differentiation competitive advantage the provision of a unique benefit that is valuable to buyers beyond simply offering a low price. p. 40

production orientation a focus on manufacturing and production quantity in which customers are meant to choose based on what is most abundantly available. p. 4

professional services pricing used by people with experience, training, and often certification, fees are typically charged at an hourly rate, but may be based on the solution of a problem or performance of an act. p. 244

profit revenue minus expenses. p. 232

programmatic buying using an automated system to make media buying decisions in real time. p. 322

promotion communication by marketers that informs, persuades, reminds, and connects potential buyers to a product for the purpose of influencing an opinion or eliciting a response. p. 296

promotional mix the combination of promotional tools—including advertising, publicity, sales promotion, personal selling, direct-response communication, and social media—used to reach the target market and fulfill the organization's overall goals. p. 302

promotional strategy a plan for the use of the elements of promotion: advertising, public relations, personal selling, sales promotion, direct-response communication, and social media. p. 296

psychographic segmentation market segmentation on the basis of personality, motives, lifestyles, and geodemographics categories. p. 140

psychological factors tools that consumers use to recognize, gather, analyze, and self-organize to aid in decision making. p. 108

public relations the marketing function that evaluates public attitudes, identifies areas within the organization the public may be interested in, and executes a program of action to earn public understanding and acceptance. p. 303

public service advertisement (PSA) an announcement that promotes a program of a nonprofit organization or of a federal, provincial or territorial, or local government. p. 226

publicity public information about a company, a product, a service, or an issue appearing in the mass media as a news item. p. 303

pull strategy a marketing strategy that stimulates consumer demand to obtain product distribution. p. 313

pulsing media schedule a media scheduling strategy that uses continuous scheduling throughout the year coupled with a flighted schedule during the best sales periods. p. 329

purchasing power a comparison of income versus the relative cost of a set standard of goods and services in different geographic areas. p. 19

push money money offered to channel intermediaries to encourage them to push products—that is, to encourage other members of the channel to sell the products. p. 344

push strategy a marketing strategy that uses aggressive personal selling and trade advertising to convince a wholesaler or a retailer to carry and sell particular merchandise. p. 313

pyramid of corporate social responsibility a model that suggests corporate social responsibility is composed of economic, legal, ethical, and philanthropic responsibilities and that the firm's economic performance supports the entire structure. p. 27

quantity discount a unit price reduction offered to buyers buying either in multiple units or at more than a specified dollar amount. p. 242

random error type of sampling error in which the selected sample is an imperfect representation of the overall population. p. 84

random sample a sample arranged in such a way that every element of the population has an equal chance of being selected as part of the sample. p. 83

reach the number of target consumers exposed to a commercial at least once during a specific period, usually four weeks. p. 327

real self-image the way an individual actually perceives himself or herself to be. p. 107

rebates cash refunds given for the purchase of a product during a specific period. p. 341

receivers the people who decode a message. p. 299

recency-frequency-monetary (RFM) analysis the analysis of customer activity by recency, frequency, and monetary value. p. 163

recession a period of economic activity characterized by negative growth, which reduces demand for goods and services. p. 19

reciprocity a practice where business purchasers choose to buy from their own customers. p. 123

reference group a group in society that influences an individual's purchasing behaviour. p. 104

referrals recommendations to a salesperson from a customer or business associate. p. 347

relationship commitment a firm's belief that an ongoing relationship with another firm is so important that the relationship warrants maximum efforts at maintaining it indefinitely. p. 118

relationship marketing a strategy that focuses on keeping and improving relationships with current customers. p. 6

relationship selling (consultative selling) a multistage sales process that involves building, maintaining, and enhancing interactions with customers for the purpose of developing long-term satisfaction through mutually beneficial partnerships. p. 345

reliability the ability to perform a service dependably, accurately, and consistently. p. 215

repositioning changing consumers' perceptions of a brand in relation to competing brands. p. 149

resale price maintenance attempts by a producer to control a store's retail price for the product. p. 248

research design a plan that specifies how to answer the research question and achieve the research objectives by laying out the research tools and techniques necessary to collect and analyze data. p. 74

response list a customer list that includes the names and addresses of individuals who have responded to an offer of some kind, such as by mail, telephone, direct-response television, product rebates, contests or sweepstakes, or billing inserts. p. 161

responsiveness the ability to provide prompt service. p. 215

retailer the market intermediary that sells goods and services to the final consumer. pp. 259, 274

retailing all the activities directly related to the sale of goods and services to the ultimate consumer for personal, nonbusiness use. p. 274

retailing mix a combination of the six Ps—product, place, promotion, price, presentation, and personnel—to sell goods and services to the ultimate consumer. p. 284

return on investment (ROI) net profits divided by the investment. p. 235

revenue the price per unit charged to customers multiplied by the number of units sold. p. 232

review sites websites that allow consumers to post, read, rate, and comment on opinions regarding all kinds of products and services. p. 366

routine response behaviour the type of decision making exhibited by consumers buying frequently purchased, low-cost goods and services; requires little search and decision time. p. 99

sales orientation hard selling to the customer, who has greater choice thanks to more competition in the marketplace. p. 4

sales presentation a formal meeting in which the salesperson presents a sales proposal to a prospective buyer. p. 349

sales process (sales cycle) the set of steps a salesperson goes through to sell a particular product or service. p. 346

sales promotion marketing activities—other than personal selling, advertising, direct-response marketing, and public relations—that stimulate consumer buying and dealer effectiveness. p. 303

sales proposal a formal written document or professional presentation that outlines how the salesperson's product or service will meet or exceed the prospect's needs. p. 349

sample a subset from a larger population. p. 83

sampling a promotional program that allows the consumer the opportunity to try a product or service for free. p. 343

sampling error error that occurs when a sample does not represent the target population. p. 84

satisficers business customers who place their order with the first familiar supplier to satisfy their product and delivery requirements. p. 143

scaled-response question a closed-ended question designed to measure the intensity of a respondent's answer. p. 81

scrambled merchandising the tendency to offer a wide variety of nontraditional goods and services under one roof. p. 277

screening the first filter in the product development process, which eliminates ideas that are inconsistent with the organization's new-product strategy or are obviously inappropriate for some other reason. p. 199

search quality a characteristic that can be easily assessed before purchase. p. 213

seasonal discount a price reduction for buying merchandise out of season. pp. 213, 242

seasonal media schedule a media scheduling strategy that runs advertising only during times of the year when the product is most likely to be purchased. p. 329

secondary data data previously collected for any purpose other than the one at hand. p. 75

secondary membership groups groups with which individuals interact less consistently and more formally than with primary membership groups. p. 104

segmentation bases (variables) characteristics of individuals, groups, or organizations. p. 135

selective distortion a process whereby consumers change or distort information that conflicts with their feelings or beliefs. p. 108

selective distribution a form of distribution achieved by screening dealers to eliminate all but a few in any single area. p. 265

selective exposure the process whereby a consumer decides which stimuli to notice and which to ignore. p. 108

selective retention a process whereby consumers remember only information that supports their personal beliefs. p. 108

self-concept how consumers perceive themselves in terms of attitudes, perceptions, beliefs, and self-evaluations. p. 107

self-regulation programs voluntarily adopted by business groups to regulate the activities of their members. p. 17

self-service technologies (SST) technological interfaces that allow customers to provide themselves with products and/or services without the intervention of a service employee. p. 280

sender the originator of the message in the communication process. p. 298

service the result of applying human or mechanical efforts to people or objects. p. 212

service mark a trademark for a service. p. 186

shop-at-home television network a specialized form of direct-response marketing whereby television shows display merchandise, with the retail price, to home viewers. p. 281

shopper analytics searching for and discovering meaningful patterns in shopper data for the purpose of fine-tuning, developing, or changing market offerings. p. 289

shopper marketing understanding how one's target consumers behave as shoppers, in different channels and formats, and leveraging this intelligence to generate sales or other positive outcomes. pp. 289, 343

shopping product a product that requires comparison shopping because it is usually more expensive than a convenience product and is found in fewer stores. p. 178

showrooming searching for a product in a store and then going online to try to find it at a better price. p. 282

simulated (laboratory) market testing the presentation of advertising and other promotion materials for several products, including a test product, to members of the product's target market. p. 202

single-price tactic offering all goods and services at the same price (or perhaps two or three prices). p. 243

social acceleration the concept of exponentially rapid growth starting with human desire for improved products, spurring competitive pursuit of market share, driving innovation and technology, resulting in higher standard of living, but with new socio-environmental problems. p. 27

social class a group of people who are considered nearly equal in status or community esteem, who regularly socialize among themselves both formally and informally, and who share behavioural norms. p. 103

social commerce a subset of e-commerce that involves the interaction and user contribution aspects of social media to assist in the online buying and selling of products and services. p. 357

social gaming playing an online game that allows for social interaction between players on a social media platform. p. 327

social media a collection of online communication tools that facilitate conversations online; when used by marketers, social media tools encourage consumer empowerment. pp. 305, 354

social networking sites websites that allow individuals to connect—or network—with friends, peers, and business associates. p. 364

social news sites websites that allow users to decide which content is promoted on a given website by voting that content up or down. p. 365

social selling leveraging social networks to find the right prospects and build trusted relationships to achieve sales goals. p. 348

socialization process the passing down of cultural values and norms to children. p. 106

societal marketing orientation looking not only at the customer but expanding marketing efforts to include aspects from the external environment. p. 5

sociometric leader a low-profile, well-respected collaborative professional who is socially and professionally well connected. p. 105

spatial discrepancy the difference between the location of a producer and the location of widely scattered markets. p. 257

specialty discount stores retail stores that offer a nearly complete selection of single-line merchandise and use self-service, discount prices, high volume, and high turnover. p. 279

specialty product a particular item with unique characteristics for which consumers search extensively and for which they are very reluctant to accept substitutes. p. 179

specialty store a retail store specializing in a given type of merchandise. p. 277

sponsorship a public relations strategy in which a company spends money to support an issue, a cause, or an event that is consistent with corporate objectives, such as improving brand awareness or enhancing corporate image. p. 332

status quo pricing a pricing objective that maintains existing prices or meets the competition's prices. p. 236

stimulus any unit of input affecting one or more of the five senses: sight, smell, taste, touch, hearing. p. 96

straight rebuy a situation in which the purchaser reorders the same goods or services without looking for new information or new suppliers. p. 128

strategic business unit (SBU) a subgroup of a single business or a collection of related businesses within the larger organization. p. 35

strategic channel alliances cooperative agreements between business firms to use one of the manufacturer's already established distribution channels. p. 263

strategic planning the managerial process of creating and maintaining a fit between the organization's objectives and resources and evolving market opportunities. p. 34

subculture a homogeneous group of people who share elements of the overall culture and also have their own unique cultural elements. p. 103

supercentres retail stores that combine groceries and general merchandise goods with a wide range of services. p. 278

supermarkets large, departmentalized, self-service retailers that specialize in food and some nonfood items. p. 277

supplementary services a group of services that support or enhance the core service. p. 218

supply chain the connected chain of all the business entities, both internal and external to the company, that perform or support the marketing channel functions. p. 256

supply chain management a management system that coordinates and integrates all the activities performed by supply chain members into a seamless process, from the source to the point of consumption, resulting in enhanced customer and economic value. p. 267

supply chain team an entire group of individuals who orchestrate the movement of goods, services, and information from the source to the consumer. p. 268

survey research the most popular technique for gathering primary data, in which a researcher interacts with people to obtain facts, opinions, and attitudes. p. 79

sustainable competitive advantage an advantage that cannot be copied by the competition. p. 41

SWOT analysis identifying internal environment of strengths (S) and weaknesses (W) as well as external opportunities (O) and threats (T). p. 37

tangibles the physical evidence of a service, including the physical facilities, tools, and equipment used to provide the service. p. 215

target market a group of people or organizations for which an organization designs, implements, and maintains a marketing mix intended to meet the needs of that group, resulting in mutually satisfying exchanges. pp. 14, 144

telemarketing the use of telecommunications to sell a product or service; involves both outbound and inbound calls. pp. 281, 334

temporal discrepancy a product is produced but a customer is not ready to buy it. p. 257

test marketing the limited introduction of a product and a marketing program to determine the reactions of potential customers in a market situation. p. 201

touch points all possible areas of a business where customers have contact with that business. p. 159

trade allowance a price reduction offered by manufacturers to intermediaries, such as wholesalers and retailers. p. 344

trade sales promotion sales promotion activities targeting a marketing channel member, such as a wholesaler or retailer. p. 339

trademark the exclusive right to use a brand or part of a brand. p. 186

triple bottom line a business philosophy seen as the pursuit of profit while also benefiting society and the environment. p. 26

trust confidence in an exchange partner's reliability and integrity. p. 118

two-part pricing charging two separate amounts to consume a single good or service. p. 247

unbundling reducing the bundle of services that comes with the basic product. p. 246

undifferentiated targeting strategy a marketing approach that views the market as one big market with no individual segments and thus uses a single marketing mix. p. 144

uniform delivered pricing the seller pays the actual freight charges and bills every purchaser an identical, flat freight charge. p. 243

unique selling proposition a desirable, exclusive, and believable advertising appeal selected as the theme for a campaign. p. 320

universal product codes (UPCs) a series of thick and thin vertical lines (bar codes), readable by computerized optical scanners that match the codes to brand names, package sizes, and prices. p. 188

unsought product a product unknown to the potential buyer or a known product that the buyer does not actively seek. p. 179

Uruguay Round an agreement created by the World Trade Organization to dramatically lower trade barriers worldwide. p. 55

usage-rate segmentation dividing a market by the amount of product bought or consumed. p. 141

value the enduring belief shared by a society that a specific mode of conduct is personally or socially preferable to another mode of conduct. p. 102

value-based pricing setting the price at a level that seems to the customer to be a good price compared with the prices of other options. p. 242

vertical conflict a channel conflict that occurs between different levels in a marketing channel, most typically between the manufacturer and wholesaler or between the manufacturer and retailer. p. 266

warehouse membership clubs limited-service merchant wholesalers that sell a limited selection of brand-name appliances, household items, and groceries to members, small businesses, and groups. p. 279

warranty a confirmation of the quality or performance of a good or service. p. 190

webrooming researching a product online and then going to a store to buy it. p. 282

World Bank an international bank that offers low-interest loans, advice, and information to developing nations. p. 58

World Trade Organization (WTO) a trade organization that replaced the old General Agreement on Tariffs and Trade (GATT). p. 55

zone pricing a modification of uniform delivered pricing that divides the total market into segments or zones and charges a flat freight rate to all customers in a given zone. p. 243

Chapter 1

1. Andrew Hampp, "Saatchi CEO Kevin Roberts Declares Death of Marketing, Future of Movements @ MIDEM," *Billboard*, January 30, 2012, www.billboard.com/biz/articles/news/branding/1099158/saatchi-ceo-kevin-roberts-declares-death-of-marketing-future-of (accessed April 2017).

2. Ibid.

3. William L. Wilkie and Elizabeth S. Moore, "Scholarly Research in Marketing: Exploring the '4 Eras' of Thought Development," *Journal of Public Policy & Marketing*, 22, 2, 2003, 116–146.

4. Internet Movie Database, *Mad Men*, "For Those Who Think Young" (2008), www.imdb.com/title/tt1118051/quotes (accessed April 2017).

5. Scott Stein, "McDonald's Happy Meal Step-It Fitness Trackers Officially Recalled," August 23, 2016, www.cnet.com/news/mcdonalds-fitness-trackers-officially-recalled/.

6. Andrew Hampp, "Saatchi CEO Kevin Roberts Declares Death of Marketing, Future of Movements @ MIDEM," *Billboard*, January 30, 2012, www.billboard.com/biz/articles/news/branding/1099158/saatchi-ceo-kevin-roberts-declares-death-of-marketing-future-of (accessed April 2017).

7. Valarie A. Zeithaml, Mary Jo Bitner, and Dwayne D. Gremler, *Services Marketing*, 4th ed. (New York: McGraw-Hill Irwin, 2006), 110.

8. "Building Business Around Customers: Know Thy Customer," *BusinessWeek*, September 12, 2005, 8.

9. Vadim Kotelnikov, "Customer Retention: Driving Profits Through Giving Customers Lots of Reasons to Stay," e-COACH, www.1000ventures.com/business_guide/crosscuttings/customer_retention.html (accessed April 2017).

10. Christine Moorman, "Why Apple Is a Great Marketer," *Forbes*, October 7, 2012, www.forbes.com/sites/christinemoorman/2012/07/10/why-apple-is-a-great-marketer/ (accessed April 2017).

11. W. Brett Wilson, "Best Business Advice from W. Brett Wilson," *Financial Post*, June 10, 2013, http://business.financialpost.com/2013/06/10/best-business-advice-from-w-brett-wilson/ (accessed April 2017).

12. "W. Brett Wilson's Top 10 Tips for Small Businesses and Startups," CBC News, October 9, 2009, www.cbc.ca/news/business/w-brett-wilson-s-top-10-tips-for-small-businesses-and-startups-1.859309 (accessed April 2017).

Chapter 2

1. Quote Addicts, https://www.linkedin.com/pulse/thought-provoking-quotes-from-simon-sinek-slava-khabovets-mba (accessed August 14, 2017).

2. Michael E. Porter, "How Competitive Forces Shape Strategy," *Harvard Business Review*, March 1979 (accessed May 30, 2017).

3. Competition Bureau, www.competitionbureau.gc.ca (accessed September 15, 2014).

4. "The Canadian Code of Advertising Standards," Advertising Standards Canada, www.adstandards.com/en/Standards/canCodeOfAdStandards.aspx (accessed December 3, 2016).

5. "Median Total Income by Family," Statistics Canada, www.statcan.gc.ca/tables-tableaux/sum-som/l01/cst01/famil108a-eng.htm (accessed December 3, 2016).

6. "Special Reports—What Difference Does Learning Make to Financial Security?", Employment and Social Development Canada, January 2008, www4.hrsdc.gc.ca/.3ndic.1t.4r@-eng.jsp?iid=54 (accessed August 28, 2011).

7. "Canada's Debt-to-Income Ratio Sets New Record High at 165%," CBC News, March 11, 2016, www.cbc.ca/news/business/debt-income-1.3486811 (accessed December 3, 2016).

8. Matthew McClearn, "Prediction: Canada Will Slip Back into Recession in 2013," *Canadian Business*, January 28, 2013, www.canadianbusiness.com/economy/canada-will-slip-back-into-recession-in-2013/ (accessed October 24, 2013).

9. Bertrand Marotte, "Majority of Rich Canadians Feel Better Off Than before the Recession," *Globe and Mail*, October 3, 2013, www.theglobeandmail.com/report-on-business/majority-of-rich-canadians-feel-better-off-than-before-the-recession/article14660866/ (accessed October 24, 2013).

10. John Gibson, "Alberta Recession, One of the Most Severe Ever, TD Report Finds," CBC News, July 18, 2016, www.cbc.ca/news/canada/calgary/td-economics-report-alberta-recession-gdp-forecast-1.3684056 (accessed December 3, 2016).

11. "Nearly $1 Billion of Oils Sands Activity Lost Due to Fort McMurray Fires So Far, Report Estimates," *Financial Post*, May 17, 2016, http://business.financialpost.com/news/energy/nearly-1-billion-of-oilsands-production-lost-due-to-fort-mcmurray-fires-so-far-report-estimates?__lsa=af8a-8573 (accessed December 3, 2016).

12. "Definition of Family," The Vanier Institute of the Family, www.vanierinstitute.ca/definition_of_family#.Umhz7Pkqhng (accessed October 22, 2013).

13. "Thinking about Families: An Interview with Katherine Scott, Director of Programs, Vanier Institute of the Family," *Transition Magazine*, Winter 2010, 5–7, http://vanierinstitute.ca/include/get.php?nodeid=220 (accessed October 21, 2013).

14. Ibid.

15. Aaron Saltzman, "Smartphones and Children: Unstoppable Trend Leaves Parents with Questions and Fears," CBC News, November 17, 2015, www.cbc.ca/news/business/children-smartphones-1.3321564 (accessed December 3, 2016).

16. Karen Mazurkewich, "Tweens & Technology," *National Post*, August 10, 2010, www.mhoneill.com/106B/articles/tween%20power.pdf (accessed August 29, 2011).

17. Michael Oliveira, "25% of Grade 4 Students Have Cell Phone: Canadian Survey," *Toronto Star*, January 22, 2014, www.thestar.com/news/canada/2014/01/22/25_of_grade_4_students_have_cellphone_canadian_survey.html (accessed December 3, 2017).

18. Doug Norris, PhD, "Millennials: The Generation DuJour," Environics Analytics, January 22, 2016, www.environicsanalytics.ca/blog-details/ea-blog/2016/01/22/millennials-the-generation-du-jour (accessed December 4, 2016).

19. Karen Kroll, "Yes, Millennials and Boomers Can Work Together," *Forbes*, www.forbes.com/sites/zurich/2015/07/31/yes-millennials-and-boomers-can-work-together-heres-how-to-help/#6df9b98d7d36 (accessed December 4, 2016).

20. "Myths, Exaggerations, and Uncomfortable Truths: The real story behind Millenials in the workplace," IBM Institute for Business Value, February 19, 2015, https://www-935.ibm.com/services/us/gbs/thoughtleadership/millennialworkplace/ (accessed December 4, 2016).

21. Karen Akers, "Generation Y: Marketing to the Young and the Restless," *Successful Promotions*, January/February 2005, 33–38.

22. Sarah Boesveld, "Gen Y and Millennial Moms Having More Kids and Abandoning Helicopter Parenting," *National Post*, April 24, 2014, http://news.nationalpost.com/news/gen-y-and-millennial-moms-having-more-kids-and-abandoning-helicopter-parenting (accessed December 5, 2016).

23. Layton Han, "Gen X: The New Luxury Buyers and How to Reach Them," MediaPost, May 30, 2012, www.mediapost.com/publications/article/175754/gen-x-the-new-luxury-buyers-and-how-to-reach-them.html (accessed February 18, 2014).

24. Timothy Dewhirst, "Who Is Generation X? If Only Marketers Knew," *Globe and Mail*, January 25, 2016, www.theglobeandmail.com/report-on-business/rob-commentary/who-is-generation-x-if-only-marketers-knew/article28365604/ (accessed December 5, 2016).

25. "More Canadians Are 65 and over Than under Age 15, Statscan Says," CBC News, September 29, 2015, www.cbc.ca/news/business/statistics-canada-seniors-1.3248295 (accessed December 5, 2016).

26. Julian Beltrame, "Unemployed Kids a Burden for Boomer Parents: Report," HuffPost Business, July 5, 2013, www.huffingtonpost.ca/2013/05/07/baby-boomers-children-money_n_3230204.html (accessed October 23, 2012).

27. Ibid.

28. "Census Metropolitan Area and Census Agglomeration Definitions," Statistics Canada, September 17, 2010, www.statcan.gc.ca/pub/93-600-x/2010000/definitions-eng.htm (accessed October 23, 2013).

29. "Canada's Population Tops 36 Million for First Time," CBC News, March 16, 2016, www.cbc.ca/news/canada/stats-can-36-million-canada-population-1.3494677 (accessed December 5, 2016).

30. Martin Turcotte and Mireille Vézina, "Migration from Central to Surrounding Municipalities in Toronto, Montréal and Vancouver," *Canadian Social Trends*, Statistics Canada catalogue no. 11-008-X, 90, Winter 2010, www.statcan.gc.ca/pub/11-008-x/2010002/article/11159-eng.pdf (accessed October 23, 2013).

31. "Canada's Population Tops 36 Million, as Immigrants, Refugees Swell Numbers," CBC News, September 29, 2016, www.cbc.ca/news/business/canada-population-2016-1.3783959 (accessed December 5, 2016).

32. "Young, Suburban and Mostly Asian: Canada's Immigrant Population Surges," *National Post*, May 8, 2013, news.nationalpostcom/2013/05/08/young-suburban-and-mostly-asian-canadas-immigrant-population-surges/ (accessed October 25, 2013).

33. "Canada Census: One in Five Speaks a Foreign Language at Home," *National Post*, October 24, 2012 http://news.nationalpost.com/news/canada/canada-census-one-in-five-speaks-a-foreign-language-at-home (accessed December 6, 2016).

34. Susan Krashinksy Robertson, "More Companies Taking Multicultural Marketing to Mainstream Levels," *National Post*, October 8, 2015, http://www.theglobeandmail.com/report-on-business/industry-news/marketing/more-companies-taking-multicultural-marketing-to-mainstream-levels/article26727716/ (accessed August 7, 2017).

35. FROG Reporters, "12 Tech Trends That Will Shape Our Lives in 2017," Co.Design, *Fast Company Magazine*, December 6, 2016, https://www.fastcodesign.com/3066275/12-tech-trends-that-will-shape-our-lives-in-2017 (accessed December 6, 2016).

36. This section is adapted from Archie B. Carroll, "The Pyramid of Corporate Social Responsibility: Toward the Moral Management of Organizational Stakeholders," *Business Horizons*, July–August 1991, 39–48. See also Kirk Davidson, "Marketers Must Accept Greater Responsibilities," *Marketing News*, February 2, 1998, 6.

37. Kasturi Rangan, Lisa Chase, and Sohel Karim, "The Truth About CSR," *Harvard Business Review*, January–February 2015, https://hbr.org/2015/01/the-truth-about-csr (accessed December 7, 2016).

38. Julia Howell, "The Bottom Line of Corporate Community Giving," Imagine Canada, October 22, 2012, https://www-935.ibm.com/services/us/gbs/thoughtleadership/millennialworkplace/ (accessed December 7, 2016).

39. "Greenlist™," S. C. Johnson, www.scjohnson.ca/en/scj_greenlist.aspx (accessed October 25, 2013).

40. Based on Edward Stevens, *Business Ethics* (New York: Paulist Press, 1979). Used with permission of Paulist Press.

41. Anusorn Singhapakdi, Scott J. Vitell, and Kenneth L. Kraft, "Moral Intensity and Ethical Decision-Making of Marketing Professionals," *Journal of Business Research*, 36, 3, 1996, 245–255; and Ishmael P. Akaah and Edward A. Riordan, "Judgments of Marketing Professionals about Ethical Issues in Marketing Research: A Replication and Extension," *Journal of Marketing Research*, XXVI, 1989, 112–120.

Chapter 3

1. https://www.layerpoint.com/memorable-travis-kalanick-quotes/ (accessed August 14, 2017).

2. "Eat. Energize," Freshii, http://ir.freshii.com/home/default.aspx (accessed February 20, 2017).

Chapter 4

1. "Ethan Zuckerman Quotes," Brainy Quotes, https://www.brainyquote.com/quotes/quotes/e/ethanzucke554839.html (accessed October 15, 2016).

2. "Trade in 2016 to Grow at Slowest Pace since the Financial Crisis," World Trade Organization, press release, September 27, 2016, https://www.wto.org/english/news_e/pres16_e/pr779_e.htm (accessed October 15, 2016).

3. Shane Dingman, "Ten Canadian Firms Search for Overseas Success: Com Dev International," *Globe and Mail*, June 23, 2015, http://www.theglobeandmail.com/report-on-business/rob-magazine/top-1000/ten-canadian-firms-in-search-of-overseas-success/article25078712/ (accessed October 15, 2016).

4. "Our Business," McCain, www.mccain.com/GoodBusiness/business/Pages/default.aspx (accessed October 15, 2016).

5. Joe Castaldo, "What Really Went Wrong with Target Canada," *Marketing*, January 22, 2016, http://www.marketingmag.ca/brands/what-really-went-wrong-with-target-canada-166300 (accessed October 15, 2016).

6. "Canada's State of Trade: Trade and Investment Update—2015," Global Affairs Canada, http://www.international.gc.ca/economist-economiste/performance/state-point/state_2015_point/index.aspx?lang=eng ().accessed October 15, 2016

7. "Doors Open for Canada's SME Exporters," RBC Economics—Research, October 2015, http://www.rbc.com/economics/economic-reports/pdf/other-reports/sme-oct15.pdf (accessed October 15, 2016).

8. "5 Canadian Consumer Trends to Shape the Future of Retail," CBC News, October 21, 2013, http://www.cbc.ca/news/business/5-canadian-consumer-trends-to-shape-the-future-of-retail-1.2129072 (accessed October 15, 2016).

9. "Value of Exports for Job Creation, Economic Growth and Long-term Prosperity," Global Affairs Canada, http://www.international.gc.ca/strategy-strategie/export_fs-fd_exportation.aspx?lang=eng, (accessed July 19, 2017).

10. Daniel Workman, "Canada's Top 10 Exports," World's Top Exports, July 13, 2017, http://www.worldstopexports.com/canadas-top-exports/ (accessed October 16, 2016).

11. "Bangladesh Factory Collapse," Huffington Post, January 11, 2015, www.huffingtonpost.com/news/bangladesh-factory-collapse (accessed January 26, 2015).

12. "5by20: What We're Doing," Coca-Cola Company, http://www.coca-colacompany.com/our-company/5by20-what-were-doing (accessed October 16, 2016).

13. Nicole Webb, "Why Sleeping in Ikea Is Perfectly Acceptable, in China," Huffpost, http://www.huffingtonpost.com/nicole-webb/why-sleeping-in-ikea-is-p_1_b_9677464.html (accessed October 17, 2016).

14. "Mistakes in Advertising," LEO Network, www.learnenglish.de/mistakes/HorrorMistakes.html (accessed September 15, 2014).

15. "GNI per Capita Ranking, Atlas Method and PPP Based," The World Bank, http://data.worldbank.org/data-catalog/GNI-per-capita-Atlas-and-PPP-table (accessed October 18, 2016).

16. Ibid.

17. "Cost of Living in Singapore" Expatistan, https://www.expatistan.com/cost-of-living/singapore?currency=USD (accessed July 19, 2017).

18. Christine Birkner, "In Search of the Middle," American Marketing Association, https://www.ama.org/publications/MarketingNews/Pages/in-search-of-the-middle.aspx, (accessed October 23, 2016).

19. Ibid.

20. Christopher Horton, "When It Comes to Luxury, China Still Leads," *New York Times*, April 5, 2016, http://www.nytimes.com/2016/04/05/fashion/china-luxury-goods-retail.html?_r=0 (accessed October 29, 2016).

21. "Canada's Merchandise Trade with China," Asia Pacific Foundation of Canada, https://www.asiapacific.ca/statistics/trade/bilateral-trade-asia-product/canadas-merchandise-trade-china (accessed October 29, 2016).

22. http://www.doingbusiness.org/reports/global-reports/~/media/GIAWB/Doing%20Business/Documents/Annual-Reports/English/DB14-Chapters/DB14-Overview.pdf (accessed October 29, 2016).

23. Kaveh Waddell, "Why Google Quit China—and Why It's Heading Back," *The Atlantic*, January 19, 2016, http://www.theatlantic.com/technology/archive/2016/01/why-google-quit-china-and-why-its-heading-back/424482/ (accessed October 29, 2016).

24. Andy Blatchford, "Russian Sanctions Starting to Bite into Canadian Export Outlook," CBC News, January 2, 2015, http://www.cbc.ca/news/business/russian-sanctions-starting-to-bite-into-canadian-export-outlook-1.2888500 (accessed October 19, 2016).

25. Tanya Talaga, "Made in Canada: Our National Garment Industry Faces Huge Challenges," *Toronto Star*, October 25, 2013, https://www.thestar.com/news/world/clothesonyourback/2013/10/25/made_in_canada_our_national_garment_industry_faces_huge_challenges.html (accessed October 19, 2016).

26. "Canada's Free Trade Agreements," Foreign Affairs, Trade and Development Canada, www.international.gc.ca/trade-agreements-accords-commerciaux/agr-acc/fta-ale.aspx?lang=eng#ongoing (accessed November 3, 2016).

27. "CETA—A Trade Deal That Sets a New Standard for Global Trade: A Fact Sheet," European Commission (Trade), October 29, 2016, http://trade.ec.europa.eu/doclib/press/index.cfm?id=1567 (November 3, 2016).

28. Alex Hunt and Brian Wheeler, "Brexit: All You Need to Know about the UK Leaving the EU," BBC News, July 13, 2017, http://www.bbc.com/news/uk-politics-32810887 (accessed July 20, 2017).

29. "Canada Pledges $20M for Women's Entrepreneurship Program," CBC News, July 8, 2017, http://www.cbc.ca/news/politics/g20-hamburg-female-entrepreneur-program-1.4196164 (accessed July 19, 2017).

30. World Wealth Reports, https://www.worldwealthreport.com (accessed November 3, 2016).

31. Workman, "Canada's Top 10 Exports."

32. "Canadian Icewine Exports 2011–2015," Canadian Vintners Association, http://www.canadianvintners.com/wp-content/uploads/2016/08/Canadian-Icewine-Exports-by-Country-2011-2015.pdf (accessed November 3, 2016).

33. "Skechers Launches Joint Venture in South Korea," Business Wire, November 10, 2016, http://www.businesswire.com/news/home/20161110005045/en/SKECHERS-Launches-Joint-Venture-South-Korea (accessed November 3, 2016).

34. "How Procter & Gamble Is Conquering Emerging Markets," The Motley Fool, www.fool.com/investing/general/2013/10/27/how-procter-gamble-is-conquering-emerging-markets.aspx. (accessed November 6, 2016).

35. Jonathan Asher, "Capturing a Piece of the Global Market," *Brandweek*, June 20, 2005, 20.

36. "What Is Selling Where? Pringles Chips," *Wall Street Journal*, April 24, 2013, D3.

37. Eva Dou and Jenny W. Hsu, "How Convenient: In Taiwan the 24/7 Store Does It All," *Wall Street Journal*, May 16, 2014, http://www.wsj.com/articles/SB10001424052702304518704579520371243903680.

38. Hayley Peterson, "5 Ways Starbucks Is Different in China," Business Insider, August 8, 2014, http://www.businessinsider.com/how-starbucks-is-different-in-china-2014-8 (accessed November 20, 2016).

39. Peterson, "5 Ways Starbucks Is Different in China."

40. Gordon G. Chang, "Very Uncool in China—Will Starbucks Become Mundane," *Forbes*, May 29, 2016, http://www.forbes.com/sites/gordonchang/2016/05/29/very-uncool-in-china-will-starbucks-become-mundane/#d58cd57aeda4 (accessed November 20, 2016).

41. "Countertrade," http://allaboutcountertrade.blogspot.ca (accessed November 20, 2016).

42. Lauren La Rose, "More Canadians Choosing Credit Cards, Mobile Payments over Cash, Study Says," *Globe and Mail*, February 3, 2016,

http://www.theglobeandmail.com/report-on-business/economy/more-canadians-choosing-credit-cards-mobile-payments-over-cash-study-says/article28545469/ (accessed November 20, 2016).

43. Dave Chaffey, "Social Media Research Summary 2017," Smart Insights, April 27, 2017, http://www.smartinsights.com/social-media-marketing/social-media-strategy/new-global-social-media-research/ (accessed July 20, 2017).

44. Will Yakowicz, "The 7 Biggest Social Media Disasters of 2015," *Inc.*, http://www.inc.com/will-yakowicz/the-top-social-media-fails-2015.html (accessed November 20, 2016).

Chapter 5

1. Tamer El Araby, "Market Research in the Digital World," July 7, 2015, Nielsen Insights, http://www.nielsen.com/eg/en/insights/news/2015/market-research-in-the-digital-age.html.

2. "Research Quotes," QFINANCE, www.qfinance.com/finance-and-business-quotes/research (accessed February 2017).

3. "Definition of Marketing: About AMA," American Marketing Association, www.ama.org/AboutAMA/Pages/Definition-of-Marketing.aspx (accessed February 1, 2017).

4. Scott M. Smith and Gerald S. Albaum, *Basic Marketing Research: Volume 1, Handbook for Research Professionals Official Training Guide from Qualtrics* (Provo, UT: Qualtrics Labs, 2012), http://cloudfront.qualtrics.com/q1/wp-content/uploads/2012/02/BasicMarketingResearch.pdf (accessed February 2017); Avery M. Abernethy and George R. Franke, "FTC Regulatory Activity and the Information Content of Advertising," *Journal of Public Policy & Marketing*, 17, Fall 1998, 239–256, www.jstor.org/stable/30000774 (accessed February 2, 2017).

5. Prairie Research Associates, "Response Rates on Mail Surveys," http://www.pra.ca/resources/pages/files/technotes/rates_e.pdf (accessed February 2017).

6. Tony L. Whitehead, "Basic Classical Ethnographic Research Methods," Cultural Ecology of Health and Change, July 17, 2005, https://www.scribd.com/document/164547014/Classical-Ethno-Methods (accessed February 2017).

7. Jo Bowman, "The Rise of People-Watching Research Carried out by Brands," Raconteur, September 1, 2016, http://www.raconteur.net/business/the-rise-of-people-watching-research-carried-out-by-brands (accessed February 2017).

8. Robert Harris, "Evaluating Internet Research Sources," Virtual Salt, December 27, 2013, www.virtualsalt.com/evalu8it.htm (accessed January 31, 2017).

9. Jacob Poushter, "Smartphone Ownership and Internet Usage Continues to Climb in Emerging Economies," Pew Research Center, February 22, 2016, http://www.pewglobal.org/2016/02/22/smartphone-ownership-and-internet-usage-continues-to-climb-in-emerging-economies/ (accessed February 2017).

10. "Most Canadians Still Happy after Four Years without the Penny," Insights West, February 21, 2017, http://www.insightswest.com/news/most-canadians-still-happy-after-four-years-without-the-penny/ (accessed February 2017).

11. "Online Panels," TNS Canada, 2009, www.tnscanada.ca/our-expertise/onlinepanels.html (accessed February 2017).

12. "Communications Monitoring Report 2015: Canada's Communication System: An Overview for Citizens, Consumers, and Creators," October 22, 1025, http://www.crtc.gc.ca/eng/publications/reports/policymonitoring/2015/cmr2.htm.

13. Jasper Lim, "Challenges and Opportunities Facing Mobile Research on a Global Scale," HeraldBoy News, October 20, 2013, www.heraldboy.com/challenges-and-opportunities-facing-mobile-research-on-a-global-scale/ (accessed February 2017).

14. Knowlton Thomas, "Canadians Can't Go One Day without Checking Social Media, Study Says," Techvibes, May 8, 2013, www.techvibes.com/blog/canadians-cant-go-one-day-without-checking-social-media-study-says-2013-05-08 (accessed February 2017).

15. "Our Mobile Planet: Canada—Understanding the Mobile Consumer," Google, May 2013, http://services.google.com/fh/files/misc/omp-2013-ca-en.pdf (accessed February 2017).

16. David Gewirtz, "Volume, Velocity, and Variety: Understanding the Three V's of Big Data," ZDNet, April 20, 2016, http://www.zdnet.com/article/volume-velocity-and-variety-understanding-the-three-vs-of-big-data/.

17. Tom Boellstorff and G.E. Marcus, Ethnography and Virtual Worlds: A Handbook of Method (Princeton, NJ: Princeton University, 2012).

18. "Research Is Creating New Knowledge," C3 Metrics, http://c3metrics.com/research-is-creating-new-knowledge/ (accessed February 2017).

Chapter 6

1. Jeff Dunn, "The Model 3 Will Be Tesla's Biggest Test Yet," Business Insider, March 16, 2017, http://www.businessinsider.com/tesla-model-3-production-deliveries-chart-2017-3 (accessed July 29, 2017).

2. "What's Hot in the Living Spaces of Young Adults?" *American Demographics*, 25, 7, 2003, 14.

3. Ronald Alsop, "The Best Corporate Reputations in America: Johnson & Johnson (Think Babies!) Turns Up Tops," *Wall Street Journal*, September 23, 1999, B1; and Alsop, "Survey Rates Companies' Reputations, and Many Are Found Wanting," *Wall Street Journal*, February 7, 2001, B1.

4. Cathleen Egan, "Kellogg, General Mills Battle over Bars," *Wall Street Journal*, March 26, 2001, B10.

5. Jessica Allen, "Should Canada's Next Prime Minister Be Bilingual?" The Social, January 18, 2017, www.thesocial.ca/thejessfiles/should-canada%E2%80%99s-next-prime-minister-be-bilingual (accessed March 31, 2017).

6. Canadian Press, "Bilingualism Growing, but Not in French and English," CBC News, October 24, 2012, http://www.cbc.ca/news/canada/bilingualism-growing-but-not-in-french-and-english-1.1176469 (accessed July 29, 2017).

7. Raju Mudhar, "Hockey Night in Punjabi Goal Calls Garner Plenty of Attention," *Toronto Star*, June 5, 2016, www.thestar.com/sports/2016/06/05/hockey-night-in-punjabi-goal-calls-garner-plenty-of-attention.html (accessed March 31, 2017).

8. David Sali, "Ottawa Firms Look to Score Big with Celebrity Endorsement Deals," *Ottawa Business Journal*, February 6, 2017, http://www.obj.ca/Local/Sports-and-entertainment/2017-02-06/article-4732049/Ottawa-firms-look-to-score-big-with-celebrity-endorsement-deals (accessed July 29, 2017).

9. "The Buzz Starts Here: Finding the First Mouth for Word-of-Mouth Marketing," Knowledge@Wharton, March 4, 2009.

10. "21 under 21: Music's Hottest Young Starts," *Billboard*, September 29, 2016, www.billboard.com/photos/7519026/21-under-21-desiigner-fifth-harmony-shawn-mendes (accessed March 31, 2017).

11. Marion Chan, "Look Who's Buying Grocieries Now," *Canadian Grocer*, July 8, 2015, http://www.canadiangrocer.com/blog/look-who%E2%80%99s-buying-groceries-now-55466 (accessed March 31, 2017).

12. Linda Crane, "YouthPulseSM 2010," *Trends & Tudes*, November 2010.

13. Nora J. Rifon and Molly Catherine Ziske, "Using Weight Loss Products: The Roles of Involvement, Self-Efficacy and Body Image," in *1995 AMA Educators' Proceedings*, ed. Barbara B. Stern and George M. Zinkhan (Chicago: American Marketing Association, 1995), 90–98.

14. Keith Naughton, "In Car Buying, Baby Boomers Surpass the Young," *Bloomberg Business-Week*, August 29, 2013, www.businessweek.com/articles/2013-08-29/in-car-buying-baby-boomers-surpass-the-young (accessed November 9, 2013).

15. "PRIZMC2 Segmentation," Environics Analytics, www.environicsanalytics.ca/environics-analytics/data/consumer-segmentation/prizmc2 (accessed November 9, 2013).

16. Sarah Hall, "What Color Is Your Cart?" *Self*, September 1999, www.godiva.com (accessed January 2006).

17. Joshua Rosenbaum, "Guitar Maker Looks for a New Key," *Wall Street Journal*, February 11, 1998, B1, B5.

18. Elizabeth J. Wilson, "Using the Dollarmetric Scale to Establish the Just Meaningful Difference in Price," in *1987 AMA Educators' Proceedings*, ed. Susan Douglas et al. (Chicago: American Marketing Association, 1987), 107.

19. Sunil Gupta and Lee G. Cooper, "The Discounting of Discounts and Promotion Thresholds," *Journal of Consumer Research*, December 1992, 401–411.

20. Mark Stiving and Russell S. Winer, "An Empirical Analysis of Price Endings with Scanner Data," *Journal of Consumer Research*, June 1997, 57–67; and Robert M. Schindler and Patrick N. Kirby, "Patterns of Rightmost Digits Used in Advertised Prices: Implications for Nine-Ending Effects," *Journal of Consumer Research*, September 1997, 192–201.

21. Lindsay Myers, "The Self-Help Industry Helps Itself to Billions of Dollars," BrainBlogger, May 23, 2014, http://brainblogger.com/2014/05/23/the-self-help-industry-helps-itself-to-billions-of-dollars/ (accessed April 1, 2017).

Chapter 7

1. "The Henry Ford: America's Greatest History Attraction—Annual Report 2004," The Henry Ford, 2, www.thehenryford.org/images/AnnualReport04.pdf (accessed February 2017).

2. Industry Canada, "Consumer Trends: Chapter 2—Consumers and Changing Retail Markets," July 27, 2012, www.ic.gc.ca/eic/site/oca-bc.nsf/eng/ca02096.html (accessed February 2017).

3. "Shaping the Future of Marketing: B2B," Canadian Marketing Association, www.the-cma.org/disciplines/b2b (accessed February 2017).

4. Robert M. Morgan and Shelby D. Hunt, "The Commitment-Trust Theory of Relationship Marketing," *Journal of Marketing*, 58, 3, 1994, 23.

5. Ibid.

6. Javier Marcos Cuevas, Saara Julkunen, and Mika Gabrielsson, "Power Symmetry and the Development of Trust in Interdependent Relationships: The Mediating Role of Goal Congruence," *Industrial Marketing Management*, 48, July 2015, 149–159, http://dx.doi.org/10.1016/j.indmarman.2015.03.015.

7. Andrew Hampp, "Saatchi CEO Kevin Roberts Declares Death of Marketing, Future of Movements @ MIDEM," *Billboard*, January 30, 2012, www.billboard.com/biz/articles/news/branding/1099158/saatchi-ceo-kevin-roberts-declares-death-of-marketing-future-of (accessed February 2017).

8. "About the IMP Group," Industrial Marketing and Purchasing Group, www.impgroup.org/about.php (accessed February 2017).

9. Scott C. Hammond and Lowell M. Glenn, "The Ancient Practice of Chinese Social Networking: Guanxi and Social Network Theory," *E:CO*, 6, 1–2, 2004, 24–31, http://emergentpublications.com/ECO/eco_other/issue_6_1-2_6_ac.pdf?AspxAutoDetectCookieSupport=1 (accessed February 2017).

10. "Delivering Results That Matter to Canadians," Network of Centres of Excellence of Canada, 2012, www.nce-rce.gc.ca/_docs/reports/annual-annuel/Annual_Report_2011-2012_Rapport_Annuel_eng.pdf (accessed September 16, 2014).

11. Lin Ai and Michael Burt, "Walking the Silk Road: Understanding Canada's Changing Trade Patterns," The Conference Board of Canada, December 2012, www.conferenceboard.ca/e-library/abstract.aspx?did=5266 (accessed February 2017).

12. Government of Canada, "Summary—Canadian Industry Statistics," www.ic.gc.ca/app/scr/app/cis/summary-sommaire/41 (February 2017).

13. Government of Canada, Public Services and Procurement Canada, "Overview of the Department," https://www.tpsgc-pwgsc.gc.ca/apropos-about/cdi-mbb/1/survol-overview-eng.html (February 2017).

14. Statistics Canada, "Employment by Class of Worker and Industry, Canada, Seasonally Adjusted," http://www.statcan.gc.ca/pub/71-001-x/2017004/tbl/tbl-2-eng.htm (accessed February 2017).

15. Matevž Rašković and Barbara Mörec, "Determinants of Supplier-Buyer Relationship Competitiveness in Transnational Companies," *Economic and Business Review*, 15 (1), 2013, 5–31, www.ebrjournal.net/ojs/index.php/ebr/article/download/211/pdf (accessed February 2017).

16. Canadian Internet Registration Authority (CIRA), "The State of E-Commerce in Canada: CIRA Internet Factbook," March 2016, https://cira.ca/sites/default/files/public/Ecommerce-Factbook-March-2016.pdf (accessed February 2017).

17. Ibid.

18. David Sweet, "E-commerce in Canada: Pursuing the Promise—Report of the Standing Committee on Industry, Science and Technology," May 2012, www.parl.gc.ca/content/hoc/Committee/411/INDU/Reports/RP5535392/indurp01/indurp01-e.pdf (accessed February 2017).

19. Ibid.

20. Oracle, "2013 B2B Commerce Trends," April 2013, www.oracle-downloads.com/b2b_commercetrends.pdf (accessed February 2017).

21. Content Marketing Institute and Marketing Profs, "2016 B2B Content Marketing Benchmarks, Budgets, and Trends," http://contentmarketinginstitute.com/wp-content/uploads/2015/09/2016_B2B_Report_Final.pdf (accessed February 2017).

22. Dom Nicastro, "B2B Marketing Stats: CEOs Don't Trust CMOs, Social Doesn't Work, Banner Ads Aren't Dead," CMSWire.com, October 17, 2013, www.cmswire.com/cms/digital-marketing/b2b-marketing-stats-ceos-dont-trust-cmos-social-doesnt-work-banner-ads-arent-dead-022832.php (accessed February 2017).

23. B2B News Network, "The Basics of Great B2B Social Media Policy," August 2, 2016, http://www.b2bnn.com/2016/08/basics-great-b2b-social-media-policy/ (accessed February 2017).

Chapter 8

1. "Case Studies: Manufacturing Case Study: Arc'teryx," Environics Analytics, http://www.environicsanalytics.ca/arc'teryx (accessed January 14, 2017).

2. "Case Studies: Retail Case Study: Carlton Cards," Environics Analytics, http://www.environicsanalytics.ca/carlton-cards (accessed January 14, 2017).

3. "CrossFit Kids," CrossFit, https://kids.crossfit.com (accessed January 14, 2017).

4 "How Marketers Target Kids," MediaSmarts, http://mediasmarts.ca/marketing-consumerism/how-marketers-target-kids (accessed November 8, 2013).

5. "Population by Sex and Age Group," Statistics Canada, November 25, 2013, www.statcan.gc.ca/tables-tableaux/sum-som/l01/cst01/demo10a-eng.htm (accessed November 8, 2013).

6. Issie Lapowsky, "Why Teens Are the Most Elusive and Valuable Customers in Tech," *Inc.*, March 3, 2014, http://www.inc.com/issie-lapowsky/inside-massive-tech-land-grab-teenagers.html (accessed January 14, 2017).

7. "R U Ready 4 Us? An Introduction to Canadian Millennials," Issue, January 19, 2012, https://issuu.com/david.abacus/docs/r_u_ready_for_us_-_an_introduction_to_canadian_mil (accessed January 15, 2017).

8. David Parkinson, Janet McFarland, and Barrie McKenna, "Boom, Bust and Economic Headaches," *Globe and Mail*, January 5, 2017, http://www.theglobeandmail.com/globe-investor/retirement/the-boomer-shift-how-canadas-economy-is-headed-for-majorchange/article27159892/ (accessed January 15, 2017).

9. Nicole Bogart, "More Seniors Are Online, but Tech Adoption Remains Slow for Some," Global News, April 4, 2014, http://globalnews.ca/news/1251264/more-seniors-are-online-but-tech-adoption-remains-slow-for-some/ (accessed January 17, 2017).

10. Julie Rusciolelli, "An Agency President's Advice for Marketing to Women," *Marketing*, August 15, 2016, http://www.marketingmag.ca/brands/an-agency-presidents-advice-for-marketing-to-women-181193/ (accessed January 17, 2017).

11. Marion Chan, "Look Who's Buying Groceries Now," *Canadian Grocer*, July 8, 2015, http://www.canadiangrocer.com/blog/look-who's-buying-groceries-now-55466/ (accessed January 17, 2017).

12. Mark Burgess, "What Unilever's #unstereotype Means for Canada," Strategy, June 27, 2016, http://strategyonline.ca/2016/06/27/what-unilevers-unstereotype-means-for-canada/ (accessed January 17, 2017).

13. Bruce Campion-Smith, "Canadian Families Growing More Diverse, Census Data Shows," *Toronto Star*, September 20, 2012, www.thestar.com/news/canada/2012/09/20/canadian_families_growing_more_diverse_census_data_shows.html (accessed November 9, 2013).

14. Ibid.

15. Charles W. Lamb, Jr., Joe F. Hair, Jr., Carl McDaniel, A. J. Faria, and William J. Wellington, *Marketing*, 4th Canadian Edition (Toronto: Nelson Education Ltd., 2009), 169–170.

16. "The Evolving Canadian Population," Environics Analytics, July 7, 2016, http://www.environicsanalytics.ca/footer/news/2016/07/07/the-evolving-canadian-population/ (accessed January 17, 2017).

17. Environics Analytics, http://www.environicsanalytics.ca/prizm5/ (accessed January 18, 2017).

18. "Luna Protein FAQs," LUNA, www.lunabar.com/products/faqs/luna-protein (accessed September 16, 2014).

19. "Canadian Food Trends to 2020: A Long Range Consumer Outlook," Agriculture and Agri-Food Canada, July 2005, www.weldenscott.ca/pdf/ft-ta_e.pdf (accessed November 8, 2013).

20. "About," The Chickenburger, www.thechickenburger.com/content/about (accessed November 9, 2013).

21. "My Custom Mix," Infinit Nutrition, https://www.infinitnutrition.us/create-a-formula (accessed January 18, 2017).

22. Harmeet Singh, "Toyota Touts 'Safety for Everyone' Message," Strategy, January 27, 2017, http://strategyonline.ca/2017/01/27/toyota-touts-safety-for-everyone-message/ (accessed January 18, 2017).

23. Danny Kucharsky, "Mega Bloks Target Kids at Retail," *Marketing*, November 12, 2001, 4.

24. Josh Kolm, "Fido Delves Deeper into Millennial Life," Strategy, February 7, 2017, http://strategyonline.ca/2017/02/07/fido-delves-deeper-into-the-millennial-life/ (accessed February 9, 2017).

25. Susan Gunelius, "Kia Rolls out Brand Repositioning Ad Campaign," Corporate Eye, January 9, 2015, http://www.corporate-eye.com/main/kia-rolls-out-brand-repositioning-ad-campaign/ (accessed February 9, 2017).

26. Alice Tybout and Brian Sternthal, "Brand Positioning," in *Kellogg on Branding: The Marketing Faculty of The Kellogg School of Management*, ed. Tim Calkins et al. (Hoboken, NJ: John Wiley & Sons, Inc., 2005).

27. Ibid.

Chapter 9

1. "Customer Relationship Management (CRM) Quotes," SmallBizCRM, www.smallbizcrm.com/crm-quotes.html#sthash.DdnmhRvl.dpuf (accessed September 18, 2014).

2. Darrell K. Rigby and Dianne Ledingham, "CRM Done Right," *Harvard Business Review*, November 2004, 2, www.google.ca/url?sa=t&rct=j&q=&esrc=s&source=web&cd=2&ved=0CDQQFjAB&url=http%3A%2F%2Fdownload.microsoft.com%2Fdownload%2F8%2F8%2F2F8%2F8B8106EE-B72C-4B14-96B9-69633E92A0A4%2FCRM_Done_Right.pdf&ei=I776U5rnLseayATv6oHgCg&usg=AFQjCNHwVWxdo0IaIyYd7opiqhXw_4vkQg (accessed August 5, 2014).

3. Adrian Payne and Pennie Frow, "A Strategic Framework for Customer Relationship Management," *Journal of Marketing*, 69, 2005, 167–176, http://ns2.academicroom.com/sites/default/files/article/118/files_articles_Strategic%20Framework%20for%20Customer%20Relationship%20Management.pdf (accessed September 18, 2014).

4. OnDemand5.com, www.ondemand5.com (accessed September 18, 2014).

5. Jeff Sweat, "Keep 'Em Happy," *Internet Week.com*, January 28, 2002.

6. Sony PlayStation, www.playstation.ca/; and "SAP Customer Success Story: Playstation.com Chooses mySAP CRM," http://h71028.www7.hp.com/enterprise/downloads/playstation.pdf (accessed August 3, 2011).

7. SPC, "120+ Retailers. One Card," https://www.spccard.ca/purchase (accessed November 25, 2016).

8. SPC, "Get the Card," www.spccard.ca/about.aspx (accessed August 31, 2011).

9. Sony PlayStation, www.playstation.ca/; and "SAP Customer Success Story: Playstation.com Chooses mySAP CRM," http://h71028.www7.hp.com/enterprise/downloads/playstation.pdf (accessed August 3, 2011).

10. Office of the Privacy Commissioner of Canada, "2015–2016 Annual Report to Parliament on the *Personal Information Protection and Electronic Documents Act* and the *Privacy* Act," https://www.priv.gc.ca/en/opc-actions-and-decisions/reports-to-parliament/201516/ar_201516/.

11. Random House, *Random House Webster's Unabridged Dictionary*, 2nd ed. (New York: Random House Reference, 2005).

12. Ian Munroe, "Bell Data Collection Part of 'Disturbing Trend,'" CBC News, October 30, 2013,

www.cbc.ca/news/technology/bell-data-collection
-part-of-disturbing-trend-1.2223949 (accessed
August 4, 2014); and Ishmael N. Daro, "Questions
Remain about Bell's New Data Mining Plan,"
Canada.com, October 23, 2013, http://o.canada
.com/technology/questions-remain-about-bells
-new-data-mining-plan/ (accessed August 4, 2014).

13. Susan Fournier and Jill Avery, "Putting the
'Relationship' Back into CRM," *MIT Sloan
Management Review,* March 23, 2011, http://
sloanreview.mit.edu/article/putting-the-relationship
-back-into-crm/ (accessed August 5, 2014).

14. Bond Brand Loyalty, "Executive Summary: The 2016
Bond Loyalty Report," http://info.bondbrandloyalty
.com/hubfs/Resources/2016_Bond_Loyalty_Report
_Executive_Summary_US_Launch_Edition.pdf?t
=1467293927651 (accessed November 10, 2016).

15. "Loyalty Cards: Where's the Love?" Strategy,
http://strategyonline.ca/2016/06/08/loyalty-cards
-wheres-the-love/ (accessed November 17, 2016).

16. "Ingersoll-Rand Company Limited Maximizes
Customer Focus with Expanded CRM Capabil-
ities," Oracle, June 2006, www.ediguys.net/pages
/SCIS/ingersoll-rand-siebel-casestudy.pdf (accessed
August 5, 2014); and Darrell K. Rigby and Dianne
Ledingham, "CRM Done Right," *Harvard Business
Review,* November 2004, 2, https://hbr.org/2004/11
/crm-done-right (accessed August 5, 2014).

17. Insights taken from a conversation with
Campion CEO Brock Elliot, June 13, 2008.

18. Kit Davis, "Track Star," *Consumer Goods
Technology,* June 1, 2003, http://consumergoods
.edgl.com/old-magazine%5CTrack-Star52676
(accessed September 18, 2014).

19. "Strength in Numbers: Gigya Introduces Network
Protected Identity, Blocking Account Takeovers
across a Network of 1.1. Billion Digital Identities,"
Market Wired, www.marketwired.com/press-release
/strength-numbers-gigya-introduces-network
-protected-identity-blocking-account-takeovers
-2178976.htm (accessed November 29, 2016).

20. Warwick Ashford, "Gigya Is Consumer Identity
Leader, Finds KuppingerCole," www.computerweekly
.com/news/450403494/Gigya-is-consumer-identify
-leader-finds-KuppingerCole (accessed November
29, 2016).

21. Clara Shih, "Customer Relationship Automation Is the New CRM," *Harvard Business Review,*
October 28, 2016, https://hbr.org/2016/10/customer
-relationship-automation-is-the-new-crm (accessed
November 23, 2016).

Chapter 10

1. "Tesla Motors CEO Elon Musk: 'Great Companies Are Built on Great Products'," Wharton
School, University of Pennsylvania, http://
knowledge.wharton.upenn.edu/article/tesla
-motors-ceo-elon-musk-great-companies-are
-built-on-great-products/

2. "Life on the Digital Edge," Accenture, 2014,
www.accenture.com/t20150523T040714__w__
/us-en/_acnmedia/Accenture/Conversion-Assets
/Microsites/Documents14/Accenture-Augmented
-Reality-Customer-Experience-Drive-Growth.pdf, 6.

3. Todd Wasserman, "P&G Tries to Absorb More
Low-End Sales," *BrandWeek,* September 26, 2005, 4.

4. Todd Wasserman, "P&G Seeks Right Ingredient
to Wash Out Laundry Woes," *BrandWeek,*
August 8, 2005, 5.

5. "The 2016 Best New Product Awards—Winners in
the Beset Kids Products Category," *Canadian Living,*
July 5, 2016, www.canadianliving.com/life-and
-relationships/mediagallery/the-2016-best-new-product
-awards-winners-in-the-best-kids-products-category;
and "21016 Best New Product Award Winners
Announced from Survey of 39,000 Canadians by
Market Research Firm BrandSpark International,"
March 2, 2016, www.bestnewproductawards.biz
/canada/pdf/News-Release-2016-Best-New-Product
-Awards-02-MAR-16.pdf (accessed March 2017).

6. Janet Adamy, "Heinz Sets Overhaul Plans in
Motion," *Wall Street Journal,* September 20, 2005, A4.

7. "Dictionary," American Marketing Association,
www.marketingpower.com/_layouts/dictionary
.aspx?dLetter=B (accessed, March 2017).

8. Brad VanAuken, "What Is a Global Brand?"
Branding Strategy Insider, February 19, 2010,
www.brandingstrategyinsider.com/2010/02/what-is
-a-global-brand.html#.WMLSGhgZNok (accessed
March 2017).

9. "Nielsen: Store Brand Consumers Evolving
in Canada," www.pgstorebrands.com/top-story
-nielsen__store_brand_consumers_evolving_in
_canada-7010.html (accessed March 2017).

10. Chris Powell, "Store Brands Losing Their
Lustre: Study," *Marketing,* July 21, 2011, www
.marketingmag.ca/news/marketer-news/store-brands
-losing-their-lustre-study-32536 (accessed March 2017).

11. Ibid.

12. Deborah L. Vence, "Product Enhancement,"
Marketing News, May 1, 2005, 110.

13. Ibid.

14. Omar El Akkad, "Canadian Court Clears Way to
Trademark Sounds," *Globe and Mail,* March 28, 2012,
http://www.theglobeandmail.com/globe-investor
/canadian-court-clears-way-to-trademark-sounds
/article4096387/ (accessed March 2017).

15. Erin White, "Burberry Wants the Knockoffs to
Knock It Off," *Fort Worth Star Telegram,* May 28,
2003, 6F.

16. Deborah Ball, "The Perils of Packaging: Nestlé
Aims for Easier Openings," *Wall Street Journal,*
November 17, 2005, B1.

17. "Unilever All in for 100 Percent Recyclable
Plastics Packaging by 2025," *Canadian Packaging,*
www.canadianpackaging.com/sustainability
/unilever-100-per-cent-recyclable-plastics
-packaging-2025-149716/.

18. Government of Canada, Competition Bureau,
"Guide to the *Consumer Packaging and Labelling*
Act," www.competitionbureau.gc.ca/eic/site/cb-bc
.nsf/eng/01248.html#sec2.4.1.

Chapter 11

1. C. Gallo, *The Innovation Secrets of Steve Jobs:
Insanely Different: Principles for Breakthrough
Success* (New York: McGraw-Hill, 2011).

2. Nielsen, *Looking to Achieve New Product
Success?,* June 2015, http://www.nielsen.com
/content/dam/nielsenglobal/eu/nielseninsights/pdfs
/Nielsen%20Global%20New%20Product%20
Innovation%20Report%20June%202015.pdf
(accessed February 2017).

3. Ibid., 4.

4. https://www.forbes.com/innovative-companies
/#258357d01d65 (accessed August 2017).

5. Patricia Sellers, "P&G: Teaching an Old Dog
New Tricks," *Fortune,* May 31, 2004, 168.

6. Rebecca Harris, "Activia Brand Positioning Shifts
from Function to Emotion," *Marketing,* September
26, 2016, http://www.marketingmag.ca/brands
/activia-brand-positioning-shifts-from-function
-to-emotion-183672 (accessed February 2017).

7. Darrell Etherington, "Apple's New Product
Strategy," Crunch Network, May 30, 2013, https://
techcrunch.com/2013/05/30/apples-new-product
-strategy/ (accessed February 2017).

8. Gary Fraser and Bryan Mattimor, "Slow Down,
Speed Up New Product Growth," *Brandweek,*
January 11, 2005, 18.

9. Anne Fisher, "How Adobe Kickstarts Innovation
from Its Employees," *Fortune,* February 17, 2015,
http://fortune.com/2015/02/17/adobe-innovation
/(accessed March 2017).

10. Sellers, "P&G: Teaching an Old Dog New
Tricks," 174.

11. Ryan Tate, "Google Couldn't Kill 20 Percent
Time Even if It Wanted To," *Wired,* August 21,
2013, www.wired.com/business/2013/08/20-percent
-time-will-never-die/ (accessed March 2017).

12. Sellers, "P&G: Teaching an Old Dog New
Tricks," 174.

13. Chris Penttila, "Keeping It Fresh," *Entrepreneur,*
April 2005, 88.

14. Aaron Tilley, "Google Acquires Smart Thermostat Maker Nest for $3.2 Billion," *Forbes,*
January 13, 2014, www.forbes.com/sites/aaron-
tilley/2014/01/13/google-acquires-nest-for-3-2
-billion/ (accessed March 2017).

15. Sarah Ellison and Charles Forelle, "Gillette's
Smooth Bet: Men Will Pay More for Five-Blade
Razor," *Wall Street Journal,* September 15, 2005,
B1, B5.

16. Paul Lukas, "How Many Blades Is Enough?",
Fortune, October 31, 2005, 40.

17. David Drake, "6 Ways to Use Crowdfunding
for Product Development," *Entrepreneur,* June
24, 2015, www.entrepreneur.com/article/247668
(accessed March 2017).

18. Kira Vermond, "Why London, Ontario
Is the Perfect Test Market," *Globe and Mail,*
October 19, 2015, www.theglobeandmail.com
/report-on-business/small-business/sb-managing
/london-test-market/article26846284/ (accessed
March 2017).

19. Jeremy Lloyd, "Rory Capern to Lead Twitter
Canada, but U.S. Office in Flux," *Marketing,*
January 25, 2016, http://www.marketingmag.ca
/media/rory-capern-to-lead-twitter-canada-but
-u-s-office-in-flux-166386 (accessed
March 2017).

20. Sami Mughal, "Gillette R&D—A Journey
through Innovation and Implementation,"
OxGadgets, March 28, 2015, www.oxgadgets
.com/2015/03/gillette-rd-a-journey-through
-innovation-and-implementation.html
(accessed March 2017).

21. Chris Gayomali, "I Shaved with Gillette's New
Fusion ProGlide with FlexBall™ Technology Razor,
and Lived to Bloodily Tell about It," FastCompany,
April 30, 2014, www.fastcompany.com/3029800/i
-shaved-with-gillettes-new-fusion-proglide-with
-flexball-technology-razor-and-lived-to-bloo
(accessed March 2017).

22. "How to Market Your New Product to Early
Adopters," BDC, www.bdc.ca/en/articles-tools
/marketing-sales-export/marketing/pages/identifying
-early-adopters.aspx (accessed March 2017).

23. Kevin J. Clancy and Peter C. Krieg, "Product
Life Cycle: A Dangerous Idea," *Brandweek,*
March 1, 2004, 26.

24. "When Will it Fly?", *The Economist,* August 9,
2003, 332.

25. James Daly, "Restart, Redo, Recharge,"
Business 2.0, May 1, 2001, 11.

Chapter 12

1. "Table 282-0008: Labour Force Survey Estimates
(LFS), by North American Industry Classification
System (NAICS), Sex and Age Group," Statistics

Canada, http://www5.statcan.gc.ca/cansim/a26?lang=eng&retrLang=eng&id=2820008&&pattern=&stByVal=1&p1=1&p2=37&tabMode=dataTable&csid= (accessed January 17, 2017).

2. "The Canadian Economy at a Glance," Investors Friend, April 2017, http://www.investorsfriend.com/canadian-gdp-canadian-imports-and-exports/ (accessed January 17, 2017).

3. "Actual Hours Worked per Week by Industry, Seasonally Adjusted (Monthly)," Statistics Canada, http://www.statcan.gc.ca/tables-tableaux/sum-som/l01/cst01/labr68a-eng.htm (accessed January 17, 2017).

4. Jacqueline Palladini, "Spotlight on High-Value Services: Canada's Hidden Export Strength," Conference Board of Canada, May 26, 2015, http://www.conferenceboard.ca/e-library/abstract.aspx?did=7029 (accessed January 21, 2017).

5. Glen Hodgson and Danielle Goldfarb, "Service Exports: Canada's Quiet Growth Engine," Conference Board of Canada, May 6, 2015, http://www.conferenceboard.ca/press/speech_oped/15-05-08/services_exports_canada_s_quiet_growth_engine.aspx (accessed January 21, 2017).

6. Maria Alejandro Lopez, "Saje Natural Wellness: Family Business That Brings Plant-Based Remedies," Forbes, December 13, 2016, http://www.forbes.com/sites/meggentaylor/2016/12/12/saje-natural-wellness-the-family-business-that-brings-plant-based-remedies-to-millions/#7b347f882fff (accessed January 21, 2017).

7. "The Saje Story," Saje Natural Wellness, http://www.saje.com/ca/saje-story.html (accessed January 21, 2017).

8. Valarie A. Zeithaml, Mary Jo Bitner, and Dwayne D. Gremler, Services Marketing: Integrating Customer Focus across the Firm, 4th ed. (New York: McGraw Hill, 2006).

9. "Caring for Our Colleagues: Corporate Responsibility Issue Report 2015/2016," https://thrive.hyatt.com/content/dam/Minisites/hyattthrive/reports/Colleagues-2015.pdf (accessed August 14, 2017).

10. Zeithaml, Bitner, and Gremler, Services Marketing: Integrating Customer Focus across the Firm.

11. "Caring for Our Colleagues: Corporate Responsibility Issue Report 2015/2016."

12. "Consumers Demand a More Personalized Experience and Human Interaction," Accenture Strategy, https://www.accenture.com/ca-en/insight-canadian-consumer-demand-personalized-experience (accessed February 3, 2017).

13. Much of the material in this section is based on Christopher H. Lovelock and Jochen Wirtz, Services Marketing, 5th ed. (Upper Saddle River, NJ: Prentice Hall, 2004).

14. "The 7 Pillars," Moksha Yoga International, www.mokshayoga.ca/about/the_7_pillars/ (accessed December 2013).

15. "Our Commitment," Goodfood, https://makegoodfood.ca/en/our-commitment (accessed February 3, 2017).

16. Lovelock and Wirtz, Services Marketing.

17. Much of the material in this section is based on Dwayne Gremler, Mary Jo Bitner, and Valarie Zeithamel, Services Marketing (New York: McGraw Hill), 2012.

18. "Key Facts about Canada's Charities," Imagine Canada, http://www.imaginecanada.ca/resources-and-tools/research-and-facts/key-facts-about-canada's-charities (accessed February 3, 2017).

19. "Sector Impact," Imagine Canada, http://sectorsource.ca/research-and-impact/sector-impact accessed (February 3, 2017).

20. "What Is a Social Enterprise?", Toronto Enterprise Fund, http://www.torontoenterprisefund.ca/about-tef/what-is-a-social-enterprise (accessed February 3, 2017).

Chapter 13

1. Warren Buffett, Letter to Berkshire Hathaway Shareholders, February 27, 2009, http://www.berkshirehathaway.com/letters/2008ltr.pdf (accessed August 14, 2017).

2. Tyler McNaughton, personal interview, conducted by David Gaudet, November 18, 2016

3. "Broadhead Knowledge," Brewing Brewing Company, http://broadheadbeer.com/about-us/ (accessed August 14, 2017).

4. Thomas T. Nagle and George Cressman, "Don't Just Set Prices, Manage Them," Marketing Management, November/December 2002, 29–33; Jay Klompmaker, William H. Rogers, and Anthony Nygren, "Value, Not Volume," Marketing Management, June 2003, 45–48; and Alison Wellner, "Boost Your Bottom Line by Taking the Guesswork Out of Pricing," Inc., June 2005, 72–82.

5. "Out-Discounting the Discounter," BusinessWeek, May 9, 2004, 78–79; an interesting article on shoppers who use penetration pricing to their advantage is Edward J. Fox and Stephen J. Hoch, "Cherry-Picking," Journal of Marketing, 69, 1, 2005, 46–62.

6. Bruce Alford and Abhijit Biswas, "The Effects of Discount Level, Price Consciousness, and Sale Proneness on Consumers' Price Perception and Behavioral Intention," Journal of Business Research, September 2002, 775–783. See also V. Kumar, Vibhas Madan, and Srini Srinivasan, "Price Discounts or Coupon Promotions: Does It Matter?", Journal of Business Research, September 2004, 933–941.

7. "Price War in Aisle 3," Wall Street Journal, May 27, 2003, B1, B16. See also Kathleen Seiders and Glenn Voss, "From Price to Purchase," Marketing Management, December 2004, 38–43; "Grocery Stores Cut Out the Weekly Specials," Wall Street Journal, July 20, 2005, D1, D3; and Gerald E. Smith and Thomas Nagle, "A Question of Value," Marketing Management, July/August 2005, 39–44.

8. To learn more about pricing fairness, see Lan Xia, Kent B. Monroe, and Jennifer L. Cox, "The Price Is Unfair! A Conceptual Framework of Price Fairness Perceptions," Journal of Marketing, 68, 2004, 1–15.

9. David Bell, Ganesh Iyer, and V. Padmanabhar, "Price Competition under Stockpiling and Flexible Consumption," Journal of Marketing Research, 49, 2002, 292–303.

10. Dilip Soman and John Gourville, "Transaction Decoupling: The Effects of Price Bundling on the Decision to Consume," MSI Report, 2002, 98–131; Stefan Stremersch and Gerard J. Tellis, "Strategic Bundling of Products and Prices: A New Synthesis for Marketing," Journal of Marketing, January 2002, 55–71; and "Forget Prices and Get People to Use the Stuff," Wall Street Journal, June 3, 2004, A2.

11. Dilip Soman and John Gourville, "Transaction Decoupling: How Price Bundling Affects the Decision to Consume," Journal of Marketing Research, 38, 2001, 30–44.

12. "Gas Stations Busted for Price Fixing in Quebec," Kelowna Daily Courier, June 13, 2008, A1, A5; "Quebec Gas Companies Charged with Price Fixing," CTV News, June 12, 2008, www.ctvnews.ca/quebec-gas-companies-charged-with-price-fixing-1.301955 (accessed September 2008).

Chapter 14

1. Matt Ackerson, "Would LinkedIn Founder, Reid Hoffman, Invest in Your Business? Here's the Answer…", autogrow.ca, https://autogrow.co/would-linkedin-founder-reid-hoffman-invest-in-your-business-heres-the-answer/ (accessed February 2017).

2. Marsham International Food Brokers Inc. web page, http://marsham.ca (accessed February 2017).

3. Nicole Harris, "'Private Exchanges' May Allow B-to-B Commerce to Thrive after All," Wall Street Journal, March 16, 2001, B1; Michael Totty, "The Next Phase," Wall Street Journal, May 21, 2001, B8

4. "Pot Vending Machines Coming to Canada, Medbox Promises," Huffington Post, October 17, 2014, www.huffingtonpost.ca/2014/10/17/pot-vending-machines-canada_n_4116533.html (accessed February 2017).

5. "Pepsi, Starbucks Teaming Up," Supermarket News, October 31, 1994, 31; "Starbucks Corporation Fiscal 2006 Annual Report," Starbucks, 2006, http://media.corporate-ir.net/media_files/irol/99/99518/reports/StarbucksAnnualReport.pdf (accessed February 2017).

6. Toyota Industrial Equipment, www.toyotaforklift.com (accessed February 2017); www.toyotaforklift.com/about_us/company_profile/toyotaphilosophy.aspx; Elena Eptako Murphy, "Buying on Price Alone Can Lead to High Operating Costs," Purchasing.com, September 4, 2003.

7. "About Brokerhouse," Brokerhouse Distributors Inc., www.brokerhousedist.com/About.aspx (accessed February 2017).

8. Cassie Howard, "How Does Dollarama Get Name Brand Items?", DollarStoreHouse.com, www.dollarstorehouse.com/dollarama-name-brands/ (accessed February 2017).

9. Leigh Muzslay, "Shoes That Morph from Sneakers to Skates Are Flying out of Stores," Wall Street Journal, July 26, 2001, B1; Heelys, www.heelys.com (accessed February 2017).

10. "Angela Ahrendts to Join Apple as Senior Vice President of Retail and Online Stores," Apple Press Info, October 14, 2014, www.apple.com/pr/library/2014/10/15Angela-Ahrendts-to-Join-Apple-as-Senior-Vice-President-of-Retail-and-Online-Stores.html (accessed February 2017).

11. "Apple, AT&T Hail Decade Long Partnership," Mobile World Live, October 29, 2015, https://www.mobileworldlive.com/featured-content/home-banner/apple-att-hail-decade-long-partnership/ (accessed February 2017).

12. Jon Brodkin, "AT&T Says Its Merger with Time Warner Is Exactly What Customers Want," Ars Technica, February 21, 2017, https://arstechnica.com/tech-policy/2017/02/att-says-youll-love-more-relevant-advertising-after-time-warner-merger/ (accessed February 2017).

13. Jonathan Welsh, "Auto Makers Now 'Slam' Cars Right in the Factory," Wall Street Journal, October 30, 2001, B1.

14. Clara Lu, "Zara Supply Chain Analysis—The Secret behind Zara's Retail Success," TradeGecko, December 4, 2014, https://www.tradegecko.com/blog/zara-supply-chain-its-secret-to-retail-success (accessed February 2017).

15. Kevin O'Marah, "Zara Uses Supply Chain to Win Again," Forbes, March 9, 2016, https://www.forbes.com/sites/kevinomarah/2016/03/09/zara-uses-supply-chain-to-win-again/#29362cb51256 (accessed February 2017).

16. Julie Schlosser, "Just Do It," Fortune, December 14, 2004, http://archive.fortune.com/magazines/fortune/fortune_archive/2004/12/14/8214244/index.htm (accessed February 2017).

17. Jack Wilson, "Real-Life Examples of Successful JIT Systems," Bright Hub Project Management, July 22, 2015, http://www.brighthubpm.com/methods-strategies/71540-real-life-examples-of-successful-jit-systems/ (accessed February 2017).

18. "The Bay EDI Solutions via the Web," Covalent Works, https://www.covalentworks.com/partner?id=794 (accessed February 2017).

19. Toby Herscovitch, "Wide Range: Cutting the Cost of Crossing Borders," *ExportWise*, Winter 2006, 8–9.

20. Kevin Hogan, "Borderline Savings," *Business 2.0*, May 17, 2001, 34.

Chapter 15

1. "Disruption in Retail: From Product to Pixels," Deloitte and the Retail Council of Canada, https://www.retailcouncil.org/sites/default/files/documents/Deloitte-RCC-2015-BC-Retail-Study.pdf (accessed February 5, 2017).

2. "Retail and Wholesale Trade," Statistics Canada, http://www.statcan.gc.ca/pub/11-402-x/2012000/chap/retail-detail/retail-detail-eng.htm?fpv=60000 (accessed February 6, 2017).

3. Tavia Grant, "Canadian Employers Shed Jobs as Retail Sector Contracts," *Globe and Mail*, May 8, 2015, http://www.theglobeandmail.com/report-on-business/economy/jobs/canada-sheds-20000-jobs-in-april/article24326675/ (accessed February 7, 2017).

4. "Survey Reveals List of Canada's Most Trusted Retailers," Retail Insider, April 11, 2016, http://www.retail-insider.com/retail-insider/2016/4/survey (accessed February 7, 2017).

5. "Industry Fact Sheet," Canadian Convenience Stores Association, http://theccsa.ca/content/industry-fact-sheet accessed February 7, 2017

6. "The Industry: Profile of Direct Sellers," Direct Sellers Association, http://dsa.ca/the-industry/industry-stats/ (accessed February 7, 2017).

7. "Market Research on Digital Media, Internet Marketing," eMarketer, www.emarketer.com (accessed February 7, 2017).

8. *The State of E-Commerce in Canada*, CIRA, March 2016, https://cira.ca/sites/default/files/public/Ecommerce-Factbook-March-2016.pdf (accessed February 5, 2017).

9. Hollie Shaw, "Online Retail Sales to Hit $34-billion in Canada by 2018," *Financial Post*, July 23, 2013, http://business.financialpost.com/2013/07/23/online-retail-sales-to-hit-40-billion-in-canada-by-2018/ (accessed October 2013).

10. Stephanie Vozza, "7 Ways to Make Your Brick-and-Mortar Store Mobile Friendly," Shopify Blogs, June 17, 2016, https://www.shopify.ca/retail/127504771-7-ways-to-make-your-brick-and-mortar-store-mobile-friendly (accessed February 5, 2017).

11. *The State of E-Commerce in Canada*.

12. Michelle da Silva, "10 New Year's Resolutions Every Retailer Should Keep," Shopify Blogs, December 15, 2016, https://www.shopify.ca/retail/10-new-year-s-resolutions-every-retailer-should-keep (accessed February 7, 2017).

13. *The State of E-Commerce in Canada*.

14. Melody McKinnon, "2016 Holiday Season—Canadian Online Shopping Forecast Data," Canadian's Internet Business, November 7, 2016, http://canadiansinternet.com/2016-holiday-season-canadian-online-shopping-forecast-data/ (accessed February 9, 2017).

15. Josh Kolm, "How Canadians Decide What to Buy," Strategy, March 29, 2016, http://strategyonline.ca/2016/03/29/how-canadians-decide-what-to-buy-in-2016/.pdf (accessed July 31, 2017).

16. "CFA 2016 Accomplishments Report," Canadian Franchise Association, https://www.cfa.ca/wp-content/uploads/2016/04/CFAAccomplishments Report_2016.pdf (accessed February 9, 2017).

17. "About Gilt," Gilt, https://www.gilt.com/company/main (accessed February 9, 2017).

18. Savaya Shinkaruk, "What's Popping up around Calgary: The New Retail Trend," *Calgary Journal*, March 31, 2016, http://www.calgaryjournal.ca/index.php/living/3211-what-s-popping-up-around-calgary-the-new-retail-trend (accessed February 9, 2017).

19. "Retail Trends and Predictions," Vend, https://www.vendhq.com/university/retail-trends-and-predictions-2016 (accessed February 9, 2017).

20. Marina Strauss, "In E-Commerce Battle, Grocery Stores Perfect 'Click and Collect'," *Globe and Mail*, April 22, 2016, http://www.theglobeandmail.com/report-on-business/on-the-frontlines-of-the-online-grocery-shopping-battle/article29726909/ (accessed February 9, 2017).

21. Grant, "Canadian Employers Shed Jobs as Retail Sector Contracts."

22. "Retail Trends and Predictions."

23. "12 Forecasts for the Retail Industry in 2017," Vend, https://www.vendhq.com/university/retail-trends-and-predictions-2017 (accessed February 10, 2017).

Chapter 16

1. "Quotes," http://www.quotes.net/quote/6791 (accessed March 16, 2017).

2. Harmeet Singh, "Koodo Goes Deeper into 'Choose Happy'," Strategy, March 16, 2017, http://strategyonline.ca/2017/03/16/koodo-goes-deeper-into-choose-happy/ (accessed March 16, 2017).

3. "Growing Our Tourism Industry," Newfoundland and Labrador, January 18, 2016, http://www.releases.gov.nl.ca/releases/2016/btcrd/0118n01.aspx (accessed March 16, 2017).

4. Sheila Shayon, "Buzz Marketing: Honey Nut Cheerios Pulls Mascot for #BringBacktheBees," March 20, 2017, http://brandchannel.com/2017/03/20/honey-nut-cheerios-bring-back-the-bees-032017/ (accessed March 22, 2016).

5. Tim Nudd, "60 Years Late, Heinz Approves Don Draper's 'Pass the Heinz' Ads and Is Actually Running Them," *Adweek*, March 13, 2017, http://www.adweek.com/creativity/50-years-later-heinz-approves-don-drapers-pass-the-heinz-ads-and-is-actually-running-them/ (accessed March 23, 2016).

6. Harmeet Singh, "Check It Out: KFC Delivers the Love," Strategy, February 9, 2017, http://strategyonline.ca/2017/02/09/check-it-out-kfc-delivers-the-love/ (accessed March 23, 2016).

7. Tim Nudd, "Nike's 'Better for It' Women's Campaign Gets Brand's First-Ever Scripted YouTube Series," *Adweek*, January 28, 2016, http://www.adweek.com/brand-marketing/nikes-better-it-womens-campaign-gets-brands-first-ever-scripted-youtube-series-169245/ (accessed April 4, 2016).

8. The AIDA concept is based on the classic research of E. K. Strong, Jr., as theorized in *The Psychology of Selling and Advertising* (New York: McGraw-Hill Book Co., 1925); and "Theories of Selling," *Journal of Applied Psychology*, 9, 1, 75–86.

9. Harmeet Singh, "A New Concept, New Strategy, New Target for Sears," Strategy, April 7, 2017, http://strategyonline.ca/2017/04/07/a-new-concept-new-strategy-new-target-for-sears/ (April 8, 2017).

10. Daniel J. Howard and Thomas E. Barry, "A Review and Critique of the Hierarchy of Effects in Advertising," *International Journal of Advertising*, 9, 2, 1990, 121–135.

11. Tea and Herbal Association of Canada, http://www.tea.ca/wp-content/uploads/2016/08/2015-Tea-Fact-Sheet.pdf (accessed April 9, 2017).

12. Josh Kolm. "Tetley Seeks out Balance," Strategy, January 17, 2017, http://strategyonline.ca/2017/01/17/tetley-seeks-out-balance/ (accessed April 9, 2017).

Chapter 17

1. Bree Rody-Mantha, "Growth in Canadian Ad Spend to Slow across Most Media: Study," Media in Canada, April 13, 2017, http://mediaincanada.com/2017/04/13/growth-in-canadian-ad-spend-to-slow-across-most-media-study/ (accessed April 27, 2017).

2. Todd Spangler, "Super Bowl 2017: 16% of Viewers Plan to Watch via Online Streaming," *Variety*, January 27, 2017, http://variety.com/2017/digital/news/super-bowl-51-free-live-streaming-survey-1201971662/ (accessed April 27, 2017).

3. Todd Spangler, "Fox's Super Bowl LI Free Live-Stream Online Will Include Local Ads," *Variety*, January 17, 2017, http://variety.com/2017/digital/news/super-bowl-li-free-live-stream-fox-local-ads-1201961179/ (accessed April 27, 2017).

4. Canadian Business staff and Bruce Philp, "Canada's Best Brands, 2017," *Canadian Business*, October 11, 2016, http://www.canadianbusiness.com/lists-and-rankings/best-brands/canadas-best-brands-2017-the-top-25/image/2/ (accessed April 28, 2017).

5. Jessica Vomiero, "Rogers, Bell, Telus Are among Canada's Most Valuable Brands," MobileSyrup, February 1, 2017, http://mobilesyrup.com/2017/02/01/rogers-bell-telus-most-valuable-brands/ (accessed April 28, 2017).

6. "Does Humor Make Ads More Effective?", Knowledge Point, www.millwardbrown.com/Libraries/MB_Knowledge_Points_Downloads/Millward-Brown_KnowledgePoint_HumorInAdvertising.sflb.ashx (accessed September 18, 2014).

7. Tom Duncan, *Integrated Marketing Communications* (Burr Ridge, IL: McGraw-Hill, 2002), 257.

8. Harmeet Singh, "Kellogg Canada Bets on Ketchup," *Strategy*, April 26, 2017, http://strategyonline.ca/2017/04/26/kellogg-canada-bets-on-ketchup/(accessed April 29, 2017).

9. Sharon Groom and Brett Stewart, "Comparative Advertising—The Basics," Canadian Marketing Association, https://www.the-cma.org/disciplines/advertising/archive/comparative-advertising (accessed April 29, 2017).

10. Harmeet Singh, "Behind Canadian Tire's (Old) Viral Spot," Strategy, February 28, 2017, http://strategyonline.ca/2017/02/28/behind-canadian-tires-old-viral-spot/ (accessed April 30, 2017).

11. Russell O'Sullivan, "What Is Programmatic Marketing, Buying and Advertising?", State of Digital, October 26, 2015, http://www.stateofdigital.com/what-is-programmatic-marketing-buying-and-advertising/ (accessed May 8, 2017).

12. Rody-Mantha, "Growth in Canadian Ad Spend to Slow across Most Media: Study."

13. "Mobile Captures Nearly Half of Canada's Digital Ad Spend," eMarketer, March 16, 2016, https://www.emarketer.com/Article/Mobile-Captures-Nearly-Half-of-Canadas-Digital-Ad-Spend/1013706 (accessed May 1, 2017).

14. Chris Powell, "Newspaper Advertising Outpaces Time Spent Reading Them," *Marketing*, September 7, 2016, http://marketingmag.ca/media/newspaper-advertising-outpaces-time-spent-reading-them-182551/(accessed May 1, 2017).

15. "Industry Profiles: Magazine Publishing—Interim Update," Ontario Media Development Corporation, November 2016, http://www.omdc.on.ca/collaboration/research_and_industry_information/industry_profiles/Magazine_Industry_Profile.htm (accessed May 1, 2017).

16. Kristine Lyrette, "Media Channels: Out of Home," *Media Digest*, 2017, p. 144.

17. Susan Krashinsky Robertson, "Molson Canadian Ad Gets Second Life in Light of Trump Immigration Ban," *Globe and Mail*, February 8, 2017, http://www.theglobeandmail.com/report-on-business/industry-news/marketing/molson-canadian-ad-gets-second-life-in-light-of-trump-immigration-ban/article33957985/ (accessed May 2, 2017).

18. "Sponsorship Spending Forecast: Continued Growth around the World," IEG Sponsorship Report, January 4, 2017, http://www.sponsorship.com/iegsr/2017/01/04/Sponsorship-Spending-Forecast--Continued-Growth-Ar.aspx (accessed May 2, 2017).

19. Russ Martin, "WestJet's Expert Social Media Response to Bomb Hoaxes," *Marketing*, July 2, 2015, http://marketingmag.ca/brands/westjets-expert-social-media-response-to-bomb-hoaxes-151231/.

Chapter 18

1. "McDonald's Restaurants of Canada—McCafé Cinema," Promo Awards, 2017, https://promoawards.strategyonline.ca/Winners/Winner/2016/?w=mcdonalds-mccafecinema (accessed April 16, 2017).

2. Mark Cardwell, "London Drugs Creates LDExtras Loyalty Program," *Marketing*, October 18, 2016, http://marketingmag.ca/consumer/london-drugs-creates-ldextras-loyalty-program-185370/ (accessed April 16, 2017).

3. www.ipsos-na.com/news-polls/pressrelease.aspx?id=7071 (accessed April 16, 2017).

4. Josh Kolm, "Burning Questions: Seeking the Best in Digital Coupons," Strategy, April 13, 2017, http://strategyonline.ca/2017/04/13/burning-questions-seeking-the-best-in-digital-coupons/ (accessed April 16, 2017).

5. Kelvin Claveria, "13 Stunning Customer Loyalty Stats, Including the Surprising Ineffectiveness of Loyalty Programs," Vision Critical, November 22, 2016, www.visioncritical.com/customer-loyalty-stats/ (accessed April 16, 2017).

6. *The 2016 Bond Loyalty Report*, Brand Loyalty and Visa, http://info.bondbrandloyalty.com/hubfs/Resources/2016_Bond_Loyalty_Report_Executive_Summary_US_Launch_Edition.pdf?t=1492093294940 (accessed April 16, 2017).

7. Clay Pearn, "Loyalty Case Study: Loblaws' PC Plus," Smile.io, February 28, 2017, www.sweettoothrewards.com/blog/loyalty-case-study-loblaws-pc-plus/ (accessed April 17, 2017).

8. Josh Kolm, "Minute Rice Targets Time-Strapped Moms," Strategy, February 6, 2017, http://strategyonline.ca/2017/02/06/minute-rice-targets-time-strapped-moms/ (accessed April 18, 2017).

9. Michael Beverland, "Contextual Influences and the Adoption and Practice of Relationship Selling in a Business-to-Business Setting: An Exploratory Study," *Journal of Personal Selling and Sales Management*, 21, 3, 2001, 207.

10. Denise Deveau, "Cultural Barriers, Perceptions Keeping Canadians from Exploring Hot Global Markets," *Financial Post*, October 28, 2013, http://business.financialpost.com/2013/10/28/cultural-barriers-perceptions-keeping-canadians-from-exploring-hot-global-markets/ (accessed September 18, 2014).

Chapter 19

1. Siddharth Dwivedi, "7 Best Content Marketing Quotes from Experts That Will Make You Serious about Content," XORLabs, March 12, 2016, https://www.xorlabs.in/blog/7-best-content-marketing-quotes-from-experts-that-will-make-you-serious-about-content/ (accessed August 14, 2017).

2. "The Trump Tweet Tracker," *The Atlantic*, www.theatlantic.com/liveblogs/2016/12/donald-trump-twitter/511619/.

3. Ibid.

4. Megan Haynes, "Trending in 2014," Strategy, December 12, 2013, http://strategyonline.ca/2013/12/12/trending-in-2014/ (accessed January 2014).

5. "Internet Use in Canada," *CIRA Internet Factbook 2016*, Canadian Internet Registration Authority, https://cira.ca/factbook/domain-industry-data-and-canadian-Internet-trends/internet-use-canada (accessed June 12, 2017).

6. "2017: Canadians Love Social Media, But Canadian Businesses Hate to Embrace It!" Rapid Boost Marketing, November 20, 2016, http://rapidboost-marketing.com/canadians-love-social-media-but-canadian-businesses-hate-to-embrace-it/ (accessed June 12, 2017).

7. "Penetration of Leading Social Networks in Canada as of 4th Quarter 2016," Statista, 2017, www.statista.com/statistics/284426/canada-social-network-penetration/ (accessed June 9, 2017).

8. Penetration of Leading Social Media networks in Canada as of 4th Quarter."

9. "Most Digital Buyers Will Make Purchases via Smartphone by 2017," eMarketer, February 16, 2016, http//:www.emarketer.com/Article/Most-Digital-Buyers-Will-Make-Purchases-via-Smartphone-by-2017/1013590 (accessed June 16, 2017).

10. "10 Brands Doing an Amazing Job on Social Media," *Adweek*, July 30, 2015, www.adweek.com/digital/michael-patterson-10-brands-amazing-social-media/ (accessed March 28, 2017).

11. Netflix Twitter feed, https://twitter.com/netflix?ref_src=twsrc%5Etfw&ref_url=http%3A%2F%2F (accessed March 28, 2017).

12. [[CATCH note—online vs TV spending]]

13. Jeff Howe, *Crowdsourcing: Why the Power of the Crowd Is Driving the Future of Business* (New York, NY: Three Rivers Press, 2009), 32.

14. "The 2010 Canada Digital Year in Review," comScore, March 8, 2011, www.comscore.com/Insights/Presentations-and-Whitepapers/2011/2010-Canada-Digital-Year-in-Review (accessed January 2014).

15. "Facebook Forges Ahead into Social Commerce," *Business Insider*, August 5, 2016, www.businessinsider.com/facebook-forges-ahead-into-social-commerce-2016-8 (accessed June 16, 2016).

16. Sean Corcoran, "Defining Earned, Owned, and Paid Media," Forrester, December 16, 2009, http://

blogs.forrester.com/interactive_marketing/2009/12/defining-earned-owned-and-paid-media.html; and Brian Solis, "Why Brands Are Becoming Media," Mashable, February 11, 2010, http://mashable.com/2010/02/11/social-objects/#LTEhq98IBkqc (accessed September 18, 2014).

17. Eric Siu, "10 Ways to Use Snapchat for Business," Social Media Examiner, June 27, 2016, http://www.socialmediaexaminer.com/10-ways-to-use-snapchat-for-business/.

18. "Hootsuite," Wikipedia, https://en.wikipedia.org/wiki/Hootsuite (accessed March 28, 2017).

19. Sarah Dawley, "A Comprehensive Guide to Social Media ROI" (blog), Hootsuite, May 16, 2017, https://blog.hootsuite.com/measure-social-media-roi-business/(accessed June 16, 2017).

20. David Berkowitz, "100 Ways to Measure Social Media," Marketers Studio, November 17, 2009, www.marketersstudio.com/2009/11/100-ways-to-measure-social-media-.html (accessed January 2014).

21. Charlene Li and Josh Bernoff, *Groundswell: Winning in a World Transformed by Social Technologies*, expanded and revised ed. (Boston: Harvard Business Press, 2011).

22. David Brown, "Canadian Olympic Committee Launches Large-Scale Sochi Campaign," *Marketing*, December 31, 2013, www.marketingmag.ca/news/marketer-news/canadian-olympic-committee-launches-large-scale-sochi-campaign-97425 (accessed January 2014).

23. Pete Kallas, "Top 15 Most Popular Social Networking Sites and Apps (June 2017)," DreamGrow, June 7, 2017, www.dreamgrow.com/top-15-most-popular-social-networking-sites/ (accessed June 12, 2017).

24. "WestJet Airlines Ltd. Performs Christmas Marketing Miracle with Viral Video," *Financial Post*, December 11, 2013, http://business.financialpost.com/2013/12/11/westjet-airlines-ltd-performs-christmas-marketing-miracle-with-viral-video/ (accessed January 2014).

25. "Make This a Season of Warm Wishes," TimHortons.com, http://www.timhortons.com/ca/en/promos/warm-wishes.php (accessed November 30, 2016).

26. "Periscope," Wikipedia, https://en.wikipedia.org/wiki/Periscope_(app).

27. "Smartphone Behaviour in Canada and the Implications for Marketers in 2016," Catalyst, http://catalyst.ca/2016-canadian-smartphone-behaviour/ (accessed June 12, 2017).

28. "Our Mobile Planet: Canada—Understanding the Mobile Consumer," Google, May 2013, http://services.google.com/fh/files/misc/omp-2013-ca-en.pdf (accessed January 2014).

29. "Canada Spent Nearly $1B in Mobile Ads in 2014: EMarketer," *Marketing*, December 2014 (accessed March 28, 2017).

30. Eleanor Goldberg, "Donors Want to Be Able to Give More Via Text Message: Study," Huffington Post, July 26, 2013, www.huffingtonpost.com/2013/07/26/text-message-donation-limit_n_3653296.html. June 16, 2017

31. Portia Crowe, "Snap Is Going Public at a $24 Billion Valuation," March 1, 2017, Business Insider, http://www.businessinsider.com/snapchat-ipo-price-2017-3/.

KEY CONCEPTS

1-1 Define marketing. Marketing is about understanding the needs of the customer. No other aspect of business has this focus. Marketing helps to shape a firm's products and services based on an understanding of what the customer is looking for. Marketing is about engaging in a conversation with that customer and guiding the delivery of what is required to satisfy those needs.

1-2 Describe the evolution of marketing. Marketing has been created by an evolution in the use and application of marketing techniques in firms over many decades. The five orientations of marketing are the production orientation, the sales orientation, the marketing company orientation, the societal marketing orientation, and the relationship marketing orientation. Each one developed a new aspect of what we now know as marketing and contributed to how many view marketing today.

1-3 Define key marketing terms. An understanding of the following terms is fundamental for anyone learning about marketing:

- **Exchange:** people giving up one thing to receive another thing they would rather have
- **Customer value:** the relationship between benefits and the sacrifice necessary to obtain those benefits
- **Market segments:** groups of individuals, families, or companies that are placed together because it is believed that they share similar needs
- **Relationship building:** companies can expand their market share in three ways: attracting new customers, increasing business with existing customers, and retaining current customers
- **The marketing mix:** also known as the four Ps of marketing, these are product, price, place, and promotion. Each of the four Ps must be studied and developed to create a proper strategy to attract a market segment.

KEY TERMS

1-1

marketing the activities that develop an offering in order to satisfy a customer need

need a state of being where we desire something that we do not possess but yearn to acquire

1-2

production orientation a focus on manufacturing and production quantity in which customers are meant to choose based on what is most abundantly available

sales orientation hard selling to the customer, who has greater choice thanks to more competition in the marketplace

marketing company orientation a strong emphasis on the marketing concept and development of a more comprehensive approach to understanding the customer

societal marketing orientation looking not only at the customer but expanding marketing efforts to include aspects from the external environment that go beyond a firm's customers, suppliers, and competitors

customer satisfaction customers' evaluation of a good or service in terms of whether it has met their needs and expectations

relationship marketing a strategy that focuses on keeping and improving relationships with current customers

1-3

exchange people giving up one thing to receive another thing they would rather have

customer value the relationship between benefits and the sacrifice necessary to obtain those benefits

1-4 Explain why marketing matters. Marketing is not just about sales and advertising within a firm; it permeates the whole firm. There are rewarding careers in marketing, with compensation that is competitive with other fields of business, along with opportunities that go well beyond the cubicle. Successfully understanding marketing means having an ability to analyze and communicate findings, important skill sets for anyone in business. An understanding of marketing allows people to be informed consumers, ones who are not afraid to demand more from the products and services they rely on every day.

Marketing affects you every day!

KEY CONCEPTS

2-1 Discuss the external environment of marketing, and explain how it affects a firm. The external marketing environment consists of competitive, regulatory, economic, social, and technological variables. Marketers cannot control the external environment, but they must understand how it is changing and the effect on the target market. Marketing managers can then create a marketing mix to effectively meet the needs of target customers.

2-2 Describe the competitive factors that affect marketing.
Companies face competition from five different areas: direct competitors, who most closely match their value proposition; substitutes, who satisfy similar needs but in different ways; new entrants, who can emerge from nowhere as start-ups challenging for the same market; suppliers, who provide firms with required products, but typically charge as much as they can for said products; and buyers, who buy from firms, but typically want to pay as little as possible.

2-3 Describe the regulatory factors that affect marketing. All organizations must operate within legal boundaries. In most cases this is in the best interest of all involved; however, marketers must be on top of regulations as they evolve so that they're not blindsided by new laws and regulations that could help (opportunities) or hinder (threats) a business.

2-4 Describe the economic factors that affect marketing. Much like marketers must anticipate external forces of competition and regulations, they must also be the first to see the onset of contractions and expansions in the economy. Signs can be obvious, such as news coverage of changes in economic indicators such as jobs, GDP, and housing. Other times marketers must literally survey their business microscopically, looking for trends in sales. Any combination of shifts in consumer income or recessionary or inflationary trends in the economy will signal to firms that it is time to make adjustments to their strategies.

KEY TERMS

2-1
target market a group of people or organizations for which an organization designs, implements, and maintains a marketing mix intended to meet the needs of that group, resulting in mutually satisfying exchanges

2-3
Competition Bureau the federal department charged with administering most marketplace laws

self-regulation programs voluntarily adopted by business groups to regulate the activities of their members

2-4
purchasing power a comparison of income versus the relative cost of a set standard of goods and services in different geographic areas

discretionary income the amount of money people have to spend on nonessential items

inflation a measure of the decrease in the value of money, expressed as the percentage reduction in value since the previous year

recession a period of economic activity characterized by negative growth, which reduces demand for goods and services

environmental factors noncontrollable factors caused by natural disasters, which negatively or positively affect organizations

2-5
component lifestyles mode of living that involves choosing goods and services that meet one's diverse needs and interests rather than conforming to a single, traditional lifestyle

2-6
demography the study of people's vital statistics, such as their age, race and ethnicity, and location

Generation Z people born between 1995 and 2009

Generation Y people born between 1979 and 2000

Generation X people born between 1966 and 1978

baby boomers people born between 1947 and 1965

multiculturalism refers to the peaceful and equitable coexistence of different cultures, rather than one national culture, in a country

2-7
basic research pure research that aims to confirm an existing theory or to learn more about a concept or phenomenon

applied research an attempt by marketers to use research to develop new or improved products

2-8

corporate social responsibility a business's concern for society's welfare

triple bottom line a business philosophy seen as the pursuit of profit while also benefiting society and the environment

social acceleration the concept of exponentially rapid growth starting with human desire for improved products, spurring competitive pursuit of market share, driving innovation and technology, resulting in higher standard of living, but with new socio-environmental problems

pyramid of corporate social responsibility a model that suggests corporate social responsibility is composed of economic, legal, ethical, and philanthropic responsibilities and that the firm's economic performance supports the entire structure

green marketing the development and marketing of products designed to minimize negative effects on the physical environment

2-9

ethics the moral principles or values that generally govern the conduct of an individual or a group

morals the rules people develop as a result of cultural values and norms

code of ethics a guideline to help marketing managers and other employees make better decisions

2-5 Describe social factors that affect marketing. Social factors are the most difficult, yet most fascinating of environmental forces to predict. Whether its change or behaviour in demographics, attitudes, values, or lifestyles, social forces are at the base of just about all other factors. Moreover, they are ultimately at the base of marketing and business as a whole—as marketing, at its simplest level, is the discovery and satisfaction of human needs.

2-6 Explain the importance to marketing managers of current demographic trends. Today, several basic demographic patterns are influencing marketing mixes. Each generation enters a life stage with its own tastes and biases, and tailoring products to what customers value is key to sales. The cohorts, called Generation Z, Generation Y/Millennials, Generation X, and Baby Boomers, each has its own needs, values, and consumption patterns. Canada's cultural diversity will increasingly require multicultural marketing.

2-7 Describe technological factors that affect marketing. Monitoring new technology is essential to keeping up with competitors in today's marketing environment. Canada excels in basic research and, in recent years, has dramatically improved its track record in applied research. Innovation is increasingly becoming a global process. Without innovation, Canadian companies can't compete in global markets.

2-8 Discuss corporate social responsibility. Corporate social responsibility (CSR) is a business's concern for social and environmental welfare, often demonstrated by its adherence to the triple bottom line: financial (profit), social (people), and environmental (planet). It could be asserted that the social need for CSR resulted from decades of social needs. Our desire for bigger, faster, and stronger fuelled our competitive pursuit for business, thereby fuelling the economic furnace, necessitating both technological and regulatory expansion along the way. And so we arrive full circle, back to human needs—only now we want the same things, but only when they don't hurt society or the environment.

2-9 Describe the role of ethics and ethical decisions in business. Business ethics may be viewed as a subset of the values of society as a whole. The ethical conduct of business people is shaped by societal elements, including family, education, religion, and social movements. As members of society, business people are morally obligated to consider the ethical implications of their decisions.

Ethical decision making is approached in three basic ways. The first approach examines the consequences of decisions. The second approach relies on rules and laws to guide decision making. The third approach is based on a theory of moral development that places individuals or groups in one of three developmental stages: preconventional morality, conventional morality, or postconventional morality.

Many companies develop a code of ethics to help their employees make ethical decisions. A code of ethics can help employees identify acceptable business practices, be an effective internal control on behaviour, help employees avoid confusion when determining whether decisions are ethical, and facilitate discussion about what is right and wrong.

KEY CONCEPTS

3-1 Explain the importance of strategic planning. Strategic marketing planning is the basis for all marketing strategies and decisions. The marketing plan acts as a guidebook of marketing activities for the marketer. By specifying objectives and defining the actions required to attain them, a marketing plan provides the basis on which actual and expected performance can be compared.

Although there is no set formula, a marketing plan should include such elements as stating the business mission, setting objectives, performing a situation analysis of internal and external environmental forces, selecting target markets, delineating a marketing mix (product, price, place, and promotion) and establishing ways to implement, evaluate, and control the plan.

3-2 Develop an appropriate business mission statement. The mission statement is based on a careful analysis of benefits sought by present and potential customers and an analysis of existing and anticipated environmental conditions. The firm's mission statement establishes boundaries for all subsequent decisions, objectives, and strategies. It should focus on the market the organization is attempting to serve rather than on the good or service offered.

3-3 Describe how to conduct business portfolio analysis. In the situation (or SWOT) analysis, the firm should identify its internal strengths (S) and weaknesses (W) and also examine external opportunities (O) and threats (T). When examining external opportunities and threats, marketing managers must analyze aspects of the marketing environment in a process called environmental scanning. The six macroenvironmental forces studied most often are social, demographic, economic, technological, political and legal, and competitive.

3-4 Summarize how business planning is used for competitive advantage. A competitive advantage is a set of unique features of a company and its products that are perceived by the target market as significant and superior to those of the competition. Competitive advantages can be divided into three types: cost, product differentiation, and niche strategies. Sources of cost competitive advantages include experience curves, efficient labour, no-frills goods and services, government subsidies, product design, re-engineering, product innovations, and new methods of service delivery. A product/service differentiation competitive advantage exists when a firm provides something unique that is valuable to buyers beyond just low price. Niche competitive advantages result from targeting unique segments that have specific needs and wants. The goal of all sources of competitive advantage is to be sustainable.

KEY TERMS

3-1

planning the process of anticipating future events and determining strategies to achieve organizational objectives in the future

strategic planning the managerial process of creating and maintaining a fit between the organization's objectives and resources and evolving market opportunities

marketing environment the entire set of situational conditions, both internal (strengths and weaknesses) and external (opportunities and threats), within which a business operates

strategic business unit (SBU) a subgroup of a single business or a collection of related businesses within the larger organization

3-2

mission statement a statement of the firm's value based on a careful analysis of benefits sought by present and potential customers and an analysis of existing and anticipated environmental conditions

3-3

SWOT analysis identifying internal environment of strengths (S) and weaknesses (W) as well as external opportunities (O) and threats (T)

environmental scanning the collection and interpretation of information about forces, events, and relationships in the external environment that may affect the future of the organization or the implementation of the marketing plan

market penetration a marketing strategy that tries to increase market share among existing customers, using existing products

market development a marketing strategy that involves attracting new customers to existing products

product development a marketing strategy that entails the creation of new products for current customers

diversification a strategy of increasing sales by introducing new products into new markets

3-4

core competencies key unique strengths that are hard to imitate and underlie the functioning of an organization

competitive advantage the set of unique features of a company and its products that are perceived by the target market as significant and superior to the competition

cost competitive advantage being the low-cost competitor in an industry while maintaining satisfactory profit margins

experience curves curves that show costs declining at a predictable rate as experience with a product increases

product/service differentiation competitive advantage the provision of a unique benefit that is valuable to buyers beyond simply offering a low price

niche competitive advantage the advantage achieved when a firm seeks to target and effectively serve a single segment of the market

sustainable competitive advantage an advantage that cannot be copied by the competition

3-5

marketing strategy the activities of selecting and describing one or more target markets and developing and maintaining a marketing mix that will produce mutually satisfying exchanges with target markets

marketing objective a statement of what is to be accomplished through marketing activities

market opportunity analysis (MOA) the description and estimation of the size and sales potential of market segments that are of interest to the firm and the assessment of key competitors in these market segments

3-6

marketing mix a unique blend of product, price, place, and promotion, strategies designed to produce mutually satisfying exchanges with a target market

four Ps product, price, place, and promotion, which together make up the marketing mix

3-7

implementation the process that turns a marketing plan into action assignments and ensures that these assignments are executed in a way that accomplishes the plan's objectives

evaluation gauging the extent to which the marketing objectives have been achieved during the specified period

control provides the mechanisms both for evaluating marketing results in light of the plan's objectives and for correcting actions that do not help the organization reach those objectives within budget guidelines

marketing audit a thorough, systematic, periodic evaluation of the objectives, strategies, structure, and performance of the marketing organization

3-5 Discuss marketing planning and identification of target markets.

The target market strategy identifies which market segment or segments to focus on. A market opportunity analysis (MOA) describes and estimates the size and sales potential of market segments that are of interest to the firm. In addition, an assessment of key competitors in these market segments is performed. After the market segments are described, one or more may be targeted by the firm by (1) appealing to the entire market with one marketing mix, (2) concentrating on one segment, or (3) appealing to multiple market segments by using multiple marketing mixes.

Target Market Options

Entire Market	Multiple Markets	Single Market

3-6 Describe the elements of the marketing mix.
The marketing mix (or four Ps) is a blend of product, price, place, and promotion—strategies designed to produce mutually satisfying exchanges with a target market. The starting point of the marketing mix is the product offering. Products can be tangible goods, ideas, or services. Price is what a buyer must give up to obtain a product and is often the easiest to change of the four marketing mix elements. Place (distribution) strategies are concerned with making products available when and where customers want them. Elements of the promotional mix include advertising, direct marketing, public relations, sales promotion, personal selling, and online marketing.

3-7 Explain why implementation, evaluation, and control of the marketing plan are necessary.
Before a marketing plan can work, it must be implemented. The plan should also be evaluated to determine whether it has achieved its objectives. Poor implementation can be a major factor in a plan's failure. Control provides the mechanisms for evaluating marketing results in light of the plan's objectives and for correcting actions that do not help the organization reach those objectives within budget guidelines.

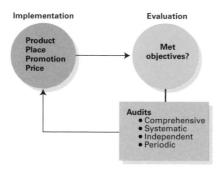

3-8 Identify several techniques that help make strategic planning effective.
First, management must realize that strategic planning is an ongoing process and not a once-a-year exercise. Second, good strategic planning involves a high level of creativity. The last requirement is top management's support and cooperation.

KEY CONCEPTS

4-1 Discuss the importance of global marketing. Business people who adopt a global vision are better able to identify global marketing opportunities, understand the nature of global networks, create effective global marketing strategies, and compete against foreign competition in domestic markets. Large corporations have traditionally been the major global competitors, but more and more small businesses are entering the global marketplace. Despite fears of job losses to other countries with cheaper labour, there are many benefits to globalization, including the reduction of poverty and increased standards of living.

4-2 Discuss the impact of multinational firms on the world economy. Multinational corporations are international traders that regularly operate across national borders. Because of their vast size and financial, technological, and material resources, multinational corporations have a great influence on the world economy. They have the ability to overcome trade problems, save on labour costs, and tap new technology. There are critics and supporters of multinational corporations, and the critics question the actual benefits of bringing capital-intensive technology to impoverished nations. Many countries block foreign investment in factories, land, and companies to protect their economies.

4-3 Describe the external environment facing global marketers. Global marketers face the same environmental factors as they do domestically: cultural; economic and technological development; political structure and actions; demography; and natural resources. Cultural considerations include societal values, attitudes and beliefs, language, and customary business practices. A country's economic and technological status depends on its stage of industrial development, which, in turn, affects average family incomes. The political structure is shaped by political ideology and such policies as tariffs, quotas, boycotts, exchange controls, trade agreements, and market groupings. Demographic variables include the size of a population and its age and geographic distribution. A shortage of natural resources also affects the external environment by dictating what is available and at what price.

4-4 Identify the various ways of entering the global marketplace. Firms use the following strategies to enter global markets, in descending order of risk and profit: direct investment, joint venture, contract manufacturing, licensing and franchising, and exporting.

KEY TERMS

4-1

global marketing marketing that targets markets throughout the world

global vision a recognition of and reaction to international marketing opportunities using effective global marketing strategies and being aware of threats from foreign competitors in all markets

gross domestic product (GDP) the total market value of all goods and services produced in a country for a given period

outsourcing the practice of using an outside supplier, generally where the productions costs are lower, to complete the work

inshoring returning jobs to Canada

4-2

multinational corporations companies that are heavily engaged in international trade, beyond exporting and importing

capital intensive using more capital than labour in the production process

global marketing standardization production of uniform products that can be sold the same way all over the world

4-3

gross national income (GNI) per capita one measure of the ability of a country's citizens to buy various goods and services

Mercosur the largest Latin American trade agreement, made up of Argentina, Bolivia, Brazil, Chile, Colombia, Ecuador, Paraguay, Peru, Uruguay, and Venezuela

Uruguay Round an agreement created by the World Trade Organization to dramatically lower trade barriers worldwide

World Trade Organization (WTO) a trade organization that replaced the old General Agreement on Tariffs and Trade (GATT)

General Agreement on Tariffs and Trade (GATT) a trade agreement that contained loopholes that enabled countries to avoid trade-barrier reduction agreements

North American Free Trade Agreement (NAFTA) an agreement among Canada, the United States, and Mexico that created the world's largest free trade zone at that time

Canadian-European Union Comprehensive Economic and Trade Agreement (CETA) a progressive free trade agreement, which covers almost all sectors, and aspects of Canada-EU trade in order to eliminate or reduce barriers

European Union (EU) a free trade zone encompassing 28 European countries

World Bank an international bank that offers low-interest loans, advice, and information to developing nations

International Monetary Fund (IMF) an international organization that acts as a lender of last resort, providing loans to troubled nations, and also works to promote trade through financial cooperation

Group of Twenty (G20) a forum for international economic development that promotes discussion between industrial and emerging-market countries on key issues related to global economic stability

high-net-worth individuals (HNWI) individuals who have $1 million in liquid financial assets

4-4

exporting selling domestically produced products to buyers in another country

buyer for export an intermediary in the global market that assumes all ownership risks and sells globally for its own account

export broker an intermediary who plays the traditional broker's role by bringing buyer and seller together

export agents intermediaries who act like manufacturers' agents for exporters; the export agents live in the foreign market

licensing the legal process whereby a licensor agrees to let another firm use its manufacturing process, trademarks, patents, trade secrets, or other proprietary knowledge

contract manufacturing private-label manufacturing by a foreign company

joint venture a domestic firm's purchase of part of a foreign company or a domestic firm joining with a foreign company to create a new entity

direct foreign investment active ownership of a foreign company or of overseas manufacturing or marketing facilities

4-5

floating exchange rates prices of different currencies move up and down based on the demand for and the supply of each currency

dumping the sale of an exported product at a price lower than that charged for the same or a like product in the home market of the exporter

countertrade a form of trade in which all or part of the payment for goods or services is in the form of other goods or services

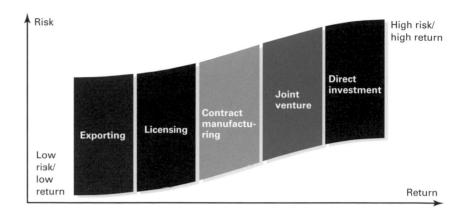

4-5 List the basic elements involved in developing a global marketing mix. A firm's major consideration is how much it will adjust the four Ps—product, promotion, place (distribution), and price—within each country. One strategy is to use one product and one promotion message worldwide. A second strategy is to create new products for global markets. A third strategy is to keep the product basically the same but alter the promotional message. A fourth strategy is to slightly alter the product to meet local conditions.

Global Marketing Mix		
Product + Promotion	**Place (Distribution)**	**Price**
One product, one message	Channel choice	Dumping
Product invention	Channel structure	Countertrade
Product adaption	Country infrastructure	Exchange rates
Message adaption		Purchasing power

4-6 Discover how the Internet is affecting global marketing. Simply opening an e-commerce site can open the door to international sales. International carriers, such as UPS, can help solve logistics problems. Language translation software can help an e-commerce business become multilingual. Yet cultural differences and old-line rules, regulations, and taxes hinder rapid development of e-commerce in many countries. Not only do global marketers use social media for understanding consumers, but they also use social media to build their brands as they expand internationally.

KEY CONCEPTS

5-1 Explain the role of marketing research. Marketing research is about using information-gathering processes to discover the needs of customers and how to better serve those needs. Marketing research is a process, like any other kind of research, and it needs guidelines to follow and direction. Marketing research helps decision makers not by solving the problem but by providing information on which decisions can be made. In a firm, marketing research can take on any one of three roles: descriptive, diagnostic and predictive.

Why marketing research?

- ☑ Improve quality of decision making
- ☑ Trace problems
- ☑ Focus on keeping existing customers
- ☑ Understand changes in marketplace

5-2 List the steps in the marketing research process. Marketing research is a process of collecting and analyzing data to use in solving specific marketing problems. There are six steps in the process of properly gathering data and creating information used to make marketing decisions. The first step, the most important and strategic decision in the research process, is to identify the problem. The second step is to choose the research design and determine whether to use an exploratory, a descriptive, or a causal approach. The third

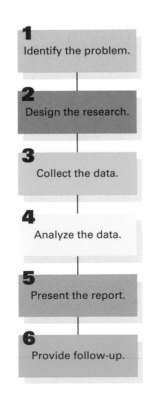

1 Identify the problem.

2 Design the research.

3 Collect the data.

4 Analyze the data.

5 Present the report.

6 Provide follow-up.

KEY TERMS

5-1

marketing research the process of planning, collecting, and analyzing data relevant to a marketing decision

5-2

marketing research objective specific statement about the information needed to solve the research question

research design a plan that specifies how to answer the research question and achieve the research objectives by laying out the research tools and techniques necessary to collect and analyze data

exploratory research an informal discovery process that attempts to gain insights and a better understanding of the management and research problems

conclusive research a more specific type of research that attempts to provide clarity to a decision maker by identifying specific courses of action

descriptive research a type of conclusive research that attempts to describe marketing phenomena and characteristics

causal research a type of conclusive research that focuses on the cause and effect of two variables and attempts to find some correlation between them

secondary data data previously collected for any purpose other than the one at hand

primary data information that is collected for the first time and is used for solving the particular problem under investigation

depth interview an interview that involves a discussion between a well-trained researcher and a respondent who is asked about attitudes and perspectives on a topic

focus group a small group of recruited participants engaged in a nonstructured discussion in a casual environment

survey research the most popular technique for gathering primary data, in which a researcher interacts with people to obtain facts, opinions, and attitudes

mall intercept interview interviewing people in the common areas of shopping malls

computer-assisted personal interviewing technique in which the interviewer reads the questions from a computer screen and enters the respondent's data directly into a computer

computer-assisted self-interviewing technique in which the respondent reads questions on a computer screen and directly keys his or her answers into a computer

central-location telephone (CLT) facility a specially designed phone room used to conduct telephone interviewing

open-ended question an interview question that encourages an answer phrased in the respondent's own words

closed-ended question an interview question that asks the respondent to make a selection from a limited list of responses

scaled-response question a closed-ended question designed to measure the intensity of a respondent's answer

observation research watching people or phenomena in a controlled manner, through either human or machine methods.

mystery shoppers researchers posing as customers who gather observational data about a store

ethnographic research the study of human behaviour in its natural context; involves observation of behaviour and physical setting

experiment a method a researcher uses to gather primary data to determine cause and effect

sample a subset from a larger population

probability sample a sample in which every element in the population has a known statistical likelihood of being selected

random sample a sample arranged in such a way that every element of the population has an equal chance of being selected as part of the sample

nonprobability sample any sample in which little or no attempt is made to have a representative cross-section of the population

convenience sample a form of nonprobability sample using respondents who are convenient, or readily accessible, to the researcher—for example, employees, friends, or relatives

measurement error an error that occurs when the information desired by the researcher differs from the information provided by the measurement process

sampling error an error that occurs when a sample does not represent the target population

frame error a sample drawn from a population that differs from the target population

random error a type of sampling error in which the selected sample is an imperfect representation of the overall population

cross-tabulation a method of analyzing data that shows the analyst the responses to one question in relation to the responses to one or more other questions

5-3

big data large amounts of data collected from interactions with customers that reveal trends and patterns

5-4

competitive intelligence (CI) an intelligence system that helps managers assess their competition and vendors in order to become more efficient and effective competitors

step is to decide how much secondary and primary data will be collected and then to collect the data. The fourth step is to analyze the data. Technology can provide a lot of help to researchers, and analysis goes well beyond the basic pie chart or bar graph. The fifth step is for researchers to present their report, taking the reams of data and turning them into something actionable for a company's decision makers. The last step is to follow up, and because marketing research is about helping make decisions, it's important that marketing researchers be able to see how their data and information are used in those decisions.

5-3 Discuss the impact of technology on marketing research. Technology has an impact on many aspects of our lives, both at home and at work. Marketing researchers are using technology to help make decisions at work and to gather information from people at home and on the go. Online surveys have become a staple of most companies' marketing research efforts because of the ease of implementation. There are also online research panels and online focus groups that provide access to respondents with just a click. Mobile technology tools allow people to answer questions on the go, and social networks have created excellent potential pools of respondents. Big data may sound intimidating, but technology has allowed companies to mine information about consumers long thought impossible or unreachable.

5-4 Describe when to conduct marketing research. The marketing research process provides an overview of what to research. But the questions of when to research and even if research should be done are just as valuable. Technology has given many people the tools to write a great survey and disseminate research quickly and easily, but it is still important to determine the right situation in which to take on the marketing research process.

KEY CONCEPTS

6-1 Explain why marketing managers should understand consumer behaviour. Consumer behaviour describes how consumers make purchase decisions and how they use and dispose of the products they buy. An understanding of consumer behaviour reduces marketing managers' uncertainty when they are defining a target market and designing a marketing mix.

6-2 Analyze the components of the consumer decision-making process. The consumer decision-making process begins with need recognition, when stimuli trigger awareness of an unfulfilled want. If additional information is required to make a purchase decision, the consumer may engage in an internal or external information search. The consumer then evaluates the additional information and establishes purchase guidelines. Finally, a purchase decision is made.

Consumer postpurchase evaluation is influenced by prepurchase expectations, the prepurchase information search, and the consumer's general level of self-confidence. Cognitive dissonance is the inner tension that a consumer experiences after recognizing a purchased product's disadvantages.

6-3 Identify the types of consumer buying decisions and discuss the significance of consumer involvement. Consumer decision making falls into three broad categories. First, consumers exhibit routine response behaviour for frequently purchased, low-cost items that require very little decision effort; routine response behaviour is typically characterized by brand loyalty. Second, consumers engage in limited decision making for occasional purchases or for unfamiliar brands in familiar product categories. Third, consumers practise extensive decision making when making unfamiliar, expensive, or infrequent purchases. The main factors affecting the level of consumer involvement are previous experience, interest, perceived risk of negative consequences (financial, social, and psychological), situation, and social visibility.

6-4 Identify and understand the cultural factors that affect consumer buying decisions. Cultural influences on consumer buying decisions include culture and values, subculture, and social class. Culture is the essential character of a society that distinguishes it from other cultural groups. The underlying elements of every culture are the values, language, myths, customs, rituals, laws, and the artifacts, or products, transmitted from one generation to the next. The most defining element of a culture is its values—the enduring beliefs shared by a society that a specific mode of conduct is personally or socially preferable to another mode of conduct. A culture can be divided into subcultures on the basis of demographic characteristics, geographic regions, national and ethnic background, political beliefs, and religious beliefs.

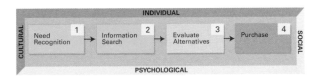

6-5 Identify and understand the social factors that affect consumer buying decisions. Social factors include such external influences as reference groups, opinion leaders, and family. Consumers seek out others' opinions for guidance on new products, on services and products with image-related attributes, or for those on which attribute information is lacking or uninformative. Consumers may use products or brands to identify with or become a member of a reference group. Opinion leaders are members

KEY TERMS

6-1

consumer behaviour how consumers make purchase decisions and how they use and dispose of purchased goods or services; also includes the factors that influence purchase decisions and product use

6-2

consumer decision-making process a five-step process used by consumers when buying goods or services

need recognition the result of an imbalance between actual and desired states

stimulus any unit of Input affecting one or more of the five senses: sight, smell, taste, touch, hearing

engineered demand where firms, led by marketers, discover a marketable need not yet known by the consumer

need a state of being where we desire something that we do not possess but yearn to acquire

internal information search the process of recalling information stored in one's memory

external information search the process of seeking information in the outside environment

nonmarketing-controlled information source a product information source not associated with advertising or promotion

marketing-controlled information source a product information source that originates with marketers promoting the product

consumer-to-consumer (C2C) reviews consumers' reviews of products on the vendors' sites where the products were purchased

platform a business model, usually digital, where producers and buyers exchange value

evoked set (consideration set) a group of the most preferred alternatives resulting from an information search, which a buyer can further evaluate to make a final choice

decision confirmation the reaffirmation of the wisdom of the decision a consumer has made

cognitive dissonance the inner tension that a consumer experiences after recognizing an inconsistency between behaviour and values or opinions

6-3

involvement the amount of time and effort a buyer invests in the search, evaluation, and decision processes of consumer behaviour

routine response behaviour the type of decision making exhibited by consumers buying frequently purchased, low-cost goods and services; requires little search and decision time

limited decision making the type of decision making that requires a moderate amount of time for gathering information and deliberating about an unfamiliar brand in a familiar product category

extensive decision making the most complex type of consumer decision making, used when considering the purchase of an unfamiliar, expensive product or an infrequently purchased item; requires the use of several criteria for evaluating options and much time for seeking information

6-4

culture the set of values, norms, attitudes, and other meaningful symbols that shape human behaviour and the artifacts, or products, of that behaviour as they are transmitted from one generation to the next

value the enduring belief shared by a society that a specific mode of conduct is personally or socially preferable to another mode of conduct

subculture a homogeneous group of people who share elements of the overall culture and also have their own unique cultural elements

social class a group of people who are considered nearly equal in status or community esteem, who regularly socialize among themselves both formally and informally, and who share behavioural norms

6-5

reference group a group in society that influences an individual's purchasing behaviour

primary membership groups groups with which individuals interact regularly in an informal, face-to-face manner

secondary membership groups groups with which individuals interact less consistently and more formally than with primary membership groups

aspirational reference groups groups that an individual would like to join

norms the values and attitudes deemed acceptable by a group

nonaspirational reference groups (dissociative groups) groups that influence our behaviour because we try to maintain distance from them

opinion leader an individual who influences the opinions of others

sociometric leader a low-profile, well-respected collaborative professional who is socially and professionally well connected

socialization process the passing down of cultural values and norms to children

6-6

personality a way of organizing and grouping the consistency of an individual's reactions to situations

self-concept how consumers perceive themselves in terms of attitudes, perceptions, beliefs, and self-evaluations

ideal self-image the way an individual would like to be

real self-image the way an individual actually perceives himself or herself to be

of reference groups who influence others' purchase decisions. Family members also influence purchase decisions; children tend to shop in patterns similar to those of their parents.

6-6 Identify and understand the individual factors that affect consumer buying decisions.

Individual factors that affect consumer buying decisions include gender, age, family life-cycle stage, personality, self-concept, and lifestyle. Beyond obvious physiological differences, men and women differ in their social and economic roles, which affect their consumer buying decisions. A consumer's age generally indicates what products he or she may be interested in purchasing. Marketers often define their target markets by consumers' life-cycle stage, following changes in consumers' attitudes and behavioural tendencies as they mature. Finally, certain products and brands reflect consumers' personality, self-concept, and lifestyle.

6-7 Identify and understand the psychological factors that affect consumer buying decisions.

Psychological factors include perception, motivation, learning, values, beliefs, and attitudes. These factors allow consumers to interact with the world around them, recognize their feelings, gather and analyze information, formulate thoughts and opinions, and take action. Perception allows consumers to recognize their consumption problems. Motivation is what drives consumers to take action to satisfy specific consumption needs. Almost all consumer behaviour results from learning, which is the process that creates changes in behaviour through experience. Consumers with similar beliefs and attitudes tend to react alike to marketing-related inducements.

lifestyle a mode of living as identified by a person's activities, interests, and opinions

6-7

psychological factors tools that consumers use to recognize, gather, analyze, and self-organize to aid in decision making

perception the process by which people select, organize, and interpret stimuli into a meaningful and coherent picture

selective exposure the process whereby a consumer decides which stimuli to notice and which to ignore

selective distortion a process whereby consumers change or distort information that conflicts with their feelings or beliefs

selective retention a process whereby consumers remember only information that supports their personal beliefs

motives driving forces that cause a person to take action to satisfy specific needs

Maslow's hierarchy of needs a method of classifying human needs and motivations into five categories in ascending order of importance: physiological, safety, social, esteem, and self-actualization

learning a process that creates changes in behaviour, immediate or expected, through experience and practice

belief an organized pattern of knowledge that an individual holds as true about his or her world

attitude a learned tendency to respond consistently toward a given object

KEY CONCEPTS

7-1 Describe business marketing. Business-to-business (B2B) marketing is more than simply using the same aspects of consumer marketing and putting the word *business* in front of the concepts and terms. B2B marketing is about making matches between the capabilities of firms and focusing on active cooperation between parties.

7-2 Explain the differences between consumer and business marketing. Business marketing is about an active buyer and active seller. Often consumer marketing focuses on a customer that passively waits for a business to develop an offering based on the 4Ps. The Canadian Marketing Association's definition of business marketing is particularly relevant to our understanding of B2B: "What makes B-to-B different than consumer marketing is the complex nature of *relationships* and *interactions* that form a buying process and customer life cycle that lasts months or years. It involves a network of individuals from buyer, seller, and even third-party partners who have different needs and interests."

7-3 Summarize the network and relationship approach to business marketing. Given the importance of relationships and interactions, it is important to stress that trust and commitment form the foundation of solid business-to-business relationships. We talk here about interaction, not transaction. Much of consumer marketing's focus is on getting customers to buy once and hoping they will buy again—a single transaction. With business marketing, the focus shifts to a series of transactions over time that build trust and establish commitment—an interaction. Traditional sales and marketing management approaches rely more on transactions, while a network model looks at interactions. The term *networks* has become a familiar one, given the growth of mobile technologies and social media. The network model in business marketing stresses the interaction among various parties looking for individual gain but not at the expense of the larger network of interconnected firms. Networks have been present in many cultures, including Japan and China, in various forms. What each incarnation of networks shows is the importance of firms working together for mutual gain while ensuring success at the company level.

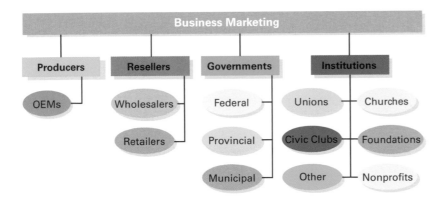

7-4 State the fundamental aspects of business marketing. One of the most important and unique aspects of business marketing is how demand is treated, whether derived, inelastic, or joint. Compared with consumer marketing, in business marketing the number of customers is fewer, the location of businesses is strategic, negotiations are important, and understanding reciprocity is essential to learning about business relationships. Business products that are offered as part of a business relationship are varied, ranging from major equipment purchases to basic supplies. Services to business are unique and more prevalent than in consumer marketing.

KEY TERMS

7-1
business-to-business (B2B) marketing the process of matching capabilities between two nonconsumer entities to create value for both organizations and the "customer's customer"; also referred to as *business marketing*

7-3
relationship commitment a firm's belief that an ongoing relationship with another firm is so important that the relationship warrants maximum efforts at maintaining it indefinitely

trust confidence in an exchange partner's reliability and integrity

7-4
derived demand demand in the business market that comes from demand in the consumer market

joint demand the demand for two or more items used together in a final product

multiplier effect (accelerator principle) the phenomenon in which a small increase or decrease in consumer demand can produce a much larger change in demand for the facilities and equipment needed to make the consumer product

reciprocity a practice where business purchasers choose to buy from their own customers

business services complementary and ancillary actions that companies undertake to meet business customers' needs

7-5
original equipment manufacturers (OEMs) individuals and organizations that buy business goods and incorporate them into the products that they produce for eventual sale to other producers or to consumers

North American Industry Classification System (NAICS) an industry classification system developed by the United States, Canada, and Mexico to classify North American business establishments by their main production processes

7-6

buying centre all those people in an organization who become involved in the purchase decision

new task buy a situation requiring the purchase of a product for the first time

modified rebuy a situation where the purchaser wants some change in the original good or service

straight rebuy a situation in which the purchaser reorders the same goods or services without looking for new information or new suppliers

7-5 Classify business customers. To understand the customer landscape in business marketing, it is helpful to categorize business customers into different groups. Most businesses that would be considered major players in business marketing are producers and resellers. However, government, MASH, and nonprofits are also important in business marketing. A well-established system to classify companies in North America is the North American Industrial Classification System (NAICS). The NAICS provides a way to identify, analyze, segment, and target business and government markets. Organizations can be identified and compared by using the NAICS numeric codes, which indicate the business sector, subsector, industry group, industry, and country industry. NAICS is a valuable tool for analyzing, segmenting, and targeting business markets.

7-6 Identify aspects of business buying behaviour. Business buying involves a much larger group of individuals working together to make a decision. While consumers can make decisions on their own or with the aid of the reference group, a business often will have a buying centre from which decisions are made. A buying centre has six types of members: initiator, influencer, gatekeeper, decider, purchaser, and user. Buying also involves understanding the situation in which a company is making a purchase. Companies may be in a new task buy situation: this is the first time they have made this type of purchase. Otherwise, business buyers are in a straight rebuy situation in which they are generally satisfied and buy the same offering again or in a modified rebuy in which some element of the previous offering was unsatisfactory and they are seeking some improvement. Finally, most business purchases are made based on the evaluative criteria of quality, service, and price.

7-7 Describe the ways in which business marketing has gone online. While much discussion of business marketing is focused on how it differs from consumer marketing, much of what is happening online is similar for both B2B and B2C. Mobile marketing and content marketing are strong trends for business marketers, providing opportunity for both new markets and new relationships but also making it necessary to understand the needs of a more informed marketplace. Social media are another area of growth for business marketing, as seen by the increased use of LinkedIn and other tools.

KEY CONCEPTS

8-1 Describe the characteristics of markets and market segments.
A market is composed of individuals or organizations that have both the ability and the willingness to make purchases to fulfill their needs or wants. A market segment is a group of individuals or organizations with similar product needs because of one or more common characteristics.

8-2 Explain the importance of market segmentation. Before the 1960s, few businesses targeted specific market segments. Today, segmentation is a crucial marketing strategy for nearly all successful organizations. Market segmentation enables marketers to tailor marketing mixes to meet the needs of particular population segments. Segmentation helps marketers identify consumer needs and preferences, areas of declining demand, and new marketing opportunities.

8-3 Describe the bases commonly used to segment consumer markets. Five bases are commonly used for segmenting consumer markets. Geographic segmentation is based on region, size, density, and climate characteristics. Demographic segmentation is based on age, gender, income level, ethnicity, and family life-cycle characteristics. Psychographic segmentation includes personality, motives, and lifestyle characteristics. Benefits sought is a type of segmentation that identifies customers according to the benefits they seek in a product. Finally, usage segmentation divides a market by the amount of product purchased or consumed. To enhance the outcome, database-driven analytics are often used.

8-4 Discuss criteria for successful market segmentation. Successful market segmentation depends on four basic criteria: (1) a market segment must be substantial and have enough potential customers to be viable; (2) a market segment must be identifiable and measurable; (3) members of a market segment must be accessible to marketing efforts; and (4) a market segment must respond to particular marketing efforts in a way that distinguishes it from other segments.

Geography	Demographics	Psychographics	Benefits	Usage Rate
• Region • Market size • Market density • Climate	• Age • Gender • Income • Race/ethnicity • Family life cycle	• Personality • Motives • Lifestyle • Geodemo-graphics	• Benefits sought	• Former • Potential • First time • Light or irregular • Medium • Heavy

8-5 Describe the bases for segmenting business markets. Business markets can be segmented on two general bases. First, businesses segment markets on the basis of company characteristics, such as customers' geographic location, type of company, company size, and product use. Second, companies may segment customers on the basis of the buying processes those customers use.

KEY TERMS

8-1

market people or organizations with needs or wants and the ability and willingness to buy

market segment a subgroup of people or organizations sharing one or more characteristics that cause them to have similar product needs

market segmentation the process of dividing a market into meaningful, relatively similar, and identifiable segments or groups

8-3

segmentation bases (variables) characteristics of individuals, groups, or organizations

geographic segmentation segmenting markets by region of a country or the world, market size, market density, or climate

demographic segmentation segmenting markets by age, gender, income, ethnic background, and family life cycle

family life cycle (FLC) a series of stages determined by a combination of age, marital status, and the presence or absence of children

psychographic segmentation market segmentation on the basis of personality, motives, lifestyles, and geodemographic categories

geodemographic segmentation segmenting potential customers into neighbourhood lifestyle categories

benefit segmentation the process of grouping customers into market segments according to the benefits they seek from the product

usage-rate segmentation dividing a market by the amount of product bought or consumed

Pareto Principle a principle holding that 20 percent of all customers generate 80 percent of the demand

8-5

satisficers business customers who place their order with the first familiar supplier to satisfy their product and delivery requirements

optimizers business customers who consider numerous suppliers, both familiar and unfamiliar, solicit bids, and study all proposals carefully before selecting one

8-7

target market a group of people or organizations for which an organization designs, implements, and maintains a marketing mix intended to meet the needs of that group, resulting in mutually satisfying exchanges

undifferentiated targeting strategy a marketing approach that views the market as one big market with no individual segments and thus uses a single marketing mix

concentrated targeting strategy a strategy used to select one segment of a market to target marketing efforts

niche one segment of a market

multisegment targeting strategy a strategy that chooses two or more well-defined market segments and develops a distinct marketing mix for each

cannibalization a situation that occurs when sales of a new product cut into sales of a firm's existing products

one-to-one marketing an individualized marketing method that uses customer information to build long-term, personalized, and profitable relationships with each customer

8-8

positioning a process that influences potential customers' overall perception of a brand, a product line, or an organization in general

position the place a product, brand, or group of products occupies in consumers' minds relative to competing offerings

product differentiation a positioning strategy that some firms use to distinguish their products from those of competitors

perceptual mapping a means of displaying or graphing, in two or more dimensions, the location of products, brands, or groups of products in customers' minds

repositioning changing consumers' perceptions of a brand in relation to competing brands

8-6 List the steps involved in segmenting markets. Six steps are involved when segmenting markets: (1) selecting a market or product category for study; (2) choosing a basis or bases for segmenting the market; (3) selecting segmentation descriptors; (4) profiling and evaluating segments; (5) selecting target markets; and (6) designing, implementing, and maintaining appropriate marketing mixes.

Note that steps 5 and 6 are actually marketing activities that follow market segmentation (steps 1 through 4).

8-7 Discuss alternative strategies for selecting target markets. Marketers select target markets by using four different strategies: undifferentiated targeting, concentrated targeting, multisegment targeting and one-to-one targeting. An undifferentiated targeting strategy assumes that all members of a market have similar needs that can be met by using a single marketing mix. A concentrated targeting strategy focuses all marketing efforts on a single market segment. Multisegment targeting is a strategy that uses two or more marketing mixes to target two or more market segments. One-to-one marketing is an individualized marketing method that uses customer information to build long-term, personalized, and profitable relationships with each customer. Successful one-to-one marketing comes from understanding customers and collaborating with them, rather than using them as targets for generic messages. Database technology makes it possible for companies to interact with customers on a personal, one-to-one basis.

8-8 Explain how and why firms implement positioning strategies and how product differentiation plays a role. Positioning is used to influence consumer perceptions of a particular brand, product line, or organization in relation to competitors. The term *position* refers to the place that the offering occupies in consumers' minds. To establish a unique position, many firms use product differentiation, emphasizing the real or perceived differences between competing offerings. Products may be differentiated on the basis of attribute, price and quality, use or application, product user, product class, or competitor.

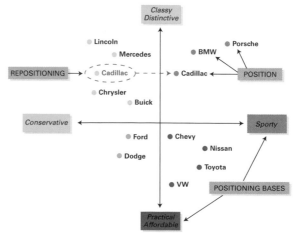

Each car occupies a position in consumers' minds.
Cars can be positioned according to attribute (sporty, conservative, etc.),
to price/quality (affordable, classy, etc.), or other bases.
With edgier ads, Cadillac has repositioned itself as a car for younger drivers.

KEY CONCEPTS

9-1 Summarize customer relationship management. In customer relationship management (CRM), a company gathers information about its customers and then uses that information to build loyalty and long-term commitments with those customers. CRM started out as a technology solution for companies looking for data on customers. Much of what was developed was strong from the technology side but did not have the loyalty focus necessary for a true CRM system. CRM must be differentiated from customer relationship marketing, which is more of a customer database than a comprehensive system of tracking and maintaining customer loyalty.

9-2 Explain the CRM cycle. The Government of Canada has taken the lead on customer relationship management by releasing an important report on CRM in Canada. The focus of the report was on developing a system of CRM that was not too strongly based in information technology but did use those tools to help create customer loyalty. What was developed was a three-stage CRM cycle. The first stage is focused on using marketing research and general marketing tools to help design and structure a system to keep track of customer information. The second stage is called business development, and here the IT tools are used to help track and establish an efficient system of data collection. Finally, the third stage takes action on the data collected and determines what systems of customer retention and loyalty could be established to not only track customers but begin a two-way interaction that will lead to long-term benefits for both parties.

9-3 Describe Stage 1 in the CRM cycle: marketing research. In the first stage of the cycle, there is a renewed focus on marketing as part of CRM. Much of what had been developed for CRM concerned technology solutions and systems rather than what needed to go into these systems. Marketing research techniques, such as competitive intelligence, focus groups, and surveys, are all possible inputs to this first stage of the CRM cycle. As the CRM cycle begins, it becomes clear that CRM is about cross-functional integration of activities in a firm that will lead to customer loyalty. The drivers of this process are those with knowledge of marketing strategy.

9-4 Describe Stage 2 in the CRM cycle: business development. Stage 2 begins with the assumption that we understand the needs of our customers and have developed an offering that should satisfy them. The first activity in this stage, then, is to identify customer relationships. Using such tools as learning and knowledge management, those relationships are identified, and the nature of the relationships and interactions is used to build a knowledge base. The action then moves to the technology side of CRM by tackling the data needs. Companies need to figure out at this stage how to capture data, store them, and determine which IT tools will best mine them.

KEY TERMS

9-1

customer relationship management (CRM) a system that gathers information about customers that can help to build customer loyalty and retain those loyal customers

9-4

data mining an analytical process that compiles actionable data on the purchase habits of a firm's current and potential customers

customer-centric a philosophy under which the company customizes its product and service offerings based on data generated through interactions between the customer and the company

learning (CRM) in a CRM environment, the informal process of collecting customer data through customer comments and feedback on product or service performance

knowledge management the process by which learned information from customers is centralized and shared for the purpose of enhancing the relationship between customers and the organization

empowerment delegation of authority to solve customers' problems quickly—usually by the first person who learns of the customer's problem

interaction the point at which a customer and a company representative exchange information and develop learning relationships

touch points all possible areas of a business where customers have contact with that business

point-of-sale interactions communications between customers and organizations that occur at the point of sale, usually in a store

data warehouse a central repository of data from various functional areas of the organization that are stored and inventoried on a centralized computer system so that the information can be shared across all functional departments of the business

database an organized system of data collection that allows for assessment, usually by computer

response list a customer list that includes the names and addresses of individuals who have responded to an offer of some kind, such as by mail, telephone, direct-response television, product rebates, contests or sweepstakes, or billing inserts

compiled lists customer lists that are developed by gathering names and addresses gleaned from telephone directories and membership rosters, sometimes enhanced with information from public records, such as census data, auto registrations, birth announcements, business start-ups, or bankruptcies

recency-frequency-monetary (RFM) analysis the analysis of customer activity by recency, frequency, and monetary value

CHAPTER REVIEW 9

lifetime value (LTV) analysis a data manipulation technique that projects the future value of the customer over a period of years by using the assumption that marketing to repeat customers is more profitable than marketing to first-time buyers

predictive modelling a data manipulation technique in which marketers try to determine, based on some past set of occurrences, the odds that some other occurrence, such as an inquiry or a purchase, will take place in the future

9-5

campaign management developing product or service offerings customized for the appropriate customer segment and then pricing and communicating these offerings to enhance customer relationships

9-5 Describe Stage 3 in the CRM cycle: customer feedback. Even after the data have been collected and mined, they will only get us so far in developing effective CRM. At this stage, companies need to look beyond the reams of data and see in there the people and companies that make up their customer base. CRM must be focused on relationship development, not just database development. Companies can use different methods and applications to build customer loyalty. Companies can develop campaigns and loyalty programs, they can try to cross-sell, and they can target their communications. They can look at product trials and distribution channel marketing. All these tools must have one goal: to truly change the way in which customers are managed and build a loyal customer base from a foundation of customer service.

9-6 Identify privacy issues in CRM. The three-stage process of CRM offers numerous options and great potential for data collection, but companies must incorporate strong policies on privacy to protect their customers. Online options are enticing, given the potential access to data, as discussed in Chapter 5 on marketing research, but big data and online options can be a dangerous mix if not managed properly. When developing CRM systems, companies should familiarize themselves with legislation such as the Personal Information Protection and Electronic Documents Act (PIPEDA) and the Privacy Act.

9-7 Determine the future challenges for CRM. The future of CRM is all about looking forward and being proactive. Firms using CRM can no longer rely on CRM to provide historical data and offer suggestions from the past to instruct the future. The future lies in predictive technologies like one would see in Amazon and other online retailers that are able to predict future purchases based on previous interactions with the customer. CRM might become "CRA" with the management of customers turning into the automation of the relationship. This re-think of CRM will take a number of years to be implemented across industries and companies. But as more companies like Amazon and Facebook gain great advantage by predictive and advanced technologies, the greater chances that this future will not be a Hollywood dystopia with machines taking over, but rather machines being use to help improve the relationship between customer and company.

KEY CONCEPTS

10-1 Define the term *product*. A product is anything, desired or not, that a person or organization receives in an exchange. The basic goal of purchasing decisions is to receive the tangible and intangible benefits associated with a product. Tangible aspects include packaging, style, colour, size, and features. Intangible qualities include service, the retailer's image, the manufacturer's reputation, and the social status associated with a product. An organization's product offering is the crucial element in any marketing mix.

10-2 Classify consumer products. Consumer products are classified into four categories: convenience products, shopping products, specialty products, and unsought products. Convenience products are relatively inexpensive and require limited shopping effort. Shopping products are of two types: homogeneous and heterogeneous. Because of the similarity of homogeneous products, they are differentiated mainly by price and features. In contrast, heterogeneous products appeal to consumers because of their distinct characteristics. Specialty products possess unique benefits that are highly desirable to certain customers. Finally, unsought products are either new products or products that require aggressive selling because they are generally avoided or overlooked by consumers.

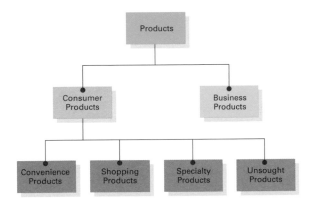

10-3 Define the terms *product item*, *product line*, and *product mix*. A product item is a specific version of a product that can be designated as a distinct offering among an organization's products. A product line is a group of closely related products offered by an organization. An organization's product mix includes all the products it sells. Product mix width refers to the number of product lines an organization offers. Product line depth is the number of product items in a product line. Firms modify existing products by changing their quality, functional characteristics, or style. Product line extension occurs when a firm adds new products to existing product lines.

10-4 Describe marketing uses of branding. A brand is a name, term, or symbol that identifies and differentiates a firm's products. Established brands encourage customer loyalty and help new products succeed. Branding strategies require decisions about individual, family, manufacturers', and private brands.

KEY TERMS

10-1

product anything, both favourable and unfavourable, received by a person in an exchange for possession, consumption, attention, or short-term use

10-2

business product a product used to manufacture other goods or services, to facilitate an organization's operations, or to resell to other customers

consumer product a product bought to satisfy an individual's personal wants

convenience product a relatively inexpensive item that merits little shopping effort

shopping product a product that requires comparison shopping because it is usually more expensive than a convenience product and is found in fewer stores

specialty product a particular item with unique characteristics for which consumers search extensively and for which they are very reluctant to accept substitutes.

unsought product a product unknown to the potential buyer or a known product that the buyer does not actively seek

10-3

product item a specific version of a product that can be designated as a distinct offering among an organization's products

product line a group of closely related product items

product mix all products that an organization sells

product mix width the number of product lines an organization offers

product line length the number of product items in a product line

product line depth the different versions of a product item in a product line

product modification changing one or more of a product's characteristics

planned obsolescence the practice of modifying products so those that have already been sold become obsolete before they actually need replacement

product line extension adding products to an existing product line to compete more broadly in the industry

10-4

brand a name, term, symbol, design, or combination thereof that identifies a seller's products and differentiates them from competitors' products

brand name that part of a brand that can be spoken, including letters, words, and numbers

brand mark the elements of a brand that cannot be spoken

brand equity the value of company and brand names

global brand a brand with at least 20 percent of the product sold outside its home country or region

brand loyalty a consistent preference for one brand over all others

generic product a no-frills, no-brand-name, low-cost product that is simply identified by its product category

manufacturer's brand the brand name of a manufacturer

private brand a brand name owned by a wholesaler or a retailer

individual branding the use of different brand names for different products

family brand the marketing of several different products under the same brand name

cobranding placing two or more brand names on a product or its package

trademark the exclusive right to use a brand or part of a brand

service mark a trademark for a service

generic product name a term that identifies a product by class or type and cannot be trademarked

10-5

persuasive labelling package labelling that focuses on a promotional theme or logo; consumer information is secondary

informational labelling package labelling designed to help consumers make proper product selections and to lower their cognitive dissonance after the purchase

universal product codes (UPCs) a series of thick and thin vertical lines (bar codes), readable by computerized optical scanners that match the codes to brand names, package sizes, and prices

10-7

warranty a confirmation of the quality or performance of a good or service

express warranty a written guarantee

implied warranty an unwritten guarantee that the good or service is fit for the purpose for which it was sold

10-5 Describe marketing uses of packaging and labelling. Packaging has four functions: containing and protecting products; promoting products; facilitating product storage, use, and convenience; and facilitating recycling and reducing environmental damage. As a tool for promotion, packaging identifies the brand and its features. It also serves the critical function of differentiating a product from competing products and linking it with related products from the same manufacturer. The label is an integral part of the package and has persuasive and informational functions. In essence, the package is the marketer's last chance to influence buyers before they make a purchase decision.

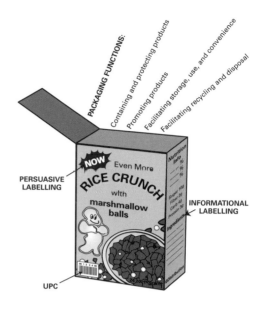

10-6 Discuss global issues in branding and packaging. In addition to brand piracy, international marketers must address a variety of concerns regarding branding and packaging, including choosing a brand-name policy, translating labels and meeting host-country labelling requirements, making packages aesthetically compatible with host-country cultures, and offering the sizes of packages preferred in host countries.

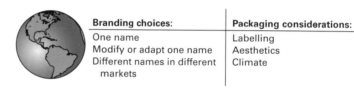

	Branding choices:	Packaging considerations:
	One name	Labelling
	Modify or adapt one name	Aesthetics
	Different names in different markets	Climate

10-7 Describe how and why product warranties are important marketing tools. Product warranties are important tools because they offer consumers protection and help them gauge product quality.

Express warranty = Written guarantee

Implied warranty = Unwritten guarantee

KEY CONCEPTS

11-1 Explain the importance of developing new products and describe the six categories of new products. New products are important to sustain growth and profits and to replace obsolete items. New products can be classified as new-to-the-world products (discontinuous innovations), new product lines, additions to existing product lines, improvements or revisions of existing products, repositioned products, or lower-priced products. To sustain or increase profits, a firm must innovate.

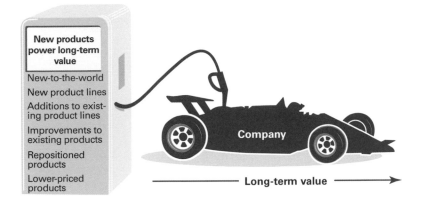

New products power long-term value
- New-to-the-world
- New product lines
- Additions to existing product lines
- Improvements to existing products
- Repositioned products
- Lower-priced products

Company → Long-term value →

11-2 Explain the steps in the new-product development process. First, a firm forms a new-product strategy by outlining the characteristics and roles of future products. Then new-product ideas are generated by customers, employees, distributors, competitors, vendors, and internal R&D personnel. Once a product idea has survived initial screening by an appointed screening group, it undergoes business analysis to determine its potential profitability. If a product concept seems viable, it progresses into the development phase, in which the technical and economic feasibility of the manufacturing process is evaluated. The development phase also includes laboratory and use testing of a product for performance and safety. Following initial testing and refinement, most products are introduced in a test market to evaluate consumer response and marketing strategies. Finally, test market successes are propelled into full commercialization. The commercialization process involves starting up production, building inventories, shipping to distributors, training a sales force, announcing the product to the trade, and advertising to consumers.

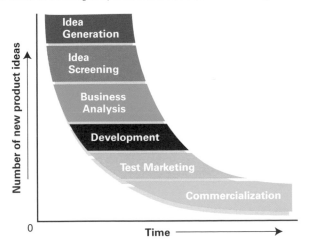

Idea Generation
Idea Screening
Business Analysis
Development
Test Marketing
Commercialization

Number of new product ideas → Time →

KEY TERMS

11-1
new product a product new to the world, new to the market, new to the producer or seller, or new to some combination of these

11-2
new-product strategy a plan that links the new-product development process with the objectives of the marketing department, the business unit, and the corporation

product development a marketing strategy that entails the creation of new products for current customers

brainstorming the process of getting a group to think of unlimited ways to vary a product or solve a problem

screening the first filter in the product development process, which eliminates ideas that are inconsistent with the organization's new-product strategy or are obviously inappropriate for some other reason

concept test evaluation of a new-product idea, usually before any prototype has been created

business analysis the second stage of the screening process, where preliminary figures for demand, cost, sales, and profitability are calculated

development the stage in the product development process in which a prototype is developed and a marketing strategy is outlined

test marketing the limited introduction of a product and a marketing program to determine the reactions of potential customers in a market situation

simulated (laboratory) market testing the presentation of advertising and other promotion materials for several products, including the test product, to members of the product's target market

commercialization the decision to market a product

11-4
adopter a consumer who was satisfied enough with his or her trial experience with a product to use it again

innovation a product perceived as new by a potential adopter

diffusion the process by which the adoption of an innovation spreads

11-5
product life cycle (PLC) a concept that traces the stages of a product's acceptance, from its introduction (birth) to its decline (death)

product category all brands that satisfy a particular type of need

introductory stage the full-scale launch of a new product into the marketplace

growth stage the second stage of the product life cycle when sales typically grow at an increasing rate, many competitors enter the market, large companies may start to acquire small pioneering firms, and profits are healthy

maturity stage a period during which sales increase at a decreasing rate

decline stage a long-run drop in sales

11-3 Discuss global issues in new-product development. A marketer with global vision seeks to develop products that can easily be adapted to suit local needs. The goal is not simply to develop a standard product that can be sold worldwide. Smart global marketers also look for good product ideas worldwide.

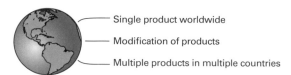

— Single product worldwide

— Modification of products

— Multiple products in multiple countries

11-4 Explain the diffusion process through which new products are adopted. The diffusion process is the spread of a new product from its producer to its ultimate adopters. Adopters in the diffusion process belong to five categories: innovators, early adopters, the early majority, the late majority, and laggards. Product characteristics that affect the rate of adoption include product complexity, compatibility with existing social values, relative advantage over existing substitutes, visibility, and trialability. The diffusion process is facilitated by word-of-mouth communication and communication from marketers to consumers.

Diffusion of Innovations—Adopter Categories

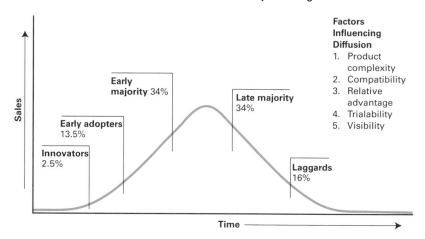

Factors Influencing Diffusion
1. Product complexity
2. Compatibility
3. Relative advantage
4. Trialability
5. Visibility

11-5 Explain the concept of product life cycles. All brands and product categories have a life cycle with four stages: introduction, growth, maturity, and decline. The rate at which products move through these stages varies dramatically. Marketing managers use the product life-cycle concept as an analytical tool to forecast a product's future and devise effective marketing strategies.

Marketing Mix Strategy	Product Life Cycle Stage			
	Introductory	Growth	Maturity	Decline
Product Strategy	Limited number of models; frequent product modifications	Expanded number of models; frequent product modifications	Large number of models	Elimination of unprofitable models and brands
Distribution Strategy	Distribution usually limited, depending on product; intensive efforts and high margins often needed to attract wholesalers and retailers	Expanded number of dealers; intensive efforts to establish long-term relationships with wholesalers and retailers	Extensive number of dealers; margins declining; intensive efforts to retain distributors and shelf space	Unprofitable outlets phased out
Promotion Strategy	Develop product awareness; stimulate primary demand; use intensive personal selling to distributors; use sampling and couponing for consumers	Stimulate selective demand; advertise brand aggressively	Stimulate selective demand; advertise brand aggressively; promote heavily to retain dealers and customers	Phase out all promotion
Pricing Strategy	Prices are usually high to recover development costs (see the appendix to Chapter 12)	Prices begin to fall toward end of growth stage as result of competitive pressure	Prices continue to fall	Prices stabilize at relatively low level; small price rises are possible if competition is negligible

KEY CONCEPTS

12-1 Discuss the importance of services to the economy. The service sector plays a crucial role in the Canadian economy, employing more than 78 percent of the workforce and accounting for a similar percentage of the gross domestic product.

12-2 Discuss the differences between services and goods. Services are distinguished by four characteristics. Services are intangible performances because they lack clearly identifiable physical characteristics, making it difficult for marketers to communicate their specific benefits to potential customers. The production and consumption of services occur simultaneously. Services quality is inconsistent because the service depends on such elements as the service provider, individual consumer, location, and so on. Finally, services cannot be inventoried. As a result, synchronizing supply with demand is particularly challenging in the service industry.

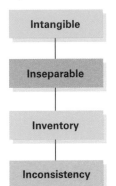

12-3 Describe the components of service quality and the gap model of service quality.
Service quality has five components: reliability (ability to perform the service dependably, accurately, and consistently), responsiveness (providing prompt service), assurance (knowledge and courtesy of employees and their ability to convey trust), empathy (caring, individualized attention), and tangibles (physical evidence of the service).

The gap model identifies five key discrepancies that can influence customer evaluations of service quality. When the gaps are large, service quality is low. As the gaps shrink, service quality improves. Gap 1, the knowledge gap, is found between customers' expectations and management's perceptions of those expectations. Gap 2, the standard gap, is found between management's perception of what the customer wants and the specifications for service quality. Gap 3, the delivery gap, is found between service quality specifications and delivery of the service. Gap 4, the communications gap, is found between service delivery and what the company promises to the customer through external communication. Gap 5, the perception gap, is found between customers' service expectations and their perceptions of service performance.

12-4 Develop marketing mixes for services using the eight Ps of services marketing. The marketing mix for services adds people, process, productivity, and physical environment to the traditional four Ps of product, price, promotions and place.

KEY TERMS

12-1
service the result of applying human or mechanical efforts to people or objects

12-2
intangibility the inability of services to be touched, seen, tasted, heard, or felt in the same manner that goods can be sensed

search quality a characteristic that can be easily assessed before purchase

experience quality a characteristic that can be assessed only after use

credence quality a characteristic that consumers may have difficulty assessing even after purchase because they do not have the necessary knowledge or experience

inseparability the inability of the production and consumption of a service to be separated; consumers must be present during the production

inconsistency the inability of service quality to be consistent each time it is delivered because the service depends on the people who provide it

inventory the inability of services to be stored for future use

12-3
reliability the ability to perform a service dependably, accurately, and consistently

responsiveness the ability to provide prompt service

assurance the knowledge and courtesy of employees and their ability to convey trust

empathy caring, individualized attention paid to customers

tangibles the physical evidence of a service, including the physical facilities, tools, and equipment used to provide the service

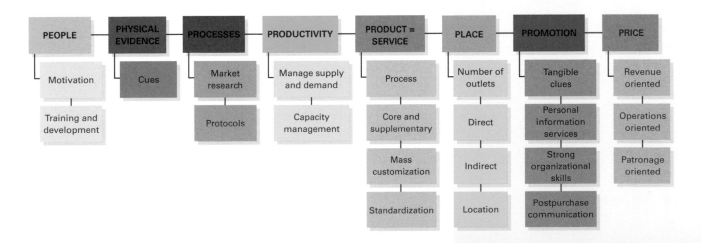

gap model a model identifying five gaps that can cause problems in service delivery and influence customer evaluations of service quality

12-4

core service the most basic benefit the consumer is buying

supplementary services a group of services that support or enhance the core service

mass customization a strategy that uses technology to deliver customized services on a mass basis

12-6

internal marketing treating employees as customers and developing systems and benefits that satisfy their needs

12-7

nonprofit organization an organization that exists to achieve some goal other than the usual business goals of profit, market share, or return on investment

nonprofit organization marketing the effort by nonprofit organizations to bring about mutually satisfying exchanges with target markets

public service advertisement (PSA) an announcement that promotes a program of a nonprofit organization or of a federal, provincial or territorial, or local government

12-5 Discuss relationship marketing in services. Relationship marketing in services involves attracting, developing, and retaining customer relationships. Relationship marketing has four levels: level 1 focuses on pricing incentives; level 2 uses pricing incentives and social bonds with customers; level 3 uses intimate knowledge of the customer to create one-to-one solutions; and level 4 uses pricing, social bonds, and structural bonds to build long-term relationships.

12-6 Explain internal marketing in services. Internal marketing means treating employees as customers and developing systems and benefits that satisfy their needs. Employees who like their jobs and are happy with the firm they work for are more likely to deliver good service and be brand ambassadors.

12-7 Describe nonprofit organization marketing. Nonprofit organizations pursue goals other than profit, market share, and return on investment.

Nonprofit Organization Marketing

PRODUCT
- Benefit complexity
- Benefit strength
- Involvement

PLACE
- Special facilities

TARGET
- Apathetic or strongly opposed
- Undifferentiated segmentation
- Complementary positioning

PROMOTION
- Professional volunteers
- Sales
- Public service advertising

PRICE
- Nonfinancial
- Indirect payment
- Separation between payers and users
- Below-cost pricing

KEY CONCEPTS

13-1 Explain the importance of price. Of the four Ps, price is special. Price is a source of revenue for the firm, not a cost centre like many promotional activities. Price involves an understanding of revenues, expenses, and the resulting profit. Many economic factors go into pricing a product or service, but there are also many other factors that are more psychological.

13-2 Describe the four-step pricing process. The four-step pricing process allows for a true understanding of the many factors included in and decisions that must be made in setting a price. The first step is to establish pricing goals. Companies must determine if they are profit oriented, focused on meeting a profit objective or a target return, or will look to sales as a way to create their pricing goals. The second step is to estimate demand, costs, and profit. This step is tied in with calculating demand at various price levels, calculating fixed and variable costs, and then determining unit price and quantities required to break even—and to make a profit. There is also a relationship here between the product and specifically the product life cycle. The third step is to establish a pricing strategy. Companies can decide to price higher (skimming), lower (penetration), or about the same (status quo) as the competition. Finally, the fourth step is to establish a pricing tactic. Pricing tactics tend to be used once the base price has been established. Tactics include discounts, geographic pricing, flexible pricing, price lining, loss leaders, and odd–even pricing (though that last one might be dying out).

KEY TERMS

13-1

price that which is given up in an exchange to acquire a good or service

revenue the price per unit charged to customers multiplied by the number of units sold

costs the combined financial value of all inputs that go into the production of a company's products, both directly and indirectly

profit revenue minus expenses

13-2

return on investment (ROI) net profits divided by the investment

market share a company's product sales as a percentage of total sales for that industry

status quo pricing a pricing objective that maintains existing prices or meets the competition's prices

price sensitivity consumers' varying levels of desire to buy a given product at different price levels

price elasticity of demand a measurement of change in consumer demand for a product relative to the changes in its price

break-even analysis the calculation of number of units sold, or total revenue required, a firm must meet to cover its costs, beyond which profit occurs

price strategy a basic, long-term pricing framework that establishes the initial price for a product and the intended direction for price movements over the product life cycle

price skimming a high introductory price, often coupled with heavy promotion

penetration pricing a relatively low price for a product initially as a way to reach the mass market

experience curves curves that show costs declining at a predictable rate as experience with a product increases

base price the general price level at which the company expects to sell the good or service

quantity discount a unit price reduction offered to buyers buying either in multiple units or at more than a specified dollar amount

cumulative quantity discount a deduction from list price that applies to the buyer's total purchases made during a specific period

noncumulative quantity discount a deduction from list price that applies to a single order rather than to the total volume of orders placed during a certain period

cash discount a price reduction offered to a consumer, an industrial user, or a marketing intermediary in return for prompt payment of a bill

functional discount (trade discount) a discount to wholesalers and retailers for performing channel functions

seasonal discount a price reduction for buying merchandise out of season

value-based pricing setting the price at a level that seems to the customer to be a good price compared with the prices of other options

FOB origin pricing the buyer absorbs the freight costs from the shipping point ("free on board")

uniform delivered pricing the seller pays the actual freight charges and bills every purchaser an identical, flat freight charge

zone pricing a modification of uniform delivered pricing that divides the total market into segments or zones and charges a flat freight rate to all customers in a given zone

freight absorption pricing the seller pays all or part of the actual freight charges and does not pass them on to the buyer

basing-point pricing charging freight from a given (basing) point, regardless of the city from which the goods are shipped

single-price tactic offering all goods and services at the same price (or perhaps two or three prices)

flexible pricing (variable pricing) different customers pay different prices for essentially the same merchandise bought in equal quantities

professional services pricing used by people with experience, training, and often certification, fees are typically charged at an hourly rate, but may be based on the solution of a problem or performance of an act

price lining offering a product line with several items at specific price points

loss-leader pricing a product is sold near or even below cost in the hope that shoppers will buy other items once they are in the store

odd–even pricing (psychological pricing) odd-numbered prices connote bargains, and even-numbered prices imply quality

price bundling marketing two or more products in a single package for a special price

unbundling reducing the bundle of services that comes with the basic product

two-part pricing charging two separate amounts to consume a single good or service

13-3

bait pricing a price tactic that tries to get consumers into a store through false or misleading price advertising and then uses high-pressure selling to persuade consumers to buy more expensive merchandise instead

deceptive pricing promoting a price or price saving that is not actually available

price fixing an agreement between two or more firms on the price they will charge for a product

predatory pricing the practice of charging a very low price for a product with the intent of driving competitors out of business or out of a market

resale price maintenance attempts by a producer to control a store's retail price for the product

13-3 Recognize the legalities and ethics of setting a price. This darker side of pricing introduces us to the concepts of bait pricing, bait and switch, and other deceptive practices. Some firms try to influence the price of their products by making agreements with competitors or by using discriminatory practices to influence the price on the shelves. All of these methods are problematic, and some well-known firms have run afoul of these legal and ethical issues with pricing.

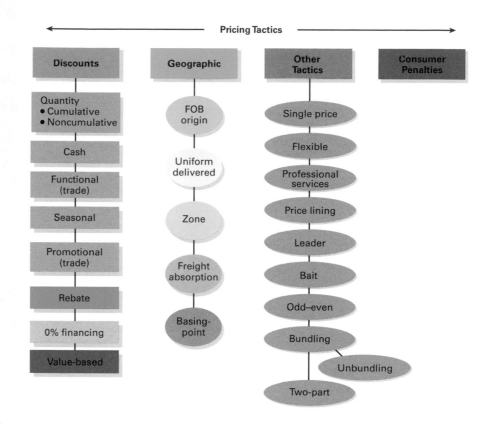

KEY CONCEPTS

14-1 Explain the nature of marketing channels. Sometimes referred to as the "forgotten P" of the four Ps, place is an important, albeit overshadowed, element of the marketing mix. The focus of place is on marketing channels (channels of distribution) that guide products from the companies producing them to the consumers or business customers purchasing and using them. The supply chain covers all companies that are responsible for some aspect of developing and distributing a product. Supply chains have intermediaries that end up performing a number of important tasks, including specialization, division of labour, the overcoming of discrepancies, and contact efficiency.

14-2 Identify different channel intermediaries and their functions. The intermediaries in a channel system and supply chain undertake important tasks that are key to a properly functioning distribution system. Intermediaries work with other firms while also ensuring their own firms' success. In determining what type of intermediary to use, a producer should look at a number of factors, including product characteristics, buyer considerations, and market characteristics. Retailers sell mainly to customers. Wholesalers help move goods through the supply chain. Agents and brokers facilitate the exchange of ownership between buyers and sellers.

14-3 Describe the types of marketing channels. Marketing channels are paths to move goods from producer to customer. The most straightforward is called the direct channel: a producer has direct contact with the end customer and does not have to rely on intermediaries. Business channels focus on B2B interactions. In multiple channels, two different types of channels are used to deliver the same product. Nontraditional channels, like vending machines, are intriguing options but with potential risk to the brand and company image. In strategic channel alliances, companies decide to work together to achieve certain supply chain goals.

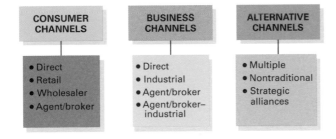

CONSUMER CHANNELS	BUSINESS CHANNELS	ALTERNATIVE CHANNELS
• Direct • Retail • Wholesaler • Agent/broker	• Direct • Industrial • Agent/broker • Agent/broker–industrial	• Multiple • Nontraditional • Strategic alliances

14-4 Summarize how to make channel strategy decisions. To make the correct decisions when selecting the overall makeup of a channel, companies look at several important factors. The market factors relate to the customer to determine the likely behaviours and patterns that they will display. Product factors deal with the product on offer and, depending on the complexity of the product, will determine how the product moves through the channel system. Finally, producer factors connect to the company behind the product and whether it has the necessary size and capabilities to manage a certain type of channel system. Distribution intensity is another important consideration. The three main types of distribution intensity are intensive, selective, and exclusive; each has its own benefits and drawbacks.

14-5 Recognize how to handle channel relationships. The importance of relationships was made evident in Chapter 7 in the discussion of business marketing. With place and distribution, we are once again talking about the need for businesses to work together. However, because business is focused on profit and growth-oriented goals,

KEY TERMS

14-1

marketing channel (channel of distribution) a set of interdependent organizations that ease the transfer of ownership as products move from producer to business user or consumer

channel members all parties in the marketing channel that negotiate with one another, buy and sell products, and facilitate the change of ownership between buyer and seller as they move the product from the manufacturer into the hands of the final consumer

supply chain the connected chain of all the business entities, both internal and external to the company, that perform or support the marketing channel functions

discrepancy of quantity the difference between the amount of product produced and the amount an end-user wants to buy

discrepancy of assortment the lack of all the items a customer needs to receive full satisfaction from a product or products

temporal discrepancy a product is produced but a customer is not ready to buy it

spatial discrepancy the difference between the location of a producer and the location of widely scattered markets

14-2

retailer a channel intermediary that sells mainly to consumers and business customers

14-3

direct channel a distribution channel in which producers sell directly to customers

dual distribution (multiple distribution) the use of two or more channels to distribute the same product to target markets

strategic channel alliances cooperative agreements between business firms to use one of the manufacturer's already established distribution channels

14-4

intensive distribution a form of distribution aimed at having a product available in every outlet where target customers might want to buy it

coverage ensuring product availability in every outlet where potential customers might want to buy it

selective distribution a form of distribution achieved by screening dealers to eliminate all but a few in any single area

exclusive distribution a form of distribution that involves only one or a few dealers within a given area

14-5

channel power a marketing channel member's capacity to control or influence the behaviour of other channel members

channel control one marketing channel member intentionally affects another member's behaviour

channel leader (channel captain) a member of a marketing channel who exercises authority and power over the activities of other channel members

channel conflict a clash of goals and methods among distribution channel members

horizontal conflict a channel conflict that occurs among channel members on the same level

vertical conflict a channel conflict that occurs between different levels in a marketing channel, most typically between the manufacturer and wholesaler or between the manufacturer and retailer

channel partnering (channel cooperation) the joint effort of all channel members to create a supply chain that serves customers and creates a competitive advantage

14-6

supply chain management a management system that coordinates and integrates all the activities performed by supply chain members into a seamless process, from the source to the point of consumption, resulting in enhanced customer and economic value

logistics the process of strategically managing the efficient flow and storage of raw materials, in-process inventory, and finished goods from point of origin to point of consumption

logistics information system the link that connects all the logistics functions of the supply chain

supply chain team an entire group of individuals who orchestrate the movement of goods, services, and information from the source to the consumer

procurement the process of buying goods and services for use in the operations of an organization

mass customization (build-to-order) a production method whereby products are not made until an order is placed by the customer; products are made according to customer specifications

just-in-time production (JIT) a process that redefines and simplifies manufacturing by reducing inventory levels and delivering raw materials just when they are needed on the production line

order processing system a system whereby orders are entered into the supply chain and filled

electronic data interchange (EDI) information technology that replaces the paper documents that usually accompany business transactions, such as purchase orders and invoices, with electronic transmission of the needed information to reduce inventory levels, improve cash flow, streamline operations, and increase the speed and accuracy of information transmission

inventory control system a method of developing and maintaining an adequate assortment of materials or products to meet a manufacturer's or a customer's demand

there is bound to be conflict when companies interact in a marketing channel. Issues of power and control are not surprising in channels, and managing them, along with taking a leadership role, is an important step for any company in a channel. Conflict in a channel can be horizontal, meaning at the same level of intermediary (e.g., distributor versus distributor) between different channels. Conflict can also be vertical within a channel (e.g., distributor versus retailer). But with all of this conflict comes some positive cooperation, and firms work together to make things easier for the entire channel, which also benefits individual firms in the process.

14-6 Learn about supply chain management. Supply chain management strives to coordinate and integrate all the activities involved in getting a product to market. This includes everything from raw materials all the way to the managing of the delivery of the final product to a customer. Logistics is often described as the grease in the wheels of supply chain management, offering the flow and storage necessary for supplies and products to make their way to the necessary points in a channel system. Purchasing and procuring the right items is a vital task in supply chain management.

14-7 List channel and distribution challenges in global markets. Globalization of markets has led to innovations and changes in every market, and channels and distribution are certainly not immune. World markets continue to open up, and with more agreements being ratified by the World Trade Organization, companies now have access to markets and partners that can potentially provide improvements to the existing supply chain.

KEY CONCEPTS

15-1 Discuss the importance of retailing in the Canadian economy.
Retailing plays a vital role in the Canadian economy for two main reasons. First, retail businesses contribute to our high standard of living by providing a vast number and diversity of goods and services. Second, retailing employs a large portion of the Canadian working population.

15-2 Explain the dimensions by which retailers can be classified.
Many different kinds of retailers exist. A retail establishment can be classified according to its ownership, level of service, product assortment, and price. On the basis of ownership, retailers can be broadly differentiated as independent retailers, chain stores, or franchise outlets. The level of service retailers provide can be classified along a continuum of high to low. Retailers also classify themselves by the breadth and depth of their product assortments. Last, general price levels also classify a store, from discounters offering low prices to exclusive specialty stores where high prices are the norm.

15-3 Describe the major types of retail operations. The major types of retail stores are department stores, specialty retailers, supermarkets, drugstores, convenience stores, discount stores, and restaurants. Department stores carry a wide assortment of shopping and specialty goods, are organized into relatively independent departments, and offset higher prices by emphasizing customer service and decor. Specialty retailers typically carry a narrower but deeper assortment of merchandise, emphasizing distinctive products and a high level of customer service. Supermarkets are large self-service retailers that offer a wide variety of food products and some nonfood items. Drugstores are retail formats that sell mostly prescription and over-the-counter medications, health and beauty aids, cosmetics, and specialty items. Convenience stores carry a limited line of high-turnover convenience goods. Discount stores offer low-priced general merchandise and consist of four types: full-line discounters, specialty discount retailers, warehouse clubs, and off-price retailers. Finally, restaurants straddle the line between the retailing and services industries; although restaurants sell a product, food and drink, to final consumers, they can also be considered service marketers because they provide consumers with the service of preparing food and providing table service.

15-4 Discuss nonstore retailing techniques. Nonstore retailing, which is shopping outside a store setting, has 4 major categories: automatic vending machines, direct retailing, direct marketing and online or e-tailing. The latest developments in retailing have occurred in the area of online retailing.

15-5 Define franchising and describe its two basic forms. Franchising is a continuing relationship in which a franchiser grants to a franchisee the business rights to operate or to sell a product. Modern franchising takes two basic forms: product or trade-name franchising and business-format franchising.

15-6 List the major tasks involved in developing a retail marketing strategy. Retail management begins with defining the target market, typically on the basis of demographic, geographic, or psychographic characteristics. After determining the target market, retail managers must develop the six variables of the retailing mix: product, promotion, place, price, presentation, and personnel.

15-7 Discuss retail product and service failures and means to improve. In spite of retailers' best intentions and efforts to satisfy each and every customer, consumer dissatisfaction can occur. No retailer can be everything to every customer. The best retailers have plans in place to recover from lapses in service. These plans hinge on honest communication with the customer as often and in as timely a fashion as possible. Good retailers treat customer disappointments as opportunities to improve.

KEY TERMS

15-1

retailing all the activities directly related to the sale of goods and services to the ultimate consumer for personal, nonbusiness use

retailer the market intermediary that sells goods and services to the final consumer

15-2

independent retailers retailers owned by a single person or partnership and not operated as part of a larger retail institution

chain stores stores owned and operated as a group by a single organization

gross margin the amount of money the retailer makes as a percentage of sales after the cost of goods sold is subtracted

15-3

department store a store housing several departments under one roof

specialty store a retail store specializing in a given type of merchandise

supermarkets large, departmentalized, self-service retailers that specialize in food and some nonfood items

scrambled merchandising the tendency to offer a wide variety of nontraditional goods and services under one roof

drugstores retail stores that stock pharmacy-related products and services as their main draw

convenience store a miniature supermarket, carrying only a limited line of high-turnover convenience goods

discount store a retailer that competes on the basis of low prices, high turnover, and high volume

full-line discount stores retailers that offer consumers very limited service and carry a broad assortment of well-known, nationally branded hard goods

mass merchandising a retailing strategy using moderate to low prices on large quantities of merchandise and lower levels of service to stimulate high turnover of products

supercentres retail stores that combine groceries and general merchandise goods with a wide range of services

specialty discount stores retail stores that offer a nearly complete selection of single-line merchandise and use self-service, discount prices, high volume, and high turnover

category killers specialty discount stores that heavily dominate their narrow merchandise segment

warehouse membership clubs limited-service merchant wholesalers that sell a limited selection of brand-name appliances, household items, and groceries to members, small businesses, and groups

off-price retailer a retailer that sells brand-name merchandise at considerable discounts

factory outlet an off-price retailer that is owned and operated by a manufacturer

15-4

nonstore retailing provides shopping without visiting a store

automatic vending the use of machines to offer goods for sale

self-service technologies (SST) technological interfaces that allow customers to provide themselves with products and/or services without the intervention of a service employee

direct retailing the selling of products by representatives who work door-to-door, office-to-office, or at in-home parties

direct marketing (direct-response marketing) techniques used to get consumers to make a purchase from their home, office, or another non-retail setting

direct mail a printed form of direct-response communication that is delivered directly to consumers' homes

telemarketing the use of telecommunications to sell a product or service; involves both outbound and inbound calls

shop-at-home television network a specialized form of direct-response marketing whereby television shows display merchandise, with the retail price, to home viewers

online retailing (e-tailing) a type of shopping available to consumers with personal computers and access to the Internet

omni channel retailing an approach that combines the advantages of the physical store experience with the information-rich experience of online shipping, providing the consumer with a seamless experience through all available shopping channels

webrooming researching a product online and then going to a store to buy it

showrooming searching for a product in a store and then going online to try to find it at a better price

15-5

franchise a relationship in which the business rights to operate and sell a product are granted by the franchisor to the franchisee

franchiser the originator of a trade name, product, methods of operation, and so on, that grants operating rights to another party to sell its product

franchisee an individual or a business that is granted the right to sell a franchiser's product

15-6

retailing mix a combination of the six Ps—product, place, promotion, price, presentation, and personnel—to sell goods and services to the ultimate consumer

product offering the mix of products offered to the consumer by the retailer; also called the product assortment or merchandise mix

brand cannibalization the reduction of sales for one brand as the result of the introduction of a new product or promotion of a current product or brand

15-8 Discuss retailer and retail consumer trends that will affect retailing in the future. Both small retailers and national chains are using technology to enhance engagement with the consumer and improve their competitiveness. In particular, mobile and social media are the biggest disruptive forces in the industry now.

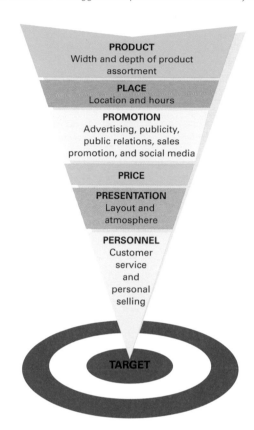

destination stores stores that consumers purposely plan to visit

pop-up shop temporary retail space that sells merchandise of any kind

atmosphere the overall impression conveyed by a store's physical layout, decor, and surroundings

15-8

shopper marketing understanding how one's target consumers behave as shoppers, in different channels and formats, and leveraging this intelligence to generate sales or other positive outcomes

shopper analytics searching for and discovering meaningful patterns in shopper data for the purpose of fine-tuning, developing, or changing market offerings

big data analytics the process of discovering patterns in large data sets for the purposes of extracting knowledge and understanding human behaviour

click-and-collect the practice of buying something online and then travelling to a physical store location to take delivery of the merchandise

KEY CONCEPTS

16-1 Discuss the role of promotion in the marketing mix. Promotion is communication by marketers that informs, persuades, reminds, and connects potential buyers of a product to influence their opinion or elicit a response. Promotional strategy is the plan for using the elements of promotion—advertising, public relations, sales promotion, direct response communication, personal selling, and social media—to meet the firm's overall objectives and marketing goals. Using these objectives, marketers combine the elements of the promotional strategy to form a coordinated promotion plan. The promotion plan then becomes an integral part of the total marketing strategy for reaching the target market, in addition to product, distribution, and price.

16-2 Describe the communication process. The communication process has several steps. It begins with encoding the message using language and symbols familiar to the receiver. The message is sent through a message channel to the receiver, who decodes the message and provides feedback to the source. Noise in the message channel can distort the message.

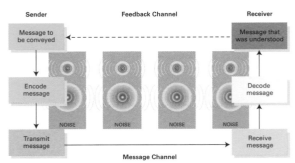

16-3 Outline the goals and tasks of promotion. The fundamental goals of promotion are to induce, modify, or reinforce behaviour by informing, persuading, reminding, and connecting. Informative promotion explains a good's or service's purpose and benefits. Promotion that informs the consumer is typically used to increase demand for a general product category or to introduce a new good or service. Persuasive promotion is designed to stimulate a purchase or an action. Promotion that persuades the consumer to buy is essential during the growth stage of the product life cycle, when competition becomes fierce. Reminder promotion is used to keep the product and brand name in the public's mind. Promotions that remind are generally used during the maturity stage of the product life cycle. To create loyal consumers and trade on established consumers, promotion today makes a connection. Social media tools are perfect for creating connection.

16-4 Discuss the elements of the promotional mix. The elements of the promotional mix include advertising, public relations, sales promotion, personal selling, direct-response communication, and social media. Advertising is a form of impersonal, one-way mass communication paid for by the source. Public relations is concerned with a firm's public image. Sales promotion is typically used to back up other components of the promotional mix by stimulating immediate demand. Personal selling typically involves direct communication, in person or by telephone. Direct-response communication is targeted communications to a specific audience. Social media are promotional tools that facilitate conversations online and encourage consumer empowerment. Social media include the creation of branded content that builds credibility for a brand and encourages the sharing of messages.

16-5 Discuss the AIDA concept and its relationship to the promotional mix. The AIDA model outlines the four basic stages in the purchase

KEY TERMS

16-1

promotion communication by marketers that informs, persuades, reminds, and connects potential buyers to a product for the purpose of influencing an opinion or eliciting a response

promotional strategy a plan for the use of the elements of promotion: advertising, public relations, personal selling, sales promotion, direct-response communication, and social media

competitive advantage the set of unique features of a company and its products that are perceived by the target market as significant and superior to the competition

16-2

communication the process by which we exchange or share meanings through a common set of symbols

interpersonal communication direct, fact-to-face communication between two or more people

mass communication the communication of a concept or message to large audiences

sender the originator of the message in the communication process

encoding the conversion of the sender's ideas and thoughts into a message, usually in the form of words or signs

channel a medium of communication—such as a voice, radio, or newspaper—used for transmitting a message

noise anything that interferes with, distorts, or slows down the transmission of information

receivers the people who decode a message

decoding interpretation of the language and symbols sent by the source through a channel

feedback the receiver's response to a message

16-4

promotional mix the combination of promotional tools—including advertising, publicity, sales promotion, personal selling, direct-response communication, and social media—used to reach the target market and fulfill the organization's overall goals

advertising impersonal, one-way mass communication about a product or an organization that is paid for by a marketer

public relations the marketing function that evaluates public attitudes, identifies areas within the organization the public may be interested in, and executes a program of action to earn public understanding and acceptance

publicity public information about a company, a product, a service, or an issue appearing in the mass media as a news item

sales promotion marketing activities—other than personal selling, advertising, direct-response marketing, and public relations—that stimulate consumer buying and dealer effectiveness

CHAPTER REVIEW 16

personal selling a purchase situation involving a personal, paid-for communication between two people in an attempt to influence each other

direct-response communication communication of a message directly from a marketing company and directly to an intended individual target audience

online marketing two-way communication of a message delivered through the Internet to the consumer

social media a collection of online communication tools that facilitate conversations online; when used by marketers, social media tools encourage consumer empowerment

consumer-generated content any form of publicly available online content created by consumers; also referred to as user-generated content

paid media a category of promotional tactic based on the traditional advertising model whereby a brand pays for advertising space

earned media a category of promotional tactic based on a public relations model that gets customers talking about products or services

owned media a category of promotional tactic based on brands becoming publishers of their own content to maximize the brands' value to consumers

branded content creation of engaging bespoke content as a way to promote a particular brand that attracts and builds relationships with consumers

16-5

AIDA concept a model that outlines the process for achieving promotional goals in terms of stages of consumer involvement with the message; the acronym stands for *attention, interest, desire,* and *action*

16-6

integrated marketing communications (IMC) the careful coordination of all promotional messages for a product or a service to ensure the consistency of messages at every contact point where a company meets the consumer

16-7

push strategy a marketing strategy that uses aggressive personal selling and trade advertising to convince a wholesaler or a retailer to carry and sell particular merchandise

pull strategy a marketing strategy that stimulates consumer demand to obtain product distribution

decision-making process, which are initiated and propelled by promotional activities: (1) attention, (2) interest, (3) desire, and (4) action. The components of the promotional mix have varying levels of influence at each stage of the AIDA model.

	Attention	Interest	Desire	Action
Advertising	✓+	✓+	✓	✓−
Direct-response Communication	✓+	✓	✓	✓+
Public Relations	✓+	✓+	✓+	✓−
Sales Promotion	✓	✓	✓+	✓
Personal Selling	✓	✓+	✓+	✓+
Social Media	✓+	✓+	✓	✓−

16-6 Discuss the concept of integrated marketing communications.

Integrated marketing communications is the careful coordination of all promotional messages for a product or service to ensure the consistency of messages at every contact point at which a company meets the consumer—advertising, sales promotion, personal selling, public relations, and social media, as well as direct marketing, packaging, and other forms of communication. Marketing managers carefully coordinate all promotional activities to ensure that consumers see and hear one message. Integrated marketing communications has received more attention in recent years because of the proliferation of media choices, the fragmentation of mass markets into segmented niches, and the decrease in advertising spending in favour of promotional techniques that generate an immediate sales response.

16-7 Know the factors that affect the promotional mix.

Promotion managers consider many factors when creating promotional mixes. These factors include the nature of the product, the product life-cycle stage, the target market characteristics, the type of buying decision involved, the availability of funds, and the feasibility of push or pull strategies.

KEY CONCEPTS

17-1 Define advertising and understand the effect of advertising.

Advertising is any form of impersonal, paid communication in which the sponsor or company is identified. Advertising helps marketers increase or maintain brand awareness and, subsequently, market share.

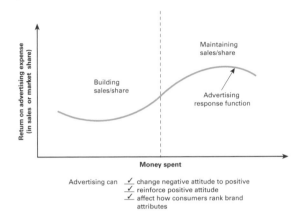

Advertising can:
- ✓ change negative attitude to positive
- ✓ reinforce positive attitude
- ✓ affect how consumers rank brand attributes

17-2 Identify the major types of advertising.
The two major types of advertising are institutional advertising and product advertising. The purpose of institutional advertising is to foster a positive company image with all stakeholders. Product advertising is designed mainly to promote goods and services, and it is classified into three main categories: pioneering, competitive, and comparative.

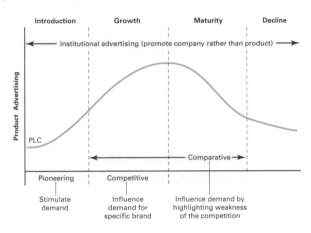

17-3 Discuss the creative decisions in developing an advertising campaign.
Once the goals and objectives of the advertising are defined, creative work can begin. Creative decisions include identifying the product's benefits, developing possible advertising appeals, evaluating and selecting the advertising appeals, executing the advertising message, and evaluating the effectiveness of the campaign.

17-4 Describe media evaluation and selection techniques and how media are purchased.
Media evaluation and selection make up a crucial step in the advertising campaign process. Major types of advertising media include newspapers; magazines; radio; television; outdoor advertising, such as billboards and bus panels; and

KEY TERMS

17-1
advertising response function a phenomenon in which spending for advertising and sales promotion increases sales or market share up to a certain level but then produces diminishing returns

17-2
institutional advertising a form of advertising designed to enhance a company's image rather than promote a particular product

product advertising a form of advertising that promotes the benefits of a specific good or service

advocacy advertising a form of advertising in which an organization expresses its views on a particular issue or cause

pioneering advertising a form of advertising designed to stimulate primary demand for a new product or product category

competitive advertising a form of advertising designed to influence demand for a specific brand

17-3
advertising campaign a series of related advertisements focusing on a common theme, slogan, and set of advertising appeals

advertising objective a specific communication task that a campaign should accomplish for a specified target audience during a specified period

advertising appeal a reason for a person to buy a product

unique selling proposition a desirable, exclusive, and believable advertising appeal selected as the theme for a campaign

programmatic buying using an automated system to make media buying decisions in real time

17-4
medium the channel used to convey a message to a target market

media planning the series of decisions advertisers make regarding the selection and use of media, allowing the marketer to optimally and cost-effectively communicate the message to the target audience

cooperative advertising an arrangement in which the manufacturer and the retailer split the costs of advertising the manufacturer's brand

cord cutting discontinuing or never committing to a TV cable or satellite provider

infomercial a 30-minute or longer advertisement that looks more like a TV talk show than a sales pitch

mobile advertising advertising that displays text, images, and animated ads via mobile phones or other mobile devices that are data enabled

advergaming placing advertising messages in Web-based or video games to advertise or promote a product, a service, an organization, or an issue

social gaming playing an online game that allows for social interaction between players on a social media platform

media mix the combination of media to be used for a promotional campaign

cost per contact the cost of reaching one member of the target market

cost per click the cost associated with a consumer clicking on a display or banner ad

reach the number of target consumers exposed to a commercial at least once during a specific period, usually four weeks

frequency the number of times an individual is exposed to a given message during a specific period

audience selectivity the ability of an advertising medium to reach a precisely defined market

media schedule designation of the media, the specific publications or programs, and the insertion dates of advertising

continuous media schedule a media scheduling strategy in which advertising is run steadily throughout the advertising period; used for products in the later stages of the product life cycle

flighted media schedule a media scheduling strategy in which ads are run heavily every other month or every two weeks, to achieve a greater impact with an increased frequency and reach at those times

pulsing media schedule a media scheduling strategy that uses continuous scheduling throughout the year coupled with a flighted schedule during the best sales periods

seasonal media schedule a media scheduling strategy that runs advertising only during times of the year when the product is most likely to be purchased

17-5

product placement a public relations strategy that involves getting a product, service, or company name to appear in a movie, television show, radio program, magazine, newspaper, video game, video or audio clip, book, or commercial for another product; on the Internet; or at special events

sponsorship a public relations strategy in which a company spends money to support an issue, a cause, or an event that is consistent with corporate objectives, such as improving brand awareness or enhancing corporate image

cause-related marketing a type of sponsorship involving the association of a for-profit company with a nonprofit organization; through the sponsorship, the company's product or service is promoted, and money is raised for the nonprofit

ambush marketing when an advertiser attempts to position itself with an event but is not sanctioned as an official sponsor

the Internet. Promotion managers choose the advertising campaign's media mix on the basis of the following variables: cost per contact, reach, frequency, characteristics of the target audience, flexibility of the medium, noise level, and lifespan of the medium. After choosing the media mix, a media schedule designates when the advertisement will appear and the specific vehicles it will appear in. Media are purchased using negotiation and while rates are published the cost of various media is based on supply and demand.

17-5 Discuss the role of public relations in the promotional mix.

Public relations is a vital part of a firm's promotional mix. Popular public relations tools include new-product publicity, product placement, consumer education, event sponsorship, issue sponsorship, and websites. An equally important aspect of public relations is managing unfavourable publicity in a way that is least damaging to a firm's image.

17-6 Discuss the role of direct-response communication in the promotional mix.

Direct-response communication is often referred to as direct marketing. It involves the development of relevant messages and offers that can be tracked, measured, analyzed, stored, and leveraged. Popular direct-marketing tools are direct-response broadcast, direct-response print, telemarketing, and direct mail. Direct-response communication is designed to generate an immediate response from the consumer through the inclusion of a key element—the offer.

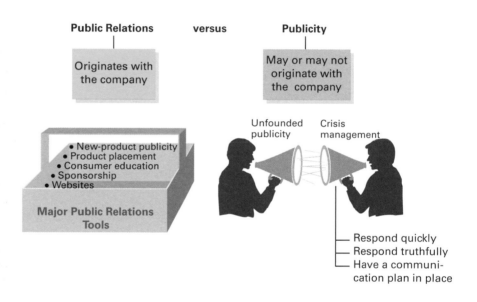

experiential marketing a form of advertising that focuses on helping consumers experience a brand such that a memorable and emotional connection is formed between the consumer and the brand

crisis management a coordinated effort to handle all the effects of either unfavourable publicity or an unexpected unfavourable event

17-6

direct-response broadcast advertising that uses television or radio and includes a direct call to action asking the consumer to respond immediately

direct-response television (DRTV) advertising that appears on television and encourages viewers to respond immediately

direct-response print advertising in a print medium that includes a direct call to action

telemarketing the use of telecommunications to sell a product or service; involves both outbound and inbound calls

Do Not Call List (DNCL) a free service whereby Canadians register their telephone number to reduce or eliminate phone calls from telemarketers

direct mail a printed form of direct-response communication that is delivered directly to consumers' homes

KEY CONCEPTS

18-1 Define and state the objectives of sales promotion. Sales promotion consists of those marketing communication activities in which a short-term incentive motivates consumers or members of the distribution channel to purchase a good or service immediately, through either by lowering the price or by adding value. The main objective of sales promotion is to increase trial purchases, consumer inventories, and repeat purchases. Sales promotion is also used to encourage brand switching and to build brand loyalty. Sales promotion supports advertising activities.

18-2 Discuss the most common forms of consumer sales promotion. Consumer forms of sales promotion include coupons and rebates, premiums, loyalty marketing programs, contests and sweepstakes, sampling, and point-of-purchase displays. Coupons are certificates entitling consumers to an immediate price reduction when they purchase a product or service. Coupons are a particularly good way to encourage product trial and brand switching. Similar to coupons, rebates provide purchasers with a price reduction, although it is not immediate. Premiums offer an extra item or incentive to the consumer for buying a product or service. Loyalty programs are extremely effective at building long-term, mutually beneficial relationships between a company and its key customers. Contests and sweepstakes are generally designed to create interest, often to encourage brand switching. Sampling is an effective method of gaining new customers. Finally, point-of-purchase displays set up at the retailer's location build traffic, advertise the product, and induce impulse buying.

18-3 Discuss the most common forms of trade sales promotion. Manufacturers use many of the same sales promotion tools used in consumer promotions, such as sales contests, premiums, and point-of-purchase displays. In addition, manufacturers and channel intermediaries use several unique promotional strategies: trade allowances, push money, training programs, free merchandise, store demonstrations, and meetings, conventions, and trade shows.

18-4 Describe personal selling. Personal selling is direct communication between a sales representative and one or more prospective buyers in an attempt to influence each other in a purchase situation. Personal selling offers several advantages over other forms of promotion. Personal selling allows salespeople to thoroughly explain and demonstrate a product. Salespeople have the flexibility to tailor a sales proposal to the needs and preferences of targeted qualified prospects. Personal selling affords greater managerial control over promotion costs and is the most effective method of closing a sale and producing satisfied customers.

KEY TERMS

18-1
consumer sales promotion sales promotion activities targeting the ultimate consumer

trade sales promotion sales promotion activities targeting a marketing channel member, such as a wholesaler or retailer

18-2
coupon a certificate that entitles consumers to an immediate price reduction when they buy the product

rebates cash refunds given for the purchase of a product during a specific period

premium an extra item offered to the consumer, usually in exchange for some proof of purchase of the promoted product

loyalty marketing program a promotional program designed to build long-term, mutually beneficial relationships between a company and its key customers

frequent-buyer program a loyalty program in which loyal consumers are rewarded for making multiple purchases of a particular good or service

sampling a promotional program that allows the consumer the opportunity to try a product or service for free

shopper marketing promotion set up at the retailer's location to build traffic, advertise the product, or induce impulse buying

18-3
trade allowance a price reduction offered by manufacturers to intermediaries, such as wholesalers and retailers

push money money offered to channel intermediaries to encourage them to push products—that is, to encourage other members of the channel to sell the products

18-5
relationship selling (consultative selling) a multistage sales process that involves building, maintaining, and enhancing interactions with customers for the purpose of developing long-term satisfaction through mutually beneficial partnerships

18-6
sales process (sales cycle) the set of steps a salesperson goes through to sell a particular product or service

lead generation (prospecting) identification of those firms and people most likely to buy the seller's offerings

cold calling a form of lead generation in which the salesperson approaches potential buyers without any prior knowledge of the prospects' needs or financial status

referrals recommendations to a salesperson from a customer or business associate

networking the use of friends, business contacts, co-workers, acquaintances, and fellow members in professional and civic organizations to identify potential clients

social selling leveraging social networks to find the right prospects and build trusted relationships to achieve sales goals

lead qualification determination of a sales prospect's (1) recognized need, (2) buying power, and (3) receptivity and accessibility

preapproach a process that describes the research a salesperson must do before contacting a prospect

needs assessment a determination of the customer's specific needs and wants and the range of options the customer has for satisfying them

sales proposal a formal written document or professional presentation that outlines how the salesperson's product or service will meet or exceed the prospect's needs

sales presentation a formal meeting in which the salesperson presents a sales proposal to a prospective buyer

negotiation the process during which both the salesperson and the prospect offer concessions in an attempt to arrive at a sales agreement

follow-up the final step of the selling process, in which the salesperson ensures that delivery schedules are met, that the goods or services perform as promised, and that the buyer's employees are properly trained to use the products

18-5 Discuss the key differences between relationship selling and traditional selling. Relationship selling is the practice of building, maintaining, and enhancing interactions with customers to develop long-term satisfaction through mutually beneficial partnerships. Traditional selling, on the other hand, is transaction focused. That is, the salesperson is most concerned with making one-time sales and moving on to the next prospect. In contrast, salespeople who practise relationship selling typically spend more time understanding a prospect's needs and developing solutions to meet those needs.

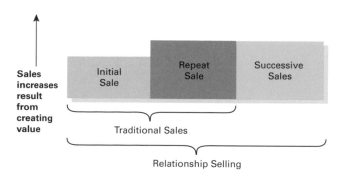

18-6 List the steps in the selling process and discuss key issues. The selling process is composed of seven basic steps: (1) generating leads, (2) qualifying leads, (3) approaching the customer and probing needs, (4) developing and proposing solutions, (5) handling objections, (6) closing the sale, and (7) following up.

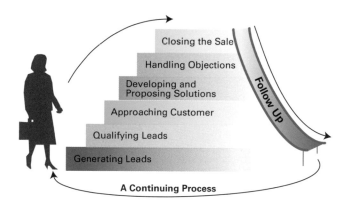

KEY CONCEPTS

19-1 Describe social media's role in an integrated marketing communication plan. Social media include social networks, microblogs, and media-sharing sites, all of which are used by the majority of adults. Smartphones and tablet computers have given consumers greater freedom to access social media on the go, which has increased the use of social media sites. Many advertising budgets are allotting more money to online marketing, including social media, mobile marketing, and search marketing. Social media represent a way for marketers to communicate one-on-one with consumers and measure the effects of those interactions. Like any other promotional component (e.g., advertising, public relations, sales promotions, and personal selling), it must be integrated into common themes and messages when used together as part of an IMC plan.

19-2 Explain how to create a social media campaign. A social media campaign should take advantage of the three media categories: *inbound media, earned media,* and *paid media.* To use these types of media in a social media campaign, first set clear, SMART objectives, then implement an effective listening system. Marketers can interact with negative feedback, make changes, and effectively manage their online presence. Paying attention to the ways that competing brands attract and engage with their customers can be particularly enlightening for both small businesses and global brands. Third, develop strategies that fulfill objectives and reflect how social media dynamically communicate with customers and build relationships.

CATEGORIES OF MEDIA TYPES

Inbound Media	Earned Media	Paid Media
Blogs	Word of mouth	Newspapers
Websites	Online buzz	Television
Facebook pages	Viral videos	Radio
	Retweets	Magazines
	Comments on blogs	Out of home
	Publicity	Direct mail
		Display
		Paid search
		Other direct online advertising

SOCIAL MEDIA STRATEGIES

Listen, learn, respond—repeat
Build relationships and trust
Promote products and services
Manage reputation
Improve customer service
Champion those who champion you

KEY TERMS

19-1
social media collection of online communication tools that facilitate conversations online; when used by marketers, social media tools encourage consumer empowerment

crowdsourcing the use of consumers to develop and market products

social commerce a subset of e-commerce that involves the interaction and user contribution aspects of social media to assist in the online buying and selling of products and services

19-5
blogs publicly accessible Web pages that function as interactive journals, whereby readers can post comments on the authors' entries

corporate or professional blogs blogs that are sponsored by a company or one of its brands and maintained by one or more of the company's employees

noncorporate blogs independent blogs that are not associated with the marketing efforts of any particular company or brand

microblogs blogs with strict post length limits

social networking sites websites that allow individuals to connect—or network—with friends, peers, and business associates

media-sharing sites websites that allow users to upload and distribute multimedia content, such as videos and photos

social news sites websites that allow users to decide which content is promoted on a given website by voting that content up or down

location-based social networking sites websites that combine the fun of social networking with the utility of location-based GPS technology

review sites websites that allow consumers to post, read, rate, and comment on opinions regarding all kinds of products and services

19-6
apps short for applications; free or purchased software programs that are downloaded to run on smartphones, tablet computers, and other mobile devices

19-3 Evaluate the various methods of measurement for social media.

Hundreds of metrics have been developed to measure social media's value, but these metrics are meaningless unless they are tied to key performance indicators. Common measurement activities used today are these:

1. **Buzz:** Volume of consumer-related buzz for a brand based on posts and impression, by social channel, by stage in the purchase channel, by season, and by time of day
2. **Interest:** Number of likes, fans, followers, and friends; growth rates; rate of virality or pass-along; and change in pass-along over time
3. **Participation:** Number of comments, ratings, social bookmarks, subscriptions, page views, uploads, downloads, embeds, retweets, Facebook posts, pins, and time spent with social media platforms
4. **Search engine ranks and results:** Increases and decreases on searches and changes in key words
5. **Influence:** Media mentions, influences of bloggers reached, influences of customers reached, and second-degree reach based on social graphs
6. **Sentiment analysis:** Positive, neutral, and negative sentiment; trends of sentiment; and volume of sentiment
7. **Website metrics:** Clicks, click-through rates, and percentage of traffic. The main issue is to start with good measurable objectives, determine what needs to be measured, and figure it out.

However, only two of these activities produce quantifiable results (search engine ranks and website metrics), which makes it difficult, if not impossible, to determine a true ROI on social media strategies.

19-4 Explain consumer behaviour on social media.

To effectively leverage social media, marketers must understand who uses social media and how they use it. If a brand's target market does not use social media, a social media campaign might not be useful. There are six categories of social media users: creators, critics, collectors, joiners, spectators, and inactives. A more recent study segmented social media users into the following groups: no shows, newcomers, onlookers, cliquers, mix-n-minglers, and sparks.

19-5 Describe the social media tools in a marketer's toolbox, and explain how they are useful.

A marketer has many tools to implement a social media campaign. However, new tools emerge daily, so these resources will change rapidly. Some of the strongest social media platforms are blogs, microblogs, social networks, media creation and sharing sites, social news sites, location-based social networking sites, and virtual worlds and online gaming. Blogs allow marketers to create content in the form of posts, which ideally build trust and a sense of authenticity in customers. Microblogs, such as Twitter, allow brands to follow, retweet, and respond to potential customers' tweets, and to tweet content that inspires customers to engage the brand, laying a foundation for meaningful two-way conversation. Social networks allow marketers to increase awareness, target audiences, promote products, forge relationships, attract event participants, perform research, and generate new business. Media sharing sites give brands an interactive channel in which to disseminate content. Social news sites are useful to marketers to promote campaigns, create conversations, and build website traffic. Location-based social networking sites can forge lasting relationships and loyalty in customers. Review sites allow marketers to respond to customer reviews and comments about their brand. Virtual worlds are fertile ground for branded content, and online gaming allows marketers to integrate their message into a game platform.

- Blogs
- Microblogs
- Social networks
- Media creation and sharing sites
- Location-based social networking sites
- Virtual worlds and online gaming

19-6 Describe the impact of mobile technology on social media.

While much of the excitement in social media has been based on websites and new technology uses, much of the growth lies in new platforms. These platforms include smartphones, tablets, and phablets. The major implication of this development is that consumers now have a multitude of access points for websites.

19-7 Understand the aspects of developing a social media plan.

The social media plan is linked to larger plans, such as a promotional plan or marketing plan, and should fit appropriately into the objectives and steps in those plans. There are six stages involved in creating an effective social media plan: (1) listen, (2) identify the target audience, (3) set social media objectives, (4) define strategies, (5) select the tools and platforms, and (6) implement and monitor the strategy.

NOTES

NOTES